Bibliophiling Tejano Scholarship: Secondary Sources on Hispanic Texans

Bibliophiling Tejano Scholarship: Secondary Sources on Hispanic Texans

Bruce A. Glasrud
and
Arnoldo De León

Center for Big Bend Studies
Occasional Papers No. 8
Alpine, Texas

Sul Ross State University
A Member of the Texas State University System

2003

ISBN 0-9707709-1-X

Center for Big Bend Studies
Occasional Papers No. 8

Kelly S. García, Technical Editor
Robert J. Mallouf, Series Editor

Table of Contents

FOREWORD

The mission of the Center for Big Bend Studies stresses the importance of interdisciplinary and multicultural approaches to cultural studies. We were, therefore, excited by Bruce Glasrud's original prospectus for such a sorely needed reference volume, and we now are honored to make this impressive compendium of Tejano scholarship available to researchers and the general public. Through determination and Herculean effort, Glasrud and Arnoldo De León—both eminent historians and highly respected scholars of minority studies—have assembled a reference volume that speaks forcefully to the origins, development, diversity, manifestations, and implications of Tejano lifeways.

Bibliophiling Tejano Scholarship is dedicated to the understanding and wider diffusion of the Tejano experience. This volume facilitates and greatly enhances research potentials for a unique part of American culture. In so doing, it provides insights into the mental processes and methodologies of the many authors who have—knowingly or unwittingly—constructed and defined the boundaries of a shared ethnic consciousness. If ethnicity is indeed subject to circumstance, then the pages of this volume have much to say about how individuals and groups shape their identities within multicultural settings.

The sheer magnitude of references on Tejano culture is enlightening for researcher and layman alike, and is revealing in terms of the dynamic essence of Hispanic Texas. Clearly, the authors were faced with an intimidating task in seeking out and structuring such an enormous collection of pertinent works. The inherent difficulties of data presentation mastered by Glasrud and De León are of course hidden from the reader, who will find the volume well organized and easy to use.

Bibliophiling Tejano Scholarship invites you to step into the unique world of Tejano culture. You most certainly will exit with a much stronger awareness and clearer understanding of the cultural diversity and multicultural dynamic that makes Texas—well..., Texas!

Robert J. Mallouf
Director
Center for Big Bend Studies

PREFACE: BIBLIOPHILING TEJANO SCHOLARSHIP

Bibliophiling Tejano Scholarship is designed to be a comprehensive and path-breaking bibliography of Texas Hispanics. It was a cooperative endeavor by two west Texas colleagues—Bruce A. Glasrud and Arnoldo De León—who have known and respected each other for years, but who, due to their prior differences in residence and in their respective fields of minority history, had not worked together before this effort. All that is exhilarating about a collaborative study was realized by the two authors: an increased awareness of the complexities of preparing a thorough bibliography, an appreciation of the work of one another, the joy of discovering an ensconced citation, and the fun of challenging, inquiring, and responding to each other as they acted as sleuths. De León clearly spoke on behalf of both authors when he wrote, "I am thoroughly enjoying being part of this project!"[1] Our enjoyment and our efforts can be noted in another manner by historian Robin Winks. Even though he focused principally upon primary sources as "evidence," certainly Winks' imaginative book, *The Historian as Detective*,[2] spoke about our efforts, our approach, and us.

All sleuths (including historians) need some clues; for Glasrud, early ones came from looking at the scholarship of co-author Arnoldo De León. Not only has De León published widely on Tejano history, he also prepared a first-rate Tejano bibliographical article for the *Southwestern Historical Quarterly* (January 1995), and has followed that article with yearly updates in that journal.[3] Since those early efforts, our clues have come from prodding each other, from messages sent via both e-mail and snail mail, from perusing countless bibliographies and footnotes (in books, articles, theses, and dissertations), and from discussions with other scholars of Tejano history and culture. Both Glasrud and De León have become even more aware of the substantial accomplishments of Tejano scholarship as a result of preparing this work. We hope, and assume, that the readers and users of *Bibliophiling Tejano Scholarship*, whether scholars, students, or general practitioners, will come away with this same understanding and appreciation.

Several motivations prompted this compilation of secondary works on Tejano scholarship (which we define as those academic works that have Texas as a focus, setting, or theme, and have Mexican-descent people as their subjects). First, we recognized the need for cataloguing the huge outpouring of works written in the field during the course of our own professional careers. Actually, literature on Tejanos did not first start appearing during the 1970s; numerous studies were underway by the early 1900s—many of them theses and dissertations written by educators, anthropologists, and folklorists—and we wanted to provide a survey or inventory showing the magnitude of the scholarship. Further, we sought to indicate that this body of writings ranged far beyond our own field of specialization (history). During the last thirty years or so, a cadre of scholars in fields such as (but not limited to) psychology, demography, religion, gender studies, and literature has indeed contributed substantially to the understanding of a people once considered ahistoric. Another inducement for the compilation of this bibliography was our belief that a compendium or handbook was long over due. As Emilio Zamora, Cynthia Orozco, and Rodolfo Rocha noted in their anthology, *Mexican Americans in Texas History*, "there is no such [Tejano history] bibliography in book form."[4] The result is a much needed reference tool useful to academicians and lay people alike.

Personal incentives also drove our research. Bruce Glasrud's publication of *Exploring the Afro-Texas Experience: A Bibliography of Secondary Sources About Black Texans* (2000),[5] naturally led him to consider doing something similar for Mexican Americans in Texas (although he quickly realized that he needed professional collaboration and help), and the frequent bibliographic/historiographic publications of Arnoldo De León indicate that he has always maintained an interest in Tejano scholarship as well as Tejano history. Both authors have held a commitment to minority studies and consider it a duty to stay current on that literature: bibliographies are a common accompaniment to the books and articles that we have published. That sense of duty derives from the responsibility cast upon us during our formative years in the 1960s—a time of student revolts, civil rights movements, and more specifically, of calls for research and writing on the history of ordinary people. We were among those who first responded to the need for minority studies and we have since continued making contributions to the subject. A last personal motivation for compiling this work has been our love for scholarship, which takes us to the title of this monograph. *Webster's Collegiate Dictionary* defines **bibliophile** as "a lover of books," or "a book collector." Though the dictionary does not include the word "bibliophiling," we feel that we have approached and accomplished our task with the same passion as would any one who is a "lover of books." Taking that interest in scholarship and organizing it into a bibliography with love and care might well constitute the act of bibliophiling; hence we coined the term and use it in that context.[6]

How to arrange what very quickly amounted to thousands of entries soon perplexed us. Our model for categorizing the many books, articles, dissertations, and other publications was *Exploring the Afro-Texas Experience,* but the mass of literature we encountered on Tejanos became so unwieldy that it called for more precise organization. Thus we have divided the bibliography into three parts, each with a set of chapters (which vary in number). Part I includes a chapter titled "General" (it consists of historical literature that could not be precisely placed in any particular time period, or was not specifically Tejano literature but touched on Tejanos nonetheless) and another one on Bibliography/Historiography. Part II is the historical section of the bibliography and is divided chronologically into eight epochs. It sets the background for Part III, the most extensive section of the book. This latter component includes the literature from cultural and gender studies, the social sciences, and other disciplines.

Periodization also emerged as an issue to be resolved. What time periods should be used to divide the chapters in Part II, the historical listings in *Bibliophiling?* Recent scholarship that questions the delineation established by the first generation of Chicano scholars led us to rethink chronology. Especially under scrutiny is the generational model that divides Mexican-American history into "generations," and more specifically the twentieth century into the Immigrant (1900–1930), Mexican American (1930–1960), Chicano (1966–1975), and Hispanic Generations (post-Chicano, 1975 to the present). According to critics, this schema places too much emphasis on political moments or pivotal events in U.S. history (and thereby skews Mexican-American history, for it overlooks other more important events that impact the community internally) and it takes greater interest on the elites within Mexican-American society. Advocates of postmodernism, Marxist approaches, the world-systems model, and a more recent thesis that posits Mexican-

American history to be that of twentieth-century immigrants from Mexico whose experience has been molded by life under corporate capitalism, further question the old scholarship's divisions.[7]

Yet, such observers are not in agreement over specific watershed dates, and history must have some structure along time lines. There do in fact exist monumental events that take history in one direction or another, and for purposes of organizing Part II, we have settled on eight identifiable epochs that do seem to indicate difference with other distinct eras in Tejano history. They are as follows (an explanation for the time frame is given in the introduction to each chapter of Part II):

1. A Province of New Spain, 1716–1821
2. A Mexican Borderland, 1821–1836
3. New Identity, Old Community, 1836–1880
4. Into the Twentieth Century, 1880–1920
5. Natives and Immigrants, 1920–1945
6. Many Histories, 1945–1966
7. *El Movimiento,* 1966–1975
8. Once Forgotten, 1975 to the Present.

As to Part III—the bulk of the work—the hundreds of citations from fields other than history posed challenging questions. Were we up to the task of handling the new and multidisciplinary research that has made magnificent strides over the last decades towards explicating Tejano society and culture? How could we distinguish among disparate topics to properly determine classification? Should *corridos* fall under "Folklore" or "Music," for instance? What of women as labor activists? Would it be proper to list them under "Economics/Labor" or "Tejanas"? Compounding matters is the inclination by modern-day researchers to borrow from companion disciplines: literary critics adapt insights from anthropological models, demographers from cultural studies, and so on. We can only plead sincerity in attempting to deal with such vexations, and as academicians, to resolve in placing topics where we thought they fit best.

Concerns over chronology, periodization, and categorization were not the only questions/issues that we contemplated. At one time or another we also worried over copyright questions, bibliographic form, the title, approach, duplication, division of labor, culture, historiography, and Tejano identity as well as the complex and perplexing considerations: When do we stop? Will we ever finish the project? Where do we go from here? What we discovered was best exemplified in De León's remark, "To repeat, the more we look the more we find."[8] This comment is music to the ears of any bibliophile, certainly to us.

We enjoyed and learned from the process of putting together *Bibliophiling Tejano Scholarship*. Our expectation is that you also will enjoy and learn from this volume and that we all will have a clearer understanding of the nature of Tejanos, their history, and their scholarship in multicultural Texas. Despite our best efforts, we realize that we could not have located every source; please send any corrections or additions to Arnoldo De León, C. J. "Red" Davidson Professor of History, Box 10897, ASU Station, San Angelo, Texas 76909; arnoldo.deleon@angelo.edu; or Bruce A. Glasrud, 434 Rudeloff Road, Seguin, Texas 79155; bglasrud@sulross.edu.

Notes

1 Arnoldo De León to Bruce Glasrud, August 28, 2002 (e-mail).

2 Robin W. Winks, ed., *The Historian as Detective: Essays on Evidence* (New York: Harper Torchbooks, 1969). Winks asserted that "I have compiled this book of essays for fun, and I claim no other high purpose for it" (xiii).

3 Arnoldo De León, "Estudios Tejanos: A List of Historical Literature on Mexican Americans in Texas," *Southwestern Historical Quarterly* 98 (January 1995): 447–470. Updates were published in the *Southwestern Historical Quarterly* for the years (1995): 253–254, (1996): 242–244, (1997): 253–255, (1998): 234–235, (1999): 248–249, (2000): 296–298, (2001): 362–363, and (2002): 303–305. Select Tejano historiographical articles by De León include "Tejano History Scholarship: A Review of the Recent Literature," *West Texas Historical Association Year Book* 61 (1985): 116–133; "Texas Mexicans: Twentieth–Century Interpretations," in *Texas Through Time: Evolving Interpretations*, edited by Walter L. Buenger and Robert A. Calvert (College Station: Texas A&M University Press, 1991): 20–49; and most recently, "Whither Tejano History: Origins, Development, and Status," *Southwestern Historical Quarterly* 106 (January 2003): 349–364.

4 Emilio Zamora, Cynthia Orozco, and Rodolfo Rocha eds., *Mexican Americans in Texas History: Selected Essays* (Austin: Texas State Historical Association, 2000): 187.

5 Bruce A. Glasrud and Laurie Champion, eds., *Exploring the Afro-Texas Experience: A Bibliography of Secondary Sources About Black Texans* (Alpine, Tex.: SRSU Center for Big Bend Studies, 2000).

6 For more on bibliophiles, see Tom Raabe, "Bibliomaniacs and Bibliophiles," in *Biblioholism: The Literary Addiction* (Golden, Colo.: Fulcrum Publishing, 1991): 53–57.

7 Louis Gerard Mendoza, *Historia: The Literary Making of Chicana and Chicano History* (College Station: Texas A&M University Press, 2001): 12–36, 44, 63–70, 129–143, 198–202, 236, 275–276; Dennis N. Valdés and Refugio I. Rochín, "The Fruitless Search for A Chicana/o Paradigm," in *Voices of a New Chicana/o History*, edited by Refugio I. Roxhín and Dennis N. Valdés (East Lansing: Michigan State University Press, 2000): viii–ix; Dennis N. Valdés, "Region, Nation, and World-System: Perspectives on Midwestern Chicana/o History," *ibid.,* 130–131; and Gilbert G. González and Raúl Fernández, "Chicano History: Transcending Cultural Models," *Pacific Historical Review* 63 (November 1994): 485–497.

8 Arnoldo De León to Bruce Glasrud, September 12, 2002 (e-mail).

ACKNOWLEDGMENTS

Putting together a book-length bibliography is a daunting task though it does have its stimulating aspects, many of which derive from our experiences with those individuals who have given time, advice, and encouragement to the completion of this compilation. We appreciate and acknowledge those generous souls who have gone out of their way to assist us.

We would like to thank the library staff at Angelo State University. Maurice G. Fortin, ASU Library Director, helped us track down obscure theses and dissertations; Sharon Weber of the Interlibrary Loan department assisted us in completing bibliographic information for many of the entries; and Mark A. Allan, ASU Head of Reference, cheerfully permitted De León to check out "Reference Materials" from the ASU library to work with at home. The personnel at the Mary and Jeff Bell Library at Texas A&M University-Corpus Christi were unstinting in their professional services. During a special visit to the library, Dr. Thomas H. Kreneck, the archivist there, gave De León (following De León's visit to the library) a comprehensive overview of the library's Special Collections on Texas Mexicans, and Grace G. Charles followed up by sending him a long list of books and articles that turned out to be of much value.

We also thank the library staff at Sul Ross State University. Dean Donald W. Dowdey offered encouragement and support, librarians Eleanor Wilson and Pam Spooner never failed to answer one more question or to locate one more source, and interlibrary loan librarian Mike Robinson cheerfully and diligently searched for just the right edition and fulfilled the other numerous requests that we asked him. We have visited and been treated courteously by additional librarians in preparing this work; we extend our appreciation to library staffs at the University of Texas at El Paso, Texas Tech University, and Southwest Texas State University as well as libraries on the campus of the University of Texas at Austin (Perry-Castañeda Library, Benson Latin American Collection, and the Center for American History).

Other individuals assisted us, with our heartfelt thanks, in varied ways. Joe Labatt, the publisher at Corona Publishing, courteously provided us with a copy of *New Growth*, one of only a couple extant. James Lee at Texas Christian University Press and Mark Busby, editor of *Southwestern American Literature*, answered our queries promptly and guided us in the right direction. Carolyn Poulter and Donna Walker-Nixon at Mary Hardin Baylor University aided us in locating copies of *New Texas* stories. The dean of Texas colonial Tejano scholarship, don Félix D. Almaráz, Jr., took time from his hectic schedule, replied to questions, and sent along the bibliography of his writings. Mark S. Saka, a historian at Sul Ross State University, loaned us a bibliography and opened his collection and knowledge to the effort. University of Texas, Austin, professor Peter Ward (while Ward was in Mexico) and his assistant, Pedro Villarreal, located a citation for us, offered to send a copy of the memotria, and wished us well. Tatcho Mindiola from the University of Houston expeditiously provided page numbers, suggestions, and bibliographic items for our Tejano undertaking. Father Robert Wright of the Oblate School of Theology in San Antonio, after "talking shop" with De León at the 2003 WTHA meeting in Lubbock, sent us a substantial bibliography on Tejanos and religion. Guadalupe San Miguel Jr., from the University of Houston, abetted our Tejano effort by responding kindly to citation inquiries.

Not least, by any means, was the staff at the Center for Big Bend Studies at Sul Ross State University. From the first exploration of the idea for this compilation, Kelly García enthusiastically has given her knowledge, expertise, and support to *Bibliophiling Tejano Scholarship.* The book is much better than it might have become otherwise thanks to her careful editing. Robert J. Mallouf, the Director of the Center for Big Bend Studies, upon hearing the initial proposal/suggestion, immediately said "yes," and has helped in many ways since. Becky Hart, administrative secretary with the CBBS, and Kelly García spent many hours searching for photographs at the Institute of Texan Cultures in San Antonio. Ellen Kelley, with the assistance of Troy Solis and Melleta Bell, combed the Archives of the Big Bend for appropiate photographs.

Even with all this help and encouragement, we realize that errors may occur; they remain our own regretful responsibility.

Bruce A. Glasrud
Arnoldo De León

Part I: General and Bibliography/Historiography

1. GENERAL

This section contains materials of national or regional scale that are significant enough to warrant noting for those with an interest in Tejano scholarship. Listed are several survey history texts that touch on Mexican Americans in Texas in the context of the larger Mexican-American experience in the U.S. Included also are publications broader in scope than the chapter divisions we have established; for example, ones that cover the entire nineteenth century. Overview articles, county histories, border studies, encyclopedias, and handbooks are part of this chapter. A third group of publications that do not fit exactly into our chapter designations, perhaps due to a paucity of scholarship in that area, are categorized as "general," such as works on cultural geography.

Acuña, Rodolfo. *Occupied America: The Chicano Struggle for Liberation*. New York: Harper and Row, 1972.

________. *Occupied America: A History of Chicanos*. Fourth edition. New York: Addison-Wesley Longman, 1999.

________."Freedom in a Cage: The Subjugation of the Chicano in the United States." In *The Reinterpretation of American History and Culture*, edited by William H. Cartwright and Richard L. Watson Jr., 113–137. Washington, D.C.: National Council for the Social Studies, 1973.

Almaráz, Félix D. Jr. "Contributions of Mexican Americans to Texas Historiography." In *A Guide to the History of Texas*, edited by Light Townsend Cummins and Alvin R. Bailey Jr., 101–106. New York: Greenwood Press, 1988.

________. "Take the High Road: A Senior Scholar's Advice to Tejano Historians." *South Texas Studies* 11 (2000): 153–156.

________. "Texas History." In *Borderlands Sourcebook: A Guide to the Literature on Northern Mexico and the American Southwest,* edited by Ellwyn R. Stoddard, Richard L. Nostrand, and Jonathan P. West, 46–48. Norman: University of Oklahoma Press, 1983.

Almaráz, Félix D. Jr., and Hubert J. Miller. "Four Centuries of Shared Experience in the Borderlands." In *Borderlands: The Heritage of the Lower Rio Grande Valley through the Art of José Cisneros*, edited by Félix D. Almaráz, 17–49. Edinburg, Tex.: Hidalgo County Historical Museum, 1998.

Álvarez, Rodolfo. "The Psycho-Historical and Socioeconomic Development of the Chicano Community of the United States." *Social Science Quarterly* 53 (March 1973): 920–942.

Amberson, Mary Margaret, James A. McAllen, and Margaret H. McAllen. *I Would Rather Sleep in Texas: A History of the Lower Rio Grande Valley and the People of the Santa Anita Land Grant*. Austin: Texas State Historical Association, 2003.

Arreola, Daniel D. *Tejano South Texas: A Mexican American Cultural Province*. Austin: University of Texas Press, 2002.

________. "Beyond the Nueces: The Early Geographical Identity of South Texas." *Río Bravo: A Journal of Research and Issues* 2 (Spring 1993): 46–60.

________. "Mexican Origins of South Texas Mexican Americans, 1930." *Journal of Historical Geography* 19 (1993): 48–63.

________. "Mexican Texas: A Distinctive Borderland." In *A Geographic Glimpse of Central Texas and the Borderlands: Images and Encounters*, edited by James F. Peterson and Julie A. Tuason, 3–9. Indiana, Penn.: National Council for Geographic Education, 1995.

________. "The Texas-Mexican Homeland." *Journal of Cultural Geography* 13 (Spring/Summer 1993): 61–74.

________. "*La Tierra Tejana*: A South Texas Homeland." In *Homelands in the United States: A Geography of Culture and Place Across America*, edited by Richard L. Nostrand and Lawrence E. Estaville Jr., 101–124. Baltimore: Johns Hopkins University Press, 2001.

Benavides, Adán Jr. "Tejano." In *The New Handbook of Texas*, edited by Ron Tyler, Douglas E. Barnett, Roy R. Barkley, Penelope C. Anderson, and Mark F. Odintz, vol. 6, 238–239. Austin: Texas State Historical Association, 1996.

Binder, Norman, and Frank J. García. "Winning Political Office in Cameron County, 1876–1988: The Mexican American Case." In *More Studies in Brownsville History*, edited by Milo Kearney, 423–438. Brownsville, Tex.: Pan American University, 1989.

Calderón, Roberto R. "Tejano Politics." In *The New Handbook of Texas*, edited by Ron Tyler, Douglas E. Barnett, Roy R. Barkley, Penelope C. Anderson, and Mark F. Odintz, vol. 6, 239–242. Austin: Texas State Historical Association, 1996.

Canales, J. T. *Bits of Texas History in the Melting Pot of America*. 2 vols. San Antonio: Artes Gráficas, 1950, 1957.

Castañeda, Carlos E. *Our Catholic Heritage in Texas, 1519–1936: The Finding of Texas, 1519–1693*. Austin: Von Boeckmann-Jones, 1936.

________. *Our Catholic Heritage in Texas, 1519–1936: The Winning of Texas, 1693–1731*. Austin: Von Boeckmann-Jones, 1936.

________. *Our Catholic Heritage in Texas, 1519–1936: The Missions at Work, 1731–1761*. Austin: Von Boeckmann-Jones, 1938.

________. *Our Catholic Heritage in Texas, 1519–1936: The Passing of the Missions, 1762–1782*. Austin: Von Boeckmann-Jones, 1939.

________. *Our Catholic Heritage in Texas, 1519–1936: The End of the Spanish Regime, 1780–1810*. Austin: Von Boeckmann-Jones, 1942.

________. *Our Catholic Heritage in Texas, 1519–1936: The Fight for Freedom, 1810–1836*. Austin: Von Boeckmann-Jones, 1950.

________. *Our Catholic Heritage in Texas, 1519–1936: The Church in Texas Since Independence, 1836–1950*. Austin: Von Boeckmann-Jones, 1958.

Collins, Gladys Irene. "A History of Spanish West Texas." Master's thesis, University of Oklahoma, 1929.

Cortés, Carlos E. "Mexicans." In *Harvard Encyclopedia of American Ethnic Groups*, edited by Stephan Thernstrom, 697–719. Cambridge, Mass.: Belknap Press of Harvard University Press, 1980.

________, ed. *The Mexican Experience in Texas*. New York: Arno Press, 1976.

Crimm, Ana Carolina Castillo. "Success in Adversity: The Mexican Americans of Victoria County, Texas, 1800–1880." Ph.D. dissertation, University of Texas at Austin, 1994.

________. "Finding Their Way." In *Tejano Journey, 1770–1850*, edited by Gerald E. Poyo, 111–123. Austin: University of Texas Press, 1996.

De León, Arnoldo. *Apuntes San Angeleños: An Index of Newspaper Items Extracted from the San Angelo* Standard Times, *1884–1984*. San Angelo: Fort Concho Museum Press, 1987.

________. *Apuntes Tejanos*. 2 vols. Austin: Texas State Historical Association, 1978.

________. *Las Fiestas Patrias: Biographic Notes on the Hispanic Presence in San Angelo, Texas*. San Antonio: Caravel Press, 1978.

________. *Mexican Americans in Texas: A Brief History*. Second edition. Arlington Heights, Ill.: Harlan Davidson, 1999.

________. *The Mexican Image in Nineteenth-Century Texas*. Boston: American Press, 1982.

________. *Nuestra Historia: Our Hispanic Heritage.* Dallas: Dallas Historical Society, 1997.

________. *They Called Them Greasers: Anglo Attitudes Towards Mexicans in Texas, 1821–1900*. Austin: University of Texas Press, 1983.

________. *The Tejano Community, 1836–1900*. Albuquerque: University of New Mexico Press, 1982. Reprinted, Dallas: Southern Methodist University Press, 1997.

________. "Chicano." In *The New Handbook of Texas*, edited by Ron Tyler, Douglas E. Barnett, Roy R. Barkley, Penelope C. Anderson, and Mark F. Odintz, vol. 2, 69. Austin: Texas State Historical Association, 1996.

________. "Mexican Americans." In *The New Handbook of Texas*, edited by Ron Tyler, Douglas E. Barnett, Roy R. Barkely, Penelope C. Anderson, and Mark F. Odintz, vol. 4, 664–670. Austin: Texas State Historical Association, 1996.

________. "Los Tejanos: An Overview of Their History." In *The Texas Heritage*, edited by Ben Procter and Archie P. McDonald, 133–144. St. Louis: Forum Press, 1980.

________. "Our Gringo Amigos: Anglo Americans and the Tejano Experience." *East Texas Historical Journal* 32 (Fall 1993): 72–79.

________. "A People with Many Histories: Mexican Americans in Texas." In *The Texas Heritage*, edited by Ben Procter and Archie P. McDonald, 204–233. Fourth edition. Arlington Heights, Ill.: Harlan Davidson, 2003.

________. "The Tejano Experience in Six Texas Regions." *West Texas Historical Association Yearbook* 65 (1989): 36–49.

Dobie, J. Frank. *A Vaquero of the Brush Country*. Austin: University of Texas Press, 1965.

Foley, Douglas E., Clarice Mota, Donald E. Post, and Ignacio Lozano. *From Peones to Politicos: Class and Ethnicity in a South Texas Town, 1900–1987*. Revised edition. Austin: University of Texas Press, 1988.

________. *From Peones to Politicos: Ethnic Relations in a South Texas Town, 1900–1977*. Austin: University of Texas Press, 1977.

Galván, Jesse Jr. *The Way Back: The Autobiography of Jesse Galván Jr.: Businessman, Comedian, Federal Employee*. San Antonio: Watercress Press, 1993.

García, Mario T. "In Search of History: Carlos E. Castañeda and the Mexican American Generation." In *Renato Rosaldo Lecture Series Monographs*, No. 4, edited by Ignacio García, 1–18. Tucson: Mexican American Studies and Research Center, University of Arizona, 1988.

García, Richard A. *The Chicanos in America, 1540–1974: A Chronology and Fact Book*. Dobbs Ferry, N.Y.: Oceana Publications, 1977.

Gómez-Quiñones, Juan. "Pre-Twentieth Century Mexicans North of the Rio Bravo: Selected Social and Economic Sources." In *Development of the Mexican Working Class North of the Río Bravo: Work and Culture Among Laborers and Artisans, 1600–1900,* by Juan Gómez-Quiñones. Los Angeles: UCLA Chicano Studies Research Center, 1982.

Gonzales, Manuel G. *Mexicanos: A History of Mexicans in the United States*. Bloomington: Indiana University Press, 1999.

González de Mireles, Jovita. "Latin Americans." In *Our Racial and National Minorities: Their History, Contributions, and Present Problems*, edited by Francis J. Brown and Joseph Slabez Roucek, 497–509. New York: Prentice-Hall, 1939.

Graham, Don. *King of Texas: The 150–Year Saga of an American Ranching Empire*. New York: John Wiley and Sons, 2003.

Graham, Joe S., ed. *Hecho en Tejas*. Denton: University of North Texas Press, 1991.

Gregg, John Ernest. "The History of Presidio County." Master's thesis, University of Texas, Austin, 1933.

Grimes, Roy, ed. *300 Years in Victoria County*. Victoria, Tex.: The Victoria Advocate Publishing Co., 1968.

Griswold del Castillo, Richard, and Arnoldo De León. *North to Aztlán: A History of Mexican Americans in the United States*. New York: Twayne Publishers, 1996.

Guerra, Mary Ann Noonan. *The History of San Antonio's Market Square*. San Antonio: The Alamo Press, 1988.

Gutiérrez, David G. "Significant to Whom?: Mexican Americans and the History of the American West." *Western Historical Quarterly* 24 (November 1993): 519–539.

Herrera-Sobek, María. "Américo Paredes: A Tribute." *Mexican Studies/Estudios Mexicanos* 16 (Summer 2000): 239–266.

Hinojosa, Gilberto M. "Charting a Border Culture." *Texas Journal of Ideas, History and Culture* 20 (Fall/Winter 1997): 4–5.

________. "Texas Mexico Border: A Turbulent History." *Texas Humanist* 6 (March/April 1984): 6–9.

________. "Texas-Mexico Border: A Turbulent History." *Texas Journal of Ideas, History and Culture* 20 (Fall/Winter 1997): 10–15.

Huson, Hobart. *Refugio: A Comprehensive History of Refugio County from Aboriginal Times to 1953*. 2 vols. Woodsboro, Tex.: The Rooke Foundation, 1953.

Jordan, Terry G. "A Century and a Half of Ethnic Change in Texas, 1836–1986." *Southwestern Historical Quarterly* 89 (April 1982): 385–422.

Kibbe, Pauline R. *Latin Americans in Texas*. Albuquerque: University of New Mexico Press, 1946.

Kingrea, Nellie W. *History of the First Ten Years of the Texas Good Neighbor Commission*. Fort Worth: Texas Christian University Press, 1954.

Larralde, Carlos. *Mexican Americans: Movements and Leaders*. Los Alamitos, Calif.: Hwong Publishing, 1976.

________. "Chicano Jews in South Texas." Ph.D. dissertation, University of California at Los Angeles, 1978.

Lea, Tom. *The King Ranch*. 2 vols. Boston: Little, Brown and Co., 1957.

López, Ian F. Haney. "Race and Erasure: The Salience of Race to Latinos." In *The Latino Condition: A Critical Reader*, edited by Richard Delgado and Jean Stefancic, 180–195. New York: New York University Press, 1998.

Lott, Virgil, and Mercurio Martínez. *The Kingdom of Zapata*. San Antonio: The Naylor Company, 1953.

Madsen, William. *The Mexican-Americans of South Texas*. New York: Holt, Rinehart, and Winston, 1964.

Maril, Robert Lee. *Living on the Edge of America: At Home on the Texas Mexican Border*. College Station: Texas A&M University Press, 1992.

Martínez, Oscar J. "A History of Chicanos/Mexicanos Along the U.S. Mexico Border." In *Handbook of Hispanic Cultures in the United States*, edited by Nicolas Kanellos and Claudio Esteva-Fabregat, vol. 4, 261–280. Houston: Arte Público Press and Instituto de Cooperación Iberoamericana, 1994.

McCrary, Mallie E. "These Minorities in Our Midst: With Emphasis on Latin Americans in Texas." Master's thesis, University of Texas, Austin, 1953.

McLemore, S. Dale. "The Origins of Mexican-American Subordination in Texas." *Social Science Quarterly* 53 (March 1973): 656–670.

McWilliams, Carey. *North from Mexico: The Spanish Speaking People of the United States*. New York: Greenwood Press, 1968.

Meier, Matt S. *Mexican American Biographies: A Historical Dictionary, 1836–1987*. New York: Greenwood Press, 1988.

Meier, Matt S., and Margo Gutiérrez. *Encyclopedia of the Mexican American Civil Rights Movement*. Westport, Conn.: Greenwood Press, 2000.

Meier, Matt S., with Conchita Franco Serri, and Richard A. García. *Notable Latino Americans: A Biographical Dictionary*. Westport, Conn.: Greenwood Press, 1997.

Meier, Matt S., and Feliciano Rivera. *The Chicanos: A History of Mexican Americans*. New York: Hill and Wang, 1972.

________, eds. *Dictionary of Mexican American History*. Westport, Conn.: Greenwood Press, 1981.

Melville, Margarita B. *Twice a Minority: Mexican American Women*. St. Louis: C.V. Mosby, 1980.

Mendoza, Louis Gerard. *Historia: The Literary Making of Chicana and Chicano History*. College Station: Texas A&M University Press, 2001.

The Mexican Texans. San Antonio: Institute of Texan Cultures, 1975. Reprinted, College Station: Texas A&M University Press, 2003.

Miller, Hubert J. "Oral History: A Tool for the Study of Mexican American History in the Lower Rio Grande Valley." *Oral History Review* 15 (Fall 1987): 80–95.

Montejano, David. *Anglos and Mexicans in the Making of Texas, 1836–1986*. Austin: University of Texas Press, 1987.

________. "Old Roads, New Horizons: Texas History and the New World Order." In *Mexican Americans in Texas History*, edited by Emilio Zamora, Cynthia

Orozco, and Rodolfo Rocha, 19–33. Austin: Texas State Historical Association, 2000.

Newcomb, Pearson. *The Alamo City*. San Antonio: Standard Printing Co., 1926.

Olvera, J. Montiel. *Year Book of the Mexican Population of Texas*. San Antonio: Privately printed, 1939.

Ortego y Gasca, Philip D., and Arnoldo De León. *The Tejano Yearbook, 1519–1978: A Selective Chronicle of the Hispanic Presence in Texas*. San Antonio: Caravel Press, 1978.

Pierce, Frank G. *A Brief History of the Lower Rio Grande Valley*. Menasch, Wisc.: George Banta Publishing, 1917.

Raht, Carlyle Graham. *The Romance of the Davis Mountains and Big Bend Country*. El Paso: The Raht Books Company, 1919.

Robertson, Brian. *Wild Horse Desert: The Heritage of South Texas*. Edinburg, Tex.: New Santander Press, 1985.

Rocha, Rodolfo. "The Sting of Power and Rebellion." *Texas Journal of Ideas, History and Culture* 20 (Fall/Winter 1997): 22–27.

________. "The Tejano Experience." In *The Texas Heritage*, edited by Ben H. Procter and Archie P. McDonald, 213–229. Second edition. Arlington Heights, Ill.: Harlan Davidson, 1992.

________. "The Tejanos of Texas." In *Texas: A Sesquicentennial Celebration*, edited by Donald W. Whisenhunt, 339–352. Austin: Eakin Press, 1984.

Rosales, F. Arturo. *Chicano!: The History of the Mexican American Civil Rights Movement*. Houston: Arte Público Press, 1996.

Rosenbaum, Robert J. *Mexicano Resistance in the Southwest: "The Sacred Right of Self-Preservation."* Austin: University of Texas Press, 1981.

Ruiz, Vicki L. *From Out of the Shadows: A History of Mexican Women in the United States, 1900–1995*. New York: Oxford University Press, 1998.

Salmón, Roberto Mario. "The Texas-Mexican Legacy: Puro Tejano." *Borderlands Journal* 10 (Fall 1986): 39–50.

Samora, Julián, Joe Bernal, and Albert Peña. *Gunpowder Justice: A Reassessment of the Texas Rangers*. Notre Dame: University of Notre Dame Press, 1979.

Sánchez, George I. "Mexican Americans in Texas." In *The Handbook of Texas: A Supplement*, edited by Eldon Stephen Branda, 595–596. Austin: Texas State Historical Association, 1976.

Saunders, Lyle. "The Spanish-Speaking Population of Texas." In *The Mexican Experience in Texas*, edited by Carlos E. Cortés, 1–56. New York: Arno Press, 1976.

Saunders, Lyle, and Olen E. Leonard. "The Wetback in the Lower Rio Grande Valley of Texas." In *Mexican Migration to the United States*, edited by Carlos E. Cortés, 3–92. New York: Arno Press, 1976.

Scobee, Barry. *Fort Davis, Texas: 1583–1965*. Fort Davis, Tex.: Barry Scobee, 1963.

________. *Old Fort Davis*. San Antonio: The Naylor Company, 1947.

Scott, Florence Johnson. *Historical Heritage of the Lower Rio Grande*. San Antonio: The Naylor Company, 1937.

Simmons, Ozzie G. *Anglo-Americans and Mexican Americans in South Texas*. New York: Arno Press, 1974.

________. "Anglo-Americans and Mexican-Americans in South Texas: A Study in Dominant-Subordinate Group Relations." Ph.D. dissertation, Harvard University, 1952.

Simons, Helen, and Cathryn A. Hoyt, eds. *Hispanic Texas: A Historical Guide*. Austin: University of Texas Press, 1992.

Smith, L. Walden. *Saddles Up*. San Antonio: The Naylor Company, 1937.

"South Texas: A Tragic Paradox." *La Luz* 7 (Special Issue: April 1978): 9–23.

Stambaugh, J. Lee, and Lillian J. Stambaugh. *The Lower Rio Grande of Texas*. San Antonio: The Naylor Company, 1954.

Talbert, Robert H. *Spanish-Name People in the Southwest and West*. Fort Worth: Texas Christian University Press, 1955.

Taylor, Paul S. *An American-Mexican Frontier: Nueces County, Texas*. Chapel Hill: University of North Carolina Press, 1934.

Thompson, Jerry D. *A Wild and Vivid Land: An Illustrated History of the South Texas Border*. Austin: Texas State Historical Association, 1998.

Tijerina, Andrés A. *Tejano Empire: Life on the South Texas Ranchos*. College Station: Texas A&M University Press, 1998.

A Twentieth Century History of Southwest Texas. 2 vols. Chicago: The Lewis Publishing Company, 1907.

Vento, Arnoldo Carlos. *Mestizo: The History, Culture and Politics of the Mexican and the Chicano*. Lanham, Md.: University Press of America, 1998.

Waugh, Julia. *The Silver Cradle: Las Posadas, los Pastores, and other Mexican American Traditions*. Austin: University of Texas Press, 1988.

Weber, David J., ed. *Foreigners in Their Native Land*. Albuquerque: University of New Mexico Press, 1973.

Ximénes, Ben Cuéllar. *Gallant Outcasts*. San Antonio: The Naylor Company, 1963.

Zamora, Emilio. "The Américo Paredes Papers." *Journal of South Texas* 15 (Fall 2002): 14–31.

Zamora, Emilio, Cynthia Orozco, and Rodolfo Rocha, eds. *Mexican Americans in Texas History*. Austin: Texas State Historical Association, 2000.

Zurfluh, Hattie E. "The Spanish Heritage in Texas." Master's thesis, Baylor University, 1933.

2. BIBLIOGRAPHY/ HISTORIOGRAPHY

Bibliographies and historiographical essays that focus on Tejanos, either in general or specifically, constitute this chapter. Some of the bibliographies logged herein were compiled as early as the 1940s, though most go back only to the 1970s. More recently, computerized lists have augmented the vast literature on Tejanos and made it easier to locate it electronically. Whatever the quality of these several bibliographies, they illustrate the growing interest on the subject, for they cover the spectrum of the Tejano experience, including fields such as religion, material culture, health, and family. Historiographical essays are valuable unto themselves, as they list and evaluate countless books and articles; they also suggest topics for further study and thus prompt scholars to conduct new research in neglected areas. Certainly, all published bibliographies and historiographical essays we found proved indispensable to the compilation of *Bibliophiling Tejano Scholarship.*

Carmen Aguilar, librarian for the Mexican Library of San Antonio, Texas.
Published October 31, 1935.
The Institute of Texan Cultures at UTSA, No. L-08440A
The San Antonio Light *Collection*

Almaráz, Félix D. Jr. "The Status of Borderlands Studies: History." *Social Science Journal* 12–13 (October 1975/January 1976): 9–18.

Bannon, John Francis. "The Mission as a Frontier Institution: Sixty Years of Interest and Research." *Western Historical Quarterly* 10 (July 1979): 303–322.

Barton, Paul, and David Maldonado, eds. *Hispanic Christianity within Mainline Protestant Traditions: A Bibliography*. Decatur, Ga.: Asociación para la Educación Teológica Hispana, 1998.

Benavides, Adán Jr. *Primary Source Material for the Study of Texas and Northeastern New Spain (Later, Mexico) in San Antonio, Texas*. Paper No. 91–03. Austin: Institute of Latin American Studies at the University of Texas at Austin, 1991.

________, comp. *The Béxar Archives, 1717–1836: A Name Guide.* Austin: University of Texas Press for the University of Texas Institute of Texan Cultures at San Antonio, 1989.

Camarillo, Albert, ed. *Latinos in the United States: A Historical Bibliography.* Santa Barbara: ABC-CLIO, 1986.

Castañeda, Antonia I. "Women of Color and the Rewriting of Western History: The Discourse, Politics, and Decolonization of History." *Pacific Historical Review* 61 (November 1992): 501–533.

Castro, Donald F. "Chicano Literature: A Bibliographical Essay." *English in Texas* 7 (Summer 1976): 14–19.

Chipman, Donald E. "The Status of Biography in the Historiography of New Spain." *The Americas* 27 (January 1971): 327–339.

________. "Spanish Texas." In *Texas Through Time: Evolving Interpretations*, edited by Walter L. Buenger and Robert A. Calvert, 102–133. College Station: Texas A&M University Press, 1991.

Cruz, Gilberto R., and James H. Irby, eds. *Texas Bibliography: A Manual on History Research Materials*. Austin: Eakin Press, 1982.

Cummins, Light Townsend. "Texas under Spain and Mexico." In *A Guide to the History of Texas*, edited by Light Townsend Cummins and Alvin R. Bailey Jr., 3–16. New York: Greenwood Press, 1988.

De León, Arnoldo. "Estudios Tejanos: A List of Historical Literature on Mexican Americans in Texas." *Southwestern Historical Quarterly* 98 (January 1995): 447–470. Reprinted in *Mexican Americans in Texas History,* edited by Emilio Zamora, Cynthia Orozco, and Rodolfo Rocha, 189–209. Austin: Texas State Historical Association, 2000.

________. "Tejano History Scholarship: A Review of the Recent Literature." *West Texas Historical Association Yearbook* 61 (1985): 116–133.

________. "Texas Mexican Bibliography." In Will Howard ed. "A Sesquicentennial Reading List." *Texas Libraries* 46 (Winter 1985–1986): 84–85.

________. "Texas Mexicans: Twentieth-Century Interpretations." In *Texas Through Time: Evolving Interpretations*, edited by Walter L. Buenger and Robert A. Calvert, 20–49. College Station: Texas A&M University Press, 1991.

________. "Whither Tejano History: Origins, Development, and Status." *Southwestern Historical Quarterly* 106 (January 2003): 349–364.

Etulain, Jacqueline J. *Mexican Americans in the Twentieth Century American West: A Bibliography.* Albuquerque: University of New Mexico Press, 1990.

Flores, María G., comp., and Laura Gutiérrez Witt, ed. *Mexican American Archives at the Benson Collection: A Guide for Users.* Austin: General Libraries, University of Texas at Austin, 1981.

Gonzales, Manuel G. "Select Bibliography of Works after 1965." In *Mexicanos: A History of Mexicans in the United States*, by Manuel G. Gonzales, 281–313. Bloomington: Indiana University Press, 1999.

Graham, Joe S. "Bibliography of Texas-Mexican Material Culture." In *Hecho en Tejas: Texas-Mexican Folk Arts and Crafts*, edited by Joe S. Graham, 335–343. Denton: University of North Texas Press, 1991.

Griswold del Castillo, Richard. "Tejanos and California Chicanos: Regional Variations in Mexican American History." *Mexican Studies/Estudios Mexicanos* 1 (1985): 134–139.

Hinojosa, Gilberto M. "The Enduring Hispanic Faith Communities: Spanish and Texas Church Historiography." *Journal of Texas Catholic History and Culture* 1 (March 1990): 20–35.

Korrol, Virginia Sánchez, and Vicki L. Ruiz, eds. *Latinas in the United States: A Historical Encyclopedia.* Bloomington: Indiana University Press, 2003.

Kreneck, Thomas H. "Recovering the 'Lost' Manuscripts of Jovita González." *Texas Library Journal* 74 (Summer 1998): 76–79.

________. "The Dr. Hector P. García Papers: A Research Resource for Texas and More." *Texas Library Journal* 72 (Summer 1996): 80–83.

Loeb, Catherine. "La Chicana: A Bibliographic Survey." *Frontiers* 5 (Summer 1980): 59–74.

Maciel, David R., and James B. Speer. "Related Studies on the Chicano in Texas." *Aztlán* 6 (Fall 1975): 459–461.

McDonald, Dedra S., Evelyn A. Schlatter, and Juneal Leversee. "Selected Bibliographies, Latinas/Hispanas." In *Writing the Range, Class and Culture in the Women's West*, edited by Elizabeth Jameson and Susan Armitage, 621–630. Norman: University of Oklahoma Press, 1997.

Meier, Matt S., comp. *Bibliography of Mexican American History.* Westport, Conn.: Greenwood Press, 1984.

Meier, Matt S., and Feliciano Rivera. *A Selective Bibliography for the Study of Mexican American History.* San Jose: Spartan Bookstore, San José State College, 1971.

Mowry, James N. "A Bibliography of George I. Sánchez." In *Humanidad: Essays in Honor of George I. Sánchez*, edited by Américo Paredes, 134–141. Los Angeles: Chicano Studies Center Publications, 1977.

Orozco, Cynthia E. "Mexican American, Tejana, and Tejano History: An Instructional Bibliography." In *Mexican Americans in Texas History,* edited by Emilio Zamora, Cynthia Orozco, and Rodolfo Rocha, 211–217. Austin: Texas State Historical Association, 2000.

________. "Beyond Machismo, La Familia, and Ladies Auxiliaries: A Historiography of Mexican-Origin Women's Participation in Voluntary Associations and Politics in the United States, 1870–1990." In *Perspectives in Mexican American Studies*, vol. 5, edited by Juan R. García, 1–34. Tucson: Mexican American Studies and Research Center, University of Arizona, 1995.

Ortego, Philip D. *Selective Mexican American Bibliography*. El Paso: Border Regional Library Association and Chicano Research Institute, 1972.

Poyo, Gerald E., and Gilberto M. Hinojosa. "Selective Bibliography on Spanish Texas, 1685–1821." In *Tejano Origins in Eighteenth-Century San Antonio*, edited by Gerald E. Poyo and Gilberto M. Hinojosa, 169–189. Austin: University of Texas Press, 1991.

________. "Spanish Texas and Borderlands Historiography in Transition: Implications for United States History." *Journal of American History* 75 (September 1988): 393–416.

Romero, Yolanda G. "Discovering Tejano History." *Journal of American Ethnic History* 16 (Spring 1997): 128–132.

Ruiz, Vicki L. "Chicano History." In *Women's History: Reading Lists and Course Outlines from American Colleges and Universities,* edited by Annette K. Baxter, 143–145. Bridgeport, Conn.: Markus Weiner Publishing, 1984.

________. "La Chicana." In *Women's History: Reading Lists and Course Outlines from American Colleges and Universities,* edited by Annette K. Baxter, 139–142. Bridgeport, Conn.: Markus Weiner Publishing, 1984.

________. "Mexican American Women." In *Women's History: Reading Lists and Course Outlines from American Colleges and Universities*, edited by Louise Stevenson, 262–266. Princeton, N.J.: Markus Weiner Publishing, 1998.

________. "Mexican Women in the United States: A Bibliography." In *Selected Reading Lists and Course Outlines from American Colleges and Universities, Women's History*, edited by Annette K. Baxter and Louise L. Stevenson, 136–139. New York: Markus Wiener Publishing, 1987.

Samora, Julián, Joseph Bernal, and Alberto Peña Jr. "The Brutal Truth About the Texas Rangers." *Nuestro* 2 (August 1978): 57–58.

Sánchez, George I., and Howard Putnam. *Materials Relating to the Education of Spanish-speaking People in the United States: An Annotated Bibliography.* Westport, Conn.: Greenwood Press, 1971.

Saragoza, Alex M. "The Significance of Recent Chicano-Related Historical Writing: An Appraisal." *Ethnic Affairs* 1 (Fall 1987): 24–62.

Snapp, Elizabeth, and Harry F. Snapp. "Mexican American Women." In *Read all About Her: Texas Women's History: A Working Bibliography*, compiled and edited by Elizabeth Snapp and Harry F. Snapp, 602–603. Denton: Texas Woman's University, 1995.

Vigil, Ralph H. "Inequality and Ideology in Borderlands Historiography." *Latin American Research Review* 29 (1994): 155–171.

Weber, David J. "The Spanish Legacy and Historical Imagination." In *The Spanish Frontier in North America*, by David J. Weber, 335–360. New Haven: Yale University Press, 1992.

Whittenburg, Clarice T., and George I. Sánchez. *Materials Relating to the Education of Spanish-speaking People: A Bibliography.* Austin: University of Texas Press, 1948.

Wilson, James A., comp. *Tejanos, Chicanos and Mexicanos: A Partially Annotated, Historical Bibliography for Texas Public Schools.* San Marcos, Tex.: Bilingual-Bicultural Education Program, 1974.

Wright, Robert E. "Local Church Emergence and Mission Decline: The Historiography of the Catholic Church in the Southwest During the Spanish and Mexican Periods." *U.S. Catholic Historian* 9 (Winter/Spring 1990): 27–48.

Zinn, Maxine Baca. "Mexican Heritage Women: A Bibliographic Essay." *Sage Race Relations Abstracts* 9 (August 1984): 1–12.

Part II: Historical Sections

3. A PROVINCE OF NEW SPAIN, 1716–1821

The Hispanic presence became permanent in Texas in 1716 when Nacogdoches was founded (followed quickly by San Antonio and La Bahía). The focus of this chapter is not on Spain in Texas, but rather on ordinary people, most of whom were *mestizos*, that is of Spanish-Indian parentage. Those who were native born, or ones who were born elsewhere but stayed in Texas for a prolonged period, are also Tejanos. Under these assumptions, Álvar Nuñez Cabeza de Vaca (the first European to set foot on Texas soil) would not be considered a Tejano but the Canary Islanders who came to Texas as permanent settlers would be. Martín Perfectos de Cós (the commander of Mexico's military forces in Texas in 1835) would not be a Tejano, but Ignazio Zaragosa (the hero of the Battle of Puebla on May 5, 1862) would be labeled as such, as he was born in Goliad. The early *pobladores* (settlers) were the first to import and perpetuate the Spanish language, Spanish/Indian customs and legends, and give Texas its Spanish/Mexican flavor. Around 1800, these *pobladores* in Texas numbered about 4,000.

Photograph of historical marker on the founding of Laredo, Texas, by Tomás Sánchez.
The Institute of Texan Cultures at UTSA, No. 72-797

Abernethy, Francis Edward. "María de Agreda: The Lady in Blue." In *Legendary Ladies of Texas*, edited by Francis Edward Abernethy, 9–14. Second edition. Denton: University of North Texas Press, 1994.

________. "The Y'Barbo Legend in Early Spanish Settlement." *East Texas Historical Journal* 25.1 (Fall 1987): 30–43.

Acosta, Teresa Palomo. "María Gertrudis Pérez Cassiano." In *The New Handbook of Texas*, edited by Ron Tyler, Douglas E. Barnett, Roy R. Barkley, Penelope C. Anderson, and Mark F. Odintz, vol. 1, 1016. Austin: Texas State Historical Association, 1996.

Adams, David B. "Borderlands Communities in Conflict: Saltillo, San Esteban, and the Struggle for Municipal Autonomy, 1591–1838." *Locus: Regional and Local History of the Americas* 6 (Fall 1993): 39–51.

Allen, Henry E. "The Parrilla Expedition to the Red River in 1759." *Southwestern Historical Quarterly* 43 (July 1939): 53–71.

Allen, Winnie. "The History of Nacogdoches, 1691–1830." Master's thesis, University of Texas, Austin, 1925.

Almaráz, Félix D. Jr. *Crossroad of Empire: The Church and State on the Rio Grande Frontier of Coahuila and Texas, 1700–1821*. San Antonio: University of Texas at San Antonio, 1980.

________. *Empty Echos in a Howling Wind: Myths and Realities in the Tejano Community, from Cabeza de Vaca to Santa Anna*. El Paso: Texas Western Press, 1986.

________. *Governor Antonio Martínez and Mexican Independence in Texas: An Orderly Transition*. San Antonio: Bexar County Historical Commission, 1979.

________. *The San Antonio Missions and Their System of Land Tenure*. Austin: University of Texas Press, 1989.

________. *Tragic Cavalier: Governor Manuel Salcedo of Texas, 1803–1813.* Austin: University of Texas Press, 1971.

________. "Alonso De León in South Texas: An Early Chapter in Spanish-French Colonial Rivalry." *South Texas Studies* 8 (1997): 1–17.

________. "Franciscan Evangelization in Spanish Frontier Texas: Apex of Social Contact, Conflict, and Confluence, 1751–1761." *Colonial Latin American Historical Review* 2 (Summer 1993): 253–287.

________. "Franciscan Missions Along the Coahuila-Texas Corridor: The Formative Years, 1700–1720." *Catholic Social Science Review* 1 (1996): 137–145.

________. "Governor Manuel de Salcedo of Hispanic, Texas, 1808–1813." *Texana* 6 (1968): 12–31.

________. "Harmony, Discord, and Compromise in Spanish Colonial Texas: The Rio San Antonio Experience, 1691–1741." *New Mexico Historical Review* 67 (October 1992): 329–356.

________."Hispanic Imprints on the Texas Landscape." In *Hispanic Texas: A Historical Guide*, edited by Helen Simons and Cathryn A. Hoyt, 3–12. Austin: University of Texas Press, 1992.

________. "Independence: The Spanish Borderlands." In *Encyclopedia of North American Colonies*, edited by Jacob Ernest Cooke, 146–148. New York: Charles Scribner's Sons, 1993.

________. "The Legacy of Columbus: Spanish Mission Policy in Texas." *Journal of Texas Catholic History and Culture* 3 (1992): 17–36.

________. "Misiones Franciscanas de Nuevo México y El Paso del Norte a Través del Camino Real." In *El Camino Real de Tierra Adentro: Historia y Cultura*, 223–229. Chihuahua: Instituto Nacional de Antropología e Historia, 1997.

________. "The Rio Grande Missions: Precursors of San Antonio's Hispanic Franciscan Spiritual-Temporal Centers—The First Half Century." In *Contemporary Perspectives of the Old Spanish Missions of San Antonio*, edited by Felipe Ortego y Gasca, 49–80. San Antonio: Institute for Intercultural Studies and Research, Our Lady of the Lake University, 1979.

________. "San Antonio's Old Franciscan Missions: Material Decline and Secular Avarice in the Transition from Hispanic to Mexican Control." *The Americas* 44 (July 1987): 1–22.

________. "Social Interactions Between Civil, Military, and Mission Communities in Spanish Colonial Texas During the Height of the Bourbon Reforms, 1763–1772." *Revista Complutense de Historia de América* 21 (1995): 11–28.

________. "Spain's Cultural Legacy in Texas." In *The Texas Heritage*, edited by Ben Procter and Archie P. McDonald, 5–17. Arlington Heights, Ill.: Forum Press, 1980.

________."Spain's Heritage in South Texas: Celebrating the Past, Charting the Future." *Journal of South Texas* 16 (Spring 2003): 1–11.

________. "Texas Governor Manuel Salcedo and the Court-Martial of Padre Miguel Hidalgo, 1810–1811." *Southwestern Historical Quarterly* 99 (April 1996): 435–464.

________. "An Uninviting Wilderness: The Plains of West Texas, 1521–1821." *Great Plains Quarterly* 12 (Summer 1992): 169–180. Reprinted as "An Uninviting Land: El Llano Estacado, 1534–1821," in *Spain and the Plains: Myths and Realities of Spanish Exploration and Settlement on the Great Plains*, edited by Ralph H. Vigil, Frances W. Kaye, and John R. Wunder, 70–85. Niwot, Colo.: University Press of Colorado, 1994.

________. "The Warp and the Weft: An Overview of the Social Fabric of Mexican Texas." *East Texas Historical Journal* 27.2 (1989): 13–22.

Alonzo, Armando. *Tejano Legacy: Rancheros and Settlers in South Texas, 1734–1900.* Albuquerque: University of New Mexico Press, 1998.

________. "A Brief History of Hispanic Settlement and Ranching in South Texas, 1730–1850." *South Texas Studies* 11 (2000): 139–152.

Applegate, Howard G., and C. Wayne Hanselka. *La Junta de los Ríos del Norte y Conchos*. El Paso: Texas Western Press, 1974.

Arneson, Edwin P. "Early Irrigation in Texas." *Southwestern Historical Quarterly* 25 (October 1921): 121–130.

Ashford, Gerald. *Spanish Texas: Yesterday and Today.* Austin: Pemberton Press, 1971.

Austin, Mattie Alice (Hatcher). "The Municipal Government of San Fernando de Béxar, 1730–1800." *Quarterly of the Texas State Historical Association* 8 (1905): 277–352.

Baade, Hans W. "The Form of Marriage in Spanish North America." *Cornell Law Review* 61 (November 1975): 1–89.

Bannon, John Francis. *The Spanish Borderlands Frontier, 1513–1821*. New York: Holt, Rinehart, and Winston, 1970.

________. *The Spanish Conquistadores: Men or Devils?* New York: Holt, Rinehart and Winston, 1960.

________. "The Mission as a Frontier Institution: Sixty Years of Interest and Research." *Western Historical Quarterly* 10 (July 1979): 303–322.

Barcarisse, Charles A. "The Union of Coahuila and Texas." *Southwestern Historical Quarterly* 61 (January 1958): 341–349.

Barker, Eugene C., ed. "Minutes of the Ayuntamiento of San Felipe de Austin, 1828–1832." *Southwestern Historical Quarterly* 21 (January 1918): 299–326.

________. "Minutes of the Ayuntamiento of San Felipe de Austin, 1828–1832, II." *Southwestern Historical Quarterly* 21 (April 1918): 395–423.

Baquera, Richard. "El Paso del Norte: Regional Election Center, 1813–1821." *Password* 36 (Fall 1991): 107–116.

Benson, Nettie Lee. "Bishop Marin de Porras and Texas." *Southwestern Historical Quarterly* 51 (July 1947): 16–40.

________. "The Plan of Casa Mata." *Hispanic American Historical Review* 25 (February 1945): 45–56.

________. "Texas Failure to Send a Deputy to the Spanish Cortes, 1810–1812." *Southwestern Historical Quarterly* 64 (July 1960): 14–35.

________, ed. *Mexico and the Spanish Cortes, 1810–1822*. Austin: University of Texas Press, 1966.

________, ed. "A Governor's Report on Texas in 1809." *Southwestern Historical Quarterly* 71 (April 1968): 603–616.

Birge, Mamie. "The Casas Revolution, 1811: The First Period of Independence in Texas." Master's thesis, University of Texas, Austin, 1911.

Blake, Robert Bruce. "Antonio Gil Ibarvo." In *The New Handbook of Texas*, edited by Ron Tyler, Douglas E. Barnett, Roy R. Barkley, Penelope C. Anderson, and Mark F. Odintz, vol. 3, 812. Austin: Texas State Historical Association, 1996.

________. "Antonio Leal." In *The New Handbook of Texas*, edited by Ron Tyler, Douglas E. Barnett, Roy R. Barkley, Penelope C. Anderson, and Mark F. Odintz, vol. 4, 133. Austin: Texas State Historical Association, 1996.

________. "Locations of the Early Spanish Missions and Presidios in Nacogdoches County." *Southwestern Historical Quarterly* 41 (January 1938): 212–224.

Blyth, Lance C. "Fugitives from Servitude: American Deserters and Runaway Slaves in Spanish Nacogdoches, 1803–1808." *East Texas Historical Journal* 38.2 (2000): 3–14.

Bolton, Herbert E. *Coronado: Knight of Pueblos and Plains*. Albuquerque: University of New Mexico Press, 1949.

________. *Texas in the Middle Eighteenth Century: Studies in Spanish Colonial History and Administration*. Berkeley: University of California Press, 1915.

________. "The Beginnings of Mission Nuestra Señora del Refugio." *Southwestern Historical Quarterly* 19 (April 1916): 400–404.

________. "The Founding of Mission Rosario: A Chapter in the History of the Gulf Coast." *Quarterly of the Texas State Historical Association* 10 (October 1906): 113–139.

________. "The Founding of Missions on the San Gabriel River, 1748–1749." *Southwestern Historical Quarterly* 17 (April 1914): 323–378.

________. "The Jumano Indians in Texas, 1650–1771." *Quarterly of the Texas State Historical Association* 15 (July 1912): 66–84.

________. "The Native Tribes about the East Texas Missions." *Quarterly of the Texas State Historical Association* 11 (April 1908): 249–276.

________. "The Spanish Abandonment and Re-Occupation of East Texas, 1773–1779." *Quarterly of the Texas State Historical Association* 9 (October 1905): 67–137.

________. "Spanish Activities on the Lower Trinity River, 1746–1771." *Southwestern Historical Quarterly* 16 (April 1913): 339–377.

________. "The Spanish Occupation of Texas, 1519–1690." *Southwestern Historical Quarterly* 16 (July 1912): 1–26.

Brown, Elise D. "The History of Spanish Settlements at Orcoquisac, 1746–1772." Master's thesis, University of Texas, Austin, 1925.

Buck, Samuel M. *Yanaguana's Successors; The Story of the Canary Islanders' Immigration into Texas in the Eighteenth Century*. San Antonio: The Naylor Company, 1949.

Buerkle, Ruth Cowie. "The Continuing Military Presence." In *San Antonio in the Eighteenth Century*, edited by Esther MacMillan, 47–72. San Antonio: San Antonio Bicentennial Heritage Committee, 1976.

Burckhardt, Marc. "Doña María: Rancher of Las Cabras." *Texas Highways* 49 (August 2002): 26–29.

Butler, Robert. "The Cabildo and the Intendant." Master's thesis, University of Texas, Austin, 1967.

Caldwell, Laura. "Casas Revolt." In *The New Handbook of Texas*, edited by Ron Tyler, Douglas E. Barnett, Roy R. Barkley, Penelope C. Anderson, and Mark F. Odintz, vol. 1, 1009–1010. Austin: Texas State Historical Association, 1996.

Campbell, T. N. "Origins of Pottery Types from the Coastal Bend Region of Texas." *Bulletin of the Texas Archeological Society* 32 (1962): 331–336.

Castañeda, Carlos E. *Our Catholic Heritage in Texas, 1519–1936: The Finding of Texas, 1519–1693*. Austin: Von Boeckmann-Jones, 1936.

________. *Our Catholic Heritage in Texas, 1519–1936: The Winning of Texas, 1693–1731*. Austin: Von Boeckmann-Jones, 1936.

________. *Our Catholic Heritage in Texas, 1519–1936: The Missions at Work, 1731–1761*. Austin: Von Boeckmann-Jones, 1938.

________. *Our Catholic Heritage in Texas, 1519–1936: The Passing of the Missions, 1762–1782*. Austin: Von Boeckmann-Jones, 1939.

________. *Our Catholic Heritage in Texas, 1519–1936: The End of the Spanish Regime, 1780–1810*. Austin: Von Boeckmann-Jones, 1942.

________. *A Report on the Spanish Archives in San Antonio, Texas*. San Antonio: Artes Gráficas and theYanaguana Society, 1937.

________. "Morfi's History of Texas." Ph.D. dissertation, University of Texas, Austin, 1935.

________. "A Chapter in Frontier History." *Southwest Review* 28 (Autumn 1942): 31–52.

________. "The Coming of the Augustinians to the New World." *Records of the American Catholic Historical Society of Philadelphia* 60 (December 1949): 189–196.

________. "Communications between Santa Fe and San Antonio in the Eighteenth Century." *Texas Geographic Magazine* 5 (Spring 1941): 17–38.

________. "The Corregidor in Spanish Colonial Administration." *Hispanic American Historical Review* 9 (November 1929): 446–470.

________. "Customs and Legends of Texas Indians." *Mid-America* 3 (July 1931): 48–56.

________. "Documents for the History of the Gulf Coast Region from the Sabine to the Rio Grande: Joachim de Orabia y Bazterra and the Exploration of the Gulf Coast." *Journal of South Texas* 12 (1999): 1–22.

________. "Don Carlos de Sigúenza y Góngora." *Catholic Historical Review* 16 (April 1930): 86–89.

________. "The Early Missionary Movement in Texas." *Missionary* 35 (December 1921): 360–361.

________. "The First American Play." *Catholic World* 134 (January 1932): 429–437.

________. "The First Chartered Bank West of the Mississippi: Banco Nacional de Texas." *Business History Review* 25 (December 1951): 242–256.

________. "First European Settlement on the Rio Grande." *Texas Geographic* 9 (August 1945): 28–31.

________. "The First Pan-American Congress." *North American Review* 223 (June 1926): 248–255.

________. "Fr. Antonio Margil de Jesús." *Missionary* 38 (1924): 163–164, 197–199.

________. "Fray Juan de Zumárraga and Indian Policy in New Spain." *The Americas* 5 (1949): 296–310.

________. "God's Work in the Southwest." *Extension* 48 (November 1953): 18–19, 56.

________. "José de Escandon—Empire Builder." *Journal of South Texas* 13 (2000): 5–18.

________. "Latin America's First Great Educator." *Current History* 22 (May 1925): 223–225.

________. "Modern Language Instruction in American Colleges, 1779–1800." *Catholic Educational Review* 23 (January 1925): 3–9, 92–106.

________. "The Oldest University in America." *Pan-American Magazine* 43 (July 1930): 54–57.

________. "Pioneers in Sackcloth." *Catholic Historical Review* 25 (October 1939): 309–326.

________. "Pioneers of the Church in Texas." In *Diamond Jubilee, 1874–1949: Archdiocese of San Antonio*, edited by M. J. Gilbert, 1–16. San Antonio: Schneider Printing Company, 1949.

________. "Relations of General Scott with Santa Anna." *Hispanic American Historical Review* 29 (1949): 455–473.

________. "Silent Years in Texas History." *Southwestern Historical Quarterly* 38 (October 1934): 122–134.

________. "Social Developments and Movements in Latin America." In *Church and Society: Catholic Social and Political Thought and Movements, 1789–1950*, edited by Joseph N. Moody, 733–773. New York: Arts, Inc., 1953.

________. "Some of Our Earliest Americans Await the Magic Touch." *Texas Outlook* 37 (January 1937): 22–23.

________. "The Sons of St. Francis in Texas." *The Americas* 1 (January 1945): 289–302.

________. "Sources for Spanish American Church History." *Catholic Literary World* 10 (December 1938): 99–102.

________. "Spanish Medieval Institutions in Overseas Administration: The Prevalence of Medieval Concepts." *The Americas* 15 (October 1954): 115–129.

________. "Why I Chose History." *The Americas* 8 (April 1952): 475–492.

________. "The Woman in Blue." *Age of Mary* (January-February 1958): 22–29.

Caughey, John W. "The Spanish Southwest: An Example of Subconscious Regionalism." In *Regionalism in America*, edited by Merrill Jensen, 173–186. Madison: University of Wisconsin Press, 1952.

Celíz, Francisco. *Diary of the Alarcón Expedition into Texas, 1718–1719*, translated by Fritz Leo Hoffman. Los Angeles: Quivira Society, 1935.

Chabot, Frederick C. *San Antonio and Its Beginnings*. San Antonio: The Naylor Company, 1931.

________. *San Fernando: The Villa, Capital of the Province of Texas*. San Antonio: The Naylor Company, 1930.

________. *With the Makers of San Antonio*. San Antonio: Artes Gráficas, 1937.

________, ed. *Texas in 1811: The Las Casas and Sambrano Revolutions*. San Antonio: Yanaguana Society, 1941.

Chabrán, Richard, and Rafael Chabrán, eds. "Alonza Álvarez de Piñeda." In *The Latino Encyclopedia*, edited by Richard Chabrán and Rafael Chabrán, vol. 1, 53. New York: Marshall Cavendish, 1996.

________. "Álvar Nuñez Cabeza de Vaca." In *The Latino Encyclopedia*, edited by Richard Chabrán and Rafael Chabrán, vol. 1, 221. New York: Marshall Cavendish, 1996.

Chapa, Juan Bautista. *Texas and Northeastern Mexico, 1630–1690*, edited by William C. Foster. Austin: University of Texas Press, 1997.

Chipman, Donald E. *Spanish Texas, 1519–1821*. Austin: University of Texas Press, 1992.

________. "Alonso Álvarez de Pineda and the Río de las Palmas: Scholars and the Mislocation of a River." *Southwestern Historical Quarterly* 98 (January 1955): 369–385.

________. "'Alonso de León': Pathfinder in East Texas, 1686–1690." *East Texas Historical Journal* 33 (Spring 1995): 3–17.

________. "José González." In *The New Handbook of Texas*, edited by Ron Tyler, Douglas E. Barnett, Roy R. Barkley, Penelope C. Anderson, and Mark F. Odintz, vol. 3, 233–234. Austin: Texas State Historical Association, 1996.

________. "Juan José de Ganzabal." In *The New Handbook of Texas*, edited by Ron Tyler, Douglas E. Barnett, Roy R. Barkley, Penelope C. Anderson, and Mark F. Odintz, vol. 3, 81. Austin: Texas State Historical Association, 1996.

________. "In Search of Cabeza de Vaca's Route across Texas: An Historiographical Survey." *Southwestern Historical Quarterly* 91 (October 1987): 127–148.

________. "Spanish Texas." In *Texas Through Time: Evolving Interpretations*, edited by Walter L. Buenger and Robert A. Calvert, 102–133. College Station: Texas A&M University Press, 1991.

________. "The Status of Biography in the Historiography of New Spain." *The Americas* 27 (January 1971): 327–339.

Chipman, Donald E., and Harriett Denise Joseph. "José Bernardo Gutiérrez de Lara/Joaquin de Arredondo." In *Notable Men and Women of Spanish Texas*, edited by Donald E. Chipman and Harriett Denise Joseph, 226–249. Austin: University of Texas Press, 1999.

________, eds. *Notable Men and Women of Spanish Texas*. Austin: University of Texas Press, 1999.

Clark, Robert Carlton. "The Beginnings of Texas." *Quarterly of the Texas State Historical Association* 5 (January 1902): 189–201.

________. "Lois Juchereau de Saint-Denis and the Reestablishment of the Tejas Missions." *Quarterly of the Texas State Historical Association* 6 (July 1902): 1–26.

Clayton, Lawrence. "Some South Texas Contributions to Ranching." *South Texas Studies* 7 (1996): 1–17.

Coker, William S., ed. "Research in the Spanish Borderlands." *Latin American Historical Review* 7 (Summer 1972): 1–94.

Collins, Gladys. "Spanish West Texas, 1735–1769." *West Texas Historical Association Yearbook* 7 (1931): 95–114.

Collins, Noelle C. "A Spanish Colonial Christmas." *American Heritage* 48 (December 1997): 24–26.

Conger, Roger N. "The Tomás de la Vega Eleven League Grant on the Brazos." *Southwestern Historical Quarterly* 61 (January 1958): 370–382.

Connally, Ernest Allen. "The Ecclesiastical and Military Architecture of the Spanish Province of Texas." Ph.D. dissertation, Harvard University, 1955.

Conroy, William B. "The Llano Estacado in 1541: Spanish Perception of a Distinctive Physical Setting." In *The Spanish Borderlands—A First Reader*, edited by Oakah L. Jones, 24–32. Los Angeles: Lorrin L. Morrison, 1974.

Contreras, Roberto. "José Bernardo Gutiérrez de Lara: The Forgotten Hero." Master's thesis, Pan American University, 1975.

Cook, Gertrude, and Esther MacMillan. "San Antonio in 1776." In *San Antonio in the Eighteenth Century*, edited by Esther MacMillan, 129–135. San Antonio: San Antonio Bicentennial Heritage Committee, 1976.

Cox, Isaac J. "The Early Settlers of San Fernando." *Quarterly of the Texas State Historical Association* 5 (October 1901): 142–160.

________. "Educational Efforts in San Fernando de Béxar." *Quarterly of the Texas State Historical Association* 6 (July 1902): 27–63.

________. "The Founding of the First Texas Municipality." *Quarterly of the Texas State Historical Association* 2 (January 1899): 217–226.

Crawford, Polly Pearl. "The Beginning of Spanish Settlement in the Lower Rio Grande Valley." Master's thesis, University of Texas, Austin, 1925.

Cruz, Gilberto R. *Let There Be Towns: Spanish Municipal Origins in the American Southwest, 1610–1810*. College Station: Texas A&M University Press, 1988.

________. "Spanish Town Patterns in the Borderlands: Municipal Origins in Texas and the Southwest, 1610–1810." Ph.D. dissertation, St. Louis University, 1974.

________. "The Cabildo in Texas under the Spanish Bourbons: The Origin and Development of Municipal Life at the Villa de San Fernando, San Antonio, Texas, 1731–1800." Master's thesis, St. Mary's University, 1970.

________. "City Ordinances for the Municipal Government of San Antonio of Béjar." *Texana* 7 (Summer 1969): 95–116.

________. "Habemus Regem: San Antonio Festivities on the Occasion of the Accession of Ferdinand VI to the Spanish Crown, 1747." In *From the Mississippi to the Pacific: Essays in Honor of John Francis Bannon, S.J.*, edited by Russell M. Magnaghi, 32–42. Marquette, Mich.: Northern Michigan University Press, 1982.

Cummins, Light Townsend. "Texas under Spain and Mexico." In *A Guide to the History of Texas*, edited by Light Townsend Cummins and Alvin R. Bailey Jr., 3–16. New York: Greenwood Press, 1988.

Dabbs, J. Autrey, ed. "The Texas Missions of 1785." *Mid-America* 22 (January 1940): 38–58.

Dabney, Lancaster E. "Louis Aurey: The First Governor of Texas under the Mexican Republic." *Southwestern Historical Quarterly* 42 (October 1938): 108–116.

Daniel, James M. "The Advance of the Spanish Frontier and the Despoblado." Ph.D. dissertation, University of Texas, Austin, 1955.

________. "La Junta de los Rios and the Despoblado, 1680–1760." Master's thesis, University of Texas, Austin, 1948.

________. "The Spanish Frontier in West Texas and Northern Mexico." *Southwestern Historical Quarterly* 71 (1968): 481–495.

Davis, William Robert. "The Spanish Borderlands of Texas and Chihuahua." *Texana* 9 (1971): 142–155.

de Elguézabal, Juan Bautista. "A Description of Texas in 1803," edited by Odie B. Faulk. *Southwestern Historical Quarterly* 66 (April 1963): 513–515.

de la Teja, Jesús F. *San Antonio de Béxar: A Community on New Spain's Northern Frontier*. Albuquerque: University of New Mexico Press, 1995.

________. "Land and Society in Eighteenth Century San Antonio de Béxar: A Community on New Spain's Northern Frontier." Ph.D. dissertation, University of Texas at Austin, 1988.

________. "Discovering the Tejano Community in 'Early' Texas." *Journal of the Early Republic* 18 (Spring 1988): 73–98, 135–139. Reprinted in *En Aquel Entonces: Readings in Mexican-American History*, edited by Manuel G. Gonzales and Cynthia M. Gonzales, 38–44. Bloomington: Indiana University Press, 2000.

________. "El Camino Real: Lifeline of Colonial Texas." *Gulf Coast Historical Review* 8 (Fall 1992): 64–72.

________. "Fernando Veramendi." In *The New Handbook of Texas*, edited by Ron Tyler, Douglas E. Barnett, Roy R. Barkley, Penelope C. Anderson, and Mark F. Odintz, vol. 6, 722. Austin: Texas State Historical Association, 1996.

________. "'A Fine Country with Broad Plains—the Most Beautiful in New Spain': Colonial Views of Land and Nature." In *On the Border: An Environmental History of San Antonio*, edited by Char Miller, 41–55. Pittsburgh: University of Pittsburgh Press, 2001.

________. "Forgotten Founders: The Military Settlers of Eighteenth-Century San Antonio de Béxar." In *Tejano Origins in Eighteenth-Century San Antonio*, edited by Gerald E. Poyo and Gilberto M. Hinojosa, 27–38. Austin: University of Texas Press, 1991.

________. "Indians, Soldiers, and Canary Islanders: The Making of a Texas Frontier Community." *Locus* 3 (Fall 1990): 81–96.

________. "'Only Fit for Raising Stock': Spanish and Mexican Land and Water Rights in the Tamaulipan Cession." In *Fluid Arguments: Five Centuries of Western Water Conflict*, edited by Char Miller, 3–27. Tucson: University of Arizona Press, 2001.

________. "Rebellion on the Frontier." In *Tejano Journey, 1770–1850,* edited by Gerald E. Poyo, 15–30. Austin: University of Texas Press, 1996.

________. "Sobrevivencia económica en la frontera de Texas: los ranchos ganaderos del siglo *xviii* en San Antonio de Béxar." *Historia Mexicana* 42 (1993): 837–865.

________. "Spanish Colonial Texas." In *New Views of Borderlands History*, edited by Robert H. Jackson, 107–130. Albuquerque: University of New Mexico Press, 1998.

________. "Spanish North America." In *Grolier Multimedia Encyclopedia*. Danbury, Conn.: Grolier Electronic Publishing, 2001.

________. "The Structure of Society: The Spanish Borderlands." In *Encyclopedia of the North American Colonies*, edited by Jacob E. Cooke, 379–380. New York: Charles Scribner's Sons, 1993.

De León, Arnoldo. "The Mixed-Bloods and the Texas Missions: Un-Sung Heroes of the Spanish Borderlands." In *Contemporary Perspectives of the Old Spanish Missions of San Antonio*, edited by Philip D. Ortego, 23–32. San Antonio: Our Lady of the Lake University, 1979.

Devereaux, Linda E. "The Magee-Gutiérrez Expedition." *Texana* 11 (1973): 52–63.

De Zavala, Adina. *History and Legends of the Alamo and Other Missions in and Around San Antonio*. San Antonio: privately printed, 1917.

Dixon, Helen. "The Middle Years of the Administration of Juan María Barón de Ripperdá, Governor of Texas, 1773–1775." Master's thesis, University of Texas, Austin, 1934.

Dobkins, Betty E. *The Spanish Element in Texas Water Law*. Austin: University of Texas Press, 1959.

Donahue, William H. "The Missionary Activities of Fray Antonio de Jesús in Texas, 1716–1727." *The Americas* 14 (July 1959): 45–55.

Downs, Fane. "Governor Antonio Martínez and the Defense of Texas from Foreign Invasion, 1817–1822." *Texas Military History* 7 (Spring 1968): 27–43.

Dunn, William E. "The Apache Mission on the San Sabá River: Its Founding and Failure." *Southwestern Historical Quarterly* 17 (April 1914): 379–414.

________. "Apache Relations in Texas, 1718–1750." *Quarterly of the Texas State Historical Association* 14 (January 1911): 198–274.

________."The Founding of Nuestra Señora del Refugio, the Last Spanish Mission in Texas." *Southwestern Historical Quarterly* 25 (January 1922): 174–184.

Duty, Tony E. "The Coronado Expedition (1540–1542)." *Texana* 8 (1970): 121–139.

Eckhart, George B. "Spanish Missions of Texas, 1680–1800: An Outline of Spanish Mission History in Texas." *Kiva* 32 (February 1937).

Epperson, Jean L. *Lost Spanish Towns: Atacosito and Trinidad de Salcido*. Woodville, Tex.: Dogwood Press, 1996.

Evans, Kenneth. "The Administration of Manuel de Sandoval, Governor of Texas, 1734–1736." Master's thesis, University of Texas, Austin, 1928.

Faulk, Odie B. *The Last Years of Spanish Texas, 1778–1821*. The Hague: Mouton, 1964.

________. *A Successful Failure: The Saga of Texas, 1519–1810*. Austin: Steck-Vaughn, 1965.

________. "The Presidio: Fortress or Farce?" In *New Spain's Far Northern Frontier: Essays on Spain in the American West, 1540–1821,* edited by David J. Weber, 67–76. Albuquerque: University of New Mexico Press, 1979.

________. "Ranching in Spanish Texas." *Hispanic American Historical Review* 45 (May 1965): 257–266.

________. "Texas During the Administration of Governor Domingo Cabello y Robles, 1778–1786." Master's thesis, Texas Technological College, 1960.

________, ed. "Description of Texas in 1803." *Southwestern Historical Quarterly* 66 (April 1963): 513–515.

Fish, Jean Y. *José Vásquez Borrego and La Hacienda de Nuestra Señora de Dolores*. Zapata, Tex.: Zapata County Historical Society, 1991.

Foik, Paul J. "Captain Don Domingo Ramón's Diary of His Expedition into Texas in 1716." *Preliminary Studies of the Texas Catholic Historical Society* 2 (1933): 3–23.

________. "Fray Juan Padilla." *Mid-America* 13.2 (1930): 132–140.

Foster, William C. *Spanish Expeditions into Texas, 1689–1768*. Austin: University of Texas Press, 1995.

Foster, William C., and Jack Johnson. "The 1663 Expedition of Gregorio de Salinas Varona to Sustain the Missionaries among the Texas . . . ." *Southwestern Historical Quarterly* 97 (October 1993): 264–311.

Fox, Daniel E. "The Identification of a Lithic Component from Spanish Colonial Missions in San Antonio, Texas." Master's thesis, Texas Tech University, 1977.

García, Clotilde P. *Captain Alonso Álvarez de Pineda and the Exploration of the Texas Coast and the Gulf of Mexico*. Austin: San Felipe Press, 1982.

________. *Captain Blás María de la Garza Falcón: Colonizer of South Texas*. Austin: San Felipe Press, 1984.

________. *Captain Enrique Villareal and Rincón del Oso Land Grant*. Corpus Christi, Tex.: C. P. García, 1986.

________. "Blas María de la Garza Falcón." In *The New Handbook of Texas*, edited by Ron Tyler, Douglas E. Barnett, Roy R. Barkley, Penelope C. Anderson, and Mark F. Odintz, vol. 3, 110. Austin: Texas State Historical Association, 1996.

________. "José Antonio de la Garza Falcón." In *The New Handbook of Texas*, edited by Ron Tyler, Douglas E. Barnett, Roy R. Barkley, Penelope C. Anderson, and Mark F. Odintz, vol. 3, 110–111. Austin: Texas State Historical Association, 1996.

________. "Juan José de la Garza Montemayor." In *The New Handbook of Texas*, edited by Ron Tyler, Douglas E. Barnett, Roy R. Barkley, Penelope C. Anderson, and Mark F. Odintz, vol. 3, 112. Austin: Texas State Historical Association, 1996.

________. "María Gertrudis de la Garza Falcón." In *The New Handbook of Texas*, edited by Ron Tyler, Douglas E. Barnett, Roy R. Barkley, Penelope C. Anderson, and Mark F. Odintz, vol. 3, 111. Austin: Texas State Historical Association, 1996.

________. "Miguel de la Garza Falcón." In *The New Handbook of Texas*, edited by Ron Tyler, Douglas E. Barnett, Roy R. Barkley, Penelope C. Anderson, and Mark F. Odintz, vol. 3, 111–112. Austin: Texas State Historical Association, 1996.

________. "Rosa María Hinojosa de Balli." In *The New Handbook of Texas*, edited by Ron Tyler, Douglas E. Barnett, Roy R. Barkley, Penelope C. Anderson, and Mark F. Odintz, vol. 3, 629. Austin: Texas State Historical Association, 1996.

Garrett, Julia Kathryn. *Green Flag Over Texas: A Story of the Last Years of Spain in Texas*. Austin: Córdova Press, 1939.

________. "The War of Independence in Texas, 1811–1813." Ph.D. dissertation, University of California, Berkeley, 1935.

________. "The First Constitution of Texas, April 17, 1813." *Southestern Historical Quarterly* 40 (April 1937): 290–308.

________. "The First Newspaper of Texas: *Gaceta de Texas*." *Southwestern Historical Quarterly* 40 (January 1937): 200–215.

________. "*Gaceta de Texas*: Translation of the First Number." *Southwestern Historical Quarterly* 42 (July 1938): 21–27.

Garza, Juanita Elizondo. "Indian and Spanish-Mexican Cultural Influences in the Lower Rio Grande Valley." Master's thesis, Pan American University, 1984.

Gerald, Rex E. "BRAVO 1795: An Inventory of the Missions of Senecli, Ysleta, and Socorro by Fray José Bravo in the Year 1795." Translated by Rex E. Gerald and Olympia Caudillo. *Password* 33 (1988): 19–40.

________. "An Introduction to the Missions of the Paso del Norte Area." *Password* 20 (Summer 1975): 47–58.

Gerhard, Peter. "Texas." In *The North Frontier of New Spain*, by Peter Gerhard, 335–343. Princeton: Princeton University Press, 1982.

Gilbert, Minnie. "Mexico's First Ambassador." In *Roots by the River*, by Valley By-Liners, 31–38. Mission, Tex.: Border Kingdom Press, 1978.

________."Texas' First Cattle Queen." In *Roots by the River*, by Valley By-Liners, 15–25. Mission, Tex.: Border Kingdom Press, 1978.

________. "The Valley's Earliest Pioneer." In *Roots by the River*, by Valley By-Liners, 9–14. Mission, Tex.: Border Kingdom Press, 1978.

Gilmore, Kathleen. "The Indians of Rosario Mission." In *The Scope of Historical Archeology: Essays in Honor of John L. Cotter*, edited by David Orr and Daniel Crozier, 163–191. Philadelphia: University of Pennsylvania Press, 1984.

________. "Spanish Colonial Settlement in Texas." In *Texas Archeology: Essays Honoring R. King Harris*, edited by Kurt D. House, 132–145. Dallas: Southern Methodist University Press, 1978.

Guedea, Virginia. "Autonomía e independencia en la provincia de Texas: La junta de gobierno de San Antonio de Béjar, 1813." In *La independencia de México y el proceso autonomista novohispano, 1808–1824*, edited by Virginia Guedea, 135–183. México: Universidad Nacional Autónoma de México, 2001.

________. "The Process of Mexican Independence." *American Historical Review* 105 (February 2000): 116–130.

Guerra, Dora Elizondo. "Whose Water Is This Anyway, and Keep Your Plow Out of My Corn Field: Men, Women and Culture in Spanish Colonial Texas." *South Texas Studies* 11 (2000): 181–192.

Guerrero, Mario Salcedo. "Vicente Guerrero's Struggle for Mexican Independence, 1810–1821." Ph.D. dissertation, University of California, Santa Barbara, 1977.

"Gutiérrez de Lara, José Bernardo Maximilliano." In *The New Handbook of Texas*, edited by Ron Tyler, Douglas E. Barnett, Roy R. Barkley, Penelope C. Anderson, and Mark F. Odintz, vol. 3, 392–393. Austin: Texas State Historical Association, 1996.

Habig, Marion A. *The Alamo Chain of Missions: A History of San Antonio's Five Old Missions*. Chicago: Franciscan Herald Press, 1968.

________. *The Alamo Mission: San Antonio de Valero, 1718–1793*. Chicago: Franciscan Herald Press, 1977.

________. "Benito Fernández de Santa Ana." In *The New Handbook of Texas*, edited by Ron Tyler, Douglas E. Barnett, Roy R. Barkley, Penelope C. Anderson, and Mark F. Odintz, vol. 2, 984–985. Austin: Texas State Historical Association, 1996.

________. "Mission San José y San Miguel de Aguayo, 1720–1824." *Southwestern Historical Quarterly* 71 (April 1968): 496–516.

Hackett, Charles Wilson. "The Retreat of the Spaniards from New Mexico in 1680, and the Beginnings of El Paso." *Southwestern Historical Quarterly* 16 (October 1912): 137–168, (January 1913): 259–276.

Haggard, J. Villasaña. "The Counter-Revolution of Béxar, 1811." *Southwestern Historical Quarterly* 62 (October 1939): 222–235.

Harrison, James Christopher. "The Failure of Spain in East Texas: The Occupation and Abandonment of Nacogdoches, 1779–1821." Ph.D. dissertation, University of Nebraska, 1980.

Hatcher, Mattie Austin. *The Opening of Texas to Foreign Settlement, 1801–1821*. Austin: University of Texas Press, 1927.

________. "Conditions in Texas Affecting the Colonization Problem, 1795–1801." *Southwestern Historical Quarterly* 25 (October 1921): 81–97.

________, ed. "Texas in 1820." *Southwestern Historical Quarterly* 23 (July 1919): 47–68.

Henderson, Harry McCorry. "The Magee-Gutiérrez Expedition." *Southwestern Historical Quarterly* 55 (July 1951): 43–61.

Henderson, Mary Virginia. "Minor Empresario Contracts for the Colonizaton of Texas, 1825–1834." *Southwestern Historical Quarterly* 32 (July 1928): 1–28.

Hendricks, Rick. "The Church in El Paso del Norte in the Eighteenth Century." In *Seeds of Struggle/Harvest of Faith: The Papers of the Archdiocese of Santa Fe Catholic Cuarto Centennial Conference*, edited by Thomas J. Steele, Paul Rhetts, and Barbe Awalt, 101–118. Albuquerque: LPD Press, 1999.

________."Massacre in the Organ Mountains." *Password* 39 (Winter 1994): 169–177.

________. "A Muster of the Presidio of San Elizario." *Password* 39 (Fall 1994): 135–140.

________. "Santa María de las Caldas and the Hacienda de San Antonio: Diligencias Matrimoniales from the Lost Curacy, 1733-1739." *Nuestras Raices* 6 (Fall 1994): 115–125.

________. "Searching for Lost Padre: Eighteenth Century Mining Claims in the Organ Mountain and Greater El Paso del Norte Area." *Password* 46 (Summer 2001): 55–78.

________. "Tabardillo: The 1764 Typhus Epidemic in the El Paso del Norte Area." *Password* 38 (Summer 1993): 55–64.

Hendricks, Rick, and W. H. Timmons. *San Elizario: The Spanish Presidio to Texas County Seat*. El Paso: University of Texas at El Paso, 1998.

Henson, Margaret Swett. "'El Orcoquisac': 1756–1771: The Mission Nuestra Señora de la Luz del Orcoquisac, the Presidio San Agustin Ahumada, and the Rivalry Between the Spanish and the French for the Indian Trade in Southeastern Texas." *The Houston Review* 13 (1991): 115–126.

________. "Hispanic Texas, 1519–1836." In *Texas: A Sesquicentennial Celebration*, edited by Donald W. Whisenhunt, 33–57. Austin: Eakin Press, 1984.

Hester, Thomas Roy, and T. C. Hill Jr. "An Initial Study of a Prehistoric Ceramic Tradition in Southern Texas." *Plains Anthropologist* 16 (1971): 195–203.

________. "Mogollon Ceramics from Southern Texas." *The Artifact, El Paso Archeological Society* 7 (1969): 11–15.

Hill, Lawrence F. *José de Escandon and the Founding of Nuevo Santander: A Study in Spanish Colonization*. Columbus: Ohio State University Press, 1926.

Hinojosa, Gilberto M. *A Borderlands Town in Transition: Laredo, Texas, 1755–1870*. College Station: Texas A&M University Press, 1983.

________. "The Enduring Hispanic Faith Communities: Spanish and Texas Church Historiography." *Journal of Texas Catholic History and Culture* 1.1 (March 1990): 20–41.

________. "Friars and Indians: Towards a Perspective of Cultural Interaction in the San Antonio Mission." *U.S. Catholic Historian* 9 (Spring 1990): 203–234.

________. "The Religious-Indian Communities: The Goals of the Friars." In *Tejano Origins of Eighteenth-Century San Antonio*, edited by Gerald E. Poyo and Gilberto M. Hinojosa, 61–83. Austin: University of Texas Press, 1991.

________. "Settlers and Sojourners in the 'Chaparral': A Demographic Study of a Borderlands Town in Transition, Laredo, 1755–1870." Ph.D dissertation, University of Texas at Austin, 1979.

Hinojosa, Gilberto M., and Anne A. Fox. "Indians and Their Culture in San Fernando de Béxar." In *Tejano Origins in Eighteenth-Century San Antonio*, edited by Gerald E. Poyo and Gilberto M. Hinojosa, 105–120. Austin: University of Texas Press, 1991.

Hipp, Joe Wreford. *The Oldest Ranch in Texas: A Ranch on the Road to History*. Austin: Eakin Press, 2000.

Hoffman, Fritz Leo. "The First Three Years of the Administration of Juan María Barón de Ripperdá, Governor of Texas, 1770–1773." Master's thesis, University of Texas, Austin, 1930.

________. "Martín de Alarcón and the Founding of San Antonio, Texas." In *Essays in Mexican History: The Charles Wilson Hackett Memorial Volume*, edited by

Robert C. Cotner and Carlos E. Castañeda, 21–30. Austin: University of Texas Press, 1958.

Holmes, Jack D. L. "Interpretations and Trends in the Study of the Spanish Borderlands: The Old Southwest." *Southwestern Historical Quarterly* 74 (April 1971): 461–477.

Holmes, William H. "The Acequias of San Antonio." Master's thesis, St. Mary's University, 1962.

Hoyt, Cathryn A. "Riches, Religion, and Politics: Early Exploration in Texas." In *Hispanic Texas: A Historical Guide*, edited by Helen Simons and Cathryn A. Hoyt, 13–23. Austin: University of Texas Press, 1992.

Hughes, Anne E. *The Beginning of Spanish Settlement in the El Paso District*. Berkeley: University of California Press, 1914.

Hutchins, Wells A. "The Community Acequia: Its Origin and Development." *Southwestern Historical Quarterly* 31 (January 1928): 261–284.

Inglis, G. Douglas. "The Men of Cibola: New Investigations on the Francisco Vásquez de Coronado Expedition." *Panhandle Plains Historical Review* 55 (1982): 1–24.

Jackson, Jack. *Los Mesteños: Spanish Ranching in Texas, 1721–1821*. College Station: Texas A&M University Press, 1986.

________. "The Great Roundup of 1787." *Journal of South Texas* 13 (2000): 19–51.

________. "José Menchaca." In *The New Handbook of Texas*, edited by Ron Tyler, Douglas E. Barnett, Roy R. Barkley, Penelope C. Anderson, and Mark F. Odintz, vol. 4, 616–617. Austin: Texas State Historical Association, 1996.

________. "Juan Ignacio Pérez." In *The New Handbook of Texas*, edited by Ron Tyler, Douglas E. Barnett, Roy R. Barkley, Penelope C. Anderson, and Mark F. Odintz, vol. 5, 149–150. Austin: Texas State Historical Association, 1996.

________. "Juan José Flores." In *The New Handbook of Texas*, edited by Ron Tyler, Douglas E. Barnett, Roy R. Barkley, Penelope C. Anderson, and Mark F. Odintz, vol. 2, 1036. Austin: Texas State Historical Association, 1996.

________."Luis Antonio Menchaca." In *The New Handbook of Texas*, edited by Ron Tyler, Douglas E. Barnett, Roy R. Barkley, Penelope C. Anderson, and Mark F. Odintz, vol. 4, 617. Austin: Texas State Historical Association, 1996.

________. "Miguel Menchaca." In *The New Handbook of Texas*, edited by Ron Tyler, Douglas E. Barnett, Roy R. Barkley, Penelope C. Anderson, and Mark F. Odintz, vol. 4, 617–618, Austin: Texas State Historical Association, 1996.

________. "Simon de Arocha." In *The New Handbook of Texas*, edited by Ron Tyler, Douglas E. Barnett, Roy R. Barkley, Penelope C. Anderson, and Mark F. Odintz, vol.1, 253–254. Austin: Texas State Historical Association, 1996.

________. "Vicente Álvarez Travieso." In *The New Handbook of Texas*, edited by Ron Tyler, Douglas E. Barnett, Roy R. Barkley, Penelope C. Anderson, and Mark F. Odintz, vol.1, 137–138. Austin: Texas State Historical Association, 1996.

Jackson, Robert H. "Congregation and Population Change in the Mission Communities of Northern New Spain: Cases from the Californias and Texas." *New Mexico Historical Review* 69.2 (1994): 163–183.

________. “The Formation of Frontier Indigenous Communities: Missions in California and Texas.” In *New Views of Borderlands History*, edited by Robert H. Jackson, 131–156. Albuquerque: University of New Mexico Press, 1998.

Janicek, Ricki S. “The Development of Early Mexican Land Policy: Coahuila and Texas, 1810–1825.” Ph.D. dissertation, Tulane University, 1985.

________. “Spanish and Mexican Land Laws in Early Texas.” Master’s thesis, University of Houston, 1977.

Jarratt, Rie. *Gutiérrez de Lara, Mexican Texan: The Story of a Creole Hero*. Austin: Creole Texana, 1949.

John, Elizabeth A. H. *Storms Brewed in Other Men’s Worlds: The Confrontation of Indians, Spanish, and French in the Southwest, 1540–1795*. College Station: Texas A&M University Press, 1975.

________. “Francisco Xavier Chaves: Soldier-Interpreter.” In *The Human Tradition in Texas*, edited by Ty Cashion and Jesús F. de la Teja, 21–33. Wilmington, Del.: Scholarly Resources, 2001.

________. “Independent Indians and the San Antonio Community.” In *Tejano Origins in Eighteenth-Century San Antonio*, edited by Gerald E. Poyo and Gilberto M. Hinojosa, 123–135. Austin: University of Texas Press, 1991.

________. “Spanish-Indian Relations in the Big Bend Region during the Eighteenth and Early Nineteenth Centuries.” *Journal of Big Bend Studies* 3 (1991): 71–80.

Johnson, John G. “Juan Galván.” In *The New Handbook of Texas*, edited by Ron Tyler, Douglas E. Barnett, Roy R. Barkley, Penelope C. Anderson, and Mark F. Odintz, vol. 3, 51. Austin: Texas State Historical Association, 1996.

Jones, Oakah L. Jr. *Los Paisanos: Spanish Settlers on the Northern Frontier of New Spain*. Norman: University of Oklahoma Press, 1979.

________. “San José del Parral: Colonial Trade of Parralenses with Nuevo México and El Paso del Río del Norte.” *Journal of Big Bend Studies* 13 (2001): 11–25.

________. “Settlements and Settlers at La Junta de los Rios, 1759–1822.” *Journal of Big Bend Studies* 3 (1991): 43–70.

Jones, O. Garfield. “Local Government in the Spanish Colonies as Provided by the *Recopilación de leyes de los reinos de las Indias*.” *Southwestern Historical Quarterly* 19 (July 1915): 65–90.

Kelley, J. Charles. “Jumano and Patarabueye: Relations at La Junta de los Rios.” Ph.D. dissertation, Harvard University, 1947.

________. “Juan Sabeata and Diffusion in Aboriginal Texas.” *American Anthropologist* 57 (October 1955): 981–995.

Kimbrough, Birch Duke. “The Spanish Regime in Texas.” Master’s thesis, East Texas State Teachers College, 1939.

King, Nyal C. “Captain Antonio Gil Y’barbo: Founder of Modern Nacogdoches, 1729–1809.” Master’s thesis, Stephen F. Austin State College, 1949.

Kinsall, Al. “The Lady in Blue: María De Agreda of Spain.” *Journal of South Texas* 8 (1995): 80–96.

Kramer, V. Paul. "The Spanish Borderlands of Texas and Tamaulipas." *Texana* 10 (1972): 260–272.

Kress, Margaret Kenny. "Diary of a Visit of Inspection of the Texas Missions made by Fray Gaspar José Solis in the Year 1767–68." *Southwestern Historical Quarterly* 35 (July 1931): 28–76.

Laquest, Katherine Watson. "A Social History of the Spaniards in Nacogdoches." Master's thesis, Baylor University, 1941.

Lemée, Patricia R. "Tíos and Tantes: Familial and Political Relationships of Natchitoches and the Spanish Colonial Frontier." *Southwestern Historical Quarterly* 101 (January 1998): 340–358.

Leutenegger, Benedict, and Carmen Perry. "The Establishment of the Missions and the Work of the Missionary Fathers." In *San Antonio in the Eighteenth Century*, edited by Esther MacMillan, 22–34. San Antonio: San Antonio Bicentennial Heritage Committee, 1976.

Leutenegger, Benedict, Marion A. Habig, and Barnabas Diekemper. "Memorial of Father Benito Fernández Concerning the Canary Islanders, 1741." *Southwestern Historical Quarterly* 82 (January 1979): 265–296.

Love, Christene Moore. "The Spanish Missions of Texas." Master's thesis, Sam Houston State Teachers College, 1940.

Lynch, Margaret A. "Colonial Texas as a Frontier Problem." Ph.D. dissertation, Boston College, 1935.

MacMillan, Esther. "Government and Life in San Antonio, 1731–1784." In *San Antonio in the Eighteenth Century*, edited by Esther MacMillan, 84–98. San Antonio: San Antonio Bicentennial Heritage Committee, 1976.

________, ed. *San Antonio in the Eighteenth Century*. San Antonio: San Antonio Bicentennial Heritage Committee, 1976.

Maril, Elizabeth. "Spanish Ranching Women." *South Texas Studies* 10 (1999): 143–153.

Marshall, C. E. "The Birth of the Mestizo in New Spain." *Hispanic American Historical Review* 19 (1939): 161–184.

Matovina, Timothy M. "New Frontiers of Guadalupanismo." *Journal of Hispanic/Latino Theology* 5.1 (August 1997): 20–36.

M'Caleb, Flavius. "Some Obscure Points in the Mission Period of Texas History." *Quarterly of the Texas State Historical Association* 1 (January 1898): 216–225.

McAlister, Lyle N. "The Reorganization of the Army of New Spain, 1763–1767." *Hispanic American Historical Review* 30 (February 1953): 1–32.

________. "Social Structure and Social Change in New Spain." *Hispanic American Historical Review* 43 (1963): 349–370.

McCaa, Robert. "*Calidad, Clase,* and Marriage in Colonial Mexico: The Case of Parral, 1788–90." *Hispanic American Historical Review* 64 (August 1984): 477–501.

McCaleb, Walter F. *The Spanish Missions of Texas.* San Antonio: The Naylor Company, 1954.

McCollum, Dudley Foster. "Spanish Texas." Ph.D. dissertation, New York University, 1931.

McCorkle, James L. Jr. "Los Adaes and the Borderlands Origins of East Texas." *East Texas Historical Journal* 22.2 (1984): 3–12.

McCoy, Dorothy Abbott. "Some Valley Descendants of the Grantees." In *Roots by the River*, by Valley By-Liners, 26–29. Mission, Tex.: Border Kingdom Press, 1978.

McDonald, David. "La Bahía in 1780: Descriptions of a Mestizo Community." *South Texas Studies* 11 (2000): 119–129.

McGill, Margaret."The Administration of Carlos Franquis de Lugo, Governor of Texas, 1736–1737." Master's thesis, University of Texas, Austin, 1928.

McKnight, Joseph W. "Law without Lawyers on the Hispano-Mexican Frontier." *West Texas Historical Association Yearbook* 66 (1990): 51–65.

McMillan, Node. "The Seeds of Discontent: Legal, Historical, and Economic Aspects of Commercial Agriculture in Spanish Texas, 1779–1821." Master's thesis, Southwest Texas State University, 1981.

Meacham, Tina Laurel. "The Population of Spanish and Mexican Texas, 1716–1836." Ph.D. dissertation, University of Texas at Austin, 2000.

Menchaca, Martha. "The Spanish Settlement of Texas and Arizona." In *Recovering History, Constructing Race*, by Martha Menchaca, 97–126. Austin: University of Texas Press, 2001.

Milligan, James Clark. "José Bérnardo Gutiérrez de Lara, Mexican Frontiersman, 1811–1841." Ph.D. dissertation, Texas Tech University, 1975.

Moorhead, Max L. *The Presidio: Bastion of the Spanish Borderlands*. Norman: University of Oklahoma Press, 1975.

________. "The *Soldado de Cuera*: Stalwart of the Spanish Borderlands." In *The Spanish Borderlands—A First Reader*, edited by Oakah L. Jones, 87–105. Los Angeles: Lorrin L. Morrison, 1974.

Morey, Elizabeth May. "Attitude of the Citizens of San Fernando Toward Independence Movements in New Spain, 1811–1813." Master's thesis, University of Texas, Austin, 1930.

Morfí, Juan Agustín. *History of Texas: 1673–1779*, translated by Carlos Eduardo Castañeda. Albuquerque: University of New Mexico Press, 1935.

Morris, John Miller. "Alvar Núnez Cabeza de Vaca: An Epic Encounter." In *The Human Tradition in Texas*, edited by Ty Cashion and Jesús F. de la Teja, 1–19. Wilmington, Del.: Scholarly Resources, 2001.

Mounger, M. A. "Mission Espiritu Santo of Coastal Texas: An Example of Historic Site Archeology." Master's thesis, University of Texas, Austin, 1959.

Murphy, Henrietta. "Spanish Presidial Administration as Exemplified by the Inspection of Pedro de Rivera, 1724–1728." Ph.D. dissertation, University of Texas, Austin, Austin, 1938.

Myers, Sandra L. *The Ranch in Spanish Texas, 1691–1800*. El Paso: Texas Western Press, 1969.

________. "The Ranching Frontier: Spanish Institutional Backgrounds of the Plains Cattle Industry." In *New Spain's Far Northern Frontier: Essays on Spain in the American West, 1540–1821*, edited by David J. Weber, 79–96. Albuquerque: University of New Mexico Press, 1979.

________. "The Spanish Cattle Kingdom in the Province of Texas." *Texana* 4 (1966): 233–246.

Narrett, David E. "José Bernardo Gutiérrez de Lara: *Caudillo* of the Mexican Republic in Texas." *Southwestern Historical Quarterly* 106 (October 2002): 194–228.

Nelson, Al B. "Juan de Ugalde and the Río Grande Frontier, 1779–1816." Ph.D. dissertation, University of California, Berkeley, 1937.

Newman, Bud. "Fray García de San Francisco, Founder of El Paso." *Password* 29 (Winter 1984): 179–186.

Nunley, Carol Elaine. "Translation of Spanish Documents Pertaining to Mission Nuestra Señora del Rosario." Master's thesis, Texas Woman's University, 1975.

O'Connor, Kathryn Stoner. *The Presidio La Bahia del Espiritu Santo de Zuñiga, 1721–1846*. Austin: Von Boeckmann-Jones, 1966.

O'Rourke, Thomas P. *The Franciscan Missions in Texas, 1690–1793*. Washington, D.C.: Catholic University of America, 1927.

Park, Joseph F. "Spanish Indian Policy in Northern Mexico, 1765–1810." In *New Spain's Far Northern Frontier: Essays on Spain in the American West, 1540–1821*, edited by David J. Weber, 217–234. Albuquerque: University of New Mexico Press, 1979.

Patten, Roderick B., ed. "Miranda's Inspection of Los Almagres: His Journal, Report, and Petition." *Southwestern Historical Quarterly* 74 (October 1970): 223–254.

Persons, Billie. "Secular Life in the San Antonio Missions." *Southwestern Historical Quarterly* 62 (1958): 45–62.

Potter, Reuben. "The Colonization of Texas." *Magazine of American History* 8 (March 1882).

Powell, Lydia O. "A Study of the Influence on and Changes in Sixteenth, Seventeenth and Eighteenth Century Spanish Cartography of Texas." Master's thesis, St. Mary's University, 1985.

Poyo, Gerald E. "The Canary Islands Immigrants of San Antonio: From Ethnic Exclusivity to Community in Eighteenth-Century Béxar." In *Tejano Origins in Eighteenth-Century San Antonio*, edited by Gerald E. Poyo and Gilberto M. Hinojosa, 41–58. Austin: University of Texas Press, 1991.

________. "Community and Autonomy." In *Tejano Journey, 1770–1850*, edited by Gerald E. Poyo, 1–13. Austin: University of Texas Press, 1996.

________. "Immigrants and Integration in Late Eighteenth-Century Béxar." In *Tejano Origins in Eighteenth-Century San Antonio*, edited by Gerald E. Poyo and Gilberto M. Hinojosa, 85–104. Austin: University of Texas Press, 1991.

________. "Social Identity on the Hispanic Texas Frontier." In *Recovering the U.S. Hispanic Literary Heritage*, edited by María Herrera-Sobek and Virginia Sánchez Korrol, vol. 3, 384–401. Houston: Arte Público Press, 2000.

________, ed. *Tejano Journey, 1770–1850*. Austin: University of Texas Press, 1996.

Poyo, Gerald E., and Gilberto M. Hinojosa. "Selective Bibliography on Spanish Texas, 1685–1821." In *Tejano Origins in Eighteenth-Century San Antonio,* edited by Gerald E. Poyo and Gilberto M. Hinojosa, 169–189. Austin: University of Texas Press, 1991.

________. "Spanish Texas and Borderlands Historiography in Transition: Implications for United States History." *Journal of American History* 75 (September 1988): 393–416.

________, eds. *Tejano Origins in Eighteenth Century San Antonio*. Austin: University of Texas Press, 1991.

Price, Catherine. "The Comanches' Threat to Texas and New Mexico in the Eighteenth Century and the Development of Spanish Indian Policy." *Journal of the West* 24 (April 1985): 34–45.

Ramsdell, Charles. "Espíritu Santo: An Early Texas Cattle Ranch." *Texas Geographic Magazine* 13 (January 1949): 21–25.

Ríos McMillan, Nora E. "*Siendo Mi Derecho . . .*: The Hispanic Woman's Legal Identity in the Spanish Southwest." *South Texas Studies* 10 (1999): 102–142.

Rocha, Rodolfo. "Early Ranching Along the Rio Grande." In *At Home on the Range: Esays on the History of Western Social and Domestic Life*, edited by John R. Wunder, 3–18. Westport, Conn.: Greenwood Press, 1985.

Rock, Rosalind Zichek. "Dying Quijote: Nemesio Salcedo and the Last Years of Spain in the Internal Provinces." Ph.D. dissertation, University of New Mexico, 1981.

Rowe, Edna. "The Disturbances at Anahuac in 1832." *Southwestern Historical Quarterly* 6 (April 1903): 265–299.

Santos, Richard G. "The Quartel de San Antonio de Bexar." *Texana* 5 (1967): 187–202.

________. "Spanish Archives of Laredo." *Texana* 4 (Spring 1966): 41–46.

Schuetz, Mardith K. "The Indians of the San Antonio Missions, 1718–1821." Ph.D. dissertation, University of Texas at Austin, 1980.

________. "Indians of the San Antonio Area." In *San Antonio in the Eighteenth Century*, edited by Esther MacMillan, 1–21. San Antonio: San Antonio Bicentennial Heritage Committee, 1976.

________. "The Mission Indians." In *San Antonio in the Eighteenth Century*, edited by Esther MacMillan, 35–46. San Antonio: San Antonio Bicentennial Heritage Committee, 1976.

________. "The People of San Antonio, in the Period 1718–1731." In *San Antonio in the Eighteenth Century*, edited by Esther MacMillan, 73–83. San Antonio: San Antonio Bicentennial Heritage Committee, 1976.

Schuetz, Mardith K., and Robert K. Winn. "The Art of the Era." In *San Antonio in the Eighteenth Century*, edited by Esther MacMillan, 118–128. San Antonio: San Antonio Bicentennial Heritage Committee, 1976.

Schwarz, Ted. *The Forgotten Battlefield of the First Texas Revolution: The Battle of Medina, August 18, 1813*. Austin: Eakin Press, 1985.

Scott, Del. "The Significance of Adobe to the Spanish Colonization of the Southwest." Master's thesis, Abilene Christian College, 1962.

Scott, Florence J. *Historical Heritage of the Lower Rio Grande: A Historical Record of Spanish Exploration, Subjugation, and Colonization of the Lower Rio Grande Valley and the Activities of José Escandón, Count of Sierra Gorda . . . 1747–1848*. San Antonio: The Naylor Company, 1937.

________. *Royal Land Grants North of the Rio Grande, 1777–1821: Early History of Land Grants Made by Spain to Families in Jurisdiction of Reynosa.* Rio Grande City, Tex.: La Retama Press, 1969.

________. "The Colonial Period: Spanish Colonization of the Lower Rio Grande, 1747–1767." In *Essays in Mexican History: The Charles Wilson Hackett Memorial Volume*, edited by Robert C. Cotner and Carlos E. Casteñeda, 3–20. Austin: University of Texas Press, 1958.

________. "Spanish Land Grants in the Lower Rio Grande Valley." Master's thesis, University of Texas, Austin, 1935.

Sheffy, L. F. "The Spanish Horse on the Great Plains." *Panhandle Plains Historical Review* 6 (1933): 80–101.

Shields, Mrs. Ima Ener. "The Expansion of Spanish Missions in Texas, 1690–1794." Master's thesis, Sam Houston State Teachers College, 1950.

Smith, Ralph A. "The Spanish 'Piece' Policy in West Texas." *West Texas Historical Association Yearbook* 68 (1992): 7–24.

Solís, Gaspar José de. "Diary of a Visit of Inspection of the Texas Missions made by Fray Gaspar José de Solís in the Year 1767–1768." *Southwestern Historical Quarterly* 35 (July 1931): 68–69.

Starnes, Gary B. "Juan de Ugalde (1729–1816) and the *Provincias Internas* of Coahuila and Texas." Ph.D. dissertation, Texas Christian University, 1971.

________. "Juan de Ugalde." In *The New Handbook of Texas*, edited by Ron Tyler, Douglas E. Barnett, Roy R. Barkley, Penelope C. Anderson, and Mark F. Odintz, vol. 6, 616–617. Austin: Texas State Historical Association, 1996.

________. "Juan de Ugalde and the Coahuila-Texas Frontier." *Texana* 10 (1972): 116–128.

________. "The Spanish Borderlands of Texas and Coahuila." *Texana* 10 (1972): 20–29.

Steck, Francis B. "Forerunners of Captain De León's Expedition to Texas, 1670–1675." *Southwestern Historical Quarterly* 36 (July 1932): 1–28.

Stephenson, W. A. "Spanish Exploration and Settlement of West Texas Before the Eighteenth Century." *West Texas Historical Association Yearbook* 2 (1926): 64–84.

Stern, Peter Alan. "Social Marginality and Acculturation on the Northern Frontier of New Spain." Ph.D. dissertation, University of California, Berkeley, 1984.

________. "Marginals and Acculturation in Frontier Society." In *New Views of Borderlands History*, edited by Robert H. Jackson, 157–188. Albuquerque: University of New Mexico Press, 1998.

Stovenour, Robert E. "A History of San Antonio under Spanish Rule." Master's thesis, Southern Methodist University, 1963.

Stuntz, Jean A. "Spanish Laws for Texas Women: The Development of Marital Property Laws to 1850." *Southwestern Historical Quarterly* 104 (April 2001): 543–559.

Tarin, Randell G. "Joaquin Leal." In *The New Handbook of Texas*, edited by Ron Tyler, Douglas E. Barnett, Roy R. Barkley, Penelope C. Anderson, and Mark F. Odintz, vol. 4, 133. Austin: Texas State Historical Association, 1996.

________. "Juan Leal Goraz." In *The New Handbook of Texas*, edited by Ron Tyler, Douglas E. Barnett, Roy R. Barkley, Penelope C. Anderson, and Mark F. Odintz, vol. 4, 133–134. Austin: Texas State Historical Association, 1996.

Taylor, Virginia H., ed. *The Letters of Antonio Martínez, Last Spanish Governor of Texas, 1817–1822*. Austin: Texas State Library, 1957.

Thonhoff, Robert H. "The First Ranch in Texas." *West Texas Historical Association Yearbook* 40 (October 1964): 90–97.

________. "Joaquín de Arredondo." In *The New Handbook of Texas*, edited by Ron Tyler, Douglas E. Barnett, Roy R. Barkley, Penelope C. Anderson, and Mark F. Odintz, vol.1, 255. Austin: Texas State Historical Association, 1996.

________. "Our Spanish Legacy of Ranching in Texas." *South Texas Studies* 4 (1993): 1–11.

Timmons, W. H. "The Population of the El Paso Area: A Census of 1784." *New Mexico Historical Review* 52 (1977): 311–316.

________. "The Presidio of San Elizario, 1789–1851." *Password* 33 (Fall 1988): 107–116.

Tjarks, Alicia V. "Comparative Demographic Analysis of Texas, 1777–1793." *Southwestern Historical Quarterly* 77 (January 1974): 291–338. Reprinted in *New Spain's Far Northern Frontier: Essays on Spain in the American West, 1540–1821*, edited by David J. Weber, 137–169. Albuquerque: University of New Mexico Press, 1979.

Tunnell, Curtis, and Enrique Madrid. "Exploring the West Texas Borderlands." In *Hispanic Texas: A Historical Guide*, edited by Helen Simons and Cathryn A. Hoyt, 77–93. Austin: University of Texas Press, 1992.

Tunnell, Curtis, and W. W. Newcomb. "A Lipan Apache Mission: San Lorenzo de la Santa Cruz, 1762–1771." *Bulletin of the Texas Memorial Museum* 14 (1969): 165–167.

Tutino, John Mark. "Creole Mexico: Spanish Elites, Haciendas, and Indian Towns, 1750–1810." Ph.D. dissertation, University of Texas at Austin, 1976.

Valerio-Jiménez, Omar Santiago. "'Indios bárbaros', Divorcees, and Flocks of Vampires: Identity and Nation on the Rio Grande, 1749–1894." Ph.D. dissertation, University of California, Los Angeles, 2001.

Vigness, David M. *The Revolutionary Decades: The Saga of Texas, 1810–1836.* Austin: Steck-Vaughn, 1965.

________. "Don Hugo Oconor and New Spain's Northeastern Frontier, 1764–1776." In *The Spanish Borderlands—A First Reader*, edited by Oakah L. Jones, 170–183. Los Angeles: Lorrin L. Morrison, 1974.

Vigness, Winifred W. "Tomás Sánchez de la Barrera y Garza." In *The New Handbook of Texas*, edited by Ron Tyler, Douglas E. Barnett, Roy R. Barkley, Penelope C. Anderson, and Mark F. Odintz, vol. 5, 828. Austin: Texas State Historical Association, 1996.

Walters, Paul Hugh. "Survey of the History of La Bahía del Espiritu Santo, 1721–1821." Master's thesis, University of Texas, Austin, 1944.

________. "The Secularization of the La Bahía Missions." *Southwestern Historical Quarterly* 54 (January 1951): 287–300.

Walz, Vina E. "A History of the El Paso Area, 1680–1692." Ph.D. dissertation, University of New Mexico, 1951.

Warren, Harris Gaylord. "New Spain and the Filibusters, 1812–1821." Ph.D. dissertation, Northwestern University, 1937.

________. "Gutiérrez-Magee Expedition." In *The New Handbook of Texas*, edited by Ron Tyler, Douglas E. Barnett, Roy R. Barkley, Penelope C. Anderson, and Mark F. Odintz, vol. 3, 393–394. Austin: Texas State Historical Association, 1996.

________. "José Álvarez de Toledo's Initiation as a Filibuster, 1811–1813." *Hispanic American Historical Review* 20 (February 1940): 58–82.

Warren, Harris Gaylord, and Jack D. L. Holmes. "Simón de Herrera." In *The New Handbook of Texas*, edited by Ron Tyler, Douglas E. Barnett, Roy R. Barkley, Penelope C. Anderson, and Mark F. Odintz, vol. 3, 576. Austin: Texas State Historical Association, 1996.

Weber, David J. *Myth and the History of the Hispanic Southwest*. Albuquerque: University of New Mexico Press, 1988.

________, ed. *Foreigners in Their Native Land: Historical Roots of the Mexican Americans*. Albuquerque: University of New Mexico Press, 1973.

________, ed. *New Spain's Far Northern Frontier: Essays on Spain in the American West, 1540–1821*. Dallas: Southern Methodist University Press, 1989.

Weddle, Robert S. *San Juan Bautista: Gateway to Spanish Texas*. Austin: University of Texas Press, 1968.

________. *The San Sabá Mission: Spanish Pivot in Texas*. Austin: University of Texas Press, 1964.

________. "Cross and Crown: The Spanish Missions in Texas." In *Hispanic Texas: A Historical Guide*, edited by Helen Simons and Cathryn A. Hoyt, 25–35. Austin: University of Texas Press, 1992.

________. "Diego Jiménez." In *The New Handbook of Texas*, edited by Ron Tyler, Douglas E. Barnett, Roy R. Barkley, Penelope C. Anderson, and Mark F. Odintz, vol. 3, 941. Austin: Texas State Historical Association, 1996.

________. "Juan Domínguez de Mendoza." In *The New Handbook of Texas*, edited by Ron Tyler, Douglas E. Barnett, Roy R. Barkley, Penelope C. Anderson, and Mark F. Odintz, vol. 2, 673–674. Austin: Texas State Historical Association, 1996.

________. "San Juan Bautista: Mother of Texas Missions." *Southwestern Historical Quarterly* 71 (April 1968): 542–570.

________. "The San Sabá Mission: Approach to the Great Plains." *Great Plains Journal* 4 (Spring 1965): 29–38.

Weddle, Robert S., and Robert H. Thonhoff. *Drama and Conflict: The Texas Saga of 1776*. Austin: Madrona Press, 1976.

Weniger, Del. "Wilderness, Farm, and Ranch." In *San Antonio in the Eighteenth Century*, edited by Esther MacMillan, 99–117. San Antonio: San Antonio Bicentennial Heritage Committee, 1976.

West, Elizabeth H. "Bonilla's Brief Compendium of the History of Texas, 1772." *Quarterly of the Texas State Historical Association* 8 (July 1904): 3–78.

________. "Governor Alonso de León's 1689 Expedition Diary." *Quarterly of the Texas State Historical Association* 8 (January 1905): 199–224.

________, ed. "Diary of José Bérnardo Gutiérrez de Lara, 1811–1812." *American Historical Review* 34 (October 1928): 55–77; 34 (January 1929): 281–294.

Williams, J. W. "Coronado: From the Río Grande to the Concho." *Southwestern Historical Quarterly* 63 (October 1959): 190–220.

Woldert, Albert. "The Location of the Tejas Indian Village (San Pedro) and the Spanish Missions in Houston County, Texas." *Southwestern Historical Quarterly* 38 (January 1935): 203–212.

Wolff, Henry Jr. "Mission Espiritu Santo: First Great Cattle Ranch of Texas." *Journal of South Texas* 12 (1999): 108–120.

Wright, Robert E. "Popular and Official Religiosity: A Theoretical Analysis and a Case Study of Laredo-Nuevo Laredo, 1755–1857." Ph.D. dissertation, University of California, Berkeley, 1992.

________. "Catholic Diocesan Church of Spanish and Mexican Texas." In *The New Handbook of Texas*, edited by Ron Tyler, Douglas E. Barnett, Roy R. Barkely, Penelope C. Anderson, and Mark F. Odintz, vol. 1, 1030–1031. Austin: Texas State Historical Association, 1996.

________. "The Hispanic Church in Texas under Spain and Mexico." *U.S. Catholic Historian* 20.4 (Fall 2002): 15–33.

________. "José Antonio Valdez." In *The New Handbook of Texas*, edited by Ron Tyler, Douglas E. Barnett, Roy R. Barkely, Penelope C. Anderson, and Mark F. Odintz, vol. 6, 688–689. Austin: Texas State Historical Association, 1996.

________. "José Dario Zambrano." In *The New Handbook of Texas*, edited by Ron Tyler, Douglas E. Barnett, Roy R. Barkley, Penelope C. Anderson, and Mark F. Odintz, vol. 6, 1140–1141. Austin: Texas State Historical Association, 1996.

________. "Local Church Emergence and Mission Decline: The Historiography of the Catholic Church in the Southwest during the Spanish and Mexican Periods." *U.S. Catholic Historian* 9 (Winter/Spring 1990): 27–48.

________. "The Parish of San Agustín, Laredo, 1760–1857." In *San Agustín Parish of Laredo, Abstracts of Marriage Book I, 1790–1857*, by Angel Sepúlveda Brown and Gloria Villa Cadena, 1–46. San Antonio: privately printed, 1989.

Zamora O'Shea, Elena. *El Mesquite: A Story of the Early Spanish Settlements between the Nueces and the Rio Grande as Told by "La Posta del Palo Alto."* Dallas: Mathis Publishing, 1935.

Zavala, Silvio. *New Viewpoints on the Spanish Colonization of America*. Philadelphia: University of Pennsylvania Press, 1943.

________. "The Frontiers of Hispanic America." In *The Frontier in Perspective*, edited by Walker D. Wyman and Clifton B. Kroeber, 43–58. Madison: University of

Wisconsin Press, 1957. Reprinted in *Where Cultures Meet: Frontiers in Latin American History*, edited by David J. Weber and Jane M. Rausch, 42–50. Wilmington, Del.: Scholarly Resources, 1994.

Zobisch, Clara M. "American Interests in Spanish Texas, 1783–1814." Master's thesis, University of Oklahoma, 1936.

4. A MEXICAN BORDERLAND, 1821–1836

People now lived under a different sovereignty, as Mexico won independence from Spain in 1821. New forces drove history, among them changing governments in Mexico and the increasing presence of Anglo Americans who came to exert powerful influence on the fate of Texas and its Mexican citizens. In 1836, Anglo-Texans and their allies, among them Tejanos, successfully broke away from Mexico, and established the Republic of Texas. Citizenship under Mexico ended.

Group drawing of the eleven Mexican presidents of Texas by Gene Bustamante.
The Presidential Museum, Odessa, Texas, No. ITC-73-1197

Ahlborn, Richard E. "European Dress in Texas, 1830: As Rendered by Lino Sánchez y Tapia." *American Scene* (1972): 1–20.

Almaráz, Félix D. Jr. *Governor Antonio Martínez and Mexican Independence in Texas: An Orderly Transition*. San Antonio: Bexar County Historical Commission, 1979.

________. "Aspects of Mexican Texas: A Focal Point in Southwest History." *Red River Valley Historical Review* 2 (Fall 1975): 363–379.

________. "Governor Antonio Martínez and Mexican Independence in Texas: An Orderly Transition." *Permian Historical Annual* 15 (1975): 44–55.

________. "Río Pecos Under the Mexican Eagle." In *Pecos: Gateway to Pueblos and Plains, The Anthology*, edited by John V. Bezy and Joseph P. Sánchez, 86–92. Tucson: Southwestern Parks and Monuments Association, 1988.

________. "San Antonio's Old Franciscan Missions: Material Decline and Secular Avarice in the Transition from Hispanic to Mexican Control." *The Americas* 44 (July 1987): 1–22.

________. "Texas as a Mexican Borderland: A Review and Appraisal of Salient Events." *Journal of the West* 24 (April 1985): 108–112.

Barker, Eugene C. "Declaration of Causes for Taking Up Arms against Mexico." *Quarterly of the Texas State Historical Association* 15 (January 1912): 173–185.

________. "Native Latin American Contribution to the Colonization and Independence of Texas." *Southwestern Historical Quarterly* 46 (January 1943): 317–335.

________, ed. "Minutes of the *Ayuntamiento* of San Felipe de Austin, 1828–1832." *Southwestern Historical Quarterly* 21 (January 1918): 299–326.

Barnes, Charles Merritt. "Enrique Esparza: A Survivor from the Alamo." *La Luz* 3.6 (September 1974): 27–29.

Barrera, Manuel. *Then the Gringos Came: The Story of Martin De León and the Texas Revolution.* Laredo, Tex.: Barrera Publications, 1992.

Becerra, Francisco, as told to John S. Ford. *A Mexican Sergeant's Recollection of the Alamo and San Jacinto*. Austin: Jenkins Publishing, 1980.

Benson, Nettie Lee. "The Plan of Casa Mata." *Hispanic American Historical Review* 25 (February 1945): 45–56.

________. "Texas as Viewed from Mexico, 1820–1834." *Southwestern Historical Quarterly* 90 (January 1987): 219–291.

Berger, Max. "Education in Texas during the Spanish and Mexican Periods." *Southwestern Historical Quarterly* 51 (July 1947): 41–53.

Blevins, Don. "Francita Alavez: The Angel of Goliad." In *From Angels to Hellcats: Legendary Texas Women, 1836 to 1880*, by Don Blevins, 23–40. Missoula, Mont.: Mountain Press Publishing, 2001.

Brack, Gene. "Mexican Opinion and the Texas Revolution." *Southwestern Historical Quarterly* 72 (October 1968): 170–182.

Brear, Holly. *Inherit the Alamo*. Austin: University of Texas Press, 1995.

Bueno, Anastacio Jr. "In Storms of Fortune: José Antonio Navarro of Texas, 1821–1846." Master's thesis, University of Texas at Austin, 1978.

Bugbee, Lester G. "The Texas Frontier, 1820–1845." *Publications of the Southern History Association* 4 (March 1900): 102–121.

Campbell, Camilla. "Ángel Navarro." In *The New Handbook of Texas*, edited by Ron Tyler, Douglas E. Barnett, Roy R. Barkley, Penelope C. Anderson, and Mark F. Odintz, vol. 4, 953. Austin: Texas State Historical Association, 1996.

________. "José Ángel Navarro." In *The New Handbook of Texas*, edited by Ron Tyler, Douglas E. Barnett, Roy R. Barkley, Penelope C. Anderson, and Mark F. Odintz, vol. 4, 953–954. Austin: Texas State Historical Association, 1996.

________. "José Ángel Navarro." In *The New Handbook of Texas*, edited by Ron Tyler, Douglas E. Barnett, Roy R. Barkley, Penelope C. Anderson, and Mark F. Odintz, vol. 4, 954. Austin: Texas State Historical Association, 1996.

________. "José Eugenio Navarro." In *The New Handbook of Texas*, edited by Ron Tyler, Douglas E. Barnett, Roy R. Barkley, Penelope C. Anderson, and Mark F. Odintz, vol. 4, 955. Austin: Texas State Historical Association, 1996.

________. "José Gaspar María Flores de Abrego." In *The New Handbook of Texas*, edited by Ron Tyler, Douglas E. Barnett, Roy R. Barkley, Penelope C. Anderson, and Mark F. Odintz, vol. 2, 1037–1038. Austin: Texas State Historical Association, 1996.

________. "José Luciano Navarro." In *The New Handbook of Texas*, edited by Ron Tyler, Douglas E. Barnett, Roy R. Barkley, Penelope C. Anderson, and Mark F. Odintz, vol. 4, 955–956. Austin: Texas State Historical Association, 1996.

Campbell, Elsie. "Spanish Records of the Civil Government of Ysleta, 1835." Master's thesis, Texas Western College, 1950.

Casso, Raúl. "Damacio Jiménez." In *The New Handbook of Texas*, edited by Ron Tyler, Douglas E. Barnett, Roy R. Barkley, Penelope C. Anderson, and Mark F. Odintz, vol. 3, 940. Austin: Texas State Historical Association, 1996.

________. "Damacio Jiménez: The Lost and Found Alamo Defender." *Southwestern Historical Quarterly* 96 (July 1992): 89–93.

Castañeda, Carlos E. *Our Catholic Heritage in Texas, 1519–1936: The Fight for Freedom, 1810–1836*. Austin: Von Boeckmann-Jones, 1950.

________. "The Agony of the Church in Texas, 1821–1836." In *Our Catholic Heritage in Texas, 1519–1936*, by Carlos E. Castañeda, vol. 6: 307–355. Austin: Von Boeckmann-Jones, 1950.

________. "Statistical Report on Texas by Juan N. Almonte, 1835." *Southwestern Historical Quarterly* 28 (January 1925): 177–222.

________. "A Trip to Texas in 1828: José María Sánchez." *Southwestern Historical Quarterly* 29 (April 1926): 249–288.

________, ed. *The Mexican Side of the Texas Revolution by the Chief Mexican Participants, 1836*. Dallas: P. L. Turner Company, 1928.

Clark, John W. Jr. "Manuel de los Santos Coy." In *The New Handbook of Texas*, edited by Ron Tyler, Douglas E. Barnett, Roy R. Barkley, Penelope C. Anderson, and Mark F. Odintz, vol. 5, 892. Austin: Texas State Historical Association, 1996.

Cleaves, Wilbur S. "The Political Career of Lorenzo de Zavala." Master's thesis, University of Texas, Austin, 1931.

________. "Lorenzo De Zavala in Texas." *Southwestern Historical Quarterly* 36 (July 1932): 29–40.

Coalson, George O. "Andrea Castanon Villanueva." In *The New Handbook of Texas*, edited by Ron Tyler, Douglas E. Barnett, Roy R. Barkley, Penelope C. Anderson, and Mark F. Odintz, vol. 6, 752. Austin: Texas State Historical Association, 1996.

________. "Francita Alavez." In *The New Handbook of Texas*, edited by Ron Tyler, Douglas E. Barnett, Roy R. Barkley, Penelope C. Anderson, and Mark F. Odintz, vol. 1, 91. Austin: Texas State Historical Association, 1996.

________. "Texas Mexicans in the Texas Revolution." In *From Colony to Republic: Readings on American History to 1877*, edited by Terrence J. Barragy and Harry Russell Huebel, 163–177. Houston: Cayo Del Grullo Press, 1983.

________. "Texas Mexicans in the Texas Revolution." In *The American West: Essays in Honor of W. Eugene Hollon*, edited by Ronald Lora, 209–230. Toledo, Ohio: University of Toledo, 1980.

Cooper, Madie. "Texas Colonization Under Mexican Restrictions, 1821–1835." Master's thesis, Sam Houston State Teachers College, 1940.

Crane, R. C. "Santa Anna and the Aftermath of San Jacinto." *West Texas Historical Association Yearbook* 11 (1935): 56–61.

Crimm, Ana Carolina Castillo. "Success in Adversity: The Mexican Americans of Victoria County, Texas, 1800–1880." Ph.D. dissertation, University of Texas at Austin, 1994.

________. "Finding Their Way." In *Tejano Journey, 1770–1850,* edited by Gerald E. Poyo, 111–123. Austin: University of Texas Press, 1996.

Crisp, James E. "Anglo-Texan Attitudes Toward the Mexican, 1821–1845." Ph.D. dissertation, Yale University, 1976.

________. "An Incident in San Antonio: The Contested Iconology of Davy Crockett's Death at the Alamo." *Journal of the West* 40.2 (2001): 67–77.

________. "The Little Book That Wasn't There: The Myth and Mystery of the de la Peña Diary." *Southwestern Historical Quarterly* 97 (October 1994): 260–296.

________. "A Reply: When Revision Becomes Obsession, Bill Groneman and the de la Peña Diary." *Military History of the West* 25.2 (1995): 143–155.

Crook, Elaine Carland. "San Antonio, Texas, 1846–1861." Master's thesis, Rice University, 1964.

Cruz, Gilberto Ralph, ed. "The City Ordinances for the Internal Management and Administration of the Municipal Government of San Antonio of Béjar, 1829." *Texana* 7 (1969): 95–116.

Cruz, Gilberto R. *Let There Be Towns: Spanish Municipal Origins in the American Southwest, 1610–1810*. College Station: Texas A&M University Press, 1988.

Cummins, Light Townsend. "Texas under Spain and Mexico." In *A Guide to the History of Texas*, edited by Light Townsend Cummins and Alvin R. Bailey Jr., 3–16. New York: Greenwood Press, 1988.

Cutrer, Thomas W. "Ambrosio Rodríguez." In *The New Handbook of Texas*, edited by Ron Tyler, Douglas E. Barnett, Roy R. Barkley, Penelope C. Anderson, and Mark F. Odintz, vol. 5, 651–652. Austin: Texas State Historical Association, 1996.

Dabney, Lancaster E. "Louis Aury: The First Governor of Texas under the Mexican Republic." *Southwestern Historical Quarterly* 42 (October 1938): 108–116.

Davenport, Herbert. "Captain Jesús Cuéllar, Texas Cavalry, Otherwise 'Comanche.'" *Southwestern Historical Quarterly* 30 (July 1926): 56–62.

________. "General Juan María Jesús Carbajal." *Southwestern Historical Quarterly* 55 (April 1952): 475–483.

Davis, Graham. "The Province of Texas in Newly Independent Mexico." In *Land! Irish Pioneers in Mexican and Revolutionary Texas*, by Graham Davis, 9–38. College Station: Texas A&M University Press, 2002.

de la Peña, José Enríque. *With Santa Anna in Texas: A Personal Narrative of the Revolution*, edited by Carmen Perry. College Station: Texas A&M University Press, 1975.

de la Teja, Jesús F. *A Revolution Remembered: the Memoirs and Selected Correspondence of Juan N. Seguín*. Austin: State House Press, 1991.

________. "The Colonization and Independence of Texas: A Tejano Perspective." In *Myths, Misdeeds, and Misunderstandings: The Roots of Conflict in U.S.-Mexican Relations*, edited by Jaime E. Rodríguez O. and Kathryn Vincent, 79–96. Wilmington, Del.: Scholarly Resources Press, 1997.

________. "Discovering the Tejano Community in 'Early' Texas." *Journal of the Early Republic* 18.1 (1998): 73–98, 135–139.

________. "José Francisco Madero." In *The New Handbook of Texas,* edited by Ron Tyler, Douglas E. Barnett, Roy R. Barkley, Penelope C. Anderson, and Mark F. Odintz, vol. 4, 454. Austin: Texas State Historical Association, 1996.

________. "José Refugio Guadalupe de la Garza." In *The New Handbook of Texas,* edited by Ron Tyler, Douglas E. Barnett, Roy R. Barkely, Penelope C. Anderson, and Mark F. Odintz, vol. 3, 108. Austin: Texas State Historical Association, 1996.

________. "Juan Antonio Padilla." In *The New Handbook of Texas,* edited by Ron Tyler, Douglas E. Barnett, Roy R. Barkley, Penelope C. Anderson, and Mark F. Odintz, vol. 5, 6–7. Austin: Texas State Historical Association, 1996.

________. "Juan José María Erasmo Seguín." In *The New Handbook of Texas,* edited by Ron Tyler, Douglas E. Barnett, Roy R. Barkley, Penelope C. Anderson, and Mark F. Odintz, vol. 5, 965–966. Austin: Texas State Historical Association, 1996.

________. "Juan Nepomuceno Seguín." In *American National Biography*, edited by John A. Garraty and Mark C. Carnes, vol. 19, 602–603. New York: Oxford University Press, 1999.

________."Juan Nepomuceno Seguín." In *The New Handbook of Texas,* edited by Ron Tyler, Douglas E. Barnett, Roy R. Barkley, Penelope C. Anderson, and Mark F. Odintz, vol. 5, 966–967. Austin: Texas State Historical Association, 1996.

________. "'Only Fit for Raising Stock': Spanish and Mexican Land and Water Rights in the Tamaulipan Cession." In *Fluid Arguments: Five Centuries of Western Water Conflict*, edited by Char Miller, 3–27. Tucson: University of Arizona Press, 2001.

________. "St. James at the Fair: Religious Ceremony and Civic Boosterism on the Colonial Mexican Frontier." *The Americas* 57.3 (2001): 395–416.

________. "Tejano and Texian: Seguín and Houston in the Making of Texas." *South Texas Studies* 2 (1992): 24–36.

de la Teja, Jesús F., and John Wheat. "Béxar: Profile of a Tejano Community, 1820–1832." *Southwestern Historical Quarterly* 89 (July 1985): 7–34. Reprinted in *Tejano Origins in Eighteenth-Century San Antonio*, edited by Gerald E. Poyo and Gilberto M. Hinojosa, 1–24. Austin: University of Texas Press, 1991.

De León, Arnoldo. "Initial Contacts: Redeeming Texas from Mexicans, 1821–1836." In *They Called Them Greasers: Anglo Attitudes Towards Mexicans in Texas, 1821–1900*, by Arnoldo De León, 1–13. Austin: University of Texas Press, 1983.

________. "Mexican Texas." In *The New Handbook of Texas*, edited by Ron Tyler, Douglas E. Barnett, Roy R. Barkley, Penelope C. Anderson, and Mark F. Odintz, vol. 4, 689–695. Austin: Texas State Historical Association, 1996.

________. "Tejanos and the Texas War for Independence: Historiography's Judgment. *New Mexico Historical Review* 61 (April 1986): 137–146.

De Zavala, Adina. *History and Legends of the Alamo and Other Missions In and Around San Antonio*. San Antonio: privately published, 1917. Reprint, edited by Richard R. Flores. Houston: Arte Público Press, 1996.

Downs, Fane. "The History of Mexicans in Texas, 1820–1845." Ph.D. dissertation, Texas Tech University, 1970.

________. "Governor Antonio Martínez and the Defense of Texas from Foreign Invasion, 1817–1822." *Texas Military History* 7 (Spring 1968): 27–43.

Dyreson, Jodella K. "Sporting Activities in the American-Mexican Colonies of Texas, 1821–1835." *Journal of Sport History* 24.3 (1997): 269–284.

Edmondson, J. R. *The Alamo Story: From Early History to Current Conflicts*. Plano, Tex.: Republic of Texas Press, 2000.

Esparza, Reynaldo J. "Enrique Esparza." In *The New Handbook of Texas*, edited by Ron Tyler, Douglas E. Barnett, Roy R. Barkley, Penelope C. Anderson, and Mark F. Odintz, vol. 2, 893. Austin: Texas State Historical Association, 1996.

________. "José María Esparza." In *The New Handbook of Texas*, edited by Ron Tyler, Douglas E. Barnett, Roy R. Barkley, Penelope C. Anderson, and Mark F. Odintz, vol. 2, 893. Austin: Texas State Historical Association, 1996.

Estep, Raymond. "The Life of Lorenzo de Zavala." Ph.D. dissertation, University of Texas, Austin, 1942.

________. "José Antonio Mexía." In *The New Handbook of Texas,* edited by Ron Tyler, Douglas E. Barnett, Roy R. Barkley, Penelope C. Anderson, and Mark F. Odintz, vol. 4, 651–652. Austin: Texas State Historical Association, 1996.

________. "Lorenzo de Zavala and the Texas Revolution." *Southwestern Historical Quarterly* 57 (January 1954): 322–335.

________. "Lorenzo de Zavala." In *The New Handbook of Texas*, edited by Ron Tyler, Douglas E. Barnett, Roy R. Barkley, Penelope C. Anderson, and Mark F. Odintz, vol. 6, 1147–1148. Austin: Texas State Historical Association, 1996.

Fernández, Angela Salinas. "José María de Jesús Salinas." In *The New Handbook of Texas*, edited by Ron Tyler, Douglas E. Barnett, Roy R. Barkley, Penelope C. Anderson, and Mark F. Odintz, vol. 5, 777. Austin: Texas State Historical Association, 1996.

Fitzmorris, Mary Angela. *Four Decades of Catholicism in Texas, 1820–1860*. Washington, D.C.: Catholic University of America, 1926.

Flores, Richard R. *Remembering the Alamo: Memory, Modernity, and the Master Symbol*. Austin: University of Texas Press, 2002.

________. "The Alamo: Myth, Public History, and the Politics of Inclusion." *Radical History Review* 77 (2000): 91–103.

________. "Memory-Place, Meaning, and the Alamo." *American Literary History* 10.3 (1998): 428–445.

________. "Mexicans, Modernity, and Martyrs of the Alamo." In *Reflexiones 1998: New Directions in Mexican American Studies*, edited by Yolanda C. Padilla, 1–20. Austin: CMAS Books, 1999.

Fregoso, Rosa Linda. "Seguín: The Same Side of the Alamo." *Bilingual Review/La Revista Bilingüe* 10 (1983): 146–152.

Gambrell, Herbert P. *Mirabeau Buonaparte Lamar: Troubadour and Crusader*. Dallas: Southern Methodist University Press, 1934.

García, Clotilde P. *Padre Island and Padre José Nicolas Ballí: Application for Historical Marker*. Corpus Christi, Tex.: Grunwald Publishing, 1979.

________. "Enrique Villarreal." In *The New Handbook of Texas*, edited by Ron Tyler, Douglas E. Barnett, Roy R. Barkley, Penelope C. Anderson, and Mark F. Odintz, vol. 6, 752–753. Austin: Texas State Historical Association, 1996.

________. "José Nicolas Ballí." In *The New Handbook of Texas*, edited by Ron Tyler, Douglas E. Barnett, Roy R. Barkley, Penelope C. Anderson, and Mark F. Odintz, vol. 1, 358–359. Austin: Texas State Historical Association, 1996.

Garrett, Julia Kathryn. "The War of Independence in Texas, 1811–1813." Ph.D. dissertation, University of California, Berkeley, 1935.

Garza, Alicia. "José Vázquez Borrego." In *The New Handbook of Texas*, edited by Ron Tyler, Douglas E. Barnett, Roy R. Barkley, Penelope C. Anderson, and Mark F. Odintz, vol. 6, 716. Austin: Texas State Historical Association, 1996.

Glaser, Tom W. "Victory or Death." In *Alamo Images: Changing Perceptions of a Texas Experience*, by Susan Prendergast Schoelwer with Tom W. Glaser, 61–103. Dallas: Southern Methodist University Press, 1985.

Gómez, María O. "Francisco Antonio Ruiz." In *The New Handbook of Texas*, edited by Ron Tyler, Douglas E. Barnett, Roy R. Barkley, Penelope C. Anderson, and Mark F. Odintz, vol. 5, 710–711. Austin: Texas State Historical Association, 1996.

Gonzales, José Rafael. "The State of Coahuila y Tejas in 1824: A Governor's View from Saltillo," edited by Andrés Tijerina and David J. Weber. *Southwestern Historical Quarterly* 100 (October 1996): 187–206.

González, Anibal A. "José Antonio Díaz De León." In *The New Handbook of Texas*, edited by Ron Tyler, Douglas E. Barnett, Roy R. Barkley, Penelope C. Anderson, and Mark F. Odintz, vol. 2, 631–632. Austin: Texas State Historical Association, 1996.

Gracy, David B. II. "'Just as I Have Written It': A Study of the Authenticity of the Manuscript of José Enrique de la Peña's Account of the Texas Campaign." *Southwestern Historical Quarterly* 105 (October 2001): 254–291.

Graf, LeRoy P. "Colonizing Projects in Texas South of the Nueces, 1820–1845." *Southwestern Historical Quarterly* 50 (April 1947): 431–448.

Graham, Don. "Remembering the Alamo: The Story of the Texas Revolution in Popular Culture." *Southwestern Historical Quarterly* 89.1 (1985): 35–66.

Greaser, Galen D., and Jesús F. de la Teja. "Quieting Title to Spanish and Mexican Land Grants in the Trans-Nueces: The Bourland and Miller Commission, 1850–1852." *Southwestern Historical Quarterly* 95 (April 1992): 445–464.

Green, Stanley C. *The Mexican Republic: The First Decade, 1823–1832*. Pittsburgh: University of Pittsburgh Press, 1987.

Groneman, Bill. *Defense of a Legend: Crockett and the de la Peña Diary*. Plano, Tex.: Republic of Texas Press, 1994.

________. "Andrés Nava." In *The New Handbook of Texas,* edited by Ron Tyler, Douglas E. Barnett, Roy R. Barkley, Penelope C. Anderson, and Mark F. Odintz, vol. 4, 951. Austin: Texas State Historical Association, 1996.

________. "Antonio Fuentes." In *The New Handbook of Texas*, edited by Ron Tyler, Douglas E. Barnett, Roy R. Barkley, Penelope C. Anderson, and Mark F. Odintz, vol. 3, 22–23. Austin: Texas State Historical Association, 1996.

________. "Brigido Guerrero." In *The New Handbook of Texas*, edited by Ron Tyler, Douglas E. Barnett, Roy R. Barkley, Penelope C. Anderson, and Mark F. Odintz, vol. 3, 369. Austin: Texas State Historical Association, 1996.

________. "Carlos Espalier." In *The New Handbook of Texas*, edited by Ron Tyler, Douglas E. Barnett, Roy R. Barkley, Penelope C. Anderson, and Mark F. Odintz, vol. 2, 892. Austin: Texas State Historical Association, 1996.

________. "The Controversial Alleged Account of José Enrique de la Peña." *Military History of the West* 25.2 (1994): 129–142.

________. "The Diary of José Enrique de la Peña." *Journal of South Texas* 7 (1994): 28–51.

________. "Galba Fuqua." In *The New Handbook of Texas*, edited by Ron Tyler, Douglas E. Barnett, Roy R. Barkley, Penelope C. Anderson, and Mark F. Odintz, vol. 3, 33–34. Austin: Texas State Historical Association, 1996.

________. "Juan Abamillo." In *The New Handbook of Texas*, edited by Ron Tyler, Douglas E. Barnett, Roy R. Barkley, Penelope C. Anderson, and Mark F. Odintz, vol.1, 3–4. Austin: Texas State Historical Association, 1996.

Haggard, J. Villasaña. "Epidemic Cholera in Texas, 1833–1834." *Southwestern Historical Quarterly* 40 (January 1937): 216–230.

Hammet, Arthur B. *The Empresario Don Martin De León: The Richest Man in Texas*. Waco, Tex.: Texian Press, 1973.

Hardin, Stephen L. "Battle of the Alamo." In *The New Handbook of Texas*, edited by Ron Tyler, Douglas E. Barnett, Roy R. Barkley, Penelope C. Anderson, and Mark F. Odintz, vol.1, 83–87. Austin: Texas State Historical Association, 1996.

________. "Efficient in the Cause." In *Tejano Journey, 1770–1850,* edited by Gerald E. Poyo, 49–71. Austin: University of Texas Press, 1996.

________. "A Vatir y Perseguir: Tejano Deployment in the War of Texas Independence, 1835–1836." In *The E. C. Barksdale Student Lectures, 1985–1986*, edited by Lisa T. Davis, 160–176. Arlington: University of Texas at Arlington, 1986.

________, ed. "The Félix Nuñez Account and the Siege of the Alamo: A Critical Appraisal." *Southwestern Historical Quarterly* 94 (July 1990): 65–84.

Harris, Helen Willits. "Almonte's Inspection of Texas in 1834." *Southwestern Historical Quarterly* 41 (January 1938): 195–211.

Hendricks, Rick. "Fraud in the Lower Valley: The Rancho de Ysleta Grant Claim." *Password* 41 (Fall 1996): 135–149.

Henson, Margaret Swett. *Lorenzo de Zavala: The Pragmatic Idealist*. Fort Worth: Texas Christian University Press, 1996.

________. "Understanding Lorenzo de Zavala: Signer of the Texas Declaration of Independence." *Southwestern Historical Quarterly* 102 (July 1998): 1–17.

Herrera, Adolph Casías. "Blas María Herrera." In *The New Handbook of Texas*, edited by Ron Tyler, Douglas E. Barnett, Roy R. Barkley, Penelope C. Anderson, and Mark F. Odintz, vol. 3, 575. Austin: Texas State Historical Association, 1996.

Hinojosa, Gilberto M. "War and Social Change, Prosperity and Recession, 1810–1835." In *A Borderlands Town in Transition: Laredo, Texas, 1755–1870*, by Gilberto M. Hinojosa, 25–46. College Station: Texas A&M University Press, 1983.

Howrene, Alleine. "Causes and Origins of the Decree of April 6, 1830." *Southwestern Historical Quarterly* 16 (April 1913): 378–422.

Huson, Hobart. "José Miguel Aldrete." In *The New Handbook of Texas*, edited by Ron Tyler, Douglas E. Barnett, Roy R. Barkley, Penelope C. Anderson, and Mark F. Odintz, vol.1, 97–98. Austin: Texas State Historical Association, 1996.

Jackson, Jack. "Nicholas Trammel's Difficulties in Mexican Texas." *East Texas Historical Journal* 38.2 (2000): 15–39.

________, ed. *Texas by Terán: The Diary kept by General Manuel de Mier y Terán on his 1828 Inspection of Texas*. Austin: University of Texas Press, 2000.

Janicek, Ricki S. "The Development of Early Mexican Land Policy: Coahuila and Texas, 1810–1825." Ph.D. dissertation, Tulane University, 1985.

Jarratt, Rie. *Gutiérrez de Lara, Mexican-Texan: The Story of a Creole Hero*. Austin: Creole Texana, 1949. Reprinted in *The Mexican Experience in Texas*, edited by Carlos E. Cortés. New York: Arno Press, 1976.

Jennings, Frank. "Adina De Zavala: Alamo Crusader." *Texas Highways* 42 (March 1995): 15–21.

Johnson, John G. "José Miguel de Arciniega." In *The New Handbook of Texas*, edited by Ron Tyler, Douglas E. Barnett, Roy R. Barkley, Penelope C. Anderson, and Mark F. Odintz, vol.1, 234–235. Austin: Texas State Historical Association, 1996.

Jonas, Peter Mark. "United States Citizens vs. Mexico, 1821–1848." Ph.D. dissertation, Marquette University, 1989.

Kelly, Edith Louise, and Mattie Austin Hatcher, eds. "Tadeo Ortiz de Ayala and the Colonization of Texas, 1822–1833." *Southwestern Historical Quarterly* 32 (October 1928): 223–224.

Kemp, L. W. *The Signers of the Texas Declaration of Independence*. Houston: Anson Jones Press, 1944.

Kerr, Rita. *Juan Seguín*. Austin: Eakin Press, 1985.

Kite, Jodella Dorothea. "A Social History of the Anglo-American Colonies in Mexican Texas, 1821–1835." Ph.D. dissertation, Texas Tech University, 1990.

Lack, Paul D. "East Texas Mexicans and the Texas Revolution, 1835–1836." *Locus* 3.2 (1991): 141–155.

________. "Occupied Texas: Bexar and Goliad, 1835–1836." In *Mexican Americans in Texas History,* edited by Emilio Zamora, Cynthia Orozco, and Rodolfo Rocha, 35–49. Austin: Texas State Historical Association, 2000.

Levine, Paul G. "Remember the Alamo?" *American Film* 7 (January/February 1982): 47–48.

Long, Jeff. *Duel of Eagles: The Mexican and U.S. Fight for the Alamo*. New York: Quill, 1990.

Lowrie, Samuel H. *Culture Conflict in Texas, 1821–1835*. New York: Columbia University Press, 1932.

Lozano, Rubén Rendón. *Viva Tejas: The Story of the Mexican-Born Patriots of the Republic of Texas.* San Antonio: Southern Literary Institute, 1936.

Marsh, Gloria Candelaria. "Miguel Delgado." In *The New Handbook of Texas*, edited by Ron Tyler, Douglas E. Barnett, Roy R. Barkley, Penelope C. Anderson, and Mark F. Odintz, vol. 2, 574. Austin: Texas State Historical Association, 1996.

Matovina, Timothy M. *The Alamo Remembered: Tejano Accounts and Perspectives*. Austin: University of Texas Press, 1995.

________. "San Antonio Tejanos, 1821–1860: A Study of Religion and Ethnicity." Ph.D. dissertation, Catholic University of America, 1993.

________. "Between Two Worlds." In *Tejano Journey, 1770–1850,* edited by Gerald E. Poyo, 73–87. Austin: University of Texas Press, 1996.

________. "Religion and Ethnicity in San Antonio: Germans and Tejanos in the Wake of United States Annexation." *Catholic Southwest: A Journal of History and Culture* 10 (1999): 29–49.

________. "Tejano Accounts of the Alamo." *South Texas Studies* 5 (1994): 1–16.

McElhannon, Joseph C. "Imperial Mexico and Texas, 1821–1823." *Southwestern Historical Quarterly* 53 (1949): 117–150.

McLean, Malcolm D. "Tenoxtitlán: Dream Capital of Texas." *Southwestern Historical Quarterly* 70 (July 1966): 23–43.

McReynolds, James Michael. "Family Life in a Borderland Community: Nacogdoches, Texas, 1779–1861." Ph.D. dissertation, Texas Tech University, 1978.

Meacham, Tina Laurel. "The Population of Spanish and Mexican Texas, 1716–1836." Ph.D. dissertation, University of Texas at Austin, 2000.

Meyer, Nicholas E. "Juan Seguín." In *The Biographical Dictionary of Hispanic Americans*, by Nicholas E. Meyer, 205–206. New York: Facts on File, 1997.

________. "Lorenzo de Zavala." In *The Biographical Dictionary of Hispanic Americans*, by Nicholas E. Meyer, 235. New York: Facts on File, 1997.

Miller, Randall M. "After San Jacinto: Santa Anna's Role in Texas Independence." *East Texas Historical Journal* 9.1 (1971): 50–59.

Miller, Thomas Lloyd. "Mexican Texans at the Alamo." *Journal of Mexican American History* 2 (Fall 1971): 33–44.

________. "Mexican Texans in the Texas Revolution." *Journal of Mexican American History* 3 (1973): 105–130.

Milligan, James Clark. "José Bernardo Gutiérrez de Lara, Mexican Frontiersman, 1811–1841." Ph.D. dissertation, Texas Tech University, 1975.

Morton, Ohland. *Terán and Texas: A Chapter in Texas-Mexican Relations*. Austin: Texas State Historical Association, 1948.

Nathan, Debbie. "Forget the Alamo." *Texas Monthly* 26 (April 1998): 105–109.

O'Neal, John William. "Texas, 1791–1835: A Study in Manifest Destiny." Master's thesis, East Texas State University, 1969.

Osburn, Mary McMillan. "The Atacosito Census of 1826." *Texana* 1 (Fall 1963): 299–321.

Paredes, Raymund A. "The Origins of Anti-Mexican Sentiment in the United States." *New Scholar* 6 (1977): 139–165.

Patten, Roderick B. "José Antonio Menchaca." In *The New Handbook of Texas*, edited by Ron Tyler, Douglas E. Barnett, Roy R. Barkley, Penelope C. Anderson, and Mark F. Odintz, vol. 4, 617. Austin: Texas State Historical Association, 1996.

________. "Manuel Flores." In *The New Handbook of Texas*, edited by Ron Tyler, Douglas E. Barnett, Roy R. Barkley, Penelope C. Anderson, and Mark F. Odintz, vol. 2, 1036–1037. Austin: Texas State Historical Association, 1996.

________. "Manuel Flores." In *The New Handbook of Texas*, edited by Ron Tyler, Douglas E. Barnett, Roy R. Barkley, Penelope C. Anderson, and Mark F. Odintz, vol. 2, 1037. Austin: Texas State Historical Association, 1996.

Pohl, James W., and Stephen L. Hardin. "The Military History of the Texas Revolution: An Overview." *Southwestern Historical Quarterly* 89 (January 1986): 269–308.

Potter, Reuben M. "The Fall of the Alamo." *Magazine of American History* 2 (January 1878).

________. "The Prisoners of Matamoras: A Reminiscence of the Revolution of Texas." *Magazine of American History* 3 (May 1879).

________. "The Texas Revolution: Distinguished Mexicans Who Took Part in the Revolution of Texas, with Glances at Its Early Events." *Magazine of American History* 2 (October 1878).

Presley, James. "Santa Anna in Texas: A Mexican Viewpoint." *Southwestern Historical Quarterly* 62 (April 1959): 489–512.

Ragsdale, Crystal Sasse. *The Women and Children of the Alamo*. Austin: State House Press, 1994.

Ramos, Raúl Alberto. "From Norteño to Tejano: The Roots of Borderlands Ethnicity, Nationalism, and Political Identity in Bexar, 1811–1861." Ph.D. dissertation, Yale University, 1999.

Reichstein, Andreas; Dinorah Márquez, transl. "¿Era realmente inevitable? ¿Por que Mexico perdió Texas en 1836? Was It Really Inevitable? Why Did Mexico Lose Texas in 1836?" *Historia Mexicana* 42.4 (1993): 867–887.

Riley, John Denny. "Santos Benavides: His Influence on the Lower Rio Grande, 1823–1891." Ph.D. dissertation, Texas Christian University, 1976.

Ríos, Norma Elia Cantú. "José Francisco Ruiz: Signer of the Texas Declaration of Independence." Master's thesis, Texas Tech University, 1970.

Robinson, Cecil. "Flag of Illusion: The Texas Revolution Viewed as a Conflict of Cultures." *American West* 5.3 (1968): 10–17.

Rodríguez O., Jaime E. "La Constitución de 1824 y la formación del Estado Mexicano." *Historia Mexicana* 40 (1991): 507–535.

Roell, Craig H. "De León's Colony." In *The New Handbook of Texas*, edited by Ron Tyler, Douglas E. Barnett, Roy R. Barkley, Penelope C. Anderson, and Mark F. Odintz, vol. 2, 573–574. Austin: Texas State Historical Association, 1996.

________. "Fernando De León." In *The New Handbook of Texas*, edited by Ron Tyler, Douglas E. Barnett, Roy R. Barkley, Penelope C. Anderson, and Mark F. Odintz, vol. 2, 570–571. Austin: Texas State Historical Association, 1996.

________. "José Antonio Vásquez." In *The New Handbook of Texas,* edited by Ron Tyler, Douglas E. Barnett, Roy R. Barkley, Penelope C. Anderson, and Mark F. Odintz, vol. 6, 713. Austin: Texas State Historical Association, 1996.

________. "Plácido Benavides." In *The New Handbook of Texas*, edited by Ron Tyler, Douglas E. Barnett, Roy R. Barkley, Penelope C. Anderson, and Mark F. Odintz, vol. 1, 484. Austin: Texas State Historical Association, 1996.

________. "Rafael Antonio Manchola." In *The New Handbook of Texas*, edited by Ron Tyler, Douglas E. Barnett, Roy R. Barkley, Penelope C. Anderson, and Mark F. Odintz, vol. 4, 482–483. Austin: Texas State Historical Association, 1996.

________. "Silvestre De León." In *The New Handbook of Texas*, edited by Ron Tyler, Douglas E. Barnett, Roy R. Barkley, Penelope C. Anderson, and Mark F. Odintz, vol. 2, 572. Austin: Texas State Historical Association, 1996.

Rogers, Lisa Waller. *Angel of the Alamo: A True Story of Texas*. Austin: W. S. Benson, 2000.

Ruiz, José Francisco. *José Francisco Ruiz: Report on the Indian Tribes of Texas in 1828*, edited by John C. Ewers. New Haven: Yale University Library, 1972.

Salinas, Jesse. "The Political Career of Augustín Viesca, 1825–1835." Master's thesis, Southwest Texas State University, 1970.

Sánchez, José María. "A Trip to Texas in 1828." Transated by Carlos E. Castañeda. *Southwestern Historical Quarterly* 29 (April 1926): 249–288.

Santos, Richard G. *Santa Anna's Campaign Against Texas, 1835–1836.* Waco: Texian Press, 1968.

Schoelwer, Susan Prendergast. "Forgotten Heroes of the Alamo." *Journal of the West* 25.2 (1986): 73–80.

________, ed. *Alamo Images: Changing Perceptions of a Texas Experience*. Dallas: Southern Methodist University Press, 1985.

Schultz, Marvin Edward. "For the Better Administration of Justice: The Legal Culture of Texas, 1820–1836." Ph.D. dissertation, Texas Christian University, 1994.

Seguín, Juan N. *Personal Memoirs of Juan N. Seguín from the Year 1834 to the Retreat of General Woll from the City of San Antonio in 1842.* San Antonio: Ledger Book and Job Office, 1858.

Smith, Ralph A. "Mexican and Anglo-Saxon Traffic in Scalps, Slaves, and Livestock, 1835–1841." *West Texas Historical Association Yearbook* 36 (1960): 98–115.

Smith, Suzanne Joan. "Mexican Policy toward Texas, 1821–1825." Master's thesis, University of Texas at Austin, 1987.

Standifer, Mary M. "Luis Sánchez." In *The New Handbook of Texas,* edited by Ron Tyler, Douglas E. Barnett, Roy R. Barkley, Penelope C. Anderson, and Mark F. Odintz, vol. 5, 827–828. Austin: Texas State Historical Association, 1996.

________. "Manuel Antonio Santiago Tarín." In *The New Handbook of Texas*, edited by Ron Tyler, Douglas E. Barnett, Roy R. Barkley, Penelope C. Anderson, and Mark F. Odintz, vol. 6, 203–204. Austin: Texas State Historical Association, 1996.

________. "Nepomuceno Navarro." In *The New Handbook of Texas*, edited by Ron Tyler, Douglas E. Barnett, Roy R. Barkley, Penelope C. Anderson, and Mark F. Odintz, vol. 4, 956. Austin: Texas State Historical Association, 1996.

Strong, Bernice. "José Francisco Ruiz." In *The New Handbook of Texas,* edited by Ron Tyler, Douglas E. Barnett, Roy R. Barkley, Penelope C. Anderson, and Mark F. Odintz, vol. 4, 711–712. Austin: Texas State Historical Association, 1996.

Tanner, Eric. "The Texas Border and the Mexican Revolution." Master's thesis, Texas Tech University, 1970.

Tarin, Randell G. "José Toribio Losoya." In *The New Handbook of Texas*, edited by Ron Tyler, Douglas E. Barnett, Roy R. Barkley, Penelope C. Anderson, and Mark F. Odintz, vol. 4, 296–297. Austin: Texas State Historical Association, 1996.

________. "Pedro Herrera." In *The New Handbook of Texas*, edited by Ron Tyler, Douglas E. Barnett, Roy R. Barkley, Penelope C. Anderson, and Mark F. Odintz, vol. 3, 575–576. Austin: Texas State Historical Association, 1996.

Tarin, Randell G., and Robert L. Tarin Jr. "Vizente Tarin." In *The New Handbook of Texas*, edited by Ron Tyler, Douglas E. Barnett, Roy R. Barkley, Penelope C. Anderson, and Mark F. Odintz, vol. 6, 204. Austin: Texas State Historical Association, 1996.

Tatum, Inez. "Mexican Missions in Texas." Master's thesis, Baylor University, 1938.

Taylor, Mary D. "Cura de la Frontera, Ramón Ortiz." *U.S. Catholic Historian* 9.1–2 (Winter/Spring 1990): 67–85.

Taylor, Virginia H. *Index to Spanish and Mexican Land Grants*. Austin: General Land Office, 1976.

Texas General Land Office. *Guide to Spanish and Mexican Land Grants in South Texas*. Austin: Texas General Land Office, 1988.

Tijerina, Andrés A. *Tejanos and Texas Under the Mexican Flag, 1821–1836*. College Station: Texas A&M University Press, 1994.

________. "Tejanos and Texas: The Native Mexicans of Texas, 1820–1850." Ph.D. dissertation, University of Texas at Austin, 1977.

________. "Under the Mexican Flag." In *Tejano Journey, 1770–1850,* edited by Gerald E. Poyo, 33–47. Austin: University of Texas Press, 1996.

Tijerina, Andrés, and David J. Weber. "The State of Coahuila y Tejas in 1824: A Governor's View from Saltillo." *Southwestern Historical Quarterly* 100 (October 1996): 186–204.

Timmons, W. H. "The El Paso Area in the Mexican Period, 1821–1848." *Southwestern Historical Quarterly* 84 (July 1980): 1–28.

________. "Tadeo Ortiz and Texas." *Southwestern Historical Quarterly* 72 (July 1968): 21–33.

Tyler, Daniel. "The Mexican Teacher." *Red River Valley Historical Review* 1 (1974): 207–221.

Urbano, David. "The Saga of a Revolutionary Family: The Martin De León Family of Texas." Master's thesis, University of Texas at San Antonio, 1990.

________. "Placido Benavides in the Texas Revolution." *Journal of South Texas* 3 (1991): 1–32.

Valerio-Jiménez, Omar Santiago. "'Indios Bárbaros', Divorcees, and Flocks of Vampires: Identity and Nation on the Rio Grande, 1749–1894." Ph.D. dissertation, University of California, Los Angeles, 2001.

Vásquez, Josefina Zoraida. "The Colonization and Loss of Texas: A Mexican Perspective." In *Myths, Misdeeds, and Misunderstandings: The Roots of Conflict in U.S.-Mexican Relations*, edited by Jaime E. Rodríguez O. and Kathryn Vincent, 47–78. Wilmington, Del.: Scholarly Resources Press, 1997.

________. "The Texas Question in Mexican Politics, 1836–1845." *Southwestern Historical Quarterly* 89 (January 1986): 309–344.

Vernon, Ida S. "Activities of the Seguíns in Early Texas History." *West Texas Historical Association Yearbook* 25 (October 1949): 11–38.

Vigness, Winifred W. "Juan Nepomuceno Almonte." In *The New Handbook of Texas*, edited by Ron Tyler, Douglas E. Barnett, Roy R. Barkley, Penelope C. Anderson, and Mark F. Odintz, vol.1, 128–129. Austin: Texas State Historical Association, 1996.

Weber, David J. *The Mexican Frontier: The American Southwest Under Mexico, 1821–1846*. Albuquerque: University of New Mexico Press, 1982.

________. "The Church in Jeopardy." In *The Mexican Frontier, 1821-1846: The American Southwest under Mexico*, by David J. Weber, 69–82. Albuquerque: University of New Mexico Press, 1982.

________. "Failure of a Frontier Institution: The Secular Church in the Borderlands under Independent Mexico." *Western Historical Quarterly* 13 (April 1981): 125–143.

________. "Refighting the Alamo: Mythmaking and the Texas Revolution." In *Myth and the History of the Hispanic Southwest: Essays*, by David J. Weber, 133–151. Albuquerque: University of New Mexico Press, 1988.

________. "'Scarce More than Apes': Historical Roots of Anglo American Stereotypes of Mexican Americans." In *Bridging Two Cultures: Multidisciplinary Readings in Bicultural Education*, edited by Martha Cotera and Larry Hufford, 226–238. Austin: National Education Laboratory Publishers, 1980.

Weber, David J., ed., and Conchita Hassell Winn, trans. *Troubles in Texas, 1832: A Tejano Viewpoint from San Antonio.* Dallas: DeGolyer Library, Southern Methodist University, 1983.

Weddle, Robert S. "Damacio Jiménez." In *The New Handbook of Texas*, edited by Ron Tyler, Douglas E. Barnett, Roy R. Barkley, Penelope C. Anderson, and Mark F. Odintz, vol. 3, 940. Austin: Texas State Historical Association, 1996.

Williams, Amelia W. "A Critical Study of the Siege of the Alamo and Personnel of Its Defenders." Ph.D. dissertation, University of Texas, Austin, 1931.

________. "Alamo." In *The New Handbook of Texas*, edited by Ron Tyler, Douglas E. Barnett, Roy R. Barkley, Penelope C. Anderson, and Mark Odintz, vol. 1, 82–83. Austin: Texas State Historical Association, 1996.

________. "A Critical Study of the Siege of the Alamo and Personnel of Its Defenders." *Southwestern Historical Quarterly* 36 (April 1933): 251–287.

________. "A Critical Study of the Siege of the Alamo and Personnel of Its Defenders." *Southwestern Historical Quarterly* 36 (July 1933): 1–44.

________. "A Critical Study of the Siege of the Alamo and Personnel of Its Defenders." *Southwestern Historical Quarterly* 37 (October 1933): 79–115.

________. "A Critical Study of the Siege of the Alamo and Personnel of Its Defenders." *Southwestern Historical Quarterly* 37 (January 1934): 157–184.

________. "A Critical Study of the Siege of the Alamo and Personnel of Its Defenders." *Southwestern Historical Quarterly* 37 (April 1934): 237–312.

Wright, Robert E. "Catholic Diocesan Church of Spanish and Mexican Texas." In *The New Handbook of Texas*, edited by Ron Tyler, Douglas E. Barnett, Roy R.

Barkely, Penelope C. Anderson, and Mark F. Odintz, vol. 1, 1030–1031. Austin: Texas State Historical Association, 1996.

________. "The Hispanic Church in Texas under Spain and Mexico." *U.S. Catholic Historian* 20.4 (Fall 2002): 15–33.

________. "José Antonio Valdez." In *The New Handbook of Texas,* edited by Ron Tyler, Douglas E. Barnett, Roy R. Barkley, Penelope C. Anderson, and Mark F. Odintz, vol. 6, 688–689. Austin: Texas State Historical Association, 1996.

________. "The Parish of San Agustín, Laredo, 1760–1857." *San Agustín Parish of Laredo, Abstracts of Marriage Book I, 1790–1857*, by Angel Sepúlveda Brown and Gloria Villa Cadena, 1–46. San Antonio: privately printed, 1989.

________. "Popular and Official Religiosity: A Theoretical Analysis and A Case Study of Laredo-Nuevo Laredo, 1755–1857." Ph.D. dissertation, Graduate Theological Union, Berkeley, 1992.

5. NEW IDENTITY, OLD COMMUNITY, 1836–1880

According to the Texas Constitution of 1836, Mexicans who had been living in Texas at the time of the declaration of independence (March 2, 1836) became citizens of the Republic of Texas. The Constitution of 1845 (for the state of Texas) recognized the same citizenship status. Though Mexican Americans accepted Anglo-American politics and the new capitalism, they remained loyal to old Mexican customs and traditions. Most lived in semi-autonomous communities, either in the rural regions or in barrios (segregated sections in the urban landscape). As Texas remained basically rural and preoccupied with financial problems, sectionalism, and the Civil War and Reconstruction during this time period, mainstream society did little to disrupt the cultural ties that Tejanos maintained to their Spanish/Mexican past. But efforts to subordinate Tejanos socially seemed unrelenting. Violence, lynching, segregation, and charges of disloyalty acted as mechanisms of control.

Woman and three girls posed outside jacal, San Antonio, Texas, 1884–1889.
The Institute of Texan Cultures at UTSA, No. 83-100
Courtesy of T. K. Treadwell

Acosta, Teresa Palomo. "Basilio Benavides." In *The New Handbook of Texas*, edited by Ron Tyler, Douglas E. Barnett, Roy R. Barkley, Penelope C. Anderson, and Mark F. Odintz, vol. 1, 483. Austin: Texas State Historical Association, 1996.

________. "Gregorio García." In *The New Handbook of Texas*, edited by Ron Tyler, Douglas E. Barnett, Roy R. Barkley, Penelope C. Anderson, and Mark F. Odintz, vol. 3, 84. Austin: Texas State Historical Association, 1996.

________. "Thomas A. Rodríguez." In *The New Handbook of Texas*, edited by Ron Tyler, Douglas E. Barnett, Roy R. Barkely, Penelope C. Anderson, and Mark F. Odintz, vol. 4, 664–670. Austin: Texas State Historical Association, 1996.

Almaráz, Félix D. Jr. "The Historical Heritage of the Mexican American in Nineteenth Century Texas: An Interpretation." In *The Role of the Mexican American in the History of the Southwest*, Inter-American Institute, 12–23. Edinburg, Tex.: Pan American College, 1969.

Alonzo, Armando C. *Tejano Legacy: Rancheros and Settlers in South Texas, 1734–1900*. Albuquerque: University of New Mexico Press, 1998.

________. "Tejano Rancheros and Changes in Land Tenure, Hidalgo County, Texas, 1850–1900." Ph.D. dissertation, Indiana University, 1991.

________. "Change and Continuity in Tejano Ranches in the Trans-Nueces, 1848–1900." In *Ranching in South Texas: A Symposium*, edited by Joe S. Graham, 53–68. Kingsville, Tex.: John E. Conner Museum and Texas A&M University, 1992.

________."Mexican American Land Grant Adjudication." In *The New Handbook of Texas*, edited by Ron Tyler, Douglas E. Barnett, Roy R. Barkley, Penelope C. Anderson, and Mark F. Odintz, vol. 4, 656–659. Austin: Texas State Historical Association, 1996. Reprinted in *An Aquel Entonces: Readings in Mexican American History*, edited by Manuel C. Gonzales and Cynthia A. Gonzales, 64–71. Bloomington: Indiana University Press, 2000.

Ash, Betty Gay Hunter. "The Mexican Texan in the Civil War." Master's thesis, East Texas State University, 1972.

Austerman, Wayne R. "José Policarpo Rodríguez: Chicano Plainsman." *West Texas Historical Association Yearbook* 59 (1983): 52–74.

Baird, Robert. *The Life of Ramón Monsalvatge, a Converted Spanish Monk of the Order of the Capuchins*. New York: N.p., 1845.

Beecher, Dale Floyd. "Incentive to Violence: Political Exploitations of Lawlessness on the United States-Mexican Border, 1866–1886." Ph.D. dissertation, University of Utah, 1982.

"Benavides, Santos." In *The Handbook of Texas*, edited by Walter Prescott Webb and H. Bailey Carroll, vol. 1, 146. Austin: Texas State Historical Association, 1976.

Bennett, Eliana Guerreiro Ramos. "Frank Yturria: Profile of a Citizen." In *Studies in Matamoros and Cameron County History*, edited by Milo Kearney, Anthony Knopp, and Antonio Zavaleta, 191–194. Brownsville, Tex.: The University of Texas at Brownsville and Texas Southmost College, 1997.

Blackburn, George M., and Sherman L. Richards. "A Demographic History of the West: Nueces County, Texas, 1850." *Prologue* 4 (Spring 1972): 3–20.

Blake, R. B. "Córdova Rebellion." In *The Handbook of Texas*, edited by Walter Prescott Webb and H. Bailey Carroll, vol. 1, 412. Austin: Texas State Historical Association, 1976.

________. "Vicente Córdova." In *The New Handbook of Texas*, edited by Ron Tyler, Douglas E. Barnett, Roy R. Barkley, Penelope C. Anderson, and Mark F. Odintz, vol. 2, 324. Austin: Texas State Historical Association, 1996.

Brackenridge, R. Douglas, Francisco O. García, and John Stover. "Presbyterian Missions to Mexican Americans in Texas in the Nineteenth Century." *Journal of Presbyterian History* 49 (Summer 1971): 103–132.

Buenger, Walter L. "Orthodoxy and Ethnicity." In *Secession and the Union in Texas*, by Walter L. Buenger, 80–105. Austin: University of Texas Press, 1984.

Calderón, Roberto R. "Mexican Politics in the American Era, 1846–1900: Laredo, Texas." Ph.D. dissertation, University of California at Los Angeles, 1993.

________. "Tejano Politics." In *The New Handbook of Texas*, edited by Ron Tyler, Douglas E. Barnett, Roy R. Barkely, Penelope C. Anderson, and Mark F. Odintz, vol. 6, 239–242. Austin: Texas State Historical Association, 1996.

Canales, J. T. *Juan Cortina Presents His Motion for a New Trial.* San Antonio: Artes Gráficas, 1951.

"Carlos Rancho." In *The Handbook of Texas*, edited by Walter Prescott Webb and H. Bailey Carroll, vol. 1, 297. Austin: Texas State Historical Association, 1976.

Carpenter, Stephen M. "Search for the San Elizario Salt Road." *Journal of Big Bend Studies* 14 (2002): 141–162.

Carroll, Mark M. "Eros and Dominion: Indians, Tejanos, and Anglos." In *Homesteads Ungovernable: Families, Sex, Race, and the Law in Frontier Texas, 1823–1860*, by Mark M. Carroll, 22–50. Austin: University of Texas Press, 2001.

Chabrán, Richard, and Rafael Chabrán, eds. "Cart War." In *The Latino Encyclopedia*, edited by Richard Chabrán and Rafael Chabrán, vol. 1, 253. New York: Marshall Cavendish, 1996.

________. "Juan Cortina." In *The Latino Encyclopedia*, edited by Richard Chabrán and Rafael Chabrán, vol. 2, 388. New York: Marshall Cavendish, 1996.

________. "Republic of the Rio Grande." In *The Latino Encyclopedia*, edited by Richard Chabrán and Rafael Chabrán, vol. 5, 1383. New York: Marshall Cavendish, 1996.

________. "Salt War." In *The Latino Encyclopedia*, edited by Richard Chabrán and Rafael Chabrán, vol. 5, 1420. New York: Marshall Cavendish, 1996.

________. "Santos Benavides." In *The Latino Encyclopedia*, edited by Richard Chabrán and Rafael Chabrán, vol. 1, 155. New York: Marshall Cavendish, 1996.

Chance, Joseph E. "José María Carbajal, 1830–1874: The Life and Times of a Mexican Revolutionary." *South Texas Studies* 12 (2001): 1–20.

Connor, Seymour V. "Melinda Rankin." In *The New Handbook of Texas*, edited by Ron Tyler, Douglas E. Barnett, Roy R. Barkely, Penelope C. Anderson, and Mark F. Odintz, vol. 5, 445. Austin: Texas State Historical Association, 1996.

Crimm, Ana Carolina Castillo. "Success in Adversity: The Mexican Americans of Victoria County, Texas, 1800–1880." Ph.D. dissertation, University of Texas at Austin, 1994.

________. "Finding Their Way." In *Tejano Journey, 1770–1850*, edited by Gerald E. Poyo, 111–123. Austin: University of Texas Press, 1996.

Crook, Elaine Carland. "San Antonio, Texas, 1846–1861." Master's thesis, Rice University, 1964.

Cuéllar, Carlos E. "Laredo Small Pox Riot." In *The New Handbook of Texas*, edited by Ron Tyler, Douglas E. Barnett, Roy R. Barkely, Penelope C. Anderson, and Mark F. Odintz, vol. 4, 77–78. Austin: Texas State Historical Association, 1996.

________. "Raymond Martin." In *The New Handbook of Texas*, edited by Ron Tyler, Douglas E. Barnett, Roy R. Barkely, Penelope C. Anderson, and Mark F. Odintz, vol. 4, 531. Austin: Texas State Historical Association, 1996.

Curtis, Albert. *Fabulous San Antonio*. San Antonio: The Naylor Company, 1955.

Daddysman, James W. "Octaviano Zapata." In *The New Handbook of Texas*, edited by Ron Tyler, Douglas E. Barnett, Roy R. Barkely, Penelope C. Anderson, and Mark F. Odintz, vol. 6, 1142–1143. Austin: Texas State Historical Association, 1996.

Davenport, Herbert. "General José María Jésus Carbajal." *Southwestern Historical Quarterly* 55 (April 1952): 457–483.

________. "Captain Jesús Cuéllar, Texas Cavalry, Otherwise 'Comanche.'" *Southwestern Historical Quarterly* 30 (July 1926): 56–62.

Dawson, Joseph M. *José Antonio Navarro: Co-Creator of Texas.* Waco: Baylor University Press, 1969.

de la Teja, Jesús F. "Tejano and Texian: Seguín and Houston in the Making of Texas." *South Texas Studies* 3 (1992): 24–36.

________. "Discovering the Tejano Community in 'Early' Texas." *Journal of the 'Early' Republic* 18 (Spring 1988): 73–98.

________. "Juan Nepomuceno Seguín." In *The New Handbook of Texas*, edited by Ron Tyler, Douglas E. Barnett, Roy R. Barkley, Penelope C. Anderson, and Mark F. Odintz, vol. 5, 966–967. Austin: Texas State Historical Association, 1996.

De León, Arnoldo. *Benavides: The Town and Its Founder*. Benavides, Tex.: Benavides Centennial Committee, 1980.

________. *Social History of Mexican Americans in Nineteenth Century Duval County*. San Diego, Tex.: Commissioners' Court, 1978.

________. *They Called Them Greasers: Anglo Attitudes Towards Mexicans in Texas, 1821–1900*. Austin: University of Texas Press, 1983.

________. *The Tejano Community, 1836–1900*. Albuquerque: University of New Mexico Press, 1982.

________. "White Racial Attitudes toward Mexicanos in Texas, 1821–1900." Ph.D. dissertation, Texas Christian University, 1974.

________. "*Rancheros, Comerciantes,* and *Trabajadores* in South Texas, 1848–1900." In *Reflections of the Mexican Experience in Texas*, edited by Margarita B. Melville, 58–91. Houston: Mexican American Studies Center, University of Houston, 1979.

________. "Wresting a Competence in Nineteenth-Century Texas: The Case of the Chicanos." *Red River Valley Historical Review* 4 (Fall 1979): 52–64.

De León, Arnoldo, and Kenneth L. Stewart. *Tejanos and the Numbers Game: A Socio–Historical Profile from the Federal Censuses, 1850–1900*. Albuquerque: University of New Mexico Press, 1989.

________. "Age and Sex Composition Among *Inmigrantes* in Texas." *La Red/The Net* (February 1983): 2.

________. "Lost Dreams and Found Fortunes: Mexican and Anglo Immigrants to South Texas, 1850–1900." *Western Historical Quarterly* 14 (July 1983): 291–311.

________. "A Tale of Three Cities: A Comparative Analysis of the Socio–Economic Conditions of Mexican Americans in Los Angeles, Tucson, and San Antonio, 1850–1900." *Journal of the West* 24 (April 1985): 64–74.

________. "Tejano Demographic Patterns and Socio-Economic Development." *Borderlands Journal* 7 (Fall 1983): 1–9.

Dickens, E. Larry. "Mestizaje in Nineteenth-Century Texas." *Journal of Mexican American History* 2 (Spring 1972): 57–70.

Domenech, [Emmanuel]. *Missionary Adventures in Texas and Mexico: A Personal Narrative of Six Years' Sojourn in Those Regions*. London: Longman, Brown, Green, Longmans, and Roberts, 1858.

Douglas, James Ridley. "Juan Cortina: El Caudillo de la Frontera." Master's thesis, University of Texas at Austin, 1987.

Downing de Juana, Ana Cristina. "Intermarriage in Hidalgo County, 1860–1900." Master's thesis, University of Texas–Pan American, 1998.

Doyon, Bernard. *The Cavalry of Christ on the Rio Grande, 1849–1883*. Milwaukee: Bruce, 1956.

Dugan, Frank H. "The 1850 Affair of the Brownsville Separatists." *Southwestern Historical Quarterly* 61 (October 1957): 270–287.

Elam, Earl H. "Acculturation on the Rio Grande Frontier: The Founding of San José de Polvo and the Family of Lucía Rede Madrid." *Journal of Big Bend Studies* 5 (1993): 79–95.

"El Sauz, Texas." In *The Handbook of Texas*, edited by Walter Prescott Webb and H. Bailey Carroll, vol. 1, 564. Austin: Texas State Historical Association, 1976.

Fritz, Naomi. "José Antonio Navarro." Master's thesis, St. Mary's University, 1941.

García, Frank Jr. "José de Guadalupe García." In *The New Handbook of Texas*, edited by Ron Tyler, Douglas E. Barnett, Roy R. Barkley, Penelope C. Anderson, and Mark F. Odintz, vol. 3, 363. Austin: Texas State Historical Association, 1996.

Goldfinch, Charles W. "Juan N. Cortina, 1824–1892: A Reappraisal." Master's thesis, University of Chicago, 1949.

________. *Juan N. Cortina, 1824–1892: A Reappraisal*. Brownsville, Tex.: Bishop Print Shop, 1950.

________. "Juan N. Cortina, 1824–1892: A Reappraisal." In *Furia y Muerte: Los Bandidos Chicanos*, edited by Pedro Castillo and Albert Camarillo, 84–112. Los Angeles: Aztlán Publications, 1973.

Goldfinch, Charles W., and José T. Canales. *Juan N. Cortina: Two Interpretations*. New York: Arno Press, 1974.

González Quiroga, Miguel A. "Mexicanos in Texas During the Civil War." In *Mexican Americans in Texas History*, edited by Emilio Zamora, Cynthia Orozco, and Rodolfo Rocha, 51–62. Austin: Texas State Historical Association, 2000.

________. "Trabajadores Mexicanos en Texas (1850–1865); Los Carreteros y el Transporte de Carga." *Siglo XIX: Cuadernos de Historia* 3.9 (1994): 51–81.

Goodwyn, Frank. "Manuel Flores." In *The Handbook of Texas*, edited by Walter Prescott Webb and H. Bailey Carroll, vol. 1, 611–612. Austin: Texas State Historical Association, 1976.

Graf, LeRoy P. "The Economic History of the Lower Rio Grande, 1829–1875." Ph.D. dissertation, Harvard University, 1942.

Graham, Joe Stanley. *El Rancho in South Texas: Continuity and Change from 1750.* Denton: University of North Texas Press, 1994.

Greaser, Galen D., and Jesús F. de la Teja. "Quieting Title to the Spanish and Mexican Land Grants in the Trans–Nueces: The Bourland and Miller Commission, 1850–1852." *Southwestern Historical Quarterly* 95 (April 1992): 445–464.

Grimm, Agnes G. "Pablo Pérez." In *The New Handbook of Texas*, edited by Ron Tyler, Douglas E. Barnett, Roy R. Barkely, Penelope C. Anderson, and Mark F. Odintz, vol. 5, 150. Austin: Texas State Historical Association, 1996.

Griswold del Castillo, Richard. "'Only for My Family': Historical Dimensions of Chicano Family Solidarity—The Case of San Antonio in 1860." *Aztlán* 16 (1985): 145–176.

Gutmann, Myron P., Kristine Hopkins, Kenneth H. Fliess, and Gabriela Montes de Oca Vega, trans. "Matrimonio y Migración en la Frontera: Patrones de Nupcialidad en Texas, 1850–1910/Marriage and Migration at the Border: Patterns of Nuptiality in Texas, 1850–1910." *Historia Mexicana* 42 (julio-septiembre 1992): 45–76.

Hager, William M. "The Nueces Town Raid of 1875: A Border Incident." *Arizona and the West* 1 (Spring 1959): 258–270.

Hendricks, Rick. "Antonio Severo Borrajo: Hispano-Mexican Patriot Priest." *Southern New Mexico Historical Review* 9.1 (January 2002): 1–5.

Hernández, Sonia. "The Legacy of the Treaty of Guadalupe Hidalgo on *Tejanos'* Land." *Journal of Popular Culture* 35 (Fall 2001): 101–109.

Herrera, Adolph Casías. "Blas María Herrera." In *The New Handbook of Texas*, edited by Ron Tyler, Douglas E. Barnett, Roy R. Barkley, Penelope C. Anderson, and Mark F. Odintz, vol. 3, 575. Austin: Texas State Historical Association, 1996.

Herring, Rebecca J. "Córdova Rebellion." In *The New Handbook of Texas*, edited by Ron Tyler, Douglas E. Barnett, Roy R. Barkley, Penelope C. Anderson, and Mark F. Odintz, vol. 2, 324–325. Austin: Texas State Historical Association, 1996.

Hinojosa, Gilberto M. *A Borderlands Town in Transition: Laredo, Texas, 1755–1870*. College Station: Texas A&M University Press, 1983.

________. "Settlers and Sojourners in the Chaparral: A Demographic Study of a Borderlands Town in Transition, Laredo, 1755–1870." Ph.D dissertation, University of Texas at Austin, 1979.

Horton, Hamilton G. "Beginnings of the Mexican Work." *Texas Methodist Historical Quarterly* 1.3 (January 1910): 289–291.

Hunt, David Glenn, ed. "Vito Alessio Robles' *Coahuila y Texas Desde la Consumación de la Independencia Hasta el Tratado de Paz de Guadalupe Hidalgo* (Vol. II)." Master's thesis, Southern Methodist University, 1950.

Huson, Hobart. "Antonio Canales." In *The Handbook of Texas: A Supplement*, edited by Eldon Stephen Branda, vol. 3, 141–142. Austin: Texas State Historical Association, 1976.

________. "Carlos de la Garza." In *The New Handbook of Texas*, edited by Ron Tyler, Douglas E. Barnett, Roy R. Barkley, Penelope C. Anderson, and Mark F. Odintz, vol. 3, 105–106. Austin: Texas State Historical Association, 1996.

Jorda, Laron Donald, ed. "Vito Alessio Robles' *Coahuila y Texas Desde la Consumación de la Independencia Hasta el Tratado de Paz de Guadalupe Hidalgo* (Vol. I)." Master's thesis, Southern Methodist University, 1950.

Jordan, Terry G. "The 1887 Census of Texas' Hispanic Population." *Aztlán* 7 (August 1981): 271–278.

________. "Population Origins in Texas, 1850." *Geographical Review* 59 (January 1969): 83–103.

Juárez, José Roberto. "La Iglesia Católica y el Chicano en Sud Texas, 1836–1911." *Aztlán* 4.2 (Fall 1973): 217–254.

Kearney, Milo. "De la Garzas, Ballís, and the Political History of the Region that would later become Cameron County." In *More Studies in Brownsville History*, edited by Milo Kearney, 39–68. Brownsville, Tex.: Pan American University at Brownsville, 1989.

Knight, Lawrence Phillip. "Becoming a City and Becoming American: San Antonio, Texas, 1848–1861." Ph.D. dissertation, Texas A&M University, College Station, 1997.

Lack, Paul D. "The Córdova Revolt." In *Tejano Journey, 1770–1850*, edited by Gerald E. Poyo, 89–109. Austin: University of Texas Press, 1996.

________. "Los tejanos leales a México del este de Texas, 1838–1839." *Historia Mexicana* 42 (abril-junio 1993): 889–917.

Larralde, Carlos. *Carlos Esparza: A Chicano Chronicle*. San Francisco: R&E Research Associates, 1977.

________. "Carlos Esparza." In *The New Handbook of Texas*, edited by Ron Tyler, Douglas E. Barnett, Roy R. Barkley, Penelope C. Anderson, and Mark F. Odintz, vol. 2, 892–893. Austin: Texas State Historical Association, 1996.

________. "Juan Cortina's Spy: Elena Villarreal de Ferrer." *Journal of South Texas* 11 (1998): 104–124.

________. "Texts, by Carlos Esparza." *Critica: A Journal of Critical Essays* 1 (Spring 1984): 91–109.

Larralde, Carlos, and José Rodolfo Jacobo. *Juan N. Cortina and the Struggle for Justice in Texas*. Dubuque, Iowa: Kendall/Hunt Publishing, 2000.

Liddick, Morgan C. "Tejanos and Anglos in the Republic of Texas: Perceptions and External Factors in the Relationship." Master's thesis, California State University, Domínguez Hills, 1999.

Lott, Virgil N., and Virginia M. Fenwick. *People and Plots on the Rio Grande*. San Antonio: The Naylor Company, 1953.

Maretta, John. "José María Carvajal: United States Foreign Policy and the Filibustering Spirit in Texas, 1846–1853." *East Texas Historical Journal* 33 (1995): 3–20.

Marsh, Gloria Candelaria. "Juan Moya." In *The New Handbook of Texas*, edited by Ron Tyler, Douglas E. Barnett, Roy R. Barkely, Penelope C. Anderson, and Mark F. Odintz, vol. 4, 873–874. Austin: Texas State Historical Association, 1996.

Martínez, Juan Francisco. "Origins and Development of Protestantism among Latinos in the Southwestern United States, 1836–1900." Ph.D. dissertation, Fuller Theological Seminary, 1996.

Matovina, Timothy M. *Tejano Religion and Ethnicity: San Antonio, 1821–1860.* Austin: University of Texas Press, 1995.

________. "San Antonio Tejanos, 1821–1860: A Study of Religion and Ethnicity." Ph.D. dissertation, Catholic University of America, 1993.

________. "Between Two Worlds." In *Tejano Journey, 1770–1850,* edited by Gerald E. Poyo, 73–87. Austin: University of Texas Press, 1996.

________. "Guadalupan Devotion in a Borderlands Community." *Journal of Hispanic/Latino Theology* 4.1 (August 1996): 6–26.

________. "Lay Initiatives in Worship on the Texas *Frontera*, 1830–1860." *U.S. Catholic Historian* 12.4 (Fall 1994): 107–120.

________. "Our Lady of Guadalupe Celebrations in San Antonio, Texas, 1840–41. *Journal of Hispanic/Latino Theology* 1.1 (November 1993): 77–96.

________. "Religion and Ethnicity in San Antonio: Germans and Tejanos in the Wake of United States Annexation." *Catholic Southwest: A Journal of History and Culture* 10 (1999): 29–49.

McCoy, Dorothy Abbott. "Francisco Yturria and Heirs." In *Roots by the River*, by Valley By-Liners, 91–94. Mission, Tex.: Border Kingdom Press, 1978.

McDaniel, Ruel. "The Day They Hanged Chipita." *Texas Parade* (September 1962): 18–19.

McKenna, Verna J. "Francisco Yturria." In *The New Handbook of Texas*, edited by Ron Tyler, Douglas E. Barnett, Roy R. Barkely, Penelope C. Anderson, and Mark F. Odintz, vol. 5, 1134–1135. Austin: Texas State Historical Association, 1996.

McNeely, John H. "Juan María Ponce De León." In *The Handbook of Texas*, edited by Walter Prescott Webb and H. Bailey Carroll, vol. 1, 484. Austin: Texas State Historical Association, 1976.

Meier, Matt S. with Conchita Franco Serri and Richard A. García. "Juan Cortina." In *Notable Latino Americans: A Biographical Dictionary*, by Matt S. Meier, 103–106. Westport, Conn.: Greenwood Press, 1997.

"Menchaca, José Antonio." In *The Handbook of Texas*, edited by Walter Prescott Webb and H. Bailey Carroll, vol. 2, 172. Austin: Texas State Historical Association, 1976.

Meyer, Nicholas E. "Juan Nepomuceno Cortina." In *Biographical Dictionary of Hispanic Americans*, by Nicholas E. Meyer, 61–63. New York: Facts on File, 1997.

Meza, Rene Raymond. "Darío Sánchez." In *The New Handbook of Texas*, edited by Ron Tyler, Douglas E. Barnett, Roy R. Barkely, Penelope C. Anderson, and Mark F. Odintz, vol. 5, 826. Austin: Texas State Historical Association, 1996.

Miller, Thomas Lloyd. "José Antonio Navarro, 1795–1871." *Journal of Mexican American History* 2 (Spring 1972): 70–89.

Morris, Leopold. "The Mexican Raid of 1875 on Corpus Christi." *Quarterly of the Texas State Historical Association* 4 (October 1900): 128–139.

Nance, John Milton. *After San Jacinto: The Texas-Mexican Frontier, 1836–1841*. Austin: University of Texas Press, 1962.

________. *Attack and Counterattack: The Texas-Mexican Frontier, 1842*. Austin: University of Texas Press, 1965.

"Navarro, Angel." In *The Handbook of Texas*, edited by Walter Prescott Webb and H. Bailey Carroll, vol. 2, 262. Austin: Texas State Historical Association, 1976.

Navarro, José Antonio. *Defending Mexican Valor in Texas: José Antonio Navarro's Historical Writings, 1853–1857*, edited by David R. McDonald and Timothy M. Matovina. Austin: State House Press, 1995.

Negrete Salas, Martaelena. "La Frontera Texana y el Abigeato (1848–1872)/The Texas Border and Cattle Stealing: 1848–1872." *Historia Mexicana* 31 (julio-septiembre 1981): 79–100.

Ochoa, Ernest R. "Texas, First Dismemberment of Mexico; A Translation of Carlos Pereyra's 'Tejas, La Primera Dismembración de Méjico.'" Master's thesis, Southern Methodist University, 1948.

Odintz, Mark. "José Rafael Calixto de la Garza." In *The New Handbook of Texas*, edited by Ron Tyler, Douglas E. Barnett, Roy R. Barkley, Penelope C. Anderson, and Mark F. Odintz, vol. 3, 108. Austin: Texas State Historical Association, 1996.

Orozco, Cynthia. "Petra Vela de Vidal Kenedy." In *The New Handbook of Texas*, edited by Ron Tyler, Douglas E. Barnett, Roy R. Barkley, Penelope C. Anderson, and Mark F. Odintz, vol. 3, 1065. Austin: Texas State Historical Association, 1996.

Parra, José Antonio. "The Battle for the Salt of the Earth." *Nuestro* 3 (August 1979): 54–56.

Pate, J'Nell. "United States-Mexican Border Conflicts, 1870–1880." *West Texas Historical Association Yearbook* 38 (October 1962): 175–194.

Patten, Roderick B. "José Antonio Menchaca." In *The Handbook of Texas: A Supplement*, edited by Eldon Stephen Branda, vol. 3, 586–587. Austin: Texas State Historical Association, 1976.

________. "Manuel Flores." In *The Handbook of Texas: A Supplement*, edited by Eldon Stephen Branda, vol. 3, 300. Austin: Texas State Historical Association, 1976.

Pingenot, Ben E. "Colonel 'Winker' Valdés: 'El Azote de los Indios.'" *Journal of Big Bend Studies* 9 (1997): 33–43.

Primera, Joe C. "Los Hermanos Torres: Early Settlers of Pecos County." *Permian Historical Annual* 20 (1980): 89–96.

Ramírez, Laura Lamar. "Bartolomé García." In *The New Handbook of Texas*, edited by Ron Tyler, Douglas E. Barnett, Roy R. Barkley, Penelope C. Anderson, and Mark F. Odintz, vol. 3, 82–83. Austin: Texas State Historical Association, 1996.

Ramos, Raúl Alberto. "From Norteño to Tejano: The Roots of Borderlands Ethnicity, Nationalism, and Political Identity in Béxar, 1811–1861." Ph.D. dissertation, Yale University, 1999.

Rankin, Melinda. *Twenty Years Among the Mexicans: A Narrative of Missionary Labor*. Third edition. Cincinnati: Central Book Concern, 1881.

Rayburn, John C. "Melinda Rankin—Crusader of the Rio Grande." *Journal of Presbyterian History* 40 (September 1962): 160–180.

Reily, John Denny. "Santos Benavides: His Influence on the Lower Rio Grande, 1823–1891." Ph.D. dissertation, Texas Christian University, 1976.

Remy, Caroline M. "Hispanic-Mexican San Antonio: 1836–1861." *Southwestern Historical Quarterly* 71 (1968): 564–582.

Reséndez, Andrés. "National Identity on a Shifting Border: Texas and New Mexico in the Age of Transition, 1821–1848." *Journal of American History* 86 (September 1999): 668–688.

Rippy, J. Fred. "Border Troubles along the Rio Grande, 1848–1860." *Southwestern Historical Quarterly* 33 (October 1919): 91–111.

Robinson, Robert L. "The U.S. Navy vs. Cattle Rustlers: The *U.S.S. Río Bravo* on the Rio Grande, 1875–1879." *Military History of Texas and the Southwest* 15 (1979): 43–52.

Robinson, Robin. "Accommodation to Domination: Demise of the Tejano Elite in the Lower Rio Grande." *Journal of South Texas* 10 (1997): 69–87.

"Rodríguez, José María." In *The Handbook of Texas*, edited by Walter Prescott Webb and H. Bailey Carroll, vol. 2, 497. Austin: Texas State Historical Association, 1976.

"Rodríguez, José Policarpo." In *The Handbook of Texas*, edited by Walter Prescott Webb and H. Bailey Carroll, vol. 2, 497. Austin: Texas State Historical Association, 1976.

Roebuck, Field. "Cheno Cortina: Red Robber of the Rio Grande." *True West* 36 (September 1989): 16–21.

Romero, Mary. "El Paso Salt War: Mob Action or Political Struggle." *Aztlán* 16 (1985): 119–143.

Salmón, Roberto Mario. "Antonio Canales and the Republic of the Rio Grande, 1839–1850." In *Still More Studies on Brownsville History,* edited by Milo Kearney, 175–180. Brownsville, Tex.: The University of Texas at Brownsville, 1991.

________. "Antonio Canales Rosillo." In *The New Handbook of Texas*, edited by Ron Tyler, Douglas E. Barnett, Roy R. Barkley, Penelope C. Anderson, and Mark F. Odintz, vol. 1, 954–955. Austin: Texas State Historical Association, 1996.

________. "Antonio Zapata." In *The New Handbook of Texas*, edited by Ron Tyler, Douglas E. Barnett, Roy R. Barkely, Penelope C. Anderson, and Mark F. Odintz, vol. 6, 1142. Austin: Texas State Historical Association, 1996.

________. "The Brownsville Protest Movement of January 1866." In *Still More Studies on Brownsville History*, edited by Milo Kearney, 219–226. Brownsville, Tex.: The University of Texas at Brownsville, 1991.

________. "Don José San Román as Brownsville Capitalist, 1822–1879." *South Texas Studies* 1 (1990): 54–68.

Sánchez, Juan O. "Alberto Garza." In *The New Handbook of Texas*, edited by Ron Tyler, Douglas E. Barnett, Roy R. Barkley, Penelope C. Anderson, and Mark F. Odintz, vol. 3, 104–105. Austin: Texas State Historical Association, 1996.

________. "Darío Gonzales." In *The New Handbook of Texas*, edited by Ron Tyler, Douglas E. Barnett, Roy R. Barkley, Penelope C. Anderson, and Mark F. Odintz, vol. 3, 227. Austin: Texas State Historical Association, 1996.

Schneider, Ellen, and Paul H. Carlson. "Gunnysackers, *Carreteros*, and Teamsters: The South Texas Cart War of 1857." *Journal of South Texas* 1 (Spring 1988): 1–9.

Screws, David E. "Hispanic Texas Rangers Contribute to Peace on the Texas Frontier, 1838–1880." *Journal of Big Bend Studies* 13 (2001): 27–36.

Segovia, José Francisco. "Cristóbal Benavides." In *The New Handbook of Texas*, edited by Ron Tyler, Douglas E. Barnett, Roy R. Barkley, Penelope C. Anderson, and Mark F. Odintz, vol. 1, 483–484. Austin: Texas State Historical Association, 1996.

Shearer, Ernest C. "The Caravajal Disturbances." *Southwestern Historical Quarterly* 55 (October 1951): 201–230.

Siegel, Stanley E. "José Antonio Navarro." In *The New Handbook of Texas*, edited by Ron Tyler, Douglas E. Barnett, Roy R. Barkely, Penelope C. Anderson, and Mark F. Odintz, vol. 4, 954–955. Austin: Texas State Historical Association, 1996.

Simmen, Edward. "Thomas Gonzales." In *The New Handbook of Texas*, edited by Ron Tyler, Douglas E. Barnett, Roy R. Barkley, Penelope C. Anderson, and Mark F. Odintz, vol. 3, 228. Austin: Texas State Historical Association, 1996.

Sisneros, Samuel E. "El Paseño, Padre Ramón Ortíz: 1814–1896." *Password* 44 (Fall 1999): 107–121.

Smith, Anita Torres, and Donald E. Smith. "The Life and Times of Valeriano Torres, 1844–1898." *Journal of Big Bend Studies* 13 (2001): 37–64.

Sneed, Edgar P., and Grace Edman. "José San Román." In *The Handbook of Texas: A Supplement*, edited by Eldon Stephen Branda, vol. 3, 851–852. Austin: Texas State Historical Association, 1976.

Sonnichsen, C. L. *The El Paso Salt War*. El Paso: Texas Western Press, 1961.

________. "The El Paso Salt War." In *Ten Texas Feuds*, by C. L. Sonnichsen, 108–156. Albuquerque: University of New Mexico Press, 1957.

________. "The El Paso Salt War." In *The Handbook of Texas*, edited by Walter Prescott Webb and H. Bailey Carroll, vol. 2, 536–537. Austin: Texas State Historical Association, 1976.

________. "The El Paso Salt War." In *The New Handbook of Texas*, edited by Ron Tyler, Douglas E. Barnett, Roy R. Barkely, Penelope C. Anderson, and Mark F. Odintz, vol. 5, 783. Austin: Texas State Historical Association, 1996.

Tafoya, Carmen. "The Church in Texas." In *Fronteras: A History of the Latin American Church in the USA since 1513*, edited by Moisés Sandoval, 183–194. San Antonio: Mexican American Cultural Center, 1983.

Thompson, James H. "A Nineteenth Century History of Cameron County, Texas." Master's thesis, University of Texas, Austin, 1965.

Thompson, Jerry D. *Mexican Texans in the Union Army*. El Paso: Texas Western Press, 1986.

________. *Sabers on the Rio Grande*. Austin: Presidial Press, 1974.

________. *Vaqueros in Blue and Gray: Mexican Texans in the Civil War*. Austin: Presidial Press, 1976.

________. "Adrián J. Vidal." In *The New Handbook of Texas*, edited by Ron Tyler, Douglas E. Barnett, Roy R. Barkely, Penelope C. Anderson, and Mark F. Odintz, vol. 6, 743–744. Austin: Texas State Historical Association, 1996.

________. "Juan Nepomuceno Cortina." In *The New Handbook of Texas*, edited by Ron Tyler, Douglas E. Barnett, Roy R. Barkley, Penelope C. Anderson, and Mark F. Odintz, vol. 2, 343–344. Austin: Texas State Historical Association, 1996.

________. "The Many Faces of Juan Nepomuceno Cortina." *South Texas Studies* 2 (1991): 85–98.

________. "Mexican-Americans in the Civil War: The Battle of Valverde." *Texana* 10 (1972): 1–19.

________. "Mexican-Texans in the Civil War." In *The New Handbook of Texas*, edited by Ron Tyler, Douglas E. Barnett, Roy R. Barkely, Penelope C. Anderson, and Mark F. Odintz, vol. 4, 688–689. Austin: Texas State Historical Association, 1996.

________. "Mutiny and Desertion on the Rio Grande: The Strange Saga of Captain Adrián J. Vidal." *Military History of Texas and the Southwest* 12 (1975): 159–169.

________. "Refugio Benavides." In *The New Handbook of Texas*, edited by Ron Tyler, Douglas E. Barnett, Roy R. Barkley, Penelope C. Anderson, and Mark F. Odintz, vol. 1, 484–485. Austin: Texas State Historical Association, 1996.

________. "Santos Benavides." In *The New Handbook of Texas*, edited by Ron Tyler, Douglas E. Barnett, Roy R. Barkley, Penelope C. Anderson, and Mark F. Odintz, vol. 1, 485–486. Austin: Texas State Historical Association, 1996.

________. "A Stand Along the Border: Santos Benavides and the Battle for Laredo." *Civil War Times Illustrated* 19 (August 1980): 26–33.

________, ed. *Juan Cortina and the Texas-Mexico Frontier, 1859–1877*. El Paso: Texas Western Press, 1994.

Tijerina, Andrés. "A Tejano Prayer." In *Tejano Empire: Life on the South Texas Ranchos*, by Andrés Tijerina, 107–121. College Station: Texas A&M University Press, 1998.

Turner, Oreta. "Border Troubles Along the Rio Grande from 1848–1878." Master's thesis, East Texas State Teachers College, 1940.

Valerio-Jiménez, Omar Santiago. "'Indios Bárbaros', Divorcees, and Flocks of Vampires: Identity and Nation on the Rio Grande, 1749–1894." Ph.D. dissertation, University of California, Los Angeles, 2001.

Vest, Deed L. "The Chihuahuan Road." *Texana* 5 (Spring 1967): 1–10.

Vigness, David M. "The Lower Rio Grande Valley of Texas." Master's thesis, University of Texas, Austin, 1948.

________. "Antonio Zapata." In *The Handbook of Texas*, edited by Walter Prescott Webb and H. Bailey Carroll, vol. 2, 950. Austin: Texas State Historical Association, 1952.

________."Juan Nepomuceno Cortina." In *The Handbook of Texas*, edited by Walter Prescott Webb and H. Bailey Carroll, vol. 1, 416. Austin: Texas State Historical Association, 1976.

Wagner, Frank. "Cecilio Balerio." In *The New Handbook of Texas*, edited by Ron Tyler, Douglas E. Barnett, Roy R. Barkley, Penelope C. Anderson, and Mark F. Odintz, vol. 1, 356. Austin: Texas State Historical Association, 1996.

________. "Domínguez Mexican Company." In *The New Handbook of Texas*, edited by Ron Tyler, Douglas E. Barnett, Roy R. Barkley, Penelope C. Anderson, and Mark F. Odintz, vol. 2, 674. Austin: Texas State Historical Association, 1996.

Walraven, Edward Lee. "Ambivalent Americans: Selected Spanish Language Newspapers' Response to Anglo Domination in Texas, 1830–1910." Ph.D. dissertation, Texas A&M University, College Station, 1999.

Ward, Charles Francis. "The Salt War of San Elizario." Master's thesis, University of Texas, Austin, 1932.

Washington, Ann Reed. "South Texas' Greatest Folk Healer." In *Roots by the River*, by Valley By-Liners, 95–98. Mission, Tex.: Border Kingdom Press, 1978.

________. "Three Restless Men of Violent Times: Carbajal, Cortina and Ford." In *Roots by the River*, by Valley By-Liners, 39–44. Mission, Tex.: Border Kingdom Press, 1978.

Webster, Michael G. "Texas Manifest Destiny and the Mexican Border Conflict, 1865–1880." Ph.D. dissertation, University of Indiana, 1972.

________. "Juan N. Cortina, defensor de la raza." In *El México Olvidado: La Historia del Pueblo Chicano*, coordinated by David R. Maciel, tomo 1, 145–163. Ciudad Juárez and El Paso: Universidad Autónoma de Ciudad Juárez and University of Texas at El Paso, 1996.

Webster, Mike. "Juan N. Cortina, defensor de la raza." In *Aztlán: historia del pueblo chicano (1848–1910)*, edited by David R. Maciel and Patricia Bueno. Mexico: Secretaría de Educación Público, 1975.

Woodman, Lyman L. *Cortina, the Rogue of the Rio Grande*. San Antonio: The Naylor Company, 1950.

Wright, Robert E. "Anglo Protestant Denominations and Mexicans in the Border Zone, 1836–1875." In "Popular and Official Religiosity: A Theoretical Analysis and a Case Study of Laredo-Nuevo Laredo, 1755–1857," by Robert E. Wright, 279–331. Ph.D. dissertation, Graduate Theological Union, Berkeley, 1992.

________. "Building Churches and Communities in 19th Century South Texas." *Heritage: A Publication of the Texas Historical Foundation* 17.1 (Spring 1999): 16–20.

________. "The Catholic Church in Laredo-Nuevo Laredo, 1858–1881." In *San Agustín Parish of Laredo: Abstracts of Marriage Book II, 1858–1881*, by Angel Sepúlveda Brown and Gloria Villa Cadena, ix–xxxiii. San Antonio: privately printed, 1993.

Wunder, John R., and Rebecca J. Herring. "Frontier Conspiracy: Law, History, Turner and the Córdova Rebellion." *Red River Valley Historical Review* 7 (Summer 1982): 51–67.

"Zaragosa, Ignacio." In *The Handbook of Texas: A Supplement*, edited by Eldon Stephen Branda, vol. 3, 1142–1143. Austin: Texas State Historical Association, 1976.

6. INTO THE TWENTIETH CENTURY, 1880–1920

Demonstrable forces took Texas and Texans in new directions for about forty years after 1880. During this time period, as one recent scholar has noted, there occurred "a series of economic changes, social processes, discursive articulations, and cultural forms that resulted in the transformation of Texas from a largely Mexican, cattle-based society into an industrial and agricultural social complex . . . ."[1] The transformation energized some elements within the Tejano community, as evident in increased involvement in the politics and the economic dynamism of the era. On the other hand, change accelerated the pace of land loss, threw Tejanos into the migrant stream, cemented racist ideas about Mexicans, engendered culture conflict, provoked a Tejano rebellion in 1915, led to renewed campaigns to disenfranchise Mexican Americans, and otherwise arrested upward mobility. Simultaneously, Tejanos retained a loyalty to their Mexican heritage, and great waves of immigration from Mexico buttressed "*lo mexicano*."

---

[1]Richard R. Flores, *Rembering the Alamo: Memory, Modernity, and the Master Symbol.* (Austin: University of Texas Press, 2002), p. xvii.

Workers in a tailoring company, San Antonio, Texas ca. 1910s.
The Institute of Texan Cultures at UTSA, No. 87-385
Courtesy of Mrs. Robert Rubio

Ables, L. Robert. "Adina Emilia de Zavala." In *The Handbook of Texas: A Supplement*, edited by Eldon Stephen Branda, vol. 3, 242–243. Austin: Texas State Historical Association, 1976.

________. "The Second Battle for the Alamo." *Southwestern Historical Quarterly* 70 (January 1967): 372–413.

Acosta, Teresa Palomo. "Cleofas Calleros." In *The New Handbook of Texas*, edited by Ron Tyler, Douglas E. Barnett, Roy R. Barkley, Penelope C. Anderson, and Mark F. Odintz, vol. 1, 910. Austin: Texas State Historical Association, 1996.

________. "Congreso Mexicanista." In *The New Handbook of Texas*, edited by Ron Tyler, Douglas E. Barnett, Roy R. Barkley, Penelope C. Anderson, and Mark F. Odintz, vol. 2, 267. Austin: Texas State Historical Association, 1996.

________. "*In Re Ricardo Rodríguez*." In *The New Handbook of Texas*, edited by Ron Tyler, Douglas E. Barnett, Roy R. Barkley, Penelope C. Anderson, and Mark F. Odintz, vol. 3, 856. Austin: Texas State Historical Association, 1996.

________. "Santiago A. Brito." In *The New Handbook of Texas*, edited by Ron Tyler, Douglas E. Barnett, Roy R. Barkley, Penelope C. Anderson, and Mark F. Odintz, vol. 1, 743–744. Austin: Texas State Historical Association, 1996.

________. "Victor L. Ochoa." In *The New Handbook of Texas*, edited by Ron Tyler, Douglas E. Barnett, Roy R. Barkely, Penelope C. Anderson, and Mark F. Odintz, vol. 4, 1104–1105. Austin: Texas State Historical Association, 1996.

Alamía, Teresa Chapa. "Laguna Seca Pioneers: Vela Family History." In *Roots by the River*, by Valley By-Liners, 194–199. Mission, Tex.: Border Kingdom Press, 1978.

________. "The Mark of the River." In *Roots by the River*, by Valley By-Liners, 200–204. Mission, Tex.: Border Kingdom Press, 1978.

Anders, Evan M. *Boss Rule in South Texas: The Progressive Era*. Austin: University of Texas Press, 1982.

________. "Bosses Under Siege: The Politics of South Texas During the Progressive Era." Ph.D. dissertation, University of Texas at Austin, 1978.

________. "José Tomás Canales." In *The New Handbook of Texas*, edited by Ron Tyler, Douglas E. Barnett, Roy R. Barkley, Penelope C. Anderson, and Mark F. Odintz, vol. 1, 953–954. Austin: Texas State Historical Association, 1996.

________. "Manuel Guerra." In *The New Handbook of Texas*, edited by Ron Tyler, Douglas E. Barnett, Roy R. Barkley, Penelope C. Anderson, and Mark F. Odintz, vol. 3, 369. Austin: Texas State Historical Association, 1996.

Anderson, H. Allen. "Pastores." In *The New Handbook of Texas*, edited by Ron Tyler, Douglas E. Barnett, Roy R. Barkely, Penelope C. Anderson, and Mark F. Odintz, vol. 5, 84–85. Austin: Texas State Historical Association, 1996.

Baulch, Joe. "Garza War." In *The New Handbook of Texas*, edited by Ron Tyler, Douglas E. Barnett, Roy R. Barkley, Penelope C. Anderson, and Mark F. Odintz, vol. 3, 113. Austin: Texas State Historical Association, 1996.

________. "The Murder of Stanley Welch and the 1906 Starr County Election." *Journal of South Texas* 4 (1991): 33–46.

Belfiglio, Valentine J. "Public Policy and the Mexican Italians of El Paso County, Texas, 1880–1920." *West Texas Historical Association Yearbook* 68 (1992): 25–43.

Bryson, Conrey. "A Man Named Aoy." *Password* 35 (Summer 1990): 95–99.

Calcott, Frank. "The Mexican Peon in Texas." *Survey* 44 (June 26, 1920): 437–438.

Calderón, Roberto R. "Unión, Paz y Trabajo: Laredo's Mexican Mutual Aid Societies, 1890s." In *Mexican Americans in Texas History*, edited by Emilio Zamora, Cynthia Orozco, and Rodolfo Rocha, 63–77. Austin: Texas State Historical Association, 2000.

Cannon, Tina Nicole. "Bordering on Trouble: Conflict between Tejanos and Anglos in South Texas, 1880–1920." Master's thesis, Baylor Univeristy, 2001.

Chabrán, Richard, and Rafael Chabrán, eds. "Catarino Garza." In *The Latino Encyclopedia*, edited by Richard Chabrán and Rafael Chabrán, vol. 3, 684. New York: Marshall Cavendish, 1996.

________. "La Gran Liga Mexicanista de Beneficencia y Protectora." In *The Latino Encyclopedia*, edited by Richard Chabrán and Rafael Chabrán, vol. 3, 705. New York: Marshall Cavendish, 1996.

________. "Lucia González Parsons." In *The Latino Encyclopedia*, edited by Richard Chabrán and Rafael Chabrán, vol. 3, 702. New York: Marshall Cavendish, 1996.

Chatfield, W. H. *The Twin Cities of the Border (Brownsville and Matamoros) and the Country of the Lower Rio Grande*. New Orleans: E.P. Brandao, 1893.

Chávez, Ernesto. "Octaviano Ambrosio Larrazolo." In *The New Handbook of Texas*, edited by Ron Tyler, Douglas E. Barnett, Roy R. Barkely, Penelope C. Anderson, and Mark F. Odintz, vol. 4, 81–82. Austin: Texas State Historical Association, 1996.

Christian, Carole E. "Joining the American Mainstream: Texas' Mexican Americans During World War I." *Southwestern Historical Quarterly* 92 (April 1989): 559–595.

Coerver, Don M. "Plan of San Diego." In *The New Handbook of Texas*, edited by Ron Tyler, Douglas E. Barnett, Roy R. Barkely, Penelope C. Anderson, and Mark F. Odintz, vol. 5, 228. Austin: Texas State Historical Association, 1996.

Coerver, Don M., and Linda B. Hall. *Texas and the Mexican Revolution: A Study in State and National Border Policy*. San Antonio: Trinity University Press, 1984.

Córdova, Alfred C. *Octaviano Larrazolo: A Political Portrait.* Albuquerque: University of New Mexico Press, 1954.

Cruz, Gilberto R. "The Vicariate Apostolic of Brownsville, 1874–1912: An Overview of Its Origins and Development." In *From the Mississippi to the Pacific: Essays in Honor of John Francis Bannon, S.J.*, edited by Russell M. Magnaghi, 79–104. Marquette, Mich.: Northern Michigan University Press, 1982.

Cuéllar, Carlos E., and Stan Green. *Mexican Revolutionaries in Laredo, 1890–1891*. Laredo: Border Studies, 1991.

Cumberland, Charles C. "Border Raids in the Lower Rio Grande Valley—1915." *Southwestern Historical Quarterly* 57 (January 1954): 285–311.

________. "Mexican Revolutionary Movements from Texas, 1907–1912." *Southwestern Historical Quarterly* 52 (January 1949): 301–324.

Cuthbertson, Gilbert M. "Catarino E. Garza and the Garza War." *Texana* 12 (1974): 335–348.

________. "Catarino Erasmo Garza." In *The New Handbook of Texas*, edited by Ron Tyler, Douglas E. Barnett, Roy R. Barkley, Penelope C. Anderson, and Mark F. Odintz, vol. 3, 106–107. Austin: Texas State Historical Association, 1996.

Dameron, Chip. "The Bloody Bandit War of 1915." In *Still More Studies in Brownsville History*, edited by Milo Kearney, 253–256. Brownsville, Tex.: The University of Texas at Brownsville, 1991.

de la Garza, Beatriz Eugenia. *A Law for the Lion: Two South Texas Killings in 1912 and the Perseverance of Justice.* Austin: University of Texas Press, 2003.

de la Garza-Treviño, Ciro R. *El Plan de San Diego.* Ciudad Victoria: Universidad Autónoma de Tamualipas, 1970.

De León, Arnoldo. *In Re Ricardo Rodríguez: An Attempt at Chicano Disfranchisement in San Antonio, Texas*. San Antonio: Caravel Press, 1978. Reprinted in *En Aquel Entonces: Readings in Mexican American History*, edited by Manuel G. Gonzales and Cynthia A. Gonzales, 57–63. Bloomington: Indiana University Press, 2000.

________. "Acomodacionistas: defensores del barrio." *Caracol* 3 (December 1976): 12, 16–17.

________. "Blowout 1910 Style: A Chicano School Boycott in West Texas, 1910." *Texana* 12 (1974): 124–140.

________. "Mexicans and Mexican Americans in Texas, 1910–1920." Master's thesis, Texas Christian University, 1971.

________. "San Antonio and the Diez y Seis de Septiembre." *Caracol* 3 (October 1976): 6–7.

________. "San Diego, Texas. The Chicano City in the Woods." *Caracol* 3 (April 1977): 14–15.

________. "School Days Muchos Años Pasados." *Caracol* 3 (July 1977): 14–15.

De León, Arnoldo, and Kenneth L. Stewart. "Fertility Among Mexican Americans and Anglos in Texas, 1900." *Borderlands Journal* 9 (Spring 1986): 61–67.

________. "To Stay or Not To Stay: Naturalization Patterns in Texas, 1900." In *Chicano Social and Political History in the Nineteenth Century*, edited by Richard Griswold del Castillo and Manuel Hidalgo, 138–142. Encino, Calif.: Floricanto Press, 1992.

________. "Work Force Participation Among Mexican Immigrant Women in Texas, 1900." *Borderlands Journal* 9 (Spring 1986): 69–74.

De Wetter, Mardee. "Revolutionary El Paso, 1910–1917." Master's thesis, Texas Western College, 1946.

di Stefano, Onofre. "*La Prensa* of San Antonio and Its Literary Pages, 1913–1915." Ph.D. dissertation, University of California, Los Angeles, 1983.

________. "'Venimos a Luchar': A Brief History of *La Prensa's* Founding." *Aztlán* 16 (1985): 95–118.

Dodson, Ruth. *Don Pedrito Jaramillo: Curandero*. San Antonio: Casa Editorial Lozano, 1934.

________. "Don Pedrito Jaramillo: The *Curandero* of Los Olmos." In *The Healer of Los Olmos and Other Mexican Lore*, edited by Wilson M. Hudson, 9–70. Dallas: Texas Folklore Society, 1951.

Downing, Charles G. "José Policarpo Rodríguez." In *The New Handbook of Texas*, edited by Ron Tyler, Douglas E. Barnett, Roy R. Barkely, Penelope C. Anderson, and Mark F. Odintz, vol. 5, 654. Austin: Texas State Historical Association, 1996.

Downing de Juana, Ana Cristina. "Intermarriage in Hidalgo County, 1860–1900." Master's thesis, University of Texas–Pan American, 1998.

Espinosa, Michelle M. "José María Rodríguez." In *The New Handbook of Texas*, edited by Ron Tyler, Douglas E. Barnett, Roy R. Barkely, Penelope C. Anderson, and Mark F. Odintz, vol. 5, 653–654. Austin: Texas State Historical Association, 1996.

Estrada, Richard Medina. "Border Revolution: The Mexican Revolution in the Ciudad Juárez–El Paso Area, 1906–1915." Master's thesis, University of Texas at El Paso, 1975.

________. "The Mexican Revolution in the Ciudad Juárez–El Paso Area, 1910–1920." *Password* 24 (Summer 1979): 55–69.

Foley, Neil. "Chicanos and the Culture of Cotton in Central Texas, 1880–1900: Reshaping Class Relations in the South." In *Community Empowerment and Chicano Scholarship*, edited by Mary Romero and Cordelia Candelaria, 111–126. Berkeley: National Association for Chicano Studies, 1992.

García, Mario T. "Porfirian Diplomacy and the Administration of Justice in Texas, 1877–1900." *Aztlán* 16 (1985): 1–25.

________. "Racial Dualism in the El Paso Labor Market, 1880–1920." *Aztlán* 6 (Summer 1975): 197–218.

Garza, Alicia. "Manuel Marius García." In *The New Handbook of Texas*, edited by Ron Tyler, Douglas E. Barnett, Roy R. Barkley, Penelope C. Anderson, and Mark F. Odintz, vol. 3, 856. Austin: Texas State Historical Association, 1996.

________. "Norias Ranch Raid." In *The New Handbook of Texas*, edited by Ron Tyler, Douglas E. Barnett, Roy R. Barkely, Penelope C. Anderson, and Mark F. Odintz, vol. 4, 1033. Austin: Texas State Historical Association, 1996.

________. "Rio Grande City Riot of 1888." In *The New Handbook of Texas*, edited by Ron Tyler, Douglas E. Barnett, Roy R. Barkely, Penelope C. Anderson, and Mark F. Odintz, vol. 5, 585. Austin: Texas State Historical Association, 1996.

Garza, Refugio S. "En el Nombre de Díos y Don Pedrito Jaramillo (In the Name of God and Don Pedrito Jaramillo)." Master's thesis, Texas College of Arts and Industries, 1952.

Garza Guajardo, Celso. *En busca de Catarino Garza, 1859–1895.* Monterrey: Universidad Autónoma de Nuevo León, 1989.

Gerlach, Allen. "Conditions Along the Border—1915, the Plan de San Diego." *New Mexico Historical Review* 43 (July 1968): 192–212.

Gilliland, Maude T. *Rincón: A Story of Life on a South Texas Ranch at the Turn of the Century*. Brownsville, Tex.: Springman Lithograph, 1964.

Gómez, Arthur R. "The Glen Springs-Boquillas Raid Reconsidered: Diplomatic Intrigue on the Rio Grande." *Journal of Big Bend Studies* 4 (1992): 97–113.

Gómez-Quiñones, Juan. *Sembradores: Ricardo Flores Magón and the Partido Liberal Mexicano*. Los Angeles: Chicano Studies Research Center, 1976.

________. "The First Steps: Chicano Labor Conflict and Organizing, 1900–1920." *Aztlán* 3 (Spring 1972): 13–50.

________. "The Plan de San Diego Reviewed." *Aztlán* 1 (Spring 1970): 124–132.

Gomilla, Michelle Lorraine. "Los Refugiados y los Comerciantes: Mexican Refugees and Businessmen in Downtown El Paso, 1910–1920." Master's thesis, University of Texas at El Paso, 1990.

Gregory, Gloria X. "Manuel Jesús Jiménez." In *The New Handbook of Texas*, edited by Ron Tyler, Douglas E. Barnett, Roy R. Barkely, Penelope C. Anderson, and Mark F. Odintz, vol. 6, 1104. Austin: Texas State Historical Association, 1996.

Green, Ford. "The Infamous Plan of San Diego." *Old West* 12 (Winter 1975): 8–19.

Grimm, Agnes G. *Llanos Mesteños, Mustang Plains*. Waco: Texian Press, 1968.

________. "Peña Station." In *The Handbook of Texas: A Supplement*, edited by Eldon Stephen Branda, vol. 3, 718. Austin: Texas State Historical Association, 1976.

________. "Trinidad Salazar." In *The Handbook of Texas: A Supplement*, edited by Eldon Stephen Branda, vol. 3, 831. Austin: Texas State Historical Association, 1976.

Griswold del Castillo, Richard. "The Mexican Revolution and the Spanish-Language Press in the Borderlands." *Journalism History* 4 (Summer 1977): 42–47.

Gutiérrez-Witt, Laura. "Cultural Continuity in the Face of Change: Hispanic Printers in Texas." In *Recovering the U.S. Hispanic Literary Heritage*, II, edited by Erlinda Gonzales-Berry and Chuck Tatum, 260–278. Houston: Arte Público Press, 1996.

Gutmann, Myron P., Robert McCaa, Rodolfo Gutiérrez-Montes, and Brian Gratton. "The Demographic Impact of the Mexican Revolution in the United States." *Historia Mexicana* 50 (julio-septiembre 2000): 145–165.

Hager, William M. "The Plan of San Diego: Unrest on the Texas Border in 1915." *Arizona and the West* 5 (Winter 1963): 327–335.

Harris, Charles H., and Louis R. Sadler. "The Plan of San Diego and the Mexican-United States Crisis of 1916: A Reexamination." *Hispanic American Historical Review* 58 (August 1978): 381–408.

________. "The 1911 Reyes Conspiracy: The Texas Side." *Southwestern Historical Quarterly* 83 (April 1980): 325–348.

Hedgpeth, Donald R. "The Plan of San Diego: A Border Conspiracy." Master's thesis, Southwest Texas State University, 1969.

Henderson, H. Allen. "Casimero Romero." In *The New Handbook of Texas*, edited by Ron Tyler, Douglas E. Barnett, Roy R. Barkely, Penelope C. Anderson, and Mark F. Odintz, vol. 5, 671–672. Austin: Texas State Historical Association, 1996.

Henderson, Peter V. *Mexican Exiles in the Borderlands. 1901–1913*. El Paso: Texas Western Press, 1979.

________. "Mexican Rebels in the Borderlands, 1910–1912." *Red River Valley Historical Review* 2 (Summer 1975): 207–219.

Hernández, José Amaro. "The Proliferation of Mutual Aid Societies in the Chicano Community and the Attempt to Integrate Them: The *Primer Congreso Mexicanista de Texas*." In *Mutual Aid for Survival: The Case of the Mexican American*, by José Amaro Hernández, 60–74. Malabar, Fla.: Robert E. Krieger Publishing, 1983.

Hernández, Mary Ester. "Some Connections Between San Antonio and the Mexican Revolution." Master's thesis, University of Texas at Austin, 1973.

Hinojosa, Gilberto M. "Antecedents to the Twentieth Century." In *Mexican Americans and the Catholic Church, 1900–1965*, edited by Jay P. Dolan and Gilberto M. Hinojosa, 13–30. Notre Dame: University of Notre Dame Press, 1994.

Hinojosa-Smith, Rolando. "River of Blood." *Texas Monthly* 14 (January 1986): 196.

Hodges, B. A. *A History of the Mexican Mission Work Conducted by the Presbyterian Church in the United States of America in the Synod of Texas*. Waxahachie, Tex.: Woman's Synodical of Texas, 1931.

Johnson, Alvin S. "Mexico in San Antonio." *New Republic* 7 (June 24, 1916): 190–191.

Johnson, Benjamin H. "Sedition and Citizenship in South Texas, 1900–1930." Ph.D. dissertation, Yale University, 2000.

Justice, Glenn. *Revolution on the Rio Grande: Mexican Raids and Army Pursuits, 1916–1919*. El Paso: Texas Western Press, 1992.

________. "Revolution on the Rio Grande: The Border Raids of the Upper Big Bend and the Last American Punitive Expedition of 1919." Master's thesis, University of Texas at El Paso, 1989.

Koenig, Rebecca Anne Todd. "Antonio Rodríguez." In *The New Handbook of Texas*, edited by Ron Tyler, Douglas E. Barnett, Roy R. Barkely, Penelope C. Anderson, and Mark F. Odintz, vol. 5, 652. Austin: Texas State Historical Association, 1996.

Larralde, Carlos. "Aniceto Pizaña." In *The New Handbook of Texas*, edited by Ron Tyler, Douglas E. Barnett, Roy R. Barkely, Penelope C. Anderson, and Mark F. Odintz, vol. 5, 223–234. Austin: Texas State Historical Association, 1996.

________. "Ismael Montalvo." In *The New Handbook of Texas*, edited by Ron Tyler, Douglas E. Barnett, Roy R. Barkely, Penelope C. Anderson, and Mark F. Odintz, vol. 4, 797. Austin: Texas State Historical Association, 1996.

________. "J. T. Canales and the Texas Rangers." *Journal of South Texas* 10 (1997): 38–68.

________. "Luis de la Rosa and his Quest for Justice in Texas." *Journal of South Texas* 9 (1996): 50–78.

________. "Luis de la Rosa." In *The New Handbook of Texas*, edited by Ron Tyler, Douglas E. Barnett, Roy R. Barkley, Penelope C. Anderson, and Mark F. Odintz, vol. 2, 568. Austin: Texas State Historical Association, 1996.

________. "Santa Teresa: A Chicana Mystic." *Grito del Sol* 3 (April/June 1978): 1–114.

Lea, Tom. "So Close, So Far." *Texas Monthly* 14 (January 1986): 200, 202.

Leyva, Yolanda Chávez. "I Go to Fight for Social Justice: Children as Revolutionaries in the Mexican Revolution, 1910-1920." *Peace and Change* (October 1998): 423–439.

Limón, José E. "El Primer Congreso Mexicanista de 1911: A Precursor to Contemporary Chicanismo." *Aztlán* 5 (Spring/Fall 1974): 85–118.

Lindsay, Marcia. "A Study of the Hispanic Population of Tom Green County, Texas, in 1910." *Fort Concho Report* 19 (Fall 1987): 3–18.

Lockhart, William W. "Antonio Trujillo: Constable of San Elizario." *Password* 39 (Winter 1994): 179–186.

________. "Gregorio Nacianceno García: First Lawman and Politician of San Elizario." *Password* 40 (Fall 1995): 126–128.

Luna, Jesús. "Francisco I. Madero's Organization of the Mexican Revolution in San Antonio, Texas." Master's thesis, East Texas State University, 1969.

Maroney, James C. "The Unionization of Thurber, 1903." *Red River Valley Historical Review* 4 (Spring 1979): 17–32.

Martínez, Oscar. "The Mexicano Experience Along the Texas-Chihuahua Border: Oral Collections of the Period 1910–1920." *The Texas Humanist* 2 (February 1980): 4–5.

Martínez, Oscar J. "Pedro González Remembers the Revolution." *Password* 25 (Spring 1980): 29–37.

McClung, John Busby. "Texas Rangers Along the Rio Grande, 1910–1919." Ph.D. dissertation, Texas Christian University, 1981.

McKiernan, John Raymond. "Fevered Measures: Race, Communicable Disease and Community Formation on the Texas-Mexico Border, 1880–1923." Ph.D. dissertation, University of Michigan, 2002.

Means, Joyce F. "Joe Sitter and Chico Cano: What Really Happened?" *West Texas Historical Association Yearbook* 72 (1996): 86–104.

Meier, Matt S. with Conchita Franco Serri and Richard A. García. "Gregorio Cortéz." In *Notable Latino Americans: A Biographical Dictionary*, by Matt S. Meier, 100–103. Westport, Conn.: Greenwood Press, 1997.

Mertz, Richard J. "The Gregorio Cortéz Case." Master's thesis, Texas A&I University, 1971.

________. "'No One Can Arrest Me': The Story of Gregorio Cortéz." *Journal of South Texas* 1 (1974): 1–17.

Orozco, Cynthia E. "Gregorio Cortéz Lira." In *The New Handbook of Texas*, edited by Ron Tyler, Douglas E. Barnett, Roy R. Barkley, Penelope C. Anderson, and

Mark F. Odintz, vol. 2, 342–343. Austin: Texas State Historical Association, 1996.

________. "Porvenir Massacre." In *The New Handbook of Texas*, edited by Ron Tyler, Douglas E. Barnett, Roy R. Barkely, Penelope C. Anderson, and Mark F. Odintz, vol. 5, 285–286. Austin: Texas State Historical Association, 1996.

Porter, Joseph. "'The American Congo': Captain John G. Bourke and the Texas Military Experience." In *The Texas Military Experience From the Texas Revolution Through World War II,* edited by Joseph G. Dawson, 113–128. College Station: Texas A&M University Press, 1995.

Preuss, Gene B. "Clemente Vergara." In *The New Handbook of Texas*, edited by Ron Tyler, Douglas E. Barnett, Roy R. Barkely, Penelope C. Anderson, and Mark F. Odintz, vol. 6, 724–725. Austin: Texas State Historical Association, 1996.

Prewitt, Steven W. "'We Didn't Ask to Come to this Party': Self-Determination Collides with the Federal Government in the Public Schools of Del Rio, Texas, 1890–1971." Ph.D. dissertation, University of Houston, 2000.

Pycior, Julie Leininger. "Mexican Protective League." In *The New Handbook of Texas*, edited by Ron Tyler, Douglas E. Barnett, Roy R. Barkely, Penelope C. Anderson, and Mark F. Odintz, vol. 4, 686. Austin: Texas State Historical Association, 1996.

________. "Sociedades Mutualistas." In *The New Handbook of Texas*, edited by Ron Tyler, Douglas E. Barnett, Roy R. Barkely, Penelope C. Anderson, and Mark F. Odintz, vol. 5, 1131–1132. Austin: Texas State Historical Association, 1996.

Raat, W. Dirk. *Revoltosos: Mexico's Rebels in the United States, 1903–1923*. College Station: Texas A&M University Press, 1981.

________. "Ricardo Flores Magón." In *The New Handbook of Texas*, edited by Ron Tyler, Douglas E. Barnett, Roy R. Barkley, Penelope C. Anderson, and Mark F. Odintz, vol. 2, 1038–1039. Austin: Texas State Historical Association, 1996.

Ramírez, Adolfo. "An Historical Note: 'El Plan de San Diego.'" In *Hojas: A Chicano Journal of Education*, edited by Victor Guerra-Garza, 25–26. Austin: Juárez-Lincoln Press, 1976.

Raun, Gerald G. "Seventeen Days in November: The Lynching of Antonio Rodríguez and American-Mexican Relations, November 3–19, 1910." *Journal of Big Bend Studies* 7 (1995): 157–179.

Regis, Raúl R. "The Santa Isabel Episode, January 10, 1916: Ethnic Repercussions in El Paso and Ciudad Juárez." *Password* 42 (Summer 1997): 55–77.

Ribb, Richard. "José Tomás Canales and the Texas Rangers: Myth, Identity, and Power in South Texas, 1900–1920." Ph.D. dissertation, University of Texas at Austin, 2001.

________. "Patrician as Redeemer: José Tomás Canales and the Salvation of South Texas, 1910–1919." *Journal of South Texas* 14 (2001): 189–203.

Rice, Harvey. "The Lynching of Antonio Rodríguez." Master's thesis, University of Texas at Austin, 1990.

Richmond, Douglas W. "La Guerra en Tejas se Renova: Mexican Insurrection and Carrancista Ambitions, 1900–1920." *Aztlán* 11 (Spring 1980): 1–32.

Ríos McMillan, Nora. "A Biography of a Man and His Newspaper." *The Americas Review* 17 (Fall-Winter 1989): 136–149.

Rocha, Rodolfo. "The Influence of the Mexican Revolution on the Mexico-Texas Border, 1910–1916." Ph.D. dissertation, Texas Tech University, 1981.

________. "Background to Banditry in the Lower Rio Grande Valley of Texas." Master's thesis, Pan American University, 1974.

________. "Banditry in the Lower Rio Grande Valley of Texas, 1915." *Studies in History* 6 (1976): 55–73.

________. "The Sting and Power of Rebellion." *Texas Humanist* 6 (March/April 1984): 18–20.

________. "The Tejano Revolt of 1915." In *Mexican Americans in Texas History*, edited by Emilio Zamora, Cynthia Orozco, and Rodolfo Rocha, 103–119. Austin: Texas State Historical Association, 2000.

Rodríguez, José Policarpo. *"The Old Guide," Surveyor, Scout, Hunter, Indian Fighter, Ranchman, Preacher: His Life in His Own Words*. Nashville/Dallas: Publishing House of the Methodist Episcopal Church, South, 1897.

Romano, Octavio. "Don Pedrito Jaramillo: The Emergence of a Mexican American Folk Saint." Ph.D. dissertation, University of California at Berkeley, 1964.

Sáenz, J. Luz. *Los méxico-americanos en la gran guerra: y su contingente en pro de la democracia, la humanidad y la justicia*. San Antonio: Artes Gráficas, 1933.

Samponaro, Frank N., and Paul J. Vanderwood. *War Scare on the Rio Grande: Robert Runyon's Photographs of the Border Conflict, 1913–1916.* Austin: Texas State Historical Association, 1992.

Sandos, James A. *Rebellion in the Borderlands: Anarchism and the Plan of San Diego, 1904–1923*. Norman: University of Oklahoma Press, 1992.

________. "The Mexican Revolution and the United States, 1915–1917: The Impact of Conflict in the Tamaulipas-Texas Frontier upon the Emergence of Revolutionary Government in Mexico." Ph.D. dissertation, University of California, Berkeley, 1978.

________. "The Plan of San Diego: War and Diplomacy on the Texas Border, 1915–1916." *Arizona and the West* 14 (Summer 1972): 5–24.

Segovia, José Francisco. "Botas and Guaraches." In *The New Handbook of Texas*, edited by Ron Tyler, Douglas E. Barnett, Roy R. Barkley, Penelope C. Anderson, and Mark F. Odintz, vol. 1, 658–659. Austin: Texas State Historical Association, 1996.

Sonnichsen, C. L. "Boots and Sandals: The Laredo Election Riot." In *Ten Texas Feuds*, by C. L. Sonnichsen, 159–166. Albuquerque: University of New Mexico Press, 1957.

Taylor, Anna J. "Hispanic Settlement of the Texas Panhandle-Plains, 1876–1884." *Panhandle Plains Historical Review* 70 (1997): 36–58.

________. "New Mexican *Pastores* and Priests in the Texas Panhandle, 1876–1915." *Panhandle Plains Historical Review* 57 (1984): 65–80.

Thompson, Jerry D. *Warm Weather and Bad Whiskey: The 1886 Laredo Election Riot*. El Paso: Texas Western Press, 1994.

Vowell, Jack C. "Politics at El Paso: 1850–1920." Master's thesis, Texas Western College, 1952.

Walraven, Edward Lee. "Ambivalent Americans: Selected Spanish-Language Newspapers' Response to Anglo Domination in Texas, 1830–1910." Ph.D. dissertation, Texas A&M University at College Station, 1999.

Walter, Paul A. "Octaviano Ambrosio Larrazolo." *New Mexico Historical Review* 7 (April 1932): 97–104.

Washington, Ann Reed. "Judge Juan Manuel de la Vina." In *Roots by the River*, by Valley By-Liners, 82–84. Mission, Tex.: Border Kingdom Press, 1978.

Watts, Jake. "The Plan of San Diego and the Lower Rio Grande Valley." In *More Studies in Brownsville History*, edited by Milo Kearney, 322–345. Brownsville, Tex.: Pan American University at Brownsville, 1989.

Wharton, L. H. "The Plan de San Diego: Background and Selected Documents." *Journal of South Texas* 12 (1999): 125–155.

White, Robert Rankin. "Félix Martínez: A Borderlands Success Story." *El Palacio* 87 (Winter 1981–1982): 12–17.

________. "Félix Martínez." In *The New Handbook of Texas*, edited by Ron Tyler, Douglas E. Barnett, Roy R. Barkely, Penelope C. Anderson, and Mark F. Odintz, vol. 4, 535–536. Austin: Texas State Historical Association, 1996.

Whittington, Lona Teresa. "The Road to Sorrow: Mexican Refugees who fled Pancho Villa through Presidio, Texas, 1913–1914." Master's thesis, Sul Ross State University, 1976.

Wilcox, Sebron S. "The Laredo City Election and Riot of April, 1886." *Southwestern Historical Quarterly* 45 (July 1941): 1–23.

Wilkinson, William V. "Lawlessness in Cameron County and the City of Brownsville: 1900–1912." In *More Studies in Brownsville History*, edited by Milo Kearney, 295–305. Brownsville, Tex.: Pan American University at Brownsville, 1989.

________. "The Mexican Revolution and the Bandit Wars: The Lower Rio Grande Valley in 1915." In *More Studies in Brownsville History*, edited by Milo Kearney 245–252. Brownsville, Tex.: Pan American University at Brownsville, 1989.

Woolridge, Ruby A. "The 1891 Rio Grande Railroad Robbery." In *Studies in Brownsville History*, edited by Milo Kearney, 201–203. Brownsville, Tex.: Pan American University at Brownsville, 1986.

Woolridge, Ruby A., and Robert D. Vazzetti. "The Founding of Charro Days." In *More Studies in Brownsville History*, edited by Milo Kearney, 390–393. Brownsville: Pan American University at Brownsville, 1989.

Wright, Paul. "Life on both Sides of the Tracks in Early Alpine." *West Texas Historical Association Yearbook* 73 (1997): 96–112.

________. "Residential Segregation in Two Early West Texas Towns." *Southwestern Historical Quarterly* 102 (January 1999): 295–320.

________. "A Tumultuous Decade: Changes in the Mexican-Origin Population of the Big Bend, 1910–1920." *Journal of Big Bend Studies* 10 (1998): 163–186.

Young, Elliott. "Twilight on the Texas-Mexican Border: Catarino Garza and Identity at the Cross-Roads, 1880–1915." Ph.D. dissertation, University of Texas at Austin, 1997.

________. "Crossing Borders: Race, Nation, Class and Gender on the South Texas Border, 1877–1911." Master's thesis, University of Texas at Austin, 1997.

________. "Before the Revolution: Catarino Garza as Activist/Historian." In *Recovering the U.S. Hispanic Literary Heritage II*, edited by Erlinda Gonzales-Berry and Chuck Tatum, 213–236. Houston: Arte Público Press, 1996.

________. "Justo Sabor Penn." In *The New Handbook of Texas*, edited by Ron Tyler, Douglas E. Barnett, Roy R. Barkely, Penelope C. Anderson, and Mark F. Odintz, vol. 5, 139. Austin: Texas State Historical Association, 1996.

________. "Nemesio García." In *The New Handbook of Texas*, edited by Ron Tyler, Douglas E. Barnett, Roy R. Barkley, Penelope C. Anderson, and Mark F. Odintz, vol. 3, 87. Austin: Texas State Historical Association, 1996.

________. "Red Men, Princess Pocahontas, and George Washington: Harmonizing Race Relations in Laredo at the Turn of the Century." *Western Historical Quarterly* 29 (Spring 1998): 48–85.

________. "Remembering Catarino Garza's Revolution: An Aborted Border Insurrection." *Mexican Studies/Estudios Mexicanos* 12 (Summer 1996): 231–272.

Zamora, Emilio Jr. *El Movimiento Obrero Mexicano en el Sur de Texas, 1900–1920.* México, D.F.: Secretaría de Educación Pública, 1986.

________. "Mexican Labor Activity in South Texas, 1900–1920." Ph.D. dissertation, University of Texas at Austin, 1983.

________. "Chicano Socialist Labor Activity in Texas, 1900–1920." *Aztlán* 6 (Summer, 1975): 221–238.

________. "Sindicalismo Socialista de los Chicanos en Texas, 1900–1920." In *Orígenes del Movimiento Obrero Chicano*, edited by Luis Leobardo Arroyo and Juan Gómez-Quiñones, 92–110. México, D.F.: Ediciones Era, 1978.

7. NATIVES AND IMMIGRANTS, 1920–1945

Immigration from Mexico from circa the 1890s to 1930 overwhelmed the native-born Tejano population. During the 1920s, about one-half of Mexican-origin people were foreign-born. Though the immigrants' offspring would know no other country except Texas, these second-generation Tejanos were raised in a "Mexican" home setting. What resulted from this interplay of Mexico-born people, their U.S.-born sons and daughters, and the presence of native-born Tejanos who had acclimated to U.S. society was a process that involved internecine friction due to differences over class, generations, nationalist outlooks, politics, and identity. In major cities such as Houston and San Antonio, Mexican social and recreative clubs often existed alongside chapters of the League of United Latin American Citizens (a civic organization that excluded the foreign-born). But the common experience of discrimination, a shared ethnicity, the customs of language, religion, and folklore held communities together. An admiration for American institutions would also produce cohesiveness as loyalty for most Tejanos was to the U.S. and not Mexico.

Chili stand in Haymarket Plaza, San Antonio, Texas, 1933.
The Institute of Texan Cultures at UTSA, No. L-1433-E
The San Antonio Light *Collection*

Acosta, Teresa Palomo. "Confederación de Organizaciones Mexicanas y Latino Americanas." In *The New Handbook of Texas*, edited by Ron Tyler, Douglas E. Barnett, Roy R. Barkley, Penelope C. Anderson, and Mark F. Odintz, vol. 2, 263–264. Austin: Texas State Historical Association, 1996.

________. "Mexican Circuses." In *The New Handbook of Texas*, edited by Ron Tyler, Douglas E. Barnett, Roy R. Barkely, Penelope C. Anderson, and Mark F. Odintz, vol. 4, 683–684. Austin: Texas State Historical Association, 1996.

________. "Settlement Houses." In *The New Handbook of Texas*, edited by Ron Tyler, Douglas E. Barnett, Roy R. Barkely, Penelope C. Anderson, and Mark F. Odintz, vol. 5, 977–978. Austin: Texas State Historical Association, 1996.

Allen, Ruth. *The Labor of Women in the Production of Cotton*. University of Texas Bulletin No. 3134: September 8, 1931, Bureau of Research in the Social Sciences Study No. 3. Austin: University of Texas, Austin, 1931.

________. "Mexican Peon Women in Texas." *Sociology and Social Research* 16 (November/December 1931): 131–142.

Almaráz, Félix D. Jr. *Knight Without Armor: Carlos Eduardo Castañeda, 1896–1958*. College Station: Texas A&M University Press, 1999.

________. "Carlos E. Castañeda: The Historian and the Critics." In *Mexican Americans in Texas History*, edited by Emilio Zamora, Cynthia Orozco, and Rodolfo Rocha, 157–174. Austin: Texas State Historical Association, 2000.

________. "Carlos E. Castañeda, Mexican American Historian: The Formative Years, 1896–1927." *Pacific Historical Review* 42 (August 1973): 319–334.

________. "Carlos E. Casteñeda and *Our Catholic Heritage*: The Initial Volumes (1933–1943)." *Social Science Journal* 13 (April 1976): 27–37.

________. "Carlos E. Castañeda's Rendezvous with a Library: The Latin American Collection, 1920–1927: The Final Phase." *Journal of Library History* 16 (Spring 1981): 315–328.

________. "The Making of a Boltonian: Carlos E. Castañeda of Texas—The Early Years." *Red River Valley Historical Review* 1 (Winter 1974): 329–350.

Badillo, David A. "Between Alienation and Ethnicity: The Evolution of Mexican-American Catholicism in San Antonio, 1910–1940." *Journal of American Ethnic History* 16.4 (Summer 1997): 62–83.

Balderrama, Francisco E. "Carlos Eduardo Castañeda." In *Historians of the American Frontier: A Bio–Bibliographical Sourcebook*, edited by John R. Wunder, 171–182. New York: Greenwood Press, 1988.

Balderrama, Francisco E., and Raymond Rodríguez. *Decade of Betrayal: Mexican Repatriation in the 1930s*. Albuquerque: University of New Mexico Press, 1995.

Barnes, Roger C., and James W. Donovan. "The Southern Pecan Shelling Company: A Window to Depression Era San Antonio." *South Texas Studies* 11 (2000): 49–64.

Barrera, Elena Farías. "A Gentle Pioneer Businessman." In *Roots by the River*, by Valley By-Liners, 214–217. Mission, Tex.: Border Kingdom Press, 1978.

________. "A Legendary Figure: El Doctor Palomo." In *Roots by the River*, Valley By-Liners, 212–214. Mission, Tex.: Border Kingdom Press, 1978.

Barsun, Helen W. "Los Pastores: A Remnant of Medieval Drama in San Antonio." Master's thesis, St. Mary's University, 1943.

Bogardus, Emory. "The Mexican Immigrant and Segregation." *American Journal of Sociology* 36 (July 1930): 76–77.

Bruce-Novoa, Juan. "La Prensa and the Chicano Community." *The Americas Review* 17 (Winter 1989): 149–156.

Buitron, Richard Arthur Jr. "Who are We? The Quest for Tejano Identity in San Antonio, Texas, 1913–the Present." Ph.D. dissertation, Florida State University, 2002.

Cárdenas, Cipriano. "Hispanic Journalism in Brownsville, Texas." In *Studies in Matamoros and Cameron County History*, edited by Milo Kearney, Anthony Knopp, and Antonio Zavaleta, 227–236. Brownsville, Tex.: University of Texas at Brownsville and Texas Southmost College, 1997.

Carroll, Patrick J. "Tejano Living and Educational Conditions in World War II South Texas." *South Texas Studies* 5 (1994): 82–103.

Chabrán, Richard, and Rafael Chabrán, eds. "Alonso S. Perales." In *The Latino Encyclopedia*, edited by Richard Chabrán and Rafael Chabrán, vol. 4, 1220. New York: Marshall Cavendish, 1996.

________. "Carlos E. Castañeda." In *The Latino Encyclopedia*, edited by Richard Chabrán and Rafael Chabrán, vol. 1, 256. New York: Marshall Cavendish, 1996.

________. "George Isidore Sánchez." In *The Latino Encyclopedia*, edited by Richard Chabrán and Rafael Chabrán, vol. 5, 1433. New York: Marshall Cavendish, 1996.

________. "Ignacio Eugenio Lozano Sr." In *The Latino Encyclopedia*, edited by Richard Chabrán and Rafael Chabrán, vol. 4, 924. New York: Marshall Cavendish, 1996.

________. "Plan de San Diego." In *The Latino Encyclopedia*, edited by Richard Chabrán and Rafael Chabrán, vol. 5, 1241. New York: Marshall Cavendish, 1996.

________. "Primer Congreso Mexicanista." In *The Latino Encyclopedia*, edited by Richard Chabrán and Rafael Chabrán, vol. 5, 1304. New York: Marshall Cavendish, 1996.

________. "Sons of America." In *The Latino Encyclopedia*, edited by Richard Chabrán and Rafael Chabrán, vol. 5, 1508. New York: Marshall Cavendish, 1996.

Chavarría, Jesús. "On Chicano History: In Memoriam, George I. Sánchez 1906–1972." In *Humanidad: Essays in Honor of George I. Sánchez*, edited by Américo Paredes, 41–57. Los Angeles: Chicano Studies Center Publications, 1977.

Chávez, David. "World War II and El Paso's Second War." *Password* 40 (Summer 1995): 55–60.

Cisneros, Victor B. Nelson. "La Clase Trabajadora en Tejas, 1920–1940." *Aztlán* 6 (Summer 1975): 239–268.

________. "UCAPAWA Organizing Activities in Texas, 1935–1950." *Aztlán* 9 (Spring/Summer 1978): 71–84.

Coalson, George O. *The Development of the Migrant Farm Labor System in Texas, 1900–1954*. San Francisco: R&E Research Associates, 1977.

________. "The Development of the Migratory Farm Labor System in Texas, 1900–1954." Ph.D. dissertation, University of Oklahoma, 1955.

Croxdale, Richard. "Pecan-Shellers' Strike." In *The New Handbook of Texas*, edited by Ron Tyler, Douglas E. Barnett, Roy R. Barkely, Penelope C. Anderson, and Mark F. Odintz, vol. 6, 752. Austin: Texas State Historical Association, 1996.

Davis, Matthew Donald. "Hershel T. Manuel: 'The Doyen of Mexican American Education.'" Ph.D. dissertation, University of Texas at Austin, 2000.

De León, Arnoldo. "*Los Tasinques* and the Sheep Shearers' Union of North America: A Strike in West Texas, 1934." *West Texas Historical Association Yearbook* 55 (1979): 3–16.

De León, Arnoldo, and Robert A. Calvert. "Segregation." In *The New Handbook of Texas*, edited by Ron Tyler, Douglas E. Barnett, Roy R. Barkley, Penelope C. Anderson, and Mark F. Odintz, vol. 5, 965. Austin: Texas State Historical Association, 1996.

Filewood, David Lewis. "Tejano Revolt: The Significance of the 1938 Pecan Shellers Strike." Master's thesis, University of Texas at Arlington, 1994.

Flores, María Eva. "St. Joseph's Parish, Fort Stockton, Texas, 1875–1945: The Forging of an Identity and Community." *U.S. Catholic Historian* 21.1 (Winter 2003): 13–31.

García, Clotilde. "José Antonio García." In *The New Handbook of Texas*, edited by Ron Tyler, Douglas E. Barnett, Roy R. Barkley, Penelope C. Anderson, and Mark F. Odintz, vol. 3, 85. Austin: Texas State Historical Association, 1996.

García, María-Cristina. "Agents of Americanization: Rusk Settlement and the Houston Mexican Community, 1907–1950." In *Mexican Americans in Texas History*, edited by Emilio Zamora, Cynthia Orozco, and Rodolfo Rocha, 121–137. Austin: Texas State Historical Association, 2000.

________. "Félix Hessbrook Morales." In *The New Handbook of Texas*, edited by Ron Tyler, Douglas E. Barnett, Roy R. Barkley, Penelope C. Anderson, and Mark F. Odintz, vol. 4, 828–829. Austin: Texas State Historical Association, 1996.

________. "Fernando Salas Aldáz." In *The New Handbook of Texas*, edited by Ron Tyler, Douglas E. Barnett, Roy R. Barkely, Penelope C. Anderson, and Mark F. Odintz, vol. 5, 774. Austin: Texas State Historical Association, 1996.

________. "Isidro García." In *The New Handbook of Texas*, edited by Ron Tyler, Douglas E. Barnett, Roy R. Barkley, Penelope C. Anderson, and Mark F. Odintz, vol. 3, 85. Austin: Texas State Historical Association, 1996.

________. "Macario García." In *The New Handbook of Texas*, edited by Ron Tyler, Douglas E. Barnett, Roy R. Barkley, Penelope C. Anderson, and Mark F. Odintz, vol. 3, 86. Austin: Texas State Historical Association, 1996.

________. "Primitivo Leijo Niño." In *The New Handbook of Texas*, edited by Ron Tyler, Douglas E. Barnett, Roy R. Barkely, Penelope C. Anderson, and Mark F. Odintz, vol. 4, 1019. Austin: Texas State Historical Association, 1996.

________. "Ramón Fernández." In *The New Handbook of Texas*, edited by Ron Tyler, Douglas E. Barnett, Roy R. Barkley, Penelope C. Anderson, and Mark F. Odintz, vol. 2, 983. Austin: Texas State Historical Association, 1996.

________. "Refugio Gómez." In *The New Handbook of Texas*, edited by Ron Tyler, Douglas E. Barnett, Roy R. Barkley, Penelope C. Anderson, and Mark F. Odintz, vol. 2, 983. Austin: Texas State Historical Association, 1996.

García, Mario T. *Mexican Americans: Leadership, Ideology, and Identity, 1930–1960*. New Haven: Yale University Press, 1989.

________. "Mexican Americans and the Politics of Citizenship: The Case of El Paso, 1936." *New Mexico Historical Review* 59 (April 1984): 187–204.

García, Richard A. *Rise of the Mexican American Middle Class: San Antonio, 1929–1941*. College Station: Texas A&M University Press, 1991.

________. "The Making of the Mexican American Mind, San Antonio, Texas, 1929–1941: A Social and Intellectual History of an Ethnic Community." 2 vols. Ph.D. dissertation, University of California at Irvine, 1980.

________. "Class, Consciousness, and Ideology—The Mexican Community in San Antonio, Texas: 1930–1940." *Aztlán* 9 (Fall 1978): 23–70.

________. "The Mexican American Mind: A Product of the 1930s." In *History, Culture, and Society: Chicano Studies in the 1980s*, edited by Mario T. García, 67–93. Ypsilanti, Mich.: Bilingual Press/Editorial Bilingüe, 1983.

Garnett, William E. "Immediate and Pressing Race Problems of Texas." *Proceedings of the Southwestern Political and Social Science Association, Austin* (1925): 31–48.

Garza, Alicia. "Raymondville Peonage Cases." In *The New Handbook of Texas*, edited by Ron Tyler, Douglas E. Barnett, Roy R. Barkely, Penelope C. Anderson, and Mark F. Odintz, vol. 4, 1033–1034. Austin: Texas State Historical Association, 1996.

González de Mireles, Jovita. "Social Life in Cameron, Starr, and Zapata Counties." Master's thesis, University of Texas, Austin, 1930.

________. "America Invades the Border Towns." *Southwest Review* 15 (Summer 1930): 469–477.

González, Rosalinda M. "Chicanas and Mexican Immigrant Families, 1920–1940: Women's Subordination and Family Exploitation." In *Decades of Discontent: The Women's Movement, 1920–1940*, edited by Lois Scharf and Joan M. Jensen, 59–84. Westport, Conn.: Greenwood Press, 1983.

Green, George N. "ILGWU in Texas, 1930–1970." *Journal of Mexican American History* 1 (Spring 1971): 144–169.

Green, Stan, ed. *Border Biographies*. Laredo: Border Studies Publication, 1991.

Guerrero, Rosa. "Childhood Memories: World War II and El Paso." *Password* 40 (Summer 1995): 61–64.

Handman, Max Sylvius. "The Mexican Immigrant in Texas." *Southwestern Political and Social Science Quarterly* 7 (June 1926): 33–41.

________. "San Antonio: The Old Capital City of Mexican Life and Influence." *Survey* (May 1, 1931): 163–166

Hasdorff, James C. "The *Southern Messenger* and the Mexican Church-State Controversy, 1917–1941." *Journal of Texas Catholic History and Culture* 5 (1994): 25–46.

Hinojosa, Gilberto M. "The Immigrant Church, 1910–1940." In *Mexican Americans and the Catholic Church, 1900–1965*, edited by Jay P. Dolan and Gilberto M. Hinojosa, 31–83. Notre Dame: University of Notre Dame Press, 1994.

Hufford, Charles H. *The Social and Economic Effects of Mexican Migration into Texas.* R&E Research Associates, 1971.

________. "The Social and Economic Effects of Mexican Migration into Texas." Master's thesis, University of Colorado, 1929.

Johnson, Marjorie. "The Language of Love: Salvador M. Hinojosa (1901–1976)." In *Roots by the River*, by Valley By-Liners, 217–222. Mission, Tex.: Border Kingdom Press, 1978.

Knopp, Anthony Keith. "After the Boss: Twentieth Century Political Trends of Brownsville City Government." In *Studies in Matamoros and Cameron County History*, edited by Milo Kearney, Anthony Knopp, and Antonio Zavaleta, 85–88. Brownsville, Tex.: The University of Texas at Brownsville and Texas Southmost College, 1997.

Larralde, José. "Carlos Castañeda." *La Luz* (January–February 1975): 27.

Ledesma, Irene. "The New Deal Public Works Program and the Mexican Americans in McAllen, Texas, 1933–1936." Master's thesis, Pan American University, 1977.

Leyva, Yolanda Chávez. "Años de Desesperación: The Great Depression and the Mexican American Generation in El Paso, Texas, 1929–1935." Master's thesis, University of Texas at El Paso, 1989.

Limón, José E. "Stereotyping and Chicano Resistance: An Historical Dimension." *Aztlán* 4 (Fall 1973): 257–270.

Lynch, Michael J. III. "South Texas Renaissance Man: The Humanitarian, Political, and Philanthropic Activities of Judge J. T. Canales." Master's thesis, Texas A&M University-Kingsville, 1996.

________. "Castañeda and Canales: Collaborators, Academics, Friends." *Journal of South Texas* 13 (Spring 2000): 94–115.

________. "The Role of J. T. Canales in the Development of Tejano Identity and Mexican American Integration in Twentieth Century South Texas." *Journal of South Texas* 13 (2000): 220–259.

Manuel, Herschel T. "The Mexican Population of Texas." *Southwestern Social Science Quarterly* 15 (June 1934–March 1935): 29–51.

________. "The Mexican Population of Texas." *Southwest Review* 17 (October 1932): 290–302.

Márquez, Benjamín. *LULAC: The Evolution of a Mexican American Political Organization*. Austin: University of Texas Press, 1993.

________. "League of United Latin American Citizens and the Politics of Ethnicity." In *Latino Empowerment*, edited by Roberto E. Villareal, Norma G. Hernández, and Howard D. Neighbor, 11–24. New York: Greenwood Press, 1988.

________. "The Politics of Race and Assimilation: The League of United Latin American Citizens, 1929–1940." *Western Political Quarterly* 42 (June 1989): 355–375.

McCaffery, Isias James. "Organizing las Costureras: Life, Labor, and Unionization among Mexican Garment Workers in Two Borderland Cities, Los Angeles and San Antonio, 1933–1941." Ph.D. dissertation, University of Kansas, 1999.

McCain, Johnny M. "Texas and the Mexican Labor Question, 1942–1947." *Southwestern Historical Quarterly* 85 (July 1981): 45–64.

McDonald, Dedra S. "'The Labor Movement Was the Way': Mexican-American Women's Solidarity and Political Power in Depression-Era San Antonio." Master's thesis, University of Wisconsin, Madison, 1993.

McKay, R. Reynolds. "Texas Mexican Repatriation During the Great Depression." Ph.D. dissertation, University of Oklahoma, 1982.

________. "The Federal Deportation Campaign in Texas: Mexican Deportation from the Lower Rio Grande Valley During the Great Depression." *Borderlands Journal* 5 (Fall 1981): 95–120.

________. "The Impact of the Great Depression on Immigrant Mexican Labor: Repatriation of the Bridgeport, Texas, Coalminers." *Social Science Quarterly* 65 (June 1984): 354–363.

________. "Mexican Americans and Repatriation." In *The New Handbook of Texas*, edited by Ron Tyler, Douglas E. Barnett, Roy R. Barkely, Penelope C. Anderson, and Mark F. Odintz, vol. 4, 676–679. Austin: Texas State Historical Association, 1996.

________. "Mexican Repatriation from South Texas During the Great Depression." *Journal of South Texas* 3 (1990): 1–17.

________. "The Texas Cotton Acreage Control Law of 1931 and Mexican Repatriation." *West Texas Historical Association Yearbook* 59 (1983): 143–155.

Medrano, Manuel. "El Chubasco del '33." In *More Studies in Brownsville History*, edited by Milo Kearney, 375–380. Brownsville, Tex.: Pan American University at Brownsville, 1989.

Meier, Matt S. with Conchita Franco Serri and Richard A. García. "Carlos Castañeda." In *Notable Latino Americans: A Biographical Dictionary*, by Matt S. Meier, 66–70. Westport, Conn.: Greenwood Press, 1997.

________. "George I. Sánchez." In *Notable Latino Americans: A Biographical Dictionary*, by Matt S. Meier, 348–351. Westport, Conn.: Greenwood Press, 1997.

Meyer, Nicholas E. "Carlos E. Castañeda." In *The Biographical Dictionary of Hispanic Americans*, by Nicholas E. Meyer, 42–44. New York: Facts on File, 1997.

________. "Macario García." In *The Biographical Dictionary of Hispanic Americans*, by Nicholas E. Meyer, 92–93. New York: Facts on File, 1997.

________. "José López." In *The Biographical Dictionary of Hispanic Americans*, by Nicholas E. Meyer, 128–129. New York: Facts on File, 1997.

Miller, Hubert J. "Leo J. Leo." In *The New Handbook of Texas*, edited by Ron Tyler, Douglas E. Barnett, Roy R. Barkely, Penelope C. Anderson, and Mark F. Odintz, vol. 4, 159. Austin: Texas State Historical Association, 1996.

________. "The Story of Dr. Octavio García." In *Preparing Teachers for Bilingual Education: Basic Readings*, edited by Octavio A. Ballesteros, 171–184. Washington, D.C.: University Press of the Americas, 1979.

Monday, Jane Clements, and Betty Bailey Colley. *Voices from the Wild Horse Desert: The Vaquero Families of the King and Kenedy Ranches*. Austin: University of Texas Press, 1997.

Montejano, David. "A Journey Through Mexican Texas, 1900–1930: The Making of a Segregated Society." Ph.D. dissertation, Yale University, 1982.

________. "Frustrated Apartheid: Race, Repression, and Capitalist Agriculture in South Texas, 1920–1930." In *The World System of Capitalism, Past and Present,* edited by Walter Goldfrank, 131–168. Beverly Hills: Sage Publications, 1979.

________. "Race, Labor Repression, and Capitalist Agriculture: Notes from South Texas, 1920–1930." Berkeley: Institute for the Study of Social Change, 1977.

Montgomery, Robert H. "Keglar Hill." *Survey* 66 (May 1, 1931): 193–195.

Morín, Raúl. *Among the Valiant: Mexican Americans in World War II and Korea*. Los Angeles: Border Publishing, 1963.

Munguía, Rubén. "*La Prensa*: Memories of a Boy . . . Sixty Years Later." *The Americans Review* 17 (Winter 1989): 130–135.

Orozco, Cynthia E. "The Origins of the League of United Latin American Citizens (LULAC) and the Mexican American Civil Rights Movement in Texas with an Analysis of Women's Political Participation in a Gendered Context, 1910–1929." Ph.D. dissertation, University of California at Los Angeles, 1992.

________. "Alice Dickerson Montemayor: Feminism and Mexican American Politics in the 1930s." In *Writing the Range: Race, Class, and Culture in the Women's West*, edited by Elizabeth Jameson and Susan Armitage, 435–456. Norman: University of Oklahoma Press, 1997.

________. "Alonso S. Perales." In *The New Handbook of Texas*, edited by Ron Tyler, Douglas E. Barnett, Roy R. Barkely, Penelope C. Anderson, and Mark F. Odintz, vol. 5, 148–149. Austin: Texas State Historical Association, 1996.

________. "Antonio Victor Navarro." In *The New Handbook of Texas*, edited by Ron Tyler, Douglas E. Barnett, Roy R. Barkely, Penelope C. Anderson, and Mark F. Odintz, vol. 4, 953. Austin: Texas State Historical Association, 1996.

________. "Bernardo Garza." In *The New Handbook of Texas*, edited by Ron Tyler, Douglas E. Barnett, Roy R. Barkley, Penelope C. Anderson, and Mark F. Odintz, vol. 3, 105. Austin: Texas State Historical Association, 1996.

________. "Clemente Nicasio Idar." In *The New Handbook of Texas*, edited by Ron Tyler, Douglas E. Barnett, Roy R. Barkely, Penelope C. Anderson, and Mark F. Odintz, vol. 3, 813–814. Austin: Texas State Historical Association, 1996.

________. "Cleto Rodríguez." In *The New Handbook of Texas*, edited by Ron Tyler, Douglas E. Barnett, Roy R. Barkely, Penelope C. Anderson, and Mark F. Odintz, vol. 5, 652. Austin: Texas State Historical Association, 1996.

________. "Comisión Honórifica Mexicana." In *The New Handbook of Texas*, edited by Ron Tyler, Douglas E. Barnett, Roy R. Barkley, Penelope C. Anderson, and

Mark F. Odintz, vol. 2, 248–249. Austin: Texas State Historical Association, 1996.

________. "Gilberto A. Garza." In *The New Handbook of Texas*, edited by Ron Tyler, Douglas E. Barnett, Roy R. Barkley, Penelope C. Anderson, and Mark F. Odintz, vol. 3, 107. Austin: Texas State Historical Association, 1996.

________. "Gustavo Guerra." In *The New Handbook of Texas*, edited by Ron Tyler, Douglas E. Barnett, Roy R. Barkley, Penelope C. Anderson, and Mark F. Odintz, vol. 3, 368–369. Austin: Texas State Historical Association, 1996.

________. "Hidalgo County Rebellion." In *The New Handbook of Texas*, edited by Ron Tyler, Douglas E. Barnett, Roy R. Barkley, Penelope C. Anderson, and Mark F. Odintz, vol. 3, 593. Austin: Texas State Historical Association, 1996.

________. "Higinio Garza." In *The New Handbook of Texas*, edited by Ron Tyler, Douglas E. Barnett, Roy R. Barkley, Penelope C. Anderson, and Mark F. Odintz, vol. 3, 107. Austin: Texas State Historical Association, 1996.

________. "John C. Solis." In *The New Handbook of Texas*, edited by Ron Tyler, Douglas E. Barnett, Roy R. Barkely, Penelope C. Anderson, and Mark F. Odintz, vol. 5, 1140–1141. Austin: Texas State Historical Association, 1996.

________. "League of United Latin American Citizens." In *The New Handbook of Texas*, edited by Ron Tyler, Douglas E. Barnett, Roy R. Barkely, Penelope C. Anderson, and Mark F. Odintz, vol. 4, 129–131. Austin: Texas State Historical Association, 1996.

________. "Lino Pérez, Sr." In *The New Handbook of Texas*, edited by Ron Tyler, Douglas E. Barnett, Roy R. Barkely, Penelope C. Anderson, and Mark F. Odintz, vol. 5, 150. Austin: Texas State Historical Association, 1996.

________. "María L. de Hernández." In *The New Handbook of Texas*, edited by Ron Tyler, Douglas E. Barnett, Roy R. Barkley, Penelope C. Anderson, and Mark F. Odintz, vol. 3, 572–573. Austin: Texas State Historical Association, 1996.

________. "Order of the Sons of America." In *The New Handbook of Texas*, edited by Ron Tyler, Douglas E. Barnett, Roy R. Barkely, Penelope C. Anderson, and Mark F. Odintz, vol. 4, 1166–1167. Austin: Texas State Historical Association, 1996.

________. "Regionalism, Politics, and Gender in Southwest History: The League of United Latin American Citizens' Expansion into New Mexico from Texas, 1929–1945." *Western Historical Quarterly* 29 (Winter 1998): 459–483.

Paredes, Américo, ed. *Humanidad: Essays in Honor of George I. Sánchez.* Los Angeles: Aztlán Publications, 1977.

Paschall, Mark. "Professional Baseball in the Lower Rio Grande Valley." *Journal of Borderland Studies* 11.2 (1996): 51–68.

Peavey, John R. *Echoes from the Rio Grande, 1905 to N-O-W.* Brownsville, Tex.: Springman-King, 1963.

Perales, Alonso S. *En Defensa de Mi Raza.* 2 vols. San Antonio: Artes Gráficas, 1937.

________. *El México Americano y la politica del sur de Tejas.* San Antonio: Artes Gráficas, 1931.

Pycior, Julie Leininger. "Hijos de Texas." In *The New Handbook of Texas*, edited by Ron Tyler, Douglas E. Barnett, Roy R. Barkely, Penelope C. Anderson, and Mark F. Odintz, vol. 3, 608–609. Austin: Texas State Historical Association, 1996.

________. "Mexican American Organizations." In *The New Handbook of Texas*, edited by Ron Tyler, Douglas E. Barnett, Roy R. Barkely, Penelope C. Anderson, and Mark F. Odintz, vol. 4, 660–662. Austin: Texas State Historical Association, 1996.

________. "La Raza Organizes: Mexican American Life in San Antonio, 1915–1930, as Reflected in Mutualista Activities." Ph.D. dissertation, University of Notre Dame, 1979.

________. "Sociedad de la Unión." In *The New Handbook of Texas*, edited by Ron Tyler, Douglas E. Barnett, Roy R. Barkely, Penelope C. Anderson, and Mark F. Odintz, vol. 5, 1133. Austin: Texas State Historical Association, 1996.

Quezada, J. Gilberto. *Border Boss: Manuel B. Bravo and Zapata County*. College Station: Texas A&M University Press, 1999.

________. "The Box Family Roots and South Texas Politics: Judge Manuel Box Bravo." *East Texas Historical Journal* 34 (Fall 1996): 17–24.

________. "Judge Manuel B. Bravo: A Political Leader in South Texas, 1935–1957." *Journal of South Texas* 5 (1992): 51–67.

________. "Toward a Working Definition of Social Justice: Father Carmelo A. Tranchese, S.J., and Our Lady of Guadalupe Parish, 1932–1953." *Journal of Texas Catholic History and Culture* 4 (1993): 44–64.

Rhinehart, Marilyn, and Thomas H. Kreneck. "'In the Shadow of Uncertainty': Texas Mexicans and Repatriation in Houston During the Great Depression." *The Houston Review* 10 (1988): 21–33.

Ríos McMillan, Nora. "A Biography of a Man and His Newspaper." *The Americas Review* 17 (Fall-Winter 1989): 136–149.

________. "Colonia Diez y Ocho de Marzo." In *Studies in Matamoros and Cameron County History*, edited by Milo Kearney, Anthony Knopp, and Antonio Zavaleta, 213–218. Brownsville, Tex.: The University of Texas at Brownsville and Texas Southmost College, 1997.

________. "The Immigration Issue between 1929 and 1954 as seen through *La Prensa*." *South Texas Studies* 6 (1995): 20–52.

________. "The Repatriation of Mexicans during the Great Depression." *Journal of South Texas* 11 (1998): 44–73.

Rogers, Thomas Guy. "The Housing Situation of the Mexican in San Antonio, Texas." Master's thesis, University of Texas, Austin, 1927.

Romo, Ricardo. "George I. Sánchez and the Civil Rights Movement, 1940–1960." *La Raza Law Journal* 1 (1986): 342–362.

Rosales, Francisco Arturo. "Mexicans in Houston: The Struggle to Survive, 1908–1975." *The Houston Review* 3 (Summer 1981): 224–248.

________. "Shifting Self-Perceptions and Ethnic Consciousness Among Mexicans in Houston, 1908–1946." *The Americas Review* 16 (Spring 1988): 71–94.

San Miguel, Guadalupe Jr. "The Struggle Against Separate and Unequal Schools: Middle Class Mexican Americans in the Desegregation Campaign in Texas, 1929–1957." *History of Education Quarterly* 23 (Fall 1983): 343–359.

Schlossman, Steven. "Self-Evident Remedy: George I. Sánchez, Segregation, and Enduring Dilemmas in Bilingual Education." *Teachers' College Record* 84 (Summer 1983): 871–907.

Scotford, John R. "Mexico in Texas." In *Within These Borders: Spanish-Speaking Peoples in the U.S.A.*, by John R. Scotford, 31–55. New York: Friendship Press, 1953.

Shapiro, Harold A. "The Workers of San Antonio, Texas, 1900–1940." Ph.D. dissertation, University of Texas, Austin, 1952.

Shelton, Edgar Greer Jr. *Political Conditions among Texas-Mexicans along the Rio Grande*. San Francisco: R&E Research Associates, 1974.

________. "Political Conditions among Texas-Mexicans along the Rio Grande." Master's thesis, University of Texas, Austin, 1946.

Sloss-Vento, Adela. *Alonso S. Perales: His Struggle for the Rights of Mexican Americans*, edited by Arnold C. Vento. San Antonio: Artes Gráficas, 1977.

Smith, L. Glenn, and Joan K. Smith. "George I. Sánchez, 1906–1972." In *Lives in Education: A Narrative of People and Ideas*, by L. Glenn Smith and Joan K. Smith, 345–351. Second Edition. New York: St. Martin's Press, 1994.

Spell, Lota M. "Carlos Eduardo Castañeda." In *The Handbook of Texas: A Supplement*, edited by Eldon Stephen Branda, vol. 3, 150. Austin: Texas State Historical Association, 1976.

Stevenson, Coke R., and Ezequiel Padilla. "The Good Neighbor Policy and Mexicans in Texas." *National and International Problems Series* 17 (1943): 7–13, 17–22.

Tafoya, Carmen. "Expansion of the Church in Texas." In *Fronteras: A History of the Latin American Church in the USA since 1513*, edited by Moisés Sandoval, 225–237. San Antonio: Mexican American Cultural Center, 1983.

Taylor, Paul S. "Deportados." In *Texas Folk and Folklore*, edited by Mody C. Boatright and Wilson M. Hudson, 157–158. Dallas: Southern Methodist University Press, 1954.

"Texas Mexican Industrial Institute." In *The Handbook of Texas*, edited by Walter Prescott Webb and H. Bailey Carroll, vol. 2, 747. Austin: Texas State Historical Association, 1952.

Treviño, Roberto R. "In Their Own Way: Parish Funding and Mexican-American Ethnicity in Catholic Houston, 1911–1972." *Latino Studies Journal* 5.3 (September 1994): 87–107.

________. "La Fe: Catholicism and Mexican Americans in Houston, 1911–1972." Ph.D. dissertation, Stanford University, 1993.

Young, Elliott. "Deconstructing *La Raza*: Identifying the *Gente Decente* of Laredo, 1904–1994." *Southwestern Historical Quarterly* 98 (October 1994): 227–259.

Weeks, Douglas O. "The League of United Latin-American Citizens: A Texas-Mexican Civic Organization." *Southwestern Political and Social Science Quarterly* 10 (December 1929): 257–278.

________. "The Texas Mexicans and the Politics of South Texas." *American Political Science Review* 24 (August 1930): 606–627.

Zamora, Emilio. "The Failed Promise of Wartime Opportunity for Mexicans in the Texas Oil Industry." *Southwestern Historical Quarterly* 95 (January 1992): 323–350.

Zamora, Emilio Jr., and Roberto R. Calderón. "Manuela Solis Sager and Emma Tenayuca: A Tribute." In *Chicana Voices: Interaction of Class, Race, and Gender.* Proceedings of the National Association for Chicano Studies, edited by Teresa Córdova, Norma Cantú, Gilberto Cárdenas, Juan García, and Christine M. Sierra, 30–41. Austin: Center for Mexican American Studies Publications, University of Texas at Austin, 1986.

Zelman, Donald L. "Alazán-Apache Courts: A New Deal Response to Mexican American Housing Conditions in San Antonio." *Southwestern Historical Quarterly* 87 (October 1983): 123–150.

8. MANY HISTORIES, 1945–1966

A good segment of Mexican-American folks during the mid-twentieth century still lived in dire poverty, made their living as migrant workers, and struggled to get proper schooling. But disadvantage was not the only feature associated with Mexican-American life in that period, as communities were much more diversified than ever before. After 1945, Mexican Americans joined the influx into the cities, just as did other Americans. Many found employment in urban industry—an improvement over farm wages. Additionally, Mexican-American communities felt the full impact of American advances, eagerly embracing the fashions, music, and youth ideology of the day. Mexican-American leaders, many of them inspired by the cause of World War II, meanwhile challenged old laws (such as those requiring the purchase of poll taxes for the right to vote) and social customs that had heretofore limited ethnic progress. By the early 1960s, many of these activists called on Mexican Americans for increased electoral participation to force the national government into addressing the special problems that plagued Texas barrios.

Luz Díaz de León with his garbage pushcart.
The Institute of Texan Cultures at UTSA, No. L-3432-G
The San Antonio Light *Collection*

Acosta, Teresa Palomo. "American G.I. Forum Women's Auxiliary." In *The New Handbook of Texas*, edited by Ron Tyler, Douglas E. Barnett, Roy R. Barkley, Penelope C. Anderson, and Mark F. Odintz, vol. 1, 148. Austin: Texas State Historical Association, 1996.

________. "Bishops' Committee for Hispanic Affairs." In *The New Handbook of Texas*, edited by Ron Tyler, Douglas E. Barnett, Roy R. Barkely, Penelope C. Anderson, and Mark F. Odintz, vol. 1, 554. Austin: Texas State Historical Association, 1996.

________. "Cristóbal Alderete." In *The New Handbook of Texas*, edited by Ron Tyler, Douglas E. Barnett, Roy R. Barkley, Penelope C. Anderson, and Mark F. Odintz, vol. 1, 97. Austin: Texas State Historical Association, 1996.

________. "Political Association of Spanish-speaking Organizations." In *The New Handbook of Texas*, edited by Ron Tyler, Douglas E. Barnett, Roy R. Barkley, Penelope C. Anderson, and Mark F. Odintz, vol. 5, 256. Austin: Texas State Historical Association, 1996.

Alexander, L. "Texas Helps Her Little Latins." *Saturday Evening Post* 243 (August 5, 1961): 30–31.

Allsup, V. Carl. *The American G.I. Forum: Origins and Evolution.* Austin: Center for Mexican American Studies, University of Texas Press, 1982.

________. "The American G.I. Forum: A History of a Mexican American Organization." Ph.D. dissertation, University of Texas at Austin, 1976.

________. "The American G.I. Forum." In *The New Handbook of Texas*, edited by Ron Tyler, Douglas E. Barnett, Roy R. Barkley, Penelope C. Anderson, and Mark F. Odintz, vol. 1, 147–148. Austin: Texas State Historical Association, 1996.

________. "*Delgado* v. *Bastrop ISD*." In *The New Handbook of Texas*, edited by Ron Tyler, Douglas E. Barnett, Roy R. Barkely, Penelope C. Anderson, and Mark F. Odintz, vol. 2, 574–575. Austin: Texas State Historical Association, 1996.

________. "Education is Our Freedom: The American G.I. Forum and the Mexican American School Segregation in Texas, 1948–1957." *Aztlán* 8 (Spring/Summer/Fall 1977): 27–50.

________. "Félix Longoria Affair." In *The New Handbook of Texas*, edited by Ron Tyler, Douglas E. Barnett, Roy R. Barkely, Penelope C. Anderson, and Mark F. Odintz, vol. 2, 975–976. Austin: Texas State Historical Association, 1996.

________. "*Hernández* v. *State of Texas*." In *The New Handbook of Texas*, edited by Ron Tyler, Douglas E. Barnett, Roy R. Barkely, Penelope C. Anderson, and Mark F. Odintz, vol. 3, 574. Austin: Texas State Historical Association, 1996.

________. "A Soldier's Burial." *Revista Chicano-Riqueña* 4 (Fall 1976): 77–87.

"American G.I. Forum." In *The Handbook of Texas: A Supplement*, edited by Eldon Stephen Branda, vol. 3, 26. Austin: Texas State Historical Association, 1976.

American G.I. Forum. *What Price Wetbacks*? Austin: American G.I. Forum of Texas and Texas State Federation of Labor, 1953.

Anderson, Lynn F. "League of United Latin American Citizens (LULAC)." In *The Handbook of Texas*, edited by Walter Prescott Webb and H. Bailey Carroll, vol. 2, 27. Austin: Texas State Historical Association, 1952.

Barahona Israel, María de los Angeles. "The Lifeworld of Dwelling Experiences of Hispanic Migrant Workers: From Southern Michigan to Southern Texas." Arch.D. dissertation, University of Michigan, 1990.

Barrera, Humberto. *My Journey Through the 1960s Olympic Games*. New York: Carlton Press, 1995.

Beard, Marty. "The Right to Learn: Desegregation in West Texas Towns." *Texas Historian* 52 (May 1992): 9–12.

Binder, Norman, and Frank J. García. "Winning Political Office in Cameron County, 1876–1988: The Mexican American Case." In *More Studies in Brownsville History*, edited by Milo Kearney, 423–437. Brownsville, Tex.: Pan American University at Brownsville, 1989.

Bronder, Saul E. "Robert Emmet Lucey." In *The New Handbook of Texas*, edited by Ron Tyler, Douglas E. Barnett, Roy R. Barkely, Penelope C. Anderson, and Mark F. Odintz, vol. 4, 328–329. Austin: Texas State Historical Association, 1996.

________. *Social Justice and Church Authority: The Public Life of Archbishop Robert E. Lucey*. Philadelphia: Temple University Press, 1982.

Brookshire, Marjorie S. "Some Notes on the Integration of Mexican Americans since 1929, Nueces County, Texas." Industrial Relations Research Association *Annual Proceedings* 8 (December 1955): 356–361.

Buitron, Richard Arthur Jr. "Who are We? The Quest for Tejano Identity in San Antonio, Texas, 1913–Present." Ph.D. dissertation, Florida State University, 2002.

Carroll, Patrick J. *Félix Longoria's Wake: Bereavement, Racism, and the Rise of Mexican American Activism*. Austin: University of Texas Press, 2003.

Cavazos, Sylvia. "The Disposable Mexican: Operation Wetback, 1954, the Deportation of Undocumented Workers in California and Texas." Master's thesis, University of Texas–Pan American, 1997.

Chabrán, Richard, and Rafael Chabrán, eds. "American G.I. Forum." In *The Latino Encyclopedia*, edited by Richard Chabrán and Rafael Chabrán, vol. 1, 54. New York: Marshall Cavendish, 1996.

________. "Delgado v. Bastrop Independent School District." In *The Latino Encyclopedia*, edited by Richard Chabrán and Rafael Chabrán, vol. 2, 465. New York: Marshall Cavendish, 1996.

________. "Hector P. García." In *The Latino Encyclopedia*, edited by Richard Chabrán and Rafael Chabrán, vol. 3, 679. New York: Marshall Cavendish, 1996.

________. "Good Neighbor Policy." In *The Latino Encyclopedia*, edited by Richard Chabrán and Rafael Chabrán, vol. 3, 703. New York: Marshall Cavendish, 1996.

________. "Gus C. García." In *The Latino Encyclopedia*, edited by Richard Chabrán and Rafael Chabrán, vol. 3, 679. New York: Marshall Cavendish, 1996.

________. "Hernández v. Texas." In *The Latino Encyclopedia*, edited by Richard Chabrán and Rafael Chabrán, vol. 5, 1420. New York: Marshall Cavendish, 1996.

________. "Political Association of Spanish-speaking Organizations." In *The Latino Encyclopedia*, edited by Richard Chabrán and Rafael Chabrán, vol. 3, 1252. New York: Marshall Cavendish, 1996.

________. "Raymond L. Telles." In *The Latino Encyclopedia*, edited by Richard Chabrán and Rafael Chabrán, vol. 4, 1588. New York: Marshall Cavendish, 1996.

________. "Texas Good Neighbor Commission." In *The Latino Encyclopedia*, edited by Richard Chabrán and Rafael Chabrán, vol. 6, 1596. New York: Marshall Cavendish, 1996.

________. "Viva Kennedy Clubs." In *The Latino Encyclopedia*, edited by Richard Chabrán and Rafael Chabrán, vol. 6, 1587. New York: Marshall Cavendish, 1996.

Christian, Carole E. "John J. Herrera." In *The New Handbook of Texas*, edited by Ron Tyler, Douglas E. Barnett, Roy R. Barkely, Penelope C. Anderson, and Mark F. Odintz, vol. 3, 575. Austin: Texas State Historical Association, 1996.

Clark, John E. "Reflections on the Duke of Duval: The Litigation Record." *South Texas Studies* 8 (1996): 31–48.

Clinchy, Everett Ross Jr. *Equality of Opportunity for Latin-Americans in Texas*. New York: Arno Press, 1974.

________. "Equality of Opportunity for Latin Americans in Texas: A Study of the Economic, Social and Educational Discrimination against Latin Americans in Texas and of the Effects of Efforts of the State Government on Their Behalf." Ph.D. dissertation, Columbia University, 1954.

Cuéllar, Robert A. *A Social and Political History of the Mexican-American Population of Texas, 1929–1963.* San Francisco: R&E Research Associates, 1974.

________. "A Social and Political History of the Mexican-American Population of Texas, 1929–1963." Master's thesis, North Texas State University, 1969.

Curlee, Kendall. "Manuel Gregorio Acosta." In *The New Handbook of Texas*, edited by Ron Tyler, Douglas E. Barnett, Roy R. Barkley, Penelope C. Anderson, and Mark F. Odintz, vol. 1, 18–19. Austin: Texas State Historical Association, 1996.

De León, Arnoldo. "Pachucos." In *The New Handbook of Texas*, edited by Ron Tyler, Douglas E. Barnett, Roy R. Barkely, Penelope C. Anderson, and Mark F. Odintz, vol. 5, 2–3. Austin: Texas State Historical Association, 1996.

Donecker, Frances. "*La Prensa*." In *The Handbook of Texas*, edited by Walter Prescott Webb and H. Bailey Carroll, vol. 2, 27. Austin: Texas State Historical Association, 1952.

Dorsey, Emmet E. "The Political Role of Mexican Americans." In *Minority Problems*, edited by Arnold M. Rose and Caroline B. Rose, 202–204. New York: Harper and Row, 1965.

Dyer, Stanford P., and Merrell A. Knighten. "Discrimination After Death: Lyndon Johnson and Félix Longoria." *Southern Studies* 17 (Winter 1978): 411–426.

Fisch, Louise Ann. *All Rise: Reynaldo G. Garza: The First Mexican American Federal Judge*. College Station: Texas A&M University Press, 1996.

Flores-Witte, Amanda. "Benito Andrés Jiménez." In *The New Handbook of Texas*, edited by Ron Tyler, Douglas E. Barnett, Roy R. Barkely, Penelope C. Anderson, and Mark F. Odintz, vol. 3, 940. Austin: Texas State Historical Association, 1996.

Foley, Douglas E., Clarice Mota, Donald E. Post, and Ignacio Lozano. *From Peones to Politicos: Ethnic Relations in a South Texas Town, 1900–1977*. Austin: University of Texas Press, 1977.

________. *From Peones to Politicos: Class and Ethnicity in a South Texas Town, 1900–1987*. Revised edition. Austin: University of Texas Press, 1988.

García, Eduardo Fausto. "Presentation of Problems in Administering a Bracero Co-operative for the Year 1952." Master's thesis, Texas A&I University, 1955.

García, Ignacio M. *Hector P. García: In Relentless Pursuit of Justice*. Houston: Arte Público Press, 2002.

________. *Viva Kennedy: Mexican Americans in Search of Camelot*. College Station: Texas A&M University Press, 2000.

García, Juan Ramón. "The Texas Operation." In *Operation Wetback: The Mass Deportation of Mexican Undocumented Workers in 1954*, by Juan Ramón García, 206–233. Westport, Conn.: Greenwood Press, 1980.

García, Mario T. *The Making of a Mexican American Mayor: Raymond L. Telles of El Paso*. El Paso: Texas Western Press, 1999.

________. "Catholic Social Doctrine and Mexican American Political Thought." In *El Cuerpo de Cristo: The Hispanic Presence in the U.S. Catholic Church*, edited by Peter Casarella and Raul Gómez, 292–311. New York: Crossroad, 1998.

________. "The Chicano Southwest: Catholicism and its Meaning." *U.S. Catholic Historian* 18.4 (Fall 2000): 1–24.

Garza, Edward D. "LULAC (League of United Latin American Citizens)." Master's thesis, Southwest Texas State Teacher's College, 1951.

Graves, Ruth. "Migrant Labor." In *The Handbook of Texas: A Supplement*, edited by Eldon Stephen Branda, vol. 3, 487–488. Austin: Texas State Historical Association, 1976.

Green, George N. "The Félix Longoria Affair." *Journal of Ethnic Studies* 19 (Fall 1991): 23–49.

________. "The Good Neighbor Commission and Texas Mexicans." In *Ethnic Minorities in Gulf Coast Society*, edited by Jerrell H. Shofner and Linda V. Ellsworth, 111–128. Pensacola, Fla.: Gulf Coast History and Humanities Conference, 1979.

Grossman, Mitchell. *Multi-Factional Politics in San Antonio and Bexar County, Texas*. Austin: University of Texas Press, 1959.

Guerra, Rosa. "Childhood Memories: World War II and El Paso." *Password* 40 (Summer 1995): 61–64.

Harrison, David C. "A Survey of the Educational and Administrative Policies of the Baptist, Methodist, and Presbyterian Churches among Mexican-American People in Texas." Master's thesis, University of Texas, Austin, 1952.

Hinojosa, Gilberto M. "The Mexican-American Church, 1930–1965." In *Mexican Americans and the Catholic Church, 1900–1965*, edited by Jay P. Dolan and Gilberto M. Hinojosa, 84–119. Notre Dame: University of Notre Dame Press, 1994.

Houston, Ramona Allaniz. "African Americans, Mexican Americans, and Anglo Americans and the Desegregation of Texas, 1946–1957." Ph.D. dissertation, University of Texas at Austin, 2000.

Hunter, Cecilia Aros, and Leslie Gene Hunter. "'My Dear Friend': The J. T. Canales-Lyndon B. Johnson Correspondence." *Journal of South Texas* 5 (1992): 26–50.

Iber, Jorge. "Bobby Cavazos: A Vaquero in the Backfield." *College Football Historical Society* 14 (August 2001): 1–5.

________. "Mexican American South Texas Football: The Athletic and Coaching Careers of E. C. Lerma and Bobby Cavazos, 1932–1965." *Southwestern Historical Quarterly* 105 (April 2002): 617–633.

Kaplowitz, Craig Allan. "Mexican American, Ethnicity, and Federal Policy: The League of United Latin American Citizens and the Politics of Cultural Disadvantage, 1942–1975." Ph.D. dissertation, Vanderbilt University, 1999.

Kibbe, Pauline R. "The Economic Plight of Mexicans." In *Ethnic Relations in the United States*, edited by E. C. McDonough and E. S. Richards, 187–200. New York: Appleton-Century-Crofts, 1953.

Koestler, Fred L. "Bracero Program." In *The New Handbook of Texas*, edited by Ron Tyler, Douglas E. Barnett, Roy R. Barkely, Penelope C. Anderson, and Mark F. Odintz, vol. 1, 658. Austin: Texas State Historical Association, 1996.

________. "Operation Wetback." In *The New Handbook of Texas*, edited by Ron Tyler, Douglas E. Barnett, Roy R. Barkely, Penelope C. Anderson, and Mark F. Odintz, vol. 4, 1157–1158. Austin: Texas State Historical Association, 1996.

Larralde, Carlos. *José Rangel Cantú: South Texas' Fiery Radio Warrior*. MASCR Working Paper Series, No. 24. Tucson: Mexican American Studies and Research Center, University of Arizona, 1995.

________. "José Rangel Cantú: The Conscience of South Texas." In *Studies in Matamoros and Cameron County History*, edited by Milo Kearney, Anthony Knopp, and Antonio Zavaleta, 163–178. Brownsville, Tex.: The University of Texas at Brownsville and Texas Southmost College, 1997.

Lawrence, James R. "A Study of the Latin American Problem and the Growth of the LULAC Organization." Master's thesis, Texas A&I University, 1966.

Leatherwood, Art. "Benito Martínez." In *The New Handbook of Texas*, edited by Ron Tyler, Douglas E. Barnett, Roy R. Barkley, Penelope C. Anderson, and Mark F. Odintz, vol. 4, 534. Austin: Texas State Historical Association, 1996.

LULAC: Fifty Years of Serving Hispanics: Golden Anniversary 1929–1979. Corpus Christi, Tex.: Baldwin Printing, 1979.

Madla, Frank L. Jr. "The Political Impact of Latin Americans and Negroes in Texas Politics." Master's thesis, St. Mary's University, 1964.

Márquez, Benjamín. "Organizing Mexican-American Women in the Garment Industry: La Mujer Obrera." *Women and Politics* 15.1 (1995): 65–88.

________. "The Politics of Race and Class: The League of United Latin American Citizens in the Post-World War II Period." *Social Science Quarterly* 68 (March 1987): 89–101.

________. "The Problem of Organization Maintenance and the League of United Latin American Citizens." *Social Science Journal* 28 (1991): 203–225.

McMurtrey, Martin. *Mariachi Bishop: The Life Story of Patrick Flores*. San Antonio: Corona Publishing, 1987.

Meador, Bruce S. "Wetback Labor in the Lower Rio Grande Valley." Master's thesis, University of Texas, Austin, 1951.

Meecham, J. Lloyd. "Carlos Castañeda, 1896–1958." *Hispanic American Historical Review* 38 (August 1958): 383–385.

Meier, Matt S. with Conchita Franco Serri and Richard A. García. "Hector Pérez García." In *Notable Latino Americans: A Biographical Dictionary*, by Matt S. Meier, 168–173. Westport, Conn.: Greenwood Press, 1997.

Meyer, Nicholas E. "Benito Martínez." In *The Biographical Dictionary of Hispanic Americans*, by Nicholas E. Meyer, 139–140. New York: Facts on File, 1997.

________. "Félix Longoria." In *The Biographical Dictionary of Hispanic Americans*, by Nicholas E. Meyer, 127–128. New York: Facts on File, 1997.

________. "Hector Pérez García." In *The Biographical Dictionary of Hispanic Americans*, by Nicholas E. Meyer, 91–92. New York: Facts on File, 1997.

________. "Henry B. González." In *The Biographical Dictionary of Hispanic Americans*, by Nicholas E. Meyer, 101–102. New York: Facts on File, 1997.

Montejano, David. "The Demise of Jim Crow for Texas Mexicans, 1940–1970." *Aztlán* 16 (1985): 27–69.

Morgan, Thomas B. "The Texas Giant Awakens." *Look* 27 (October 8, 1963): 71–75.

Navarro, Carlos, and Rodolfo Acuña. "In Search of Community: A Comparative Essay on Mexicans in Los Angeles and San Antonio." In *20th Century Los Angeles: Power, Promotion, and Social Conflict*, edited by Norman M. Klein and Martin J. Schiesl, 195–226. Claremont, Calif.: Regina Books, 1990.

Orozco, Cynthia E. "Eduardo Idar." In *The New Handbook of Texas*, edited by Ron Tyler, Douglas E. Barnett, Roy R. Barkely, Penelope C. Anderson, and Mark F. Odintz, vol. 3, 814. Austin: Texas State Historical Association, 1996.

________. "Gustavo C. García." In *The New Handbook of Texas*, edited by Ron Tyler, Douglas E. Barnett, Roy R. Barkely, Penelope C. Anderson, and Mark F. Odintz, vol. 3, 84. Austin: Texas State Historical Association, 1996.

________. "Manuel C. Gonzales." In *The New Handbook of Texas*, edited by Ron Tyler, Douglas E. Barnett, Roy R. Barkely, Penelope C. Anderson, and Mark F. Odintz, vol. 3, 227. Austin: Texas State Historical Association, 1996.

________. "Viva Kennedy–Viva Johnson Clubs." In *The New Handbook of Texas*, edited by Ron Tyler, Douglas E. Barnett, Roy R. Barkely, Penelope C. Anderson, and Mark F. Odintz, vol. 6, 769–770. Austin: Texas State Historical Association, 1996.

Paredes, Américo. "Texas' Third Man: The Texas Mexican." *Race* 3–4 (May 1963): 49–58.

Paredes, Eleazar M. "The Role of the Mexican American in Kleberg County, Texas, 1915–1970." Master's thesis, Texas A&I University, 1973.

Perales, Alonso S. *Are We Good Neighbors?* San Antonio: Artes Gráficas, 1948.

Perry, G. S. "The Gonzalezes of San Antonio." *Saturday Evening Post* 221 (October 2, 1948): 24–25, 51, 53.

"Political Association of Spanish-speaking Organizations." In *The Handbook of Texas: A Supplement*, edited by Eldon Stephen Branda, vol. 3, 743. Austin: Texas State Historical Association, 1976.

"*La Prensa*." In *The Handbook of Texas: A Supplement*, edited by Eldon Stephen Branda, vol. 3, 505. Austin: Texas State Historical Association, 1976.

Prewitt, Steven W. "'We Didn't Ask to Come to this Party': Self-Determination Collides with the Federal Government in the Public Schools of Del Rio, Texas, 1890–1971." Ph.D. dissertation, University of Houston, 2000.

________. "Everything from Ditch Diggers to Doctors: LULAC Council 60, A Mexican American Civic Organization in Houston, Texas, 1945–1960." Master's thesis, University of Houston, 1995.

Privett, Stephen A. *The U.S. Catholic Church and Its Hispanic Members: The Pastoral Vision of Archbishop Robert E. Lucey*. San Antonio: Trinity University Press, 1988.

Pycior, Julie Leininger. *LBJ and Mexican Americans: The Paradox of Power*. Austin: University of Texas Press, 1997.

Quiroz, Rudolph Anthony. "Claiming Citizenship: Class and Consensus in a Twentieth Century Mexican American Community." Ph.D. dissertation, University of Iowa, 1998.

________. "Class and Consensus: Twentieth-Century Mexican American Ideology in Victoria, Texas." *Southwestern Historical Quarterly* 106 (July 2002): 31–54.

________. "Mexican American Struggles for Citizenship: Local Organizations in Twentieth Century, Victoria, Texas." *South Texas Studies* 7 (1996): 108–130.

Ramírez, Emilia S. "Wetback Children in South Texas." Master's thesis, University of Texas, Austin, 1951.

Rechy, John. "Jim Crow Wears a Sombrero." *The Nation* 10 (October 1950): 210–213.

"Rivera, Juan." In *The Handbook of Texas: A Supplement*, edited by Eldon Stephen Branda, vol. 3, 802. Austin: Texas State Historical Association, 1976.

Rodríguez, Eugene Jr. *Henry B. González: A Political Profile*. New York: Arno Press, 1976.

________. "Henry B. González: A Political Profile." Master's thesis, St. Mary's University, 1965.

Rollin, María F. "The Champion of Zapata: Father Edward Bestien and the Right For Just Compensation." *Catholic Southwest: A Journal of History and Culture* 12 (2001): 107–117.

________, ed. *The Fighting Padre of Zapata: Father Edward Bastien and the Falcón Dam Project*. Southwestern Studies No. 110. El Paso: Texas Western Press, 2003.

Sandoval, Moisés. *Our Legacy: The First Fifty Years*. Washington, D.C.: League of United Latin American Citizens, 1979.

________. "Effects of World War II on the Hispanic People." In *Fronteras: A History of the Latin American Church in the USA since 1513*, edited by Moises Sandoval, 341–376. San Antonio: Mexican American Cultural Center, 1983.

Scruggs, Otey M. "Texas and the Bracero Program." *Pacific Historical Review* 32 (August 1963): 251–264.

Seaholm, Megan. "Leonidas González Cigaroa." In *The New Handbook of Texas*, edited by Ron Tyler, Douglas E. Barnett, Roy R. Barkely, Penelope C. Anderson, and Mark F. Odintz, vol. 2, 110. Austin: Texas State Historical Association, 1996.

Stillwell, Hart. "Portrait of the Magic Valley." *New Republic* 116 (April 7, 1947): 14–17.

Toscano, Hercilia X. "Edward Treviño Ximénes." In *The New Handbook of Texas*, edited by Ron Tyler, Douglas E. Barnett, Roy R. Barkely, Penelope C. Anderson, and Mark F. Odintz, vol. 6, 1103. Austin: Texas State Historical Association, 1996.

Tubbs, Lowell Lester. "A Survey of the Problems of Migratory Mexicans." Master's thesis, University of Texas, Austin, 1954.

Wheelock, Ernestine. "League of United Latin American Citizens (LULAC)." In *The Handbook of Texas: A Supplement*, edited by Eldon Stephen Branda, vol. 3, 512. Austin: Texas State Historical Association, 1976.

Woods, Frances J. *Mexican Ethnic Leadership in San Antonio, Texas.* Washington, D.C.: Catholic University of America, 1949.

Zelade, Richard. "Last Rites, First Rights." *Texas Monthly* 14 (January 1986): 192, 194.

9. EL MOVIMIENTO, 1966–1975

A farmworkers' march in the summer of 1966, from the Rio Grande Valley to the state capital, sparked a Mexican-American civil rights upheaval in Texas that would last into the mid-1970s. The heyday of *El Movimiento* (called the "Chicano Movement") in the state would last from about 1968 to 1972, but the 1966 march to Austin brought attention to lingering problems that had for so long afflicted Mexican Americans. It inspired a "militant" element within Tejano society to voice newer solutions to old conditions; the Mexican American Youth Organization and the Raza Unida Party would be at the forefront of the *movimiento*. Confrontation, school boycotts, radical language, and an appeal to the grass-roots voters distinguished the strategy of this youthful cohort from that of its predecessors. Following the second electoral defeat of the Raza Unida Party at the state level in 1974, the Chicano Movement declined. But the Movement was not the most salient attraction of the 1960s and 1970s. These decades also drew Mexican Americans into the Great Society programs and inspired many to pursue higher education. At the same time, national causes led others to join antiwar protests and various student revolts.

Dr. José Angel Guitérrez giving a lecture at Sul Ross State University, 2002.
Photograph courtesy of SRSU News and Publications

Abreo, Rosa María. "A History of Rio Grande City, Texas High School, 1960–1969." Ph.D. dissertation, University of Texas at Austin, 2001.

Achor, Shirley. "Santos Rodríguez." In *The New Handbook of Texas*, edited by Ron Tyler, Douglas E. Barnett, Roy R. Barkley, Penelope C. Anderson, and Mark F. Odintz, vol. 5, 656. Austin: Texas State Historical Association, 1996.

Acosta, Teresa Palomo. "Association for the Advancement of Mexican Americans." In *The New Handbook of Texas*, edited by Ron Tyler, Douglas E. Barnett, Roy R. Barkley, Penelope C. Anderson, and Mark F. Odintz, vol. 1, 269. Austin: Texas State Historical Association, 1996.

________. "Crystal City Revolts." In *The New Handbook of Texas*, edited by Ron Tyler, Douglas E. Barnett, Roy R. Barkely, Penelope C. Anderson, and Mark F. Odintz, vol. 2, 431. Austin: Texas State Historical Association, 1996.

________. "Mexican American Legal Defense and Educational Fund." In *The New Handbook of Texas*, edited by Ron Tyler, Douglas E. Barnett, Roy R. Barkley, Penelope C. Anderson, and Mark F. Odintz, vol. 4, 659. Austin: Texas State Historical Association, 1996.

________. "Mexican American School Board Members Association." In *The New Handbook of Texas*, edited by Ron Tyler, Douglas E. Barnett, Roy R. Barkley, Penelope C. Anderson, and Mark F. Odintz, vol. 4, 670–671. Austin: Texas State Historical Association, 1996.

________. "Mexican American Youth Organization." In *The New Handbook of Texas*, edited by Ron Tyler, Douglas E. Barnett, Roy R. Barkley, Penelope C. Anderson, and Mark F. Odintz, vol. 4, 682–683. Austin: Texas State Historical Association, 1996.

________. "Raza Unida Party." In *The New Handbook of Texas*, edited by Ron Tyler, Douglas E. Barnett, Roy R. Barkley, Penelope C. Anderson, and Mark F. Odintz, vol. 5, 462–463. Austin: Texas State Historical Association, 1996.

Allsup, V. Carl. "*Cisneros* v. *Corpus Christi ISD*." In *The New Handbook of Texas*, edited by Ron Tyler, Douglas E. Barnett, Roy R. Barkely, Penelope C. Anderson, and Mark F. Odintz, vol. 2, 113. Austin: Texas State Historical Association, 1996.

Bailey, Richard. "The Starr County Strike." *Red River Valley Historical Review* 4 (Winter 1979): 42–61.

Baird, Frank L., ed. *Mexican Americans: Political Power, Influence, or Resource*. Lubbock: Texas Tech Press, 1977.

Behnken, Brian David. "On Parallel Tracks: A Comparison of the African-American and Latino Civil Rights Movements in Houston." Master's thesis, University of Houston, 2001.

Benavidez, Roy. *The Last Medal of Honor: A True Story of Unbelievable Valor*. Burnet, Tex.: Swan Publishing, 1991.

________. *Medal of Honor: A Vietnam Warrior Story*. Washington, D.C.: Brassey's, 1995.

Benavidez, Roy, and Oscar Griffin. *The Three Wars of Roy Benavidez*. San Antonio: Corona Publishing, 1985.

Branda, Eldon S. "Chicano." In *The Handbook of Texas: A Supplement*, edited by Eldon Stephen Branda, vol. 3, 166. Austin: Texas State Historical Association, 1976.

Bray, Nancy Gail. "South Texas La Raza, A Fulcrum for Revolt? The Political Socialization Experience in Two Texas Towns." Master's thesis, University of Texas at Austin, 1975.

Camejo, Antonio. "A Report from Aztlán: Texas Chicanos Forge Own Political Power." In *La Causa Politica: A Chicano Politics Reader*, edited by F. Chris García, 234–240. Notre Dame: University of Notre Dame Press, 1974.

Carranza, Vicente. "Chicanos and the Future with Raza Unida Party." *Caracol* 3 (November 1976): 18–21, 29.

Chabrán, Richard, and Rafael Chabrán, eds. "Crystal City, Texas." In *The Latino Encyclopedia*, edited by Richard Chabrán and Rafael Chabrán, vol. 2, 397. New York: Marshall Cavendish, 1996.

________. "José Angel Gutiérrez." In *The Latino Encyclopedia*, edited by Richard Chabrán and Rafael Chabrán, vol. 3, 722. New York: Marshall Cavendish, 1996.

________. "La Raza Unida Party." In *The Latino Encyclopedia*, edited by Richard Chabrán and Rafael Chabrán, vol. 5, 1354. New York: Marshall Cavendish, 1996.

________. "March to Austin." In *The Latino Encyclopedia*, edited by Richard Chabrán and Rafael Chabrán, vol. 4, 939. New York: Marshall Cavendish, 1996.

________. "Mexican American Youth Organization." In *The Latino Encyclopedia*, edited by Richard Chabrán and Rafael Chabrán, vol. 4, 988. New York: Marshall Cavendish, 1996.

Chandler, Charles R. "The Mexican-American Protest Movement in Texas." Ph.D. dissertation, Tulane University, 1968.

Clark, John E. "Reflections on the Duke of Duval: The Litigation Record." *South Texas Studies* 8 (1977): 31–48.

Clayson, William. "'The Barrios and the Ghettos Have Organized': Community Action, Political Acrimony, and the War on Poverty in San Antonio." *Journal of Urban History* 28 (January 2002): 158–183.

Clayton, Lawrence, and Susan C. Allen. "Looking Back at Crystal City." *Texas Journal of Ideas, History and Culture* 20 (Fall/Winter 1997): 38–43.

Coles, Robert, and Harry Huge. "Thorns on the Yellow Rose of Texas." In *America's Other Youth: Growing Up Poor*, edited by David Gottlieb, 73–80. Englewood Cliffs, N.J.: Prentice Hall, 1971.

________. "Thorns on the Yellow Rose of Texas." *New Republic* 160 (April 19, 1969): 13–17.

Compeán, Mario, and José Angel Gutiérrez. *La Raza Unida Party in Texas.* New York: Pathfinder Path, 1970.

"Crystal City." In *The Handbook of Texas: A Supplement*, edited by Eldon Stephen Branda, vol. 3, 212. Austin: Texas State Historical Association, 1976.

Curtis, Tom. "Politics: Raza Desunida." *Texas Monthly* 5 (February 1977): 102–107, 132, 160.

________. "Viva! La Raza!" *Texas Monthly* 14 (January 1986): 190.

de la Garza, Rudolph O. "Voting Patterns in 'Bi-cultural' El Paso: A Contextual Analysis of Chicano Voting Behavior." *Aztlán* 5 (Spring and Fall 1974): 235–260.

De León, Arnoldo. "The Sixties and El Movimiento, 1960–1976." In *Mexican Americans in Texas: A Brief History*, by Arnoldo De León, 122–135. Second Edition. Arlington Heights, Ill.: Harlan Davidson, 1999.

De León, Arnoldo, and Robert A. Calvert. "Civil Rights Movement." In *The New Handbook of Texas*, edited by Ron Tyler, Douglas E. Barnett, Roy R. Barkely, Penelope C. Anderson, and Mark F. Odintz, vol. 2, 118–121. Austin: Texas State Historical Association, 1996.

Dickens, Edwin Larry. "The Political Role of Mexican Americans in San Antonio, Texas." Master's thesis, Texas Tech University, 1969.

Erenberg, Mark. "A Story of the Political Relocation of the Texas-Mexican Migratory Farm Workers to Wisconsin." Ph.D. dissertation, University of Wisconsin, 1969.

Flores, María Eva. "Las Hermanas." In *The New Handbook of Texas*, edited by Ron Tyler, Douglas E. Barnett, Roy R. Barkely, Penelope C. Anderson, and Mark F. Odintz, vol. 4, 89–90. Austin: Texas State Historical Association, 1996.

Foley, Douglas E. "The Legacy of the *Partido Raza Unida* in South Texas: A Class Analysis." *Ethnic Affairs* 2 (Spring 1988): 47–73.

García, Dan David. "Chicano Declaration of Independence and Rebellion: Echoes of 1776." Master's thesis, University of Houston-Clear Lake, 2000.

García, Ignacio M. *Mexican American Youth Organization: Precursor of Change in Texas*. Tucson: Mexican American Studies and Research Center, University of Arizona, 1987.

________. *United We Win: The Rise and Fall of the Raza Unida Party*. Tucson: Mexican American Studies and Research Center, University of Arizona Press, 1989.

________. "Chicanismo: The Forging of a Militant Ethos Among Mexican Americans." Ph.D. dissertation, University of Arizona, 1995.

________. "Armed with a Ballot: The Rise of the La Raza Unida Party in Texas." Master's thesis, University of Arizona, 1990.

________. "How Chicanos Took Over Crystal City." *Nuestro* 3 (December 1979): 63–64.

________. "Is the Party Over for La Raza Unida?" *Nuestro* 4 (March 1980): 33–34.

________. "The Movement in Robstown." In *Chicanismo: The Forging of a Militant Ethos Among Mexican Americans*, by Ignacio M. García, 117–132. Tucson: University of Arizona Press, 1997.

________. "El Rechazo de Aztlán: la contrapolitica de los hispanícos en Robstown, Texas." *NACSS Journal* (Summer 1998).

Garza, José. "La Raza Unida in Crystal City: A Study of a Chicano Third Party Movement." Master's thesis, Trinity University, 1972.

Gelber, David. "Crystal City's Cracked Promise." *Working Papers for a New Society* 4 (1976): 30–35.

Goodman, Mary Ellen. *The Mexican American Population of Houston: A Survey in the Field, 1965–1970*. Houston: Rice University Studies, 1971.

Goodman, Mary Ellen, and Alma Beman. "Child's Eye View of Life in a Urban Barrio." In *Spanish-speaking People in the United States*. Proceedings of the 1968 Annual Spring Meeting of the American Ethnological Society, edited by June Helm, 84–103. Seattle: University of Washington Press, 1968.

Gutiérrez, Armando. "The Politics of the Texas Border: An Historical Overview and Some Contemporary Directions." In *Views Across the Border*, edited by Stanley R. Ross, 117–140. Albuquerque: University of New Mexico Press, 1978.

Gutiérrez, Armando George. "The Subjugation of Militancy: Chicanos in a South Texas Town." Ph.D. dissertation, University of Texas at Austin, 1974.

Gutiérrez, Armando G., and Herbert Hirsch. "The Militant Challenge to the Dominant Ethos: 'Chicanos' and 'Mexican Americans.'" *Social Science Quarterly* 53 (March 1973): 830–845.

________. "Political Maturation and Political Awareness: The Case of the Crystal City Chicano." *Aztlán* 5 (Spring and Fall 1974): 295–312.

Gutiérrez, José Angel. *A Chicano Manual on How to Handle Gringos*. Houston: Arte Público Press, 2003.

________. *The Making of a Chicano Militant. Lessons from Cristal.* Madison: University of Wisconsin Press, 1998.

________. "Toward a Theory of Community Organization in a Mexican American Community in South Texas." Ph.D. dissertation, University of Texas at Austin, 1977.

________. "La Raza and Revolution: The Empirical Conditions of Revolution in Four South Texas Counties." Master's thesis, St. Mary's University of San Antonio, 1968.

________. "Mexicans Need to Control Their Own Destiny." In *La Causa Politica: A Chicano Politics Reader*, edited by F. Chris García, 226–233. Notre Dame: University of Notre Dame Press, 1974.

________. "El Politico: The Mexican American Elected Official." *Prospectiva*, numero 2. El Paso: Mictla Publications, 1972.

________. "We Who Built La Raza Unida in Crystal City." *International Socialist Review* 32 (1971): 17–19, 36–37.

Hirsch, Herbert, and Armando Gutiérrez. *Learning to be Militant: Ethnic Identity and the Development of the Political Militance in a Chicano Community*. San Francisco: R&E Research Associates, 1977.

Jensen, Richard J., and John C. Hammerback. "An Interview with José Angel Gutiérrez." *Western Journal of Speech Communication* 44 (Summer 1980): 203–213.

________. "Radical Nationalism among Chicanos: The Rhetoric of José Angel Gutiérrez." *Western Journal of Speech Communication* 44 (Summer 1980): 35–41.

Kaplowitz, Craig Allan. "Mexican Americans, Ethnicity, and Federal Policy: The League of United Latin American Citizens and the Politics of Cultural Disadvantage, 1942–1975." Ph.D. dissertation, Vanderbilt University, 1999.

Leal, Ray Robert. "The 1966–1967 South Texas Farm Workers Strike." Ph.D. dissertation, Indiana University, 1983.

Leatherwood, Art, and Alicia A. Garza. "Alfredo Cantú González." In *The New Handbook of Texas*, edited by Ron Tyler, Douglas E. Barnett, Roy R. Barkely, Penelope C. Anderson, and Mark F. Odintz, vol. 3, 233. Austin: Texas State Historical Association, 1996.

Limón, José E. "The Expressive Culture of a Chicano Student Group at Austin, 1967–1975." Ph.D. dissertation, University of Texas at Austin, 1978.

Márquez, Benjamín. "Power and Politics in a Chicano Barrio." Ph.D. dissertation, University of Wisconsin, 1983.

Martínez, José Villarreal Jr. "Internal Colonialism and Decolonization in El Centro: A Sociohistorical Analysis of Chicanos in a Texas City." Ph.D. dissertation, University of Texas at Austin, 1981.

Matovina, Timothy M. "Representation and the Reconstruction of Power: The Rise of PADRES and Las Hermanas." In *What's Left? Liberal American Catholics*, edited by Mary Jo Weaver. Bloomington: Indiana University Press, 1999.

McCleskey, Clifton, and Bruce Merrill. "Mexican American Political Behavior in Texas." *Social Science Quarterly* 53 (March 1973): 783–798.

Méndez, Beatrice. "Crystal City." *Caracol* 2 (April 1976): 29.

Meyer, Nicholas E. "José Angel Gutiérrez." In *The Biographical Dictionary of Hispanic Americans*, by Nicholas E. Meyer, 102–104. New York: Facts on File, 1997.

________. "Roy Pérez Benavidez." In *The Biographical Dictionary of Hispanic Americans*, by Nicholas E. Meyer, 25–27. New York: Facts on File, 1997.

Miller, Michael V. "Chicano Community Control in South Texas: Problems and Prospects." *Journal of Ethnic Studies* 3 (Fall 1975): 70–89.

Miller, Michael V., and James D. Preston. "Vertical Ties and the Redistribution of Power in Crystal City." *Social Science Quarterly* 53 (March 1973): 772–784.

Montejano, David. "The Demise of Jim Crow for Texas Mexicans, 1940–1970." *Aztlán* 16 (1985): 27–69.

Navarro, Armando. *The Cristal Experiment: A Chicano Struggle for Community Control*. Madison: University of Wisconsin Press, 1999.

________. *Mexican American Youth Organization: Avant-Garde of the Chicano Movement in Texas*. Austin: University of Texas Press, 1995.

________. *La Raza Unida: A Chicano Challenge to the U.S. Two-Party Dictatorship*. Philadelphia: Temple University Press, 2000.

________. "El Partido de la Raza Unida in Crystal City: A Peaceful Revolution." Ph.D. dissertation, University of California, Riverside, 1974.

Nieto, Leo D. "The Chicano Movement and the Churches in the United States." *Perkins Journal* 29.1 (Fall 1975): 32–41.

O'Connor, Karen, and Lee Epstein. "A Legal Voice for the Chicano Community: The Activities of the Mexican American Legal Defense and Educational Fund, 1968–1982." *Social Science Quarterly* 65 (June 1984): 245–256.

Orozco, Cynthia E. "Intercultural Development Research Association." In *The New Handbook of Texas*, edited by Ron Tyler, Douglas E. Barnett, Roy R. Barkely, Penelope C. Anderson, and Mark F. Odintz, vol. 3, 858–859. Austin: Texas State Historical Association, 1996.

________. "Matías William García." In *The New Handbook of Texas*, edited by Ron Tyler, Douglas E. Barnett, Roy R. Barkely, Penelope C. Anderson, and Mark F. Odintz, vol. 3, 86–87. Austin: Texas State Historical Association, 1996.

________. "Mexican American Democrats." In *The New Handbook of Texas*, edited by Ron Tyler, Douglas E. Barnett, Roy R. Barkley, Penelope C. Anderson, and Mark F. Odintz, vol. 4, 654–655. Austin: Texas State Historical Association, 1996.

________. "William C. Velásquez." In *The New Handbook of Texas*, edited by Ron Tyler, Douglas E. Barnett, Roy R. Barkley, Penelope C. Anderson, and Mark F. Odintz, vol. 6, 720. Austin: Texas State Historical Association, 1996.

Parker, Benny. "Power in Conflict: A Chicano Political Party of Social Disequilibrium and Anglo Chicano Power Relationships as Expressed Through a Situational Analysis of Public Address in Crystal City, Texas, in 1972." Ph.D. dissertation, Southern Illinois University, 1974.

Peña, Albert. "La Raza." In *Practicing Texas Politics*: A Brief Survey, edited by Eugene W. Jones, Joe E. Ericson, Lyle C. Brown, Robert S. Trotter Jr., and Eileen M. Lynch, 31–32. Boston: Houghton Mifflin, 1971.

Pérez, José G. "A Big Step Forward for the Raza Unida Parties." *International Socialist Review* 34 (1973): 14–17, 39.

Procter, Ben H. "The Modern Texas Rangers: A Law Enforcement Dilemma in the Rio Grande Valley." In *The Mexican Americans: An Awakening Minority*, edited by Manuel Servín, 212–227. Beverly Hills: Glencoe Press, 1970.

Pycior, Julie Leininger. "From Hope to Frustration: Mexican Americans and Lyndon Johnson in 1967." *Western Historical Quarterly* 24 (November 1993): 469–494.

________. "Lyndon, La Raza, and the Paradox of Texas History." In *Lyndon Baines Johnson and the Exercise of Power*, edited by Bernard J. Firestone and Robert C. Vogt, 129–147. Westport, Conn.: Greenwood Press, 1988.

Quiros, Angie. *Coverage of the Raza Unida Movement as Reported by Four Texas Newspapers*. Austin: University of Texas Press, 1973.

Rada, Stephen E. "Manipulating the Media: A Case Study of a Chicano Strike in Texas." *Journalism Quarterly* 54 (Spring 1977): 109–113.

Ramos, Henry A. J. *The American G.I. Forum: In Pursuit of the Dream, 1948–1983*. Houston: Arte Público Press, 1998.

________. *A People Forgotten, A Dream Pursued: The History of the American G.I. Forum, 1948–1972*. Corpus Christi, Tex.: American G.I. Forum of the United States, 1982.

"Raza Unida Party." In *The Handbook of Texas: A Supplement*, edited by Eldon Stephen Branda, vol. 3, 782–783. Austin: Texas State Historical Association, 1976.

Rhinehart, Marilyn, and Thomas H. Kreneck. "The Minimum Wage March of 1966: A Case Study in Mexican American Politics, Labor, and Identity." *The Houston Review* 11 (1989): 27–44.

Richardson, Chad, María Olivia Villarreal-Solano, and Cruz C. Torres. "Anglo-Hispanic Relations in South Texas from 1945 to 1993: A Triangulated Profile." *Río Bravo* 3 (1994): 114–134.

Rivera, George J. "Social Change in the Barrio: The Chicano Movement in South Texas." *Aztlán* 3 (1972): 205–214.

Rodríguez, Marc Simon. "Obreros Unidos: Migration, Migrant Farm Workers Activism, and the Chicano Movement in Wisconsin and Texas, 1950–1980." Ph.D. dissertation, Northwestern University, 2000.

Romero, Juan. "Charisma and Power: An Essay on the History of PADRES." *U.S. Catholic Historian* 9.1–2 (Winter/Spring 1990): 147–163.

________. "Mexican American Priests: History of PADRES 1969–1989." In *Hispanics in the Church: Up from the Cellar*, edited by Philip E. Lampe, 71–94. San Francisco/London: Catholic Scholars Press, 1994.

Romero, Yolanda G. "Trini Gámez, The Texas Farm Workers, and Mexican American Community Empowerment: Toil and Trouble on the Texas South Plains." In *Mexican Americans in Texas History*, edited by Emilio Zamora, Cynthia Orozco, and Rodolfo Rocha, 143–155. Austin: Texas State Historical Association, 2000.

Rosales, Rodolfo. *The Illusion of Inclusion: The Untold Political Story of San Antonio*. Austin: University of Texas Press, 2000.

________. "The Rise of Chicano Middle Class Politics in San Antonio, 1951–1985." Ph.D. dissertation, University of Michigan, 1991.

Sánchez, George I. "Mexican American Joint Council." In *The Handbook of Texas: A Supplement*, edited by Eldon Stephen Branda, vol. 3, 595–596. Austin: Texas State Historical Association, 1976.

Sánchez, Juan O. "Encina: The Uvalde School Walkout." Master's thesis, Sul Ross State University, 1992.

________. "Walkout *Cabrones*: The Uvalde School Walkout of 1970." *West Texas Historical Association Yearbook* 68 (1992): 122–133.

Sandoval, Moisés. "The Church and El Movimiento." In *Fronteras: A History of the Latin American Church in the USA since 1513*, edited by Moises Sandoval, 377–412. San Antonio: Mexican American Cultural Center, 1983.

________. "Church Structures for the Hispanics." In *Fronteras: A History of the Latin American Church in the USA since 1513*, edited by Moisés Sandoval, 413–438. San Antonio: Mexican American Cultural Center, 1983.

San Miguel, Guadalupe Jr. *Brown Not White: School Integration and the Chicano Movement in Houston*. College Station: Texas A&M University Press, 2001.

Santillán, Richard. *Chicano Politics: La Raza Unida*. Los Angeles: Tlaquilo Publications, 1973.

Shockley, John S. *Chicano Revolt in a Texas Town*. Notre Dame: University of Notre Dame Press, 1974.

________. "Crystal City, Texas: Mexican Americans and Political Change." Ph.D. dissertation, University of Wisconsin, Madison, 1972.

________. "Crystal City: La Raza Unida and the Second Revolt." In *Chicano: The Beginning of Bronze Power*, edited by Renato Rosaldo, Robert A. Calvert, and Gustav L. Seligmann, 74–86. New York: Morrow, 1974.

________. "Landless Laborers and the Chicano Movement in South Texas." In *Forging Nations: A Comparative View of Rural Ferment and Revolt*, edited by Joseph Spielberg and Scott Whiteford, 128–149. Lansing: Michigan State University Press, 1976.

Smallwood, James M. "Viva Johnson: LBJ and the Transformation of the Hispanic Community in Texas." *Journal of South Texas* 15 (Fall 2002): 32–85.

Teske, Raymond H. C. Jr., and Bardin H. Nelson. "Middle Class Mexican Americans and Political Power Potential: A Dilemma." *Journal of Political and Military Sociology* 4 (1976): 107–119.

Tirado, Miguel. "Mexican American Community Political Organization." *Aztlán* 1 (Spring 1970): 53–78.

Trujillo, Armando L.*Chicano Empowerment and Bilingual Education: Movimiento Politics in Crystal City, Texas*. New York: Garland Publishing, 1998.

________. "Community Empowerment and Bilingual/Bicultural Education: A Study of the *Movimiento* in a South Texas Community." Ph.D. dissertation, University of Texas at Austin, 1993.

________."Bilingual/Bicultural Education and Politics in Crystal City, Texas: 1969–1989." In *Chicanas and Chicanos in Contemporary Society*, edited by Roberto M. De Anda, 157–178. Boston: Allyn and Bacon, 1996.

Vega, Arturo. "Mexican Americans and Internal Colonialism in Texas." Master's thesis, St. Mary's University, 1968.

Vigil, Evangelina. "El Partido Hipócrita." *Caracol* 3 (February 1977): 22–23.

Villarreal, Roberto E. "Mexican Americans in South Texas: An Inquiry into Social and Political Change." Ph.D. dissertation, University of Oklahoma, 1975.

Villarreal, Roberto E., and Olga Mapula. "Latino Participation and Municipal Politics in a Border City." In *Latinos and Political Coalitions: Political Empowerment for the 1990s*, edited by Roberto E. Villarreal and Norma G. Hernández, 14–152. New York: Praeger Publishers, 1991.

Watt, Alan J. "The Religious Dimensions in the Farm Worker Movement." Ph.D. dissertation, Vanderbilt University, 1999.

Winn, Charles Carr. "The Valley Farm Workers Movement, 1966–1967." Master's thesis, University of Texas at Arlington, 1970.

Zamora, Emilio, Jr. "Fighting on Two Fronts: José de la Luz Saenz and the Language of the Mexican American Civil Rights Movement." In *Recovering the U.S. Hispanic Literary Heritage*, edited by José F. Aranda Jr. and Silvio Torres-Saillant, vol. 4, 172–183. Houston: Arte Público Press, 2002.

10. ONCE FORGOTTEN, 1976 TO THE PRESENT

Once overlooked, viewed with contempt and disgust, or treated as second-class citizens, Tejanos since the Chicano Movement have become increasingly visible in Texas as consumers, office holders, and productive members of society. This trend toward higher visibility owes to numerous reasons including the decline of old barriers to social and economic gains, the attention brought to the Mexican-American presence by the Chicano Movement, opportunities more readily available for acquiring a higher education, appeals by political parties, increased assimilation rates, demographic trends created by higher birth rates and increased immigration from Mexico, and a number of other factors. Despite material improvement over past ages, not everyone has shared in American beneficence. There still exists a neglected "underclass" of Tejanos made up of first-generation farm workers and residents of *colonias* (generally, unincorporated areas of Texas border towns), of school dropouts, or of children of broken families.

Bust portrait of Gen. Richard E. Cavazos, the first Texas-born Mexican-American four star general in the United States Army, ca. 1982.
The Institute of Texan Cultures at UTSA, No. 85-858
Courtesy of Randolph Air Force Base

Acosta, Teresa Palomo. "Mexican American Joint Council." In *The New Handbook of Texas*, edited by Ron Tyler, Douglas E. Barnett, Roy R. Barkley, Penelope C. Anderson, and Mark F. Odintz, vol. 4, 655–656. Austin: Texas State Historical Association, 1996.

Alexander, Bobby C. "A Pentecostal-Styled Mexican Mission in Dallas: An Illustration of Religious Diversity among New Latino Immigrants." *Listening* 33.3 (Fall 1998): 175–187.

Bain, Kenneth, and Paul Travis. "South Texas Politics." *Southern Exposure* 12 (1984): 49–52.

Barahona Israel, María de los Angeles. "The Lifeworld of Dwelling Experiences of Hispanic Migrant Workers: From Southern Michigan to Southern Texas." Arch.D. dissertation, University of Michigan, 1990.

Bezdek, Robert R., David M. Billeaux, and Juan Carlos Huerta. "Latinos, At-Large Elections, and Political Change: Evidence from the 'Transition Zone.'" *Social Science Quarterly* 81 (March 2000): 207–225.

Brischetto, Robert R. *The Political Empowerment of Texas Mexicans, 1974–1988.* San Antonio: Southwest Voter Research Institute, 1988.

________. "Electoral Empowerment: The Case for Tejanos." In *Latino Empowerment: Progress, Problems, and Prospects*, edited by Roberto E. Villareal, Norma G. Hernández, and Howard D. Neighbor, 71–90. New York: Greenwood Press, 1988.

Brischetto, Robert R., Charles L. Cottrell, and R. Michael Stevens. "Conflict and Change in the Political Culture of San Antonio in the 1970s." In *The Politics of San Antonio: Community, Progress, and Power*, edited by David R. Johnson, John A. Booth, and Richard J. Harris, 75–94. Lincoln: University of Nebraska, 1983.

Brischetto, Robert R., and Richard L. Engstrom. "Cumulative Voting and Latino Representation: Exit Surveys in Fifteen Texas Communities." *Social Science Quarterly* 78 (December 1977): 973–991.

Bryson, Conrey. "Contemporary Civil Rights Issue as Affected by Events in El Paso." *Password* 27 (Spring 1982): 26–31.

Burka, Paul. "Henry B. and Henry C." *Texas Monthly* 14 (January 1986): 182–183, 218, 220, 222, 224, 226, 228, 230.

Cárdenas, Gilberto, Rodolfo O. de la Garza, and Niles Hansen. "Mexican Immigrants and the Chicano Ethnic Enterprise: Re-conceptualizing an Old Problem." In *Mexican Immigrants and Mexican Americans: An Evolving Relation*, edited by Harley L. Browning and Rodolfo O. de la Garza, 120–137. Austin: Center for Mexican American Studies and University of Texas Press, 1986.

Chabrán, Richard, and Rafael Chabrán, eds. "Henry Cisneros." In *The Latino Encyclopedia*, edited by Richard Chabrán and Rafael Chabrán, vol. 2, 321. New York: Marshall Cavendish, 1996.

________. "Humberto 'Tati' Santiesteban." In *The Latino Encyclopedia*, edited by Richard Chabrán and Rafael Chabrán, vol. 5, 1447. New York: Marshall Cavendish, 1996.

________. "Lauro E. Cavazos." In *The Latino Encyclopedia*, edited by Richard Chabrán and Rafael Chabrán, vol. 1, 270. New York: Marshall Cavendish, 1996.

________. "Mario Barrera." In *The Latino Encyclopedia*, edited by Richard Chabrán and Rafael Chabrán, vol. 1, 137. New York: Marshall Cavendish, 1996.

________. "Reynaldo Garza." In *The Latino Encyclopedia*, edited by Richard Chabrán and Rafael Chabrán, vol. 3, 685. New York: Marshall Cavendish, 1996.

________. "Ricardo Romo." In *The Latino Encyclopedia*, edited by Richard Chabrán and Rafael Chabrán, vol. 5, 1408. New York: Marshall Cavendish, 1996.

________. "Tony Bonilla." In *The Latino Encyclopedia*, edited by Richard Chabrán and Rafael Chabrán, vol. 1, 175. New York: Marshall Cavendish, 1996.

Chapa, Jorge, and Vicente A. Lazaro. "Hopwood in Texas: The Untimely Death of Affirmative Action." In *Chilling Admissions: The Affirmative Action Crisis and the Search for Alternatives*, edited by Gary Orfield and Edward Miller, 51–70. Cambridge, Mass.: Harvard University Press, 1997.

Cottrell, Charles L. *A Report on the Participation of Mexican Americans, Blacks, and Females in the Political Institutions and Process in Texas, 1968–1978.* San Antonio: Texas Advisory Committee to the United States Commission on Civil Rights, 1980.

Cruz, Adrián. "The Battle to be Mayor: A Case Study of Interethnic Conflict in the Lower Rio Grande Valley." Master's thesis, University of Texas–Pan American, 2001.

de la Garza, Rodolfo O., and Karl Schmitt. "Texas Land Grants and Chicano-Mexican Relations: A Case Study." *Latin American Research Review* 21 (March 1986): 123–138.

DeSipio, Louis. "The Dynamics of Electoral Participation in South Texas." *South Texas Studies* 4 (1993): 89–121.

Diehl, Kemper, and Jan Jarbee. *Cisneros: A Portrait of a New American.* San Antonio: Corona Publishing, 1985.

Elías De Mounce, María Elena. "Mexican Elites in the United States: An Introductory Investigation of Privileged Mexicans in South Texas." Master's thesis, University of Texas–Pan American, 1996.

Elizondo, Virgilio. "The Mexican American Cultural Center Story." *Listening* 32.3 (Fall 1997): 152–160.

Eschbach, Karl, Jacqueline Hagan, Nestor Rodríguez, and Anna Zakos. "The Houston Heights: Co-existing Communities?" *Cityscapes: A Journal of Policy Development and Research* 4 (1998): 245–259.

Finke, Eugene I. "Aldermanic Redistricting in El Paso, Texas." Ph.D. dissertation, New Mexico State University, 1984.

Finnel, Susanna. "The Hopwood Chill: How the Court Derailed Diversity Efforts at Texas A&M." In *Chilling Admissions: The Affirmative Action Crisis and the Search for Alternatives*, edited by Gary Orfield and Edward Miller, 71–82. Cambridge, Mass.: Harvard University Press, 1997.

Flores, Henry. "Deconstruction and Chicano Politics: Coalition Building During the Cisneros Era." In *Latinos and Political Coalitions: Political Empowerment for the 1990s*, edited by Roberto E. Villarreal and Norma G. Hernández, 144–152. New York: Praeger, 1991.

García, Ignacio. "COPS: Policing the System." *Nuestro* 4 (August 1980): 22, 24.

Gilles, John. *Señor Alcalde: A Biography of Henry Cisneros.* Minneapolis: Dillon Press, 1988.

Godoy, Raquel María López. "Image Versus Issues: The Appeals used to Reach Hispanic Voters in Texas—A Content Analysis of the 1982 and 1986 Gubernatorial Campaigns." Ph.D. dissertation, University of Texas at Austin, 1991.

González, Larry Justin. "Hispanic/Latino Empowerment in Houston." Ph.D. dissertation, University of Houston, 1994.

Graves, Scott, and Jongho Lee. "Ethnic Underpinnings of Voting Preferences: Latinos and the 1996 U.S. Senate Election in Texas." *Social Science Quarterly* 81 (March 2000): 226–236.

Gwynne, S. C. "Is 'Al Gonzales' Spanish for 'Stealth Liberal'?" *Texas Monthly* 31 (June 2003): 104–107, 123–124, 165–167.

Hall, Grace, and Alan Saltztein. "Equal Employment Opportunity for Minorities in Municipal Government." *Social Science Quarterly* 57 (March 1977): 864–872.

Hernández, Al Carlos. "Vilma Martínez: Una Chicana Ejemplar." *Nuestro* 5 (August-September 1981): 13–14.

Hollas, James, and Robert R. Bezdek. *Nueces County Elections: 1972–1980.* Corpus Christi, Tex.: Corpus Christi State University, 1980.

Holley, Joe. "Viva la Raza! in Crystal City." *The Texas Humanist* 2 (February 1980): 2–3.

Iber, Jorge. "Becoming Raiders Rojos: Using Sport to Claim Hispanic 'Space' at Texas Tech University." *West Texas Historical Association Yearbook* 77 (2001): 139–151.

LeFevre, Karen E. "The Family History of Senator Hector Uribe: A Study in Mexican American Heritage." In *Studies in Brownsville History*, edited by Milo Kearney, 248–274. Brownsville, Tex.: Pan American University at Brownsville, 1986.

Márquez, Benjamín. "The Industrial Area Foundation and the Mexican American Community in Texas: The Politics of Issue Mobilization." In *Minority Group Influence: Agenda Setting, Formulation, and Public Policy*, edited by Paula D. McClain, 127–146. Westport, Conn.: Greenwood Publishing, 1993.

________. "Organizing the Mexican American Community in Texas: The Legacy of Saul Alinsky." *Policy Studies Review* 9 (Winter 1990): 353–373.

Martínez, Douglas. "Hispanic Organizations: Meeting the Challenge of the 1980s." *La Luz* 8 (February-March, 1980): 8–11, 16–17, 18, 43.

Meier, Matt S. with Conchita Franco Serri and Richard A. García. "Henry Barbosa González." In *Notable Latino Americans: A Biographical Dictionary*, by Matt S. Meier, 183–186. Westport, Conn.: Greenwood Press, 1997.

________. "Henry Cisneros." In *Notable Latino Americans: A Biographical Dictionary*, by Matt S. Meier, 84–86. Westport, Conn.: Greenwood Press, 1997.

________. "Lauro Cavazos." In *Notable Latino Americans: A Biographical Dictionary*, by Matt S. Meier, 70–73. Westport, Conn.: Greenwood Press, 1997.

________. "Lee Treviño." In *Notable Latino Americans: A Biographical Dictionary*, by Matt S. Meier, 385–389. Westport, Conn.: Greenwood Press, 1997.

Melville, Margarita B. "Chicano!" *The Texas Humanist* 2 (February 1980): 1.

Meyer, Nicholas E. "Eligio 'Kika' de la Garza." In *The Biographical Dictionary of Hispanic Americans*, by Nicholas E. Meyer, 67–68. New York: Facts on File, 1997.

________. "Henry Cisneros." In *The Biographical Dictionary of Hispanic Americans*, by Nicholas E. Meyer, 53–55. New York: Facts on File, 1997.

________. "Lauro F. Cavazos." In *The Biographical Dictionary of Hispanic Americans*, by Nicholas E. Meyer, 44. New York: Facts on File, 1997.

________. "Vilma S. Martínez." In *The Biographical Dictionary of Hispanic Americans*, by Nicholas E. Meyer, 141–142. New York: Facts on File, 1997.

________. "William C. 'Willie' Velásquez." In *The Biographical Dictionary of Hispanic Americans*, by Nicholas E. Meyer, 226–228. New York: Facts on File, 1997.

Murata, Katsuyuki. "The (Re)shaping of Latino/Chicano Ethnicity Through the Inclusion/Exclusion of Undocumented Immigrants: The Case of LULAC's Ethno-Politics." *American Studies International* 39 (June 2001): 4–33.

Nathan, Debbie. "The Trials of Ray Caballero." *The Texas Observer* 95 (April 11, 2003): 4–5, 17–19, 26–28.

Navarro, Ana Cecilia. "Understanding the Mexican American Voter: Legacy and Potential of the Mexican American Community of El Paso." Master's thesis, University of Texas at El Paso, 1986.

Nixon-Méndez, Nina. "The Development of a City Preservation Plan Based on the Historical Analysis of Urban Settlement Patterns in Laredo, Texas." *Journal of Big Bend Studies* 9 (1997): 77–88.

Orozco, Cynthia E. "Mexican American Legislative Caucus." In *The New Handbook of Texas*, edited by Ron Tyler, Douglas E. Barnett, Roy R. Barkley, Penelope C. Anderson, and Mark F. Odintz, vol. 4, 659–660. Austin: Texas State Historical Association, 1996.

________. "Mexican American Republicans of Texas." In *The New Handbook of Texas*, edited by Ron Tyler, Douglas E. Barnett, Roy R. Barkley, Penelope C. Anderson, and Mark F. Odintz, vol. 4, 663–664. Austin: Texas State Historical Association, 1996.

Perigrino, Santiago. "The Political Ideology of the Mexican American in a Southwestern City." Master's thesis, University of Texas at El Paso, 1970.

Polinard, Jerry L., Robert D. Winkler, and Norman E. Binder. "Ethnicity and Political Participation in Cameron and Hidalgo Counties: Mexican American Voters and Nonvoters." In *Studies in Matamoros and Cameron County History*, edited by Milo Kearney, Anthony Knopp, and Antonio Zavaleta, 89–106. Brownsville, Tex.: The University of Texas at Brownsville and Texas Southmost College, 1997.

Polinard, Jerry L., Robert D. Winkler, and Tomás Longoria Jr. "The Impact of District Elections on the Mexican American Community: The Electoral Perspective." *Social Science Quarterly* 72 (September 1991): 608–614.

Rips, Geoffrey. "Mexican Americans *Jalaron la Palanca*, Democrats Say *Ole*." In *Practicing Texas Politics: A Brief Survey*, edited by Eugene W. Jones, Joe E. Ericson, Lyle C. Brown, Robert S. Trotter Jr., and Eileen M. Lynch, 86–88. Boston: Houghton Mifflin, 1984.

Rodríguez, Nestor P., Noelia Elizondo, David Mena, Ricardo Rojas, Adolfo Vásquez, and Frank Yeverino. "Political Mobilization in Houston's Magnolia." In *Barrio Ballots: Latino Politics in the 1990 Elections*, edited by Rodolfo O. de la Garza, Martha Menchaca, and Louis DeSipio, 83–114. Boulder, Colo.: Westview Press, 1994.

Rosales, Rodolfo. "Personality and Style in San Antonio Politics: Henry Cisneros and Bernardo Eureste, 1975–1985." In *Chicano Politics and Society in the Late Twentieth Century*, edited by David Montejano, 3–30. Austin: University of Texas Press, 1999.

Sandoval, Moisés. "The Struggle with LULAC." *Nuestro* 3 (September 1979): 30–33.

San Miguel, Guadalupe Jr. "Bitter Struggles: Mexican Americans and the Revision of the Texas Bilingual Education Bill in 1981." In *The Chicano Struggle: Analyses of Past and Present Efforts*, edited by John A. Garcia, Teresa Córdova, and Juan R. García, 111–130. Binghamton, N.Y.: Bilingual Press/Editorial Bilingüe, 1984.

Skerry, Peter N. *Mexican Americans: The Ambivalent Minority.* New York: The Free Press, 1993.

________. "The Ambivalent Minority: Emergent Styles of Mexican American Politics." Ph.D. dissertation, Harvard University, 1991.

Smith, Ann Crowley. "Whites, Blacks, and Hispanics as Candidates in Local Elections." Ph.D. dissertation, University of Texas at Arlington, 1988.

Treviño, Lee. *They Call Me Super Mex.* New York: Random House, 1982.

Vásquez, Juan. "Watch Out for Willie Velásquez." *Nuestro* 3 (March 1979): 2–24.

Villarreal, Roberto E., Norma G. Hernández, and Howard D. Neighbor. "EPISO and Political Empowerment." *Journal of Borderlands Studies* 3 (1988): 81–96.

Wrinkle, Robert D., and Lawrence W. Miller. "A Note on Mexican Voter Registration and Turnout." *Social Science Quarterly* 65 (June 1984): 308–314.

Part III: Topics

11. ECONOMICS/LABOR

The bibliographic citations in this section cover a wide range and include works that consider occupations, employment levels, livelihood, labor, and skills among Mexican Texans. Some studies focus on economic theory, others on factual data and interpretation. Noticeable is that early stereotypes of Tejanos as unskilled field workers and household servants are out of step with the research. Tejanos were found in every type of occupation, protested their lot via strikes and labor unions, and earned a living through varied jobs and opportunities.

Arthur Pérez, city policeman arresting man holding C.I.O. picket during pecan sheller strike, San Antonio, Texas, February 11, 1938. The Institute of Texan Cultures at UTSA, No. L-1759-F The San Antonio Light *Collection*

Abrams, Herbert K. "Occupational and Environmental Problems Along the U.S.-Mexico Border." *Southwest Economy and Review* 4.3 (1979): 3–17.

Acosta, Teresa Palomo. "Miguel Martínez." In *The New Handbook of Texas*, edited by Ron Tyler, Douglas K. Barnett, Roy R. Barkley, Penelope C. Anderson, and Mark F. Odintz, vol. 4, 536–537. Austin: Texas State Historical Association, 1996.

________. "Nicosia Idar." In *The New Handbook of Texas,* edited by Ron Tyler, Douglas E. Barnett, Roy R. Barkley, Penelope C. Anderson, and Mark F. Odintz, vol. 3, 815–816. Austin: Texas State Historical Association, 1996.

Allen, Carl. "Notes on Mexican Mine Labor." *Mining and Scientific Press* 94 (March 16, 1907): 345–346.

Allen, Ruth. "The Mexican Woman." In *The Labor of Women in the Production of Cotton*, by Ruth Allen, 209–240. Austin: University of Texas, Austin, 1931.

Alonzo, Armando C. *Tejano Legacy: Rancheros and Settlers in South Texas, 1734–1900*. Albuquerque: University of New Mexico Press, 1982.

________. "Tejano Rancheros and Changes in Land Tenure, Hidalgo County, Texas, 1848–1900." Ph.D. dissertation, Indiana University, 1994.

________. "A History of the Mexicans in the Lower Rio Grande Valley of Texas: Their Role in Land Development and Commercial Agriculture, 1900–1930." Master's thesis, University of Texas–Pan American, 1982.

________. "Change and Continuity in Tejano Ranches in the Trans-Nueces, 1848–1900." In *Ranching in South Texas: A Symposium*, edited by Joe S. Graham, 53–68. Kingsville, Tex.: Texas A&M University-Kingsville, 1994.

________. "Mexican-American Land Grant Adjudication." In *En Aquel Entonces: Readings in Mexican-American History*, edited by Manuel G. Gonzales and Cynthia M. Gonzales, 64–71. Bloomington: Indiana University Press, 2000.

Anders, Evan M. "Manuel Guerra." In *The New Handbook of Texas,* edited by Ron Tyler, Douglas E. Barnett, Roy R. Barkley, Penelope C. Anderson, and Mark F. Odintz, vol. 3, 369. Austin: Texas State Historical Association, 1996.

Anderson, H. Allen. "Ciboleros." In *The New Handbook of Texas,* edited by Ron Tyler, Douglas E. Barnett, Roy R. Barkley, Penelope C. Anderson, and Mark F. Odintz, vol. 2, 108. Austin: Texas State Historical Association, 1996.

Arroyo, Laura E. "Industrial and Occupational Distribution of Chicano Workers." *Aztlán* 4.2 (1973): 343–382.

August, Ray. "Cowboys v. Rancheros: The Origins of Western American Livestock Law." *Southwestern Historical Quarterly* 96.4 (1993): 457–488.

Austerman, Wayne R. "José Policarpo Rodríguez: Chicano Plainsman." *West Texas Historical Association Yearbook* 59 (1983): 52–74.

Babington, Lamar J. "Mexican-American Labor Problems in Texas." Ph.D. dissertation, University of Texas, Austin, 1965.

Bailey, Richard R. "Farm Labor in Texas and the Starr County Strike." Master's thesis, Texas Christian University, 1973.

________. "The Starr County Strike." *Red River Valley Historical Review* 4 (Winter 1976): 42–61.

Baker, Susan González. "Many Rivers to Cross: Mexican Immigrants, Women Workers, and the Structure of Labor Markets in the Urban Southwest." Ph.D. dissertation, University of Texas at Austin, 1989.

Barahona Israel, María de los Angeles. "The Lifeworld and Dwelling Experiences of Hispanic Migrant Workers: From Southern Michigan to Southern Texas." Arch.D. dissertation, University of Michigan, 1990.

Barnes, Roger C., and James W. Donovan. "The Southern Pecan Shelling Company: A Window to Depression-Era San Antonio." *South Texas Studies* 11 (2000): 49–64.

Barr, Alwyn. "Occupation and Geographic Mobility in San Antonio, 1870–1900." *Social Science Quarterly* 51 (September 1970): 396–403.

Barrera, Elena Farías. "Eva Dolores Carrizales, M.D." In *One Hundred Women of the Rio Grande Valley of Texas*, edited by the Rio Writers, 22–25. Austin: Eakin Press, 1983.

Barry, Tom. "Whatever Became of the Farah Strikers?" *Nuestro* 2 (October 1978): 36–37.

Barton, Joséf J. "Land, Labor, and Community in Nueces County: Czech Farmers and Mexican Laborers in South Texas, 1880–1930." In *Ethnicity on the Great Plains*, edited by Frederick C. Luebke, 190–209. Lincoln: University of Nebraska Press, 1980.

Bauder, Harald Sven. "Labour Market Marginalisation of Young Latinos in San Antonio, Texas: A Geographical Perspective of Neighborhood Processes." Ph.D. dissertation, Wilfrid Laurier University, 1998.

Belden, Joe. *The Latin American Market of Austin, Texas*. Dallas: Joe Belden and Associates, 1951.

Benetiz, Joseph Spielberg. "The Mexican Crisis and the Segmented Labor Market of the Lower Rio Grande Valley of Texas." *Río Bravo* 2.1 (1992): 103–119.

Betts, Dianne C., and Daniel J. Slottje. *Crisis on the Rio Grande: Poverty, Unemployment, and Economic Development on the Texas-Mexico Border*. Boulder, Colo.: Westview Press, 1994.

Black, F. Michael, ed. *Mirando City: A New Town in a New Oil Field*. Laredo: Laredo Publishing, 1972.

Blackwelder, Julia Kirk. *Women of the Depression: Caste and Culture in San Antonio, 1929–1939*. College Station: Texas A&M University Press, 1984.

________. "Emma Tenayuca: Vision and Courage." In *The Human Tradition in Texas*, edited by Ty Cashion and Jesús F. de la Teja, 191–208. Wilmington, Del.: Scholarly Resources, 2001.

________. "Women in the Work Force: Atlanta, New Orleans, and San Antonio, 1930–1940." *Journal of Urban History* 4 (May 1978): 331–358.

Blazek, Lida Frances. "Food Habits and Living Conditions of Mexican Families on Four Income Levels in the Upper Rio Grande Valley." Master's thesis, University of Texas, Austin, 1938.

Blum, Owen W. "Some Aspects of the Latin-American Market of Austin, Texas, with Emphasis on the Radio as a Means of Reaching this Market." Master's thesis, University of Texas, Austin, 1952.

Bradshaw, Benjamin Spencer. "Potential Labor Force Supply, Placement, and Migration of Mexican-American and Other Males in the Texas-Mexico Border Region." *International Migration Review* 10 (1976): 29–45.

Brand, Donald D. "The Early History of the Range Cattle Industry in Northern Mexico." *Agricultural History* 35 (1961): 132–139.

Briggs, Vernon M. Jr., Walter Fogel, and Fred H. Schmidt. *The Chicano Worker*. Austin: University of Texas Press, 1977.

Briody, Elizabeth K. *Household Labor Patterns Among Mexican Americans in South Texas: Buscando Trabajo Segura*. New York: AMS Press, 1988.

________. "Household Work/Subsistence Strategies Among Mexican Americans of the Lower Rio Grande Valley." Ph.D. dissertation, University of Texas at Austin, 1985.

________. "Patterns of Household Immigration into South Texas." *International Migration Review* 21 (Spring 1987): 27–47.

Brookshire, Marjorie S. "The Industrial Patterns of Mexican-American Employment in Nueces County, Texas." Ph.D. dissertation, University of Texas, Austin, 1954.

Broom, Perry M. "An Interpretive Analysis of the Economic and Educational Status of Latin Americans in Texas, with Emphasis on Ten Basic Factors Underlying an Approach to an Improvement Progress of Occupation, Guidance, Training, and Adjustment for Secondary Schools." Ph.D. dissertation, University of Texas, Austin, 1942.

Brown, Harold Owen. "The Building of the Texas-Mexican Railroad." Master's thesis, Texas A&I College, 1937.

Buss, Francis Ann Leeper. "An Oral History of a Chicana Farm Worker: Her Struggles and Social Visions." Ph.D. dissertation, University of Arizona, 1995.

Bustamente, Jorge, Clark Reynolds, and Raúl Hinojosa, eds. *U.S.-Mexico Relations: Labor Market Interdependence*. Stanford, Calif.: Stanford University Press, 1992.

Calcott, F. "The Mexican Peon in Texas." *Survey* 44 (June 26, 1920): 436–439.

Calderón, Roberto R. *Mexican Coal Mining Labor in Texas and Coahuila, 1880–1930*. College Station: Texas A&M University Press, 2000.

________. "Unión, Paz y Trabajo: Laredo's Mexican Mutual Aid Societies, 1890s." In *Mexican Americans in Texas History*, edited by Emilio Zamora, Cynthia Orozco, and Rodolfo Rocha, 63–77. Austin: Texas State Historical Association, 2000.

________, ed. *South Texas Coal Mining: A Community History*. Eagle Pass, Tex.: Privately printed, 1984.

Calderón, Roberto R., and Emilio Zamora. "Manuela Solis Sager and Emma Tenayuca: A Tribute." In *Chicana Voices: Intersections of Class, Race, and Gender*, edited by Teresa Córdova, Norma Cantú, Gilberto Cárdenas, Juan García, and

Christine M. Sierra, 30–41. Albuquerque: University of New Mexico Press, 1993.

Camara, Fernando. "Differential Migration Streams, Economic Growth, and Socio-Cultural Changes in Mexican Border Cities." In *Migration Across Frontiers: Mexico and the United States*, edited by Fernando Camara and Robert Van Kemper, 101–126. New York: State University of New York Press, 1979.

Cárdenas, Gilberto. "Manpower Impact and Problems of Mexican Illegal Aliens in an Urban Labor Market." Ph.D. dissertation, University of Illinois, 1976.

________. "Mexican Illegal Aliens in the San Antonio Labor Market." *Texas Business Review* 53 (1979): 187–191.

Cárdenas, Gilberto, Beth Anne Shelton, and Devon Peña. "Undocumented Immigrant Women in the Houston Labor Market." *California Sociologist* 5 (Summer 1982): 98–118.

Cárdenas, Gilberto, and Estevan T. Flores. *Social, Economic, and Demographic Characteristics of Undocumented Mexicans in the Houston Labor Market: A Preliminary Report*. Houston: Gulf Coast Legal Aid Foundation, 1980.

Cárdenas, Gilberto, Jorge Chapa, and Susan Burek. "The Changing Economic Position of Mexican Americans in San Antonio." In *Latinos in a Changing U.S. Economy*, edited by Rebecca Morales and Frank Bonilla, 160–183. Newbury Park, Calif.: Sage Publications, 1993.

Cardoso, Lawrence A. "Labor Emigration to the Southwest, 1916 to 1920: Mexican Attitudes and Policy." *Southwestern Historical Quarterly* 79 (1975): 400–416.

Carlson, Paul H. "The Panhandle Pastores." In *Texas Woolybacks: The Range Sheep and Goat Industry*, by Paul H. Carlson, College Station: Texas A&M University Press, 1982.

________. "Panhandle Pastores: Early Sheepherding in the Texas Panhandle." *Panhandle Plains Historical Review* 53 (1980): 1–15.

________. "The Texas Background—Spanish or American?" *West Texas Historical Association Yearbook* 52 (1976): 61–70.

Casstevens, Mary Anna. "The Institution of the Spanish-Mexican Ranch and Its Culture in South Texas." Master's thesis, Texas A&M University-Kingsville, 1997.

________. "Randado." In *Ranching in South Texas: A Symposium*, edited by Joe S. Graham, 44–48. Kingsville, Tex.: Texas A&M University-Kingsville, 1992.

Castañeda, Carlos E. "The First Chartered Bank West of the Mississippi: Banco Nacional de Texas." *Business History Review* 25 (December 1951): 242–256.

Chabrán, Richard, and Rafael Chabrán, eds. "Farah Strike." In *The Latino Encyclopedia*, edited by Richard Chabrán and Rafael Chabrán, vol. 2, 581. New York: Marshall Cavendish, 1996.

________. "Tex-Son Garment Strike." In *The Latino Encyclopedia*, edited by Richard Chabrán and Rafael Chabrán, vol. 6, 1597. New York: Marshall Cavendish, 1996.

Chahin, Jaime. "Reflections of a Migrant Farmworker." *Latino Studies Journal* 11 (Spring 2000): 26–36.

Chapa, J. "The Question of Mexican American Assimilation: Socio-economic Parity or Underclass Formulation?" *Public Affairs Comment* 35.1 (1988): 1–7.

Chesney, Michael Edward. "An Overview of the Mexican 'Maquiladora' Industries: History, Benefits, and Controversies, 1965–1985." Master's thesis, University of Texas at Austin, 1985.

Christiansen, John R. "Estimation of Socioeconomic Status of Spanish-Americans in Atascosa and Bexar Counties, Texas." *Rocky Mountain Social Science Journal* 2.1 (1965): 215–222.

Cisneros, Victor B. Nelson. "La Clase Trabajadora en Tejas, 1920–1930." *Aztlán* 6 (Summer 1975): 239–268.

________. "UCAPAWA Organizing Activities in Texas, 1935–1950." *Aztlán* 9 (Spring-Summer 1978): 71–84.

Clark, Madeline. "A Preliminary Survey of Employment Possibilities of the Spanish-American Girls Receiving Commercial Training in the San Antonio Secondary Schools." Master's thesis, University of Texas, Austin, 1936.

Clayton, Lawrence. "Some South Texas Contributions to Ranching." *South Texas Studies* 7 (1996): 1–17.

Clinchy, Everett Ross Jr. *Equality of Opportunity for Latin-Americans in Texas*. New York: Arno Press, 1974.

________. "Equality of Opportunity for Latin-Americans in Texas." Ph.D. dissertation, Columbia University, 1954.

Coalson, George O. *The Development of the Migratory Farm Labor System in Texas, 1900–1954*. San Francisco: R&E Research Associates, 1977.

Conley, Mariita Cecilia. "The Role of the Labor Contractor in the Farm Labor Market of South Texas: The Case of the Citrus Industry." Master's thesis, University of Texas at Austin, 1976.

Cooney, Rosario Santana. "Changing Labor Force Participation of Mexican American Wives: A Comparison with Anglos and Blacks." *Social Science Quarterly* 56.2 (1975): 252–261.

Copp, Nelson G. "Wetbacks and Braceros: Mexican Migrant Laborers and American Immigration Policy, 1930–1960." Ph.D. dissertation, St. Mary's University, 1963.

Cornwell, Tammy Bettina. "Comprehension and Miscomprehension of Selected Print Advertisements: Focus on the Hispanic Consumer." Ph.D. dissertation, University of Texas at Austin, 1988.

Coronado, Raúl Jr. "Selena's Good Buy: Texas Mexicans, History and Selena Meet Transnational Capitalism." *Aztlán* 26 (April 2001): 59–100.

Cothran, Mary L. "Occupational Patterns of Rural and Urban Spanish-Americans in Two South Texas Counties." Master's thesis, Texas A&M University, College Station, 1966.

Covacha-Quauhtlatoa. "The Coloring of Local #370: The Changing Complexion of an El Paso, Texas Printers' Union." *E. C. Barksdale Student Lectures* 15 (1997–1998): 338–356.

Cowling, Annie. "The Civil War Trade of the Lower Rio Grande Valley." Master's thesis, University of Texas, Austin, 1926.

Coyle, Laurie, Gail Hershatter, and Emily Honig. "Farah Strike." In *The New Handbook of Texas,* edited by Ron Tyler, Douglas E. Barnett, Roy R. Barkley, Penelope C. Anderson, and Mark F. Odintz, vol. 2, 950. Austin: Texas State Historical Association, 1996.

________. "Women at Farah: An Unfinished Story." In *Mexican Women in the United States: Struggles Past and Present*, edited by Magdalena Mora and Adelaida Del Castillo, 117–144. Los Angeles: Chicano Studies Research Publications, 1980.

Crain, Forest Burr. "The Occupational Distribution of Spanish-Named People of Austin, Texas." Master's thesis, University of Texas, Austin, 1948.

Cravens, John N. "Two Miners and Their Families in the Thurber-Strawn Coal Mines, 1905–1918." *West Texas Historical Association Yearbook* 45 (1969): 115–126.

Crawford, Ann Fears, and Crystal Sasse Ragsdale. "Worker for Women: Lupe Anguiano." In *Women in Texas: Their Lives, Their Experiences, Their Accomplishments*, by Crystal Sasse Ragsdale, 321–329. Burnet, Tex.: Eakin Press, 1982.

Croxdale, Richard. "The 1938 Pecan Shellers' Strike." In *Women in the Texas Workforce: Yesterday and Today*, edited by Richard Croxdale and Melissa Hield, 24–34. Austin: People's History in Texas, 1979.

Davidson, C., and C. M. Gaitz. "Are the Poor Different?: A Comparison of the Work Behavior and Attitudes Among the Urban Poor and Non-Poor." *Social Problems* 22.2 (1974): 229–245.

Davis, Edward Everett. "King Cotton Leads Mexicans into Texas." *Texas Outlook* 9 (April 1925): 1–3.

________. "Peons." In *The White Scourge*, by Edward Everett Davis, 166–175. San Antonio: The Naylor Company, 1940.

Davis, Ethelyn Clara. "Little Mexico: A Study of Horizontal and Vertical Mobility." Master's thesis, Southern Methodist University, 1936.

Dearman, Cecil J. "A Socio-Economic Study of Latin-American Farm Migrants in Texas." Master's thesis, Texas Agricultural and Mechanical College, 1947.

de Chavana, Herminia Ballí. "Carlos Manuel Ballí Tijerina." In *The New Handbook of Texas,* edited by Ron Tyler, Douglas E. Barnett, Roy R. Barkley, Penelope C. Anderson, and Mark F. Odintz, vol. 1, 361. Austin: Texas State Historical Association, 1996.

de la Garza, Rodolfo O., and Karl Schmitt. "Texas Land Grants and Chicano-Mexican Relations: A Case Study." *Latin American Research Review* 21.1 (1986): 123–138.

De la Zerda, Nancy Jane. "Employment Interviewers Reactions to Mexican American Speech." Ph.D. dissertation, University of Texas at Austin, 1977.

De León, Arnoldo. "*Los Tasinques* and the Sheep Shearers' Union of North America: A Strike in West Texas, 1934." *West Texas Historical Association Yearbook* 55 (1979): 3–16.

________. "*Rancheros, Comerciantes*, and *Trabajadores* in South Texas, 1848–1900." In *Reflections of the Mexican Experience in Texas*, edited by Margarita B. Melville, 58–91. Houston: Mexican American Studies Center, University of Houston, 1979.

________. "Wresting a Competence in Nineteenth-Century Texas: The Case of the Chicanos." *Red River Valley Historical Review* 4 (Fall 1979): 52–64.

De León, Arnoldo, and Kenneth L. Stewart. "Lost Dreams and Found Fortunes: Mexican and American Immigrants in South Texas." *Western Historical Quarterly* 14 (July 1983): 291–310.

________. "Tejano Demographic Patterns and Socio-Economic Development." *Borderlands Journal* 7 (Fall 1983): 1–9.

________. "Work Force Participation Rates Among Mexican Immigrant Women in Texas, 1900." *Borderlands Journal* 9 (Spring 1986): 69–74.

de Oliver, Miguel. "Multicultural Consumerism and Racial Hierarchy: A Case Study of Market Culture and the Structural Harmonization of Contradictory Doctrines." *Antipode* 33 (March 2001): 228–259.

Devadoss, Narayanaswamy. "Truck Transportation of Fresh Fruits and Vegetables: An Econometric Analysis of the Southwest Region's Fresh Produce Truck Service Market." Ph.D. dissertation, University of Oklahoma, 1987.

Dickerson, Ben E. "An Analysis of the Income of Rural and Urban Spanish Americans in Two South Texas Counties." Master's thesis, Texas A&M University, 1965.

Dobie, J. Frank. *A Vaquero of the Brush Country*. Austin: University of Texas Press, 1965.

________. "The Mexican Vaquero of the Texas Border." *Southwestern Political and Social Science Quarterly* 8 (June 1927): 15–26.

________. "Ranch Mexicans." *Survey* (May 1, 1931): 167–170.

________. "Versos of the Texas Vaqueros." In *Happy Hunting Ground*, edited by J. Frank Dobie, 30–43. Austin: Texas Folk-lore Society, 1925.

Donigan, Norma F. "An Occupational Study of Dallas Migratory Mexicans." Master's thesis, Southern Methodist University, 1950.

Dow, Pauline A. "Mexican Domestic Workers in Perspective: Focus on El Paso, Texas." Master's thesis, University of Texas at El Paso, 1987.

Duncan, Cameron. "The Runaway Shop and the Mexican Border Industrialization Program." *Southwest Economy and Society* 2 (October-November 1976): 4–25.

Ellis, Christine Evangeline. "The Relation of Socioeconomic Status to the Intelligence and School Success of Mexican Children." Master's thesis, University of Texas, Austin, 1932.

Farrell, Grace A. "Homemaking with the 'Other Half' along Our International Border." *Journal of Home Economics* 12 (1929): 413–418.

Felice, L. G. "Mexican-American Self-Concept and Educational Achievement: The Effects of Economic Isolation and Socio-economic Deprivation." *Social Science Quarterly* 53.4 (1973): 716–726.

Fernández-Kelly, María Patricia. *For We Are Sold, I and My People: Women and Industry in Mexico's Northern Frontier*. Albany: State University of New York Press, 1983.

________. "Mexican Border Industrialization, Female Labor Force Participation, and Migration." In *Women, Men, and the International Division of Labor*, edited by June Nash and María Patricia Fernández-Kelly, 205–223. Albany: State University of New York Press, 1983.

Filewood, David. "Tejano Revolt: The Significance of the 1938 Pecan Shellers' Strike." Master's thesis, University of Texas at Arlington, 1994.

Fish, Jean. "Nuestra Señora de los Dolores: The First Ranch in South Texas, 1750." In *Ranching in South Texas: A Symposium*, edited by Joe S. Graham, 10–14. Kingsville, Tex.: Texas A&M University-Kingsville, 1992.

Flores, Roy, and Gilberto Cárdenas. *A Study of the Demographic and Employment Characteristics of Undocumented Aliens in San Antonio, El Paso, and McAllen, Texas*. San Antonio: U.S. Commission on Civil Rights, Texas State Advisory Committee, 1978.

Foley, Douglas E. *Learning Capitalist Culture: Deep in the Heart of Tejas*. Philadelphia: University of Pennsylvania Press, 1990.

Foley, Neil F. *The White Scourge: Mexicans, Blacks, and Poor Whites in Texas Cotton Culture*. Berkeley: University of California Press, 1997.

________. "The New South in the Southwest: Anglos, Blacks, and Mexicans in Central Texas, 1880–1930." Ph.D. dissertation, University of Michigan, 1990.

________. "Chicanos and the Culture of Cotton in Central Texas, 1880–1900: Reshaping Class Relations in the South." In *Community Empowerment and Chicano Scholarship*, edited by Mary Romero and Cordelia Candelaria, 111–126. Berkeley: National Association for Chicano Studies, 1992.

________. "Mexican Migrant and Tenant Labor in Central Texas Cotton Counties, 1880–1930: Social and Economic Transformation in a Multi-Cultural Society." *Wooster Review* 9 (Spring 1989): 90–101.

________. "Mexicans, Mechanization, and the Growth of Corporate Cotton Culture in South Texas: the Taft Ranch, 1900–1930." *Journal of Southern History* 62 (May 1996): 275–302.

Form, William H., and Julius Rivera. "The Place of Returning Migrants in a Stratification System." *Rural Sociology* 23 (1958): 286–297.

________. "Work Contracts and International Evaluations: The Case of a Mexican Border Village." *Social Forces* 37 (1959): 334–338.

Foscue, Edwin J. "Agricultural History of the Lower Rio Grande Valley Region." *Agricultural History* 8.3 (1934): 124–137.

French, William Earl. "Peaceful and Working People: The Inculcation of the Capitalist Work Ethic in a Mexican Mining District (Hidalgo District, Chihuahua), 1880–1920." Ph.D. dissertation, University of Texas at Austin, 1990.

Fugate, Francis L. "Origins of the Range Cattle Industry in South Texas." *Agricultural History* 35 (1961): 155–158.

Fuller, Roden. "Occupation of the Mexican Born Population of Texas, New Mexico, and Arizona, 1900–1920." *Journal of the American Statistical Association* 23 (March 1928): 64–74.

Galván, Jesse Jr. *The Way Back: The Autobiography of Jesse Galván Jr.: Businessman, Comedian, Federal Employee.* San Antonio: Watercress Press, 1993.

García-Camarillo, Cecilio. "Las Cartas que dejó Gilberto Padilla en el Valle de Tejas." *Caracol* 2 (February 1976): 5–7.

García, Clotilde P. "Antonio García Valverde." In *The New Handbook of Texas,* edited by Ron Tyler, Douglas E. Barnett, Roy R. Barkley, Penelope C. Anderson, and Mark F. Odintz, vol. 3, 89. Austin: Texas State Historical Association, 1996.

García, Ignacio. "The Many Battles of Tony Orendain." *Nuestro* 3 (November 1979): 25–29.

García, María-Cristina. "Félix Tijerina." In *The New Handbook of Texas*, edited by Ron Tyler, Douglas E. Barnett, Roy R. Barkley, Penelope C. Anderson, and Mark F. Odintz, vol. 6, 496–497. Austin: Texas State Historical Association, 1996.

García, Mario T. "Obreros: The Mexican Workers of El Paso, 1900–1920." Ph.D. dissertation, University of California at San Diego, 1975.

________. "Border Proletariats: Mexican Americans and the International Union of Mine, Mill, and Smelter Workers." In *Mexican Americans: Leadership, Ideology, and Identity, 1930–1960*, by Mario T. García, 175–198. New Haven: Yale University Press, 1989.

________. "Racial Dualism in the El Paso Labor Market, 1880–1920." *Aztlán* 6 (Summer 1975): 197–218.

________. "Working for the Union." *Mexican Studies/Estudios Mexicanos* 9.2 (Summer 1993): 241–257.

García, Martha Xochitl. "Alberto Gonzalo García." In *The New Handbook of Texas,* edited by Ron Tyler, Douglas E. Barnett, Roy R. Barkley, Penelope C. Anderson, and Mark F. Odintz, vol. 3, 82. Austin: Texas State Historical Association, 1996.

García, Nelda C. "Language Factors in the Employment of Bilingual Mexican Americans: A Case Study Analysis." Ph.D. dissertation, Michigan State University, 1971.

García, Richard A. *Rise of the Mexican American Middle Class: San Antonio, 1929–1941*. College Station: Texas A&M University Press, 1990.

________. "Class, Class Consciousness, and Ideology—Mexican American Population of San Antonio, Texas, 1930–1940." *Aztlán* 9 (1978): 23–69.

Garza, Elisa Gorena. "The Academic and Social Adjustment of the Children of Agricultural Migratory Workers in Hidalgo County, Texas." Master's thesis, Texas Women's University, 1963.

Garza, Fernando R. "Esteban García." In *The New Handbook of Texas,* edited by Ron Tyler, Douglas E. Barnett, Roy R. Barkley, Penelope C. Anderson, and Mark F. Odintz, vol. 3, 83. Austin: Texas State Historical Association, 1996.

George, Eugene. "Spanish and Mexican Architecture on Early South Texas Ranches." In *Ranching in South Texas: A Symposium*, edited by Joe S. Graham, 49–52. Kingsville, Tex.: Texas A&M University-Kingsville, 1992.

Gilliland, Maude T. *Rincón: A Story of Life on a South Texas Ranch at the Turn of the Century*. Brownsville, Tex.: Springman-King Lithograph Company, 1964.

Gomilla, Michelle Lorraine. "Los Refugiados y los Comerciantes: Mexican Refugees and Businessmen in Downtown El Paso, 1910–1920." Master's thesis, University of Texas at El Paso, 1990.

González Quiroga, Miguel A. "Trabajadores Mexicanos en Texas (1850–1865): Los carreteros y el transporte de carga." *Siglo XIX: Cuadernos de Historia* 3.9 (1994): 51–81.

Graf, LeRoy P. "The Economic History of the Lower Rio Grande Valley, 1820–1875." 2 vols. Ph.D. dissertation, Harvard University, 1942.

Graham, Joe S. *El Rancho in South Texas: Continuity and Change From 1750*. Denton: University of North Texas Press, 1994.

________. The Spanish and Mexican Origins of Ranching in Texas." *Journal of Big Bend Studies* 10 (1998): 77–87.

________. "The Spanish-Mexican Roots of Ranching in South Texas." In *Ranching in South Texas: A Symposium*, edited by Joe S. Graham, 1–9. Kingsville, Tex.: Texas A&M University-Kingsville, 1992.

________. "Vaquero Folk Arts and Crafts in South Texas." In *Hecho en Tejas: Texas-Mexican Folk Arts and Crafts*, edited by Joe S. Graham, 93–116. Denton: University of North Texas Press, 1991.

________, ed. *Ranching in South Texas: A Symposium*. Kingsville, Tex.: Texas A&M University-Kingsville, 1992.

Graves, Ruth Parker. "A History of the Interrelationships between Imported Mexican Labor, Domestic Migrants, and the Texas Agricultural Economy." Master's thesis, University of Texas, Austin, 1960.

Green, George N. "Anti-Labor Politics in Texas, 1941–1957." In *American Labor in the Southwest: The First One Hundred Years*, edited by James C. Foster, 217–227. Tucson: University of Arizona Press, 1982.

________. "ILGWU in Texas, 1930–1970." *Journal of Mexican American History* 1 (Spring 1971): 144–169.

Guerra, Manuel. "Alberca de Arriba Ranch." In *The New Handbook of Texas*, edited by Ron Tyler, Douglas E. Barnett, Roy R. Barkley, Penelope C. Anderson, and Mark F. Odintz, vol.1, 93–94. Austin: Texas State Historical Association, 1996.

Guzmán, Jane Bock. "María Luna." *Legacies: A History Journal for Dallas and North Central Texas* (Fall 2001): 17–18.

Hale, John E. "Employability Problems for Disadvantaged Mexican Americans." Master's thesis, St. Mary's University, 1972.

Hall, William C. "A Study of 281 Farm Labor Families of South Texas." Master's thesis, Texas College of Arts and Industries, 1942.

Handman, Max S. "Economic Reasons for the Coming of the Mexican Immigrant." *American Journal of Sociology* 25 (January 1930): 601–611.

________. "The Mexican Immigrant in Texas." *National Conference of Social Work Proceedings* (1926): 332–339.

Hardesty, Scarlett G., Malcolm D. Holmes, and James D. Williams. "Economic Segmentation and Worker Earnings in a U.S.-Mexico Border Enclave." *Sociological Perspectives* 31.4 (1988): 466–489.

Harrison, Rebecca Charlene. "An Examination of Training Needs among Hispanic Entrepreneurs in Houston, Texas." Master's thesis, Lamar University-Beaumont, 1993.

Harris, Richard J. "Mexican American Occupational Attainment in San Antonio: Comparative Assessments." In *The Politics of San Antonio: Community, Progress, and Power*, edited by John A. Booth, David R. Johnson, and Richard J. Harris, 53–71. Lincoln: University of Nebraska Press, 1984.

Hawkins, Gladys, Jean Soper, and Jane Pike Henry. *Your Maid from Mexico: A Home Training Course for Maids in English and Spanish*. San Antonio: The Naylor Company, 1959.

Hernández, José Amaro. "The Proliferation of Mutual Aid Societies in the Chicano Community and the Attempt to Integrate Them: The *Primer Congreso Mexicanista de Texas*." In *Mutual Aid for Survival: The Case of the Mexican American*, 60–74. Malabar, Fla.: Robert E. Krieger, 1983.

Hield, Melissa. "Union-Minded: Women in the Texas ILGWU, 1933–1950." In *Women in the Texas Workforce: Yesterday and Today*, edited by Richard Croxdale and Melissa Hield, 1–23. Austin: People's History in Texas, 1979.

Hill, George W. *Texas-Mexican Migratory Agricultural Workers in Wisconsin*. Madison: Agricultural Experiment Station, University of Wisconsin, 1948.

Hipp, Joe Wreford. *The Oldest Ranch in Texas: A Ranch on the Road to History*. Austin: Eakin Press, 2000.

Housewright, George Maxwell. "The Changing Economic Status in Texas of the Latin American and the Negro: 1950–1960." Ph.D. dissertation, University of Arkansas, 1972.

Hufford, Charles H. "The Social and Economic Effects of Mexican Migration into Texas." Master's thesis, Howard Payne College, 1929.

Iber, Jorge. "Bidal Aguero and *El Editor* Newspaper: The Varied Roles of a Spanish Surnamed Entrepreneur in a Lubbock, Texas Barrio, 1977–1999." *West Texas Historical Association Yearbook* 75 (1999): 54–62.

________. "Vaqueros in the Western Cattle Industry." In *The Cowboy Way: An Exploration of History and Culture*, edited by Paul H. Carlson, 21–32. Lubbock: Texas Tech University Press, 2000.

Jackson, Jack. *Los Mesteños: Spanish Ranching in Texas, 1721–1821*. College Station: Texas A&M University Press, 1986.

________. "Hispanic Ranching Heritage." In *Hispanic Texas: A Historical Guide*, edited by Helen Simons and Cathryn A. Hoyt, 51–57. Austin: University of Texas Press, 1992.

________. "The Great Roundup of 1787." *Journal of South Texas* 13 (2000): 19–51.

________. "Juan José Flores." In *The New Handbook of Texas,* edited by Ron Tyler, Douglas E. Barnett, Roy R. Barkley, Penelope C. Anderson, and Mark F. Odintz, vol. 2, 1036. Austin: Texas State Historical Association, 1996.

Johnson, Marjorie. "Salvador Marcos Hinojosa." In *The New Handbook of Texas,* edited by Ron Tyler, Douglas E. Barnett, Roy R. Barkley, Penelope C. Anderson, and Mark F. Odintz, vol. 3, 628–629. Austin: Texas State Historical Association, 1996.

Johnston, Marshall C. "Past and Present Grasslands of Southern Texas and Northeastern Mexico." *Ecology* 44.3 (1963): 456–466.

Jones, Lamar B. "Mexican American Labor Problems in Texas." Ph.D. dissertation, University of Texas, Austin, 1965.

Jones, Lamar B., and C. R. Rice "Agricultural Labor in the Southwest: The Post-Bracero Years." *Social Science Quarterly* 61.1 (1980): 86–94.

Kane, Tim D. "The Effect of Labor Market Change upon the Employment of Low Income Mexican Americans: The San Antonio Experience." Ph.D. dissertation, University of Texas at Austin, 1972.

Katz, Friedrich. "Labor Conditions on Haciendas in Porfirian Mexico: Some Trends and Tendencies." *Hispanic American Historical Review* 54 (February 1974): 1–47.

Kibbe, Pauline R. "The Economic Plight of Mexicans." In *Ethnic Relations in the United States*, edited by Edward C. McDonagh and Eugene S. Richards, 189–200. New York: Appleton Century Crofts, 1953.

Kilgore, Dan. "The Spanish Missions and the Origins of the Cattle Industry in Texas." In *Proceedings of the Second Annual Mission Research Conference*, edited by Gilberto R. Cruz, 62–67. San Antonio: Missions National Historical Park, 1984.

King, Allen G., B. Lindsay Lowell, and Frank D. Bean. "The Effects of Hispanic Immigrants on the Earnings of Native Hispanic Americans." *Social Science Quarterly* 67.4 (1986): 673–689.

Knowlton, Clark S. "Changing Patterns of Segregation and Discrimination Affecting the Mexican Americans of El Paso, Texas: An Analysis of Socioeconomic Characteristics." In *Politics and Society in the Southwest: Ethnicity and Chicano Pluralism*, edited by Z. Anthony Kruszewski, Richard L. Hough, and Jacob Ornstein-Galicia, 131–154. Boulder, Colo.: Westview Press, 1982.

Knox, William John. *The Economic Status of the Mexican Immigrant in San Antonio, Texas*. San Francisco: R&E Research Associates, 1971.

________. "The Economic Status of the Mexican Immigrant in San Antonio, Texas." Master's thesis, University of Texas, Austin, 1927.

Kuvlesky, William P., and Rumaldo Z. Juárez. "Mexican American Youth and the American Dream." In *Career Behavior of Special Groups*, edited by J. S. Picou and R. E. Campbell, 241–296. Columbus, Ohio: Charles E. Merrill, 1975.

Lamare, James W., and Mary Steffey Lamare. "Sociopolitical Reactions to Public Policy: Tenant Attitudes about a Relocation Program." In *Politics and Society in the Southwest: Ethnicity and Chicano Pluralism*, edited by Z. Anthony

Kruszewski, Richard L. Hough, and Jacob Ornstein-Galicia, 237–247. Boulder, Colo.: Westview Press, 1982.

Landolt, Robert Garland. *The Mexican-American Workers of San Antonio*. New York: Arno Press, 1968.

________. "The Mexican-American Workers of San Antonio, Texas." Ph.D. dissertation, University of Texas, Austin, 1965.

Laney, John Clemens. "Vocational Needs of the Mexican-American in South Texas." Ph.D. dissertation, Texas Tech University, 1973.

Lapage, J. Preston. "A Study of the Relationship between the Political Association of Spanish-Speaking Organizations and Organized Labor in Texas." Master's thesis, University of Texas, Austin, 1965.

Larralde, Carlos M. "José Esparza." In *The New Handbook of Texas,* edited by Ron Tyler, Douglas E. Barnett, Roy R. Barkley, Penelope C. Anderson, and Mark F. Odintz, vol. 2, 839. Austin: Texas State Historical Association, 1996.

Larson, Jane E. "Free Market Deep in the Heart of Texas." *Georgetown Law Journal* 84 (1995): 179–258.

Leal, Ray Robert. "The 1966–1967 South Texas Farm Workers Strike." Ph.D. dissertation, Indiana University, 1983.

Ledesma, Irene. "Unlikely Strikers: Mexican American Women in Strike Activity in Texas, 1919–1974." Ph.D. dissertation, Ohio State University, 1992.

________. "Texas Newspapers and Chicana Workers' Activism, 1919–1974." *Western Historical Quarterly* 26 (Autumn 1995): 309–331. Reprinted in *En Aquel Entonces: Readings in Mexican-American History*, edited by Manuel G. Gonzales and Cynthia M. Gonzales, 158–164. Bloomington: Indiana University Press, 2000.

Lehmann, Val W. *Forgotten Legions: Sheep in the Rio Grande Plain of Texas*. El Paso: Texas Western Press, 1969.

Leifeste, Sam Andrew. "Characteristics of the Texas Latin American Market." Ph.D. dissertation, University of Texas, Austin, 1954.

Leyva, Yolanda Chávez. "'Faithful Hard-Working Hands': Mexican Workers During the Great Depression." *Perspectives in Mexican American Studies* 5 (1995): 63–77.

Lockhart, William W. "Antonio Trujillo: Constable of San Elizario." *Password* 39 (Winter 1994): 179–186.

________. "Gregorio Nacianceno García, 1st: Indian Fighter and Politician." *Password* 40 (Fall 1995): 119–125.

________. "Gregorio Nacianceno García, 2d: Lawman and Politician of San Elizario." *Password* 40 (Fall 1995): 126–128.

Love, Clara M. "History of the Cattle Industry in the Southwest." *Southwestern Historical Quarterly* 19 (1916): 370–399.

Luna, Guadalupe T. "'Agricultural Underdogs' and International Agreements: The Legal Context of Agricultural Workers Within the Rural Economy." *New Mexico Law Review* 26 (Winter 1996): 9–56.

Machado, Manuel A. Jr. "An Uneasy Alliance: The Hispanics' Impact on the Southwestern Cattle Industry." In *Southwestern Agriculture: Pre-Columbian to Modern*, edited by Henry C. Dethloff and Irvin M. May Jr., 49–58. College Station: Texas A&M University Press, 1982.

Macías-González, Victor M. "Mexicans of the Better Class: The Exile of Chihuahuan Upper Classes in El Paso, 1913–1930." *Password* 45 (Winter 2000): 175–195.

Maril, Elizabeth. "Spanish Ranching Women." *South Texas Studies* 10 (1999): 143–153.

Márquez, Raquel. "Chicana Labor Activists: The Case of Fuerza Unida." Master's thesis, University of Texas at Austin, 1995.

Martínez, Camilo Amado Jr. "The Mexican and Mexican American Laborers in the Lower Rio Grande Valley of Texas, 1870–1930." Ph.D. dissertation, Texas A&M University, 1987.

________. "The Mexicans' and Mexican-Americans' Contribution to the Development of the Lower Rio Grande Valley and Its Citrus Industry." Master's thesis, Pan American University, 1982.

________. "Labor in the Valley: The Development of Texas' Citrus Industry." *Journal of South Texas* 7 (1994): 1–27.

________. "Vamos Pal West: Let's Go West." *West Texas Historical Association Yearbook* 70 (1994): 40–56.

Martínez, Oscar J. "Border Boom Town: Ciudad Juárez since 1880." Ph.D. dissertation, University of California, Los Angeles, 1975.

________. "The Foreign Orientation of the Ciudad Juárez Economy." In *The Social Ecology and Economic Development of Ciudad Juárez*, edited by Young Gay, 141–151. Boulder, Colo.: Westview Press, 1986.

Martínez Torres, María Guadalupe. "Interview." In *Barrios and Borderlands: Cultures of Latinos and Latinas in the United States*, edited by Denis Lynn Daly Heyck, 240–250. New York: Routledge, 1994.

Mathews, P. L. "The Mexican as a Coal Miner." *Coal Age* 12 (August 25, 1917): 312–315.

Maunder, Marvel Lee. "Job Satisfaction of Hispanic Food Service Workers." Ph.D. dissertation, Texas Tech University, 1990.

McArthur, Daniel Evander. "The Cattle Industry of Texas, 1685–1918." Master's thesis, University of Texas, Austin, 1918.

McCaffery, Isias James. "Organizing *las Costureras*: Life, Labor, and Unionization among Mexican Garment Workers in Two Borderlands Cities, Los Angeles and San Antonio, 1933–1941." Ph.D. dissertation, University of Kansas, 1999.

McCain, Johnny Mac. "Contract Labor as a Factor in the United States-Mexican Relations, 1942–1947." Ph.D. dissertation, University of Texas at Austin, 1970.

________. "Texas and the Mexican Labor Question, 1942–1947." *Southwestern Historical Quarterly* 85 (1981): 45–64.

McDonagh, E. C. "Status Levels of Mexicans." *Sociology and Social Research* 33 (July 1949): 449–459.

McKay, R. Reynolds. "The Federal Deportation Campaign in Texas: Mexican Deportation From the Lower Rio Grande Valley During the Great Depression." *Borderlands Journal* (Fall 1981): 95–120.

________. "The Impact of the Great Depression on Immigrant Mexican Labor: Repatriation of the Bridgeport, Texas, Coal Miners." *Social Science Quarterly* 65 (June 1984): 354–363.

McMillan, Node. "The Seeds of Discontent: Legal, Historical, and Economic Aspects of Commercial Agriculture in Spanish Texas, 1779–1821." Master's thesis, Southwest Texas State University, 1981.

McQuarie, Mary Diane. "Technology and Manpower Economics—Farm Workers in the Lower Rio Grande Valley." Master's thesis, University of Texas at Austin, 1979.

Meador, Bruce S. "'Wetback' Labor in the Lower Rio Grande Valley." Master's thesis, University of Texas, Austin, 1951.

Melville, Margarita B. "Mexican Women Adapt to Migration." *International Migration Review* 12.2 (1978): 225–235.

Menefee, Selden C. *Mexican Migratory Workers of South Texas.* Washington, D.C.: Works Projects Administration, 1941.

Menefee, Selden C., and Orin C. Cassmore. *The Pecan Shellers of San Antonio: The Problem of Underpaid and Unemployed Mexican Labor.* Washington, D.C.: Works Projects Administration, 1940.

Menon, Anil, and Willard B. Platzer. "Consumer Response to Advertising along the Texas/Mexico Border." *Borderlands Journal* 8 (Spring 1985): 57–80.

Mercado Villagra, Salvador Arturo. "Purchasing Patterns, Life-Style, and Demographics among Middle Class Mexican Americans and Mexicans: A Market Segmentation Study." Ph.D. dissertation, University of Texas at Austin, 1988.

Meyer, Frederic. *Spanish Name Persons in the Labor Force in Manufacturing Industry in Texas*. Austin: University of Texas Press, 1951.

________. "Employment and Relative Earnings of Spanish-Name Persons in Texas Industries." *Southern Economics Journal* 19 (April 1953): 494–507.

Miller, Lawrence W., Jerry L. Polinard, and Robert D. Wrinkle. "Attitudes Toward Undocumented Workers: The Mexican American Perspective." In *The Mexican American Experience: An Interdisciplinary Anthology*, edited by Rodolfo O. de la Garza, Frank D. Bean, Charles M. Bonjean, Ricardo Romo, and Rodolfo Álvarez, 228–240. Austin: University of Texas Press, 1985.

Miller, Michael V. "Poverty, Development, and the Quality of Life in a Texas Border City." Ph.D. dissertation, Texas A&M University, 1981.

________. "Industrial Development and An Expanding Labor Force in Brownsville." *Texas Business Review* 55 (November-December 1981): 258–261.

Miller, Michael V., and William P. Kuvlesky. *The Farm Labor Movement in South Texas: Historical Development, Current Status, and Implications for Change*. College Station: Department of Rural Sociology, Texas A&M University, 1975.

Miller, Michael V., and Robert Lee Maril. *Poverty in the Lower Rio Grande Valley of Texas: Historical and Contemporary Dimensions*. College Station: Texas Agricultural Experiment Station, 1978.

Miller, Michael V., and Avelardo Valdez. "Immigration and Perceptions of Economic Deprivation Among Working Class Mexican American Men." *Social Science Quarterly* 65 (1984): 455–464.

Mindiola, Tatcho Jr. "Age and Income Discrimination Against Mexican Americans and Blacks in Texas, 1960–1970." *Social Problems* 27 (1979): 196–208.

________. "The Cost of Being a Mexican Female Worker in the 1970 Houston Labor Market." *Aztlán* 11.2 (Fall 1980): 231–247.

Monday, Jane Clements, and Betty Bailey Carroll. *Voices from the Wild Horse Desert: The Vaquero Families of the King and Kenedy Ranches*. Austin: University of Texas Press, 1997.

Montejano, David. *Race, Labor Repression, and Capitalist Agriculture: Notes from South Texas, 1920–1930*. Berkeley: Institute for the Study of Social Change, 1977.

________. "Frustrated Apartheid: Race, Repression, and Capitalist Agriculture in South Texas, 1920–1930." In *The World-System of Capitalism: Past and Present*, edited by Walter Goldfrank, 131–168. Beverly Hills: Sage Publications, 1979.

Morgan, George R., and Omer C. Stewart. "Peyote Trade in South Texas." *Southwestern Historical Quarterly* 87 (January 1984): 269–296.

Morris, Marion Beth. "The History of the Mexican Contract Labor Program, 1942–1966." Master's thesis, North Texas State University, 1967.

Negrete Salas, Martaelena. "La Frontera Texana y el Abigeato (1848–1872)/The Texas Border and Cattle Stealing: 1848–72." *Historia Mexicana* 31.1 (1981): 79–100.

Nelson, Eastin, and Frederic Meyers. *Labor Requirements and Labor Resources in the Lower Rio Grande Valley of Texas*. Austin: University of Texas Press, 1950.

Norquest, Carrol. *Rio Grande Wetbacks: Mexican Migrant Workers*. Albuquerque: University of New Mexico Press, 1972.

North, David. *The Border Crossers: People Who Live in Mexico and Work in the United States*. Washington, D.C.: Trans Century Corporation, 1970.

Orendain, Antonio. "La Huelga en el valle de Tejas." *Caracol* 1.11 (July 1975): 13–14.

________. "La Lucha Campesina en Texas." *Caracol* 2.8 (April 1976): 14–15, 17.

________. "Texas Farm Workers: Unión de Campesinos Statement." *Caracol* 2.5 (January 1976): 22.

________. "Campaña en contra de 14 (b) / Campaign Against 14B." *Caracol* 4.8 (April 1978): 6.

Orndorff, Helen. "History of the Development of Agriculture in the El Paso Valley." Master's thesis, Texas Western College, 1957.

Orozco, Cynthia E. "Clemente Nicasio Idar." In *The New Handbook of Texas,* edited by Ron Tyler, Douglas E. Barnett, Roy R. Barkley, Penelope C. Anderson, and

Mark F. Odintz, vol. 3, 813–814. Austin: Texas State Historical Association, 1996.

________. "Eduardo Idar." In *The New Handbook of Texas,* edited by Ron Tyler, Douglas E. Barnett, Roy R. Barkley, Penelope C. Anderson, and Mark F. Odintz, vol. 3, 814. Austin: Texas State Historical Association, 1996.

________. "Eleuterio Escobar Jr." In *The New Handbook of Texas,* edited by Ron Tyler, Douglas E. Barnett, Roy R. Barkley, Penelope C. Anderson, and Mark F. Odintz, vol. 2, 889–890. Austin: Texas State Historical Association, 1996.

________. "José Antonio de la Garza." In *The New Handbook of Texas,* edited by Ron Tyler, Douglas E. Barnett, Roy R. Barkley, Penelope C. Anderson, and Mark F. Odintz, vol. 3, 107. Austin: Texas State Historical Association, 1996.

Ortiz González, Victor Manuel. "Market Identity: 'Hispanic' Entrepreneurship and Global Economic Integration in El Paso, Texas." Ph.D. dissertation, Stanford University, 1993.

Papailias, Gerassimos. "An Economic Study about Citrus Cooperatives in South Texas." Master's thesis, Texas A&I University, 1983.

Parigi, Sam Frank. *A Case Study of Latin American Unionization in Austin, Texas*. New York: Arno Press, 1976.

________. "A Case Study of Latin American Unionization in Austin, Texas." Ph.D. dissertation, University of Texas, Austin, 1964.

Parsley, Rosa Frances. "A Study of the Expenditure for Food of Some Urban Latin American Families on Work Relief in Austin, Texas." Master's thesis, University of Texas, Austin, 1935.

Perry, Joseph H. "Economic Characteristics of Texas Intrastate Migrants." Master's thesis, University of Texas, Austin, 1961.

Pisani, Michael J., and David W. Yoskowitz. "The Maid Trade: Cross-Border Work in South Texas." *Social Science Quarterly* 83 (2002): 568–579.

Pitts, John Bost III. "Speculation in Headright Land Grants in San Antonio from 1837 to 1842." Master's thesis, Trinity University, 1966.

Plascencia, Luis F. B., Miguel Ceballos, and Robert W. Glover. *Texas Farm Worker Enumeration Project.* Austin: Center for the Study of Human Resources, 1989.

Plata, M. "Stability and Change in the Prestige Ranking of Occupation Over 49 Years." *Journal of Vocational Behavior* 6.1 (1975): 95–99.

Privett, John Delmar. "Agricultural Unionism Among Chicanos in Texas." Master's thesis, University of Texas at Austin, 1971.

Pumarejo, Faustino Jr. "Educational Attainment and Organizational Perceptions of Mexican-American Supervisors." Ph.D. dissertation, Michigan State University, 1987.

Queen, Rae Wyatt. "Characteristics Related to Career Decision Making for Hispanic Adolescents in Texas." Ph.D. dissertation, Texas A&M University, 1999.

Quiñones, Juan Gómez. *Making of the Mexican Working Class North of the Río Bravo*. Los Angeles: Aztlán Publications, 1977.

Ramírez, Cirila Quintero. "Sindicatos Agrícolas en el Norte Tamaulipas y el Sur de Texas: Antecedentes Históricos." *Río Bravo* 3.1 (1993): 86–99.

Ramírez, Emilia Schunior. *Ranch Life in Hidalgo County after 1850*. Edinburg, Tex.: New Santander Press, 1971.

Ramírez, Nora Ethel. "The Vaquero and Ranching in the Southwestern United States, 1600–1970." Ph.D. dissertation, Indiana University, 1979.

Ramos, José María. "La politica comercial y antidrogas en Laredo, Texas." *Río Bravo* 3.2 (1994): 78–88.

Ramsdell, Charles. "Espiritu Santo: An Early Texas Cattle Ranch." *Texas Geographic Magazine* 13 (Fall 1949): 21–25.

Raymond, Richard D., and Michael Sesnowitz. "Labor Market Discrimination Against Mexican American College Graduates." *Southern Economic Journal* 49.4 (1983): 1122–1136.

Reagan, Barbara B. *Mexican-American Industrial Migrants*. Dallas: Southern Methodist University, 1971.

Reavis, Dick J. "The Last of the Border Lords." In *The Late Great Mexican Border: Reports from a Disappearing Line*, edited by Bobby Byrd and Susannah Mississippi Byrd, 80–100. El Paso: Cinco Puntos Press, 1996.

Reeve, Shirley Ballard. "Comparison by Socioeconomic Class of the Power Structure of Mexican-American and Anglo-American Families in the Rio Grande Valley of South Texas." Ph.D. dissertation, Florida State University, 1975.

Reyes, Juan. "Huelga Campesina en Tejas." *Caracol* 2.1 (September 1975): 14–15.

Rhinehart, Marilyn D., and Thomas H. Kreneck. "The Minimum Wage March of 1966: A Case Study in Mexican-American Politics, Labor, and Identity." *Houston Review* 11.1 (1989): 27–44.

Rhi-Pérez, Pablo. "A Cross Cultural Study of Attitudes toward Advertising and Consumer Brand Choice Strategies among Mexicans, Mexican-Americans and Anglos." Ph.D. dissertation, University of Texas at Austin, 1989.

Rhoades, Cecilia Claudine. "The Poison Crop: South Texas Farmers Versus Toxwaste Hazardous Waste Storage Facility." Ph.D. dissertation, University of Texas at Austin, 1997.

Richardson, Chad, and Cruz C. Torres. "'Only a Maid': Undocumented Domestic Workers in South Texas." In *Batos, Bolillos, Pochos, and Pelados: Class and Culture on the South Texas Border*, by Chad Richardson, 169–194. Austin: University of Texas Press, 1999.

Richardson, Chad, Cruz C. Torres, and Juanita Valdez Cox. "'*Mamá, Nosotros Somos Migrantes*': South Texas Farmworkers, 1950–1990." In *Batos, Bolillos, Pochos, and Pelados: Class and Culture on the South Texas Border*, by Chad Richardson, 17–42. Austin: University of Texas Press, 1999.

Ríos, Diana Isabel Arredondo. "Mexican American Audiences: A Qualitative and Quantitative Study of Ethnic Subgroup Uses for Mass Media." Ph.D. dissertation, University of Texas at Austin, 1993.

Ríos McMillan, Nora E. "Leonidas González." In *The New Handbook of Texas,* edited by Ron Tyler, Douglas E. Barnett, Roy R. Barkley, Penelope C. Anderson, and

Mark F. Odintz, vol. 3, 234–235. Austin: Texas State Historical Association, 1996.

Rips, Geoffrey. "Living History: Emma Tenayuca Tells her Story." *The Texas Observer* 75 (October 28, 1983): 7–15.

Robinson, G. C. "Mustangs and Mustanging in Southwest Texas." In *Mustangs and Cow Horses*, edited by J. Frank Dobie, Mody C. Boatright, and Harry R. Ransom, 3–21. Dallas: Southern Methodist University Press, 1940.

Rocha, Rodolfo. "Background to Banditry in the Lower Rio Grande Valley of Texas." Master's thesis, Pan American University, 1974.

________. "Early Ranching Along the Rio Grande." In *At Home on the Range: Essays on the History of Western Social and Domestic Life*, edited by John R. Wunder, 3–18. Westport, Conn.: Greenwood Press, 1985.

Rodríguez, Marc Simon. "*Obreros Unidos:* Migration, Migrant Farm Workers Activism, and the Chicano Movement in Wisconsin and Texas, 1950–1980." Ph.D. dissertation, Northwestern University, 2000.

Rodríguez, Nestor. "Latino Settlement in the 'Free-Enterprise City.'" In *Residential Apartheid*, edited by Robert D. Bullard, J. Eugene Grigsby III, and Charles Lee, 201–222. Los Angeles: University of California Press, 1995.

Roell, Craig H. "Martin De León." In *The New Handbook of Texas,* edited by Ron Tyler, Douglas E. Barnett, Roy R. Barkley, Penelope C. Anderson, and Mark F. Odintz, vol. 2, 571. Austin: Texas State Historical Association, 1996.

Rojas, Arnold R. *The Vaquero*. Charlotte, N.C.: McNally and Loftin, 1964.

Romero, José Ynocencio. "Spanish Sheepmen on the Canadian at Old Tascosa," edited by Ernest R. Archambeau. *Panhandle Plains Historical Review* 19 (1946): 45–72.

Romero, Mary. "The Death of Smeltertown: A Case Study of Lead Poisoning in a Chicano Community." In *Chicano Studies: Survey and Analysis*, edited by Dennis J. Bixler-Márquez, Carlos F. Ortega, Rosalía Solórzano-Torres, and Lorenzo LaFarelle, 115–122. Dubuque, Iowa: Kendall/Hunt, 1999.

Romero, Yolanda G. "Adelante Compañeros: The Sanitation Worker's Struggle in Lubbock, Texas, 1968–1972." *West Texas Historical Association Yearbook* 69 (1993): 82–87.

Rossoudji, Sherrie A., and Susan I. Rainey. "The Labor Market Earnings of Female Migrants: The Case of Temporary Mexican Migrants to the U.S." *International Migration Review* 28 (1984): 1120–1143.

Rouse, John E. *The Criollo: Spanish Cattle in the Americas*. Norman: University of Oklahoma Press, 1977.

Rozek, Barbara J. "The Entry of Mexican Women into Urban Based Industries: Experiences in Texas during the Twentieth Century." In *Women and Texas History: Selected Essays*, edited by Fane Downs and Nancy Baker Jones, 15–33. Austin: Texas State Historical Association, 1993.

Ruiz, Vicki L. "By the Day or the Week: Mexicana Domestic Workers in El Paso." In *Women on the U.S.-Mexico Border: Responses to Change*, edited by Vicki L. Ruiz and Susan Tiano, 61–76. Boston: Allen and Unwin, 1987.

Russell, James W. "Class and Nationality Relations in a Texas Border City: The Case of El Paso." *Aztlán* 16 (1985): 217–239.

Sáenz, Andrés. *Early Tejano Ranching: Daily Life at Ranchos San José and El Fresnillo*, edited by Andrés Tijerina. College Station: Texas A&M University Press, 1999.

Sáenz, Rogelio, and Marie Ballejos. "Industrial Development and Persistent Poverty in the Lower Rio Grande Valley." In *Forgotten Places: Uneven Development in Rural America*, edited by Thomas A. Lyson and William W. Falk, 102–124. Lawrence: University Press of Kansas, 1993.

Salazar, Jaime G., and Judith M. Espinosa. "A Sociodemographic Profile of Hispanic Physicians in Three United States Metropolitan Areas." *Aztlán* 10 (1979): 111–122.

Salmón, Roberto Mario. "Don José San Ramón as Brownsville Capitalist, 1822–1879." *South Texas Studies* 1 (1990): 54–68.

Saunders, Lyle, and Olen E. Leonard. *The Wetback in the Lower Rio Grande Valley of Texas*. Inter-American Education Occasional Papers, No. 7. Austin: University of Texas, Austin, 1951. Reprinted in *Mexican Migration to the United States*, edited by Carlos E. Cortés, 3–92. New York: Arno Press, 1976.

Schlossman, Steven. "Self-Evident Remedy? George I. Sánchez, Segregation, and Enduring Dilemmas in Bilingual Education." *Teachers College Record* 84 (Summer 1983): 871–907.

Scholes, William E. "The Migrant Worker." In *La Raza: Forgotten Americans*, edited by Julian Samora, 63–94. Notre Dame: University of Notre Dame Press, 1966.

Scruggs, Otey M. "Texas and the Bracero Program, 1942–1947." *Pacific Historical Review* 32 (August 1963): 251–264. Reprinted in *Mexican Workers in the United States: Historical and Political Perspectives*, edited by George C. Kiser and Martha Woody Kiser, 85–97. Albuquerque: University of New Mexico Press, 1979.

________. "The United States, Mexico, and the Wetback." *Pacific Historical Review* 30 (1961): 149–164.

Seaholm, Megan. "Leonidas González Cigarroa." In *The New Handbook of Texas,* edited by Ron Tyler, Douglas E. Barnett, Roy R. Barkley, Penelope C. Anderson, and Mark F. Odintz, vol. 2, 110. Austin: Texas State Historical Association, 1996.

Segulia, Frances. "Mi Jacalito." *Password* 21 (Fall 1976): 97–98.

Shapiro, Harold A. "The Workers of San Antonio, Texas, 1900–1940." Ph.D. dissertation, University of Texas, Austin, 1952.

________. "The Pecan Shellers of San Antonio, Texas." *Southwestern Social Science Quarterly* 32 (1952): 229–244.

Sharpe, Patricia. "Ninfa Laurenzo." *Texas Monthly* (August 2001): 40.

Shinn, Vara D. "Social and Economic Status of the Mexicans in Texas Since 1910." Master's thesis, University of Chicago, 1930.

Shockley, John S. "Landless Laborers and the Chicano Movement in South Texas." In *Forging Nations: A Comparative View of Rural Ferment and Revolt*, edited by

Joseph Spielberg and Scott Whiteford, 128–149. Lansing: Michigan State University Press, 1976.

Sisneros, Samuel E. "The Casasola Legacy in El Paso." *Password* 47 (Spring 2002): 23–28.

Sklair, Leslie. *Assembling for Development: The Maquila Industry in Mexico and the United States*. Boston: Unwin Hyman, 1989.

________. "The Maquila Industry and the Creation of a Transnational Capitalist Class in the United States-Mexico Border Region." In *Changing Boundaries in the Americas: New Perspectives on the U.S.-Mexican, Central American, and South American Borders*, edited by Lawrence A. Herzog, 69–88. San Diego: Center for U.S.-Mexican Studies, 1992.

Skrabanek, R. L., and Aura Rapton. *Occupational Change Among Spanish Americans in Atascosa County and San Antonio, Texas*. College Station: Texas A&M University Press, 1966.

Smith, Anita Torres. "Shearing: *La Trasquila*, in the First Half of the Twentieth Century." *Journal of Big Bend Studies* 6 (1994): 99–117.

Smith, Henry M. "Farm Labor in the Lower Rio Grande Valley of Texas." Master's thesis, Texas A&I University, 1947.

Solórzano-Torres, Rosalía. "Women, Labor, and the U.S.-Mexico Border: Mexican Maids in El Paso, Texas." In *Mexicanas at Work in the United States*, edited by Margarita Melville, 75–83. Houston: Mexican American Studies Program, University of Houston, 1988.

Stewart, Kenneth L., and Arnoldo De León. *Not Room Enough: Mexicans, Anglos, and Socioeconomic Change in Texas, 1850–1900*. Albuquerque: University of New Mexico Press, 1993.

________. "Education, Literacy, and Occupational Structure in West Texas, 1860–1900." *West Texas Historical Association Yearbook* 60 (1984): 127–143.

Stoddard, Ellwyn R. *Patterns of Poverty Along the U.S.-Mexico Border*. El Paso: Center for Inter-American Studies, University of Texas at El Paso, 1978.

________. "Illegal Mexican Labor in the Borderlands: Institutionalized Support of an Unlawful Practice." *Pacific Sociological Review* 19.2 (1976): 175–210.

________. "Texas Higher Education and Border Funding Inequities: Implication for Border Universities and Transborder Cooperation." *Río Bravo* 2.1 (1992): 54–75.

Stoddard, Ellwyn R., and John Hedderson. *Patterns of Poverty along the U.S.-Mexico Border*. Las Cruces: Joint Border Research Institute, New Mexico State University, 1989.

Sturgeon, Shirley H. "Commerce in the Texan Empresario Colonies." Master's thesis, Northwestern University, 1943.

Sweeney, Paul. "AMATEX in Juárez: A Squalid Business." *Texas Observer* (June 9, 1978): 8–10.

Taylor, Anna J. "New Mexican Pastores and Priests in the Texas Panhandle, 1887–1915." *Panhandle Plains Historical Review* 57 (1984): 65–80.

________. "*Pastores* in the Texas Panhandle, 1876–1884." *Hale County History* 10.1 (1980): 1–49.

Taylor, Paul S. *Mexican Labor in the United States: Dimmit County, Winter Garden, South Texas.* Berkeley: Publications in Economics, University of California, 1930.

________. "Mexicans North of the Rio Grande." *Survey* 66 (May 1, 1931): 135–140, 197, 200–202, 205.

Thompson, John M. "Mobility, Income, and Utilization of Mexican American Manpower in Lubbock, Texas, 1960–1970." D.B.A. dissertation, Texas Tech University, 1972.

Thonhoff, Robert H. "Our Spanish Legacy of Ranching in Texas." *South Texas Studies* 4 (1993): 1–11.

Tiefenbacher, John P. "A Rio Grande 'Brew': Agriculture, Industry, and Water Quality in the Lower Rio Grande Valley." In *Fluid Arguments: Five Centuries of Western Water Conflict*, edited by Char Miller, 178–200. Tucson: University of Arizona Press, 2001.

Tinsley, Dillard B. "Cultural Keys to Understanding Mexican American Business Employees." *Journal of the American Studies Association of Texas* 13 (1982): 14–21.

Todes, Jay L. "Use of Wetbacks in Open Shop Campaigns in San Antonio." Master's thesis, University of Texas, Austin, 1949.

Torres-Raines, Rosario. "The Mexican American Woman and Work: Intergenerational Perspectives of Comparative Ethnic Groups." In *Mexicanas At Work in the United States*, edited by Margarita B. Melville, 33–46. Houston: Mexican American Studies Program, University of Houston, 1988.

Towers, George William. "Colonia Formation and Economic Restructuring in El Paso, Texas." Ph.D. dissertation, University of Arizona, 1991.

Trinidad, David. "Rebecca Flores Harrington: Life under the Texas Hot Sun." *Tejas* (Spring 1995): 37.

Tubbs, Lowell L. "A Survey of the Problems of the Migratory Mexicans." Master's thesis, University of Texas, Austin, 1952.

________. "Texas Migrants." In *Readings on La Raza: The Twentieth Century*, edited by Matt S. Meier and Feliciano Rivera, 173–182. New York: Hill and Wang, 1974.

Tunnell, Curtis. *Wax, Men, and Money: A Historical and Archeological Study of Candelilla Wax Camps along the Rio Grande Border of Texas*. Austin: Texas Historical Commission, 1981.

Ugalde, Antonio. *The Urbanization Process of a Poor Mexican Neighborhood*. Austin: University of Texas Press, 1974.

Underwood, Jerald. "The Vaquero." In *Vaqueros, Cowboys, and Buckaroos*, edited by Lawrence Clayton, Jim Hoy, and Jerald Underwood, 1–65. Austin: University of Texas Press, 2001.

________. "The Vaquero in South Texas: An Interpretation by John Houghton Allen." *West Texas Historical Association Yearbook* 68 (1992): 93–99.

Upham, W. Kennedy, and David E. Wright. *Poverty among Spanish Americans in Texas: Low-Income Families in a Minority Group*. College Station: Texas Agricultural Experiment Station, 1966.

Vaccaro, Georgiana Chenault. "Identifying and Acquiring Information Needed to Work Successfully without Formal Training: Perceptions of Selected Immigrant Latino Workers in Texas." Ph.D. dissertation, Texas A&M University, 1998.

Valdez, Avelardo. *The Impact of the North American Free Trade Agreement on Mexican American Workers in South Texas*. San Antonio: Hispanic Research Center, University of Texas at San Antonio, 1994.

Valle, Isabel. *Fields of Toil: A Migrant Family's Journey*. Pullman: Washington State University Press, 1994.

Vargas, Zaragosa. "Emma Tenayuca: Labor and Civil Rights Organizer of 1930s San Antonio." In *The Human Tradition in America Between the Wars, 1920–1945*, edited by Donald W. Whisenhunt, 169–184. Wilmington, Del.: Scholarly Resources, 2002.

________. "Tejana Radical: Emma Tenayuca and the San Antonio Labor Movement." *Pacific Historical Review* 66 (1997): 553–580.

Vassberg, David Erland. "The Use of Mexicans and Mexican Americans as an Agricultural Work Force in the Lower Rio Grande Valley of Texas." Master's thesis, University of Texas, Austin, 1966.

Vega, Arturo. "Mexican Americans and Internal Colonialism in Texas." Master's thesis, St. Mary's University, 1983.

Villarreal, Jesús. "Chicano Earnings in Texas." Master's thesis, University of Texas at Austin, 1979.

Villarreal, Roberto M. "The Mexican American Vaqueros of the Kenedy Ranch: A Social History." Master's thesis, Texas A&I University, 1972.

Waddell, Jack. "Value Orientations of Young Mexican-American Males as Reflected in Their Work Patterns and Employment Preferences." Master's thesis, University of Texas, Austin, 1962.

Walcott, Red. "The Latino Petro-Baron." *Nuestro* 1 (July 1977): 21–24.

Walker, David Wayne. "Kinship, Business, and Politics: The Martínez del Río Family in Mexico, 1824–1864." Ph.D. dissertation, University of Chicago, 1981.

Walker, Kenneth P. "The Pecan Shellers of San Antonio and Mechanization." *Southwestern Historical Quarterly* 69 (July 1965): 44–58.

Waters, Lawrence Leslie. "Transient Mexican Agricultural Labor." *Southwestern Social Science Quarterly* 22 (June 1941): 49–66.

Weaver, Charles Morris. "Comparative Study of the Job Performance of Spanish-surname Officers in San Antonio, Texas." *Phylon* 30 (Spring 1969): 27–33.

Weaver, C. M., and N. D. Glenn. "The Job Performance of Mexican Americans." *Sociology and Social Research* 54.4 (1970): 477–494.

Webb, James L., Mariita C. Conley, Luis C. de Gregorio-Rocasolano, Charles Keil, and Roy Van Cleve. *The Citrus Labor Market of the Lower Rio Grande Valley of*

Texas: A Study of Labor Utilization Problems. Austin: Center for the Study of Human Resources, University of Texas at Austin, 1975.

Welch, Carol J. "Income Inequality Among Mexican-Americans and Blacks in an El Paso Low Income Area: A Structural Analysis." Master's thesis, University of Texas at El Paso, 1978.

West, Richard. "Our Lady of the Taco (Tula Borunda Gutiérrez)." *Texas Monthly* 14 (January 1986): 198.

Whiteford, Linda. "Mexican American Women as Innovators." In *Twice a Minority: Mexican American Women*, edited by Margarita Melville, 109–126. St. Louis: C. V. Mosby Company, 1980.

Winn, Charles Carr. "Mexican Americans in the Texas Labor Movement." Ph.D. dissertation, Texas Christian University, 1972.

Wolff, Henry Jr. "Mission Espiritu Santo: First Great Cattle Ranch of Texas." *Journal of South Texas* 12 (1999): 108–120.

Wright, Paul. "Work Among Anglos and Hispanics in the Big Bend, 1910." *West Texas Historical Association Yearbook* 71 (1995): 21–35.

Young, Andrew H. "Life and Labor on the King Ranch, 1853–1900." Master's thesis, Texas A&M University-Kingsville, 1992.

________. "Life and Labor on the King Ranch: The Early Years, 1853–1865." *Journal of South Texas* 6 (1993): 54–71.

Zamora, Emilio. *The World of the Mexican Worker in Texas*. College Station: Texas A&M University Press, 1993.

________. *El Movimiento Obrero Mexicano en el Sur de Texas, 1900–1920*. Mexico, D.F.: Secretaría de Educación Público, 1986.

________. "Mexican Labor Activity in South Texas, 1900–1920." Ph.D. dissertation, University of Texas at Austin, 1983.

________. "Chicano Socialist Labor Activity in Texas, 1900–1920." *Aztlán* 6 (Summer 1976): 221–238.

________. "The Failed Promise of Wartime Opportunity for Mexicans in the Texas Oil Industry." *Southwestern Historical Quarterly* 95 (Winter 1995): 323–350.

________. "Labor Formation, Community, and Politics: The Mexican Working Class in Texas, 1900–1945." In *Border Crossings: Mexican and Mexican-American Workers*, edited by John Mason Hart, 139–162. Wilmington, Del.: Scholarly Resources, 1998.

________. "Sara Estela Ramírez: A Note on Research in Progress." *Hembra: Hermanas en Movimiento Brotando Raices de Aztlán* (Spring 1976).

________. "Sara Estela Ramírez: Una Rosa en el Movimiento." In *Mexican Women in the United States: Struggles Past and Present*, edited by Magdalena Mora and Adelaida R. Del Castillo, 163–170. Los Angeles: Chicano Studies Research Center, 1980.

Zavaleta, Antonio N. "'The Twin Cities': A Historical Synthesis of the Socio-Economic Interdependence of the Brownsville-Matamoros Border Community." In *Studies in Brownsville History*, edited by Milo Kearney, 125–173. Brownsville, Tex.: Pan American University at Brownsville, 1986.

12. EDUCATION

The studies listed in the section on education depict the gamut of Tejano educational experiences and ideas from Spanish colonial beginnings to the present. The aspects of Tejano education that are covered by the authors in this section include the battles for equity in Texas education, favorable and unfavorable educational experiences, educational philosophy, the Anglo-dominated record of inferior and separate schooling, as well as the goals of Mexican Americans for education in Texas.

Sister Superior Alma and students in classroom at Mission Espada, San Antonio, Texas, January 12, 1941.
The Institute of Texan Cultures at UTSA, No. L-2637-I
The San Antonio Light *Collection*

Abreo, Rosa María. "A History of Rio Grande City, Texas High School, 1960–1969." Ph.D. dissertation, University of Texas at Austin, 2001.

Acevedo, Baltazar A. Jr. "Socialization: The Mexican American Mid-Level Administrator in Texas Institutions of Higher Education." Ph.D. dissertation, University of Texas at Austin, 1979.

Acosta, Teresa Palomo. "*Edgewood ISD v. Kirby*." In *The New Handbook of Texas,* edited by Ron Tyler, Douglas E. Barnett, Roy R. Barkley, Penelope C. Anderson, and Mark F. Odintz, vol. 2, 784–785. Austin: Texas State Historical Association, 1996.

Adam, Michelle. "Two Decades of Energy and Vision: Pan Am President Miguel Nevarez." *Hispanic Outlook in Higher Education* 11 (December 4, 2000): 6–8.

Adams, Aida Medina. "Learning Preference and Mexican American Students: Considering the Significance of Acculturation, Socioeconomic Status, and Academic Performance." Ph.D. dissertation, Texas Tech University, 2000.

Adams, Ruth Loraine. "Inter-Group Relations in a Class in the Carrizo Springs Public Schools." Master's thesis, University of Texas, Austin, 1949.

Adkins, Patricia G. "Socio-Cultural Factors in Educating Disadvantaged Children." In *Education of the Spanish-Speaking Urban Child: A Book of Readings*, edited by Earl J. Ogletree and David García, 209–214. Springfield, Ill.: Charles C. Thomas Publisher, 1975.

Adkins, Patricia G., and R. G. Young. "Cultural Perceptions in the Treatment of Handicapped School Children of Mexican American Parentage." *Journal of Research and Development in Education* 9.4 (1976): 83–90.

Aguirre, R. W. "The Effect of a Parental Involvement Program on Self Concepts and School Attitudes of Mexican American First Grade Children." Ph.D. dissertation, University of Houston, 1972.

Akery, Nicholas. "An Exploratory Study of the Education of Spanish-speaking Children in the Primary Grades of Edinburg, Texas." Master's thesis, University of Texas, Austin, 1955.

Alanis, Iliana. "A Descriptive Analysis of a Texas Two-Way Bilingual Program and Its Effects on Fifth-Grade Academic and Linguistic Achievement." Ph.D. dissertation, University of Texas at Austin, 1998.

Alaniz, Rosalee Renee. "Self-esteem, Assertion, and Change Orientation among Hispanic College Students According to Birth Order and Gender." Master's thesis, Texas A&M University-Kingsville, 1997.

Alcalá, Carlos M., and Jorge C. Rangel. "De Jure Segregation of Chicanos in Texas Schools." *Harvard Civil Rights and Civil Liberties Law Review* 7 (March 1972): 307–391.

Alejandro, Rubén. "Influence Strategies used by an Elementary School Principal, Teachers, and Support Staff to Involve Low Socio-economic Mexican-American Parents in Their Children's Education." Ph.D. dissertation, University of Texas at Austin, 2000.

Alexander, Elizabeth Urban. "Who Pays for the Schools? *San Antonio ISD v. Rodríguez* and the Politics of School Finance." *Proteus: A Journal of Ideas* 13 (Spring 1996): 53–57.

Allsup, V. Carl. "*Cisneros v. Corpus Christi ISD*." In *The New Handbook of Texas,* edited by Ron Tyler, Douglas E. Barnett, Roy R. Barkley, Penelope C. Anderson, and Mark F. Odintz, vol. 2, 113. Austin: Texas State Historical Association, 1996.

________. "*Delgado v. Bastrop ISD*." In *The New Handbook of Texas,* edited by Ron Tyler, Douglas E. Barnett, Roy R. Barkley, Penelope C. Anderson, and Mark F. Odintz, vol. 2, 574–575. Austin: Texas State Historical Association, 1996.

________. "Education is Our Freedom: The American G.I. Forum and the Mexican American School Segregation in Texas, 1948–1957." *Aztlán,* 8 (Spring 1977): 27–50.

________. "*Hernández v. Driscoll CISD*." In *The New Handbook of Texas,* edited by Ron Tyler, Douglas E. Barnett, Roy R. Barkley, Penelope C. Anderson, and Mark F. Odintz, vol. 3, 573–574. Austin: Texas State Historical Association, 1996.

Almaráz, Félix D. Jr. "Carlos Eduardo Castañeda." In *The New Handbook of Texas,* edited by Ron Tyler, Douglas E. Barnett, Roy R. Barkley, Penelope C. Anderson, and Mark F. Odintz, vol. 1, 1016. Austin: Texas State Historical Association, 1996.

________. "Rediscovering a Forgotten Rationale [for Bilingual Education]." *Texas Outlook* 60 (November 1976): 34–35.

Almendariz, Arturo. "Profile of a School Dropout in the Odem-Edroy Independent School District." Ed.D. dissertation, Texas A&M University, 1992.

Aloglah, Omar Mustafa. "A Comparative Study of Self-esteem Between Low-income Hispanic Bilingual and Monolingual Urban Elementary Students." Ed.D. dissertation, Texas Southern University, 1993.

Alston, H. L., and E. B. Doughtie. "Correspondence of Constructs Measured by the Kindergarten Screening Inventory by Sex and Ethnic Groups." *Psychology in the Schools* 12.4 (1975): 428–429.

Álvarez, Salvador. "The Influence of Phonological Characteristics upon Orthography in Mexican-American Second Graders." Ph.D. dissertation, University of Texas at Austin, 1973.

Amastae, Jon. "Language Shift and Maintenance in the Lower Rio Grande Valley of Southern Texas." In *Bilingualism and Language Contact: Spanish, English, and Native American Languages*, edited by Florence Barkin, Elizabeth A. Brandt, and Jacob Ornstein-Galicia, 261–277. New York: Teachers College, Columbia University, 1982.

Anderson, Mary. *A Comparative Study of the English Speaking and Spanish Speaking Beginners in the Public Schools.* San Francisco: R&E Research Associates, 1976.

________. "A Comparative Study of the English Speaking and Spanish Speaking Beginners in the Public Schools." Master's thesis, University of Texas, Austin, 1951.

Andersson, Theodore. "A New Focus on the Bilingual Child." In *Educating the Mexican American*, edited by Henry Sioux Johnson and William J. Hernández-M, 235–242. Valley Forge, Penn.: Judson Press, 1970.

Armstrong, Robert Lee. "A Descriptive Comparison among Black, Brown, and White Youth in Vocational Education in Texas." Ed.D. dissertation, University of Houston, 1981.

Ashburn, Katherine Travis. "History of the Methodist Educational Work among the Mexicans in Texas." Master's thesis, Texas Christian University, 1934.

Ash, Marilyn Louise Holtze. "The Relationship of Family and School Decision-Making Structures to Political Efficacy in Anglo-American, Mexican-American, and Mexican Upper Level Grade School Children." Ph.D. dissertation, University of Arizona, 1980.

Ashton, Price R. "The Fourteenth Amendment and the Education of Latin American Children in Texas." Master's thesis, University of Texas, Austin, 1949.

Atkinson, Rosa M. "The Educational Retardation of the Spanish-speaking Child and Recommendations for Remediation." Master thesis, University of Texas, Austin, 1953.

Atwood, Patricia Beaty. "Self-Concept and Its Relation to Acculturation and Oral Language Acquisition among Secondary Mexican-American Students." Ph.D. dissertation, Texas Woman's University, 2001.

Ayala-Scheuneman, María de Jesús. "A Brief History of Three Presbyterian Educational Institutions in South Texas." *Journal of South Texas* 3 (Spring 1991): 66–82.

Baeza, Abelardo. "La Escuela Del Barrio: A History of Alpine's Centennial School, 1936–1969." *Journal of Big Bend Studies* 4 (1992): 131–145.

________. "La Escuela de Don Clemente: History of the Madero Ward Elementary School in Alpine, Texas, 1910–1936." *Journal of Big Bend Studies* 7 (1995): 41–53.

Baez, Jo Anne Marie. "Self-concept and Academic Achievement, Controlling Acculturation, in Mexican-American and Anglo Elementary Students from Texas." Ph.D. dissertation, Central Michigan University, 1997.

Barrera, María W. "A Survey on the Status of Reading in Spanish in the First Grades of Texas Schools Involved in Bilingual Education Programs, with Emphasis on Scheduling, Language Usage, Materials, and the Methodology for Initial Reading." Ed.D. dissertation, Texas A&I University, 1978.

Baugh, Lila. "A Study of Pre-School Vocabulary of Spanish-speaking Children." Master's thesis, University of Texas, Austin, 1933.

Bauman, Raquel Portillo. "A Study of Mexican American Women's Perceptions of Factors that Influence Academic and Professional Goal Attainment." Ed.D. dissertation, University of Houston, 1984.

Bean, Athena Hafner. "A Comparison of the Academic Success of Hispanic Students Who Entered Selected Texas Community Colleges with a GED or a High School Diploma." Ed.D. dissertation, Baylor University, 1999.

Beckett, Amie Ann Mitchell. "Texas Prekindergarten Teachers' Knowledge and Beliefs about the Development of Early Childhood Bilingualism: A Study of Teachers in Districts with Limited and Large Populations of Hispanic Students." Ph.D. dissertation, University of Texas at Austin, 1993.

Beherfall, Lester. "Some Linguistic Problems of the Spanish-speaking People of Texas." *Modern Language Journal* 42 (February 1958): 87–90.

Benavides, Alda Treviño. "An Analysis of Key Leadership Behaviors of the Principal in a High-performing Elementary School Serving Mexican American Children in South Texas." Ed.D. dissertation, University of Texas–Pan American, 2001.

Benefield, Linda Lee. "Determinants of Course Withdrawal and Subsequent Term Enrollment of Adult Women in a Community College: A Cross-cultural Comparison." Ph.D. dissertation, Texas A&M University, 1991.

Benítez, Carrahlee. "A Study of Some Non-Standard English Features in the Speech of Seventh-grade Mexican-Americans Enrolled in a Remedial Reading Program in an Urban Community of South Texas." Master's thesis, Texas A&I University, 1970.

Benítiz, Mario, et al. *The Status of Foreign Language Programs in the Largest Schools of South Texas during the Spring of 1967*. Kingsville, Tex.: Texas A&I University, 1968.

Bennett, Catherine. "The History of Education in Laredo, Texas, to 1870." Master's thesis, University of Texas, Austin, 1939.

Benson, Robert Alan. "Economically Disadvantaged Successful Schools: An Analysis of Teaching Practices." Ph.D. dissertation, University of Texas at Austin, 1996.

Berger, Max. "Education in Texas during the Spanish and Mexican Periods." *Southwestern Historical Quarterly* 51 (July 1947): 41–53.

Berlanga, David Jr. "The English and Spanish of Mexican-American Bilingual Teachers." Ed.D. dissertation, Texas A&I University, 1978.

Bernal, Joe J. "A Great American (George I. Sánchez)." In *Humanidad: Essays in Honor of George I. Sánchez*, edited by Américo Paredes, 14–18. Los Angeles: Chicano Studies Center Publications, 1977.

Bernal, Joseph. "The Role of the State." In *Educating the Mexican American*, edited by Henry Sioux Johnson and William J. Hernández-M, 363–368. Valley Forge, Penn.: Judson Press, 1970.

Birtchet, Amy Lee. "Albar Antonio Peña." In *The New Handbook of Texas*, edited by Ron Tyler, Douglas E. Barnett, Roy R. Barkley, Penelope C. Anderson, and Mark F. Odintz, vol. 5, 133. Austin: Texas State Historical Association, 1996.

Black, Mary S. "Historical Factors Affecting Mexican American Parental Involvement and Educational Outcomes: The Texas Environment from 1910–1996." Ed.D. dissertation, Harvard University, 1996.

Blanco, George M. "Teaching Spanish as a Standard Dialect in Grades 7–12: A Rationale for a Fundamental Skills Approach." Ph.D. dissertation, University of Texas at Austin, 1971.

Blanton, Carlos Kevin. "From Intellectual Deficiency to Cultural Deficiency: Mexican Americans, Testing, and School Policy in the American Southwest, 1920–1940." *Pacific Historical Review* 72 (February 2003): 39–62.

________. "The Strange Career of Bilingual Education: A History of the Political and Pedagogical Debate Over Language Instruction in American Public Education, 1890–1990." Ph.D. dissertation, Rice University, 1999.

Blevins, Hubert W. Jr. "A Compartive Study of Mexican American and Anglo Dropouts in a Large Metropolitan School District in Texas." Ed.D. dissertation, North Texas State University, 1975.

Bliven, Brent David. “An Integrative Model of Middle School Student Utilization of School-based Health Services.” Ph.D. dissertation, University of Texas at Austin, 1996.

Block, Billy Burel. “Analysis of Self-concepts of Selected School Personnel and Mexican-American Students in School Systems of Texas Education Agency’s Region XVII.” Ed.D. dissertation, Texas Tech University, 1977.

Bouteba, Paul M. “Designing Chicano Heritage Materials.” Ed.D. dissertation, University of Houston, 1982.

Bowen, J. Donald. “Local Standards and Spanish in the Southwest.” In *Studies in Language and Linguistics, 1972–1973*, edited by Ralph W. Ewton Jr. and Jacob Ornstein, 153–164. El Paso: Texas Western Press, 1973.

Bowers, Gladina. “Mexican Education in East Donna.” *Texas Outlook* 15 (March 1931): 29–33.

Box, W. J. “To Determine the Factors Influencing the Attendance of Spanish-Culture Children in Raymondville Elementary Schools.” Master’s thesis, Texas A&I University at Kingsville, 1952.

Boyd, Molly Henderson. “Student Satisfaction: An Evaluation of the Overall Community College Educational Experience.” Ph.D. dissertation, New Mexico State University, 1982.

Brackenridge, J. T. “Escuela Con Dos Lenguas: School, San Antonio, Texas.” *Instructor* 78 (February 1969): 56–58.

Brantley, Harold C. “The Implementation of a Program of Bilingual Instruction.” In *Educating the Mexican American*, edited by Henry Sioux Johnson and William J. Hernández-M, 250–256. Valley Forge, Penn.: Judson Press, 1970.

Brattin, Terry H. “The Impact of Mandatory Placement and Remediation on Persistence and Academic Achievement: A Study of the Texas Academic Skills Program at a State Technical College.” Ed.D. dissertation, University of Houston, 1993.

Braudaway, Douglas. “Desegregation in Del Rio.” *Journal of South Texas* 13 (2000): 240–265.

Brawner, M. R. “Migration and Educational Achievement of Mexican Americans.” *Social Science Quarterly* 53.4 (1973): 727–737.

Bredegg, Patricia Sosa. “Portrayal of Hispanics in State Adopted Textbooks, Grades One, Three, and Five: A Content Analysis.” Ed.D. dissertation, Texas A&M University-Commerce, 2001.

Brewer, Samuel Aaron Jr. “Latin Americans in Texas High Schools.” Master’s thesis, University of Texas, Austin, 1952.

Browning, Horace N. “A Comparison of the Spanish-Speaking and English-Speaking Children in Nine Schools Over a Four-Year Period.” Master’s thesis, University of Texas, Austin, 1944.

Brown, Perry M. “An Interpretive Analysis of the Economic and Educational Status of Latin Americans in Texas, with Emphasis on Ten Basic Factors Underlying an Approach to an Improvement Program of Occupational Guidance, Training, and Adjustment for Secondary Schools.” Ph.D. dissertation, University of Texas, Austin, 1942.

Brown Wrinkle, Mary H. "Pitch Improvement in Anglos and Latin American Children." Master's thesis, University of Texas, Austin, 1950.

Brussell, C. B. *Disadvantaged Mexican American Children and Early Educational Experience*. Austin: Southwest Educational Development Corporation, 1968.

Bryant, Katherine Fagan. "A Homemaking Program for Spanish Girls of Kleberg County, Planned in Accordance with Findings from a Study of Their Home Life." Master's thesis, Texas A&I University at Kingsville, 1944.

Bussey, Jo Ann Keslar. "A Comparative Study of Phonological Variation Among First, Second, and Third Grade Linguistically Different Children in Five San Antonio (Texas) Schools: 1970." Ph.D. dissertation, University of Texas at Austin, 1971.

Cabaza, Berta. "The Spanish Language in Texas, No. 2. Cameron and Willacy Counties." Master's thesis, University of Texas, Austin, 1950.

Cabrera, Vicente Vargas Jr. "Factors Influencing First-Generation Mexican-American College Students' Persistence at the University of Texas at Austin." Ph.D. dissertation, University of Texas at Austin, 1998.

Calderón, Carlos I. "The Education of Spanish-speaking Children in Edcouch-Elsa, Texas." Master's thesis, University of Texas, Austin, 1950.

Cannon, John Robert. "Si se puede!: A Critical Qualitative Study of Mexican-American Female Business Graduates." Ed.D. dissertation, University of Houston, 2000.

Cantú, I. S. "The Effects of Family Characteristics, Parental Influence, Language Spoken, School Experience, and Self-Motivation on the Level of Educational Achievement among Mexican Americans." Ph.D. dissertation, University of Michigan, 1975.

Caples, Minerva López. "A Content Analysis of the Mexican Americans in the BASAL Readers, Grades 1–6, Adopted by the State of Texas." Ed.D. dissertation, Texas A&I University, 1979.

Caples-Osorio, Ronald W. "Educational Aspirations of Selected Mexican American Elementary School Children Enrolled in Bilingual Education." Ed.D. dissertation, Texas A&I University, 1979.

Carbo, Rosie. "From Migrant Worker to Professor of the Year." *Hispanic Outlook in Higher Education* 7 (September 27, 1996): 15–16.

________. "The Politics of Caring—Or, Not Caring: The 'Subtractive Schooling' of Chicano Children." *Hispanic Outlook in Higher Education* 10 (October 8, 1999): 14–15.

Carlson, Paul Edward. "Investigation of Bias in the Diagnosis of Behaviorally-Disordered Mexican-American Children Using the Social Behavior Assessment Scale." Ph.D. dissertation, Ohio State University, 1983.

Carroll, Naomi Eleta White. "Undergraduate Retention Programs for Minorities: A Case Study." Ph.D. dissertation, University of Texas at Austin, 1998.

Carroll, Patrick J. "Tejano Living and Educational Conditions in World War II South Texas." *South Texas Studies* 5 (1994): 82–103.

Carrow, E. "Comprehension of English and Spanish by Preschool Mexican American Children." *Modern Language Journal* 55.5 (1971): 299–306.

________. "Linguistic Functions of Bilingual and Monolingual Children." *Journal of Speech and Hearing Disorders* 26.3 (1957): 371–380.

Carter, Thomas P. "Preparing Teachers for Mexican-American Children." In *Educating the Mexican American*, edited by Henry Sioux Johnson and William J. Hernández-M, 193–209. Valley Forge, Penn.: Judson Press, 1970.

Carter, Thomas P., and R. D. Segura. *Mexican Americans in School: A Decade of Change*. Princeton, N.J.: College Entrance Examination Board, 1979.

Casso, Henry J. "*Ya Basta*, The Siesta is Over." In *Educating the Mexican American*, edited by Henry Sioux Johnson and William J. Hernández-M, 93–99. Valley Forge, Penn.: Judson Press, 1970.

Castañeda, Carlos E. "Broadening the Concept of History Teaching in Texas." *Proceedings of Inter American Conference on Intellectual Exchange* (1943): 97–108.

________. "Latin America's First Great Educator." *Current History* 22 (May 1925): 223–225.

________. "Modern Language Instruction in American Colleges, 1779–1800." *Catholic Educational Review* 23 (January 1925): 3–9, 92–106.

________. "The Oldest University in America." *Pan-American Magazine* 43 (July 1930): 54–57.

Castillo, Henrietta A. "Educational Handicaps of Latin American Children in the American Schools." Master's thesis, St. Mary's University, 1941.

Cerda, Gilberto. "The Spanish Language in Texas, No. 1. Val Verde, Edwards, and Kinney Counties." Master's thesis, University of Texas, Austin, 1950.

Cerda, Gilberto, et al. *Vocabulario Español de Texas*. Austin: University of Texas Press, 1970.

Cervantes, Alfonso. "A Selected Vocabulary of Anglicisms Used by the Spanish-speaking First Grade Students of the Elementary Schools of Del Rio, Texas." Master's thesis, Southwest Texas State University, 1973.

Chabrán, Richard, and Rafael Chabrán, eds. "Cisneros v. Corpus Christi Independent School District." In *The Latino Encyclopedia*, edited by Richard Chabrán and Rafael Chabrán, vol. 2, 321. New York: Marshall Cavendish, 1996.

________. "*San Antonio Independent School District* v. *Rodríguez*." In *The Latino Encyclopedia*, edited by Richard Chabrán and Rafael Chabrán, vol. 5, 1422. New York: Marshall Cavendish, 1996.

Chaston, John M. "Aspect Choice in Preterit and Imperfect Usage in the Speech of Mexican-American College Students in Texas: A Sociolinguistic Approach." Ph.D. dissertation, University of Texas at Austin, 1987.

________. "Sociolinguistic Analysis of Gender Agreement in Article/Noun Combinations in Mexican American Spanish in Texas." *Bilingual Review/La Revista Bilingüe* 21.3 (1996): 195–202.

Chávez, David Julián. "Civic Education of the Spanish American." Master's thesis, University of Texas, Austin, 1950.

Childers, Jean. "Some Secondary Curriculum Considerations for Teaching Spanish to the Mexican Americans in Austin, Texas." Master's thesis, University of Texas at Austin, 1971.

Clark, Christian, et al. "Latino Researchers at UTEP: Using Intellect to Improve Society." *Hispanic Outlook in Higher Education* 9 (February 26, 1999): 11–13.

Clark, Madeline. "A Preliminary Survey of the Employment Possibilities of the Spanish-American Girls Receiving Commercial Training in the San Antonio Secondary Schools." Master's thesis, University of Texas, Austin, 1936.

Clayton, Frances. "A Study of the Reading of Latin and Anglo Students at Texas Western College." Master's thesis, University of Texas, Austin, 1954.

Cmajdalka, Sandra Lynn. "Problem Solving Difficulties in Mathematics: Examining Five Process Skills in Multidigit Addition for Hispanic Limited English Proficient Students." Ph.D. dissertation, Texas A&M University, 1999.

Coan, Barlett E. "A Comparative Study of the American and Mexican Children in the 'Big Bend' Area for 1935–1936." Master's thesis, University of Texas, Austin, 1936.

Cobb, Albert Folsom. "Comparative Study of the Athletic Ability of Latin American and Anglo American Boys on a Junior High School Level." Master's thesis, University of Texas, Austin, 1952.

Coers, W. C. "Comparative Achievement of White and Mexican Junior High Pupils." *Peabody Journal of Education* 12.4 (1935): 157–162.

Coiner, Cynthia Gale. "Marketing Higher Education to Mexican-Americans: Identification of Successful Marketing Strategies and Tactics." Ph.D. dissertation, Old Dominion University, 1990.

Coltharp, Lurline H. "Bilingual Onomastics: A Case Study." In *Bilingualism in the Southwest*, edited by Paul R. Turner, 131–140. Tucson: University of Arizona Press, 1975.

Conner, Ruth Patton. "Some Community-Home-School Problems of Latin American Children in Austin, Texas." Master's thesis, University of Texas, Austin, 1949.

Coole, Ruth Musgrave. "A Comparison of Anglo-American and Latin-American Girls in Grades 5–11, with Reference to their Vocational, Academic, and Recreational Preferences and Aversions." Master's thesis, University of Texas, Austin, 1937.

Coon, Ruby Irene. "A History of the Teaching of Spanish in Texas." Master's thesis, University of Texas, Austin, 1930.

Cornejo, Ricardo J. "Bilingualism: Study of the Lexicon of the Five-Year-Old Spanish-Speaking Children of Texas." Ph.D. dissertation, University of Texas at Austin, 1969.

________. "The Acquisition of Lexicon in the Speech of Bilingual Children." In *Bilingualism in the Southwest*, edited by Paul R. Turner, 67–93. Tucson: University of Arizona Press, 1975.

Cortéz, Emiliano Carlos. "Teaching the Short Story in Spanish: Literary Analysis and Commentary." Ph.D. dissertation, University of North Texas, 1995.

Cox, Isaac Joslin. “Educational Efforts in San Fernando de Béxar.” *Southwestern Historical Quarterly* 6 (July 1902): 27–63.

Cromack, Isabel C. “Latin Americans: A Minority Group in the Austin Public Schools.” Master’s thesis, University of Texas, Austin, 1949.

Cruz, Carlos Peña. “Implementation of Bilingual Education Programs in South Texas.” Ed.D. dissertation, Texas A&M University-Kingsville, 1995.

Cruz, María Angelita. “Spanish-speaking Children’s Expressed Attitudes Toward Money Values.” Master’s thesis, University of Texas, Austin, 1942.

Cruz, Pablo Arnoldo. “The Leadership Actions of Principals in Schools that have Experienced Academic Success with Hispanic Students.” Ph.D. dissertation, University of Texas at Austin, 1995.

Curiel, H., J. A. Rosenthal, and H. G. Richeck. “Impacts of Bilingual Education on Secondary School Grades, Attendance, Rebellion, and Dropouts.” *Hispanic Journal of Behavioral Sciences* 8 (December 1986): 357–367.

Curiel, H., W. F. Stenning, and P. Cooper-Stenning. “Achieved Reading Level, Self-esteem, and Grades as Related to Length Exposure to Bilingual Education.” *Hispanic Journal of Behavioral Sciences* 2 (December 1980): 389–400.

Daly, Mary Ann (Beck). “The Educational Problem of the Mexican Migrants of Texas with Specific Reference to the Average Daily Attendance.” Master’s thesis, Southwest Texas State University, 1955.

Davenport, E. Lee. “A Comparative Study of Mexican and Non-Mexican Siblings.” Master’s thesis, University of Texas, Austin, 1931.

________. “The Intelligence Quotients of Mexican and Non-Mexican Siblings.” *School and Society* 36 (1932): 304–306.

Davidson, John Porterfield. “Language of Instruction in Adult Education.” Master’s thesis, University of Texas at Austin, 1973.

Davis, Edward Everett. *A Report on Illiteracy in Texas*. Austin: University of Texas Bulletin No. 2328, 1923.

________. *A Study of Rural Schools in Travis County*. Austin: University of Texas Bulletin No. 67, 1916.

Davis, Edward Everett, and C. T. Gray. *A Study of Rural Schools in Karnes County*. Austin: University of Texas Bulletin No. 2246, 1922.

Davis, Matthew Donald. “Herschel T. Manuel: The Doyen of Mexican American Education.” Ph.D. dissertation, University of Texas at Austin, 2000.

Deanda, R., and V. Lockett. “Introducing Black and Chicano Content into A Social Work Curriculum: A Recommendation.” *Social Work Education Reporter* 20.3 (1972): 28–36.

De los Santos, Alfredo G. Jr., Joaquín Montemayor, and Enrique Solis Jr. “Chicano Students in Higher Education: Access, Attribution, and Achievement.” *Aztlán* 14 (1983): 79–100.

Dennis, Kathleen Murphy. “Factors Contributing to Successful Examinee Performance on the Spanish EXCET.” Ed.D. dissertation, East Texas State University, 1994.

De Sales, Deanna Margaret. "Do Affirmative Action Programs Pay Off? A Case Study on the University of Texas at Austin Experience." Ph.D. dissertation, University of Texas at Austin, 1997.

Desiderio, Mike Francis. "Educational Qualifications of Middle-Grade School Teachers: What Principals of Schools along the Texas-Mexico Border Seek in New Hires." Ph.D. dissertation, Texas A&M University, 1997.

Dexter, Rawlins Parker. "Background Characteristics and Matriculation Rationale of Hispanic and Non-Hispanic Students in Selected Two-Year Colleges." Ph.D. dissertation, University of North Texas, 1992.

Díaz-Disa, Ignacio. "A Speech Survey of Eighty Spanish-speaking Children in Four Elementary Schools of Austin, Texas." Master's thesis, University of Texas, Austin, 1952.

Dietz, Roger. "The Art of Healing." *Hispanic Outlook in Higher Education* 7 (October 11, 1996): 14–15.

Dillon, David Andrew. "An Analysis of the Written Syntactic Maturity in English of Mexican-American Migrant Students." Master's thesis, Southwest Texas State University, 1972.

Doan, William F. "The Effect of Response Meaningfulness of Verbal Paired-Associate Learning in Anglo-American and Mexican American Fifth Grade Children." Master's thesis, University of Texas, Austin, 1966.

Dodd, Elmer Cecil. "A Comparison of Spanish-speaking and English-speaking Children in Brownsville, Texas." Master's thesis, University of Texas, Austin, 1930.

Doerr, Marvin Ferdinand. "Problems of Elimination of Mexican Pupils from School." Master's thesis, University of Texas, Austin, 1938.

Dorsey, Georgia Lee. "A History of the Education of Spanish-Speaking People in Texas." Master's thesis, North Texas State College, 1941.

Drennan, Davy Ceolece. "The Progress in Reading of Fourth Grade Spanish-speaking Pupils." Master's thesis, University of Texas, Austin, 1937.

Drennan, Orlena Pink. "The Progress in Reading of Second-Grade Spanish-speaking Pupils." Ph.D. dissertation, University of Texas, Austin, 1939.

Durán, Yvonne. "School Board Performance as Viewed by Superintendents and School Board Members." Ed.D. dissertation, Texas A&M University-Kingsville, 1996.

Elías-Olivares, Lucía Ernestina. "Ways of Speaking in a Chicano Community: A Sociolinguistic Approach." Ph.D. dissertation, University of Texas at Austin, 1976.

________. "Study of the Oral Spanish Vocabulary of Ten High School Mexican-American Students in Austin." Master's thesis, University of Texas at Austin, 1970.

Elms, James Edwin. "Attendance of Mexican and Anglo Students in Two Austin Texas Schools." Master's thesis, University of Texas, Austin, 1950.

Emerson, Barbara Lee Priest. "Latin Americans in the Secondary Schools of Bryan, Texas." Master's thesis, University of Texas, Austin, 1955.

Emerson, Ralph Waddell. "Education for the Mexican in Texas." Master's thesis, Southern Methodist University, 1929.

Ensle, Anne Louise Labay. "Involvement in Language-Minority Parents in Elementary Education: A Case Study." Ed.D. dissertation, University of Houston, 1996.

Escamilla, Mark Steven. "Factors Affecting African-American, Anglo, and Hispanic First-generation Community College Students, who have Persisted and Graduated from Four-year Institutions between 1990 and 2000." Ph.D. dissertation, University of Texas at Austin, 2001.

Escamilla, Pedro Manuel. "A Sociolinguistic Study of Modal Selection among Mexican-American College Students in Texas." Ph.D. dissertation, University of Texas at Austin, 1982.

Esmaeili, Ghanbar Ali. "A Comparison of Mathematics Performance of Mexican-American College Students Utilizing Web-based Instruction versus Traditional Instruction." Ed.D. dissertation, Texas A&M University-Kingsville, 2001.

Estes, Dwain M., ed. *Improving Educational Opportunities of the Mexican American*. Austin: Texas Education Agency, 1967.

Estrada, Rosa Omega. "A Study of the Attitudes of Texas Mexican American Women Toward Higher Education." Ed.D. dissertation, Baylor University, 1985.

Estrada, Veronica López. "Expecting the Best: Case Studies of Resilient Mexican-American Girls in a South Texas High School." Ph.D. dissertation, Ohio State University, 1997.

Evans, Phyllis Joyce Howell. "Word-Pair Discrimination and Imitation Abilities of Pre-School Economically-Disadvantaged Native-Spanish-Speaking Children." Ph.D. dissertation, University of Texas at Austin, 1971.

Fabricus, Valeda Clareen. "A Determination, Using Super's Career Development Theory, of the Nursing Career Preferences of Twelfth Grade Students in Health Occupation Courses in Texas." Ph.D. dissertation, University of North Texas, 1982.

Fan, Banson Seelai. "A Study of Selected Status Risk and Behavioral Risk Characteristics of Students in Two Texas Secondary Alternative Education Programs." Ed.D. dissertation, Baylor University, 2000.

Fassold, Mark A. J. "Disparate Impact Analyses of TAAS Scores and School Equality." *Hispanic Journal of Behavioral Sciences* 22 (November 2000): 460–480.

Feeley, Dorothy Louise Young. "Mexican Americans in Texas: A View of Their History and Education in the Texas Public Schools." Master's thesis, University of Texas at Austin, 1970.

Felice, L. G. "Mexican-American Self-Concept and Educational Achievement: The Effects of Economic Isolation and Socio-economic Deprivation." *Social Science Quarterly* 53.4 (1973): 716–726.

Ferguson, Ruthmarie Galaviz. "Physical Attractiveness, Sex, Ethnicity, Teacher Expectancy, Student Ability, and Language Grouping Impact on School Behavioral and Academic Outcomes." Ph.D. dissertation, Texas A&M University, 1985.

Finch, Barbara L. S. "Contrasting Portraits: *San Antonio* v. *Rodríguez* and the Emergent Equal Protection Ideal." Master's thesis, Rice University, 1998.

Fiol, John Joseph. "The Status of Counseling Services Offered to Elementary Mexican American Students in Selected School Districts in the State of Texas." Ed.D. dissertation, Texas A&I University, 1984.

Fisher, Alan Thomas. "English Proficiency of Beginning Elementary Spanish-Speaking Students." Ph.D. dissertation, University of Houston, 1973.

Floca, Kathryn Pricilla Haines. "The Legality of Chicano Education." Master's thesis, University of Texas at Austin, 1971.

Flores-Feist, María Celia. "A Comparative Study of Learning Styles of Hispanic and Anglo Chemistry Students." Ed.D. dissertation, Texas Tech University, 1995.

Flores, Felipe V., Robert F. Kane, and Félix Velarde-Muñoz. "Rights of Undocumented Children to Attend Public Schools in Texas." *Chicano Law Review* 4.1 (1977): 61–93.

Flores, Noé E. "A Study on the Status of Chicano Literature in Selected Texas Secondary Schools." Ed.D. dissertation, Texas A&I University, 1979.

Flores, Steve Méndez. "The Superintendent/Board Relationship and Its Role in the Improvement of Hispanic Student Achievement in an Exemplary Rated School District in Texas." Ph.D. dissertation, University of Texas at Austin, 2001.

Fogartie, Ruth Ann Douglas. "Spanish-Name People in Texas with Special Emphasis on Those Who are Students in Texas Colleges and Universities." Master's thesis, University of Texas, Austin, 1948.

Foley, Douglas E. *Learning Capitalist Culture: Deep in the Heart of Tejas*. Philadelphia: University of Pennsylvania Press, 1990.

________. "Legalistic and Personalistic Adaptations in a South Texas School." *Journal of Research and Development in Education* 9.4 (1976): 74–82.

________. "Reconsidering Anthropological Explanations of Ethnic School Failure." *Anthropology and Education Quarterly* 22 (March 1991): 60–86.

Foley, Douglas E., and Jean Meadowcroft. "Life in a Changing Multi-ethnic School: Anglo Teachers and their Views of Mexicano Students." In *Bilingual Education*, edited by Hernan LaFontaine, Leonard H. Golubchick, and Barry Persky, 84–88. Wayne, N.J.: Avery Publishing Group, 1978.

Foster, David William. "The Phonology of Mexican-American Spanish." In *Problems in Applied Educational Sociolinguistics: Readings on Language and Culture Problems of United States Ethnic Groups*, edited by Glenn G. Gilbert and Jacob Ornstein, 85–100. The Hague: Mouton Publishers, 1978.

Franco, Stephen Leonard. "Neuropsychological Test Performance of Mexican American and Anglo American High School Students from Communities of the United States-Mexico Border Region of South Texas." Ph.D. dissertation, University of Texas at Austin, 1996.

Frank, Jean Ringler. "Income, Family Stressors, and Parent Education as Correlates of School Dropout." Ph.D. dissertation, University of Texas at Austin, 1987.

Fraser, William K. "A Study of the Abilities of Spanish-speaking and English-speaking Children of Kinney County, Texas." Master's thesis, University of Texas, Austin, 1946.

Friedman, Marjorie Scilken. "An Appraisal of the Role of the Public School as an Acculturating Agency of Mexican Americans in Texas, 1850–1968." Ph.D. dissertation, New York University, 1978.

Frontera, Lucy S., and Rosalind Horowitz. "Reading and Study Behaviors of Fourth Grade Hispanics: Can Teachers Assess Risk?" *Hispanic Journal of Behavioral Sciences* 17 (February 1995): 100–120.

Fuentes, Sylvia. "*La Pisca, La Familia, y Las Schools*: Personal Narratives of Tejana Women in the Midwest and the Nature of Adult Education." Ed.D. dissertation, Northern Illinois University, 1998.

Galindo, D. Letticia. "Linguistic Influence and Variation on the English of Chicano Adolescents in Austin, Texas." Ph.D. dissertation, University of Texas at Austin, 1987.

________. "Dispelling the Male-Only Myth: Chicanos and Caló." *Bilingual Review/La Revista Bilingüe* 17.1 (1992): 3–35.

________. "Language Attitudes toward Spanish and English Varieties: A Chicano Perspective." *Hispanic Journal of Behavioral Sciences* 17.1 (1995): 77–99.

________. "Language Use and Language Attitudes: A Study of Border Women." *Bilingual Review/La Revista Bilingüe* 21.1 (1996): 5–17.

Gallegos, L. L. "A Comparison of Social Studies Curriculum Needs as Perceived by Mexican American Parents, Students, and Teachers." Ph.D. dissertation, University of Houston, 1974.

Galligan, Martha. "Factors Related to Attrition and Retention Rates of Hispanic Female Students at the University of Texas–Pan American." Ph.D. dissertation, University of Texas at Austin, 1994.

Galloway, Irma Nell. "Trends in the Employment of Minority Women as Administrators in Texas Public Schools—1976–1981." Ed.D. dissertation, Texas Southern University, 1986.

Galván, Nicanor Jr. "A Study of Factors that influence Hispanics in their pursuit of Higher Education in Central and South Texas." Ed.D. dissertation, Texas A&I University, 1993.

Galván, Roberto A., and R. V. Teschner. *El Diccionario Español de Tejas: The Dictionary of the Spanish of Texas*. Silver Springs, Md.: Institute of Modern Languages, 1975.

Galván, R. R. "Bilingualism as it Relates to Intelligence Test Scores and School Achievement Among Culturally Deprived Spanish-American Children." Ph.D. dissertation, Texas Tech University, 1967.

Garabedian, Charles Albert. "The Wildcats vs. the Mustangs: The Consolidation of the San Felipe and Del Rio Independent School Districts." Master's thesis, Sul Ross State University, 1994.

García, Cecilia Annette. "The Difference in Helping Behavior between Hispanic versus Non-Hispanic Subjects Using the Wrong Number Technique." Master's thesis, Texas A&M University-Kingsville, 1997.

García, Ignacio. "A Coach on the Right Track." *Nuestro* 3 (October 1979): 44, 46.

García, Juan Carlos. "Predictors of Participation in Continuing Education by Hispanic Pastors in Texas." Ph.D. dissertation, Southwestern Baptist Theological Seminary, 1998.

García, María-Cristina. "Juárez-Lincoln University." In *The New Handbook of Texas,* edited by Ron Tyler, Douglas E. Barnett, Roy R. Barkley, Penelope C. Anderson, and Mark F. Odintz, vol. 3, 1011. Austin: Texas State Historical Association, 1996.

García, María Estela Peña. "Level of Involvement of Title I Parents in a South Texas School District." Ed.D. dissertation, Texas A&M University-Kingsville, 1999.

García, Mario T. "Education and the Mexican American: Eleuterio Escobar and the School Improvement League of San Antonio." In *Mexican Americans: Leadership, Ideology, and Identity, 1930–1960*, by Mario T. García, 62–83. New Haven: Yale University Press, 1989.

García, Ricardo Thomas. "The Relation among College Student Attitudes, Motivation and Aptitude to Foreign Language Achievement: A Test of Gardner's Model." Ed.D. dissertation, University of Houston, 1996.

García, Shernaz Bhathena. "Effects of Student Characteristics, School Programs and Organization on Decisionmaking for the Placement of Hispanic Students in Classes for the Learning Disabled." Ph.D. dissertation, University of Texas at Austin, 1984.

Garza, George J. "Social and Economic Status of Mexicans of San Marcos and Its Bearing upon the Education of Mexican Children." Master's thesis, Southwest Texas State University, 1940.

Garza, María Luisa. "A Study of the Use of the Inter-American Tests of General Ability in Various South Texas Title VII Bilingual/Bicultural Programs." Ed.D. dissertation, Texas A&I University, 1978.

Garza, Nora Ramírez. "A Description and Analysis of Selected Successful Developmental Reading Programs in Texas Community Colleges." Ph.D. dissertation, University of Texas at Austin, 1994.

Garza, R. T. "Affective and Associative Qualities in the Learning Styles of Chicanos and Anglos." *Psychology in the Schools* 15.1 (1978): 111–115.

Garza, R. T., and F. W. Widlak. "Antecedents of Chicano and Anglo Student Perceptions of the University Environment." *Journal of College Student Personnel* 17.4 (1976): 295–299.

Garza, Sergio. "The Effects of Learning Styles on Learning Reading Vocabulary Words in Context among Mexican-American Sixth Graders in a South Texas Middle School Campus." Ed.D. dissertation, Texas A&M University-Kingsville, 1998.

Garza, Sherryl Ana. "Linguistic Acceptability of the Laidlaw Reading Series, Grades 1–3, to the Spanish-speaking Chicano Child in Texas." Ed.D. dissertation, Texas A&I University, 1979.

Gibbs, Linda Louise. "Analysis of Developmental Mathematics Programs in Texas Community Colleges which are Successful with Black and Hispanic Students." Ph.D. dissertation, University of Texas at Austin, 1994.

Gibson, Mary Ellen. "Some Important Problems in Teaching Spanish Culture Children." Master's thesis, Texas College of Arts and Industries, 1940.

Gilbert, Ennis Hall. "Some Legal Aspects of the Education of Spanish-Speaking Children of Texas." Master's thesis, University of Texas, Austin, 1947.

Gilbert, G. G., ed. *Texas Studies in Bilingualism*. Berlin: Walter de Gruyter and Co., 1970.

Glass, Nellie May. "A Study of Reading Performance of Anglo and Latin American Children." Master's thesis, University of Texas, Austin, 1949.

Godina-Silva, Norma Baudelia. "A Study of Mexican-American Bilingual Education Teachers' Responses to the Involvement of Mexican-American Linguistic Minority Parents at Posada Elementary." Ph.D. dissertation, New Mexico State University, 1997.

Gómez, Daniel Parra. "Discouragement, Encouragement, and At Risk Hispanic Elementary Students' Self-esteem: An Ethnographic Case Study." Ed.D. dissertation, Texas Tech University, 1994.

Gómez, Severo. "Bilingual Education in Texas." *La Luz* 2.7 (November 1973): 46–48.

________. "Innovation in Education: Bilingual Education in Texas." *Educational Leadership* 28 (April 1971): 757–762.

Gonzales, Manuel C. "Our Spanish-speaking Parent-Teacher Groups and Their Problems." *Texas Outlook* 27 (June 1943): 23–24.

Gonzales, Paul Franklin. "Mexican American Culture in Bilingual Education Classrooms Grades 1 Through 3: A Description of Three Spanish/English Programs in Texas." Ph.D. dissertation, University of Texas at Austin, 1998.

González, Aurora Marjorie. "A Study of the Intelligence of Mexican Children in Relation to Their Socio-Economic Status." Master's thesis, University of Texas, Austin, 1932.

González, Emiliano. "Culturally Relevant Teaching Pedagogy and Practice: A Critical Study of Three Hispanic Teachers Working with Colonia Students." Ph.D. dissertation, Indiana University, 1998.

González, Gustavo. *The Phonology of Corpus Christi Spanish*. Austin: Southwest Educational Development Laboratory, 1969.

________. "A Linguistic Profile of the Spanish-speaking First Grader in Corpus Christi." Master's thesis, University of Texas, Austin, 1968.

________. "Some Characteristics of the English Used by Migrant Spanish-Speaking Children of Texas." *Aztlán* 7 (Spring 1976): 27–49.

González, Mary Ellen Martínez. "A Case Study of Parent Involvement in a Middle School in the Rio Grande Valley of South Texas." Ph.D. dissertation, University of Texas at Austin, 1996.

González, Simón. "Implications of the Serrano and Rodríguez Cases on the Education of Mexican Americans." *Educational Resources and Techniques* 12.2 (Summer 1972): 27–31.

Goodman, P. W., and B. S. Brooks. "A Comparison of Anglo and Mexican American Students Attending the Same University." *Kansas Journal of Sociology* 10.2 (1974): 181–203.

Goodwin, Kathryn Michele. "An Educational Tool to Help Mexican-Americans Identify Food Label Information." Master's thesis, Texas Woman's University, 1997.

Graham, Leon R. "A Comparison of the English-speaking and Latin-American Students in the Mercedes, Texas Schools." Master's thesis, Southern Methodist University, 1938.

Grout, Paul Asbury. "Trends in Scholastics, Enrollment, Average Daily Attendance, and Age-Grade Distribution of Spanish-American Pupils in Lyford, Texas Public Schools, 1933–1938." Master's thesis, Texas A&I University, 1938.

Guerra, Norma Susan. "Computer-assisted Assessment of Reading Comprehension with Hispanic Fourth Grade Pupils." Ph.D. dissertation, Texas A&M University, 1988.

Guerra, Patricia Lynn. "Hispanic Student Perceptions of Factors Contributing to Their Access and Success in Graduate Education at The University of Texas at Austin: A Case Study." Ph.D. dissertation, University of Texas at Austin, 1994.

Guerra, Yvette Rodríguez. "The Effects of the 1995 JTPA Summer TAAS Program on Reading, Math, and Writing Scores of C.H.O.E.T. High School Students in Hidalgo County, Texas." Ed.D. dissertation, Texas A&M University-Kingsville, 1998.

Guerra, Veronica. "Second Language Proficiency and Tolerance of Ambiguity: A Comparative Study." *South Texas Studies* 2 (1991): 99–125.

Guerrero, Andre L. "The Presence of Undocumented Mexican Children in Texas Public Schools." Ed.D. dissertation, Harvard University, 1990.

Guinn, H., J. A. Rosenthal, and H. G. Richeck. "Impacts of Bilingual Education on Secondary School Grades, Attendance, Retention, and Dropout." *Hispanic Journal of Behavioral Sciences* 8 (December 1986): 357–367.

Gunn, R. "Characteristics of Drug Use Among Mexican American Students." *Journal of Drug Education* 5.3 (1975): 235–247.

Gunn, R., and R. S. Hurley. "A Comparison of Drug Use Among Houston and Lower Rio Grande Valley Secondary Students." *Adolescence* 6 (1976): 455–459.

Gutiérrez, Emeterio Jr. "A Study of School Attendance of Migrant Students in La Grulla, Texas." Master's thesis, University of Texas, Austin, 1952.

Habermacher, Andrew Lee. "Physical Development of Anglo and Spanish Culture School Boys and Girls Ages 13–18, Inclusive." Master's thesis, Texas A&I University, 1940.

Hailey, Ermine Michael. "Border Crossings: Using the Rhetorical Concept of a 'Contact Zone' in Freshman Composition Classes." Master's thesis, Texas A&M University-Kingsville, 2002.

Hall, Gilbert Ennis. "Some Legal Aspects of the Education of Spanish Speaking Children of Texas." Master's thesis, University of Texas, Austin, 1947.

Hambrick, Albert Lewis. "Teacher Mobility and Student Success in Texas High Schools: A Correlational Study." Ed.D. dissertation, Texas A&M University-Commerce, 2000.

Hannel, Clarence Wayne. "An Analysis of the Retention Rate among Seventh Graders in a Random Sample of Junior High Schools in Texas." Ed.D. dissertation, Texas Tech University, 1985.

Hardgrave, Robert, and Santiago Hinojosa. *The Politics of Bilingual Education: A Study of Four Southwest Texas Communities.* Manchaca, Tex.: Sterling Swift Publishing, 1975.

Harding, Bill. "Migrant Pupils: Challenge to Texas Education." *Texas Outlook* 39 (July 1955): 6–13.

Harper, Kaye Brown. "A Comparison of Career Patterns among Minority and Non-minority Administrators in Higher Education Institutions in the State of Texas." Ed.D. dissertation, Texas Southern University, 1985.

Harris, James Kilbourne. "A Sociological Study of a Mexican School in San Antonio, Texas." Master's thesis, University of Texas, Austin, 1927.

Harrison, David C. "A Survey of the Administrative and Educational Policies of the Baptist, Methodist, and Presbyterian Churches Among Mexican American People in Texas." Master's thesis, University of Texas, Austin, 1952.

Hayes, James V. "An Analysis of Latin-American Partial Attendance and Drop-outs in the Elementary Schools of Eagle Pass, Texas, in Recent Years." Master's thesis, University of Texas, Austin, 1952.

Heiler, Barbara. "An Investigation of the Causes of Primary Stress Mislocation in the English Speech of Bilingual Mexican-American Students." Master's thesis, University of Texas at El Paso, 1966.

Heinz, Martha Clough. "Racial and Ethnic Identification, Preference, and Acceptance in Hispanic and Caucasian Preschool Children." Ph.D. dissertation, University of South Carolina, 1984.

Hendrix, Don Robert. "Influence in South Texas Schools as Impacted by the Degree of Shift from Anglo to Mexican-American Control." Ph.D. dissertation, University of Texas at Austin, 1977.

Hensey, Fritz. "Language Variation and Bilingual Education." In *Social and Educational Issues in Bilingualism and Biculturalism*, edited by Robert St. Clair, Guadalupe Valdés, and Jacob Ornstein-Galicia, 141–152. Washington, D.C.: University Press of America, 1981.

Hensley, Jim B. *Mexican Immigrant-Alien Study, 1975–76*. Edinburg, Tex.: Region I Education Service Center, Texas Education Agency, 1976.

Hernández, Carolyn. "LULAC: The History of a Grassroots Organization and Its Influence on Educational Policies, 1929–1983." Ph.D. dissertation, Loyola University of Chicago, 1995.

Hernández, Elias Vega. "Reading Retardation of Children in Zavala School, Austin, Texas." Master's thesis University of Texas, Austin, 1954.

Hernández, Magdalena. "A Study of the Relationship between Support Services and the Retention of Mexican-American and Anglo Adult Students in Three Texas Community Colleges." Ph.D. dissertation, University of Texas at Austin, 1980.

Herrington, David Earl. "Barriers, Influences, and Leadership Challenges of Selected Mexican American Administrators in South Texas Higher Education from 1970–1990." 2 vols. Ph.D. dissertation, Texas A&M University, 1993.

Herr, Selma Ernestine. "The Effect of Pre-first Grade Training Upon Reading Readiness and Reading Achievement Among Spanish American Children in the First Grade." Ph.D. dissertation, University of Texas, Austin, 1944.

Hill, Henry Carl. "A Study of the Public Two-Year Colleges in Texas in the Recruiting and Retention of Minorities from 1984–1990." Ph.D. dissertation, Texas A&M University, 1993.

Hnatek, Margaret. "A Survey of Population Factors Relating to the Education of Migrant Children in Victoria County, Texas." Master's thesis, University of Texas, Austin, 1952.

Hodgden, Aurora Sánchez. "The Importance of a Teacher's Racial/Ethnic Background as a Factor in a Student's Academic Achievement: A Study of Mexican-Americans in Laredo, Texas." Ed.D. dissertation, Oklahoma State University, 1990.

Holland, B. F., and G. McDaniel. "Teaching Latin Americans to Read by Means of Visual Aids." *Texas Outlook* 26 (July 1942): 20–22.

Hollinger, Jay Scott. "A Study of Parental Involvement at a Blue Ribbon Elementary School on the Texas-Mexico Border." Ed.D. dissertation, University of Texas–Pan American, 2001.

Holtzman, Wayne Harold Jr. "Divergent Thinking as a Function of the Degree of Bilingualism of Mexican-American and Anglo Fourth-Grade Students." Ph.D. dissertation, University of Texas at Austin, 1980.

Houston, Ramona Allaniz. "African Americans, Mexican Americans, and Anglo Americans and the Desegregation of Texas, 1946–1957." Ph.D. dissertation, University of Texas at Austin, 2000.

Howe, Anna L. "Proposals for the Organization and Administration of a Program of Special Education to Improve the English Speech of Certain Spanish-Speaking Pupils, Eagle Pass, Texas." Master's thesis, University of Texas, Austin, 1952.

Hudelson, Sarah Jane. "Male-Female Role Patterns of Mexican American Children in a South Texas School." Master's thesis, University of Texas at Austin, 1971.

Hughes, A. H. "Speaking English at School." *Texas Outlook* 28 (November 1944): 26.

Hughes, Lois S. "A Comparative Study of the Intelligence of Mexican Children and Non-Mexican Children." Master's thesis, University of Texas, Austin, 1928.

Huser, C. W. "San Antonio Educates Little Mexico." *Adult Education Bulletin* 3 (April 1939): 13–16.

Hutchison, Cornelia. "A Comparative Study of the Teaching Materials for Six-Year-Old Children in Mexico and Texas." Master's thesis, University of Texas, Austin, 1945.

Hyland, E. D. "Using Music to Teach English to Spanish-Speaking Beginners." *Texas Outlook* 29 (May 1945): 30.

Iber, Jorge. "Becoming Raiders Rojos: Using Sport to Claim Hispanic 'Space' at Texas Tech University." *West Texas Historical Association Yearbook* 77 (2001): 139–151.

________. "Mexican Americans of South Texas Football: The Athletic and Coaching Careers of E. C. Lerma and Bobby Cavazos, 1932–1965." *Southwestern Historical Quarterly* 105 (April 2002): 617–633.

________. "A Vaquero in the Backfield: The Career of Bobby Cavazos, Texas Tech's First Hispanic All American." *College Football Historical Society* 14 (August 2001): 1–5.

Isom, George Hemingway. "Comparison of Middle School Organization Pattern and Traditional School Organization Pattern Via ACT Composite Score Means within Three Racial-Ethnic Groups of Students." Ph.D. dissertation, University of Iowa, 1980.

Jackson, Dorris Goforth. "Educational Status of Mexican Children in a Texas Elementary School." Master's thesis, University of Texas, Austin, 1952.

Jackson, Lucille Prim. "An Analysis of the Language Difficulties of the Spanish-speaking Children of the Bowie High School, El Paso, Texas." Master's thesis, University of Texas, Austin, 1938.

January, William Spence. "The Chicano Dialect of the Mexican American Communities of Dallas and Ft. Worth." Master's thesis, Texas Christian University, 1970.

Jesse, Daniel Marion. "Understanding High-achieving Middle Schools for Latino Students in Poverty." Ph.D. dissertation, University of Colorado at Denver, 2001.

Johnson, D. L., et al. *Houston Parent-Child Development Center*. Houston: University of Houston, 1976.

________. "The Houston Parent-Child Development Center: A Parent Education Program for Mexican American Families." *American Journal of Orthopsychiatry* 44.1 (1974): 121–128.

Johnson, Roberta Muriel. "History of the Education of Spanish-speaking Children in Texas." Master's thesis, University of Texas, Austin, 1932.

Johnson, Vally Lou. "Survey of Spanish-speaking Scholastics in Brewster County, Texas." Ed.D. thesis, Colorado State College (Greeley), 1950.

________. "A Study to Determine the Levels in Curriculum Areas where Remedial Work is Needed Most in Elementary School for Spanish-speaking Children Shown by Correlation of Mental Age and Education Age." Ed.D. thesis, Colorado State College (Greeley), 1952.

Johnston, Edith Louise. "The Use of Mexican Folk Dances in School Activities." Master's thesis, University of Texas, Austin, 1937.

Jones, Benton McLain. "A Study of the Acculturation and Social Aspirations of Sixty Junior High School Students from the Mexican Ethnic Group." Master's thesis, University of Texas, Austin, 1962.

Jones, Charles Fleming. "Characteristics of Ethnic Minorities in Educational Technology in Higher Education in Texas." Ed.D. dissertation, East Texas State University, 1980.

Jones, Michael Hunter. "The Interrelationships between Communication Apprehension, Academic Achievement, Teacher Gender, Student Gender, and Student Perception of Teacher Immediacy among Seventh-Grade Nonnative Hispanic ESL Students in a Selected Urban Middle School Setting." Master's thesis, Stephen F. Austin State University, 1993.

Jones, Wash Antoine. "Factors Influencing Career Choice of African-American and Hispanic Graduates of the College of Agriculture and Life Sciences at Texas A&M University." Ph.D. dissertation, Texas A&M University, 1999.

Juárez, José Roberto. "Texas Association of Chicanos in Higher Education." In *The New Handbook of Texas*, edited by Ron Tyler, Douglas E. Barnett, Roy R. Barkley, Penelope C. Anderson, and Mark F. Odintz, vol. 6, 289. Austin: Texas State Historical Association, 1996.

Juárez, Rumaldo Z. "Education Status Orientation of Mexican American and Anglo American Youths in Selected Low-Income Counties of Texas." Master's thesis, Texas A&M University, College Station, 1968.

Kadechi, James U. "A Study of Mexican Education in Atascosa County with Special Reference to the Pleasanton Elementary School." Master's thesis, University of Texas, Austin, 1940.

Kaderli, Albert T. "The Educational Problem in the Americanization of Spanish-speaking Pupils of Sugarland, Texas." Master's thesis, University of Texas, Austin, 1940.

Karnath, Colin Joseph. "Factors Associated with Hispanic Student Attendance among Major Urban Middle Schools in Texas." Ed.D. dissertation, Texas A&M University-Kingsville, 2001.

Keen, Marvin Spruce. "A Comparative Study of the Motor Ability of Latin-American and Anglo-American Boys." Master's thesis, University of Texas, Austin, 1941.

Kells, Michelle Hall. "Basic Writing: A Gateway to College for Mexican Americans of South Texas." Master's thesis, Texas A&M University-Kingsville, 1995.

Kelly, Rex Robert. "Vocabulary as Used on the Mexican Border." Master's thesis, Baylor University, 1938.

Kidd, M. C. "Chance to Succeed: Program for Migratory Children." *Texas Outlook* 49 (August 1965): 16–17.

Kinnebrew, Robert Keith. "Achievement and Persistence of Postsecondary Vocational-Technical Students as a Function of Ethnicity and Sex." Ph.D. dissertation, Texas A&M University, 1984.

Kithcart, Beverly Frick. "Hispanic Students: Characteristics of Those Who Choose a Post-Secondary Education." Ed.D. dissertation, University of Houston, 1991.

Kramme, Clyde Ira. "A Comparison of Anglo Culture with Spanish Culture Elementary Students in Physical Development as Determined by Height, Weight and Vital Capacity Measurements." Master's thesis, Texas A&I University, 1939.

Kreneck, Thomas H. "Little School of the 400." In *The New Handbook of Texas,* edited by Ron Tyler, Douglas E. Barnett, Roy R. Barkley, Penelope C. Anderson, and Mark F. Odintz, vol. 6, 237–238. Austin: Texas State Historical Association, 1996.

Kuvlesky, William P., David E. Wright Jr., and Rumaldo Z. Juárez. "Status Projections and Ethnicity: A Comparison of Mexican-American, Negro and Anglo Youth." *Journal of Vocational Behavior* 1 (April 1971): 137–151.

Laible, Julie Catherine. "Educating *Muchachas de la Frontera*: Educational Practices That Promote the Success of Mexican-American Females in Texas/Mexico Border Schools." Ph.D. dissertation, University of Texas at Austin, 1995.

Lamana, Richard A., and Julián Samora. "Recent Trends in Educational Status of Mexican Americans in Texas." In *Improving Educational Opportunities of the Mexican American.* Proceedings First Texas Conference for the Mexican Americans, San Antonio, 1967, edited by Dwain M. Estes and David W. Darling, 20–41. Austin: Southwest Educational Laboratory Development, 1967.

Lampe, P. E. *A Comparative Study of Assimilation of Mexican American Parochial versus Public Schools*. San Francisco: R&E Research Associates, 1975.

Landmann, Robert S. "A Lexical Compilation of Rio Grande Valley Spanish: Aspects of Applied Research Techniques in Cross-Cultural Survey Investigation in the United States." In *Problems in Applied Educational Sociolinguistics: Readings on Language and Culture Problems of United States Ethnic Groups*, edited by Glenn G. Gilbert and Jacob Ornstein, 23–33. The Hague: Mouton Publishers, 1978.

Lang, Elaine Marie. "Successful Developmental Reading Programs at Selected Hispanic-serving Texas Community Colleges." Ph.D. dissertation, University of Texas at Austin, 2001.

Langenegger, Joyce A. "The School as a Political Tool: A Case Study of Crystal City." Master's thesis, Department of Education, Baylor University, 1993.

Lantolf, James P. "Speaker Sex and *Para* Reduction in Chicano Spanish." In *Bilingualism and Language Contact: Spanish, English and Native American Languages*, edited by Florence Barkin, Elizabeth A. Brandt, and Jacob Ornstein-Galicia, 166–176. New York: Teachers College, Columbia University, 1982.

Lara-Braud, Jorge. *Bilingualism for Texas; Education for Fraternity.* Austin: Hispanic-American Institute, 1970.

Lashaway-Bokina, Nancy. "Gifted but Gone: High Ability, Mexican-American, Female Dropouts." Ph.D. dissertation, University of Connecticut, 1996.

Lazos, Hector. "A Study of the Relationship of Language Proficiency in the Mother Tongue and Acquisition of Second Language Reading Skills in Bilingual Children at Age Twelve." Ph.D. dissertation, University of Texas at Austin, 1981.

Leff, Gladys Ruth. "George I. Sánchez: Don Quixote of the Southwest." Ph.D. dissertation, University of North Texas, 1976.

Leggett, Jo-Ann Sory. "The Relation between Self-reported Parental Behaviors and Beliefs and the Early Success of Preschool Head Start Children." Ed.D. dissertation, University of Houston, 1993.

Leo, David G. "A Historical and Political Analysis of Bilingual Education in Texas, 1974–1983: An Educator's Perspective." Ed.D. dissertation, University of Houston, 1985.

Lewis, Preston. "De León Follows Historical Path of Mexican Americans." *Hispanic Outlook in Higher Education* 11 (May 21, 2001): 25–27.

________. "Up and Coming Scholars' Program Offers Chance for College: Angelo State University Reaches Out." *Hispanic Outlook in Higher Education* 10 (May 5, 2000): 29–32.

Lieshoff, Sylvia Cobos. "The Impact of Literacy Programs: Perceptions of Selected Mexican and Mexican-American Women in Texas." Ph.D. dissertation, Texas A&M University, 1995.

Light, Jere Cook. "A Critical Analysis of Anglo and Mexican-American Cultural Patterns in Two Texas Border City Junior Colleges." Master's thesis, University of Texas at Austin, 1974.

________. "The Mexican-American and the Community-College in Texas." *South Texas Journal of Research and the Humanities* 1 (Fall 1977): 141–148.

Little, Wilson. *Spanish-Speaking Children in Texas*. Austin: University of Texas Press, 1944. Reprinted in *Education and the Mexican American*, edited by Carlos E. Cortés. New York: Arno Press, 1974.

Liu, Samuel T. "Essays on the Effects of Immigration on Education and Crime." Ph.D. dissertation, Massachusetts Institute of Technology, 2000.

Lizcano, Elpidio. "*Educación Bilingüe en Cristal*." *Caracol* 1.10 (June 1975): 10–11.

Loefler, H. W. "San Antonio's Mexican Child." *Texas Outlook* 29 (March 1945): 28.

Loftin, J. O. "Mexican Secondary Education Developed in the Sidney Lanier Junior High School of San Antonio, Texas." Master's thesis, State Teachers' College, Greeley, Colo., 1927.

López, Richard E., and Julián Samora. "George Sánchez and Testing." In *Humanidad: Essays in Honor of George I. Sánchez*, edited by Américo Paredes, 107–115. Los Angeles: Chicano Studies Center Publications, 1977.

López, Yolanda. "The Influence of Ethnicity on Management Styles of Women in Educational Administration." Ed.D. dissertation, Baylor University, 1993.

Lovato, Chris Yolanda. "Achievement Motivation, Role Stress and Individual Characteristics as Predictors of College Performance among Mexican Americans and Anglo Americans." Ph.D. dissertation, University of Texas at Austin, 1981.

Lowery, Flora. "Night School in Little Mexico." *Southwest Review* 16 (October 1930): 32–46.

Lowry, Sarah J. "A Comparison of Certain Physical Abilities of Anglo and Latin American Fifth and Sixth Grade Girls." Master's thesis, University of Texas, Austin, 1952.

Low, Wilson E. "A Study of the Failures and Withdrawals of Martin High School, Laredo, Texas." Master's thesis, University of Texas, Austin, 1954.

Lozano, Amparo. "An Experiment in Teaching Spanish and English to Spanish-Speaking Children." Master's thesis, University of Texas, Austin, 1932.

Lozano, Anthony G. "Intercambio de Español e Ingles en San Antonio, Texas." Master's thesis, University of Texas at Austin, 1972.

Luhrs, Joyce. "Chicanos Make Waves in Texas." *Hispanic Outlook in Higher Education* 6 (February 2, 1996): 7–8.

Luna, Juanita J. "A Selected Vocabulary of the Spanish Spoken in Sabinal, Texas." Master's thesis, Southwest Texas State University, 1970.

Lyons, Patricia Ann English. "Heideggerian Hermeneutic Inquiry into the Perceptions of Selected Texas Public School Beginning Minority Teachers." Ed.D. dissertation, Baylor University, 2000.

Madrid, Sandra Emilia. "The Effects of Socialization on Goal Actualization of Public School Chicana Principals and Superintendents." Ph.D. dissertation, University of Washington, 1985.

Maldonado-Colón, Elba C. "Profiles of Hispanic Students Placed in Speech, Hearing and Language Programs in a Selected School District in Texas." Ed.D. dissertation, University of Massachusetts, 1984.

Maldonado, Jesús Rubén. "The Effect of the ESEA Title-VII Program on the Cognitive Development of Mexican-American Students within a Major South Texas School District." Ed.D. dissertation, University of Houston, 1977.

Mallon, Stephen Craig. "Leadership Position and Sex Role Stereotyping of Hispanic Gifted and Talented Children." Ed.D. dissertation, East Texas State University, 1994.

Manuel, Herschel T. *The Education of Mexican and Spanish-Speaking Children in Texas*. Austin: Fund for Research in the Social Science, University of Texas, 1930. Reprinted in *Education and the Mexican American*, edited by Carlos E. Cortés. New York: Arno Press, 1974.

________. *Spanish-Speaking Children of the Southwest*. Austin: University of Texas Press, 1965.

________. "A Comparison of Spanish-speaking and English Speaking Children in Reading and Arithmetic." *Journal of Applied Psychology* 19.1 (1935): 189–202.

________. "The Educational Problem Presented by the Spanish-speaking Child of the Southwest." *School and Society* (1934): 692–695.

________. "The Intelligence and Drawing Ability of Young Mexican Children." *Journal of Applied Psychology* 16.4 (1932): 382–387.

________. "The Mexican Child in Texas." *Southwest Review* 17.3 (1932): 290–311.

________. "The Mexican Population of Texas." *Southwestern Social Science Quarterly* 15 (June 1934): 29–51.

________. "Recruiting and Training Teachers for Spanish-speaking Children in the Southwest." In *Educating the Mexican American*, edited by Henry Sioux Johnson and William J. Hernández-M, 183–192. Valley Forge, Penn.: Judson Press, 1970.

________. "The Spanish-speaking Child." *Texas Outlook* 14 (January 1930): 21.

Manuel, Herschel T., and Aline Rather. "That One Talent." *The Nation's Schools* 2 (November 1928): 27–33.

Manuel, Herschel T., and Carrie Wright. "The Language Difficulty of Mexican Children." *Journal of Genetic Psychology* 36 (September 1929): 458–466.

Marand, Delia Ríos. "The Benefits of a Language Arts Literature-Based Curriculum on Hispanic Students in the Third-, Fourth-, and Fifth-Grade." Ph.D. dissertation, University of Illinois at Urbana-Champaign, 1996.

Marshall, Carolyn Emmett. "Evaluation of a Bilingual Video-Novella Method to Teach Elderly Mexican American Non-Readers How to Decrease Their Risk of Diabetic Complications." Ph.D. dissertation, Texas A&M University, 1994.

Martínez, Arnulfo Simeón. "A Study of the Scholastic Census of the Spanish-speaking Children of Texas." Master's thesis, University of Texas, Austin, 1944.

Martínez, Elizabeth Sugar. "Ethnic Cleansing in the Barrio: A Critical Ethnography of the Politics, Practices, and Pedantry of Schooling Urban Latino Bilingual Students." Ed.D. dissertation, University of Houston, 2001.

Martínez, María Consuelo G. "The Effect of the College Exploration Early Intervention Summer Program on Performance and Retention of Hispanic Disadvantaged First-year Students in Higher Education." Ed.D. dissertation, Texas A&M University-Kingsville, 2000.

Martin, Kenneth. "A Comparative Study of Rural and Urban Community Colleges' Student Support Services Programs." Ed.D. dissertation, Baylor University, 2001.

Mata, Zelma Diana. "Anglo and Hispanic Women Administrators' Perceptions of the Conflict among Their Multiple Roles as Professional, Spouse, Parent and Self in Selected Higher Education Institutions in Texas." Ed.D. dissertation, University of Houston, 1993.

Mathis, William. "Political Socialization in a Mexican American School." Ph.D. dissertation, University of Texas at Austin, 1973.

Maville, Janice Ann. "The Relationship between Social Support and Persistence among Female Hispanic Students in an Associate Degree Nursing Program." Ed.D. dissertation, Texas A&M University, 1992.

McClendon, Juliette Jane. "Spanish-speaking Children of Big Spring: An Educational Challenge." Ph.D. dissertation, University of Texas, Austin, 1964.

McClinton, Johnnie W. "Effectiveness of a Bilingual Vocational-Technical Program." Ph.D. dissertation, University of Missouri, Columbia, 1972.

McCrary, Mallie E. "These Minorities in Our Midst with Emphasis on Latin Americans in Texas." Master's thesis, University of Texas, Austin, 1953.

McCormick, Bonnie Day. "Attitude, Achievement, and Classroom Environment in a Learner-centered Introductory Biology Course." Ph.D. dissertation, University of Texas at Austin, 2000.

McCullough, Y. Jayne. "A Comparative Analysis of Leadership Qualities of African American, Anglo American and Hispanic American Principals Regarding School Effectiveness in Selected Urban Secondary Schools." Ed.D. dissertation, Texas Southern University, 1994.

McDaniel, Gertrude D. "The Use of Visual Aids in Teaching the Mexican Beginner to Read." Master's thesis, University of Texas, Austin, 1937.

McDowell, Neil Allen. "A Status Study of the Academic Capabilities and Achievements of Three Ethnic Groups: Anglo, Negro, and Spanish Surname in San Antonio, Texas." Ph.D. dissertation, University of Texas, Austin, 1966.

McKenzie, Dylicia Avila. "A Descriptive Study of Effective Instructional Methodologies used by Selected Outstanding Bilingual Education Teachers." Ed.D. dissertation, Texas A&M University-Kingsville, 1995.

McKown, Johnette Edwards. "Critical Behaviors of Texas Community Colleges in Meeting Black and Hispanic Hiring Goals." Ed.D. dissertation, East Texas State University, 1990.

McLean, Robert J. "A Cooperative Study of Anglo-American and Spanish-Name Children in the Austin Public Schools Over a Seven-Year Period." Master's thesis, University of Texas, Austin, 1950.

McLennan, LeRoy. "A Comparison of the Spanish-Speaking and English-Speaking Children in Nine Schools Over a Three-Year Period." Master's thesis, University of Texas, Austin, 1936.

McNeil, Linda M. "Sameness, Bureaucracy, and the Myth of Educational Equality: The TAAS System of Testing in Texas Public Schools." *Hispanic Journal of Behavioral Sciences* 22 (November 2000): 508–523.

McPherson-Darrow, Elizabeth. "A Tale of Three Districts: Examining the TAAS Exit Level Reading Passing Rates of Hispanic and Hispanic Non-LEP Students in Arlington, Houston, and El Paso." Ph.D. dissertation, Texas Woman's University, 2002.

McWilliams, Carey. "George Sánchez: Teacher, Scholar, Activist." In *Humanidad: Essays in Honor of George I. Sánchez*, edited by Américo Paredes, 116–119. Los Angeles: Chicano Studies Center Publications, 1977.

Meador, Bruce S. "Minority Groups and Their Education in Hays County, Texas." Ph.D. dissertation, University of Texas, Austin, 1959.

Means, Johnny Clinton. "A Proposal for a Program of Education for the Migrant Students in the Secondary Schools of Harlingen, Texas." Master's thesis, Southwest Texas State University, 1959.

Meckel, Robert. "Native Son to Lead University of Texas at San Antonio: Ricardo Romo Goes the Distance." *Hispanic Outlook in Higher Education* 9 (July 16, 1999): 6–8.

Medel, Jesús Cantú. "Neoindigenism in the Chicano Community in Houston, Texas: A Site for Praxis in Art Education." Master's thesis, University of Houston, 2001.

Mejias, Hugo, and Pamela Anderson. "Attitude toward use of Spanish on the South Texas Border." *Hispania* 71.2 (1988): 401–406.

________. "Language Maintenance in Southern Texas." *Southwest Journal of Linguistics* 7 (1984–1987): 116–124.

Mellenbruch, Julia Ida. "Teaching Spanish to Spanish-speaking Students in Texas High Schools." Master's thesis, University of Texas, Austin, 1954.

________. "Let's Teach Spanish to Spanish-speaking Students at School." *Texas Outlook* 39.5 (July 1955): 14–15.

Mendoza, Alicia Patricia. "Stress and Coping: A Comparison of Coping Efficacy between Anglo and Mexican American University Students." Ph.D. dissertation, University of Texas at Austin, 1980.

Metke, L. Michael. "Students Who Persist: Factors Associated with the Persistence of Mexican American Students at a Two-Year Technical College." Ed.D. dissertation, University of Houston, 1993.

Michel, Joseph. "A Pilot Project for Recording the Speech of the Five-Year-Old Texas Spanish-English Pre-School Bilingual Child." *Florida Language Reporter* 20 (Fall 1969): 15–17.

Miller, Hubert J. "The Story of Dr. Octavio García." In *Preparing Teachers for Bilingual Education: Basic Readings*, edited by Octavio A. Ballesteros, 171–184. Washington, D.C.: University Press of the Americas, 1979.

Mindiola, Tatcho Jr., and Lorenzo Cano. *Higher Educational Needs of Mexican Americans and Blacks in Texas.* Houston: Mexican American Studies Program, 1986.

Mindiola, Tatcho Jr., Luis Salinas, and Karl Eschbach. *A Profile of Undocumented Seniors in Select Houston Independent School District High Schools*. Houston: Center for Mexican American Studies Research Report, University of Houston, 1996.

Mireles, Edmundo E. "A Cultural and Practical Subject—The Teaching of Spanish in Our Public Schools." *American School Board Journal* 127 (November 1953): 33.

________. "Corpus Christi Kids are Bilingual." *Texas Outlook* 35 (May 1951): 10–12.

________. "¿Habla ud. Ingles?" *Time* 43 (February 14, 1944): 71.

Missena, Esteban Guillermo. "A Study of Learning Styles and Related Factors of Adults in Selected Hispanic Baptist Churches in Tarrant County." Ph.D. dissertation, Southwestern Baptist Theological Seminary, 1997.

Mitchell, Nan Jones. "An Evaluation of Provisions for the Education of Spanish-speaking Children in San Marcos, Texas." Master's thesis, University of Texas, Austin, 1946.

Moecker, Donald Lyle Jr. "The Argyris/Schon Theoretical Model Applied to Special Education Decision Processes for Anglo and Hispanic." Ph.D. dissertation, University of Texas at Austin, 1989.

Montemayor, Elsa Diana. "A Study of the Spanish Spoken by Certain Bilingual Students of Laredo, Texas." Master's thesis, Texas Woman's University, 1966.

Montgomery, Gary T. "Comfort With Acculturation Status Among Students from South Texas." *Hispanic Journal of Behavioral Sciences* 14 (May 1992): 201–223.

Montiel, Arturo. "The Recruitment of Non-college Bound, At Risk Hispanic High School Students in Texas Community Colleges." Ed.D. dissertation, Oklahoma State University, 2001.

Moody-Kurly, Gloria. "Acculturation and Academic Achievement of Mexican-American Adolescents in the Rio Grande Valley." Ed.D. dissertation, University of Houston, 1998.

Moran, Mattie Belle. "A Study of the Oral and Reading Vocabularies of Beginning Spanish-speaking Children." Master's thesis, University of Texas, Austin, 1940.

Morrow, Victoria P., and William P. Kuvlesky. "Bilingual Patterns of Nonmetropolitan Mexican-American Youth." In *Politics and Society in the Southwest: Ethnicity and Chicano Pluralism*, edited by Z. Anthony Kruszewski, Richard L. Hough, and Jacob Ornstein-Galicia, 3–24. Boulder, Colo.: Westview Press, 1982.

Muñiz-Quiz, Miriam M. "Profiles of Mexican-American and Anglo School Board Members along the Texas-Mexico Border Region: Characteristics and Factors That Influence Them to Seek Office." Ph.D. dissertation, New Mexico State University, 2000.

Murillo, Nathan. "The Works of George I. Sánchez: An Appreciation." In *Chicano Psychology*, edited by Joe L. Martínez Jr. and Richard H. Mendoza, 23–32. Second edition. Orlando, Fla.: Academic Press, 1984.

Murray, M. E., et al. "Ethnic Group Difference: Between WISC and WAIS Scores in Delinquent Boys." *Journal of Experimental Education* 42.2 (1973): 68–72.

Nabb, David B. "Music Performance Program Enrollment and Course Availability for Educationally Disadvantaged versus Non-educationally Disadvantaged High School Students in Texas." Ph.D. dissertation, University of North Texas, 1995.

Nall, Frank C. II. "Levels of Aspiration of Mexican Americans in El Paso Schools." Ph.D. dissertation, Michigan State University, 1959.

Nami, Julia. "A Study of the Family Life, in its Relation to Education, of Pupils in the Second Grade of the Anthony Margil School, San Antonio, Texas." Master's thesis, University of Texas, Austin, 1940.

Natalicio, Luiz F. S., and Diana S. Natalicio. "The Educational Problems of Atypical Student Groups: The Native Speaker of Spanish." *Urban Education* 4 (October 1969): 262–272. Reprinted in *Education of the Spanish-Speaking Urban Child: A Book of Readings*, edited by Earl J. Ogletree and David García, 238–248. Springfield, Ill.: Charles C. Thomas Publisher, 1975.

Nicholson, Anita Lucindy Connelly. "Hispanic Females, Forty Plus Years of Age, Returning to Six South Texas Universities to Study Science and/or Math: Biases, Sources, Effects, and the Barriers Imposed." Master's thesis, Texas A&M University-Kingsville, 1997.

Nicola, Petra Castro. "The Educational Problem of the Mexican Migrants of Texas, with Specific Reference to San Marcos, Texas." Master's thesis, Southwest Texas State University, 1952.

Norwood, Nell. "Development of a Curriculum Guide for Teaching the Mexican American Culture of Texas in Spanish Language Class for Native Speakers." Master's thesis, University of Texas at Austin, 1972.

November, Abigail A. "Variables Associated with Lunch Fat Intake of Mexican-American Fifth-Graders in Two Central Texas School Districts." Ph.D. dissertation, New York University, 1993.

Nwachie, Judy Carol Flakes. "An Evaluation: The Texas Equal Educational Opportunity Plan for Higher Education on the Representation of Black and Hispanic Women Administrators." Ph.D. dissertation, University of Texas at Austin, 1993.

Ochoa, Hermelinda. "Linguistic Errors made by Spanish-speaking Children in Written English." Master's thesis, University of Texas, Austin, 1942.

Ochoa, Salvador Hector. "Experimental Classification Procedures to Address Within-group Sociometric Status Variability of Hispanic Learning Disabled Pupils for Academic and Play Activities." Ph.D. dissertation, Texas A&M University, 1989.

O'Donnell, Lorraine Gordy. "Identification, Teacher Perceptions, and Analysis of Selected Behaviors for Elementary Principals in the Texas-Mexico Border Area of El Paso County." Ed.D dissertation, New Mexico State University, 1996.

Ojeda-de la Cruz, Juanita Calderón. "Mexican and Black Americans' Sex Role Stereotyping in the School's Socialization Process." Ed.D. dissertation, Texas A&I University, 1985.

Oliveira, A. L. "A Comparison of the Verbal Teaching Behaviors of Junior High School Mexican American and Anglo American Teachers of Social Studies and Mathematics Classes of Predominantly Spanish-speaking Children." Ph.D. dissertation, University of Texas at Austin, 1970.

Ornelas, Juanita Pantoja. "Factors in Upward Mobility of Anglo and Hispanic Women in Public School Administration." Ph.D. dissertation, Texas Woman's University, 1991.

Ornstein-Galicia, Jacob. "Chicano Caló: Description and Review of a Border Variety." *Hispanic Journal of Behavioral Sciences* 9.4 (1987): 359–373.

________. "Correlating Bilingualism/Biculturalism and Socio-Educational Factors in a Survey of Mexican-American Students at a Southwestern University." In *Politics and Society in the Southwest: Ethnicity and Chicano Pluralism*, edited by Z. Anthony Kruszewski, Richard L. Hough, and Jacob Ornstein-Galicia, 197–214. Boulder, Colo.: Westview Press, 1982.

Orozco, Cynthia E. "*Del Rio ISD v. Salvaterria*." In *The New Handbook of Texas,* edited by Ron Tyler, Douglas E. Barnett, Roy R. Barkley, Penelope C. Anderson, and Mark F. Odintz, vol. 2, 578–579. Austin: Texas State Historical Association, 1996.

________. "Edmundo Eduardo Mireles." In *The New Handbook of Texas,* edited by Ron Tyler, Douglas E. Barnett, Roy R. Barkley, Penelope C. Anderson, and Mark F. Odintz, vol. 4, 770–771. Austin: Texas State Historical Association, 1996.

________. "Home Improvement League." In *The New Handbook of Texas*, edited by Ron Tyler, Douglas E. Barnett, Roy R. Barkley, Penelope C. Anderson, and Mark F. Odintz, vol. 5, 925–926. Austin: Texas State Historical Association, 1996.

________. "Intercultural Development Research Association." In *The New Handbook of Texas,* edited by Ron Tyler, Douglas E. Barnett, Roy R. Barkley, Penelope C. Anderson, and Mark F. Odintz, vol. 3, 858–859. Austin: Texas State Historical Association, 1996.

________. "*Rodríguez v. San Antonio ISD*." In *The New Handbook of Texas*, edited by Ron Tyler, Douglas E. Barnett, Roy R. Barkley, Penelope C. Anderson, and Mark F. Odintz, vol. 5, 658–659. Austin: Texas State Historical Association, 1996.

________. "Simon G. Domínguez." In *The New Handbook of Texas,* edited by Ron Tyler, Douglas E. Barnett, Roy R. Barkley, Penelope C. Anderson, and Mark F. Odintz, vol. 2, 673. Austin: Texas State Historical Association, 1996.

________. "Spanish-speaking PTA." In *The New Handbook of Texas*, edited by Ron Tyler, Douglas E. Barnett, Roy R. Barkley, Penelope C. Anderson, and Mark F. Odintz, vol. 6, 13–14. Austin: Texas State Historical Association, 1996.

________. "Texans for the Educational Advancement of Mexican Americans." In *The New Handbook of Texas*, edited by Ron Tyler, Douglas E. Barnett, Roy R. Barkley, Penelope C. Anderson, and Mark F. Odintz, vol. 6, 271. Austin: Texas State Historical Association, 1996.

Ortego, Philip D. "The Education of Mexican Americans." In *The Chicanos: Mexican American Voices*, edited by Ed Ludwig and James Santibañez, 157–172. New York: Penguin Books, 1971.

Osborne, Marie A. "The Educational Status of Intrastate Migrants in Texas, 1935." Master's thesis, University of Texas, Austin, 1954.

Ovalle, María Alicia. "The Development of Fourth-Grade Spanish Writing among Mexican-American Students in an Elementary School in South Texas." Ed.D. dissertation, Texas A&M University-Kingsville, 1998.

Overfelt, Robert. "A Non-Traditional Approach to Higher Education: Sul Ross State University Uvalde Study Center and the Older Hispanic Student." In *Proceedings of the Conference on Hispanics and Higher Education, 1987*, edited by Judith A. Parsons, 93–103. Alpine, Tex.: Sul Ross State University Press, 1988.

Owens, Keith. "Dr. Patricia Hernández." *Hispanic Outlook in Higher Education* 6 (March 15, 1986): 11–12.

Parada, Mrs. Stella (Garza). "School Attendance of Southside School (Latin-American), San Marcos, Texas." Master's thesis, Southwest Texas State University, 1945.

Paredes, Américo. "Jorge Isidoro Sánchez y Sánchez (1906–1972)." In *Humanidad: Essays in Honor of George I. Sánchez*, edited by Américo Paredes, 120–126. Los Angeles: Chicano Studies Center Publications, 1977.

Parías, María Julieta. "The Spanish Language in Texas, No. 3, Duval, Webb, and Zapata Counties." Master's thesis, University of Texas, Austin, 1950.

Parr, Eunice E. *A Comparative Study of Mexican and American Children in the Schools of San Antonio, Texas*. San Francisco: R&E Research Associates, 1971.

________. "A Comparative Study of Mexican and American Children in the Schools of San Antonio." Master's thesis, University of Chicago, 1926.

Parry, Esther Louise. "A Comparison of the Abilities of Spanish-speaking and English-Speaking Children in Ninth Grade Algebra." Master's thesis, University of Texas, Austin, 1933.

Parsons, Judith A., ed. *Proceedings of the Conference on Hispanics and Higher Education, 1987*. Alpine, Tex.: Sul Ross State University Press, 1988.

Past, Ray. "English (Only!) Spoken Here." *Password* 30 (Summer 1985): 63–78.

Patranella, Kenneth Wayne. "Academic Performance, Attendance, and Schedule Rigor of Extracurricular Participants and Nonparticipants." Ed.D. dissertation, Texas A&M University, 1987.

Pedroza, Bertha Anna. "Consequences of High-stakes Testing on Historically Disenfranchised Students: Analysis of Student Outcomes." Ph.D. dissertation, University of Texas at Austin, 1997.

Pérez, Enrique García. "Factors Associated with Recruitment and Persistence of Hispanic and White non-Hispanic Agriculture Students at a Regional University in South Texas." Ed.D. dissertation, Texas A&M University-Kingsville, 1999.

Pérez, Ernest. "Effects of Bilingual Education on Language Use and Language Preference of Fourth-Grade Mexican American Children in Four Bilingual Education Projects in Texas." Ph.D. dissertation, University of Texas at Austin, 1979.

Pérez, Ricardo Jesús. "A Quantitative Analysis on the Treatment of the Mexican American in State Adopted Texas History Textbooks." Ph.D. dissertation, University of Michigan, 1979.

Pérez, Roberto Cruz. "A Study of the Leadership Styles of Mexican American Educational Administrators in Selected Texas Public Schools." Ph.D. dissertation, University of Texas at Austin, 1981.

Peterson, Margaret W. "Curricular Preferences of Elementary School Children." Master's thesis, University of Texas, Austin, 1942.

Phemister, Linda Lightfoot. "How Disadvantaged, Hispanic, Gifted Students Perceive the Relevancy of the University of Texas Pan American New Challenge Program." Master's thesis, University of Texas–Pan American, 1994.

Phillips, B. V., et al. "A Formative and Summative Evaluation Model for Special Educational Programs." *Journal of Medical Education* 51 (1976): 836–843.

Pipes, Karl M. "A Study of the Failures and Drop-outs in the San Benito High School." Master's thesis, University of Texas, Austin, 1950.

Post, Donald E. "Ethnic Competition for Control of Schools in Two South Texas Towns." Ph.D. dissertation, University of Texas at Austin, 1975.

________. "Ethnic Conflict in Two South Texas Towns." *Journal of Integrated Education* 15 (September 1977): 10–14.

Poulter, Virgil L. "A Phonological Study of the Spanish Speech of Mexican-American College Students Native to Fort Worth-Dallas." Ph.D. dissertation, Louisiana State University, 1973.

________. "Comparison of Voiceless Stops in the English and Spanish of Bilingual Natives of Fort Worth-Dallas." In *Texas Studies in Bilingualism*, edited by G. G. Gilbert, 42–49. Berlin: Walter de Gruyter, 1970.

Preston, J. D., and P. A. Fry. "Marijuana Use Among Houston High School Students." *Social Science Quarterly* 51.1 (1971): 170–178.

Preuss, Gene B. "Cotulla Revisited: A Reassessment of Lyndon Johnson's Year as a Public School Teacher." *Journal of South Texas* 10 (1997): 20–37.

________. "Differing Perceptions: Public School Teachers and Mexican Students in Texas, 1910–1930." *West Texas Historical Association Yearbook* 72 (1996): 119–129.

Prewitt, Steven W. "'We Didn't Ask to Come to this Party': Self-Determination Collides with the Federal Government in the Public Schools of Del Rio, Texas, 1890–1971." Ph.D. dissertation, University of Houston, 2000.

Prigden, William McKinley. "A Survey and Proposed Plan of Reorganization at the Public Schools in Zavala County." Master's thesis, University of Texas at Austin, 1976.

Pruitt, Daughn Warren. "Vocational Identity, Level of Career Indecision, and Barriers of Hispanic Reentry Women in Selected Texas Community Colleges: Implications for Adult Education." Ph.D. dissertation, Texas A&M University, 1992.

Pryor, Guy C. *Evaluation of the Bi-lingual Project of Harlandale Independent School District, San Antonio, Texas, in the First Grades of Four Elementary Schools During 1966–1967 School Year*. San Antonio: Harlandale Independent School District, 1967.

Pumarejo, Faustino Jr. "Educational Attainment and Organizational Perceptions of Mexican-American Supervisors." Ph.D. dissertation, Michigan State University, 1987.

Putnam, Howard L. "The Relation of College Programs of Community Services to the Needs of the Spanish-speaking People." Ph.D. dissertation, University of Texas, Austin, 1956.

Queen, Rae Wyatt. "Characteristics Related to Career Decision Making for Hispanic Adolescents in Texas." Ph.D. dissertation, Texas A&M University, 1999.

Quilantán, María Cristina. "Mexican American Women: Unique Superintendents in Texas." Ed.D. dissertation, University of Texas–Pan American, 2002.

Quintanilla, Delia G. "Effective Schooling of Hispanic Americans: A Policy Analysis of the State Bilingual Education Statutes of Texas and Massachusetts." Ed.D. dissertation, Boston University, 1993.

Quintanilla, Guadalupe C. "The Little School of the 400 and Its Impact on Education for the Spanish Dominant Bilingual Children of Texas." Ph.D. dissertation, University of Houston, 1976.

Quiz, Fernando Zapata. "Leadership Approaches of the Public School Principalship: Hispanic and Non-Hispanic Superintendents' Perceptions along the Texas-Mexico Border Region." Ph.D. dissertation, New Mexico State University, 2000.

Ramírez, A. G., R. H. Milk, and A. Sapiens. "Intragroup Differences and Language Attitudes toward Varieties of Spanish among Bilingual Pupils from California to Texas." *Hispanic Journal of Behavioral Sciences* 5 (December 1983): 417–429.

Ramírez, Carina. "Lexical Usage of, and Attitude toward, Southwest Spanish in the Ysleta, Texas Area." In *Problems in Applied Educational Sociolinguistics: Readings on Language and Culture Problems of United States Ethnic Groups*, edited by Glenn G. Gilbert and Jacob Ornstein, 43–54. The Hague: Mouton Publishers, 1978.

Ramírez, Diana María. "Children of Mexican Immigrants: Negotiating School in a Two-way Setting on the Texas-Mexico Border." Ed.D. dissertation, University of Texas–Pan American, 2002.

Ramírez, Ernesto Jr. "The Identification of Special Problems as Perceived by Mexican-American Chief Executive Officers in Selected Community Colleges in the Southwest and Public School Districts in Texas." Ph.D. dissertation, University of Texas at Austin, 1975.

Ramírez, Gina Yvonne. "Cross-cultural Differences in Behaviors among Ninth Graders at William B. Travis High School, Austin, Texas." Master's thesis, University of Texas Graduate School of Biomedical Science at Galveston, 1992.

Ramírez, Jorge A. "The Shared Success of Adelina Silva: Alamo's Award-Winning Activist." *Hispanic Outlook in Higher Education* 9 (July 16, 1999): 12–14.

Ramírez, Karen G. "Bilingualism and Bilingual Programs in El Paso: Kindergarten and First Grade." Master's thesis, University of Texas at El Paso, 1971.

Ramírez, Manuel III. "Identification with Mexican Family Values and Authoritarianism in Mexican-Americans." *Journal of Social Psychology* 73 (1967): 3–11.

________. "Potential Contributions by the Behavioral Sciences to Effective Preparation Programs for Teachers of Mexican-American Children." In *Educating the Mexican American*, edited by Henry Sioux Johnson and William J. Hernández-M, 210–231. Valley Forge, Penn.: Judson Press, 1970.

Ramírez, María Irene. "A Comparison of Three Methods of Teaching the Spanish-speaking Student." Ed.D. dissertation, East Texas State University, 1971.

Ramírez, Norma. "An Analysis of Academic Achievement of Hispanic Students Identified as Learning-Disabled: Initial Referral and Reappraisal in a Coastal Bend Area School District." Ed.D. dissertation, Texas A&M University-Kingsville, 1997.

Ramírez, Olga M. "Some Factors Related to Mathematics Anxiety among Hispanic College Undergraduates." Ph.D. dissertation, Texas A&M University, 1985.

Ramírez, Olga M., Sylvia Rebollos Taube, and Paul Michael Taube. "Factors Influencing Mathematics Among Mexican American College Students." *Hispanic Journal of Behavioral Sciences* 12 (August 1990): 292–298.

Ramírez, Sara L. "The Educational Status and Socio-Economic Backgrounds of Latin-American Children in Waco, Texas." Master's thesis, University of Texas, Austin, 1957.

Ramírez Vida, Rosa María. "The Effect of Culturally Relevant Units of Instruction on the Attitude of Fifth Grade Social Studies Students." Ph.D. dissertation, University of Texas at Austin, 1980.

Ramón, Simón René. "Vocabulario selecto del español regional de Del Rio, Texas." Master's thesis, Southwest Texas State University, 1974.

Rangel, Jorge C., and Carlos M. Alcalá. "De Jure Segregation of Chicanos in Texas Schools." *Harvard Civil Rights—Civil Liberties Law Review* 7 (March 1972): 307–391.

Rangel, Victor Manuel. "A Study of the Relationship between Grades, Test Scores, Discipline Referrals, and Family Constellation of Middle School Students." Master's thesis, Texas A&I University, 1991.

Raynes, Joseph Lincoln. "A Descriptive Study of the Demographic Characteristics of Texas Community School Participants and Their Primary Reasons for

Participation in Community School Activities." Ph.D. dissertation, Texas A&M University, 1984.

Ray, Ruth Aileen Dunn. "Selected Graduate Programs of Professional Education in the Spanish Southwest, with Curricular Emphases on Blacks, Indians, and Spanish Americans." Ed.D. dissertation, University of North Texas, 1980.

Redden, Sharron Ann. "Self-esteem and Intrinsic Motivational Effects of Using a Constructivist and a Behaviorist Approach to Computer Usage in Fifth-grade Hispanic Classes." Ph.D. dissertation, Nova Southeastern University, 2000.

Renner, Richard R. "Some Characteristics of Spanish Name Texans and Foreign Latin Americans in Texas Higher Education." Ph.D. dissertation, University of Texas, Austin, 1957.

________. "Spanish Name University Students in Texas Outlast Others." *College and University* 38 (Spring 1963): 282–283.

Reséndez, Victor Jr. "Vocabulario español de Seguin, Texas." Master's thesis, Southwest Texas State University, 1970.

Reuthinger, Hortense. "A Comparative Study of Two Methods of Theory Instruction for Seventh Grade Latin American Girls." Master's thesis, University of Texas, Austin, 1956.

Reyes, Augustine. "Alternative Education: The Dark Side of Education or New Tools for Latinos to Achieve Self-Actualization." *Bilingual Review/La Revista Bilingüe* 25 (2000): 249–276.

Reyes, María Elena. "Female Hispanic College Students: Upper-division and Graduate Students at Four Major Public Institutions in Texas." Ph.D. dissertation, University of Texas at Austin, 1991.

Reyes, Rogelio. "The Social and Linguistic Foundations of Chicano Caló: Trends for Future Research." In *Research Issues and Problems in United States Spanish*, edited by Jacob Ornstein-Galicia, George Green, and Dennis Bixler-Márquez, 75–97. Brownsville, Tex.: Pan American University, 1988.

Reynolds, Selma F. *Some Aspects of Spanish as Spoken and Written by Spanish-speaking Students of a Junior High School in Texas*. Denton: Texas State College for Women, 1945.

________. "Some Aspects of Spanish as Spoken and Written by Spanish-speaking Students of a Junior High School in Texas." Master's thesis, Texas State College for Women, 1945.

Rice, Laurence Stewart. "Factors Related to Disproportionate Representation of Hispanics in Programs for Students with Learning Disabilities." Ph.D. dissertation, University of Texas at Austin, 1995.

Richardson, Chad, and María Olivia Villarreal-Solano. "The Pain of Gain: Fifty Years of Anglo-Hispanic Relations in South Texas Schools." In *Batos, Bolillos, Pochos, and Pelados: Class and Culture on the South Texas Border*, by Chad Richardson, 123–152. Austin: University of Texas Press, 1999.

Richardson, Chad, María Olivia Villarreal-Solano, and Cruz C. Torres. "Anglo-Hispanic Relations in South Texas Schools from 1945 to 1993: A Triangulated Profile." *Río Bravo* 3.2 (1994): 114–134.

Richter, Tellmond Herder. "Comparison of Latin-Americans and Anglo-Americans with Reference to Chronological Age, Reading Comprehension, and Arithmetic Computation in the Upper Elementary Grades in the Pearsall and Charlotte, Texas, Schools." Master's thesis, Southwest Texas University, 1951.

Riley, Frances Lucile. "A Longitudinal Evaluation of the Pre-First Grade Language Experiences in the McAllen Public Schools." Master's thesis, Texas A&I University at Kingsville, 1961.

Rivera, Carlos. "The Meaning and Implication of Bilingualism for Texas Schools." In *Improving Educational Opportunities of the Mexican-Americans.* Proceedings First Texas Conference for the Mexican-American, San Antonio, 1967, edited by Dwain M. Estes and David W. Darling, 67–79. Austin: Southwest Educational Development Laboratory, 1967.

Rivera, Daniel Joe. "A Comparative Analysis of the Leader Behavior of Texas Mexican-American Administrators in Higher Education." Ph.D. dissertation, University of Texas at Austin, 1976.

Robertson, Clyde Reeves. "A Comparative Study of the Progress of American and Mexican Pupils in Certain Elementary Schools in Texas." Master's thesis, University of Texas, Austin, 1935.

Robertson-Courtney, Phyllis Marie. "Disadvantaged Hispanic Students' Perceptions of Factors Contributing to Their Academic Success." Ph.D. dissertation, University of Texas at Austin, 1989.

Robinson, Ellen Joyce Phillips. "A Study of English Language Development in Spanish-Dominant Five-Year-Old Children in the Sweetwater Public Schools." Master's thesis, Hardin-Simmons University, 1977.

Robles, Barbara J. "Latinas in the Academy: Profiling Current and Future Scholars." *Reflexiones: New Directions in Mexican American Studies*, edited by Richard R. Flores, 91–113. Austin: University of Texas at Austin, 1999.

Rocha, Pedro Jr. "An Investigation of Performance Behaviors of Mexican and Anglo American Deans and Chairpersons as they managed Critical Incident Situations in Selected Texas Community Junior Colleges." Ph.D. dissertation, University of Texas at Austin, 1981.

Rodríguez, Concha. "An Analytical and Remedial Study of the Spanish used by Latin American Children." Master's thesis, St. Mary's University, 1949.

Rodríguez, Jason Oscar. "A Study of the Nature and Scope of Parental Involvement in Bilingual Education Programs under ESEA Title I in Two Texas School Districts." Ph.D. dissertation, University of Texas at Austin, 1987.

Rodríguez, María Dalinda. "The Attitudes of Hispanic Parents, Teachers and Administrators Regarding Bilingual Education for Students With and Without Learning Disabilities." Ph.D. dissertation, University of Texas at Austin, 1994.

Rodríguez, Rodolfo. "Bilingual Education." In *The New Handbook of Texas,* edited by Ron Tyler, Douglas E. Barnett, Roy R. Barkley, Penelope C. Anderson, and Mark F. Odintz, vol. 1, 486. Austin: Texas State Historical Association, 1996.

Rohr, Thurman G. "A Study of the Correction of English Pronunciation of Latin American Pupils." Master's thesis, University of Texas, Austin, 1948.

Rollins, E. L. "A Snellen Chart Technique Study of Visual Acuity of the Spanish Culture Pupils in the Stephen F. Austin Public Elementary School, Kingsville, Texas." Master's thesis, Texas A&I University at Kingsville, 1937.

Romero, Carlos Humberto. "The Perceptions of Guidance and Counseling of Hispanic/Non-Hispanic Students in Two Selected High Schools of South Texas." Ed.D. dissertation, Texas A&I University, 1987.

Romo, Harriett. "Contrasting Perceptions of Schooling Among the Mexican Origin Population." In *Mexican Immigrants and Mexican Americans: An Evolving Relation*, edited by Harley L. Browning and Rodolfo O. de la Garza, 175–193. Austin: CMAS Publications, 1986.

________. "The Mexican Origin Population's Differing Perceptions of their Children's Schooling." In *The Mexican American Experience: An Interdisciplinary Anthology*, edited by Rodolfo O. de la Garza, Frank D. Bean, Charles M. Bonjean, Ricardo Romo, and Rodolfo Álvarez, 377–392. Austin: University of Texas Press, 1985.

Romo, Harriett D., and Toni Falbo. *Latino High School Graduation: Defying the Odds*. Austin: University of Texas Press, 1996.

Ronda, Michelle A., and Richard R. Valencia. "'At Risk' Chicano Students: The Institutional and Communicative Life of a Category." *Hispanic Journal of Behavioral Sciences* 16 (November 1994): 363–395.

Roots, Floy. "Methods and Materials for Teaching Spanish to Spanish-Speaking Students in Texas High Schools." Master's thesis, University of Texas, Austin, 1939.

Rosales, Raúl G. "General Educational Development Certification: Effects of G.E.D. Certification on Migrant Recipients as Compared to Migrant Dropouts in South Texas." Ed.D. dissertation, University of Houston, 1975.

Roska, Linda Ann. "An Evaluation of the Accelerated Schools Process Using the Texas Assessment of Academic Skills." Ph.D. dissertation, University of Texas at Austin, 1999.

Rouse, Lura Nelson. "A Study of the Education of Spanish-speaking Children in Dimmit County, Texas." Master's thesis, University of Texas, Austin, 1948.

Russell, D. "Problems of Mexican Children in the Southwest." *Journal of Educational Sociology* 17 (December 1943): 216–222.

Salazar, Martín. "Mexican Americans' Observed Perceptions of Counselor Credibility as a Function of Language." Ed.D. dissertation, Texas Tech University, 1994.

Salinas, Alfredo. "Mexican American Persistence at a Hispanic-serving Institution: Lessons and Anomalies in a 10-Year University Cohort." Ed.D. dissertation, University of Texas–Pan American, 2002.

Salinas, Guadalupe. "Mexican Americans and the Desegregation of Schools in the Southwest." *El Onto: A Journal of Contemporary Mexican American Thought* 4 (Summer 1971): 36–69.

Salinas, Medardo Jr. "A Comparison of the Levels of Personal and Social Adjustment Between Anglo-American and Mexican-American Adolescents in 6 AAAA Schools of the Rio Grande Valley of Texas." Master's thesis, Pan American University, 1976.

Sánchez, George I. *Concerning Segregation of Spanish-speaking Children in the Public Schools*. Austin: University of Texas Press, 1951. Reprinted in *Education and the Mexican American*, edited by Carlos E. Cortés. New York: Arno Press, 1974.

________. *Forgotten People*. Albuquerque: University of New Mexico Press, 1940.

________. *"Wetback": A Preliminary Report*. Advisory Committee for the Study of Spanish-speaking People. Austin: University of Texas Press, 1949.

________. "The Education of Bilinguals in a State School System." Ph.D. dissertation, University of California, Berkeley, 1934.

________. "Scores of Spanish-speaking Children on Repeated Tests." Master's thesis, University of Texas, Austin, 1931.

________. "The American of Mexican Descent." *Chicago Jewish Forum* 20 (Winter 1961–1962): 120–124.

________. "Bilingualism and Mental Measures." *Journal of Applied Psychology* 8 (December 1934): 765–772.

________. "Child Development in the Rural Environment." In *Growth and Development: The Basis for Educational Programs*, edited by Progressive Education Association, 112–118. New York: Progressive Education Association, 1936.

________. "The Community School in the Rural Scene." In *The Community School*, edited by Samuel Everett, 164–215. New York: D. Appleton-Century, 1939.

________. "Concerning American Minorities." In *Proceedings of the Southwest Council on Education of Spanish-speaking People*, 51–55. n.p.: Council on Education of Spanish-speaking People, 1951.

________. "Cultural Relations within the Americas." *Childhood Education* (April 1942): 339–342.

________. "Educational Change in Historical Perspective." In *Mexican Americans and Educational Change*, edited by Alfredo Castañeda, 14–21. New York: Arno Press, 1974.

________. "An Educational Philosophy to Meet the Needs of a Democracy in Crisis." *Proceedings of the Texas School Administration and Supervisors*, 1–5. Austin: Texas School Administration and Supervisors, 1941.

________. "Education in Mexico." In *Comparative Education*, edited by A. V. Moehlman and J. S. Roucek, 85–108. New York: Dryden Press, 1951.

________. "The Education of Bilinguals in a State School System." In *Education and the Mexican American*, edited by Carlos E. Cortés. New York: Arno Press, 1974.

________. "Education of Minority and Special Groups in Rural Areas." In *White House Conference on Rural Education*, by the White House Conference on Rural Education, 176–177. Washington, D.C.: National Education Association of the United States, 1945.

________. "An Educator Speaks Out." *Home Missions* 18 (July 1967): 18–19.

________. "Group Differences and Spanish-speaking Children: A Critical Review." *Journal of Applied Psychology* 16 (October 1932): 549–558.

________. "History, Culture, and Education." In *La Raza: Forgotten Americans*, edited by Julian Samora, 1–26. Notre Dame, Ind.: University of Notre Dame Press, 1966.

________. "The Implication of a Basal Vocabulary to the Measurement of the Abilities of Bilingual Children." *Journal of Social Psychology* 5 (1934): 395–402.

________. "Inter American Education: The New Frontier." In *Proceedings of the 46th National Congress of Parents and Teachers*, 33–40. San Antonio: National Congress of Parents and Teachers, 1942.

________. "A New Frontier for the Americas." *The Alcalde* 19 (March 1961): 9–11.

________. "North of the Border." In *Proceedings and Transactions of the Texas Academy of Science*, 77–85. Austin: Texas Academy of Science, 1942.

________. "Pachucos in the Making." *Common Ground* 4 (Autumn 1943): 13–20.

________. "Quantitative and Objective Criteria in Education: A Delusion." *Texas Journal of Secondary Education* 13 (Spring 1960): 1–5.

________. "School Integration and Americans of Mexican Descent." *American Unity* 16.3 (1958): 9–14.

________. "Scores of Spanish-speaking Children on Repeated Tests." *Pedagogical Seminary and Journal of Genetic Psychology* (March 1932): 223–231.

________. "Spanish in the Southwest." In *Educating the Mexican American*, edited by Henry Sioux Johnson and William J. Hernández-M, 24–32. Valley Forge, Penn.: Judson Press, 1970.

________. "Spanish-Speaking People in the Southwest: A Brief Historical Review." *California Journal of Elementary Education* 12 (November 1953): 106–111.

________. "Theory and Practice in Rural Education." *Progressive Education* 13 (1936): 590–596.

________. "The United Mexican States." In *Comparative Educational Administration*, edited by Theodore L. Reller and Edgar L. Masphet, 151–165. Englewood Cliffs, N.J.: Prentice-Hall, 1962.

________, ed. *First Regional Conference on the Education of Spanish-speaking People in the Southwest*. Austin: University of Texas Press, 1946.

Sánchez, George I., and Charles L. Eastlack. *Say It the Spanish Way*. Austin: Good Neighbor Commission of Texas, 1960.

Sánchez, George I., H. J. Otto, et al. *A Guide for Teachers of Spanish-speaking Children*. Austin: Texas State Department of Education, 1946.

Sánchez, George I., and Howard Putnam. *Materials Relating to the Education of Spanish–speaking People in the United States: An Annotated Bibliography*. Westport, Conn.: Greenwood Press, 1971.

Sánchez, George I., R. C. Reindorp, and Bernice M. Boswell. *References for Teachers of English as a Foreign Language*. Austin: University of Texas Press, 1949.

Sánchez, George I., and Virgie Sánchez. "Education in Mexico in the Sixteenth Century." *New Mexico Quarterly* 4 (August 1934): 184–192.

Sánchez, George I., and Virgil E. Strickland. *Study of the Educational Opportunities Provided Spanish-surnamed Children in the Texas School System.* Austin: University of Texas Press, 1974.

________. "Spanish Name Spells Discrimination." *The Nation's Schools* 41 (January 1948): 1–7.

Sánchez, Juan O. "Walkout Cabrones: The Uvalde School Walkout of 1970." *West Texas Historical Association Yearbook* 68 (1992): 122–133.

Sánchez-Rosado, Kevin Adolfo. "Levels of Acculturation of Children of Mexican Descent as Perceived in Their Kinetic Family Drawings." Ph.D. dissertation, Andrews University, 2001.

Sánchez, Rosaura, et al. "*La Perika Tejana:* A Study of the Texas Chicano Dialect." *Magazín* 1 (January 1973): 60–66.

Sánchez, Serafín Victor. "A Descriptive and Exploratory Study of Mexican-American Dropouts." Ph.D. dissertation, Texas A&M University, 1999.

San Miguel, Guadalupe Jr. *Brown, Not White: School Integration and the Chicano Movement in Houston*. College Station: Texas A&M University Press, 2001.

________. *"Let All of Them Take Heed": Mexican Americans and the Campaign for Educational Equality in Texas, 1910–1981*. Austin: University of Texas Press, 1987.

________. "Endless Pursuits: The Chicano Educational Experience in Corpus Christi, Texas, 1880–1960." Ph.D. dissertation, Stanford University, 1979.

________. "Actors Not Victims: Chicanas/os and the Struggle for Educational Equality." In *Chicanas/Chicanos at the Crossroads: Social, Economic, and Political Change*, edited by David R. Maciel and Isidro D. Ortiz, 159–180. Tucson: University of Arizona Press, 1996.

________. "Bitter Struggles: Mexican Americans and the Revision of the Texas Bilingual Education Bill in 1981." In *The Chicano Struggle: Analyses of Past and Present Efforts*, edited by John A. García, Teresa Córdova, and Juan R. García, 111–130. Binghamton, N.Y.: Bilingual Press/Editorial Bilingüe, 1984.

________. "'The Community is Beginning to Rumble': The Origins of Chicano Educational Protest in Houston, 1965–1970." *The Houston Review* 13 (1991): 127–148.

________. "Culture and Education in the American Southwest: Towards an Explanation of Chicano School Attendance, 1850–1940." *Journal of American Ethnic History* 7 (Spring 1988): 5–21.

________. "From a Dual to a Tripartite School System: The Origins and Development of Education Segregation in Corpus Christi, Texas." *Integrated Education* 17 (September/December 1979): 27–38.

________. "Mexican American Organizations and the Changing Politics of School Desegregation in Texas, 1945–1980." *Social Science Quarterly* 63 (December 1982): 701–715.

________. "Mexican Americans and Education." In *The New Handbook of Texas*, edited by Ron Tyler, Douglas E. Barnett, Roy R. Barkley, Penelope C. Anderson, and Mark F. Odintz, vol. 4, 671–672. Austin: Texas State Historical Association, 1996.

________. "The Origins, Development, and Consequences of the Educational Segregation of Mexicans in the Southwest." In *Chicano Studies: A Multidisciplinary Approach*, edited by Eugene E. García, Francisco Lomelí, and Isidro Ortiz, 195–208. New York: Teachers' College Press, 1984.

________. "The Schooling of Mexicanos in the Southwest, 1848–1891." In *The Elusive Quest for Equality: 150 Years of Chicano/Chicana Education*, edited by José F. Moreno, 31–51. Cambridge, Mass.: Harvard Educational Review, 1999.

________. "Social and Educational Influences Shaping the Mexican American Mind." *Journal of Midwest History of Education Society* 14 (1986): 57–66.

________. "The Struggle Against Separate and Unequal Schools: Middle Class Mexican Americans and the Desegregation Campaign in Texas, 1929–1957." *History of Education Quarterly* 23 (Fall 1983): 343–359. Reprinted in *En Aquel Entonces: Readings in Mexican-American History*, edited by Manuel G. Gonzales and Cynthia M. Gonzales, 209–216. Bloomington: Indiana University Press, 2000.

San Miguel, Guadalupe Jr., and Richard R. Valencia. "From the Treaty of Guadalupe Hidalgo to Hopwood: The Educational Plight and Struggle of Mexican Americans in the Southwest." *Harvard Educational Review* 68 (1998): 353–412.

Santana, Henry A. "A Study of the Scholastic Performance and Attitudes of Mexican-American Students under the Majority to Minority Voluntary Transfer Policy within a Major South Texas School District." Ed.D. dissertation, University of Houston, 1974.

Sapp, Theresa Laima Bacenas. "An Investigation of Ethnicity, Gender, and Anxiety on the Creative Thinking Abilities of Anglo and Mexican-American College Students under Conditions of Cooperation and Competition." Ph.D. dissertation, University of Georgia, 1991.

Sauceda-Castillo, Mary Jane. "Learning Styles: A Comparative Study of Cultural Differences in African-American, Anglo-American, Asian-American, and Hispanic-American Accounting Students in Texas Public Universities." Ph.D. dissertation, Texas A&M University, 2001.

Saucedo, Leticia M. "The Legal Issues Surrounding the TAAS Case." *Hispanic Journal of Behavioral Sciences* 22 (2000): 411–422.

Sawyer, Janet Beck Moseley. *Social Aspects of Bilingualism in San Antonio, Texas.* Alabama: University of Alabama Press, 1964.

________. "Spanish-English Bilingualism in San Antonio, Texas." In *El lenguaje de los Chicanos*, edited by E. Hernández-Chávez, A. D. Cohen, and A. Beltrán, 18–41. Arlington, Vir.: Center for Applied Linguistics, 1975.

Schaefer, Thomas Edward. "The Impact of Hispanic Ascendancy on the Humanistic Curriculum in Texas Higher Education." Ed.D. dissertation, Texas Tech University, 1992.

Schaer, Bertha A. "A New Language for José." *Texas Outlook 50* (December 1966): 32–33.

Schlossman, Steven. "Self-Evident Remedy: George I. Sánchez, Segregation, and Enduring Dilemma in Bilingual Education." *Teachers' College Record* 84 (Summer 1983): 871–907.

Sedwick, Loretta Susan Wyatt. "An Analysis of Admissions Yield and Telemarketing at Texas A&M University-Kingsville." Ph.D. dissertation, Texas A&M University, 1999.

Sethuraju, Nadarajan Raj. "Race Relations on Campus: African Americans and Hispanics in Two Educational Institutions." Ph.D. dissertation, Texas Woman's University, 2000.

Shade, Cynthia Diane Specia. "Effect of Gifted and Talented Program on Hispanic High School Students in Edgewood Independent School District, San Antonio, Texas." Ed.D. dissertation, Texas A&M University, 1993.

Sharp, John M. "The Origin of Some Non-Standard Lexical Items in the Spanish of El Paso." *Studies in Language and Linguistics, 1969–70*, by University of Texas at El Paso, 207–232. El Paso: Texas Western Press, 1970.

Shaw, Bruce Walsh. "Sociometric Status and Athletic Ability of Anglo American and Latin American Boys in a San Antonio Junior High School." Master's thesis, University of Texas, Austin, 1951.

Shaw, Joanne. "On the Move with Dr. Martha Medrano." *Hispanic Outlook in Higher Education* 9 (June 4, 1999): 12–14.

Shirley, Dennis. *Valley Interfaith and School Reform: Organizing for Power in South Texas*. Austin: University of Texas Press, 2002.

Simmens, Jeff. "TACHE Determined to Boost Hispanic Faculty." *Hispanic Outlook in Higher Education* 11 (January 8, 2001): 10–12.

Simmons, Ozzie G. "The Mutual Images and Expectations of Anglo-Americans and Mexican-Americans." In *Education of the Spanish-speaking Urban Child: A Book of Readings*, edited by Earl J. Ogletree and David García, 138–153. Springfield, Ill.: Charles C. Thomas Publisher, 1975.

Simmons, Thomas Edward. "The Citizen Factories: The Americanization of Mexican Students in Texas Public Schools, 1920–1945." Ph.D. dissertation, Texas A&M University, 1976.

Sisk, William O. "The Mexican in Texas Schools." *Texas Outlook* 14 (December 1930): 10.

Skinner, Robert Eugene. "The Effects of Second Language Instruction upon the English Verbal Performance of Secondary Students as Measured by the Texas Assessment of Academic Skills." Ed.D. dissertation, Texas A&M University-Kingsville, 1997.

Smith, Elizabeth Laverne. "A Descriptive Study of the Demographic Characteristics of Texas Community School Enrollees and Their Levels of Satisfaction." Ph.D. dissertation, Texas A&M University, 1985.

Smith, J. B. Jr. "A Survey of Pupil Failure in the La Feria School with Suggested Remedial Measures." Master's thesis, University of Texas, Austin, 1939.

Smith, Josephine Whitley. "One Family and the Schools." Master's thesis, University of Texas at Austin, 1971.

Smith, Sue Ida. "Three Studies of Retarded Spanish-Culture Beginners, Edinburg, Texas." Master's thesis, Texas A&I University at Kingsville, 1947.

Smith, Walter E. "Mexicano Resistance to Schooled Ethnicity: Ethnic Student Power in South Texas, 1930–1970." Ph.D. dissertation, University of Texas at Austin, 1978.

Smith, Walter E., and Douglas E. Foley. *The Transition of Multiethnic Schooling in Model Town, Texas: 1930–1969*. National Institute of Education Project No. RO20825 and No. 3–4003. Washington, D.C.:National Institute of Education Project, 1975.

________. "Mexican Resistance to Schooling in a South Texas Colony." *Education and Urban Society* 10.2 (1978): 145–176.

Solé, Yolanda P. "Sociolinguistic Perspectives of Texas Spanish and the Teaching of the Standard Language." In *Southwest Language and Linguistics in Educational Perspective*, edited by Gina C. Harvey and M. F. Heiser, 171–185. San Diego: San Diego State University, 1975.

Sosa, Alonzo Hernández. "Bilingual-Bicultural Education in Texas Elementary Public Schools, 1930–1975." Ed.D. dissertation, East Texas State University, 1975.

Sosa-Bonilla, Rosalinda. "The Education of the Mexican American: An Annotated Bibliography." Ed.D. dissertation, Texas A&I University, 1979.

Sosa, Ismael Jr. "A Comparison of Academic Success Indicators of Middle Rio Grande GED and Traditional High School Graduates Entering Southwest Texas Junior College as Freshmen." Ph.D. dissertation, Texas A&M University, 2000.

Soto, Gilberto David. "Elementary Music Education in Laredo, Texas: A Survey of Teaching Strategies and Its Application in the Music Education of Mexican-American Children." Ph.D. dissertation, University of Southern Mississippi, 1995.

Stallings, Angela Widener. "A Study of the Implementation of a Standardized Dress Code and Student Achievement of Hispanic Students in a Suburban High School: A Companion Study." Ed.D. dissertation, Sam Houston State University, 2000.

Stedman, J. M., and R. E. McKenzie. "Family Factors Related to Competence in Young Disadvantaged Mexican American Children." *Child Development* 42.5 (1971): 1602–1607.

Stedman, J. M., and R. L. Adams. "Achievement as a Function of Language Competence, Behavior Adjustment, and Sex in Young Disadvantaged Mexican American Children." *Journal of Educational Psychology* 63.5 (1972): 411–417.

________. "Teacher Perception of Behavioral Adjustment as a Function of Linguistic Ability in Mexican American Headstart Children." *Psychology in the Schools* 10.2 (1973): 221–225.

Steubner, Josephine. "Racial Differences in Reading Achievement." *Texas Outlook* 24 (January 1940): 32.

Stewart, Kenneth L., and Arnoldo De León. "Education is the Gateway: Comparative Patterns of School Attendance and Literacy Between Anglos and Tejanos in Three Texas Regions, 1850–1900." *Aztlán* 16 (1985): 177–195.

________. "Education, Literacy, and Occupational Structure in West Texas, 1860–1900." *West Texas Historical Association Yearbook* 60 (1984): 127–143.

________. "Literacy Among *Immigrantes* in Texas, 1850–1900." *Latin American Research Review* 20 (Fall 1985): 180–187.

Stoddard, Ellwyn R. "Texas Higher Education and Border Funding Inequities: Implication for Border Universities and Transborder Cooperation." *Río Bravo* 2.1 (1992): 54–75.

Stohl, Darthula D. "A Study Treating the Teaching of Language Skills through Music to Spanish-Speaking Children." Master's thesis, University of Texas, Austin, 1954.

Streeter, Vivian. "The Development of the Teaching of Spanish in Texas Public Schools." Master's thesis, University of Texas, Austin, 1928.

Stringer, Jeffrey Lewis. "The Performance of Bilingual Interaction in a Latino Community." Ph.D. dissertation, University of Texas at Austin, 1997.

Sultemeier, Barbara Louise. "Assessing the Relationship between Hispanic Power Structure and Funding of Bilingual Education." Ph.D. dissertation, Texas A&M University, 1982.

Swope-Marrs, Suzanne Rebecca. "Factors Influencing Minority Students' Selection of Teaching as a Career Choice." Ed.D. dissertation, Texas A&M University-Commerce, 1998.

Tapia-Geitz, Olga Hope. "The Relationship between Family/Social Factors and Bilingual Proficiency of Mexican-American College Freshmen." Ph.D. dissertation, University of Oregon, 1986.

Taylor, Darlene Marie. "A Study of the Dropout Rate of Selected Rural, Urban, and Suburban School Districts in Harris and Montgomery Counties." Master's thesis, Stephen F. Austin State University, 1987.

Taylor, J. T. "Americanization of Harlingen's Mexican School Population." *Texas Outlook* 18 (September 1934): 37–38.

Telese, James A. "Mexican American High School Students' Perceptions of Mathematics and Mathematics Teaching." *Hispanic Journal of Behavioral Sciences* 21 (May 1999): 154–169.

Teschner, Richard V. "Second-Language Acquisition and Foreign Language Teaching: Spanish Language Programs at a University on the U.S.-Mexico Border." In *Bilingualism and Language Contact: Spanish, English, and Native American Languages,* edited by Florence Barking, Elizabeth A. Brandt, and Jacob Ornstein-Galicia, 228–240. New York: Teachers College, Columbia University, 1982.

Tevisk, Martha. "George Isidore Sánchez." In *The New Handbook of Texas*, edited by Ron Tyler, Douglas E. Barnett, Roy R. Barkley, Penelope C. Anderson, and Mark F. Odintz, vol. 5, 826–827. Austin: Texas State Historical Association, 1996.

Thomas, Dorina Alaniz. "Reading Achievement of Chicano Children as a Function of Language Spoken and Language Preference." Ph.D. dissertation, University of Michigan, 1980.

Thomas, Kathryn. "Who Leaves and Why: An Examination of Latino Student Attrition From a Selective Public School Thematic Choice Program in San Antonio, Texas." Ph.D. dissertation, University of North Texas, 1996.

Thompson, Merrill E., and Claude C. Dove. "A Comparison of Physical Achievement of Anglo and Spanish American Boys in Junior High School." *Research Quarterly* 13 (October 1942): 341–346.

Thormalen, Karen Chadwick. "The Impact of Primary Grade Retention on the Academic Performance and Self-perceptions of Middle School Students in an Urban/Suburban School District." Ph.D. dissertation, Texas A&M University, 1998.

Tinney, Ed. "I'll Keep My Children: The Life of Pioneer Educator Noé Lara Camúñez." *West Texas Historical Association Yearbook* 75 (1999): 23–31.

Tomás, Donald Lee. "Retention Predictors for Hispanic Students Enrolled in Developmental Courses in Rural Community Colleges." Ed.D. dissertation, Grambling State University, 1998.

Torres-Ayala, Buenaventura. "The Relationship of Spanish Language Usage and Exposure to Spanish Oral Proficiency among Mexican American College Students." Ph.D. dissertation, University of California, Los Angeles, 1994.

Torres, Belinda Mae. "The Relationship between Work Values and Job Satisfaction of Potential Minority Leaders in Community Colleges and Technical Institutes." Ph.D. dissertation, Texas A&M University, 1990.

Torres, Domitila Irma. "A Study of the Relationship among Language Maintenance, Academic Achievement, and Home Language Factors of the Mexican-American Seventh Grader in a South Texas Middle School." Ed.D. dissertation, Texas A&M University-Kingsville, 1996.

Torres, Mark Alexander. "*Edgewood* vs. *Kirby*: Tax Warfare in Texas." Ed.D. dissertation, University of Texas at El Paso, 2001.

Torres, Maryann. "Happiness and Global Self-worth among College Students: Ethnic and Gender Variables." Master's thesis, Texas A&I University, 1993.

Torres Smith, Anita. "Praxedis Mata Torres: The First Mexican American Teacher in the Public Schools in Uvalde County, Texas." *Journal of Big Bend Studies* 3 (1991): 157–179.

Townshend, D. R., and G. L. Zamora. "Differing Interaction Patterns in Bilingual Classrooms." *Contemporary Education* 46.3 (1975): 196–202.

Treviño, B. G. "Bilingual Education: A Psychological Helping Hand." *Texas Outlook* 53 (May 1969): 24–25.

________. "Bilingual Instruction in the Primary Grades." *Modern Language Journal* 54.4 (1970): 255–256.

Treviño, Mary L. "The Scales of Independent Behavior with Hispanic Elementary Age Children in Texas." Ph.D. dissertation, Texas A&M University, 1991.

Treviño, Robert Edward. "Bilingual-Bicultural Education in the Corpus Christi Independent School District: A Process Evaluation." Master's thesis, University of Texas at Austin, 1979.

Trujillo, Armando L. "Community Empowerment and Bilingual/Bicultural Education: A Study of the *Movimiento* in a South Texas Community." Ph.D. dissertation, University of Texas at Austin, 1993.

________. "Bilingual/Bicultural Education and Politics in Crystal City, Texas: 1969–1989." In *Chicanas and Chicanos in Contemporary Society*, edited by Roberto M. De Anda, 157–178. Boston: Allyn and Bacon, 1996.

Tullis, David Sherman. "A Comprehensive Study of Negro, Latin, and Anglo Children in a West Texas Community." Ed.D. dissertation, Texas Tech University, 1964.

Underwood, Marion L. "A Study of the Homes of One Hundred Latin-American Girls in Corpus Christi to be Used as a Basis for a Homemaking Education Program in the Elementary Schools." Master's thesis, University of Texas, Austin, 1937.

Valdes, Guadalupe. "Bilingualism in a Mexican Border City: A Research Agenda." In *Bilingualism and Language Contact: Spanish, English, and Native American Languages*, edited by Florence Barkin, Elizabeth Brandt, and Jacob Ornstein-Galicia, 3–17. New York: Teachers College, Columbia University, 1982.

Valencia, Karen Nell. "Dropping Out: A Regression Study of Variables Related to Attrition Rates among Hispanic Students from the *Colonias* of Hidalgo County in South Texas." Ed.D. dissertation, University of Houston, 1996.

Valencia, Richard R. "Inequalities and the Schooling of Minority Students in Texas: Historical and Contemporary Conditions." *Hispanic Journal of Behavioral Sciences* 22 (November 2000): 445–459.

Valencia, Richard R., and Ernesto M. Bernal. "An Overview of Conflicting Opinions in the TAAS Case." *Hispanic Journal of Behavioral Sciences* 22 (November 2000): 423–444.

Valenzuela, Angela. "Liberal Gender Role Attitudes and Academic Achievement Among Mexican-Origin Adolescents in Two Houston Inner City Catholic Schools." *Hispanic Journal of Behavioral Sciences* 15 (August 1993): 310–323.

________. "The Significance of the TAAS for Mexican Immigrants and Mexican American Adolescents: A Case Study." *Hispanic Journal of Behavioral Sciences* 22 (November 2000): 524–539.

________. "Subtractive Schooling: U.S.-Mexican Youth and the Politics of Caring." In *Reflexiones: New Directions in Mexican American Studies*, edited by Yolanda C. Padilla, 123–146. Austin: Center for Mexican American Studies and University of Texas Press, 1999.

Vega, José E. *Education, Politics, and Bilingualism in Texas*. Washington, D.C.: University Press of America, 1983.

________. "The Enactment of Bilingual Education Legislation in Texas: 1969–1973." Ph.D. dissertation, University of Illinois, 1980.

________. "The Enactment of Bilingual Education Legislation in Texas, 1969–1973." In *Bilingual Education and Public Policy in the United States*, edited by Raymond V. Padilla, 109–135. Ypsilanti, Mich.: Department of Foreign Languages and Bilingual Studies, Michigan State University, 1979.

Venegas, Moisés. "Educational and Occupational Aspirations and Expectations of El Paso High School Students." Ed.D. dissertation, New Mexico State University, 1973.

Verner, Zenobia, and Josue González. "English Language Teaching in a Texas Bilingual Programme." *English Language Teaching* 25 (June 1971): 296–302.

Villanueva, Myrna Evette. "De Viva Voz: Attaining Success in the Community College." Ph.D. dissertation, University of Texas at Austin, 1998.

Wages, Sherry D. "Mexican American Dropouts in the Valley—Their Reasons for Leaving School and their Educational and Occupational Status Projections. Master's thesis, Texas A&M University, 1971.

Waldrop, Revel H., and John G. Bruhn. *Health Management and Health Professions Education in South Texas*. Galveston: University of Texas Medical Branch, 1975.

Walker, Myrtle Lee Garner. "The Portrayal of Blacks, Mexican-Americans, and Indians in Selected Texas-Adopted Secondary American Literature Textbooks." Ed.D. dissertation, East Texas State University, 1982.

Walschak, Melissa Anne. "Attitudes of Students, Parents, and Teachers toward English and Spanish in a New Concurrent Approach Bilingual Education Program in San Antonio, Texas." Ph.D. dissertation, University of Texas at Austin, 1994.

Walsh, M. A. *The Development of a Rationale for a Program to Prepare Teachers for Spanish-speaking Children in a Bilingual-Bicultural Elementary School*. San Francisco: R&E Research Associates, 1976.

Watson, Scott Harris. "A Study on the Effects of Four Different Types of Mentoring Plans Using Retired Community Individuals and College Students as Mentors on Hispanic 'At Risk' Students' Grades and Attendance." Master's thesis, Stephen F. Austin State University, 1996.

Watson, Susan Kay. "The Effects of a Prekindergarten Program on the English Language Development of Four-year-old Hispanic Children." Ed.D. dissertation, Texas Tech University, 1988.

Weaver, Laurie Ruth. "A Critical Ethnography of Writing Instruction in a Bilingual Classroom." Ed.D. dissertation, University of Houston, 1995.

Weir, E. P. "The Mexican Child." *Texas Outlook* 20 (June 1936): 20–23.

Wellborne, K. Roque. "Spanish for Children of Hispano Descent." *Texas Outlook* 25 (December 1941): 33–34.

Weller, Nancy Fitzpatrick. "The Impact of School Year Work on Adolescent Development." Dr.P.H. dissertation, University of Texas Health Science Center at Houston, 1997.

Whitaker, J. M. "Survey of Socioeconomic Status of the Pupils of Franklin D. Roosevelt Elementary School." Master's thesis, University of Texas at El Paso, 1948.

Whittenburg, Clarice T., and George I. Sánchez. *Materials Relating to the Education of Spanish-speaking People: A Bibliography*. Austin: University of Texas Press, 1948.

Wilder, L. A. "Problems in the Teaching of Mexican Children." *Texas Outlook* 20 (August 1936): 9–10.

Williams, Chaney E. "A Comparative Study of Transitional Bilingual Education in an Urban School District of Texas." Ed.D. dissertation, Texas Southern University, 2001.

Williams, F., and R. C. Naremore. "Language Attitudes: An Analysis of Teacher Differences." *Speech Monographs* 41.4 (1974): 391–396.

Williams, F., et al. "Ethnic Stereotyping and Judgments of Children's Speech." *Speech Monographs* 38.3 (1971): 168–170.

Wilson, Jacques. "An Appalling Waste: Factors Affecting the Development of Mexican American Elementary School Students in Texas." *The Texas Observer* (August 23, 1963): 31.

Wilson, Joe H. "Secondary School Drop-Outs with Special Reference to Spanish-speaking Youth in Texas." Ph.D. dissertation, University of Texas, Austin, 1953.

Wooten, Kay. "The Anglo-Latin-American Spanish Class." *Texas Outlook* 25 (October 1941): 14–16.

Wortham, Sue Clark. "A Survey and Comparison of Beginning Reading Instruction Practices in English versus Spanish for Mexican-American Children in First-Grade Classrooms in Texas." Ph.D. dissertation, University of Texas at Austin, 1976.

Wright, Robert Gene. "Factors Affecting Retention of Black and Hispanic Students in a Community College System and Implications for Transfer to Senior Institutions of Higher Education in Texas." Ph.D. dissertation, Texas A&M University, 1989.

Wueste, Gladys (Riskind). "A Survey of Factors Relating to the Education of the Children of Migratory Parents of Eagle Pass, Texas." Master's thesis, University of Texas, Austin, 1950.

Yarborough, C. L. "Age and Grade Status of Texas Children of Latin American Descent." *Journal of Educational Research* 40.1 (1946): 14–27.

Ybarra, Jesse R. "A Study to Determine Why Spanish-speaking Children Drop Out of School in Junior and Senior School in a Particular Community in San Antonio, Texas." Master's thesis, Trinity University, 1955.

Yoes, Deck Jr. "Reading Programs for Mexican-American Children of Texas." *Reading Teacher* 20 (January 1967): 313–318.

Yonan, Barbara Ann. "Relationships between Student Perceptions of Parental Educational Attitudes and Support and Temperament Styles among Hispanic and Black Students Who Stay In or Drop Out of High School." Ph.D. dissertation, University of Texas at Austin, 1991.

Young, Gay. "Chicano College Students on the Texas-Mexican Border: Traditions and Transformation." *Hispanic Journal of Behavioral Sciences* 14 (August 1992): 341–352.

Zabala, José María. "Formas verbales en la producción escrita de estudiantes México-Americanos de la Universidad de Texas en El Paso." Master's thesis, University of Texas at El Paso, 1979.

Zamora, Emilio Jr. "*Las Escuelitas*: A Texas-Mexican Search for Educational Excellence." In *Los Tejanos: Children of Two Cultures*, 13–25. Edinburg, Tex.: South Texas Regional Training Office, 1978.

Zavaleta, Antonio Noé. "Teaching Sociology to the 'Border' Mexican American Student." *South Texas Journal of Research and the Humanities* 3 (Fall 1979): 53–68.

Zuñiga, Cecilia Lorraine. "Hispanic Parent Participation in School Activities and the Relationship to Student Success." Ph.D. dissertation, University of Wisconsin-Madison, 1998.

13. FAMILY

Most scholars and commentators stress the influential role of the family within the Hispanic Texas community. This section reflects that influence. Works included discuss the role of family from numerous perspectives—the overall importance of family in Tejano society and scholarship, role of gender, relationship of children to family, comparative family studies with black and white Texans, as well as changes that have occurred within Tejano family rituals, roles, and decision-making over time. The studies in this section, as in most of the topical sections, range from the Spanish period to the current period.

Group portrait taken on the José Justo Rodríguez Ranch, located four miles north of Pleasanton, Texas, 1890s. Standing (L to R): José E. Rodríguez, María Antonio Rodríguez, Catarino de Jesús Rodríguez, and Clemente Esparza. Seated (L to R): Simona Esparza Rodríguez, Conception Rodríguez, José Justo Rodríguez holding José Pedro Rodríguez, and Ana Esparza Rodríguez holding José Simón Rodríguez.
Atascosa County Historical Museum, No. ITC-93-241

Alvírez, David. "The Effects of Formal Church Affiliation and Religiosity on Fertility Patterns of Mexican Americans in Austin, Texas." Ph.D. dissertation, University of Texas at Austin, 1971.

Anderson, James G., and William Johnson. *Social and Cultural Characteristics of Mexican American Families in South El Paso, Texas.* Las Cruces, N.M.: Research Center of New Mexico State University, 1968.

Ash, Marilyn Louise Holtze. "The Relationship of Family and School Decision-Making Structures to Political Efficacy in Anglo-American, Mexican-American, and Mexican Upper Level Grade School Children." Ph.D. dissertation, University of Arizona, 1980.

Barker, E. Shannon. "Los Tejanos de San Antonio: Mexican Immigrant Family Acculturation, 1880–1929." Ph.D. dissertation, George Washington University, 1996.

Bastida, Elena. "Kinship Ties of Mexican Migrant Women on the United States/Mexico Border." *Journal of Comparative Family Studies* 32.4 (2001): 549–569.

Bean, Frank D. "Components of Income and Expected Family Size among Mexican Americans." *Social Science Quarterly* 54 (1973): 103–116.

Bean, Frank D., and Benjamin S. Bradshaw. "An Exploratory Study of Intermarriage between Mexican Americans and Anglo Americans, 1850–1960." *Southwestern Sociological Proceedings* (1970): 120–125.

________. "Intermarriage between Persons of Spanish and Non-Spanish Surname: Changes from the Mid-Nineteenth to the Mid-Twentieth Century." *Social Science Quarterly* 51 (1979): 389–395.

Black, Mary S. "Historical Factors Affecting Mexican American Parental Involvement and Educational Outcomes: The Texas Environment from 1910–1996." Ed.D. dissertation, Harvard University, 1996.

Blayeck, Leda F. "The Habits and Living Conditions of Mexican Families on Fixed Income Levels in the Upper Rio Grande Valley." Master's thesis, University of Texas, Austin, 1938.

Boldt, Joanne Shuhi. "Patterns of Intergenerational Helping among Mexican-Americans: A Three Generational Study." Ph.D. dissertation, University of Kentucky, 1985.

Bradshaw, Benjamin S. "Some Demographic Aspects of Marriage: A Comparative Study of Three Ethnic Groups." Master's thesis, University of Texas, Austin, 1960.

Briody, Elizabeth K. *Household Labor Patterns Among Mexican Americans in South Texas: Buscando Trabajo Seguro*. New York: AMS Press, 1988.

________. "Patterns of Household Immigration into South Texas." *International Migration Review* 21 (Spring 1987): 27–47.

Calvert, Glen Allen. "A Tri-Ethnic Study of Family Planning, Lubbock County, Texas." Master's thesis, Texas Tech University, 1969.

Cantú, I. S. "The Effects of Family Characteristics, Parental Influence, Language Spoken, School Experience, and Self-Motivation on the Level of Educational Achievement among Mexican Americans." Ph.D. dissertation, University of Michigan, 1975.

Cantú, Norma E. "Tejanos Along the Border." *Texas Journal of Ideas, History and Culture* 20 (Fall/Winter 1997): 6–9.

Cázares, Ralph B., Edward Murguía, and W. Parker Frisbie. "Mexican American Intermarriage in a Nonmetropolitan Context." In *The Mexican American Experience: An Interdisciplinary Anthology*, edited by Rodolfo O. de la Garza, Frank D. Bean, Charles M. Bonjean, Ricardo Romo, and Rodolfo Álvarez, 393–401. Austin: University of Texas Press, 1985.

Clements, Harold. "An Analysis of Levels of Living of Spanish-American Rural and Urban Families in Two South Texas Counties." Master's thesis, Texas A&M University, College Station, 1963.

Coan, Barlett E. "A Comparative Study of the American and Mexican Children in the 'Big Bend' Area for 1935–36." Master's thesis, University of Texas, Austin, 1936.

Colwell, Brian, Dennis Smith, and James J. Zhang. "Cambio en las escuelas: Mexican-American Parent Attitudes Toward School Health Education." *Journal of Community Health* 25 (October 2000): 427–437.

Crimm, Ana Carolina Castillo. "'*Aqui Todos Somos Primos*' ('We Are All Cousins'): Marriage and Extended Families in Victoria, 1840–1880." *South Texas Studies* 10 (1999): 65–81.

________. "Founding Families of Victoria." *South Texas Studies* 3 (1992): 1–23.

Davidson, Randy. "Outmarriage Among Hispanics: Cameron County, 1870-1970." In *Still More Studies on Brownsville History*, edited by Milo Kearney, 49–56. Brownsville, Tex.: University of Texas at Brownsville, 1991.

de Garmo, Mary Eloise [Mrs. Frank]. *Pathfinders of Texas, 1836–1846: Being the Stories of Pioneer Families that Builded Well for Nueces County and Corpus Christi*. Austin: Von Boeckmann-Jones, 1951.

Downing de Juana, Ana Cristina. "Intermarriage in Hidalgo County, 1860–1900." Master's thesis, University of Texas–Pan American, 1998.

Estrada, Marta. "Dichos from the Lower Valley." *Password* 40 (Fall 1995): 145–152.

Evans, Carol Anne. "The Transmission of Spanish as a Family Language." Ph.D. dissertation, University of Texas at Austin, 1989.

Faris, Buford, and Norval Glenn. "Fatalism and Familism Among Anglos and Mexican Americans in San Antonio." *Sociology and Social Research* 60 (July 1976): 393–402.

Flores, J. M. "A Study of Mexican American Cultural Characteristics as Perceived by Members of Impoverished Mexican American Families and Its Educational Implications." Ph.D. dissertation, University of Houston, 1972.

Francesca, Sister Mary. "Variations of Selected Cultural Patterns among Three Generations of Mexicans in San Antonio, Texas." *American Catholic Sociological Review* 19 (February 1958): 24–34.

García, Mario T. "La Familia: The Mexican Immigrant Family, 1900–1930." In *Work, Family, Sex Roles, Language: Selected Papers*, edited by Mario Barrera, Alberto Camarillo, and Francisco Hernández, 117–139. Berkeley: Tonatiuh-Quinto Sol International, 1980.

Gonzales, Kathleen May. *The Mexican Family in San Antonio, Texas*. San Francisco: R&E Research Associates, 1971.

________. "The Mexican Family in San Antonio, Texas." Master's thesis, University of Texas, Austin, 1928.

Gonzales, Manuel G. *The Hispanic Elite of the Southwest*. El Paso: Texas Western Press, 1989.

González, Genaro. *Only Sons*. Houston: Arte Público Press, 1991. **[fiction]**

Grebler, Leo, Joan W. Moore, and Ralph C. Guzman, eds. "The Family—Variations in Time and Space." In *The Mexican-American People: The Nation's Second Largest Minority*, 350–377. New York: Free Press, 1970.

Griswold del Castillo, Richard. *La Familia: Chicano Families in the Urban Southwest*. Notre Dame: University of Notre Dame Press, 1984.

________. "'Only For My Family . . .': Historical Dimensions of Chicano Family Solidarity—The Case of San Antonio in 1860." *Aztlán* 16 (1985): 145–176.

Gutmann, Myron P., Kristine Hopkins, Kenneth H. Fliess, and Gabriela Montes de Oca Vega, transl. "Matrimonio y migración en la frontera: Patrones de nupcialidad en Texas, 1850–1910/Marriage and Migration at the Border: Patterns of Nuptiality in Texas, 1850–1910." *Historia Mexicana* 42.1 (1992): 45–76.

Guzmán García, Victor M. "The Legacy of Captain Alonso García." *Password* 43 (Winter 1998): 159–174.

Hall, William C. "A Study of 281 Farm Labor Families of South Texas." Master's thesis, Texas College of Arts and Industries, 1942.

Harris, Charles H. III. *A Mexican Family Empire: The Latifundia of the Sánchez Navarro Family, 1765–1867*. Austin: University of Texas Press, 1975.

Hinojosa, Alicia. *The Hinojosa Family: From Mier, Tamaulipas, Mexico to Texas*. Somerville, Tex.: A. Hinojosa Perone, 1992.

Hispanic Children in Texas. Special Report of the Texas Kids County Project. Center for Public Policy Priorities and the School of Social Work, University of Texas at Austin. Austin: Texas Kids County Project, 1995.

Hoppe, S. K., and P. L. Heller. "Alienation, Familism, and the Utilization of Health Services by Mexican Americans." *Journal of Health and Social Behavior* 16.3 (1975): 304–314.

Hotvedt, Mary Eleanor. "Family Planning Among Mexican-Americans of South Texas." Ph.D. dissertation, Indiana University, 1976.

Imperia, Giovanna. "Family Purchasing Decisions among Mexican-Americans and Anglos." Ph.D. dissertation, University of Texas at Austin, 1982.

Johnson, D. L., et al. *Houston Parent-Child Development Center*. Houston: University of Houston, 1976.

________. "The Houston Parent-Child Development Center: A Parent Education Program for Mexican American Families." *American Journal of Orthopsychiatry* 44.1 (1974): 121–128.

Kazen, Phyllis M. "Mexican American Kinship Interaction: A Study of 20 Families at Austin." Master's thesis, University of Texas, Austin, 1966.

Larson, L. B., et al. "Nutrition Status of Children of Mexican American Migrant Parents." *Journal of American Diet Association* 64.1 (1974): 29–35.

Laurel, Noel Fernando. "An Intergenerational Comparison of Attitudes toward the Support of Aged Parents: A Study of Mexican-Americans in Two South Texas Communities." D.S.W. dissertation, University of Southern California, 1976.

LeFevre, Karen E. "The Family History of Senator Hector Uribe: A Study in Mexican-American Heritage." In *Studies in Brownsville History*, edited by Milo Kearney, 248–274. Brownsville, Tex.: Pan American University at Brownsville, 1986.

Lemée, Patricia R. "Tíos and Tantes: Familial and Political Relationships of Natchitoches and the Spanish Colonial Frontier." *Southwestern Historical Quarterly* 101 (January 1998): 340–358.

López, Linda C., Virginia V. Sánchez, and Minami Hamilton. "Immigrant and Native-Born Mexican-American Parents' Involvement in a Public School: A Preliminary Study." *Psychological Reports* 86 (April 2000): 521–525.

López-Stafford, Gloria. *A Place in El Paso: A Mexican-American Childhood.* Albuquerque: University of New Mexico Press, 1996.

Mahoney, Mary. "Spanish and English Language Usage by Rural and Urban Mexican American Families in Two South Texas Counties." Master's thesis, Texas A&M University, 1967.

Maril, Robert Lee. *Living on the Edge: At Home on the Texas-Mexico Border*. College Station: Texas A&M University Press, 1992.

Markides, Kyriakos S., Sue K. Hoppe, Harry W. Martin, and Dianne M. Timbers. "Sample Representativeness in a Three-Generation Study of Mexican Americans." *Journal of Marriage and the Family* 45 (November 1983): 911–916.

McReynolds, James Michael. "Family Life in a Borderland Community: Nacogdoches, Texas, 1779–1861." Ph.D. dissertation, Texas Tech University, 1978.

Mendoza, Lydia. *Lydia Mendoza: A Family Autobiography*, compiled by Chris Strachwitz and James Nicolopulus. Houston: Arte Público Press, 1993.

Mengden, Susan Collette. "Marital Stability: A Qualitative Psychological Study of Mexican American Couples." Ph.D. dissertation, Boston College, 1994.

Miller, Michael V. "Variations in Mexican American Family Life: A Review Synthesis of Empirical Research." *Aztlán* 9 (Fall 1978): 209–231.

Miller, Monte Christopher. "Assessment of Relative Importance of Faithfulness in Marriage among Mexican Americans." Psy.D. dissertation, Our Lady of the Lake University, 1995.

Mirandé, Alfredo. "The Chicano Family: A Reanalysis of Conflicting Views." *Journal of Marriage and the Family* 39 (1977): 747–756.

Monday, Jane Clements, and Betty Bailey Colley. *Voices from the Wild Horse Desert: The Vaquero Families of the King and Kenedy Ranches*. Austin: University of Texas Press, 1997.

Murray, Sister Mary John. *A Social-Cultural Study of 118 Mexican Families Living in a Low-Rent Public Housing Project in San Antonio, Texas*. Studies in Sociology 38. Washington, D.C.: Catholic University of America, 1954.

________. "A Socio-Cultural Study of 118 Mexican Families Living in a Low-Rent Public Housing Project in San Antonio, Texas." Ph.D. dissertation, Catholic University of America, 1954.

Murray, Winifred M. *A Socio-Cultural Study of 118 Mexican Families Living in a Low-Rent Public Housing Project in San Antonio, Texas*. New York: Arno Press, 1976.

Nami, Julia. "A Study of the Family Life, in its Relation to Education, of Pupils in the 2nd Grade of the Anthony Margil School, San Antonio, Texas." Master's thesis, University of Texas, Austin, 1940.

Nies, Charles M. "Social Psychology Variables Related to Family Planning Among Mexican American Females." Ph.D. dissertation, University of Texas at Austin, 1974.

Orozco vda. de Blanca, Serafina. "My Recollections of the Orozco Family and the Mexican Revolution of 1910." *Password* 25 (Spring 1980): 11–16.

Paredes, Américo. "The Undying Love of 'El Indio' Córdova: *Décimas* and Oral History in a Border Family." *Ernesto Galarza Commemorative Lecture*, Stanford University, 1987. Reprinted in *Folklore and Culture on the Texas-Mexican Border*, edited by Richard Bauman, 247–265. Austin: Center for Mexican American Studies, 1993.

Parsley, Rosa Frances. "A Study of the Expenditure for Food of Some Urban Latin-American Families on Work Relief in Austin." Master's thesis, University of Texas, Austin, 1935.

Perry, Elsie A. "A Comparison of the Content Material of Mexican and United States Readers." Master's thesis, University of Texas, Austin, 1931.

Ramírez, Emilia Schunior. *Ranch Life in Hidalgo County after 1850*. Edinburg, Tex.: New Santander Press, 1971.

________. "Wetback Children in South Texas." Master's thesis, University of Texas, Austin, 1951.

Reeve, Shirley Ballard. "Comparison by Socioeconomic Class of the Power Structure of Mexican-American and Anglo-American Families in the Rio Grande Valley of South Texas." Ph.D. dissertation, Florida State University, 1975.

Robertson, Clyde Reeves. "A Comparative Study of the Progress of American and Mexican Pupils in Certain Elementary Schools in Texas." Master's thesis, University of Texas, Austin, 1935.

Romano-V., Octavio Ignacio. "Donship in a Mexican-American Community in Texas." *American Anthropologist* 62 (1960): 966–976.

Rubio, Abel G. *Stolen Heritage: A Mexican-American's Rediscovery of His Family's Lost Land Grant*, edited by Thomas H. Kreneck. Austin: Eakin Press, 1986.

Sáenz, Andrés. *Early Tejano Ranching: Daily Life at Ranchos San José and El Fresnillo*, edited by Andrés Tijerina. College Station: Texas A&M University Press, 1999.

Salinas, Susan Mary. "The Effect of Domestic Values on Marriage between Anglos and Hispanics." Master's thesis, University of Texas at Arlington, 1986.

Schultz, T. E., E. Murguía, and S. K. Hoppe. "Gender Role Orientation among Three Generations of Mexican American Women." In *The 1988 Victoria College Social Sciences Symposium*, 87–100. Victoria, Tex.: Victoria College Press, 1988.

Sowards, Kathryn Ann. "Early Childbearing and the Epidemiology of Infant Death in the Mexican Ancestry and Anglo Populations of San Antonio, Texas: 1935–1984." Ph.D. dissertation, University of Texas at Austin, 1995.

Stedman, J. M., and R. E. McKenzie. "Family Factors Related to Competence in Young Disadvantaged Mexican American Children." *Child Development* 42.5 (1971): 1602–1607.

Stewart, Kenneth L., and Arnoldo De León. "Households and Families: Composition, Convergence and Cultural Perceptions." In *Not Room Enough: Mexicans, Anglos, and Socio-economic Change in Texas, 1850–1900*, by Kenneth L. Stewart and Arnoldo De León, 73–91. Albuquerque: University of New Mexico Press, 1993.

Stoddard, Ellwyn R. *The Role of Social Factors in the Successful Adjustment of Mexican American Families to Forced Housing Relocation*. El Paso: Community Renewal Program, 1970.

________. "The Adjustment of Mexican American Barrio Families to Forced Housing Relocation." *Social Science Quarterly* 53 (1973): 749–759.

Strachwitz, Chris, and James Nicolopulos, comps. *Lydia Mendoza: A Family Autobiography*. Houston: Arte Público, 1994.

Tapia-Geitz, Olga Hope. "The Relationship between Family/Social Factors and Bilingual Proficiency of Mexican-American College Freshmen." Ph.D. dissertation, University of Oregon, 1986.

Uhlengeyer, P. "Marital Instability Among Mexican Americans: Following the Pattern of Blacks?" *Social Problems* 20.1 (1972): 49–56.

Upham, W. Kennedy, and David E. Wright. *Poverty among Spanish Americans in Texas: Low-Income Families in a Minority Group*. College Station: Texas Agricultural Experiment Station, 1966.

Urbano, David. "The Saga of a Revolutionary Family: The Martin De León Family of Texas." Master's thesis, University of Texas at San Antonio, 1990.

Valdez, Avelardo. "Recent Increases in Intermarriage by Mexican American Males: Bexar County, Texas, from 1971 to 1980." *Social Science Quarterly* 64 (March 1983): 136–144.

Vargas, Jorge A. "The Other Side of the Treaty of Guadalupe Hidalgo: A Synopsis of the Case Involving 433 Land Claims by Texas Families against the Government of Mexico." *Texas Hispanic Journal of Law and Policy* 5 (Spring 2001): 41–56.

Walker, David Wayne. "Kinship, Business, and Politics: The Martínez del Río Family in Mexico, 1824–1864." Ph.D. dissertation, University of Chicago, 1981.

Walker, Deborah J. "Parental Investment and Grandparental Investment among Mexican-Americans of Laredo, Texas." Ph.D. dissertation, Pennsylvania State University, 1990.

West, Richard. "An American Family—Roots: The Mexican Version." *Texas Monthly* (March 1980): 108–119, 166–181.

Whiteford, Linda MacMillan. "Family Relations in Seco County: A Case Study of Social Change." Ph.D. dissertation, University of Wisconsin-Milwaukee, 1977.

________. "The Borderland as an Extended Community." In *Migration Across Frontiers: Mexico and the United States*, edited by Fernando Camera and Robert Van Kemper, 127–137. Albany, N.Y.: State University of New York Press, 1979.

Williams, Brett. "Why Migrant Women Feed Their Husbands Tamales: Foodways as a Basis for a Revisionist View of Tejano Family Life." In *Ethnic and Regional Foodways in the United States: The Performance of Group Identity*, edited by Linda Keller Brown and Kay Mussell, 113–126. Knoxville: University of Tennessee Press, 1984.

Williams, Coleen. "Cultural Differences and Medical Care of Ten Mexican Migrant Families in San Antonio, Texas." Master's thesis, University of Texas, Austin, 1959.

Williams, Norma. *The Mexican American Family: Tradition and Change*. Dix Hills, N.Y.: General Hall Publishers, 1990.

________. "Changing Patterns in the Mexican American Family." Ph.D. dissertation, University of Texas at Austin, 1984.

________. "Changes in Funeral Patterns and Gender Roles Among Mexican Americans." In *Women on the U.S.-Mexico Border: Responses to Change*, edited by Vicki L. Ruiz and S. Tiano, 197–217. Boston: Allen and Unwin, 1987.

________. "Role Making Among Married Mexican American Women: Issues of Class and Ethnicity." *Journal of Applied Behavioral Science* 24 (1987): 203–217.

________. "Traditional Life-cycle Rituals among Mexican Americans in Texas." In *The Mexican American Family: Tradition and Change*, by Norma Williams, 18–40. Dix Hills, N.Y.: General Hall Publishers, 1990.

Zermaño, Estela Martínez. "Mi Familia." *South Texas Studies* 11 (2000): 157–168.

Zinn, Maxine Baca. "Chicano Family Research." *Journal of Ethnic Studies* 7 (Fall 1979): 59–63.

14. TEJANAS

Only sources on the subject of Mexican-descent women are listed in this heading but the span of coverage is wide. The time period of the studies extends from the colonial era to that of the present and the disciplines range from sociology to education to family life. As the several sources in this chapter indicate, Hispanic women in Texas have been singers, literary figures, caring mothers, labor activists, among other endeavors in the Lone Star State.

Emma Tenayuca standing on the steps of the San Antonio City Hall, with fist up raised, San Antonio, Texas, ca. 1938.
The Institute of Texan Cultures at UTSA, No. L-1541-D
The San Antonio Light *Collection*

Ables, L. Robert. "Adina Emilia de Zavala." In *The New Handbook of Texas*, edited by Ron Tyler, Douglas E. Barnett, Roy R. Barkley, Penelope C. Anderson, and Mark F. Odintz, vol. 6, 1146–1147. Austin: Texas State Historical Association, 1996.

Abernethy, Francis Edward. "María de Agreda: The Lady in Blue." In *Legendary Ladies of Texas*, edited by Francis Edward Abernethy, 9–14. Second edition. Denton: University of North Texas Press, 1994.

Aceves, Melba Lucila. "Pregnancy Outcomes among Hispanic Adolescents in Relation to Uterine Growth, Weight Gain, and Prepregnant Weight." Master's thesis, University of Texas Graduate School of Biomedical Science at Galveston, 1988.

Acosta, Teresa Palomo. "Beatriz Tagle Pérez." In *The New Handbook of Texas*, edited by Ron Tyler, Douglas E. Barnett, Roy R. Barkley, Penelope C. Anderson, and Mark F. Odintz, vol. 5, 149. Austin: Texas State Historical Association, 1996.

________. "Chicana Research and Learning Center." In *The New Handbook of Texas*, edited by Ron Tyler, Douglas E. Barnett, Roy R. Barkely, Penelope C. Anderson, and Mark F. Odintz, vol. 2, 68–69. Austin: Texas State Historical Association, 1996.

________. "Conferencia de Mujeres por La Raza." In *The New Handbook of Texas*, edited by Ron Tyler, Douglas E. Barnett, Roy R. Barkely, Penelope C. Anderson, and Mark F. Odintz, vol. 2, 266. Austin: Texas State Historical Association, 1996.

________. "Conferencia Plástica Chicana." In *The New Handbook of Texas*, edited by Ron Tyler, Douglas E. Barnett, Roy R. Barkely, Penelope C. Anderson, and Mark F. Odintz, vol. 2, 266. Austin: Texas State Historical Association, 1996.

________. "Cruz Azul Mexicana." In *The New Handbook of Texas*, edited by Ron Tyler, Douglas E. Barnett, Roy R. Barkely, Penelope C. Anderson, and Mark F. Odintz, vol. 2, 337–338. Austin: Texas State Historical Association, 1996.

________. "Elida García de Falcón." In *The New Handbook of Texas*, edited by Ron Tyler, Douglas E. Barnett, Roy R. Barkely, Penelope C. Anderson, and Mark F. Odintz, vol. 3, 88. Austin: Texas State Historical Association, 1996.

________. "Flores de Andrade." In *The New Handbook of Texas*, edited by Ron Tyler, Douglas E. Barnett, Roy R. Barkely, Penelope C. Anderson, and Mark F. Odintz, vol. 2, 1038. Austin: Texas State Historical Association, 1996.

________. "Home Altars." In *The New Handbook of Texas*, edited by Ron Tyler, Douglas E. Barnett, Roy R. Barkely, Penelope C. Anderson, and Mark F. Odintz, vol. 3, 677–678. Austin: Texas State Historical Association, 1996.

________. "Josefina Augustina Flores de Barker." In *The New Handbook of Texas*, edited by Ron Tyler, Douglas E. Barnett, Roy R. Barkely, Penelope C. Anderson, and Mark F. Odintz, vol. 2, 1038. Austin: Texas State Historical Association, 1996.

________. "Josefina López de Jiménez." In *The New Handbook of Texas*, edited by Ron Tyler, Douglas E. Barnett, Roy R. Barkley, Penelope C. Anderson, and Mark F. Odintz, vol. 4, 290. Austin: Texas State Historical Association, 1996.

________. "Leonora Mendoza." In *The New Handbook of Texas*, edited by Ron Tyler, Douglas E. Barnett, Roy R. Barkley, Penelope C. Anderson, and Mark F. Odintz, vol. 4, 619. Austin: Texas State Historical Association, 1996.

________. "La Mujer Moderna." In *The New Handbook of Texas*, edited by Ron Tyler, Douglas E. Barnett, Roy R. Barkley, Penelope C. Anderson, and Mark F. Odintz, vol. 4, 52. Austin: Texas State Historical Association, 1996.

________. "María Gertrudis Pérez Cassiano." In *The New Handbook of Texas*, edited by Ron Tyler, Douglas E. Barnett, Roy R. Barkely, Penelope C. Anderson, and Mark F. Odintz, vol. 1, 1016. Austin: Texas State Historical Association, 1996.

________. "Mexican American Business and Professional Women's Association." In *The New Handbook of Texas*, edited by Ron Tyler, Douglas E. Barnett, Roy R. Barkley, Penelope C. Anderson, and Mark F. Odintz, vol. 4, 653–654. Austin: Texas State Historical Association, 1996.

________. "Paula Losoya Taylor." In *The New Handbook of Texas*, edited by Ron Tyler, Douglas E. Barnett, Roy R. Barkley, Penelope C. Anderson, and Mark F. Odintz, vol. 4, 297. Austin: Texas State Historical Association, 1996.

________. "Sara Estela Ramírez." In *The New Handbook of Texas*, edited by Ron Tyler, Douglas E. Barnett, Roy R. Barkley, Penelope C. Anderson, and Mark F. Odintz, vol. 5, 424. Austin: Texas State Historical Association, 1996.

________. "Tejana Singers." In *The New Handbook of Texas*, edited by Ron Tyler, Douglas E. Barnett, Roy R. Barkley, Penelope C. Anderson, and Mark F. Odintz, vol. 6, 237–238. Austin: Texas State Historical Association, 1996.

Acosta, Teresa Palomo, and Ruthe Winegarten. *Las Tejanas: 300 Years of History*. Austin: University of Texas Press, 2003.

Aguayo, Anna Macías. "Dolores 'Lolita' Guerrero." In *Notable Hispanic American Women*, edited by Diane Telgen and Jim Kamp, 188–189. Detroit: Gale Research, 1993.

________."Grace Martínez Tatum." In *Notable Hispanic American Women*, edited by Diane Telgen and Jim Kamp, 397. Detroit: Gale Research, 1993.

________. "Oralia Lille Corrales." In *Notable Hispanic American Women*, edited by Diane Telgen and Jim Kamp, 112–113. Detroit: Gale Research, 1993.

Alarcón, Norma. "Interview with Pat Mora." *Third Woman* 3 (1985–1986): 121–126.

Alamía, Teresa Chapa. "Sr. Mary Enriqueta Vela." In *One Hundred Women of the Rio Grande Valley of Texas* by The Rio Writers, 188–189. Austin: Eakin Press, 1983.

Allen, Ruth. "Mexican Peon Women in Texas." *Sociology and Social Research* 16 (November/December 1931): 131–142.

________. *The Labor of Women in the Production of Cotton*. University of Texas Bulletin No. 3134: September 8, 1931, Bureau of Research in the Social Sciences Study No. 3. Austin: University of Texas, Austin, 1931.

"Alsbury, (Mrs.) Horace, aka Juana Navarro." In *The Handbook of Texas*, edited by Walter Prescott Webb and H. Bailey Carroll, vol. 1, 36. Austin: Texas State Historical Association, 1952.

Andreassi, D. D. "Norma Brito Selvera." In *Notable Hispanic American Women*, edited by Diane Telgen and Jim Kamp, 383–384. Detroit: Gale Research, 1993.

Aranda-Navanjo, Barbara. "The Health-Seeking Experiences of Mexican-American Women with HIV/AIDS." Ph.D. dissertation, University of Texas at Austin, 1997.

Ashbaugh, Carolyn. *Lucy Parsons: American Revolutionary*. Chicago: Illinois Labor History Society, 1976.

Baker, Susan González. "Many Rivers to Cross: Mexican Immigrants, Women Workers, and the Structure of Labor Markets in the Urban Southwest." Ph.D. dissertation, University of Texas at Austin, 1989.

Ballí, Cecilia. "All About My Mother." *Texas Monthly* 31 (February 2003): 106–109, 128–131.

________. "Ciudad de la Muerte." *Texas Monthly* 31 (June 2003): 108–117, 170–173.

Barbash, Louis, and Frederick P. Close. "Lydia Mendoza: The Voice of a People." *Texas Humanist* (November/December 1983): 18–20.

Barrera, Elena Farías. "Deldie Sáenz García." In *One Hundred Women of the Rio Grande Valley of Texas*, by The Rio Writers, 49–51. Austin: Eakin Press, 1983.

________. "Dina Fernández Treviño." In *One Hundred Women of the Rio Grande Valley of Texas*, by The Rio Writers, 176–178. Austin: Eakin Press, 1983.

________. "Estella Minerva Cuéllar." In *One Hundred Women of the Rio Grande Valley of Texas*, by The Rio Writers, 29–30. Austin: Eakin Press, 1983.

________. "Eva Dolores Carrizales, M.D." In *One Hundred Women of the Rio Grande Valley of Texas*, by The Rio Writers, 23–25. Austin: Eakin Press, 1983.

________. "Macaria Chapa Hinojosa." In *One Hundred Women of the Rio Grande Valley of Texas*, The Rio Writers, 54–56. Austin: Eakin Press, 1983.

________. "Yolanda Chapa Hinojosa." In *One Hundred Women of the Rio Grande Valley of Texas*, by The Rio Writers, 176–178. Austin: Eakin Press, 1983.

Barry, Tom. "Whatever Became of the Farah Strikers?" *Nuestro* 2 (October 1978): 36–37.

Barton, Florence Ward. "Celia Chávez Muñoz." In *One Hundred Women of the Rio Grande Valley of Texas*, by The Rio Writers, 138–139. Austin: Eakin Press, 1983.

________. "Rosa María Serna Zapata." In *One Hundred Women of the Rio Grande Valley of Texas*, by The Rio Writers, 205–207. Austin: Eakin Press, 1983.

Bastida, Elena. "Kinship Ties of Mexican Migrant Women on the United States/Mexico Border." *Journal of Comparative Family Studies* 32 (Autumn 2001): 549–569.

Bauman, Raquel Portillo. "A Study of Mexican American Women's Perception of Factors that Influence Academic and Professional Goal Attainment." Ed.D. dissertation, University of Houston, 1984.

Beecher, Graciela. "Judy Canales." In *Notable Hispanic American Women*, edited by Diane Telgen and Jim Kamp, 70. Detroit: Gale Research, 1993.

Benefield, Linda Lee. "Determinants of Course Withdrawal and Subsequent Term Enrollment of Adult Women in a Community College: A Cross-cultural Comparison." Ph.D. dissertation, Texas A&M University, 1991.

Blackwelder, Julia Kirk. *Women of the Depression: Caste and Culture in San Antonio, 1929–1939*. College Station: Texas A&M University Press, 1984.

________."Emma Tenayuca: Vision and Courage." In *The Human Tradition in Texas*, edited by Ty Cashion and Jesús F. de la Teja, 194–206. Wilmington, Del.: Scholarly Resources, 2001.

Blevins, Don. "Francisca Alavez: The Angel of Goliad." In *From Angels to Hellcats: Legendary Texas Women, 1836–1880*, by Don Blevins, 23–40. Missoula, Mont.: Mountain Press Publishing, 2001.

Bonilla-Santiago, Gloria. "Lena Guerrero." In *Notable Hispanic American Women*, edited by Diane Telgen and Jim Kamp, 189–190. Detroit: Gale Research, 1993.

Brown, Robert W., R. Todd Jewell, and Jeffrey J. Rous. "Abortion Decisions among Hispanic Women Along the Texas-Mexican Border." *Social Science Quarterly* 81 (March 2000): 237–252.

Brune, Betty Jean. "Mexican American and Anglo-American Attitudes toward Women: An Investigation of Traditionalism, Biculturalism, and Ethnicity." Ph.D. dissertation, University of Texas at Austin, 1989.

Burciaga, Cecilia P. "The 1977 Women's Conference in Houston." *La Luz* 7 (November 1978): 8–9.

Burr, Ramiro. "Women in Conjunto Music." In *Puro Conjunto, An Album in Words and Pictures*, edited by Juan Tejeda and Avelardo Valdez, 85–95. Austin: CMAS Books, Guadalupe Cultural Arts Center, 2001.

Bussell, Robyn Ellen. "Battered Latinas and Law Enforcement: An Analysis of their Experience." Master's thesis, University of Texas at Arlington, 2001.

Buss, Francis Ann Leeper. "An Oral History of a Chicana Farm Worker: Her Struggles and Social Visions." Ph.D. dissertation, University of Arizona, 1995.

Buxton, Linda. "The Political Realities of the Rio Grande Valley Women." Master's thesis, The Univeristy of Texas-Pan American, 1999.

Calderón, Roberto R. "All Over the Map: *La Onda Tejana* and the Making of Selena." In *Chicano Renaissance: Contemporary Cultural Trends*, edited by David R. Maciel, Isidro D. Ortiz, and María Herrra-Sobek, 1–47. Tucson: University of Arizona Press, 2000.

Calderón, Roberto R., and Emilio Zamora. "Manuela Solis Sager and Emma Tenayuca: A Tribute." In *Chicana Voices: Intersections of Class, Race, and Gender*, edited by Teresa Córdova, Norma Cantú, Gilberto Cárdenas, Juan García and Christine M. Sierra, 30–41. Albuquerque: University of New Mexico Press, 1990.

Cannon, John Robert. "Si se Puede!: A Critical Qualitative Study of Mexican American Female Business Graduates." Ed.D. dissertation, University of Houston, 2000.

Cantú, Norma E. "Las Mujeres." In *The New Handbook of Texas*, edited by Ron Tyler, Douglas E. Barnett, Roy R. Barkley, Penelope C. Anderson, and Mark F. Odintz, vol. 4, 92–93. Austin: Texas State Historical Association, 1996.

________. "Pastoras and Malinches: Women in a Traditional Folk Drama of Laredo, Texas." In *Recovering the U.S. Hispanic Literary Heritage*, edited by José F. Aranda Jr. and Silvio Torres-Saillant, vol. 4, 172–183. Houston: Arte Público Press, 2002.

Cantú, Tony. "Cashing in on Selena: How the Tejano Queen's Murder Caused an Economic Phenomenon." *Hispanic* (June 1996): 18–24.

Cárdenas, Gilberto, Beth Anne Shelton, and Devon Peña. "Undocumented Immigrant Women in the Houston Labor Market." *California Sociologist* 5 (Summer 1982): 98–118.

Cardozo-Freeman, Inez. "Games Mexican Girls Play." *Journal of American Folklore* 88 (January-March 1975): 12–24.

Castañeda, Antonia I. "Women of Color and the Rewriting of Western History: The Discourse, Politics, and Decolonization of History." *Pacific Historical Review* 61 (November 1992): 501–533.

Catalano, Julie. "Gloria Rodríguez." In *Notable Hispanic American Women*, edited by Diane Telgen and Jim Kamp, 345–347. Detroit: Gale Research, 1993.

________. "Teresa Urrea." In *Notable Hispanic American Women*, edited by Diane Telgen and Jim Kamp, 405–406. Detroit: Gale Research, 1993.

Chabrán, Richard, and Rafael Chabrán, eds. "Antonia Castañeda." In *The Latino Encyclopedia*, edited by Richard Chabrán and Rafael Chabrán, vol. 1, 256. New York: Marshall Cavendish, 1996.

________. "Carmen Lomas Garza." In *The Latino Encyclopedia*, edited by Richard Chabrán and Rafael Chabrán, vol. 3, 912. New York: Marshall Cavendish, 1996.

________. "Estela Portillo Trambley." In *The Latino Encyclopedia*, edited by Richard Chabrán and Rafael Chabrán, vol. 5, 1284. New York: Marshall Cavendish, 1996.

________. "Martha P. Cotera." In *The Latino Encyclopedia*, edited by Richard Chabrán and Rafael Chabrán, vol. 2, 391. New York: Marshall Cavendish, 1996.

________. "Patricia 'Pat' Mora." In *The Latino Encyclopedia*, edited by Richard Chabrán and Rafael Chabrán, vol. 4, 1064. New York: Marshall Cavendish, 1996.

________. "Sandra Cisneros." In *The Latino Encyclopedia*, edited by Richard Chabrán and Rafael Chabrán, vol. 2, 321. New York: Marshall Cavendish, 1996.

________. "Sara Estela Ramírez." In *The Latino Encyclopedia*, edited by Richard Chabrán and Rafael Chabrán, vol. 5, 1351. New York: Marshall Cavendish, 1996.

________. "Vicki Carr." In *The Latino Encyclopedia*, edited by Richard Chabrán and Rafael Chabrán, vol. 1, 249. New York: Marshall Cavendish, 1996.

Chávez Leyva, Yolanda. "'Faithful Hard-working Mexican Hands': Mexicana Workers During the Great Depression." *Perspectives in Mexican American Studies* 5 (1995): 63–77.

Cisneros, Sandra. "Cactus Flowers: In Search of Tejana Feminist Poetry." *Third Woman* 3 (1986): 73–80.

Clark, Madeline. "A Preliminary Survey of Employment Possibilities of the Spanish-American Girls Receiving Commercial Training in the San Antonio Secondary Schools." Master's thesis, University of Texas, Austin, 1936.

Codye, Corian. *Vilma Martínez*. Milwaukee: Raintree Publishers, 1990.

Contreras, Sheila Marie. "A Mestizo Account: Teresa Paloma Acosta's Questions to a Spanish Grandmother." In *Reflexiones 1998: New Directions in Mexican American Studies*, edited by Yolanda C. Padilla, 103–122. Austin: CMAS, Books, 1999.

Coronado, Raúl Jr. "Selena's Good Buy: Texas Mexicans, History, and Selena Meet Transnational Capitalism." *Aztlán* 26 (Spring 2001): 59–100.

Cotera, María Eugenia. "Engendering a 'Dialectics of Our America': Jovita González's Pluralist Dialogue as Feminist Testimonio." In *Las Obreras: Chicana Politics of Work and Family*, edited by Vicki L. Ruiz, 237–248. Los Angeles: UCLA Chicano Studies Research Center Publications, 2000.

Cotera, Martha P. *Diosa y Hembra: The History and Heritage of Chicanas in the United States*. Austin: Information Systems Development, 1976.

Cottrell, Debbie Mauldin. "Faustina Porras Martínez." In *The New Handbook of Texas*, edited by Ron Tyler, Douglas E. Barnett, Roy R. Barkley, Penelope C. Anderson, and Mark F. Odintz, vol. 4, 534–535. Austin: Texas State Historical Association, 1996.

Coyle, Laurie, Gail Hershatter, and Emily Honig. "Women at Farah: An Unfinished Story." In *Mexican Women in the United States: Struggles Past and Present*, edited by Magdalena Mora and Adelaida R. del Castillo, 117–144. Los Angeles: Chicano Studies Research Center, 1980.

Crawford, Ann Fears, and Crystal Sasse Ragsdale. "First Chicana Legislator: Irma Rangel." In *Women in Texas: Their Lives, Their Experiences, Their Accomplishments*, by Ann Fears Crawford and Crystal Sasse Ragsdale, 330–339. Burnet, Tex.: Eakin Press, 1982.

________. "Preserver of the Heritage: Adina de Zavala." In *Women in Texas: Their Lives, Their Experiences, Their Accomplishments*, by Ann Fears Crawford and Crystal Sasse Ragsdale, 165–175. Burnet, Tex.: Eakin Press, 1982.

________. "Worker for Women: Lupe Anguiano." In *Women in Texas: Their Lives, Their Experiences, Their Accomplishments*, by Ann Fears Crawford and Crystal Sasse Ragsdale, 321–329. Burnet, Tex.: Eakin Press, 1982.

Croxdale, Richard. "The 1938 Pecan Shellers' Strike." In *Women in the Texas Workforce: Yesterday and Today*, edited by Richard Croxdale and Melissa Hield, 24–34. Austin: People's History in Texas, 1979.

Daydi-Tolson, Santiago. "La Isabela de Guadalupe y otras chucas, Carmen Tafolla." In *Five Poets of Aztlán*, edited by Santiago Daydi-Tolson, 165–210. Binghamton, N.Y.: Bilingual Press/Editorial Bilingüe, 1985.

Del Castillo, Adelaida R., ed. *Between Borders: Essays on Mexicana/Chicana History*. Encino: Floricanto Press, 1990.

De León, Arnoldo, and Kenneth L. Stewart. "Work Force Participation Rates Among Mexican Immigrant Women in Texas, 1900." *Borderlands Journal* 9 (Spring 1986): 69–74.

Detweiler, Louise. "The Question of Cultural Difference and Gender Oppression in Estela Portillo Trambley's *The Day of the Swallow.*" *Bilingual Review/La Revista Bilingüe* 21 (1996): 146–152.

Díaz-Stevens, Ana María. "The Saving Grace: The Matriarchal Core of Latino Popular Religion." *Latino Studies Journal* 4 (September 1993): 60–78.

Dudley, Jean Hogan. "Clara Zepeda." In *One Hundred Women of the Rio Grande Valley of Texas*, by The Rio Writers, 207–209. Austin: Eakin Press, 1983.

Dysart, Jane. "Mexican Women in San Antonio, 1830–1860: The Assimilation Process." *Western Historical Quarterly* 7 (October 1976): 365–375.

Edgar, Julia. "Judith Zaffirini." In *Notable Hispanic American Women*, edited by Diane Telgen and Jim Kamp, 421–422. Detroit: Gale Research, 1993.

________. "Martha P. Cotera." In *Notable Hispanic American Women*, edited by Diane Telgen and Jim Kamp, 113–115. Detroit: Gale Research, 1993.

Estrada, Rosa Omega. "A Study of the Attitudes of Texas Mexican American Women toward Higher Education." Ed.D. dissertation, Baylor University, 1985.

Estrada, Veronica López. "Expecting the Best: Case Studies of Resilient Mexican-American Girls in a South Texas High School." Ph.D. dissertation, Ohio State University, 1997.

Evans, Bill. "Christine Hernández." In *Notable Hispanic American Women*, edited by Diane Telgen and Jim Kamp, 199. Detroit: Gale Research, 1993.

Fernández-Kelly, María Patricia. *For We are Sold, I and My People: Women and Industry in Mexico's Northern Frontier.* Albany: State University of New York Press, 1983.

________. "Mexican Border Industrialization, Female Labor Force Participation, and Migration." In *Women, Men, and the International Division of Labor*, edited by June Nash and María Patricia Fernández-Kelly, 205–223. Albany: State University of New York Press, 1983.

Firestone, Juanita M., and Richard J. Harris. "Hispanic Women in Texas: An Increasing Portion of the Underclass." *Hispanic Journal of Behavioral Sciences* 16 (May 1994): 176–185.

Flores, Elena. "Sexual Attitudes and Behavior Among Mexican-Origin Adolescent Females." Ph.D. dissertation, The Wright Institute, 1992.

Foster, Sally. "Carmen Lomas Garza." In *Notable Hispanic American Women*, edited by Diane Telgen and Jim Kamp, 174–175. Detroit: Gale Research, 1993.

________. "Juliet Villarreal García." In *Notable Hispanic American Women*, edited by Diane Telgen and Jim Kamp, 170–172. Detroit: Gale Research, 1993.

________. "María Latino Hernández." In *Notable Hispanic American Women*, edited by Diane Telgen and Jim Kamp, 200–202. Detroit: Gale Research, 1993.

Franks, Jeff. "Mizzoner: Councilwoman María Berriozabal Succeeded Henry Cisneros Once, Can She Do it Again?" *San Antonio Monthly* (March 1987): 25–29, 64–66.

Fries, Elaine Kaye. "Leadership Skills Possessed and Attitudes Toward Individual or Group-Centered Leadership as Perceived by Hispanic Women with Limited

Resources in the Lower Rio Grande Valley of Texas." Ph.D. dissertation, Texas A&M University, 2001.

Fuentes, Sylvia. "*La Pisca, La Familia, y Las* Schools: Personal Narratives of Tejana Women in the Midwest and the Nature of Adult Education." Ed.D. dissertation, Northern Illinois University, 1998.

Galindo, D. Letticia. "Dispelling the Male-Only Myth: Chicanos and Caló." *Bilingual Review/La Revista Bilingüe* 17 (January-April 1992): 3–35.

________. "Language Use and Language Attitudes: A Study of Border Women." *Bilingual Review/La Revista Bilingüe* 21 (May-August 1996): 5–17.

Galligan, Martha. "Factors Related to Attrition and Retention Rates of Hispanic Female Students at the University of Texas–Pan American." Ph.D. dissertation, University of Texas at Austin, 1994.

Galloway, Irma Nell. "Trends in the Employment of Minority Women as Administrators in Texas Public Schools—1976–1981." Ed.D. dissertation, Texas Southern University, 1986.

García, Clotilde. "María Gertrudis de la Garza Falcón." In *The New Handbook of Texas*, edited by Ron Tyler, Douglas E. Barnett, Roy R. Barkley, Penelope C. Anderson, and Mark F. Odintz, vol. 3, 111. Austin: Texas State Historical Association, 1996.

________. "Rosa María Hinojosa de Ballí." In *The New Handbook of Texas*, edited by Ron Tyler, Douglas E. Barnett, Roy R. Barkley, Penelope C. Anderson, and Mark F. Odintz, vol. 3, 629. Austin: Texas State Historical Association, 1996.

García-Johnson, Ronie-Richelle. "Angela de Hoyos." In *Notable Hispanic American Women*, edited by Diane Telgen and Jim Kamp, 122–124. Detroit: Gale Research, 1993.

________. "Pat Mora." In *Notable Hispanic American Women*, edited by Diane Telgen and Jim Kamp, 281–282. Detroit: Gale Research, 1993.

________. "Sara Estela Ramírez." In *Notable Hispanic American Women*, edited by Diane Telgen and Jim Kamp, 330–331. Detroit: Gale Research, 1993.

García, María Cristina. "Consuelo González Amezcua." In *The New Handbook of Texas*, edited by Ron Tyler, Douglas E. Barnett, Roy R. Barkley, Penelope C. Anderson, and Mark F. Odintz, vol. 3, 235–236. Austin: Texas State Historical Association, 1996.

________. "Liga Feminil Mexicanista." In *The New Handbook of Texas*, edited by Ron Tyler, Douglas E. Barnett, Roy R. Barkley, Penelope C. Anderson, and Mark F. Odintz, vol. 4, 194. Austin: Texas State Historical Association, 1996.

________. "María Torres Reyna." In *The New Handbook of Texas*, edited by Ron Tyler, Douglas E. Barnett, Roy R. Barkley, Penelope C. Anderson, and Mark F. Odintz, vol. 5, 554–555. Austin: Texas State Historical Association, 1996.

________. "Mujeres Artistas del Suroeste." In *The New Handbook of Texas*, edited by Ron Tyler, Douglas E. Barnett, Roy R. Barkley, Penelope C. Anderson, and Mark F. Odintz, vol. 4, 878. Austin: Texas State Historical Association, 1996.

García, Mario T. "The Chicana in American History: The Mexican Women of El Paso, 1880–1920: A Case Study." *Pacific Historical Review* 49 (May 1980): 315–337.

Garza-Falcón, Leticia M. "The Historical Fiction of Jovita González: Complex and Competing Class Identities." In *Gente Decente: A Borderlands Response to the Rhetoric of Dominance*, by Leticia M. Garza-Falcón, 74–132. Austin: University of Texas Press, 1998.

________. "María Cristina Mena's Elite, Fermina Guerra's 'Folk': The Struggles of Their Distinct and Converging Worlds." In *Gente Decente: A Borderlands Response to the Rhetoric of Dominance*, by Leticia M. Garza-Falcón, 133–155. Austin: University of Texas Press, 1998.

________. "The Texas History of Beatriz de la Gaza's Narratives: Sustaining Women, Hispanic Heroes, and a Sense of Place." In *Gente Decente: A Borderlands Response to the Rhetoric of Dominance*, by Leticia M. Garza-Falcón, 215–238. Austin: University of Texas Press, 1998.

Gilbert, Minnie. "Texas' First Cattle Queen." In *Roots by the River*, by Valley By-Liners, 15–25. Mission, Tex.: Border Kingdom Press, 1978.

Gil, Carlos B. "Lydia Mendoza: Houstonian and First Lady of Mexican American Song." *The Houston Review* 3 (Summer 1981): 249–260. Reprinted in *Chicano Border Culture and Folklore*, edited by José Villarino and Arturo Ramírez, 181–194. San Diego: Marín Publications, 1993.

Gómez, Sarah Ann. "Experiences and Opinions about Fiber and Breast Cancer in Older Hispanic Women in the Houston Area." Master's thesis, Texas Woman's University, 2001.

Gonsior, Marían C. "Carmen Tafolla." In *Notable Hispanic American Women*, edited by Diane Telgen and Jim Kamp, 395. Detroit: Gale Research, 1993.

________. "Estela Portillo Trambley." In *Notable Hispanic American Women*, edited by Diane Telgen and Jim Kamp, 323–324. Detroit: Gale Research, 1993.

González, John M. "Terms of Engagement: Nation or Patriarchy in Jovita González's and Eve Raleigh's *Caballero*." In *Recovering the U.S. Hispanic Literary Heritage*, edited by José F. Aranda, Jr. and Silvio Torres-Saillant, vol. 4, 264–276. Houston: Arte Público Press, 2002.

González, Rosalinda M. "Chicanas and Mexican Immigrant Families 1920–1940: Women's Subordination and Family Exploitation." In *Decades of Discontent: The Women's Movement, 1920–1940*, edited by Lois Scharf and Joan M. Jensen, 59–84. Westport, Conn.: Greenwood Press, 1983.

Griffith, Albert J. "The Scion, The Señorita, and the Texas Ranch Epic: Hispanic Images in Film." *Bilingual Review/La Revista Bilingüe* 16 (September-December 1991): 15–22.

Guerra, Dora Elizondo. "Whose Water Is This Anyway, and Keep Your Plow Out of My Corn Field: Men, Women and Culture in Spanish Colonial Texas." *South Texas Studies* 11 (2000): 181–192.

Gulley, Irene Treviño. "Hispanic Women in Positions of Leadership." Ed.D. dissertation, University of Houston, 1995.

Guthrie, Keith. *The Legend of Chipita: The Only Woman Hanged in Texas*. Austin: Eakin Press, 1990.

Gutiérrez, José Angel. "Experiences of Chicana County Judges in Texas Politics: In Their Own Words." *Frontiers* 20.1 (1999): 181–191.

Guzmán, Jane Bock. "Dallas Barrio Women of Power." Master's thesis, University of North Texas, 1992.

________. "María Luna." *Legacies: A History Journal for Dallas and North Central Texas* (Fall 2001): 17–18.

Habermacher, Andrew Lee. "Physical Development of Anglo and Spanish Culture School Boys and Girls Age 13–18, Inclusive." Master's thesis, Texas A&I University, 1940.

Hawkins, Gladys, Jean Soper, and Jane Pike Henry. *Your Maid From Mexico: A Home Training Course for Maids in English and Spanish.* San Antonio: The Naylor Company, 1959.

Hawkins, Nicole DeShaun. "Six-year Survival Analysis of African American and Hispanic Women with Breast Cancer in the State of Texas." Master's thesis, University of North Texas Health Science Center at Fort Worth, 1999.

Hebert, Rachel Bluntzer. *Shadows on the Nueces: The Saga of Chipita Rodríguez*. Atlanta: Emory University, Banner Press, 1942.

Hepburn, Ruth A. "Mujeres de Hoy: Some Feminists of Tejas." *Common Ground* (March 1974): 4.

Hernández, Al Carlos. "Vilma Martínez: Una Chicana Ejemplar." *Nuestro* 5 (August-September 1981): 13–14.

Hernández, Arthur E. "Do Role Models Influence Self Efficacy and Aspirations in Mexican American At-Risk Females?" *Hispanic Journal of Behavioral Sciences* 17 (May 1995): 256–263.

Hernández-Tovar, Inés. "Sara Estela Ramírez: The Early Twentieth Century Texas Mexican Poet." Ph.D. dissertation, University of Houston, 1984.

________. "Sara Estela Ramírez, *Sembradora*." *Legacy: A Journal of Nineteenth Century American Women Writers* 6 (1989): 13–26.

Herrera-Sobek, María. *Chicana Creativity and Criticism: Charting New Frontiers in American Literature*. Houston: Arte Público Press, 1988.

________. *The Mexican Corrido: A Feminist Analysis*. Bloomington: Indiana University Press, 1990.

Hield, Melissa. "Union-Minded: Women in the Texas ILGWU, 1933–1950." In *Women in the Texas Workforce: Yesterday and Today*, edited by Richard Croxdale and Melissa Hield, 1–23. Austin: People's History in Texas, 1979.

Holden, Frances Mayhugh. "Teresa Urrea." In *The New Handbook of Texas*, edited by Ron Tyler, Douglas E. Barnett, Roy R. Barkley, Penelope C. Anderson, and Mark F. Odintz, vol. 6, 678–679. Austin: Texas State Historical Association, 1996.

Holden, William Curry. *Teresita*. Owings Mill, Md.: Stemmer House Publishers, 1978.

Honig, Emily. "Women at Farah Revisited: Political Mobilization and Its Aftermath among Chicana Workers in El Paso, Texas, 1972–1992." *Feminist Studies* 22 (Summer 1996): 425–452.

Hurtado, Aida. "Midwife Practices in Hidalgo County, Texas." *Trabajos Monográficos: Studies in Chicana/Latina Research* 3 (1987): 1–30.

Igo, John. "Julia Mott Waugh on Los Pastores." In *Diamond Bessie and the Shepherds*, edited by Wilson M. Hudson, 15–26. Austin: Encino Press, 1972.

Jennings, Frank. "Adina de Zavala: Alamo Crusader." *Texas Highways* 42 (March 1995): 15–21.

Jerome, Annette Corrine. "An Investigation of the Effects of a Structured Group to Enhance Self-Esteem, Internal Locus of Control Orientation and Career Aspirations of Hispanic Adolescent Females." Ph.D. dissertation, Brigham Young University, 1995.

Johnson, Carmen Acosta. "Breast Feeding and Social Class Mobility: The Case of Mexican Migrant Mothers in Houston, Texas." In *Twice a Minority: Mexican American Women*, edited by Margarita B. Melville, 66–82. St. Louis: C.V. Mosby Company, 1980.

Jones, Nancy Baker. "Jovita Idar." In *The New Handbook of Texas*, edited by Ron Tyler, Douglas E. Barnett, Roy R. Barkley, Penelope C. Anderson, and Mark F. Odintz, vol. 3, 814. Austin: Texas State Historical Association, 1996.

Jones, Nancy Baker, and Ruthe Winegarten. "Irma Rangel." In *Capitol Women: Texas Female Legislators, 1923–1999,* by Nancy Baker Jones and Ruthe Winegarten, 204–206. Austin: University of Texas Press, 2000.

________. "Judith Lee Pappas Zaffirini." In *Capitol Women: Texas Female Legislators, 1923–1999,* by Nancy Baker Jones and Ruthe Winegarten, 233–235. Austin: University of Texas Press, 2000.

________."María Elena (Lena) Guerrero." In *Capitol Women: Texas Female Legislators, 1923–1999,* by Nancy Baker Jones and Ruthe Winegarten, 227–230. Austin: University of Texas Press, 2000.

________. "Sylvia Romo." In *Capitol Women: Texas Female Legislators, 1923–1999,* by Nancy Baker Jones and Ruthe Winegarten, 254–255. Austin: University of Texas Press, 2000.

________. "Yolanda Navarro Flores." In *Capitol Women: Texas Female Legislators, 1923–1999,* by Nancy Baker Jones and Ruthe Winegarten, 250–251. Austin: University of Texas Press, 2000.

Joos, Sandra Kay. "Social, Attitudinal and Behavioral Correlates of Weight Change Among Mexican American Women." Ph.D. dissertation, The University of Texas Health Science Center at Houston School of Public Health, 1984.

Jover, Margaret Anna. "Risk-Taking Propensity of Successful and Unsuccessful Hispanic Female Entrepreneurs." Ph.D. dissertation, Texas Woman's University, 1992.

Keller, Elena. "Vicki Carr." In *Notable Hispanic American Women*, edited by Diane Telgen and Jim Kamp, 74–77. Detroit: Gale Research, 1993.

Keyes, Grace Granger. "Mexican American and Anglo American Midwifery in San Antonio, Texas." Ph.D. dissertation, University of Wisconsin, Milwaukee, 1985.

Kinsall, Al. "The Lady in Blue: María de Agreda of Spain." *Journal of South Texas* 8 (1995): 80–96.

Kreneck, Thomas H. "Recovering the 'Lost' Manuscripts of Jovita González." *Texas Library Journal* 74 (Summer 1998): 76–79.

________. "The Letter From Chapultepec." *The Houston Review* 3 (Summer 1981): 268–271.

Laible, Julie Catherine. "Educating *Muchachas de la Frontera*: Educational Practices that Promote the Success of Mexican-American Females in Texas/Mexico Border Schools." Ph.D. dissertation, University of Texas at Austin, 1995.

Larralde, Carlos. "Francisca Reyes Esparza." In *The New Handbook of Texas*, edited by Ron Tyler, Douglas E. Barnett, Roy R. Barkley, Penelope C. Anderson, and Mark F. Odintz, vol. 2, 893. Austin: Texas State Historical Association, 1996.

________. "Santa Teresa: A Chicana Mystic." *Grito del Sol* 3 (April/June 1978): 1–14.

Lashaway-Bokina, Nancy. "Gifted but Gone: High Ability, Mexican-American Female Dropouts." Ph.D. dissertation, University of Connecticut, 1996.

Lawhn, Juanita Luna. "*El Regidor* and *La Prensa*: Impediments to Women's Self-Definition." *Third Woman* 4 (1989): 134–142.

________. "Victorian Attitudes Affecting the Mexican Woman Writing in *La Prensa* during the Early 1900s and the Chicana of the 1980s." In *Missions in Conflict: Essays on U.S.-Mexican Relations and Chicano Culture*, edited by Renate von Bardeleben, Dietrich Briesemeister, and Juan Bruce-Novoa, 65–71. Tubingen: Narr, 1986.

Ledbetter, Barbara A. "Black and Mexican Women Slaves in Young County, Texas, 1856–1865." *West Texas Historical Association Yearbook* 56 (1980): 100–102.

Ledesma, Irene. "Unlikely Strikers: Mexican-American Women in Strike Activity in Texas, 1919–1974." Ph.D. dissertation, Ohio State University, 1992.

________. "Texas Newspapers and Chicana Workers' Activism, 1919–1974." *Western Historical Quarterly* 26 (Autumn 1995): 309–331.

Lieshoff, Sylvia Cobos. "The Impact of Literacy Programs: Perceptions of Selected Mexican and Mexican-American Women in Texas." Ph.D. dissertation, Texas A&M University, 1995.

Limón, José E. "La vieja 'Ines,' A Mexican Folk Game: A Research Note." In *Twice a Minority: Mexican American Women*, edited by Margarita B. Melville, 88–94. St. Louis: C. V. Mosby Company, 1980.

________. "Selena: Sexuality, Performance, and the Problematic of Hegemony." In *Reflexiones 1997: New Directions in Mexican American Studies*. Austin: Center for Mexican American Studies and the University of Texas Press, 1998.

Lindstrom, Naomi. "Four Representative Hispanic Women Poets of Central Texas: A Portrait of Plurality." *Third Woman* 2 (1984): 64–70.

López-Stafford, Gloria. *A Place in El Paso: A Mexican American Childhood.* Albuquerque: University of New Mexico Press, 1996.

López, Yolanda. "The Influence of Ethnicity on Management Styles of Women in Educational Administration." Ed.D. dissertation, Baylor University, 1993.

Madrid, Sandra Emilia. "The Effects of Socialization on Goal Actualization of Public School Chicana Principals and Superintendents." Ph.D. dissertation, University of Washington, 1985.

Mahnken, Jonathan David. "A Validation Study for Self-reported Data of Recent Mammography Use Among Older Mexican-American Women in Southeast Texas." Master's thesis, University of Texas Graduate School of Biomedical Science at Galveston, 2000.

Manríquez, B. J. "Argument in Narrative: Tropology in Jovita González's *Caballero*." *Bilingual Review/La Revista Bilingüe* 25 (2000): 172–178.

Maril, Elizabeth. "Spanish Ranching Women." *South Texas Studies* 10 (1999): 143–153.

Márquez, Benjamín. "Organizing Mexican-American Women in the Garment Industry: La Mujer Obrera." *Women and Politics* 15 (May 1995): 65–87.

Márquez, Raquel. "Chicana Labor Activists: The Case of Fuerza Uida." Master's thesis, University of Texas at Austin, 1995.

Marshall, María Sandra González. "The Childbearing Beliefs and Practices of Pregnant Mexican-American Adolescents Living in Southwest Border Regions." Master's thesis, University of Arizona, 1987.

Martínez, Yleana. "María Antonietta Berriozabal." In *Notable Hispanic American Women*, edited by Diane Telgen and Jim Kamp, 56. Detroit: Gale Research, 1993.

________. "Norma García." In *Notable Hispanic American Women*, edited by Diane Telgen and Jim Kamp, 172–174. Detroit: Gale Research, 1993.

________. "Santa Barraza." In *Notable Hispanic American Women*, edited by Diane Telgen and Jim Kamp, 52–53. Detroit: Gale Research, 1993.

Mata, Zelma Diana. "Anglo and Hispanic Women Administrators' Perceptions of the Conflict among their Multiple Roles as Professional, Spouse, Parent and Self in Selected Higher Education Institutions in Texas." Ed.D. dissertation, University of Houston, 1993.

Maville, Janice Ann. "The Relationship between Social Support and Persistence among Female Hispanic Students in an Associate Degree Nursing Program." Ed.D. dissertation, Texas A&M University, 1992.

McCaffery, Isias James. "Organizing *las Costureras*: Life, Labor, and Unionization among Mexican Garment Workers in Two Borderlands Cities, Los Angeles and San Antonio, 1933–1941." Ph.D. dissertation, University of Kansas, 1999.

McClean, Cathy Heather. "Factors Affecting Compliance of Hispanic Women with Cervical Dysplasia." Master's thesis, University of Texas Graduate School of Biomedical Science at Galveston, 1990.

McCoy, Dorothy Abbott. "Andrea 'Andy' Montes." In *One Hundred Women of the Rio Grande Valley of Texas*, by The Rio Writers, 134–135. Austin: Eakin Press, 1983.

________. "Gloria Campos." In *One Hundred Women of the Rio Grande Valley of Texas*, by The Rio Writers, 21–23. Austin: Eakin Press, 1983.

________. "Mary Yturria." In *One Hundred Women of the Rio Grande Valley of Texas*, by The Rio Writers, 202–204. Austin: Eakin Press, 1983.

McDonald, Dedra S. "'The Labor Movement Was the Way': Mexican-American Women's Solidarity and Political Power in Depression-Era San Antonio." Master's thesis, University of Wisconsin, Madison, 1993.

McKenna, Teresa. "Engendering the Border: Toward a Chicana Literary Aesthetic." In *Migrant Song: Politics and Process in Contemporary Chicano Literature*, edited by Teresa McKenna, 104–125. Austin: University of Texas Press, 1997.

Meier, Matt S. with Conchita Franco Serri and Richard A. García. "Emma Tenayuca." In *Notable Latino Americans: A Biographical Dictionary*, by Matt S. Meier, 369–371. Westport, Conn.: Greenwood Press, 1997.

________. "Lydia Mendoza." In *Notable Latino Americans: A Biographical Dictionary*, by Matt S. Meier, 245–247. Westport, Conn.: Greenwood Press, 1997.

________. "Sandra Cisneros." In *Notable Latino Americans: A Biographical Dictionary*, by Matt S. Meier, 87–91. Westport, Conn.: Greenwood Press, 1997.

________. "Vicki Carr." In *Notable Latino Americans: A Biographical Dictionary*, by Matt S. Meier, 57–60. Westport, Conn.: Greenwood Press, 1997.

Melville, Margarita B. "Selective Acculturation of Female Mexican Migrants." In *Twice a Minority: Mexican American Women*, edited by Margarita B. Melville, 155–163. St. Louis: C. V. Mosby Company, 1980.

________. "Mexican Women Adapt to Migration." *International Migration Review* 12 (Winter 1978): 225–235.

Mendoza, Lydia. "The Lark of the Border." In *Ethnic Recordings in America: A Neglected Heritage, 119–132.* Washington, D.C.: American Folklife Center, Library of Congress, 1982.

Meyer, Nicholas E. "Vilma Martínez." In *The Biographical Dictionary of Hispanic Americans*, by Nicholas E. Meyer, 141–142. New York: Facts on File, 1997.

Milligan, Bryce. *Corazón del Norte: A Selection of North Texas Latino Writing.* San Antonio: Wings Press, 1996.

________. "Ever Radical: A Survey of Tejana Writers." In *Texas Women Writers: A Tradition of Their Own*, edited by Sylvia Ann Grider and Lou Halsell Rodenberger, 207–246. College Station: Texas A&M University Press, 1997.

Mindiola, Tatcho Jr. "The Cost of Being a Mexican Female Worker in the 1970 Houston Labor Market." *Aztlán* 11 (Fall 1980): 231–247.

Mitchell, Marci K. "Lived Experience and the Power of Relationships: An Ethnographic Study of Female Latina Graduates and Dropouts in a South Texas Border High School." Ed.D. dissertation, University of Houston, 1998.

Morales, Cynthia Ann. "*Todo por la raza*: Community Activism Among Mexican-American Women in San Antonio, 1920–1940." Master's thesis, Texas A&M University-Kingsville, 2001.

Moynihan, Dee Jacques. "Doña María: Rancher of Las Cabras." *Texas Highways* (August 2002): 26–29.

Nathan, Debbie. *Women and Other Aliens: Essays from the U.S. Mexico Border*. El Paso: Cinco Puntos Press, 1980.

Nicholson, Anita Lucindy Connelly. "Hispanic Females, Forty Plus Years of Age, Returning to Six South Texas Universities to Study Science and/or Math: Biases, Sources, Effects, and the Barriers Imposed." Master's thesis, Texas A&M University-Kingsville, 1997.

Niles, T. A. "Tessa Martínez Tagle." In *Notable Hispanic American Women*, edited by Diane Telgen and Jim Kamp, 396–397. Detroit: Gale Research, 1993.

Nwachie, Judy Carol Flakes. "An Evaluation: The Texas Equal Educational Opportunity Plan for Higher Education on the Representation of Black and Hispanic Women Administrators." Ph.D. dissertation, University of Texas at Austin, 1993.

Ojeda-de la Cruz, Juanita Calderón. "Mexican and Black Americans' Sex Role Stereotyping in the School's Socialization Process." Ed.D. dissertation, Texas A&I University, 1985.

Ornelas, Juanita Pantoja. "Factors in Upward Mobility of Anglo and Hispanic Women in Public School Administration." Ph.D. dissertation, Texas Woman's University, 1991.

Orozco, Aurora E. "Mexican Blood Runs Through My Veins." In *Speaking Chicana: Voice, Power, Identity*, edited by D. Letticia Galindo and María Dolores Gonzales, 106–120. Tucson: University of Arizona Press, 1999.

Orozco, Cynthia E. "The Origins of the League of United Latin American Citizens (LULAC) and the Mexican American Civil Rights Movement in Texas with an Analysis of Women's Political Participation in a Gendered Context, 1910–1929." Ph.D. dissertation, University of California at Los Angeles, 1992.

________. "Alice Dickerson Montemayor: Feminism and Mexican American Politics in the 1930s." In *Writing the Range: Race, Class, and Culture in the Women's West*, edited by Elizabeth Jameson and Susan Armitage, 435–456. Norman: University of Oklahoma Press, 1997.

________. "Alicia Guadalupe Elizondo de Lozano." In *The New Handbook of Texas*, edited by Ron Tyler, Douglas E. Barnett, Roy R. Barkley, Penelope C. Anderson, and Mark F. Odintz, vol. 4, 318. Austin: Texas State Historical Association, 1996.

________. "Ana Salazar de Esparza." In *The New Handbook of Texas*, edited by Ron Tyler, Douglas E. Barnett, Roy R. Barkley, Penelope C. Anderson, and Mark F. Odintz, vol. 5, 774–775. Austin: Texas State Historical Association, 1996.

________. "Beyond Machismo, La Familia, and Ladies Auxiliaries: A Historiography of Mexican-Origin Women's Participation in Voluntary Associations and Politics in the United States, 1870–1990." In *Perspectives in Mexican American Studies*, vol. 5, edited by Juan R. García, 1–34. Tucson: Mexican American Studies and Research Center, University of Arizona, 1995.

________. "Carolina Malpica Munguía." In *The New Handbook of Texas*, edited by Ron Tyler, Douglas E. Barnett, Roy R. Barkley, Penelope C. Anderson, and Mark F. Odintz, vol. 4, 887. Austin: Texas State Historical Association, 1996.

________. "Chicana Rights Project." In *The New Handbook of Texas*, edited by Ron Tyler, Douglas E. Barnett, Roy R. Barkley, Penelope C. Anderson, and Mark F. Odintz, vol. 2, 69. Austin: Texas State Historical Association, 1996.

________. "Círculo Cultural Isabel la Católica." In *The New Handbook of Texas*, edited by Ron Tyler, Douglas E. Barnett, Roy R. Barkley, Penelope C. Anderson, and Mark F. Odintz, vol. 2, 111–112. Austin: Texas State Historical Association, 1996.

________. "Consuelo Herrera Méndez." In *The New Handbook of Texas*, edited by Ron Tyler, Douglas E. Barnett, Roy R. Barkley, Penelope C. Anderson, and Mark F. Odintz, vol. 4, 618. Austin: Texas State Historical Association, 1996.

________. "Elvira Rodríguez de Gonzales." In *The New Handbook of Texas*, edited by Ron Tyler, Douglas E. Barnett, Roy R. Barkley, Penelope C. Anderson, and Mark F. Odintz, vol. 5, 657–658. Austin: Texas State Historical Association, 1996.

________. "Emilia Wilholmina Schunior Ramírez." In *The New Handbook of Texas*, edited by Ron Tyler, Douglas E. Barnett, Roy R. Barkley, Penelope C. Anderson, and Mark F. Odintz, vol. 5, 423–424. Austin: Texas State Historical Association, 1996.

________. "Esther Nieto Machuca." In *The New Handbook of Texas*, edited by Ron Tyler, Douglas E. Barnett, Roy R. Barkley, Penelope C. Anderson, and Mark F. Odintz, vol. 4, 410. Austin: Texas State Historical Association, 1996.

________. "Eva Carrillo de García." In *The New Handbook of Texas*, edited by Ron Tyler, Douglas E. Barnett, Roy R. Barkley, Penelope C. Anderson, and Mark F. Odintz, vol. 3, 83–84. Austin: Texas State Historical Association, 1996.

________. "Fermina Guerra." In *The New Handbook of Texas*, edited by Ron Tyler, Douglas E. Barnett, Roy R. Barkley, Penelope C. Anderson, and Mark F. Odintz, vol. 3, 368. Austin: Texas State Historical Association, 1996.

________. "Herlinda Morales Rodríguez." In *The New Handbook of Texas*, edited by Ron Tyler, Douglas E. Barnett, Roy R. Barkley, Penelope C. Anderson, and Mark F. Odintz, vol. 5, 653. Austin: Texas State Historical Association, 1996.

________. "Hispanic Women's Network of Texas." In *The New Handbook of Texas*, edited by Ron Tyler, Douglas E. Barnett, Roy R. Barkley, Penelope C. Anderson, and Mark F. Odintz, vol. 3, 631. Austin: Texas State Historical Association, 1996.

________. "Josefina Escajeda." In *The New Handbook of Texas*, edited by Ron Tyler, Douglas E. Barnett, Roy R. Barkley, Penelope C. Anderson, and Mark F. Odintz, vol. 2, 887. Austin: Texas State Historical Association, 1996.

________. "Ladies in LULAC." In *The New Handbook of Texas*, edited by Ron Tyler, Douglas E. Barnett, Roy R. Barkley, Penelope C. Anderson, and Mark F. Odintz, vol. 4, 1–2. Austin: Texas State Historical Association, 1996.

________. "María de Sada." In *The New Handbook of Texas*, edited by Ron Tyler, Douglas E. Barnett, Roy R. Barkley, Penelope C. Anderson, and Mark F. Odintz, vol. 5, 750–751. Austin: Texas State Historical Association, 1996.

________. "María Elena Zamora O'Shea." In *The New Handbook of Texas*, edited by Ron Tyler, Douglas E. Barnett, Roy R. Barkley, Penelope C. Anderson, and Mark F. Odintz, vol. 4, 1166–1167. Austin: Texas State Historical Association, 1996.

________. "María L. de Hernández." In *The New Handbook of Texas*, edited by Ron Tyler, Douglas E. Barnett, Roy R. Barkley, Penelope C. Anderson, and Mark F. Odintz, vol. 3, 572–573. Austin: Texas State Historical Association, 1996.

________. "Mexican American Women." In *The New Handbook of Texas*, edited by Ron Tyler, Douglas E. Barnett, Roy R. Barkley, Penelope C. Anderson, and Mark F. Odintz, vol. 4, 680–682. Austin: Texas State Historical Association, 1996.

________. "Petra Vela de Vidal Kenedy." In *The New Handbook of Texas*, edited by Ron Tyler, Douglas E. Barnett, Roy R. Barkley, Penelope C. Anderson, and Mark F. Odintz, vol. 3, 1065. Austin: Texas State Historical Association, 1996.

________. "Selena Quintanilla Pérez." In *The New Handbook of Texas*, edited by Ron Tyler, Douglas E. Barnett, Roy R. Barkley, Penelope C. Anderson, and Mark F. Odintz, vol. 5, 392–393. Austin: Texas State Historical Association, 1996.

Orozco, Cynthia E., and Teresa Palomo Acosta. "Jovita González de Mireles." In *The New Handbook of Texas*, edited by Ron Tyler, Douglas E. Barnett, Roy R. Barkley, Penelope C. Anderson, and Mark F. Odintz, vol. 3, 236–237. Austin: Texas State Historical Association, 1996.

Ortego y Gasca, Felipe de. "The Hispanic Woman: A Humanistic Perspective." *La Luz* (November 1977): 7–10.

"Outstanding Hispanic: Dr. Clotilde García." *La Luz* 7 (May 1978): 14.

Owens, Keith. "Dr. Patricia Hernández." *Hispanic Outlook in Higher Education* 6 (March 15, 1996): 11–12.

Palmisano, Joseph M. "Belén Robles." In *Notable Hispanic American Women. Book II*, edited by Joseph M. Palmisano, 274–276. Detroit: Gale Research, 1998.

________. "Cathi Villalpando." In *Notable Hispanic American Women. Book II*, edited by Joseph M. Palmisano, 340–341. Detroit: Gale Research, 1998.

________. "Enedina Casárez." In *Notable Hispanic American Women. Book II*, edited by Joseph M. Palmisano, 327–328. Detroit: Gale Research, 1998.

________. "Gloria Anzaldúa." In *Notable Hispanic American Women. Book II*, edited by Joseph M. Palmisano, 24–26. Detroit: Gale Research, 1998.

________. "Guadalupe Quintanilla." In *Notable Hispanic American Women. Book II*, edited by Joseph M. Palmisano, 253–256. Detroit: Gale Research, 1998.

________. "Irma Rangel." In *Notable Hispanic American Women. Book II*, edited by Joseph M. Palmisano, 259–261. Detroit: Gale Research, 1998.

________. "Jovita González." In *Notable Hispanic American Women. Book II*, edited by Joseph M. Palmisano, 134–137. Detroit: Gale Research, 1998.

________. "Lucy González Parsons." In *Notable Hispanic American Women. Book II*, edited by Joseph M. Palmisano, 243–244. Detroit: Gale Research, 1998.

________. "Minerva Pérez." In *Notable Hispanic American Women. Book II*, edited by Joseph M. Palmisano, 250–252. Detroit: Gale Research, 1998.

________. "Norma E. Cantú." In *Notable Hispanic American Women. Book II*, edited by Joseph M. Palmisano, 43–44. Detroit: Gale Research, 1998.

________. "Norma V. Cantú." In *Notable Hispanic American Women. Book II*, edited by Joseph M. Palmisano, 44–46. Detroit: Gale Research, 1998.

________. "Olivia Castellano." In *Notable Hispanic American Women. Book II*, edited by Joseph M. Palmisano, 56–58. Detroit: Gale Research, 1998.

________. "Tina Guerrero Fuentes." In *Notable Hispanic American Women. Book II*, edited by Joseph M. Palmisano, 120–122. Detroit: Gale Research, 1998.

________. "Tish Hinojosa." In *Notable Hispanic American Women. Book II*, edited by Joseph M. Palmisano, 153–155. Detroit: Gale Research, 1998.

________. "Selena." In *Notable Hispanic American Women. Book II*, edited by Joseph M. Palmisano, 297–300. Detroit: Gale Research, 1998.

Paredez, Deborah Ann. "Crossing over the Latina Body: The Selena Phenomenon and the Reproduction of Latinidad." Ph.D. dissertation, Northwestern University, 2002.

Parker, Edith Olbrich. "María Gertrudis Pérez Cordero Cassiano." In *Women in Early Texas*, edited by Evelyn M. Arrington, 49–57. Second edition. Austin: Texas State Historical Association, 1994.

Patoski, Joe Nick. *Selena: coma la flor*. Boston: Little, Brown, 1996.

Peña, Sylvia Novo. "Evangelina Vigil-Piñon." In *Notable Hispanic American Women*, edited by Diane Telgen and Jim Kamp, 460–461. Detroit: Gale Research, 1993.

________. "Lydia Mendoza." In *Notable Hispanic American Women*, edited by Diane Telgen and Jim Kamp, 271–272. Detroit: Gale Research, 1993.

Pérez, Anita Méndez. "Mexican-American Mothers' Perceptions and Beliefs About Language Acquisition Among Toddlers with Language Disabilities." Ph.D. dissertation, University of Texas at Austin, 1998.

Pérez, Emma. *Oral Narratives as Chicana (His)tory Text*. Working Paper 32. Tucson: Southwest Institute for Research on Women, University of Arizona, 1994.

________. "Tejanas: Diasporic Subjectivities and Post-Revolution Identities." In *The Decolonial Imaginary: Writing Chicanas into History*, by Emma Pérez, 76–155. Bloomington: Indiana University Press, 1999.

Pisani, Michael J., and David W. Yoskowitz. "The Maid Trade: Cross-Border Work in South Texas." *Social Science Quarterly* 83 (June 2002): 568–579.

Pospisil, JoAnn. "Women and Wax: Female Participation in the Candelilla Wax Industry." *Journal of Big Bend Studies* 8 (1996): 153–166.

Poythress, Stephanie. "Catalina Esperanza García." In *Notable Hispanic American Women*, edited by Diane Telgen and Jim Kamp, 166. Detroit: Gale Research, 1993.

Pruitt, Daughn Warren. "Vocational Identity, Level of Career Indecision, and Barriers of Hispanic Reentry Women in Selected Texas Community Colleges: Implications for Adult Education." Ph.D. dissertation, Texas A&M University, 1992.

Quilantán, María Cristina. "Mexican-American Women: Unique Superintendents in Texas." Ed.D. dissertation, University of Texas–Pan American, 2002.

Ragsdale, Crystal Sasse. *The Women and Children of the Alamo*. Austin: State House Press, 1994.

Ramírez, Elizabeth Cantú. "Concepción Hernández." In *The New Handbook of Texas*, edited by Ron Tyler, Douglas E. Barnett, Roy R. Barkley, Penelope C. Anderson, and Mark F. Odintz, vol. 3, 572. Austin: Texas State Historical Association, 1996.

________. "Hispanics and Mexican Women on the Texas Stage, 1875–1900." In *Women and Texas History: Selected Essays*, edited by Fane Downs and Nancy Baker Jones, 34–41. Austin: Texas State Historical Association, 1993.

Ramos, Luis Arturo. *Angela de Hoyos: A Critical Look*. Albuquerque: Pajarito Publications, 1979.

Reyes, María Elena. "Female Hispanic College Students: Upper-division and Graduate Students at Four Major Public Institutions in Texas." Ph.D. dissertation, University of Texas at Austin, 1991.

Reyna, Sergio. "Jovita González y su obra folklórico-literaria: Reconstrucción de la historia cultural méxico-americana." In *Recovering the U.S. Hispanic Literary Heritage*, edited by José F. Aranda Jr. and Silvio Torres-Saillant, vol. 4, 184–200. Houston: Arte Público Press, 2002.

Richardson, Chad, and Cruz C. Torres. "'Only a Maid': Undocumented Domestic Workers in South Texas." In *Batos*, *Bolillos*, *Pochos*, and *Pelados*: *Class and Culture on the South Texas Border*, by Chad Richardson, 169–194. Austin: University of Texas Press, 1999.

Richmond, Clint. *Selena: The Phenomenal Life and Tragic Death of the Tejano Music Queen*. New York: Pocket Books, 1995.

Ríos McMillan, Nora E. "Ana María del Carmen Calvillo: How an Independent Spirit Emerged." *Journal of South Texas* 13 (Fall 2000): 174–192.

________. "'*Siendo Mi Derecho . . .*': The Hispanic Woman's Legal Identity in the Spanish Southwest. *South Texas Studies* 10 (1999): 102–142.

Rips, Geoffrey. "Living History: Emma Tenayuca Tells Her Story." *Texas Observer* 75 (October 28, 1983): 7–15.

"Rodríguez, Chipita." In *The Handbook of Texas: A Supplement*, edited by Eldon Stephen Branda, vol. 3, 809. Austin: Texas State Historical Association, 1976.

Rodríguez, María Elena. "Mary Dilley, Curandera: A Modern South Texas Folk Healer." Master's thesis, Texas A&M University-Kingsville, 1993.

Rodríguez, Richard, and Gloria L. Rodríguez. "Teresa Urrea: Her Life, as it Affected the Mexican-United States Border." *El Grito: A Journal of Contemporary Mexican American Thought* 5 (Summer 1972): 48–68.

Rogers, Mary Beth, Sherry A. Smith, and Janelle D. Scott. "Women of a Revolution: Jovita Idar (1885–1955) and Leonor Villegas de Magnón (1874–1955)." In *We Can Fly: Stories of Katherine Stinson and Other Gutsy Texas Women*, by Mary Beth Rogers, Sherry A. Smith, and Janelle D. Scott, 74–87. Austin: Ellen C. Temple, 1983.

Romero, Yolanda G. "From Rebels to Immigrants to Chicanas: Hispanic Women in Lubbock County." Master's thesis, Texas Tech University, 1987.

________. "Trini Gámez, The Texas Farm Workers, and Mexican American Community Empowerment: Toil and Trouble on the Texas South Plains." In *Mexican*

Americans in Texas History, edited by Emilio Zamora, Cynthia Orozco, and Rodolfo Rocha, 143–155. Austin: Texas State Historical Association, 2000.

Rozek, Barbara J. "The Entry of Mexican Women into Urban Based Industries: Experiences in Texas During the Twentieth Century." In *Women and Texas History: Selected Essays*, edited by Fane Downs and Nancy Baker Jones, 15–33. Austin: Texas State Historical Association, 1993.

Ruiz, Vicki L. "By the Day or the Week: Domestic Workers in El Paso." In *Women on the United States-Mexico Border*, edited by Vicki L. Ruiz and Susan Tiano, 61–76. Boston: Allen and Unwin, 1987.

________. "Dead Ends or Gold Mines? Using Missionary Records in Mexican American Women's History." In *Writing the Range: Race, Class, and Culture in the Women's West*, edited by Elizabeth Jameson and Susan Armitage, 354–371. Norman: University of Oklahoma Press, 1997.

________. "Oral History and La Mujer: The Rosa Guerrero Story." In *Women on the U.S.-Mexico Border: Responses to Change*, edited by Vicki L. Ruiz and Susan Tiano, 219–231. Boston: Allen and Unwin, 1987.

Russell, A. Yvonne, Martha S. Williams, and Patricia A. Farr. "The Health Attitudes of Young Hispanic Women and the Health Status of their Children on the Texas-Mexico Border." *Journal of Community Health* 23 (June 1998): 165–179.

Saldaña, Delia, Albana M. Dassori, and Alexander L. Miller. "When is Caregiving a Burden?: Listening to Mexican American Women." *Hispanic Journal of Behavioral Sciences* 21 (August 1999): 283–301.

Saldívar-Hull, Sonia. "Feminism on the Border: From Gender Politics to Geopolitics." In *Criticism in the Borderlands: Studies in Chicano Literature, Culture, and Ideology*, edited by Héctor Calderón and José David Saldivar, 203–220. Durham: Duke University Press, 1991.

Sánchez, Olga. "Lucía Eldine González de Parson: Labor Organizer." *Imágenes de la Chicana* 1(1974): 10–12.

San Miguel, Guadalupe Jr. "Actors Not Victims: Chicanas/os and the Struggle for Educational Equality." In *Chicanas/Chicanos at the Crossroads: Social, Economic, and Political Change*, edited by David R. Maciel and Isidro D. Ortiz, 159–180. Tucson: University of Arizona Press, 1996.

Saunders, Freddie Milam. "Berta Longoria." In *One Hundred Women of the Rio Grande Valley of Texas*, by The Rio Writers, 114–116. Austin: Eakin Press, 1983.

________. "Elena Farías Barrera." In *One Hundred Women of the Rio Grande Valley of Texas*, by The Rio Writers, 3–5. Austin: Eakin Press, 1983.

________. "Rafaela G. Valverde." In *One Hundred Women of the Rio Grande Valley of Texas*, by The Rio Writers, 179–181. Austin: Eakin Press, 1983.

Sawyer-Morse, Mary Kaye. "Psychosocial and Behavioral Correlates of Disordered Eating among Young Adult Hispanic Females." Ph.D. dissertation, University of Texas at Austin, 1997.

Schultz, T. E., E. Murguía, and S. K. Hoppe. "Gender Role Orientation Among Three Generations of Mexican American Women." In *The 1988 Victoria College Social Sciences Symposium*. 87–100. Victoria, Tex.: Victoria College Press, 1988.

Scott, Glenn. "Anna Salazar de Esparza." In *Women in Early Texas*, edited by Evelyn M. Arrington, 219–222. Second edition. Austin: Texas State Historical Association, 1994.

________. "Juana Navarro de Alsbury." In *Women in Early Texas*, edited by Evelyn M. Arrington, 191–196. Second edition. Austin: Texas State Historical Association, 1994.

Serna, Melissa S. "Gender and Educational Differences in the Psychic Phenomena Beliefs of Mexican-Americans." Master's thesis, Texas A&M University-Kingsville, 1997.

Sharpe, Patricia. "Ninfa Laurenzo." *Texas Monthly* 29 (August 2001): 40.

Sifuentes, D. Ileana. "Influences on the Hispanic Woman's Selection of Work and Social Activity Apparel." Master's thesis, University of North Texas, 1994.

Smith, Pamela A., and Elizabeth C. Ramírez. "Beatriz Escalona Pérez." In *The New Handbook of Texas*, edited by Ron Tyler, Douglas E. Barnett, Roy R. Barkley, Penelope C. Anderson, and Mark F. Odintz, vol. 2, 888–889. Austin: Texas State Historical Association, 1996.

Smylie, Vernon. *A Noose for Chipita*. Corpus Christi, Tex.: Texas Syndicate Press, 1970.

Solórzano, Rosalía. "María Gullermina Valdés Villalva." In *The New Handbook of Texas*, edited by Ron Tyler, Douglas E. Barnett, Roy R. Barkley, Penelope C. Anderson, and Mark F. Odintz, vol. 6, 688. Austin: Texas State Historical Association, 1996.

Solorzano-Torres, Rosalia. "Women, Labor, and the U.S.-Mexico Border: Mexican Maids in El Paso, Texas." In *Mexicanas at Work in the United States*, edited by Margarita B. Melville, 75–83. Houston: Mexican American Studies Program, University of Houston, 1988.

Soto-Fulp, Sylvia. "Conflict Resolution Styles: Ethnic and Gender Differences." Ph.D. dissertation, New Mexico State University, 1996.

Spencer, Laura Gutiérrez. "The Desert Blooms: Flowered Songs by Pat Mora." *Bilingual Review/Revista Bilingüe* 20 (January-April 1995): 28–36.

Stephens, Richard C., George T. Oser, and Zena Smith Blau. "To Be Aged, Hispanic, and Female: The Triple Risk." In *Twice a Minority: Mexican American Women*, edited by Margarita B. Melville, 249–258. St. Louis: C. V. Mosby Company, 1980.

Stewart, Kenneth L., and Arnoldo De León. "Work Force Participation Among Mexican Immigrant Women in Texas, 1900." *Borderlands Journal* 9 (Spring 1986): 69–74.

Stewart, Paula. "Patricia de la Garza de León." In *The New Handbook of Texas*, edited by Ron Tyler, Douglas E. Barnett, Roy R. Barkley, Penelope C. Anderson, and Mark F. Odintz, vol. 2, 571–572. Austin: Texas State Historical Association, 1996.

Strachwitz, Chris, and James Nicolopulos, comps. *Lydia Mendoza: A Family Autobiography*. Houston: Arte Público Press, 1994.

Tafolla, Carmen. *Curandera*. San Antonio: M&E Editions, 1983.

________. *To Split a Human: Mitos, Machos y la Mujer Chicana*. San Antonio: Mexican American Cultural Center, 1984.

Taylor, Virginia H. "Adina de Zavala." In *Women in Early Texas*, edited by Evelyn M. Arrington, 301–308. Second edition. Austin: Texas State Historical Association, 1994.

Tejeda, Juan. "Eva Ybarra." In *Puro Conjunto: An Album in Words and Pictures*, edited by Juan Tejeda and Avelardo Valdez, 295–300. Austin: CMAS Books, Guadalupe Cultural Arts Center, 2001.

Thompson, Sharon Eileen. "An Analysis of Social Support and Prenatal Care among Low-income Women in a United States/Mexico Border City." Ph.D. dissertation, University of New Mexico, 1999.

Tijerina, Mary Sylvia. "Mexican American Women's Perspectives of End-stage Renal Disease and the Hemodialysis Regimen: Psychosocial Influences of Compliance with Treatment Recommendations." Ph.D. dissertation, University of Texas at Austin, 2000.

Tinajero, Joséfina Villamil, and Dee Ann Spencer. "Creating a Future for Hispanic Mothers and Daughters on the U.S.-Mexico Border." In *Life, Death, and In-Between on the U.S.-Mexico Border: Así es la vida*, edited by Martha Oehmke Loustaunau and Mary Sánchez-Bane, 95–112. Westport, Conn.: Bergin and Garvey, 1999.

Torres-Raines, Rosario. "The Mexican American Woman and Work: Intergenerational Perspectives of Comparative Ethnic Groups." In *Mexicanas at Work in the United States*, edited by Margarita B. Melville, 33–46. Houston: Mexican American Studies Program, 1988.

Torres Smith, Anita. "A Pioneer Medicine Woman." *Journal of Big Bend Studies* 8 (1996): 79–85.

________. "Praxedis Mata Torres: The First Mexican American Teacher in the Public Schools in Uvalde County, Texas." *Journal of Big Bend Studies* 3 (1991): 157–179.

Torrez, Lilian Marie. "Hispanic Female Superintendents: Perspectives from the Extraordinary." Ph.D. dissertation, University of New Mexico, 1998.

Tovar, Inés H. "Sara Estela Ramírez: The Early Twentieth-Century Texas Mexican Poet." Ph.D. dissertation, University of Houston, 1984.

Treviño, Roberto R. "Facing Jim Crow: Catholic Sisters and the 'Mexican Problem' in Texas." *Western Historical Quarterly* 34 (Summer 2003): 139–164.

Trinidad, David. "Rebecca Flores Harrington: Life under the Hot Texas Sun." *Tejas* (Spring 1995): 37.

Turner, Kay. "Mexican American Women's Home Altars: The Art of Relationship." Ph.D. dissertation, University of Texas at Austin, 1990.

Underwood, Marylyn. "The Ghost of Chipita: The Crying Woman of San Patricio." In *Legendary Ladies of Texas*, edited by Francis Edward Abernethy, 50–56. Second edition. Denton: University of North Texas Press, 1994.

________. "Joséfa Rodríguez." In *The New Handbook of Texas*, edited by Ron Tyler, Douglas E. Barnett, Roy R. Barkley, Penelope C. Anderson, and Mark F. Odintz, vol. 5, 654–655. Austin: Texas State Historical Association, 1996.

Urdaneta, María Luisa. "Chicana Use of Abortion: The Case of Alcalá." In *Twice A Minority: Mexican American Women*, edited by Margarita B. Melville, 33–51. St. Louis: C. V. Mosby Company, 1980.

Vachon, Michelle. "Emma Tenayuca." In *Notable Hispanic American Women*, edited by Diane Telgen and Jim Kamp, 398–399. Detroit: Gale Research, 1993.

Valdez, Avelardo, and Jeffrey A. Halley. "Why Are There So Few Women Conjunto Artists." In *Puro Conjunto: An Album in Words and Pictures*, edited by Juan Tejada and Avelardo Valdez, 229–239. Austin: CMAS Books, Guadalupe Cultural Arts Center, 2001.

Vález, María Luisa. "The Pilgrimage of Hispanics in the Sisters of Charity of the Incarnate Word." *U.S. Catholic Historian* 9 (1990): 181–194.

Vargas, Zaragosa. "Tejana Radical: Emma Tenayuca and the San Antonio Labor Movement During the Great Depression." *Pacific Historical Review* 66 (November 1998): 553–580.

Vásquez-Ajmac, Luis. "Blandina Cárdenas Ramírez." In *Notable Hispanic American Women*, edited by Diane Telgen and Jim Kamp, 328–330. Detroit: Gale Research, 1993.

Velásquez-Treviño, Gloria. "Jovita González, Una Voz de Resistencia Cultural en la Temprana Narrativa Chicana." In *Mujer y Literatura Mexicana y Chicana: Culturas en Contacto*, edited by Aralia López-González, Amelia Malagamba, and Elena Urrutia, 77–84. México: Colegio de la Frontera Norte, 1988.

Villarreal, Mary Ann. "The Synapses of Struggle: Martha Cotera and Tejana Activism." In *Las Obreras: Chicana Politics of Work and Family*, edited by Vicki L. Ruiz, 273–296. Los Angeles: UCLA Chicano Studies Research Center Publications, 2000.

Von Hatten, Carol. "Vilma Martínez." In *Notable Hispanic American Women*, edited by Diane Telgen and Jim Kamp, 261–263. Detroit: Gale Research, 1993.

Washington, Ann Reed. "Teresa Chapa Alamia." In *Notable Hispanic American Women*, edited by Diane Telgen and Jim Kamp, 1–3. Detroit: Gale Research, 1993.

Weinman, Maxine L. "United States and Mexico-Born Hispanic Teen Mothers: A Descriptive Study of Factors that Relate to Postpartum Compliance." *Hispanic Journal of Behavioral Sciences* 16 (May 1994): 186–194.

Weiss, Nancy Sue. "The Epidemiology of Uterine Cervical Cancer among Anglo and Hispanic Women in Texas." Ph.D. dissertation, University of Texas Health Science Center at Houston, 1991.

West, John O. "The Weeping Woman: *La Llorona*." In *Legendary Ladies of Texas*, edited by Francis Edward Abernethy, 30–36. Second edition: Denton: University of North Texas Press, 1994.

Whiteford, Linda. "Mexican American Women as Innovators." In *Twice a Minority: Mexican American Women*, edited by Margarita B. Melville, 109–126. St. Louis: C. V. Mosby Company, 1980.

Williams, Brett. "Why Migrant Women Feed Their Husbands Tamales: Foodways as a Basis for a Revisionist View of Tejano Family Life." In *Ethnic and Regional Foodways in the United States: The Performance of Group Identity*, edited by Linda Keller Brown and Kay Mussell, 113–126. Knoxville: University of Tennessee Press, 1984.

Williams, Norma. "Changes in Funeral Patterns and Gender Roles among Mexican Americans." In *Women on the U.S.-Mexico Border: Responses to Changes*, edited by Vicki L. Ruiz and Susan Tiano, 197–217. Boston: Allen and Unwin, 1987.

________. "Role Making Among Married Mexican American Women: Issues of Class and Ethnicity." *Journal of Applied Behavioral Science* 24 (May 1987): 203–217.

Zaffirini, Judith (as told to Joe Nick Patoski). "Pom-pom and Circumstance." *Texas Monthly* 31 (February 2003): 84, 86, 88.

Zamora, Emilio Jr. "Sara Estela Ramírez: A Note on Research in Progress." *Hembra: Hermanas en Movimiento Brotando Raices de Aztlán* (Spring 1976): 4–6.

________. "Sara Estela Ramírez: Una Rosa en el Movimiento." In *Mexican Women in the United States: Struggles Past and Present*, edited by Magdalena Mora and Adelaida R. Del Castillo, 163–169. Los Angeles: Chicano Studies Research Center, 1980.

Zamora, Emilio Jr., and Roberto R. Calderón. "Manuela Solis Sager and Emma Tenayuca: A Tribute." In *Chicano Voices: Interaction of Class, Race, and Gender*. Proceedings of the National Association for Chicana Studies, edited by Teresa Córdova, Norma Cantú, Gilberto Cárdenas, Juan García, and Christine M. Sierra, 30–41. Austin: Center for Mexican American Studies Publications, University of Texas at Austin, 1986.

15. CULTURE

The culture of a people is a broad-based term which refers to the group's literature, physical objects, music, lifestyle, folklore, religion, mores, and behavior patterns. For this study, we have separately treated (because so much has been written on the topics) the music, religion, folklore, and literature of the Mexican-American experience in Texas. Instead this section covers general considerations of Tejano culture, of depictions of the Tejano built environment, Texas Mexican food and clothes, Tejano behavior, and coverage of the celebrations and fiestas used by Tejanos to celebrate and emphasize their culture and to make it available to other Texans.

Henry A. Guerra Sr., and Downtown City Market Master hold poster for "Noches de Fiesta." Four children in Mexican costume pose in front of them. Photograph by Harvey Patteson and Son, San Antonio, Texas, ca. late 1940s. The Institute of Texan Cultures at UTSA, No. 86-63

Abernethy, Francis Edward. "Charrería: From Spain to Texas." In *Charreada: Mexican Rodeo in Texas*, edited by Francis Edward Abernethy, 1–5. Denton: University of North Texas Press, 2002.

________. "The Spanish on the Moral." In *The Folklore of Texan Cultures*, edited by Francis E. Abernethy, 27–39. Austin: Encino Press, 1974.

________. "The Y'barbo Legend in Early Spanish Settlement." *East Texas Historical Journal* 25.1 (Fall 1987): 30–43.

________, ed. *Charreada: Mexican Rodeo in Texas.* Denton: University of North Texas Press, 2002.

Achor, Shirley. *Mexican Americans in a Dallas Barrio*. Tucson: University of Arizona Press, 1978.

________. "Of Thorns and Roses: Variations in Cultural Adaptations among Mexican-Americans in an Urban Texas Barrio." Ph.D. dissertation, Southern Methodist University, 1974.

Acosta, Teresa Palomo. "Chicano Literary Renaissance." In *The New Handbook of Texas*, edited by Ron Tyler, Douglas E. Barnett, Roy R. Barkley, Penelope C. Anderson, and Mark F. Odintz, vol. 2, 71–72. Austin: Texas State Historical Association, 1996.

________. "Chicano Mural Movement." In *The New Handbook of Texas*, edited by Ron Tyler, Douglas E. Barnett, Roy R. Barkley, Penelope C. Anderson, and Mark F. Odintz, vol. 2, 72–73. Austin: Texas State Historical Association, 1996.

________. "La Crónica." In *The New Handbook of Texas*, edited by Ron Tyler, Douglas E. Barnett, Roy R. Barkley, Penelope C. Anderson, and Mark F. Odintz, vol. 3, 1187. Austin: Texas State Historical Association, 1996.

________. "Home Altars." In *The New Handbook of Texas*, edited by Ron Tyler, Douglas E. Barnett, Roy R. Barkley, Penelope C. Anderson, and Mark F. Odintz, vol. 3, 677–678. Austin: Texas State Historical Association, 1996.

________. "Mexican American Folk Arts and Crafts." In *The New Handbook of Texas*, edited by Ron Tyler, Douglas E. Barnett, Roy R. Barkley, Penelope C. Anderson, and Mark F. Odintz, vol. 4, 655. Austin: Texas State Historical Association, 1996.

________. "Quinceañeras." In *The New Handbook of Texas*, edited by Ron Tyler, Douglas E. Barnett, Roy R. Barkley, Penelope C. Anderson, and Mark F. Odintz, vol. 5, 389–390. Austin: Texas State Historical Association, 1996.

________. "Spanish-language Radio." In *The New Handbook of Texas*, edited by Ron Tyler, Douglas E. Barnett, Roy R. Barkley, Penelope C. Anderson, and Mark F. Odintz, vol. 6, 5–6. Austin: Texas State Historical Association, 1996.

________. "Spanish-language Television." In *The New Handbook of Texas*, edited by Ron Tyler, Douglas E. Barnett, Roy R. Barkley, Penelope C. Anderson, and Mark F. Odintz, vol. 6, 6. Austin: Texas State Historical Association, 1996.

Acosta, Teresa Palomo, and Kendall Curlee. "Chicano Arts Network." In *The New Handbook of Texas*, edited by Ron Tyler, Douglas E. Barnett, Roy R. Barkley, Penelope C. Anderson, and Mark F. Odintz, vol. 2, 69–71. Austin: Texas State Historical Association, 1996.

Ahlborn, Richard E. "The Hispanic Horseman: A Sampling of Horse Gear from the Fred Harvey Collection." *El Palacio* 89.2 (1983): 12–21.

Aiken, Riley. *Folktales from the Borderland*. Dallas: Southern Methodist University Press, 1980.

Alarcón, Justo. "Las metamorfosis del diablo en *El Diablo en Texas* de Aristeo Brito." *De Colores* 5 (1980): 30–44.

Albro, Ward S. *To Die on Your Feet: The Life, Times, and Writings of Práxedis G. Guerrera*. Fort Worth: Texas Christian University Press, 1996.

________. "Práxedis G. Guerrera: Revolutionary Writer or Writer as Revolutionary?" In *Recovering the U.S. Hispanic Literary Heritage*, II, edited by Erlinda Gonzales-Berry and Chuck Tatum, 199–212. Houston: Arte Público Press, 1996.

Alicea, Ines Pinto. "Dr. Jaime Chahin Produces *'Las Colonias:* The Forgotten Americans.'" *Hispanic Outlook in Higher Education* 11 (September 24, 2000): 20–22.

Almaráz, Félix D. Jr. *Knight Without Armor: Carlos Eduardo Castañeda, 1896–1958*. College Station: Texas A&M University Press, 1999.

________. "Carlos E. Castañeda and Our Catholic Heritage: The Initial Volumes (1933–1943)." *The Social Science Journal* 13 (April 1976): 27–37.

________. "Carlos E. Castañeda: The Historian and the Critics." In *Mexican Americans in Texas History: Selected Essays*, edited by Emilio Zamora, Cynthia Orozco, and Rodolfo Rocha, 157–174. Austin: Texas State Historical Association, 2000.

________. "Carlos E. Castañeda's Rendezvous with a Library: The Latin American Collection, 1920–1927—The First Phase." *Journal of Library History* 16 (Spring 1981): 315–328.

________. "Carlos Eduardo Castañeda." In *The New Handbook of Texas*, edited by Ron Tyler, Douglas E. Barnett, Roy R. Barkley, Penelope C. Anderson, and Mark F. Odintz, vol. 1, 1016. Austin: Texas State Historical Association, 1996.

________. "Carlos Eduardo Casteñeda, Mexican-American Historian: The Formative Years, 1896–1927." *Pacific Historical Review* 42 (August 1973): 319–334.

________. "Hispanic Imprints on the Texas Landscape." In *Hispanic Texas: A Historical Guide*, edited by Helen Simons and Cathryn A. Hoyt, 3–12. Austin: University of Texas Press, 1992.

________. "The Historical Heritage of the Mexican American in 19th Century Texas, An Interpretation." In *The Role of the Mexican American in the History of the Southwest*, by Inter-American Institute, 12–23. Edinburg, Tex.: Pan American College, 1969.

________. "José Cisneros: An Artist in Pursuit of a Star." In *Borderlands: The Heritage of the Lower Río Grande through the Art of José Cisneros*, edited by Félix D. Almaráz Jr., 11–16. Edinburg: Hidalgo County Historical Museum, 1998.

________. "Landmarks of the Valley: A Heritage in Review." *Proceedings – An Exploration of a Common Legacy: A Conference on Border Architecture*, 16–17. Austin: Texas Historical Commission, 1978.

________. "The Making of a Boltonian: Carlos E. Castañeda of Texas—The Early Years." *Red River Valley Historical Review* 1 (Winter 1974): 329–350.

________. "Texas History." In *Borderlands Sourcebook: A Guide to the Literature on Northern Mexico and the American Southwest*, edited by Richard L. Nostrand, Ellwyn R. Stoddard, and Jonathan P. West, 46–48. Norman: University of Oklahoma Press, 1983.

Almaráz, Félix D. Jr., and Hubert J. Miller. "Four Centuries of Shared Experience in the Borderlands." In *Borderlands: The Heritage of the Lower Río Grande through the Art of José Cisneros*, edited by Félix D. Almaráz Jr., 17–40. Edinburg, Tex.: Hidalgo County Historical Museum, 1998.

Alvarado, Rodolfo Valier. "A History of Teatro in Lubbock, Texas." Ph.D. dissertation, Texas Tech University, 1995.

Amastae, Jon. "Official English and the Learning of English." In *Chicano Studies: Survey and Analysis*, edited by Dennis J. Bixler-Márquez, Carlos F. Ortega, Rosalía Solórzano Torres, and Lorenzo LaFarelle, 229–233. Dubuque, Iowa: Kendall/Hunt, 1999.

Anzaldúa, Gloria. *Borderlands/La Frontera: The New Mestiza*. San Francisco: Aunt Lute, 1987.

Applegate, Howard G., and C. Wayne Hanselka. *La Junta de los Ríos del Norte y Conchos*. El Paso: Texas Western Press, 1974.

Arnold, Charles August. *The Folklore, Manners and Customs of the Mexicans in San Antonio, Texas*. San Francisco: R&E Research Associates, 1971.

________. "Folklore, Manners, and Customs of Mexicans in San Antonio, Texas." Master's thesis, University of Texas, Austin, 1927.

Arreola, Daniel D. "Plazas of San Diego, Texas: Signatures of Mexican-American Place Identity." *Places: A Quarterly Journal of Environmental Design* 8 (Spring 1993): 80–87.

________. "Plaza Towns of South Texas." *Geographical Review* 82 (January 1992): 56–73.

Arrizón, Alicia. "The Mexican American Stage: La Chata Noloesca and Josefina Niggli." In *Latina Performances: Traversing the Stage*, by Alicia Arrizón, 29–72. Bloomington: Indiana University Press, 1999.

Austerman, Wayne R. "Tinaja de las Palmas: A Landmark on the El Paso Road." *Password* 28 (Spring 1983): 7–16.

Baracat, Robert A. "The Bear's Son Tale in Northern Mexico." Master's thesis, Texas Western College, 1964.

Barbee, William Clayton. "A Historical and Architectural Investigation of San Ygnacio, Texas." Master's thesis, University of Texas at Austin, 1981.

Barrera, Aida. *Looking for Carrascolendas: From Child's World to Award Winning Television*. Austin: University of Texas Press, 2001.

Barrera, Alberto. "Mexican-American Roadside Crosses in Starr County." In *Hecho en Tejas: Texas-Mexican Folk Arts and Crafts,* edited by Joe S. Graham, 278–292. Denton: University of North Texas Press, 1991.

________. "Mexican-American Roadside Crosses in Starr County." In *Tejano Folk Arts and Crafts,* edited by Joe S. Graham, 35–36. Kingsville, Tex.: John E. Conner Museum, 1989.

Barsun, Helen W. "Los Pastores: A Remnant of Medieval Drama in San Antonio." Master's thesis, St. Mary's University, 1943.

Bauman, Richard. "Differential Identity and the Social Base of Folklore." In *Toward New Perspectives in Folklore*, edited by Américo Paredes and Richard Bauman, 31–41. Austin: University of Texas Press, 1972.

Baumel-Schreffler, Sandra. "Mexican-Spanish in Houston, Texas: A Study of Language Contact and Its Effects on Overt Subject Pronouns." Ph.D. dissertation, University of Florida, 1995.

Benavides, Adán Jr. "Tejano." In *The New Handbook of Texas*, edited by Ron Tyler, Douglas E. Barnett, Roy R. Barkley, Penelope C. Anderson, and Mark F. Odintz, vol. 6, 238–239. Austin: Texas State Historical Association, 1996.

Boatright, Mody C., ed. *Mexican Border Ballads and Other Lore*. Austin: Texas Folklore Society, 1946.

Bolde, Alfredo Pérez. "Unas Páginas Extraviadas de la Historia de Texas." *Borderlands Journal* 7.2 (1984): 105–125.

Bourke, John G. "The Folk-Foods of the Rio Grande Valley and of Northern Mexico." *Journal of American Folklore* 8 (January-March 1895): 41–71.

________. "Folk-Foods of the Rio Grande Valley." In *Southwestern Lore*, edited by J. Frank Dobie, 85–117. Dallas: Southwest Press, 1931.

________. "The Miracle Play of the Rio Grande." *Journal of American Folklore* 6 (1893): 89–95.

________. "Notes on the Language and Folk-Usage of the Rio Grande Valley." *Journal of American Folklore* 9 (April-June 1896): 81–116.

________. "Popular Medicine, Customs, and Superstitions of the Rio Grande." *Journal of American Folklore* 7 (1894): 119–146.

Bouteba, Paul M. "Designing Chicano Heritage Materials." Ed.D. dissertation, University of Houston, 1982.

Brennan, James Edward. "A Study of the Channels of Communication used by Spanish-Named Residents of San Antonio, Texas." Ph.D. dissertation, Louisiana State University, 1968.

Brenner, Marie. "Murder on the Border." *New Yorker* (September 13, 1993): 52–75.

Brito, Aristeo. *The Devil in Texas/El Diablo en Texas*. Tempe, Ariz.: Bilingual Review/Press, 1990.

Broyles, Yolanda Julia. "Hinojosa's *Klail City y sus alrededores*: Oral Culture and Print Culture." In *The Rolando Hinojosa Reader*, edited by José David Saldivar, 109–132. Houston: Arte Público Press, 1984.

Bruce-Novoa, Juan. "*La Prensa* and the Chicano Community." *Americas Review* 17 (1989): 150–156.

________. "Who's Killing Whom in Belken County: Rolando Hinojosa's Narrative Production." *Monographic Review/Revista Monográfica* 3 (1987): 288–297.

Bryson, Conrey. "Tribute to Abraham Chávez Jr." *Password* 26 (Winter 1981): 158–162.

Buckner, Dellos U. "Study of the Lower Rio Grande Valley as a Culture Area." Master's thesis, University of Texas, Austin, 1929.

Buitron, Richard Arthur Jr. "Who Are We? The Quest for Tejano Identity in San Antonio, Texas, 1913–the Present." Ph.D. dissertation, Florida State University, 2002.

Calderón, Roberto R., and Emilio Zamora. "Manuela Solis Sager and Emma Tenayuca: A Tribute." In *Chicana Voices: Intersections of Class, Race, and Gender*, edited by Teresa Córdova, Norma Cantú, Gilberto Cárdenas, Juan García, and Christine M. Sierra, 30–41. Originally published in 1986. Albuquerque: University of New Mexico Press, 1993.

Campa, Arthur L. *Hispanic Culture in the Southwest*. Norman: University of Oklahoma Press, 1979.

________. *The Spanish Folksong in the Southwest*. Albuquerque: University of New Mexico Bulletin, 1933.

________. "From El Paso to the Gulf." In *Hispanic Culture in the Southwest*, by Arthur L. Campa, 156–164. Norman: University of Oklahoma Press, 1979.

________. "The Lower Rio Grande." In *Hispanic Culture in the Southwest*, by Arthur L. Campa, 165–188. Norman: University of Oklahoma Press, 1979.

________. "The Spanish Language in the Southwest." In *Humanidad: Essays in Honor of George I. Sánchez*, edited by Américo Paredes, 19–40. Los Angeles: Chicano Studies Center Publications, 1977.

Cantú, Norma E. "The Offering and the Offerers: A Generic Illocation of a Laredo Pastorela in the Tradition of Shepherds' Plays." Ph.D. dissertation, University of Nebraska-Lincoln, 1982.

________. "Costume as Cultural Resistance and Affirmation: The Case of South Texas Community." In *Hecho en Tejas: Texas-Mexican Folk Arts and Crafts*, edited by Joe S. Graham, 117–131. Denton: University of North Texas Press, 1991.

________. "La Quinceañera: Towards an Analysis of a Life Cycle Ritual." *Southern Folklore* 56 (1999): 73–101.

________. "Tejanos Along the Border." *Texas Journal of Ideas, History and Culture* 20 (Fall/Winter 1997): 6–9.

Cantú, Norma, and Ofelia Zapata Vela. "The Mexican American Quilting Traditions of Laredo, San Ygnacio and Zapata." In *Hecho en Tejas: Texas-Mexican Folk Arts and Crafts*, edited by Joe S. Graham, 77–92. Denton: University of North Texas Press, 1991.

Cárdenas de Dwyer, Carlota. "Chicano Literature: A Convergence of Cultures." *English in Texas* 10 (Winter 1978): 29–31.

Cárdenas, Lupe. "Implied Violence in Tomás Rivera's Apparent Pacifism." In *Aztlán Chicano Culture and Folklore: An Anthology*, edited by José "Pepe" Villarino and Arturo Ramírez, 141–145. New York: McGraw Hill, 1998.

Cárdenas, Reyes. *I was Never a Militant Chicano*. Austin: Relampago Books Press, 1987.

Cardozo-Freeman, Inez. "Games Mexican Girls Play." *Journal of American Folklore* 88 (1975): 12–24.

Carlson, G. E. "Community Organization Turns a Corner." *Sociology and Social Research* 32 (March 1948): 782–786.

Carrasco, Sara Margarita Campos. "Mexican American Folk Medicine: A Descriptive Study of the Different Curanderismo Techniques Practiced by Curanderos or Curanderas and Used by Patients in the Laredo, Texas Area." Ph.D. dissertation, Texas Woman's University, 1984.

Carrillo, Leonardo, et al., eds. *Canto al Pueblo: An Anthology of Experiences*. San Antonio: Penca Books, 1978.

Casstevens, Mary Anna. "The Institution of the Spanish-Mexican Ranch and Its Culture in South Texas." Master's thesis, Texas A&M University-Kingsville, 1997.

________. "Randado: The Built Environment of a Texas-Mexican Ranch." In *Hecho en Tejas: Texas-Mexican Folk Arts and Crafts*, edited by Joe S. Graham, 309–334. Denton: University of North Texas Press, 1991.

Castañeda, Carlos E. "Why I Chose History." *The Americas* 8 (April 1952): 475–492.

________. "The Woman in Blue." *Age of Mary* (January-February 1958): 22–29.

Castro, Tony. "The Confessions of St. Con Safos." *Nuestro* 2 (April 1978): 49–53.

Cerda, Gilberto, Berta Cabaza, and Julieta Farios. *Vocabulario español de Texas*. Austin: University of Texas Press, 1970.

Chabot, Frederick. *With the Makers of San Antonio*. San Antonio: Artes Gráficas, 1937.

Champion, Carol Esparza. "Face-ism in Texas and Mexico." *Borderlands Journal* 3 (Spring 1980): 121–130.

Chandler, Charles R., Yung-mei Tsai, and Rene Wharton. "Twenty Years After: Replicating a Study of Anglo- and Mexican-American Cultural Values." *Social Science Journal* 36 (1999): 353–367.

Chapa, Carla. "*Las Notas De Kingsville*, 1944–1963: The Voice of the Mexican American Community." *Journal of South Texas* 9 (1996): 93–101.

"Charro Days." In *The Handbook of Texas*, edited by Walter Prescott Webb and H. Bailey Carroll, vol. 1, 331. Austin: Texas State Historical Association, 1952.

Charles de Cerda, Dora Elia. "El Uso de 'Tu' y 'Usted' en al Valle del Rio Grande." Master's thesis, Texas A&M University-Kingsville, 1997.

Chaston, John Malcolm. "Aspect Choice in Preterit and Imperfect Usage in the Speech of Mexican-American College Students in Texas: A Sociolinguistic Approach." Ph.D. dissertation, University of Texas at Austin, 1987.

________. "Sociolinguistic Analysis of Gender Agreement in Article/Noun Combinations in Mexican Americans Spanish in Texas." *Bilingual Review/La Revista Bilingüe* 21 (September-December 1996): 195–202.

Chávez, John R. *The Lost Land: The Chicano Image of the Southwest*. Albuquerque: University of New Mexico Press, 1984.

________. "The Lost Land: The Chicano Image of the Southwest." Ph.D. dissertation, University of Michigan, 1980.

________. "The Image of the Southwest in the Chicano Novel, 1970–1979." *Bilingual Review/La Revista Bilingüe* 14.3 (1987–1988): 41–56.

Chávez, Tomás Jr. *Quinceañera: A Liturgy in the Reformed Tradition*. San Angelo, Tex.: Presbytery of Tres Ríos, 1983.

Christiansen, Paul. "From Cowboys to *Curanderas*: The Cycle of Texas Literature." *Southwest Review* 73 (Spring 1988): 10–29.

Cisneros, José. *Faces of the Borderlands: Twenty One Drawings*. El Paso: Texas Western Press, 1977.

________. *Riders Across the Centuries: Horsemen of the Spanish Borderlands*. El Paso: Texas Western Press, 1984.

________. *Riders of the Border: A Selection of Thirty Drawings*. El Paso: Texas Western Press, 1971.

________. "Art By and For the Bilingual." *Password* 17 (Fall 1972): 99–105.

Cisneros, Sandra. "Do You Know Me?: I Wrote *The House on Mango Street*." *The Americas Review* 15 (Spring 1987): 77–79.

Clark, Sara. "Decoration of Graves in Central Texas with Seashells." In *Diamond Bessie and the Shepherds*, edited by Wilson M. Hudson, 33–44. Austin: Encino Press, 1972.

Cline, C. L. "The Rio Grande Valley." *Southwest Review* 25 (April 1940): 239–255.

Cochran, Robert. "The Interlude of Game: A Study of Washers." *Western Folklore* 38 (1979): 71–82.

Cole, M. R. *Los Pastores: A Mexican Miracle Play*. New York: Publications of the American Folklore Society, 1907.

Contreras, Sheila Marie. "A Mestizo Account: Teresa Paloma Acosta's Questions to a Spanish Grandmother." In *Reflexiones 1998: New Directions in Mexican American Studies*, edited by Yolanda C. Padilla, 103–122. Austin: CMAS Books, 1999.

Corbin Diane H. "Angelina." In *Legendary Ladies of Texas*, edited by Francis E. Abernethy, 15–20. Dallas: E-Heart Press, 1981.

Cornell, Rebecca. "Tex Mex Dialect or Gidget Goes to Acuña." In *Between the Cracks of History: Essays on Teaching and Illustrating Folklore*, edited by Francis Edward Abernethy, 226–234. Dallas: University of North Texas Press, 1992.

Cotera, María Eugenia. "Deconstructing the Corrido Hero: *Caballero* and Its Gendered Critique of Nationalist Discourse." *Perspectives in Mexican American Studies* 5 (1995): 151–170.

Crawford, Ann Fears, and Crystal Sasse Ragsdale. "Preserver of the Texas Heritage: Adina De Zavala." In *Women in Texas: Their Lives, Their Experiences, Their Accomplishments*, by Ann Fears Crawford and Crystal Sasse Ragsdale, 165–175. Burnet, Tex.: Eakin Press, 1982.

Crimmins, Colonel M. L. "The History of La Villita." *West Texas Historical Association Yearbook* 26 (1950): 130–134.

Crosthwaite, Luis Humberto, John William Byrd, and Bobby Byrd, eds. *Puro Border: Dispatches, Snapshots, and Graffiti from the U.S./Mexico Border.* El Paso: Cinco Puntos Press, 2003.

Cruz, Adrian. "The Battle to be Mayor: A Case Study of Interethnic Conflict in the Lower Rio Grande Valley." Master's thesis, University of Texas–Pan American, 2001.

Curlee, Kendall. "Beatrice Valdez Jiménez." In *The New Handbook of Texas*, edited by Ron Tyler, Douglas E. Barnett, Roy R. Barkley, Penelope C. Anderson, and Mark F. Odintz, vol. 6, 1103–1104. Austin: Texas State Historical Association, 1996.

________. "Dionico Rodríguez." In *The New Handbook of Texas*, edited by Ron Tyler, Douglas E. Barnett, Roy R. Barkley, Penelope C. Anderson, and Mark F. Odintz, vol. 5, 652–653. Austin: Texas State Historical Association, 1996.

________. "La Peña." In *The New Handbook of Texas*, edited by Ron Tyler, Douglas E. Barnett, Roy R. Barkley, Penelope C. Anderson, and Mark F. Odintz, vol. 4, 72. Austin: Texas State Historical Association, 1996.

________. "Manuel Gregorio Acosta." In *The New Handbook of Texas*, edited by Ron Tyler, Douglas E. Barnett, Roy R. Barkley, Penelope C. Anderson, and Mark F. Odintz, vol. 1, 18–19. Austin: Texas State Historical Association, 1996.

________. "Mexi-Arte." In *The New Handbook of Texas*, edited by Ron Tyler, Douglas E. Barnett, Roy R. Barkley, Penelope C. Anderson, and Mark F. Odintz, vol. 4, 698–699. Austin: Texas State Historical Association, 1996.

________. "Xochil Art and Culture Center." In *The New Handbook of Texas*, edited by Ron Tyler, Douglas E. Barnett, Roy R. Barkley, Penelope C. Anderson, and Mark F. Odintz, vol. 6, 1104. Austin: Texas State Historical Association, 1996.

Daniggelis, Paul Dean. "The Sculptor of Cristo Rey." *Password* 31 (Winter 1986): 186–190.

de la Garza, Beatriz. "The Border, from a Human Perspective." *Laredos: A Journal of the Borderlands* 1.2 (1995): 6.

________. "Guerrero Viejo: A Myth of Survival and Endurance." *Laredos: A Journal of the Borderlands* 1.3 (1995): 14.

de la Teja, Jesús F. "The Written Word." In *Hispanic Texas: A Historical Guide*, edited by Helen Simons and Cathryn A. Hoyt, 141–147. Austin: University of Texas Press, 1992.

De León, Arnoldo. *Las Fiestas Patrias: Biographic Notes on the Hispanic Presence in San Angelo, Texas*. San Antonio: Caravel Press, 1978.

________. "Tejano Holy Days in the Nineteenth Century." *South Texas Journal of Research and the Humanities* 2 (Spring 1978): 35–44.

De Zavala, Adina. *History and Legends of the Alamo and other Missions in and around San Antonio*, edited by Richard Flores. Houston: Arte Público Press, 1996.

________. "Religious Beliefs of the Tejas, or Hasanias, Indians." In *Round the Levee*, edited by Stith Thompson, 39–43. Austin: Texas Folk-lore Society, 1916.

Díaz De León, Efren. "Code-switching as a Strategy for Communication by Third-grade Students in Bilingual Classrooms." Ed.D. dissertation, Texas A&I University, 1986.

Dickey, Dan Williams. *The Kennedy Corridos: A Study of the Ballads of a Mexican-American Hero*. Austin: University of Texas Press, 1978.

________. "Corridos." In *The New Handbook of Texas*, edited by Ron Tyler, Douglas E. Barnett, Roy R. Barkley, Penelope C. Anderson, and Mark F. Odintz, vol. 2, 337–338. Austin: Texas State Historical Association, 1996.

Dinger, Adeline Short. *Folklife and Folklore of the Mexican Border*. Edinburgh, Tex.: Hidalgo County Historical Society, 1974.

Dingus, Anne. "Adios, Bandito." *Texas Monthly* 14 (January 1986): 186–187.

di Stefano, Onofre. "*La Prensa* of San Antonio and Its Literary Page, 1913 to 1915." Ph.D. dissertation, University of California, Los Angeles, 1983.

________. "'Venimos a luchar': A Brief History of *La Prensa's* Founding." *Aztlán* 16 (1985): 95–119.

Dodson, Ruth. *Don Pedrito Jaramillo: Curandero.* San Antonio: Casa Editorial Lozano, 1934.

________. "The Life of Don Pedro Jaramillo: Benefactor of Humanity." *Perspectives in Mexican American Studies* 1 (1988): 69–74.

Donahue, Linda Giss. "Marketing the Arts to a Multicultural Population." Ph.D. dissertation, Texas Tech University, 1992.

Dorson, Richard M. "Is There a Folk in the City?" In *The Urban Experience and Folk Tradition*, edited by Américo Paredes and Ellen J. Stekert, 21–52. Austin: University of Texas Press, 1971.

Dunn, Edward Wesley Jr. "A Factor Analysis of Communication Habits and Attitudes among Mexican-Americans in Austin and San Antonio, Texas." Ph.D. dissertation, University of Texas at Austin, 1973.

Durán, Gustavo. *14 Traditional Spanish Songs from Texas*. Washington, D.C.: Pan American Union, 1942.

Dyreson, Jodella K. "Sporting Activities in the American-Mexican Colonies of Texas, 1821–1835." *Journal of Sport History* 24 (Fall 1997): 269–289.

Elam, Earl H. "Acculturation on the Rio Grande Frontier: The Founding of San José del Polvo and the Family of Lucía Redé Madrid." *Journal of Big Bend Studies* 5 (1993): 70–95.

________. "Aspects of Acculturation in the Lower Big Bend Region of Texas, 1848–1943." *Journal of Big Bend Studies* 12 (2000): 71–91.

Ellis, John M. "Mortality Differentials for a Spanish-Surname Population Group." *Southwestern Social Science Quarterly* 39 (March 1959): 313–321.

Engstrand, Iris H. W., Richard Griswold del Castillo, and Elena Poniatowska. *Culture y Cultura: Consequences of the U.S.-Mexican War, 1846–1848*. Los Angeles: Autry Museum of Western Heritage, 1998.

Erevia, Angela. *Quinceañera*. San Antonio: Mexican American Cultural Center, 1980.

Espinosa, Aurelio M. "The Texans: A New Mexican Spanish Folk Play of the Middle Nineteenth Century." *New Mexico Quarterly Review* 12.3 (1943): 299–308.

Estrada, Marta. "Dichos from the Lower Valley." *Password* 40 (Fall 1995): 145–152.

Estrada, Miguel Enrique Soto. "Behind the Myth: Ignacio Zaragoza: The Hero of the Cinco de Mayo." *South Texas Studies* 11 (2000): 169–180.

Eyde, David B. "Pluralism in El Paso, Texas." In *Politics and Society in the Southwest: Ethnicity and Chicano Pluralism*, edited by Z. Anthony Kruszewski, Richard L. Hough, and Jacob Ornstein-Galicia, 155–167. Boulder, Colo.: Westview Press, 1982.

Fish, Jean Y. *José Vasquez Borrego and La Hacienda de Nuestra Señora de Dolores*. Zapata, Tex.: Zapata County Historical Society, 1991.

Flanagan, Sammy Lee Jr. "Gender Identity Development in Self-disclosed Gay Men in Hidalgo County, Texas." Master's thesis, University of Texas–Pan American, 2000.

Flores, J. M. "A Study of Mexican American Cultural Characteristics as Perceived by Members of Impoverished Mexican American Families and Its Educational Implications." Ph.D. dissertation, University of Houston, 1972.

Flores, Richard R. *Los Pastores: History and Performance in the Mexican Shepherd's Play of South Texas*. Washington, D.C.: Smithsonian Institution Press, 1995.

________. "The *Corrido* and the Emergence of Texas-Mexican Social Identity." *Journal of American Folklore* 105 (1992): 166–182.

________. "History, 'Los Pastores,' and the Shifting Poetics of Dislocation." *Journal of Historical Sociology* 6.2 (1993): 164–185.

________. "'Los Pastores' and the Gifting of Performance." *American Ethnologist* 21.2 (1994): 270–285.

Flynn, Ronald, Edwin Davison, and Edward Chávez. *The Golden Age of the Accordion*. Schertz, Tex.: Flynn Associates Publishing, 1992.

Foley, Neil. "How do you say 'Honey' in MexAmerica." *Journal of American Ethnic History* 19.1 (1999): 71–74.

Fowler, Gene. "History and Culture along the Rio Grande: Los Caminos del Rio." *Texas Highways* 49.9 (2002): 26–35.

Fraley, Elizabeth. "A Chronological History of the San Antonio Fiesta de San Jacinto and the Battle of Flowers." Master's thesis, Southwest Texas State Teachers College, 1943.

Francesca, S. M. "Variations of Selected Cultural Patterns Among Three Generations of Mexicans in San Antonio, Texas." *American Catholic Sociological Review* 19 (1958): 19, 24–34.

Fredericksen, Brooke. "Cuando lleguemos/When We Arrive: The Paradox of Migration in Tomás Rivera's '. . . y no se lo tragó la tierra.'" *Bilingual Review/La Revista Bilingüe* 19 (1994): 142–150.

Freeman, Joe C. "Regional Architecture and Associated Crafts." In *A Shared Experience: The History, Architectural and Historic Designation of the Lower Rio Grande Heritage Corridor*, edited by Mario L. Sánchez, 137–197. Second edition. Austin: Texas Historical Commission, 1994.

Fregoso, Rosa Linda. "Recycling Colonialist Fantasies on the Texas Borderlands." *In Home, Exile, Homeland: Film, Media, and the Politics of Place*, edited by Hamid Naficy, 169–198. New York: Routledge Press, 1998.

________. "*Seguín*: The Same Side of the Alamo." In *Chicano Cinema: Research, Reviews, and Resources*, edited by Gary D. Keller, 146–152. Binghamton, N.Y.: Bilingual Review/Press, 1985.

________. "*Zoot Suit* and *The Ballad of Gregorio Cortéz*." *Critica* 1 (Spring 1985): 126–131.

Fuentes, Rumel. "Corridos de Rumel." *El Grito: A Journal of Contemporary Mexican American Thought* 6 (Spring 1973): 3–40.

Fuson, Robert H. "The Origin of the Word *Gringo*." In *Singers and Storytellers*, edited by Mody C. Boatright, Wilson M. Hudson, and Allen Maxwell, 282–284. Dallas: Southern Methodist University Press, 1961.

"*Gaceta de Tejas*." In *The New Handbook of Texas,* edited by Ron Tyler, Douglas E. Barnett, Roy R. Barkley, Penelope C. Anderson, and Mark F. Odintz, vol. 3, 39–40. Austin: Texas State Historical Association, 1996.

Galindo, D. Letticia. "Language Use and Language Attitudes: A Study of Border Women." *Bilingual Review/La Revista Bilingüe* 21 (January-April 1996): 5–17.

Gallegos, Esperanza. "The Piñata-Making Tradition in Laredo." In *Hecho en Tejas: Texas-Mexican Folk Arts and Crafts*, edited by Joe S. Graham, 188–203. Denton: University of North Texas Press, 1991.

Galván, Roberto A. "El Dialecto Español de San Antonio, Texas." Ph.D. dissertation, Tulane University, 1955.

________. "Un Estudio Geográfico de Algunos Vocablos Usados por Los Habitantes De Habla Español de San Antonio, Texas." Master's thesis, University of Texas, Austin, 1949.

García, Ignacio. "A Coach on the Right Track." *Nuestro* 3 (October 1979): 44, 46.

García, Lionel G. *I Can Hear the Cowbells Ring*. Houston: Arte Público Press, 1994.

García, María-Cristina. "Charrería." In *The New Handbook of Texas,* edited by Ron Tyler, Douglas E. Barnett, Roy R. Barkley, Penelope C. Anderson, and Mark F. Odintz, vol. 2, 50–51. Austin: Texas State Historical Association, 1996.

________. "Comite Patriótico Mexicano." In *The New Handbook of Texas,* edited by Ron Tyler, Douglas E. Barnett, Roy R. Barkley, Penelope C. Anderson, and Mark F. Odintz, vol. 2, 249. Austin: Texas State Historical Association, 1996.

________. "Consuelo González Amezcua." In *The New Handbook of Texas,* edited by Ron Tyler, Douglas E. Barnett, Roy R. Barkley, Penelope C. Anderson, and Mark F. Odintz, vol. 3, 235–236. Austin: Texas State Historical Association, 1996.

________. "*La Gaceta Mexicana*." In *The New Handbook of Texas,* edited by Ron Tyler, Douglas E. Barnett, Roy R. Barkley, Penelope C. Anderson, and Mark F. Odintz, vol. 4, 5–6. Austin: Texas State Historical Association, 1996.

________. "Jesús Murrillo." In *The New Handbook of Texas,* edited by Ron Tyler, Douglas E. Barnett, Roy R. Barkley, Penelope C. Anderson, and Mark F. Odintz, vol. 4, 892. Austin: Texas State Historical Association, 1996.

García, Mario T. "Carlos E. Castañeda and the Search for History." In *Mexican Americans: Leadership, Ideology, and Identity, 1930–1960*, by Mario T. García, 231–251. New Haven: Yale University Press, 1989.

________. "George I. Sánchez and the Forgotten People." In *Mexican Americans: Leadership, Ideology, and Identity, 1930–1960*, by Mario T. García, 252–272. New Haven: Yale University Press, 1989.

________. "*La Frontera*: The Border as Symbol and Reality in Mexican-American Thought." *Mexican Studies/Estudios Mexicanos* 1 (Summer 1985): 196–225.

García, Ralph. "Misconceptions of Stereotyping the Chicano and Mexican Arts in San Antonio." *Caracol* 5 (June 1979): 9–10.

García, Raúl. "Mexican American Cultural Art Center." In *The New Handbook of Texas*, edited by Ron Tyler, Douglas E. Barnett, Roy R. Barkley, Penelope C. Anderson, and Mark F. Odintz, vol. 4, 654. Austin: Texas State Historical Association, 1996.

García, Richard A. "The Making of the Mexican-American Mind, San Antonio, Texas, 1929–1941." Ph.D. dissertation, University of California, Irvine, 1980.

________. Class, Consciousness, and Ideology—The Mexican Community of San Antonio, Texas: 1930–1940." *Aztlán* 9 (1978): 23–69.

________. "The Mexican American Mind: A Product of the 1930s." In *History, Culture and Society: Chicano Studies in the 1980s*, edited by Mario T. García and Francisco Lomelí, 67–93. Ypsilanti, Mich.: Bilingual Press, 1983.

Garreau, Joel. "MexAmerica." In *The Multicultural Southwest: A Reader*, edited by A. Gabriel Meléndez, M. Jane Young, Patricia Moore, and Patrick Pynes, 123–132. Tucson: University of Arizona Press, 2001.

Garza-Bigger, Gloria. "Domingo Peña—A Man of the People." *La Luz* 3 (May 1974): 14–15.

Garza, Juanita Elizondo. "Indian and Spanish-Mexican Cultural Influences in the Lower Rio Grande Valley." Master's thesis, Pan American University, 1984.

Garza, Refugio S. "En el Nombre De Díos y Don Pedrito Jaramillo." Master's thesis, Texas A&I University, 1952.

Gilbreath, Essie Maude. "Some Superstitions and Folk Tales of the Kingsville Mexicans." Master's thesis, Texas College of Arts and Industries, 1938.

Ginsberg, Judith. "La verdad sin voz: Elegy and Reparation." *The Americas Review* 14 (Summer 1986): 88–93.

Glazer, Mark. "Faith and Saints in Mexican-American Folk Religion." In *More Studies in Brownsville History*, edited by Milo Kearney, 275–283. Brownsville, Tex.: Pan American University at Brownsville, 1989.

________, ed. *Flour from Another Sack*. Edinburg, Tex.: Pan American University Press, 1982.

Goldman, Shifra M. "Artistas Chicanas Texanas." *Fem* 8 (June-July 1984): 29–31.

________. "Chicano Art Alive and Well in Texas: A 1981 Update." *Revista Chicano-Riquena* 9 (1981): 34–40.

González, Alicia María. "'Guess How Doughnuts Are Made': Verbal and Nonverbal Aspects of the *Panadero* and His Stereotype." In *"And Other Neighborly Names": Social Process and Cultural Image in Texas Folklore*, edited by Richard Bauman and Roger D. Abrahams, 104–122. Austin: University of Texas Press, 1981.

________. "Murals: Fine, Popular, or Folk Art." *Aztlán* 13 (1982): 149–163.

González de Mireles, Jovita. "Social Life in Cameron, Starr, and Zapata Counties." Master's thesis, University of Texas, Austin, 1930.

________. "America Invades the Border Towns." *Southwest Review* 15 (Summer 1930): 467–477.

________. "Among My People." In *Mexican-American Authors*, edited by Américo Paredes and Raymund Paredes, 8–15. Boston: Houghton Mifflin, 1972. Originally printed in *Tone the Bell Easy*, edited by J. Frank Dobie, 99–108. Austin: Texas Folklore Society, 1932.

________. "Latin Americans." In *Our Racial and National Minorities: Their History, Contributions, and Present Problems*, edited by Francis J. Brown and Joseph Slabez Roucek, 497–509. New York: Prentice-Hall, 1937.

González, María del Refugío. "The Spanish Folklore of Webb and Zapata Counties." Master's thesis, University of Texas, Austin, 1952.

Gorges, Kay. "The Interpretation of Latin-American and Anglo-American Cultures in the Lower Rio Grande Valley of Texas." Master's thesis, University of Texas, Austin, 1955.

Gosnell, Lynn, and Suzanne Gott. "San Fernando Cemetery: Decoration of Love and Loss in a Mexican American Community." In *Cemeteries and Gravemakers: Voices of American Culture*, edited by Richard E. Meyer, 217–236. Ann Arbor: UMI Research Press, 1989.

Gradante, William. "Art Among the Low Riders." In *Folk Art in Texas*, edited by Francis E. Abernethy, 70–77. Dallas: Southern Methodist University Press, 1985.

________. "Low and Slow, Mean and Clean." *Natural History* 91 (1982): 28–39.

Graham, Joe S. *Grandmother's Tea: Mexican Herbal Remedies—A Study Guide*. San Antonio: University of Texas Institute of Texan Cultures, 1979.

________. *The Jacal in the Big Bend: Its Origin and Evolution*, edited by Robert J. Mallouf. Alpine, Tex.: Chihuahuan Desert Research Institute, 1988.

________. *El Rancho in South Texas: Continuity and Change from 1750*. Denton: University of North Texas Press, 1994.

________. *Tejano Folk Arts and Crafts in South Texas/Artesanía Tejana*. Kingsville, Tex.: John E. Conner Museum, 1990.

________. "The 'Caso': A Study of an Emic Genre of Folk Narrative among Mexican Americans of West Texas." 2 vol. Ph.D. dissertation, University of Texas at Austin, 1981.

________. "Alberto Ramírez: Bricoleur par Excellence." In *Papers of the Chihuahuan Desert Research Institute*, edited by Robert J. Mallouf, 73–83. Alpine, Tex.: CDRI Publications, 1990.

________. "The Built Environment in South Texas: The Hispanic Legacy." In *Hispanic Texas: A Historical Guide*, edited by Helen Simons and Cathryn A. Hoyt, 58–75. Austin: University of Texas Press, 1992.

________. "Curanderismo." In *The New Handbook of Texas,* edited by Ron Tyler, Douglas E. Barnett, Roy R. Barkley, Penelope C. Anderson, and Mark F. Odintz, vol. 2, 452. Austin: Texas State Historical Association, 1996.

________. "*Descansos* (Roadside Crosses): Folk Art and Ritual in Remembrance of the Deceased." In *Out Near Phantom Hill*, edited by Darrin Cozzens and Reed Harp, 153–164. Stillwater, Okla.: Southwest and Texas Popular Culture Association, 1990.

________. "Foodways of Pioneer Texas Mexicans." In *Texana I: The Frontier*, edited by Candace M. Volz and Keith A. Drake, 11–16. Austin: Texas Historical Commission, 1983.

________. "Hecho a Mano en Tejas." In *Hecho en Tejas: Texas-Mexican Folk Arts and Crafts*, edited by Joe S. Graham, 1–47. Denton: University of North Texas Press, 1991.

________. "The *Jacal* in South Texas: The Origins and Forms of a Folk House." In *Hecho en Tejas: Texas-Mexican Folk Arts and Crafts*, edited by Joe S. Graham, 293–308. Denton: University of North Texas Press, 1991.

________. "Mexican-American Folk Housing in South and West Texas: Some Comparisons." In *An Exploration of a Common Legacy*, edited by Marlene Heck, 38–65. Austin: Texas Historical Commission, 1978.

________. "Mexican-American Lime Kilns in West Texas: The Limits of Folk Technology." In *Hoein' the Short Rows*, edited by Francis E. Abernethy, 73–92. Dallas: Southern Methodist University Press, 1988.

________. "Mexican-American Traditional Foodways at La Junta de Los Ríos." *Journal of Big Bend Studies* 2 (1990): 1–27.

________. "Mexican-American Traditional Foodways: Sources and Prospects." In *American Frontiers: Past, Present, and Future*, edited by Michael K. Schoenecke, 421–449. Oklahoma City: Oklahoma Historical Society, 1984.

________. "Southwestern Hispanics." In *America's Architectural Roots*, edited by Dell Upton and Diana Maddex, 91–98. Washington, D.C.: National Trust for Historic Preservation, 1986.

________. "Tejano Folk Arts and Crafts in South Texas: Continuity in the Midst of Change." *Texas Journal* 12.1 (1989): 44–45.

________. "Tejano Saddlemakers and the Running W Saddle Shop." In *Hecho en Tejas: Texas-Mexican Folk Arts and Crafts*, edited by Joe S. Graham, 204–221. Denton: University of North Texas Press, 1991.

________. "Texas-Mexican Vernacular Architecture." In *The New Handbook of Texas,* edited by Ron Tyler, Douglas E. Barnett, Roy R. Barkley, Penelope C. Anderson, and Mark F. Odintz, vol. 6, 362–363. Austin: Texas State Historical Association, 1996.

________. "Tex-Mex Foods." In *The New Handbook of Texas,* edited by Ron Tyler, Douglas E. Barnett, Roy R. Barkley, Penelope C. Anderson, and Mark F. Odintz, vol. 6, 451–452. Austin: Texas State Historical Association, 1996.

________. "Tradition and Mexican Candelilla Wax Makers." In *Some Still Do: Essays on Texas Customs*, edited by Francis E. Abernethy, 39–54. Austin: The Encino Press, 1975.

________. "*Vaquero* Folk Arts and Crafts in South Texas." In *Hecho en Tejas: Texas-Mexican Folk Arts and Crafts*, edited by Joe S. Graham, 93–116. Denton: University of North Texas Press, 1991.

________, ed. *Hecho en Tejas: Texas-Mexican Folk Arts and Crafts.* Denton: University of North Texas Press, 1991.

Grajeda, Ralph. "Tomás Rivera's Appropriation of the Chicano Past." In *Modern Chicano Writers: A Collection of Critical Essays*, edited by Joseph Sommers and Tomás Ybarra-Frausto, 74–85. Englewood Cliffs, N.J.: Prentice-Hall, 1979.

Green, George K. "The Corridos of Mexico and South Texas: Modern Variations on Medieval Themes." In *More Studies in Brownsville History*, edited by Milo Kearney, 69–80. Brownsville, Tex.: Pan American University at Brownsville, 1989.

Grider, Sylvia Ann. "Con Safos: Mexican Americans, Names, and Graffiti." *Journal of American Folklore* 88 (April-June 1975): 132–142.

Griego, Linda. "The 'Ojo.'" *Southwest Folklore* 1.4 (Fall 1977): 35.

Griffith, Albert J. "The Scion, the Señorita, and the Texas Ranch Epic: Hispanic Images in Film." *Bilingual Review/La Revista Bilingüe* 16 (1991): 15–22.

Grimm, Agnes G. *Llanos Mesteñas: Mustang Plains*. Waco: Texian Press, 1968.

________. "Eulalio Vásquez." In *The New Handbook of Texas*, edited by Ron Tyler, Douglas E. Barnett, Roy R. Barkley, Penelope C. Anderson, and Mark F. Odintz, vol. 6, 720. Austin: Texas State Historical Association, 1996.

________. "Pedro Jaramillo." In *The New Handbook of Texas,* edited by Ron Tyler, Douglas E. Barnett, Roy R. Barkley, Penelope C. Anderson, and Mark F. Odintz, vol. 3, 910–911. Austin: Texas State Historical Association, 1996.

Griswold del Castillo, Richard. "The Mexican Revolution and the Spanish-Language Press in the Borderlands." *Journalism History* 4 (Summer 1977): 42–47.

Guerra, Dora Elizondo. "Whose Water Is This Anyway, and Keep Your Plow Out of My Corn Field: Men, Women and Culture in Spanish Colonial Texas." *South Texas Studies* 11 (2000): 181–192.

Guerra, Fermina. *Mexican and Spanish Folklore and Incidents in Southwest Texas*. San Antonio: San Antonio Press, 1979.

________. "Mexican and Spanish Folklore and Incidents in Southwest Texas." Master's thesis, University of Texas, Austin, 1941.

________. "Rancho Buena Vista, Its Ways of Life and Traditions." In *Mexican American Authors*, edited by Américo Paredes and Raymund Paredes, 17–26. Boston: Houghton Mifflin, 1976. Originally published in *Texian Stomping Ground*, edited by J. Frank Dobie, Mody C. Boatright, and Harry H. Ransom, 59–77. Dallas: Southern Methodist University Press, 1941.

Gutiérrez, Félix. "Spanish-Language Media in America: Background, Resources, History." *Journalism History* 4 (Summer 1977): 34–67.

Gutiérrez, Rubén Flores. "Guerrero Viego: An Architectural Legacy." In *A Shared Experience: The History, Architectural and Historic Designation of the Lower Rio Grande Heritage Corridor*, edited by Mario L. Sánchez, 199–223. Second edition. Austin: Texas Historical Commission, 1994.

Hambric, Julia. "Charro Regalia." In *Charreada: Mexican Rodeo in Texas*, edited by Francis Edward Abernethy, 7–16. Denton: University of North Texas Press, 2002.

________. "The Events in the Charreada." In *Charreada: Mexican Rodeo in Texas*, edited by Francis Edward Abernethy, 37–71. Denton: University of North Texas Press, 2002.

________. "La Escaramuza." In *Charreada: Mexican Rodeo in Texas*, edited by Francis Edward Abernethy, 73–93. Denton: University of North Texas Press, 2002.

Handman, Max S. "San Antonio: The Old Capital City of Mexican Life and Culture." *Survey* 66 (May 1, 1931): 163–166.

Hardt, Annabelle. "The Bicultural Heritage of Texas." Ph.D. dissertation, University of Texas, Austin, 1968.

Harwell, Thomas Meade. *Studies in Texas Folklore—Rio Grande Valley*. Lewiston, Penn.: Edward Mellen Press, 1997.

Hawley, C. A. "Life along the Border." *West Texas Historical and Scientific Society Publications* 20 (1964): 7–88.

Heimsath, Charles H. "The Mysterious Woman in Blue." In *Legends of Texas*, edited by J. Frank Dobie, 132–135. Hatboro, Penn.: Folklore Associates, 1964.

Hernández, Macarena del Rocío. "Celebrating the Cycle of Life: El Día de los Muertos." *Texas Highways* 49.9 (2002): 22–25.

Hertzog, J. Carl. "Tribute to José Cisneros." *Password* 19 (Winter 1974): 177–183.

Hester, Paul, and Peter C. Papademetriou. *La Arquitectura: Spanish Influences on Houston's Architecture*. Houston: Houston Public Library, 1979.

Hester, Thomas Roy, and T. C. Hill Jr. "An Initial Study of a Prehistoric Ceramic Tradition in Southern Texas." *Plains Anthropologist* 16 (1971): 195–203.

________. "Mogollón Ceramics from Southern Texas." *The Artifact, El Paso Archeological Society* 7 (1969): 11–15.

Hicks, Helen. "Password Salutes Manuel Acosta." *Password* 18 (Summer 1973): 83–85.

Hiester, Miriam Webb. "*Los Paisanos*: Folklore of the Texas-Mexicans of the Lower Rio Grande Valley." Master's thesis, University of Texas, Austin, 1954.

Hinojosa, Gilberto. "Charting a Border Culture." *Texas Journal of Ideas, History and Culture* 20 (Fall/Winter 1997): 4–5.

Hinojosa-Smith, Rolando. "*La Prensa*: A Lifelong Influence on Hispanics in Texas." *The Americas Review* 17 (Fall 1989): 125–129.

________. "A Sense of Place." *Texas Journal of Ideas, History, and Culture* 17.1 (1994): 18–21.

________. "This Writer's Sense of Place." In *The Texas Literary Tradition: Fiction, Folklore, History*, edited by Don Graham, James W. Lee, and William Pilkington, 120–124. Austin: College of Liberal Arts, University of Texas at Austin, Texas State Historical Association, 1983.

Horton, Frances. "Food Habits and Living Conditions of Mexicans Dwelling in the Rio Grande Valley Between Roma and Mercedes." Master's thesis, University of Texas, Austin, 1936.

Houts, P. L. "An Interview with George I. Sánchez." *The National Elementary Principal* 50.2 (1970): 102–104.

Hudson, Wilson M., ed. *The Healer of Los Olmos and Other Mexican Lore*. Dallas: Southern Methodist University Press, 1951.

Hunter, Leslie Gene, and Cecilia Aros Hunter. "'Mother Lane' and the 'New Mooners': An Expression of *Curanderismo*." *Southwestern Historical Quarterly* 99 (January 1996): 291–325.

Igo, John. "Julia Mott Waugh on *Los Pastores*." In *Diamond Bessie and the Shepherds*, edited by Wilson M. Hudson, 15–26. Austin: Encino Press, 1972.

Ivey, Alfred Joe. "A Study of the Vocabulary of Newspapers Printed in the Spanish Language in Texas." Master's thesis, University of Texas, Austin, 1927.

Jameson, John R. "An International Peace Park on the Rio Grande: A Study of Cultural Differences." In *The American West: Essays in Honor of W. Eugene Hollon*, edited by Ronald Lora, 115–132. Toledo, Ohio: University of Toledo, 1980.

Jasper, Pat, and Kay Turner "Art Among Us/Arte Entre Nosotros: Mexican-American Folk Art in San Antonio." In *Hecho en Tejas: Texas-Mexican Folk Arts and Crafts*, edited by Joe S. Graham, 48–76. Denton: University of North Texas Press, 1991.

________. "The Artists Among Us." In *Art Among Us/Arte Entre Nosotros*, edited by Pat Jasper and Kay Turner, 60–71. San Antonio: San Antonio Museum Association, 1986.

________, eds. *Art Among Us/Arte Entre Nosotros: Mexican American Folk Art of San Antonio*. San Antonio: San Antonio Museum Association, 1986.

Jiménez, Alfredo, and Beatriz Suñe. "Society and Culture in the Spanish Borderlands." In *Handbook of Hispanic Cultures in the United States*, edited by Nicolás Kanellos and Claudio Esteva-Fabregat, vol. 4, 228–258. Houston: Arte Público Press and Instituto de Cooperación Iberoamericana, 1994.

Johnson, Michael Gregory. "Discourse Markers in Tejano Speaking: Code Switching as a Resource in Spanish-English Conversation." Ph.D. dissertation, University of Texas at Austin, 1995.

Jordan, Rosan A. "Tension and Speech Play in Mexican-American Folklore." In "*And Other Neighborly Names*": *Social Process and Cultural Image in Texas Folklore*, edited by Richard Bauman and Roger D. Abrahams, 252–265. Austin: University of Texas Press, 1981.

Jordan, Sandra. "Alice Dickerson Montemayor of Laredo." In *Folk Art in Texas*, edited by Francis Edward Abernethy, 184–187. Dallas: Southern Methodist University Press, 1985.

Juárez, Miguel. *Colors on Desert Walls: The Murals of El Paso*. El Paso: Texas Western Press, 1997.

Kanellos, Nicolás. "San Antonio." In *A History of Hispanic Theatre in the United States: Origins to 1940*, by Nicolás Kanellos, 71–103. Austin: University of Texas Press, 1990.

Kendall, Dorothy Steinbomer. *Gentilz: Artist of the Old Southwest*. Austin: University of Texas Press, 1974.

Kenmotsu, Nancy A. "Cartography of the Lower Rio Grande." In *A Shared Experience: The History, Architectural and Historic Designation of the Lower Rio Grande Heritage Corridor*, edited by Mario L. Sánchez, 225–249. Second edition. Austin: Texas Historical Commission, 1994.

Kirk, William. "Cultural Conflict in Mexican Life." *Sociology and Social Research* 15 (March-April 1931): 352–364.

Knowlton, Clark S. "Changing Patterns of Segregation and Discrimination Affecting the Mexican Americans of El Paso." In *Politics and Society in the Southwest: Ethnicity and Chicano Pluralism*, edited by Z. Anthony Kruszewski, Richard L. Hough, and Jacob Ornstein-Galicia, 131–154. Boulder, Colo.: Westview Press, 1982.

________. "Culture Conflict and Natural Resources." In *Social Behavior, Natural Resources and the Environment*, edited by William R. Burch Jr., Neil H. Cheek Jr., and Lee Taylor, 109–145. New York: Harper and Row, 1972.

________. "Patterns of Accommodation of Mexican Americans in El Paso, Texas." In *Politics and Society in the Southwest: Ethnicity and Chicano Pluralism*, edited by Z. Anthony Kruszewski, Richard L. Hough, and Jacob Ornstein-Galicia, 215–236. Boulder, Colo.: Westview Press, 1982.

Koenig, Rebecca Anne Todd. "Fiestas Patrias." In *The New Handbook of Texas,* edited by Ron Tyler, Douglas E. Barnett, Roy R. Barkley, Penelope C. Anderson, and Mark F. Odintz, vol. 2, 994–995. Austin: Texas State Historical Association, 1996.

Kreneck, Thomas H. *Del Pueblo: A Pictorial History of Houston's Hispanic Community*. Houston: Houston International University, 1989.

________. "Domingo Peña." In *The New Handbook of Texas*, edited by Ron Tyler, Douglas E. Barnett, Roy R. Barkley, Penelope C. Anderson, and Mark F. Odintz, vol. 5, 133–134. Austin: Texas State Historical Association, 1996.

________. "Jesse Murillo: Social Artist for the Houston-Galveston Region." *The Houston Review* 5 (Summer 1983): 80–83.

Lane, John Hart. "Voluntary Associations among Mexican Americans in San Antonio, Texas." Ph.D. dissertation, University of Texas, Austin, 1968.

Lara, Margarita. "Language Competence and Reading Comprehension of Mexican-American Elementary School Students." Ed.D. dissertation, University of Houston, 1986.

Larralde, Carlos M. "José Cantú." In *The New Handbook of Texas,* edited by Ron Tyler, Douglas E. Barnett, Roy R. Barkley, Penelope C. Anderson, and Mark F. Odintz, vol. 1, 963. Austin: Texas State Historical Association, 1996.

LeCompte, Mary Lou. "The Hispanic Influence on the History of Rodeo, 1823–1922." *Journal of Sport History* 12.1 (1985): 21–38.

Leff, Gladys R. "George I. Sánchez: Don Quixote of the Southwest." Ph.D. dissertation, North Texas State University, 1976.

Lehmer, Donald. "Modern *Jacales* of Presidio." *El Palacio* 46 (1939): 183–186.

Leonard, Frances. "Living on La Frontera: Borderlands in Words and Pictures." *Texas Journal of Ideas, History and Culture* 20 (Fall/Winter 1997): 16–21.

León-Portilla, Miguel. "The Norteño Variety of Mexican Culture: An Ethnohistorical Approach." In *Plural Society in the Southwest*, edited by Edward H. Spicer and Raymond H. Thompson, 77–114. Albuquerque: University of New Mexico Press, 1972.

Libretti, Tim. "'We Can Starve Too': Américo Paredes' *George Washington Gómez* and the Proletarian *Corrido*." In *Recovering the U.S. Hispanic Literary Heritage*, vol. 2, edited by Erlinda Gonzales-Berg and Chuck Taylor, 118–130. Houston: Arte Público Press, 1996.

Light, Jere Cook. "A Critical Analysis of Anglo and Mexican-American Cultural Patterns in Two Texas Border City Junior Colleges." Ph.D. dissertation, University of Texas at Austin, 1974.

Limón, José E. *American Encounters: Greater Mexico, the United States, and the Erotics of Culture*. Boston: Beacon Press, 1998.

________. *Dancing with the Devil: Society and Cultural Poetics in Mexican American South Texas*. Madison: University of Wisconsin Press, 1994.

________. *Mexican Ballads, Chicano Epic: History, Social Dramas, and Poetic Persuasions*. Stanford, Calif.: Stanford Center for Chicano Research, 1986.

________. *Mexican Ballads, Chicano Poems: History and Influence in Mexican-American Social Poetry*. Berkeley: University of California Press, 1992.

________. *Mexican Culture in South Texas: A Teaching Resource*. Laredo, Tex.: Laredo State University, 1982.

________. *Return of the Mexican Ballad: Américo Paredes and His Anthropological Text as Persuasive Political Performance*. Stanford, Calif.: Stanford Center for Chicano Research, 1986.

________. "The Expressive Culture of a Chicano Student Group at Austin, 1967–1975." Ph.D. dissertation, University of Texas at Austin, 1978.

________. "*Agringado* Joking in Texas-Mexican Society: Folklore and Differential Identity." *New Scholar* 6 (1974): 33–50.

________. "Américo Paredes: A Man from the Border." *Revista Chicano-Riqueña* 8.3 (1980): 1–5.

________. "*El Baile*: Culture and Contradiction in Mexican American Dancing." In *Puro Conjunto, An Album in Words and Pictures*, edited by Juan Tejeda and

Avelardo Valdez, 241–252. Austin: CMAS Books, Guadalupe Cultural Arts Center, 2001.

________. "Dancing with the Devil: Society, Gender, and the Political Unconsciousness in Mexican American South Texas." In *Criticism in the Borderlands: Studies in Chicano Literature, Culture, and Ideology*, edited by Héctor Calderón and José David Salvídar, 221–235. Durham: Duke University Press, 1991.

________. "Folklore, Gendered Repression, and Cultural Critique: The Case of Jovita González." *Texas Studies in Literature and Language* 35 (1993): 453–473.

________. "Folklore, Social Conflict and the United States-Mexico Border." In *Handbook of American Folklore*, edited by Richard Dorson, 216–226. Bloomington: Indiana University Press, 1983.

________. "The Folk Performance of 'Chicano' and the Cultural Limits of Political Ideology." In "*And Other Neighborly Names*": *Social Process and Cultural Image in Texas Folklore*, edited by Richard Bauman and Roger D. Abrahams, 197–225. Austin: University of Texas Press, 1981.

________. "Healing the Wounds: Folk Symbols and Historical Crisis." *Texas Humanist* 6 (March/April 1984): 21–23.

________. "Healing the Wounds: Folk Symbols and Historical Crisis." *Texas Journal of Ideas, History and Culture* 20 (Fall/Winter 1997): 44–49.

________. "History, Chicano Joking, and the Varieties of Higher Education: Tradition and Performance as Critical Symbolic Action." *Journal of the Folklore Institute* 19 (1982): 141–166.

________. "Legendry, Metafolklore, and Performance: A Mexican-American Example." *Western Folklore* 42 (July 1983): 191–208.

________. "*La Llorona*, History, and the Grief of a Nation." *Humanities* (Winter 2002): 1, 5.

________. "Mexican, Foundational Fictions, and the United States: *Caballero*, a Late Border Romance." *Modern Languages Quarterly* 57 (1996): 341–353.

________. "*El Primer Congreso Mexicanista de 1911*: A Precursor to Contemporary Chicanismo." *Aztlán* 5 (1974): 85–106.

________. "Selena, Sexuality, Greater Mexico and the Song-and-Dance with Hegemony." *ETNOFOOR* 10 (1997): 90–111.

________. "Texas Literature and the Future: Some Notes from the South." In *The Texas Literary Tradition: Fiction, Folklore, History*, edited by Don Graham, James W. Lee, and William Pilkington, 145–151. Austin: College of Liberal Arts, University of Texas at Austin, Texas State Historical Association, 1983.

________. "Texas-Mexican Popular Music and Dancing: Some Notes on History and Symbolic Process." *Latin American Music Review* 4 (Fall/Winter 1983): 229–246.

________. "With a *Corrido* in His Heart: Américo Paredes is the Top Chicano Scholar." *Nuestro* 3 (September 1979): 40–42.

Littlejohn, E. G. "The Holy Spring of Father Margil at Nacogdoches." In *Legends of Texas*, edited by J. Frank Dobie, 204–205. Hatboro, Penn.: Folklore Associates, 1964.

Lizarraga, Silvia A. "Cambio: Intento principal de . . . y lo se lo trago la tierra." *Aztlán* 7 (Fall 1976): 419–426.

________. "'La mujer doublemente explotada': On the Road to Texas: Pete Fonseca." *Aztlán* 16 (1985): 197–215.

Loa, Sijefredo. "The Use of Subject NPs by Spanish Speakers in Central Texas." Ph.D. dissertation, University of Texas at Austin, 1989.

Lockhart, William W. "Casa Ronquilo in San Elizario." *Password* 41 (Summer 1996): 71–86.

Long, Christopher. "Xavier González." In *The New Handbook of Texas,* edited by Ron Tyler, Douglas E. Barnett, Roy R. Barkley, Penelope C. Anderson, and Mark F. Odintz, vol. 3, 235. Austin: Texas State Historical Association, 1996.

Longoria, Arturo. "Breads of Los Tejanos." *Texas Highways* 49 (August 2002): 40–43.

Longoria, Mario D. "Revolution, Visionary Plan, and the Marketplace: A San Antonio Incident." *Aztlán* 12.2 (1982): 211–226.

López, Joe Raymond. "Religion in Selected Works of Chicano Literature." Master's thesis, Texas Tech University, 1975.

López, Joey. "Musica Chicana." *Caracol* 1 (June 1975): 8.

López-Stafford, Gloria. *A Place in El Paso: A Mexican-American Childhood.* Albuquerque: University of New Mexico Press, 1996.

Lowry, Jack. "Remembering Our Hispanic Legacy: ¡Viva Texas!" *Texas Highways* 49.9 (2002): 12–15.

Low, Setha M. "The Cultural Meaning of the Plaza: The History of the Spanish-American Gridplan-Plaza Urban Design." In *The Cultural Meaning of Urban Space*, edited by Robert Rotenberg and Gary McDonogh, 75–93. Westport, Conn.: Bergin and Garvey, 1993.

Lozano, Rubén Rendón. *Viva Tejas: The Story of the Mexican-born Patriots of the Republic of Texas.* San Antonio: Southern Literary Institute, 1936.

Luna Lawhn, Juanita. "*El Regidor* and *La Prensa*: Impediments to Women's Self-Definition." In *Third Woman: The Sexuality of Latinas*, edited by Norma Alarcon, Ana Castillo, and Cherrie Moraga, 134–142. Berkeley: Third Woman Press, 1989.

________. "Victorian Attitudes Affecting the Mexican Woman Writing in *La Prensa* during the Early 1900s and the Chicana of the 1980s." In *Missions in Conflict: Essays on U.S.-Mexican Relations and Chicano Culture*, edited by Renate von Bardeleben, Dietrich Briesemeister, and Juan Bruce-Novoa, 65–71. Tubingen: Narr, 1986.

Lynch, Michael J. III. "Castañeda and Canales: Collaborators, Academics, Friends." *Journal of South Texas* 13 (2000): 94–115.

Madsen, William. "The Alcoholic Agringado." *American Anthropologist* 66.2 (1964): 355–361.

________. "Anxiety and Witchcraft in Mexican American Acculturation." *Anthropology Quarterly* 39.2 (1966): 1101–1127.

________. "Value Conflict and Folk Psychology in South Texas." In *Magic, Faith, and Healing*, edited by Ari Kiev, 420–444. New York: Free Press, 1964.

Maldonado, David J. *Crossing Guadalupe Street: Growing Up Hispanic and Protestant*. Albuquerque: University of New Mexico Press, 2001.

Mallory, Randy. "Hangin' Out in South Texas' Outdoor Living Rooms: Plaza Life." *Texas Highways* 49.9 (2002): 16–21.

Manríquez, B. J. "Argument in Narrative: Tropology in Jovita González's *Caballero*." *Bilingual Review/La Revista Bilingüe* 25 (2000): 172–178.

Manuel, Herschel T. "The Mexican Population of Texas." *Southwestern Social Science Quarterly* 15 (June 1934): 29–51.

________. "The Mexican Population of Texas." *Southwest Review* 17 (1932): 290–302.

Marek, Elizabeth. "La Revolución Mexicana en el Exilo: Silvestre Terrazas y Su Periodico *La Patria*, 1919–1920." Master's thesis, University of Texas at El Paso, 1990.

Maril, Robert Lee. *Living on the Edge of America: At Home on the Texas-Mexican Border*. College Station: Texas A&M University Press, 1992.

Martínez, Camilo A. "Vamos Pal Wes; Let's Go West." *West Texas Historical Association Yearbook* 70 (1994): 40–56.

Martínez, Cervando, and Harry W. Martin. "Folk Diseases Among Mexican Americans." *Journal of the American Medical Association* 196.2 (1966): 161–164.

Mayer, Vicki Alexis. "Mexican Americans, Mass Media, and Cultural Citizenship: Cultural Affirmation and Consumer Alienation in San Antonio, Texas." Ph.D. dissertation, University of California, San Diego, 2000.

McBride, J. D. "Liga Protectora Latina." *Journal of the West* 14 (1975): 82–90.

McDowell, John Holmes. "The *Corrido* of Greater Mexico as Discourse, Music, and Event." In *"And Other Neighborly Names": Social Process and Cultural Image in Texas Folklore*, edited by Richard Bauman and Roger D. Abrahams, 44–75. Austin: University of Texas Press, 1981.

________. "The Speech Play and Verbal Art of Chicano Children: An Ethnographic and Socio-linguistic Study." Ph.D. dissertation, University of Texas at Austin, 1975.

McFarland, Ron. "Indelibly Chicano: An Interview with Ricardo Sánchez." *The Americas Review* 21 (Summer 1993): 89–101.

McKnight, Joseph W. "Law Without Lawyers on the Hispano-Mexican Frontier." *West Texas Historical Association Yearbook* 66 (1990): 51–65.

McLean, Robert N. *That Mexican As He Really Is, North and South of the Rio Grande*. New York: Fleming H. Revell, 1928.

________. "Rubbing Shoulders on the Border." *Survey* (May 1, 1924): 184–185.

McNeil, Norman Laird ("Brownie"). "Mexican Border Ballads." Master's thesis, University of Texas, Austin, 1944.

Meed, Douglas V. "Abandoned Terrazas Mansion Still Retains Its Splendor." *Password* 41 (Spring 1996): 35–38.

Melville, Margarita B. "The Mexican American and the Celebration of Fiestas Patrias." *Grito del Sol* 3 (1978): 107–118.

________. "Selective Acculturation of Female Mexican Migrants." In *Twice a Minority: Mexican American Women*, edited by Margarita B. Melville, 155–163. St. Louis: C.V. Moseby Company, 1980.

Mendoza, Louis G. "Confronting La Frontera, Identity and Gender: Poetry and Politics in *La Cronica* and *El Demócrata Fronterizo*." In *Recovering the U.S. Hispanic Literary Heritage*, edited by María Herrera-Sobek and Virginia Sánchez Korrol, vol. 3, 103–123. Houston: Arte Público Press, 2000.

Mercado-Allinger, Patricia A. "Hispanic Heritage on the High Plains: The Panhandle Perspective." In *Hispanic Texas: A Historical Guide*, edited by Helen Simons and Cathryn A. Hoyt, 37–50. Austin: University of Texas Press, 1992.

Merrill, Celia Dale. "Mexican-American English in McAllen, Texas: Features of Accentedness in the English of Native Spanish Bilinguals." Ph.D. dissertation, University of Texas at Austin, 1987.

Meyer, Nicholas E. "Lee Treviño." In *The Biographical Dictionary of Hispanic Americans*, by Nicholas E. Meyer, 216–217. New York: Facts on File, 1997.

________."Luis Jiménez." In *The Biographical Dictionary of Hispanic Americans*, by Nicholas E. Meyer, 118–119. New York: Facts on File, 1997.

________."Trini López." In *The Biographical Dictionary of Hispanic Americans*, by Nicholas E. Meyer, 130–132. New York: Facts on File, 1997.

________."Vicki Carr." In *Notable Latino Americans: A Biographical Dictionary*, by Nicholas E. Meyer, 57–60. Westport, Conn.: Greenwood Press, 1997.

Miller, W. "Latin American Child and Music." *Texas Outlook* 31 (October 1947): 26.

Mireles, E. E., Roy B. Fisher, and Jovita González de Mireles. *Mi libro español*. Austin: W. S. Benson and Company, 1941.

Moffatt, Lori. "Border Crossings: Exploring Los Dos Laredos." *Texas Highways* (May 2003): 22–29.

Montalvo, Carmela. "The Pastorela: The Missionary's Medium for Religious Instruction." *Tejidos* 2 (Fall 1975): 17–46.

Montaño, Mario. "The History of Mexican Food Folkways of South Texas: Street Vendors, Offal Foods, and Barbacoa de Cabeza." Ph.D. dissertation, University of Pennsylvania, 1992.

Montejano, David. "The Demise of 'Jim Crow' for Texas Mexicans, 1940–1970." *Aztlán* 16 (1985): 27–69.

________. "Is Texas Bigger Than the World System? A Critique From a Provincial Point of View." *Review* 4 (Winter 1981): 620–623.

Morales, Alejandro. "Expanding the Means of Chicano Cinema: *Yo Soy Chicano, Raices De Sangre, Seguín*. In *Chicano Cinema: Research, Reviews, and Resources*, edited by Gary D. Keller, 121–137. Binghamton, N.Y.: Bilingual Review/Press, 1985.

Mounce, Gary. "Popular Culture and Politics: *The Pelea de Gallo* (Cockfight) in South Texas." *South Texas Studies* 1 (1990): 1–36.

Mrak, Norma Ariana. "Cambios en el paradigma pronominal acusativo de tercera persona: los efectos de la simplificación en el español de hablantes de origen mexicano de Houston." Ph.D. dissertation, University of Houston, 2000.

Mullins, Leslie. "A Collection of Stories of Early Texas." Master's thesis, Southwest Texas State Teachers College, 1943.

Murillo, Nathan. "The Works of George I. Sánchez: An Appreciation." In *Chicano Psychology*, edited by Joe L. Martínez and Richard H. Mendoza, 1–10. Orlando, Fla.: Academic Press, 1984.

Nájera-Ramírez, Olga. "Mountain of Traditions: The Origin and Evolution of *La Escaramuza Charro*." In *Chicano Traditions: Continuity and Change,* edited by Norma E. Cantú and Olga Najera-Ramírez, 207–223. Urbana: University of Illinois Press, 2002.

Newton, Ada Louise. "The History of Architecture along the Rio Grande as Reflected in the Buildings around Rio Grande City 1749–1920." Master's thesis, Texas A&I University, 1964.

Niggli, Josefina. "Call Them Dreams." *Pax: A Journal for Peace Through Culture* 3.1–2 (1985–1986): 98–102.

Norman, Arthur. "Migration to Southwest Texas: People and Words." *Southwestern Social Science Quarterly* 37 (1956): 149–158.

Nostrand, Richard L. "The Hispanic American Borderland: Delineation of an American Culture Region." *Annals of the Association of American Geographers* 60 (1970): 638–661.

Ochoa, Rubén E. "Folk Arts and Crafts Embody a Vibrant Response to Life: *Hecho a Mano*." *Texas Highways* 49.9 (2002): 50–56.

Oden, Arthur. "Mud, Sticks, and Stones." Master's thesis, Texas Western College, 1959.

Olivares, Julián, ed. *International Studies in Honor of Tomás Rivera*. Houston: Arte Público Press, 1986.

Orozco, Aurora E. "Mexican Blood Runs Through My Veins." In *Speaking Chicana: Voice, Power, and Identity*, edited by D. Letticia Galindo and María Dolores Gonzales, 106–120. Tucson: University of Arizona Press, 1999.

Orozco, Cynthia E. "Alicia Guadalupe Elizondo de Lozano." In *The New Handbook of Texas*, edited by Ron Tyler, Douglas E. Barnett, Roy R. Barkley, Penelope C. Anderson, and Mark F. Odintz, vol. 4, 318. Austin: Texas State Historical Association, 1996.

________. "Casimiro Pérez Álvarez." In *The New Handbook of Texas*, edited by Ron Tyler, Douglas E. Barnett, Roy R. Barkley, Penelope C. Anderson, and Mark F. Odintz, vol. 5, 151. Austin: Texas State Historical Association, 1996.

________. "Eulalio Marín." In *The New Handbook of Texas*, edited by Ron Tyler, Douglas E. Barnett, Roy R. Barkley, Penelope C. Anderson, and Mark F. Odintz, vol. 4, 508. Austin: Texas State Historical Association, 1996.

________. "José Romulo Mungía Torres." In *The New Handbook of Texas*, edited by Ron Tyler, Douglas E. Barnett, Roy R. Barkley, Penelope C. Anderson, and Mark F. Odintz, vol. 4, 887–888. Austin: Texas State Historical Association, 1996.

________. "Pablo Cruz." In *The New Handbook of Texas,* edited by Ron Tyler, Douglas E. Barnett, Roy R. Barkley, Penelope C. Anderson, and Mark F. Odintz, vol. 2, 428–429. Austin: Texas State Historical Association, 1996.

O'Shea, Elena Zamora. *El Mesquite, A Story of the Early Spanish Settlements between the Nueces and the Rio Grande as Told by "La Posta del Palo Alto."* Dallas: Mathis Publishing, 1935.

Paredes, Américo. *Folklore and Culture on the Texas-Mexican Border*, edited by Richard Bauman. Austin: Center for Mexican American Studies, 1993.

________. *A Texas-Mexican Cancionero: Folksongs of the Lower Border*. Urbana: University of Illinois Press, 1976.

________. *Uncle Remus con chíle*. Houston: Arte Público Press, 1993.

________. *"With His Pistol in His Hand": A Border Ballad and Its Hero*. Austin: University of Texas Press, 1958.

________. "Ballads of the Lower Border." Master's thesis, University of Texas, Austin, 1953.

________. "The Ancestry of Mexico's *Corridos*: A Matter of Definitions." *Journal of American Folklore* 76 (1963): 231–235.

________. "The Anglo-American in Mexican Folklore." In *New Voices in American Studies*, edited by Ray B. Browne, Donald M. Winkelman, and Allen Hayman, 113–127. Lafayette, Ind.: Purdue University Studies, 1966.

________. "The Bury-Me-Not Theme in the Southwest." In *And Horns on the Toads*, edited by Mody C. Boatright, Wilson M. Hudson, and Allen Maxwell, 88–92. Dallas: Southern Methodist University Press, 1959.

________. "The Concept of the Emotional Core Applied to the Mexican *Corrido* 'Benjamin Argumendo.'" In *Folklore and Culture on the Texas-Mexican Border*, edited by Richard Bauman, 143–176. Austin: CMAS Books, 1993.

________. "Concepts about Folklore in Latin America and the United States." *Journal of the Folklore Institute* 6 (1969): 20–38.

________. "The *Corrido*: Yesterday and Today." In *Ecology and Development of the Border Region*, edited by Stanley R. Ross, 293–297. Mexico City: Asociación Nacional de Universidades e Institutos de Enseñanza Superior, 1983.

________. "'El corrido de José Mosqueda' as an Example of Pattern in the Ballad." *Western Folklore* 17 (1958): 154–162.

________. "El cowboy norteamericano en el folklore y la literature." *Cuadernos del Instituto Nacional de Antropología* 4 (1963): 227–240.

________. "The *Décima* on the Texas-Mexican Border: Folksong as an Adjunct to Legend." *Journal of the Folklore Institute* 3 (1966): 154–167.

________. "Dichos." In *Mexican American Authors*, edited by Américo Paredes and Raymund Paredes, 27–34. Boston: Houghton Mifflin, 1976.

________. "Divergencias en el concepto del folklore y el contexto cultural." *Folklore Americas* 27 (1967): 29–38.

________. "Estados Unidos, México y el machismo." *Journal of Inter-American Studies* 9 (1967): 65–84. Reprinted as "The United States, Mexico, and *Machismo*," translated by Marcy Steen. *Journal of the Folklore Institute* 8 (1971): 17–37.

________. "El folklore en los Estados Unidos durante la última década (1953–1962)." *Folklore Americano* 10 (1963): 256–262.

________. "El folklore de los grupos de origen mexicano en Estados Unidos." *Folklore Americano* 14 (1966): 146–163. Reprinted as "The Folk Base of Chicano Literature." In *Modern Chicano Writers: A Collection of Critical Essays*, edited by Joseph Sommers and Tomás Ybarra-Frausto, 4–17. Englewood Cliffs, N.J.: Prentice-Hall, 1979.

________. "The Folklore of Groups of Mexican Origin in the United States." In *Folklore and Culture on the Texas-Mexican Border*, edited by Richard Bauman, 3–18. Austin: CMAS Books, 1993.

________. "Folklore and History." In *Singers and Storytellers*, edited by Mody C. Boatright, William M. Hudson, and Allen Maxwell, 56–68. Dallas: Southern Methodist University Press, 1961.

________. "Folklore, Lo Mexicano, and Proverbs." *Aztlán* 13 (Spring/Fall 1982): 1–11.

________. "Folk Medicine and the Intercultural Jest." In *Spanish-Speaking People in the United States*, edited by June Helm, 104–119. Seattle: University of Washington Press, 1968. Reprinted in *Folk Groups and Folklore Genres: A Reader*, edited by Elliott Oring, 63–77. Logan: Utah State University Press, 1989.

________. "Gringo." *Western Folklore* 19 (1960): 277.

________. "José Mosqueda and the Folklorization of Actual Events." *Aztlán* 4 (Spring 1973): 1–30.

________. "The Legend of Gregorio Cortéz." In *Mesquite and Willow*, edited by Mody C. Boatright, Wilson M. Hudson, and Allen Maxwell, 3–22. Dallas: Southern Methodist University Press, 1957.

________. "The Love Tragedy in Texas-Mexican Balladry." In *Folk Travelers: Ballads, Tales, and Talk*, edited by Mody C. Boatright, William M. Hudson, and Allen Maxwell, 110–114. Dallas: Southern Methodist University Press, 1953.

________. "Luis Inclán: First of the Cowboy Writers." *American Quarterly* 12 (1960): 55–70.

________. "The Mexican Contribution to Our Culture." *Texas Observer* 19 (August 1960): 6–7.

________. "The Mexican *Corrido*: Its Rise and Fall." In *Madstones and Twisters*, edited by Mody C. Boatright, Wilson M. Hudson, and Allen Maxwell, 91–105. Dallas: Southern Methodist University Press, 1958.

________. "Mexican Legendry and the Rise of the Mestizo." In *American Folk Legend: A Symposium*, edited by Wayland Hand, 97–107. Berkeley: University of California Press, 1971.

________. "Mexican Riddling Wellerisms." *Western Folklore* 19 (1960): 200.

________. "The Mexico-Texan Corrido." *Southwest Review* 27 (1942): 470–481.

———. "Moochers." In *Buying the Wind: Regional Folklore in the United States*, edited by Richard M. Dorson, 453–454. Chicago: University of Chicago Press, 1964.

———. "Nearby Places and Strange-Sounding Names." In *The Texas Literary Tradition: Fiction, Folklore, History*, edited by Don Graham, James W. Lee, and William Pilkington, 130–138. Austin: University of Texas Press, 1983.

———. "No Estiendo." In *Buying the Wind: Regional Folklore in the United States*, edited by Richard M. Dorson, 452–453. Chicago: University of Chicago Press, 1964.

———. "On Ethnographic Work among Minority Groups: A Folklorist's Perspective." *New Scholar* 6 (1977): 1–32. Reprinted in *New Directions in Chicano Scholarship*, edited by Ricardo Romo and Raymund Paredes, 1–32. La Jolla: Chicano Studies Program, University of California, San Diego, 1978.

———. "On *Gringo*, *Greaser*, and Other Neighborly Names." In *Singers and Storytellers*, edited by Mody C. Boatright, Wilson M. Hudson, and Allen Maxwell, 285–290. Dallas: Southern Methodist University Press, 1961.

———. "Pastorela to Celebrate the Birth of Our Lord Jesus Christ." In *Buying the Wind: Regional Folklore in the United States*, edited by Richard M. Dorson, 466–479. Chicago: University of Chicago Press, 1964.

———. "The Problem of Identity in a Changing Culture: Popular Expressions of Culture Conflict along the Lower Río Grande Border." In *Views across the Border: The United States and Mexico*, edited by Stanley R. Ross, 68–94. Albuquerque: University of New Mexico Press, 1978.

———. "Proverbs and Ethnic Stereotypes." *Proverbium* 15 (1970): 95–97.

———. "A Selective Annotated Bibliography of Recent Works in Latin American Folklore, 1960–1967." *Handbook of Latin American Studies* 30 (1968): 385–410.

———. "Some Aspects of Folk Poetry." *Texas Studies in Literature and Language* 6 (1964): 213–225.

———. "Tag, You're It." *Journal of American Folklore* 73 (1960): 157–158.

———. "Texas' Third Man: The Texas-Mexican." *Race* 4.2 (1963): 49–58.

———. "Translations of Corridos and Calaveras." In *Corridos and Calaveras*, by Edward Larocque Tinker, 41–58. Austin: University of Texas Press, 1961.

———. "Tributaries to the Mainstream: The Ethnic Groups." In *Our Living Traditions: An Introduction to American Folklore*, edited by Tristram P. Coffin, 70–80. New York: Basic Books, 1968.

———. "The Undying Love of 'El Indio' Córdova: *Décimas* and Oral History in a Border Family." *Ernesto Galarza Commemorative Lecture*, Stanford University, 1987. Reprinted in *Folklore and Culture on the Texas-Mexican Border*, edited by Richard Bauman, 247–265. Austin: Center for Mexican American Studies Books, 1993.

———. "The United States, Mexico, and *Machismo*." In *Folklore and Culture on the Texas-Mexican Border*, edited by Richard Bauman, 3–18. Austin: CMAS Books, 1993.

________. "The Where and Why of Folklore." *Illinois History* 23.4 (1970): 75–76.

________. "Where Cultures Clashed and Merged." *Texas Observer* 12 (August 1960): 7.

________, ed. *Folktales of Mexico*. Chicago: University of Chicago Press, 1970.

________, ed. *Humanidad: Essays in Honor of George I. Sánchez*. Los Angeles: Chicano Studies Center Publications, 1977.

Paredes, Américo, and George Foss. "The *Décima Cantada* on the Texas-Mexican Border: Four Examples." *Journal of the Folklore Institute* 3 (August 1966): 91–115.

Paredes, Américo, and Raymund Paredes, eds. *Mexican-American Authors*. Boston: Houghton Mifflin, 1972.

Paredes, Américo, and Richard Bauman, eds. *Toward New Perspectives in Folklore*. Austin: University of Texas Press, 1972.

Park, Glenna M. Stearman. "Jail House Rag." In *Folk Art in Texas*, edited by Francis E. Abernethy, 167–171. Dallas: Southern Methodist University Press, 1985.

Parle, Dennis J. "Casa Editorial Lozano." In *The New Handbook of Texas,* edited by Ron Tyler, Douglas E. Barnett, Roy R. Barkley, Penelope C. Anderson, and Mark F. Odintz, vol. 1, 1008. Austin: Texas State Historical Association, 1996.

________. "The Novels of the Mexican Revolution Published by the Casa Editorial Lozano." *The Americas Review* 17 (Fall 1989): 163–168.

Paschall, Mark L. "Professional Baseball in the Lower Rio Grande Valley of South Texas, 1949–1961." Master's thesis, University of Texas–Pan American, 1982.

Peck, R. F., and Rogelio Díaz-Guerrero. "Two Core-Culture Patterns and the Diffusion of Values Across Their Border." *International Journal of Psychology* 4.2 (1967): 272–282.

Pérez, Ramón "Tianguis." *Diary of an Undocumented Immigrant*. Houston: Arte Público Press, 1991.

Pérez, Soledad. "Mexican Folklore from Austin." Master's thesis, University of Texas, Austin, 1949.

Perry, Ann. "Tejano Festivals: Celebrations of History and Community." In *Hispanic Texas: A Historical Guide*, edited by Helen Simons and Cathryn A. Hoyt, 121–129. Austin: University of Texas Press, 1992.

Phillips, Juanita Stroud. *Hispanic Folklore in the Rio Grande Valley of Texas*. Bloomington, Ind.: 1st Books Library, 2001.

________. "The Spanish Folklore of Cameron County, Texas." Master's thesis, University of Texas, Austin, 1950.

Phillips, Rebecca K. "Spanglish as a Marker of Identification among Hispanics in the United States: A Case Study of Two Tejano Radio Stations." Master's thesis, Rice University, 2002.

Pierce, James Alfred. "Sociolinguistic Relationships in Attitudes toward Anglo and Mexican-American Varieties of English in Corpus Christi, Texas." Ph.D. dissertation, University of Texas at Austin, 1989.

Plascencia, Luis F. B. "Lowriding in the Southwest: Cultural Symbols in the Mexican Community." In *History, Culture, and Society: Chicano Studies in the 1980s*, edited by Mario T. García and Francisco Lomelli, 141–175. Ypsilanti, Mich.: Bilingual Review/Press, 1983.

Pospisil, JoAnn. "Chihuahuan Desert Candelilla: Folk Gathering of a Regional Resource." *Journal of Big Bend Studies* 6 (1994): 59–73.

Potter, Cristela. "When We All Come to Rest." In *Out Near Phantom Hill,* edited by Darrin Cozzens and Reed Harp, 134–142. Stillwater, Okla.: Southwest and Texas Popular Culture Association, 1990.

________. "When We All Come to Rest." In *Tejano Folk Arts and Crafts*, edited by Joe S. Graham, 39–41. Kingsville, Tex.: John E. Conner Museum, 1989.

Powell, Lydia O. "A Study of the Influences on and Changes in Sixteenth, Seventeenth, and Eighteenth Century Spanish Cartography of Texas." Master's thesis, St. Mary's University, 1985.

Pross, Edith E. "A Chicano Play and Its Audience." *The Americas Review* 14 (Spring 1986): 71–79.

Pycior, Julie Leininger. "*La Raza* Organizes: Mexican American Life in San Antonio, 1915–1930 as reflected in *Mutualista* Activities." Ph.D. dissertation, University of Notre Dame, 1979.

Quirarte, Jacinto. *The Art and Architecture of Texas Missions*. Austin: University of Texas Press, 2002.

________. "Porfirio Salinas Jr." In *The New Handbook of Texas,* edited by Ron Tyler, Douglas E. Barnett, Roy R. Barkley, Penelope C. Anderson, and Mark F. Odintz, vol. 5, 777. Austin: Texas State Historical Association, 1996.

Ramírez, Arturo. "The Ballad of Gregorio Cortéz, A Comparative Analysis in Film and Corrido." In *Aztlán, Chicano Culture and Folklore: An Anthology*, edited by José 'Pepe' Villarino and Arturo Ramírez, 195–199. New York: McGraw Hill Company, 1998.

________. "Views of the Corrido Hero: Paradigm and Development." *The Americas Review* 18 (Summer 1990): 71–79.

Ramírez, Elena Farías. "The Remarkable Ramírez Family." In *Roots by the River*, by Valley By-Liners, 337–340. Mission, Tex.: Border Kingdom Press 1978.

Ramos, Eric. "Mexican American Yard Art in Kingsville." In *Hecho en Tejas: Texas-Mexican Folk Arts and Crafts*, edited by Joe S. Graham, 250–262. Denton: University of North Texas Press, 1991.

________. "Mexican-American Yard Art in Kingsville." In *Tejano Folk Arts and Crafts*, edited by Joe S. Graham, 37–39. Kingsville, Tex.: John E. Conner Museum, 1989.

Ramos-García, Luis A., ed. *Cuentos de Austin/Tales from Austin.* Austin: Studia Hispanica Editions, 1980.

Raymond, Howard G. "Acculturation and Social Mobility among Latin Americans in Resaca City." Master's thesis, University of Texas, Austin, 1932.

Reyna, José R. *Modismos de Tejas*. San Antonio: Penca Books, 1980.

________. *Raza Humor: Chicano Joke Tradition in Texas*. San Antonio: Penca Books, 1980.

________. "Mexican American Prose Narrative in Texas: The Jest and Anecdote." Ph.D. dissertation, University of California at Los Angeles, 1973.

________. "Chicano Folklore: Raza Humor in Texas." *De Colores* 1.4 (1975): 58–65.

________. "Raza Humor in Texas." *Revista Chicano-Requena* 4 (Winter 1976): 27–33.

________. "Tejano Music as an Expression of Cultural Nationalism." In *Chicano Border Culture and Folklore*, edited by José Villarino and Arturo Ramírez, 175–180. San Diego: Marin Publications, 1992. Reprinted in *Puro Conjunto, An Album in Words and Pictures*, edited by Juan Tejeda and Avelardo Valdez, 191–198. Austin: CMAS Books, Guadalupe Cultural Arts Center, 2001.

Richardson, Chad. *Batos, Bolillos, Pochos, and Pelados: Class and Culture on the South Texas Border*. Austin: University of Texas Press, 1999.

Ríos McMillan, Nora E. "A Biography of a Man and His Newspaper." *The Americas Review* 17 (1989): 136–149.

________. "The Immigration Issue Between 1929 and 1954 as Seen Through *La Prensa*." *South Texas Studies* 6 (1995): 20–52.

________. "Ignacio E. Lozano." In *The New Handbook of Texas*, edited by Ron Tyler, Douglas E. Barnett, Roy R. Barkley, Penelope C. Anderson, and Mark F. Odintz, vol. 4, 318. Austin: Texas State Historical Association, 1996.

________. "Leonidas González." In *The New Handbook of Texas,* edited by Ron Tyler, Douglas E. Barnett, Roy R. Barkley, Penelope C. Anderson, and Mark F. Odintz, vol. 3, 234–235. Austin: Texas State Historical Association, 1996.

________. "Nemesio García Naranjo." In *The New Handbook of Texas,* edited by Ron Tyler, Douglas E. Barnett, Roy R. Barkley, Penelope C. Anderson, and Mark F. Odintz, vol. 3, 88–89. Austin: Texas State Historical Association, 1996.

________. "La Prensa." In *The New Handbook of Texas*, edited by Ron Tyler, Douglas E. Barnett, Roy R. Barkley, Penelope C. Anderson, and Mark F. Odintz, vol. 4, 73–74. Austin: Texas State Historical Association, 1996.

Rips, Geoffrey. "Living History: Emma Tenayuca Tells her Story." *Texas Observer* 75 (October 28, 1983): 7–15.

Rivera, Jana. "Chicano Art: The Power and the Polemic." *Hispanic Outlook in Higher Education* 7 (August 30, 1996): 9–10.

Robertson, Brian. *Wild Horse Desert: The Heritage of South Texas*. Edinburg, Tex.: New Santander Press, 1985.

Robinson, Willard B. "Colonial Ranch Architecture in Spanish-Mexican Tradition." *Southwestern Historical Quarterly* 83 (October 1979): 123–150.

Rodríguez, Blanca. "Fronteras y literatura: El periódico *La Patria* (El Paso, Texas, 1919-1925)." *Mexican Studies/Estudios Mexicanos* 19 (Winter 2003): 107–125.

Rodríguez, Jesse. "Texas-Mexican Yard Shrines: Folk Art and the Public Declaration of Faith." In *Out Near Phantom Hill,* edited by Darrin Cozzens and Reed Harp, 146–153. Stillwater, Okla.: Southwest and Texas Popular Culture Association, 1990.

Rodríguez, Robert. *Rebel Without a Crew, or How a 23-year-old Film-maker with $7,000 Became a Hollywood Player*. New York: Penguin Books, 1995.

Romero, Yolanda. "Los Socios Del Sementerio (Sic): A Mexican-American Burial Society." *West Texas Historical Association Yearbook* 63 (1987): 123–130.

Romo, Ricardo. "An Insider's View of the Westside." In *Art Among Us/Arte Entre Nosotros*, edited by Pat Jasper and Kay Turner, 50–59. San Antonio: San Antonio Museum Association, 1986.

Rosaldo, Renato. "Politics, Patriarchs, and Laughter." In *The Nature and Context of Minority Discourse*, edited by Abdul R. JanMohamed and David Lloyd, 124–145. New York: Oxford University Press, 1990.

Rote, Carey. *César A. Martínez: A Retrospective*. San Antonio: Marion Koegler McNay Art Museum, University of Texas Press, 1999.

Rubel, Arthur J. "Concept of Diseases in Mexican American Culture." *American Anthropologist* 62.5 (1960): 795–814.

________. "The Mexican American *Palomilla*." *American Anthropologist* 67.4 (1965): 92–97.

Ruff, Ann. "Angel of Goliad." *Texas Highways* 33.8 (1986): 18–19.

Ruiz, Vicki L. "Oral History and La Mujer: The Rosa Guerrero Story." In *Women on the U.S.-Mexico Border: Responses to Change*, edited by Vicki L. Ruiz and Susan Tiano, 219–231. Boston: Allen and Unwin, 1987.

Russell, Rubye S. "Folklore of South Texas and Mexico." Master's thesis, Sul Ross State College, 1952.

Salcido, Joel. "Roma: Scenes From a Texas Town." *Texas Highways* 50 (January 2003): 38–45.

Salomon, Jeff. "Mex Appeal." *Texas Monthly* 27 (September 1999): 80–84.

Salvucci, Linda K. "Getting the Facts Straight: New Views of Mexico and Its Peoples in Recently Adopted U.S. History Textbooks in Texas." *Public Historian* 14.4 (1992): 57–69.

Sánchez, George I. "History, Culture, and Education." In *La Raza: Forgotten Americans*, edited by Julian Samora, 1–26. Notre Dame: University of Notre Dame Press, 1966.

Sánchez, Mario L., ed. *A Shared Experience: The History, Architecture and Historic Designations of the Lower Rio Grande Heritage Corridor*. Austin: Los Caminos del Río and Texas Historical Commission, 1991.

Sánchez, Sam Jr. "Los Portales in San Elizario." *Password* 41 (Fall 1996): 113–116.

Saunders, Lyle. *The Spanish-Speaking Population of Texas*. Austin: University of Texas Press, 1949.

Schement, Jorge Reina, and Ricardo Flores. "The Origins of Spanish Language Radio: The Case of San Antonio." *Journalism History* 4 (Summer 1977): 56–58, 61.

Schuetz, Mardith Keithly. "Professional Artisans in the Hispanic Southwest: The Churches of San Antonio, Texas." *Americas* 40.1 (July 1983): 17–71.

Schwetz, Edward M. *Spanish Missions of Texas—Views*. Austin: University of Texas Press, 1968.

Scott, Florence Johnson. *Historical Heritage of the Lower Rio Grande*. San Antonio: The Naylor Company, 1937.

________. "Customs and Superstitions among Texas Mexicans on the Rio Grande Border." In *Coffee in the Gourd*, edited by J. Frank Dobie, 75–84. Austin: Publications of the Texas Folklore Society, 1923.

Segulia, Frances. "Mi Jacalito." *Password* 21 (Fall 1976): 97–98.

Seriff, Suzanne K. "*Este soy yo*: The Politics of Representation of a Texas-Mexican Folk Artist." Ph.D. dissertation, University of Texas at Austin, 1989.

________. "Homages in Clay: The Fugural Ceramics of José Varela." In *Hecho en Tejas: Texas-Mexican Folk Arts and Crafts*, edited by Joe S. Graham, 146–171. Denton: University of North Texas Press, 1991.

Seriff, Suzanne K., and José Limón. "Bits and Pieces: The Mexican American Folk Aesthetic." In *Art Among Us/Arte Entre Nosotros*, edited by Pat Jasper and Kay Turner, 40–49. San Antonio: San Antonio Museum Association, 1986.

Silverthorne, Elizabeth. "Posadas, Pastores, and Piñatas: The Spanish-Mexican Heritage." In *Christmas in Texas*, by Elizabeth Silverthorne, 21–32. College Station: Texas A&M University Press, 1990.

Simmen, Edward. "Boyer Gonzales, Sr." In *The New Handbook of Texas,* edited by Ron Tyler, Douglas E. Barnett, Roy R. Barkley, Penelope C. Anderson, and Mark F. Odintz, vol. 3, 225–226. Austin: Texas State Historical Association, 1996.

________, ed. *North of the Rio Grande: The Mexican-American Experience in Short Fiction*. New York: Penguin Books, 1992.

Simmons, Ozzie G. "The Mutual Images as Expectations of Anglo Americans and Mexican Americans." *Daedalus* 90.2 (1961): 289–299.

Simons, Helen. "The Tex-Mex Menu." In *Hispanic Texas: A Historical Guide*, edited by Helen Simons and Cathryn A. Hoyt, 131–139. Austin: University of Texas Press, 1992.

Simons, Helen, and Roni Morales. "Churches, Chapels, and Shrines: Expressions of Hispanic Catholicism in Texas." In *Hispanic Texas: A Historical Guide*, edited by Helen Simons and Cathryn A. Hoyt, 107–119. Austin: University of Texas Press, 1992.

Sisneros, Samuel E. "The Casasola Legacy in El Paso." *Password* 47 (Spring 2002): 23–28.

Smith, Anita Torres. "*Descansos*: Markers to Heaven." *Journal of Big Bend Studies* 12 (2000): 259–269.

Smith, J. Griffis. "Flavors from Tenochtitlán to Texas: The Tejano Table." *Texas Highways* 49.9 (2002): 42–49.

Smith, Pamela A., and Elizabeth C. Ramírez. "Beatriz Escalona Pérez." In *The New Handbook of Texas,* edited by Ron Tyler, Douglas E. Barnett, Roy R. Barkley, Penelope C. Anderson, and Mark F. Odintz, vol. 2, 888–889. Austin: Texas State Historical Association, 1996.

Smith, Ralph A. "Poor Mexico, So Far From God and So Close to the Tejanos." *West Texas Historical Association Yearbook* 44 (1968): 78–105.

Spencer, Laura Gutiérrez. "The Desert Blooms: Flowered Songs by Pat Mora." *Bilingual Review/La Revista Bilingüe* 20.1 (1995): 28–36.

Spicer, Jacquelyn. "El Paso Murals." In *Folk Art in Texas*, edited by Francis E. Abernethy, 65–69. Dallas: Southern Methodist University Press, 1985.

Spielberg, Joseph. "Humor in the Mexican American *Palomilla*: Some Historical, Social, and Psychological Implications." *Revista Chicana-Riquena* 2 (1974): 41–50.

Steely, James W. Spanish Mission Revival in Twentieth-Century Architecture." In *Hispanic Texas: A Historical Guide*, edited by Helen Simons and Cathryn A. Hoyt, 95–105. Austin: University of Texas Press, 1992.

Stone, Michael C. "Lowriders." In *The New Handbook of Texas*, edited by Ron Tyler, Douglas E. Barnett, Roy R. Barkley, Penelope C. Anderson, and Mark F. Odintz, vol. 4, 316–317, Austin: Texas State Historical Association, 1996.

Studerus, Lenard H. "Mood Variability in Border Spanish." *Bilingual Review/La Revista Bilingüe* 20 (May-August 1995): 99–113.

Swenson, Ed. "Mexican American Tent Shows on Permanent Exhibit at Hertzberg Collection in San Antonio." *The White Tops* 71 (July/August 1998): 15.

Taboada, Antonio Prieto. "El Caso del la pistas culturales en *Partners in Crime*." *The Americas Review* 19 (Winter 1991): 117–132.

Tafolla, Carmen. *Curandera*. San Antonio: M&A Editions, 1983.

________. *To Split a Human: Mitos, Machos y la Mujer Chicana*. San Antonio: Mexican American Cultural Center, 1984.

Tan, Alexis S. "Evaluation of Newspapers and Television by Blacks and Mexican Americans." *Journalism Quarterly* 55.4 (1978): 673–681.

Tarver, Katherine Feild. "Los Pastores." Master's thesis, Southwestern University, 1926.

Torrans, Thomas. *The Magic Curtain: The Mexican American Border in Fiction, Film, and Song.* Fort Worth: Texas Christian University Press, 2002.

Torre, Chito de la. "Tejanos 'Main Squeeze' Turns Sixteen." *Hispanic* 10 (May 1997): 12–14.

Torres, Eliseo. *The Folk Healer: The Mexican-American Tradition of Curanderismo*. Kingsville, Tex.: Nieves Press, 1983.

Torres-Raines, Rosario. "The Mexican Origin of Rituals, Ceremonies, and Celebrations in South Texas." *South Texas Studies* 7 (1996): 131–163.

Treviño, Lee, and Sam Blair. *They Call Me Super Mex*. New York: Random House, 1983.

Treviño, Roberto R. "*Prensa y Patria*: The Spanish Language Press and the Biculturation of the Tejano Middle Class, 1920–1940." *Western Historical Quarterly* 22 (November 1991): 451–472.

Treviño, Rosa Nelia. "Home Altars in Zapata County, Texas." In *Tejano Folk Arts and Crafts*, edited by Joe S. Graham, 42–45. Kingsville, Tex.: John E. Conner Museum, 1989.

Trotter, Robert T. II, and Juan Antonio Chavira. *Curanderismo: Mexican American Folk Healing*. Athens: University of Georgia Press, 1981.

Tucker, Albert. "The Lost Communities of San Vicente." *West Texas Historical Association Yearbook* 72 (1996): 105–118.

Tunnell, Curtis, and Enrique Madrid. "*Coronas para los Muertos*: The Fine Art of Making Paper Flowers." In *Hecho en Tejas: Texas-Mexican Folk Arts and Crafts*, edited by Joe S. Graham, 131–145. Denton: University of North Texas Press, 1991.

________. "Exploring the West Texas Borderlands." In *Hispanic Texas: A Historical Guide*, edited by Helen Simons and Cathryn A. Hoyt, 77–94. Austin: University of Texas Press, 1992.

Turk, Judy Van Slyke, Jim Richstad, Robert L. Bryson Jr., and Sammye M. Johnson. "Hispanic Americans in the News in Two Southwestern Cities." *Journalism Quarterly* 66.1 (1989): 107–113.

Turner, Kay. "Mexican-American Women's Home Altars: The Art of Relationship." Ph.D. dissertation, University of Texas at Austin, 1990.

________. "The Cultural Semiotics of Religious Icons: La Virgen de San Juan de Los Lagos." *Semiotica* 47 (1983): 317–361.

________. "Mexican American Home Altars: Towards Their Interpretation." *Aztlán* 13 (1982): 309–326.

Turner, Kay, and Pat Jasper. *Day of the Dead: The Tex/Mex Tradition*. San Antonio: Guadalupe Cultural Arts Center, 1988.

________. "*La Casa, La Calle y La Esquina*: A Look at the Art Among Us." In *Art Among Us/Arte Entre Nosotros*, edited by Pat Jasper and Kay Turner, 10–39. San Antonio: San Antonio Museum Association, 1986.

Underwood, Marylyn. "The Ghost of Chipita: The Crying Woman of San Patricio." In *Legendary Ladies of Texas*, edited by Francis Edward Abernethy, 51–56. Dallas: E-Heart Press, 1981.

Vargas, George. "Border Artists in the Contemporary El Paso Mural Movement: Painting the New Frontier." In *Chicano Studies: Survey and Analysis*, edited by Dennis J. Bixler-Márquez, Carlos F. Ortega, Rosalía Solórzano Torres, and Lorenzo LaFarelle, 321–330. Dubuque, Iowa: Kendall/Hunt, 1999.

Vargas, Kathy. *Kathy Vargas: Photographs, 1971–2000*. San Antonio: Marion Koogler McNay Art Museum, 2000.

Vela, Chito. "Piñatas, Parades y Paletas: Mexican Fiestas." *Texas Highways* 49.9 (2002): 36–41.

Vela, Ofelia Z. "The Quilting Tradition in Zapata County." In *Tejano Folk Arts and Crafts*, edited by Joe S. Graham, 46–48. Kingsville, Tex.: John E. Conner Museum, 1989.

Vidaurri, Cynthia Lee. "The Mexican-American Religious Folk Arts Tradition in South Texas." Master's thesis, Texas A&I University, 1991.

________. "A Declaration of Faith." In *Tejano Folk Arts and Crafts*, edited by Joe S. Graham, 32–34. Kingsville, Tex.: John E. Conner Museum, 1989.

________. "Texas-Mexican Home Altars: Folk Art and Private Devotion." In *Out Near Phantom Hill*, edited by Darrin Cozzens and Reed Harp, 153–164. Stillwater, Okla.: Southwest and Texas Popular Culture Association, 1990.

________. "Texas-Mexican Religious Folk Art in Robstown, Texas." In *Hecho en Tejas: Texas-Mexican Folk Arts and Crafts*, edited by Joe S. Graham, 222–249. Denton: University of North Texas Press, 1991.

Vigil, Ralph H. "Inequality and Ideology in Borderlands Historiography." *Latin American Research Review* 29 (1994): 155–171.

Vila, Pablo Sergio. "Everyday Life, Culture, and Identity on the Mexican-American Border: The Ciudad Juárez–El Paso Case." Ph.D. dissertation, University of Texas at Austin, 1994.

Walraven, Edward Lee. "Ambivalent Americans: Selected Spanish-Language Newspapers' Response to Anglo Domination in Texas, 1830–1910." Ph.D. dissertation, Texas A&M University, 1999.

Watson, Walter T. "Mexicans in Dallas." *Southwest Review* 22.4 (July 1937): 406–420.

Waugh, Julia Nott. *The Silver Cradle: Las Posadas, Los Pastores, and Other Mexican American Traditions*. Originally published in 1955. Austin: University of Texas Press, 1988.

West, John O. *Mexican-American Folklore: Legends, Songs, Festivals, Proverbs, Crafts, Tales of Saints, of Revolutionaries, and More*. Little Rock: August House, 1988.

________. "Cultural Confusion on the Playground." *Journal of American Folklore* 84 (1971): 342–343.

________. "To Die Like a Man: The 'Good Outlaw' Tradition in the American Southwest." Ph.D. dissertation, University of Texas, Austin, 1964.

________. "Grutas at the Crossroads of the Spanish Southwest." *Password* 32 (Spring 1987): 3–12.

________. "Folk Grave Decorations Along the Rio Grande." In *Folk Art in Texas*, edited by Francis Edward Abernethy, 46–51. Dallas: Southern Methodist University Press, 1985.

________. "The Historian, the Folklorist, and Juan Diego." *Southwest Folklore* 4.1 (Winter 1980): 30–39.

________. "Mal Ojo." In *The Folklore of Texas Cultures*, edited by Francis Edward Abernethy, 82–83. Austin: Encino Press, 1974.

________. "The Weeping Woman: La Llorona." In *Legendary Ladies of Texas*, edited by Francis Edward Abernethy, 30–36. Second edition. Denton: University of North Texas Press, 1994.

West, John O., and Roberto González. "Adobe: Earth, Straw, and Water." In *Built in Texas*, edited by Francis E. Abernethy, 60–73. Waco: E-Heart Press, 1979.

Wheat, John. "'Los Pastores': Continuity and Change in a Texas-Mexican Nativity Drama." *Journal of Texas Catholic History and Culture* 5 (1994): 47–64.

Williams, Brett. "Why Migrant Women Feed Their Husbands Tamales: Foodways as a Basis for a Revisionist View of Tejano Family Life." In *Ethnic and Regional Foodways in the United States: The Performance of Group Identity*, edited by Linda Keller Brown and Kay Mussell, 113–126. Knoxville: University of Tennessee Press, 1984.

Williams, Norma. "Changes in Funeral Patterns and Gender Roles among Mexican Americans." In *Women on the U.S.-Mexico Border: Responses to Change*, edited by Vicki L. Ruiz and Susan Tiano, 197–217. Boston: Allen and Unwin, 1987.

Wittliff, William D., and Joe B. Frantz. "*Vaquero*: Genesis of the Texas Cowboy." In *The Folklore of Texan Cultures*, edited by Francis E. Abernethy, 65–68. Austin: Encino Press, 1974.

Winn, Conchita Hassell. "Spanish-language Newspapers." In *The New Handbook of Texas*, edited by Ron Tyler, Douglas E. Barnett, Roy R. Barkley, Penelope C. Anderson, and Mark F. Odintz, vol. 6, 4–5. Austin: Texas State Historical Association, 1996.

Wolff, Len. "*Charreada*: Rodeo Mexican-Style." *Texas Highways* 32 (April 1985): 12–15.

Woolley, Bryan. "La Vida del Charro." In *Charreada: Mexican Rodeo in Texas*, edited by Francis Edward Abernethy, 17–36. Denton: University of North Texas Press, 2002.

Wright, Pearl C. "Religious Fiestas in San Antonio." Master's thesis, St. Mary's University, 1946.

Wright, S. J. *San Antonio de Bexar: Historical, Traditional, Legendary*. Austin: Morgan Printing, 1916.

Ybarra-Frausto, Tomás. "La Chata Noloesca: Figura del Donaire." *Revista Chicano-Riquena* 11 (1983): 37–47.

Zamora, Emilio Jr. "Mutualist and Mexicanist Expressions of a Political Culture in Texas." In *Mexican Americans in Texas History,* edited by Emilio Zamora, Cynthia Orozco, and Rodolfo Rocha, 83–101. Austin: Texas State Historical Association, 2000.

Zavala, Charlcie Joan. "Bullfights on the Border: A History of Barrera Taurina, El Paso's Afficianado Club." *Password* 42 (Spring 1997): 39–52.

16. FOLKLORE

Folklore can be defined as the traditional legends, sayings, songs, tales, and customs of a people; originally they were passed on orally by song and story and captured more recently in print. Folklore can also be considered the study of these customs. For this compilation, we have selected our lists of works from folklore publications and journals, items by Tejano folklore scholars such as Américo Paredes, and works which include the word folklore (or similar name) in the title. Furthermore, the folklore must be set in Texas, or have a Texas theme, to be included in this section.

Los Pastores—photograph of the character Luzbel.
The Institute of Texan Cultures at UTSA, No. 70-293

Abernethy, Francis Edward. "Longino Guerrero's Corrido of J. Frank Dobie." In *Corners of Texas*, edited by Francis E. Abernethy, 197–200. Denton: University of North Texas Press, 1981.

________. "María de Agreda: The Lady in Blue." In *Legendary Ladies of Texas*, edited by Francis E. Abernethy, 9–14. Dallas: E-Heart Press, 1981.

________. "The Spanish on the Moral." In *The Folklore of Texan Cultures*, edited by Francis E. Abernethy, 27–39. Austin: Encino Press, 1974.

Aiken, Riley. *Folktales from the Borderland*. Dallas: Southern Methodist University Press, 1980.

________. "Fifteen Mexican Tales." In *A Good Tale and a Bonny Tune*, edited by Mody C. Boatright, Wilson M. Hudson, and Allen Maxwell, 3–56. Dallas: Southern Methodist University Press, 1964.

________. "A Pack Load of Mexican Tales." In *Puro Mexicano*, edited by J. Frank Dobie, 1–87. Austin: Texas Folklore Society, 1935.

________. "A Pack Load of Mexican Tales." In *Texas Folk and Folklore*, edited by Mody Boatright, Wilson M. Hudson, and Allen Maxwell, 24–38. Dallas: Southern Methodist University Press, 1954.

Arbuckle, H. C. III. "Don José and Don Pedrito." In *The Folklore of Texan Cultures*, edited by Francis E. Abernethy, 84–87. Austin: Encino Press, 1974.

Arnold, August. *The Folklore, Manners and Customs of the Mexicans in San Antonio, Texas*. San Francisco: R&E Research Associates, 1971.

________. "Folklore, Manners, and Customs of Mexicans in San Antonio, Texas." Master's thesis, University of Texas, Austin, 1927.

Arteaga, Alfred. "The Chicano-Mexican Corrido." *Journal of Ethnic Studies* 13 (Summer 1985): 75–107.

Azpiazu, Joseph. "Virgen de San Juan del Valle Shrine." In *The New Handbook of Texas*, edited by Ron Tyler, Douglas E. Barnett, Roy R. Barkley, Penelope C. Anderson, and Mark F. Odintz, vol. 6, 760. Austin: Texas State Historical Association, 1996.

Baracat, Robert A. "The Bear's Son Tale in Northern Mexico." Master's thesis, Texas Western College, 1964.

________. "The Bear's Son Tale in Northern Mexico." *Journal of American Folklore* 78 (October 1965): 330–336.

Bauman, Richard. "Differential Identity and the Social Base of Folklore." In *Toward New Perspectives in Folklore*, edited by Américo Paredes and Richard Bauman, 31–41. Austin: University of Texas Press, 1972.

Bloom, Maude McFie. "Holy Ghost Canyon." In *Puro Mexicano*, edited by J. Frank Dobie, 175–183. Austin: Texas Folklore Society, 1935.

Boatright, Mody C., ed. *Mexican Border Ballads and Other Lore*. Austin: Texas Folklore Society, 1946.

Carpenter, Ann. "Scratches on the Bedpost: Vestiges of the Lechuza." In *The Folklore of Texan Cultures*, edited by Francis E. Abernethy, 68–74. Austin: Encino Press, 1974.

Carrasco, Sara Margarita Campos. "Mexican American Folk Medicine: A Descriptive Study of the Different Curanderismo Techniques Practiced by Curanderos or Curanderas and Used by Patients in the Laredo, Texas Area." Ph.D. dissertation, Texas Woman's University, 1984.

Castillo, Arnulfo. "Charro Jiro Afamado." In *The Folklore of Texan Cultures*, edited by Francis E. Abernethy, 68–74. Austin: Encino Press, 1974.

Córdova, Gabriel. "Black and White Magic on the Texas-Mexican Border." In *Folk Travelers: Ballads, Tales, and Talk*, edited by Mody C. Boatright, Wilson M. Hudson, and Allen Maxwell, 195–199. Dallas: Southern Methodist University Press, 1953.

Cornell, Rebecca. "Tex Mex Dialect or Gidget Goes to Acuña." In *Between the Cracks of History: Essays on Teaching and Illustrating Folklore*, edited by Francis Edward Abernethy, 226–234. Dallas: University of North Texas Press, 1992.

Council, Kay Francine. "Exploratory Documentation of Texas Norteño-Conjunto Music." Master's thesis, University of Texas at Austin, 1978.

DeHuff, Elizabeth Willis. "The Metamorphosis of a Folk Tale." In *Puro Mexicano*, edited by J. Frank Dobie, 122–134. Austin: Texas Folklore Society, 1935.

Dinger, Adeline Short. *Folklife and Folklore of the Mexican Border*. Edinburg, Tex.: Hidalgo County Historical Society, 1974.

Dobie, J. Frank, ed. *Puro Mexicano*. Austin: Texas Folklore Society, 1935.

________. "The Battlefields of Palo Alto and Resaca de la Palma." In *Legends of Texas*, edited by J. Frank Dobie, 51–52. Hatboro, Penn.: Folklore Associates, 1964.

________. "Charm in Mexican Folktales." In *The Healer of Los Olmos and Other Mexican Lore*, edited by Wilson M. Hudson, 1–8. Austin: Texas Folklore Society, 1951.

________. "La Canción del Rancho de los Olmos." *Journal of American Folklore* 36 (1923): 192–196.

________. "How the Brazos Got Its Name." In *Legends of Texas*, edited by J. Frank Dobie, 209–217. Hatboro, Penn.: Folklore Associates, 1964.

________. "Legendary Spanish Forts Down the Nueces." In *Legends of Texas*, edited by J. Frank Dobie, 43–48. Hatboro, Penn.: Folklore Associates, 1964.

________. "The Silver Ledge on the Frio." In *Legends of Texas*, edited by J. Frank Dobie, 60–61. Hatboro, Penn.: Folklore Associates, 1964.

________. "Stories in Texas Place Names." In *Straight Texas*, edited by J. Frank Dobie, 5–27. Hatboro, Penn.: Folklore Associates, 1966.

________. "Tale of Two Companions." In *From Hell to Breakfast*, edited by Mody C. Boatright and Donald Day, 36–41. Dallas: Southern Methodist University Press, 1944.

________. "Treasure Legends of McMullen County." In *Legends of Texas*, edited by J. Frank Dobie, 28–42. Hatboro, Penn.: Folklore Associates, 1964.

________. "Versos de los Bandidos." In *Texas Folk and Folklore*, edited by Mody C. Boatright, Wilson M. Hudson, and Allen Maxwell, 143–146. Dallas: Southern Methodist University Press, 1957.

________. "Versos of the Texas Vaqueros." In *Happy Hunting Ground*, edited by J. Frank Dobie, 30–43. Originally printed 1925. Hatboro, Penn.: Folklore Associates, 1964.

________. "Weather Wisdom of the Texas-Mexican Border." In *Coffee in the Gourd*, edited by J. Frank Dobie, 87–99. Dallas: Southern Methodist University Press, 1923.

Dodson, Ruth. *Don Pedrito Jaramillo: Curandero.* San Antonio: Casa Editorial Lozano, 1934.

________. "The Curandero of Los Olmos." In *Texas Folk and Folklore*, edited by Mody C. Boatright, Wilson M. Hudson, and Allen Maxwell, 264–269. Dallas: Southern Methodist University Press, 1954.

________. "Don Pedrito Jaramillo: The Curandero of Los Olmos." In *The Healer of Los Olmos and Other Mexican Lore*, edited by Wilson M. Hudson, 9–70. Austin: Texas Folklore Society, 1951.

________. "Folk Curing Among the Mexicans." In *Cultural Differences in Medical Care*, edited by Robert H. Gemmill, 59–76. Ft. Sam Houston, Tex.: Academy of Health Sciences, 1972.

________. "Folk-Curing among the Mexicans." In *Tone the Bell Easy*, edited by J. Frank Dobie, 82–98. Austin: Texas Folklore Society, 1932.

________. "The Ghost Nun." In *Backwoods to Border*, edited by Mody C. Boatright and Donald Day, 137–139. Dallas: Southern Methodist University Press, 1943.

________. "The Ghost Nun." In *Texas Folk and Folklore*, edited by Mody C. Boatright, Wilson M. Hudson, and Allen Maxwell, 124–126. Dallas: Southern Methodist University Press, 1954.

________. "Texas-Mexican Horsebreaking." In *Mustangs and Cow Horses*, edited by J. Frank Dobie, Mody C. Boatright, and Harry H. Ransom, 269–290. Austin: Texas Folklore Society, 1940.

________. "Tortilla Making." In *In the Shadow of History*, edited by J. Frank Dobie, Mody C. Boatright, and Harry H. Ransom, 137–141. Austin: Texas Folklore Society, 1939.

Dorman, Artell. "Speak of the Devil." In *And Horns on the Toads*, edited by Mody C. Boatright, Wilson M. Hudson, and Allen Maxwell, 142–146. Dallas: Southern Methodist University Press, 1959.

Dorson, Richard M. "Southwest Mexicans." In *Buying the Wind: Regional Folklore in the United States*, edited by Richard M. Dorson, 415–495. Chicago: University of Chicago Press, 1964.

Duarte, Guadalupe. "Around the Fire with *mis Abuelitos*." In *Madstones and Twisters*, edited by Mody C. Boatright, Wilson M. Hudson, and Allen Maxwell, 154–159. Dallas: Southern Methodist University Press, 1958.

Durán, Gustavo. *14 Traditional Spanish Songs from Texas*. Washington, D.C.: Pan American Union, 1942.

Dwyer, Thomas A. "From Mustangs to Mules." In *Mustangs and Cow Horses*, edited by J. Frank Dobie, Mody C. Boatright, and Harry H. Ransom, 47–60. Austin: Texas Folklore Society, 1940.

Eddins, A. W. "La Casa de Santa Anna." In *Legends of Texas*, edited by J. Frank Dobie, 237–238. Hatboro, Penn.: Folklore Associates, 1964.

Eddins, A. W., and Mrs. Morgan Smith. "Wise Saws from Texas." In *Straight Texas*, edited by J. Frank Dobie, 239–244. Austin: Texas Folklore Society, 1937.

Escajeda, Josefina. "Tales from San Elizario." In *Puro Mexicano*, edited by J. Frank Dobie, 115–121. Austin: Texas Folklore Society, 1935.

Estrada, Marta. "Dichos from the Lower Valley." *Password* 40 (Fall 1995): 145–152.

Fuson, Robert H. "The Origin of the Word *Gringo*." In *Singers and Storytellers*, edited by Mody C. Boatright, Wilson M. Hudson, and Allen Maxwell, 282–284. Dallas: Southern Methodist University Press, 1961.

Gámiz, Everardo. "Legends from Durango." In *Puro Mexicano*, edited by J. Frank Dobie, 162–174. Austin: Texas Folklore Society, 1935.

García, Alfredo R. "Spanish Folklore from South Texas." In *Mesquite and Willow*, edited by Mody C. Boatright, Wilson M. Hudson, and Allen Maxwell, 187–191. Dallas: Southern Methodist University Press, 1957.

Garza, Humberto."Owl-Bewitchment in the Lower Rio Grande Valley." In *Singers and Storytellers*, edited by Mody C. Boatright, Wilson M. Hudson, and Allen Maxwell, 218–225. Dallas: Southern Methodist University Press, 1961.

Gilbreath, Essie Maude. "Some Superstitions and Folk Tales of the Kingsville Mexicans." Master's thesis, Texas College of Arts and Industries, 1938.

Glazer, Mark. *Flour from Another Sack and Other Proverbs, Folk Beliefs, Tales, Riddles, and Recipes*. Edinburg, Tex.: University of Texas–Pan American Press, 1994. Originally published in 1982.

________. "Continuity and Change in Legendry: Two Mexican-American Examples." In *Perspectives on Contemporary Legend*, edited by Paul Smith, 108–127. Sheffield, Eng.: Centre for English Cultural Tradition and Language, University of Sheffield, 1984.

________. "The Cultural Adaptation of a Rumour Legend: 'The Boyfriend's Death' in South Texas." In *Perspectives on Contemporary Legend*, edited by Gillian Bennett, Paul Smith, J. D. A. Widdowson, 93–108. Sheffield, Eng.: Sheffield Academy, 1987.

________. "Faith and Saints in Mexican American Folk Religion." In *More Studies in Brownsville History*, edited by Milo Kearney, 275–284. Brownsville, Tex.: Pan American University at Brownsville, 1989.

________. "'*La Llorona*' in South Texas: Tradition and Modernity in a Mexican American Legend." In *Plenary Papers: The 8th Congress for the International Society for Folk Narrative Research*, edited by Reimund Kvideland and Torunn Selberg, 205–212. Bergen, Nor.: International Society for Folk Narrative Research, 1985.

________. "The Mexican American Legend in the Lower Rio Grande Valley: An Overview." *Borderlands* 10 (Fall 1986): 143–160.

________. "The Rio Grande Folklore Archive: A Summary of Methods of Collection, Classification and of Holdings." *Southwest Folklore* 5 (Summer 1981): 16–23.

________. "'La Sirena del Mar': An Interpretation of Symbolism, Disobedience and Transformation in a Mexican-American Example." *Southwest Folklore* 5 (Winter 1981): 55–69.

González, Jovita Guerra (de Mireles). *Dew on the Thorn*, edited by José Limón. Houston: Arte Público Press, 1997.

________. *The Woman Who Lost Her Soul and Other Stories*, edited by Sergio Reyna. Houston: Arte Público Press, 1997.

________. "Among My People." In *Tone the Bell Easy*, edited by J. Frank Dobie, 99–108. Austin: Texas Folklore Society, 1932. Reprinted in *Mexican American Authors*, edited by Américo Paredes and Raymund Paredes, 8–16. Boston: Houghton Mifflin, 1976.

________. "The Bullet-Swallower." In *Puro Mexicano*, edited by J. Frank Dobie, 107–114. Austin: Texas Folklore Society, 1935.

________. "The Devil in Texas." In *A Treasury of Western Folklore*, edited by B. A. Botkin, 699–702. New York: Crown Publishers, 1951.

________. "Folklore of the Texas-Mexican Vaquero." In *Texas and Southwestern Folklore*, edited by J. Frank Dobie, 7–22. Austin: Texas Folklore Society, 1927.

________. "The Ghost of Las Chimineas." In *Texas Tales*, edited by David K. Sellars, 97–106. Dallas: Noble and Noble, 1955.

________. "The Mescal-Drinking Horse." In *Mustangs and Cow Horses*, edited by J. Frank Dobie, Mody C. Boatright, and Harry H. Ransom, 396–402. Austin: Texas Folklore Society, 1940.

________. "Shades of the Tenth Muse." In *Las obreras: Chicana Politics of Work and Family*, edited by Vicki L. Ruiz, 249–256. Los Angeles: UCLA Chicano Studies Research Center Publications, 2000.

________. "Stories of My People." In *Texas Folk and Folklore*, edited by Mody C. Boatright, Wilson M. Hudson, and Allen Maxwell, 19–24. Dallas: Southern Methodist University Press, 1954.

________. "Tales and Songs of the Texas-Mexicans." In *Man, Bird, and Beast*, edited by J. Frank Dobie, 86–116. Austin: Texas Folklore Society, 1930.

________. "With the Coming of the Barbwire Came Hunger: Folklore of the Texas-Mexican Vaquero." In *Aztlán: An Anthology of Mexican-American Literature*, edited by Luis Valdez and Stan Steiner, 81–83. New York: Alfred A. Knopf, 1972.

González, María del Refugío. "The Spanish Folklore of Webb and Zapata Counties." Master's thesis, University of Texas, Austin, 1952.

González, Rosalinda. "Work and Play on a Border Ranch." In *The Golden Log*, edited by Mody C. Boatright, Wilson M. Hudson, and Allen Maxwell, 141–155. Dallas: Southern Methodist University Press, 1962.

Goodwyn, Frank. "At a Branding Roundup." In *Backwoods to Border*, edited by Mody C. Boatright and Donald Day, 105–114. Dallas: Southern Methodist University Press, 1943.

________. "Ballad of Manuel Rodríguez." In *Mustangs and Cow Horses*, edited by J. Frank Dobie, Mody C. Boatright, and Harry H. Ransom, 304–306. Austin: Texas Folklore Society, 1940.

________. "El Toro Moro." In *Texas Folk and Folklore*, edited by Mody C. Boatright, Wilson M. Hudson, and Allen Maxwell, 147–149. Dallas: Southern Methodist University Press, 1954.

________. "Folklore of the King Ranch Mexicans." In *Southwestern Lore*, edited by J. Frank Dobie, 48–62. Dallas: Southwest Press, 1931.

Green, George K. "The *Corridos* of Mexican and South Texas: Modern Variations on Medieval Themes." In *More Studies in Brownsville History*, edited by Milo Kearney, 69–81. Brownsville, Tex.: Pan American University at Brownsville, 1989.

Guerra, Fermina. "Mexican and Spanish Folklore and Incidents in Southwest Texas." Master's thesis, University of Texas, Austin, 1941.

________. "Mexican Animals Tales." In *Backwoods to Border*, edited by Mody C. Boatright and Donald Day, 188–194. Dallas: Southern Methodist University Press, 1943.

________. "Rancho Buena Vista, Its Ways of Life and Traditions." In *Mexican American Authors*, edited by Américo Paredes and Raymund Paredes, 17–26. Boston: Houghton Mifflin, 1976. Originally published in *Texian Stomping Ground*, edited by J. Frank Dobie, Mody C. Boatright, and Harry H. Ransom, 59–77. Dallas: Southern Methodist University Press, 1941.

Guerra, Victor J. "Con Su Pluma en la Mano: The Legacy of Américo Paredes." *Hopscotch: A Cultural Review* 2.1 (2000): 86–91.

Hale, Meredith. "I Heard It on the Border." In *And Horns on the Toads*, edited by Mody C. Boatright, Wilson M. Hudson, and Allen Maxwell, 136–141. Dallas: Southern Methodist University Press, 1959.

Harwell, Thomas Meade. *Studies in Texas Folklore—Rio Grande Valley*. Lewiston, Penn.: Edward Mellen Press, 1997.

Hernández, Guillermo. "The Ballad of Gregorio Cortéz." *Critica* 1 (Spring 1985): 122–131.

Hiester, Miriam W. "*Los Paisanos*: Folklore of the Texas-Mexicans of the Lower Rio Grande Valley." Master's thesis, University of Texas, Austin, 1954.

________. "Tales of the Paisanos." In *Singers and Story Tellers*, edited by Mody C. Boatright, Wilson M. Hudson, and Allen Maxwell, 226–243. Dallas: Southern Methodist University Press, 1961.

"La Historia de Don Jacinto Treviño." *Magazin* 1 (September 1973): 14–26.

Holt, Roy. "Frijoles." In *Texian Stomping Grounds*, edited by J. Frank Dobie, Mody C. Boatright, and Harry H. Ransom, 49–58. Dallas: Southern Methodist University Press, 1941.

Hudson, Wilson M. "The Envious and the Envied *Compadres*." In *Mexican Border Ballads and Other Lore*, edited by Mody C. Boatright, Wilson M. Hudson, and Allen Maxwell, 35–42. Dallas: Southern Methodist University Press, 1946.

________. "The Fisherman and the Snake of Many Colors." In *The Healer of Los Olmos and Other Mexican Lore*, edited by Wilson M. Hudson, 132–136. Dallas: Southern Methodist University Press, 1951.

________. "To Whom God Wishes to Give He Will Give." In *The Healer of Los Olmos and Other Mexican Lore*, edited by Wilson M. Hudson, 128–132. Dallas: Southern Methodist University Press, 1951.

________, ed. *The Healer of Los Olmos and Other Mexican Lore*. Dallas: Southern Methodist University Press, 1951.

Huie, Jorge Green. "*Los Corridos Sudtejanos: Nuestra tradición milenaria*." In *Still More Studies in Brownsville History*, edited by Milo Kearney, 163–166. Brownsville, Tex.: The University of Texas at Brownsville, 1991.

Hurley, Elizabeth. "Come Buy, Come Buy." In *Folk Travelers: Ballads, Tales, and Talk*, edited by Mody C. Boatright, Wilson M. Hudson, and Allen Maxwell, 115–138. Dallas: Southern Methodist University Press, 1953.

Jiménez, Baldemar. "Cuentos de Susto." In *Golden Log*, edited by Mody C. Boatright, Wilson M. Hudson, and Allen Maxwell, 155–164. Dallas: Southern Methodist University Press, 1962.

Jordan, Rosan A. "Tension and Speech Play in Mexican-American Folklore." In "*And Other Neighborly Names*"*: Social Process and Cultural Image in Texas Folklore*, edited by Richard Bauman and Roger D. Abrahams, 252–265. Austin: University of Texas Press, 1981.

Kincaid, Edgar B. "The Mexican *Pastor*." In *Southwestern Lore*, edited by J. Frank Dobie, 63–68. Dallas: Southwest Press, 1931.

Lea, Aurora Lucero-White. *Literary Folklore of the Hispanic Southwest*. San Antonio: The Naylor Company, 1953.

Madsen, William. "Value Conflict and Folk Psychology in South Texas." In *Magic, Faith, and Healing*, edited by Ari Kiev, 420–440. New York: Free Press, 1964.

McNeil, Norman Laird ("Brownie"). "Mexican Border Ballads." Master's thesis, University of Texas, Austin, 1944.

________. "El Contrabando del Paso." In *Texas Folk and Folklore*, edited by Mody C. Boatright, Wilson M. Hudson, and Allen Maxwell, 152–156. Dallas: Southern Methodist University Press, 1954.

________. "Corrido de Kansas." In *Texas Folk and Folklore*, edited by Mody C. Boatright, Wilson M. Hudson, and Allen Maxwell, 150–151. Dallas: Southern Methodist University Press, 1954.

________. "Corridos of the Mexican Border." In *Mexican Border Ballads and Other Lore*, edited by Mody C. Boatright, 1–34. Dallas: Southern Methodist University Press, 1946.

________. "*Curanderos* of South Texas." In *And Horns on the Toads*, edited by Mody C. Boatright, Wilson M. Hudson, and Allen Maxwell, 32–44. Dallas: Southern Methodist University Press, 1959.

________. "Haymarket Plaza." In *The Sky is my Tipi*, edited by Mody C. Boatright, 168–178. Dallas: Southern Methodist University Press, 1949.

Miles, Elton. *More Tales of the Big Bend*. College Station: Texas A&M University Press, 1988.

________. *Stray Tales of the Big Bend*. College Station: Texas A&M University Press, 1993.

________. *Tales of the Big Bend*. College Station: Texas A&M University Press, 1976.

________. "Chisos Ghosts." In *Madstones and Twisters*, edited by Mody C. Boatright, Wilson M. Hudson, and Allen Maxwell, 106–122. Dallas: Southern Methodist University Press, 1958.

________. "The Corridos of the Big Bend." In *Sonovagun Stew: A Folklore Miscellany*, edited by Francis E. Abernethy, 36–47. Dallas: Southern Methodist University Press, 1985.

________. "The Devil in the Big Bend." In *Folk Travelers: Ballads, Tales, and Talk*, edited by Mody C. Boatright, Wilson M. Hudson, and Allen Maxwell, 205–216. Dallas: Southern Methodist University Press, 1953.

Mindiola, Tatcho Jr. "El Corrido de Gregorio Cortéz." *Southwest Media Review* 3 (Spring 1985): 52–56.

Mora, Joaquín. "Songs the Vaqueros Sing." In *Southwestern Lore*, edited by J. Frank Dobie, 118–123. Dallas: Southwest Press, 1931.

Nolen, Oran Warder. "Some Odd Mexican Customs." In *From Hell to Breakfast*, edited by Mody C. Boatright and Donald Day, 57–59. Dallas: Southern Methodist University Press, 1944.

Orozco, Cynthia E. "Emilia Wilhelmina Schunior Ramírez." In *The New Handbook of Texas,* edited by Ron Tyler, Douglas E. Barnett, Roy R. Barkley, Penelope C. Anderson, and Mark F. Odintz, vol. 5, 423. Austin: Texas State Historical Association, 1996.

________. "Fermina Guerra." In *The New Handbook of Texas,* edited by Ron Tyler, Douglas E. Barnett, Roy R. Barkley, Penelope C. Anderson, and Mark F. Odintz, vol. 3, 368. Austin: Texas State Historical Association, 1996.

________. "Josefina Escadeja." In *The New Handbook of Texas,* edited by Ron Tyler, Douglas E. Barnett, Roy R. Barkley, Penelope C. Anderson, and Mark F. Odintz, vol. 2, 887. Austin: Texas State Historical Association, 1996.

________. "María Elena Zamora O'Shea." In *The New Handbook of Texas,* edited by Ron Tyler, Douglas E. Barnett, Roy R. Barkley, Penelope C. Anderson, and Mark F. Odintz, vol. 4, 1176–1177. Austin: Texas State Historical Association, 1996.

Orozco, Cynthia E., and Teresa Palomo Acosta. "Jovita González de Mireles." In *The New Handbook of Texas,* edited by Ron Tyler, Douglas E. Barnett, Roy R. Barkley, Penelope C. Anderson, and Mark F. Odintz, vol. 3, 236–237. Austin: Texas State Historical Association, 1996.

O'Shea, Elena Zamora. *El Mesquite, A Story of the Early Spanish Settlements between the Nueces and the Rio Grande as Told by "La Posta del Palo Alto."* Dallas: Mathis Publishing, 1935.

Paredes, Américo. *Folklore and Culture on the Texas-Mexican Border*, edited by Richard Bauman. Austin: Center for Mexican American Studies, 1993.

________. *The Hammon and the Beans and Other Stories*. Houston: Arte Público Press, 1994.

________. *"With His Pistol in His Hand": A Border Ballad and Its Hero*. Austin: University of Texas Press, 1958.

________. *Uncle Remus con chile*. Houston: Arte Público Press, 1993.

________. "The Bury-Me-Not Theme in the Southwest." In *And Horns on the Toads*, edited by Mody C. Boatright, Wilson M. Hudson, and Allen Maxwell, 88–92. Dallas: Southern Methodist University Press, 1959.

________. "El Corrido de Gregorio Cortéz: A Ballad of Border Conflict." Ph.D. dissertaton, University of Texas, Austin, 1956.

________. "Folklore and History." In *Singers and Storytellers*, edited by Mody C. Boatright, William H. Hudson, and Allen Maxwell, 56–68. Dallas: Southern Methodist University Press, 1961.

________. "The Hammon and the Beans." In *The Chicano: From Caricature to Self-portrait*, edited by Edward Simmen, 274–278. New York: New American Library, 1971.

________. "The Legend of Gregorio Cortéz." In *Mexican American Authors*, edited by Américo Paredes and Raymund Paredes, 35–50. Boston: Houghton Mifflin, 1976. Originally published in *Mesquite and Willow*, edited by Mody C. Boatright, Wilson M. Hudson, and Allen Maxwell, 3–22. Dallas: Southern Methodist University Press, 1957.

________. "The Love Tragedy in Texas-Mexican Balladry." In *Folk Travelers: Ballads, Tales, and Talk*, edited by Mody C. Boatright, William M. Hudson, and Allen Maxwell, 110–114. Dallas: Southern Methodist University Press, 1953.

________. "The Mexican *Corrido*: Its Rise and Fall." In *Madstones and Twisters*, edited by Mody C. Boatright, Wilson M. Hudson, and Allen Maxwell, 91–105. Dallas: Southern Methodist University Press, 1958.

________. "On *Gringo, Greaser*, and Other Neighborly Names." In *Singers and Storytellers*, edited by Mody C. Boatright, Wilson M. Hudson, and Allen Maxwell, 285–290. Dallas: Southern Methodist University Press, 1961.

________. "Pastorela to celebrate the Birth of Our Lord Jesus Christ." In *Buying the Wind: Regional Folklore in the United States*, edited by Richard M. Dorson, 453–454. Chicago: University of Chicago Press, 1964.

________. "The United States, Mexico, and *Machismo*." In *Folklore and Culture on the Texas-Mexican Border*, edited by Richard Bauman, 3–18. Austin: CMAS Books, 1993.

________. "The Where and Why of Folklore." *Illinois History* 23.4 (1970): 75–76.

Paredes, Américo, and Richard Bauman, eds. *Toward New Perspectives in Folklore*. Austin: University of Texas Press, 1972.

Parks, H. B. "Buried in Bexar County." In *Southwestern Lore*, edited by J. Frank Dobie, 133–141. Hatboro, Penn.: Folklore Associates, 1965.

Perales, Alonso M. "Violeta and the Owls." In *The Folklore of Texan Cultures*, edited by Frances Edward Abernethy, 78–81. Austin: Encino Press, 1974.

Peregrino, José Flores. *Mesquitierra*. Albuquerque: Pajarito Publications, 1977.

Pérez, Soledad. "Mexican Folklore From Austin." Master's thesis, University of Texas, Austin, 1949.

________. "Dichos from Austin." In *Texas Folk and Folklore*, edited by Mody C. Boatright, Wilson M. Hudson, and Allen Maxwell, 223–229. Dallas: Southern Methodist University Press, 1954.

________. "Mexican Folklore from Austin." In *The Healer of Los Olmos and Other Mexican Lore*, edited by Mody C. Boatright, Wilson M. Hudson, and Allen Maxwell, 71–127. Dallas: Southern Methodist University Press, 1951.

________. "Ratoncito Pérez." In *Texas Folk and Folklore*, edited by Mody C. Boatright, Wilson M. Hudson, and Allen Maxwell, 77–79. Dallas: Southern Methodist University Press, 1954.

________. "Susto." In *Texas Folk and Folklore*, edited by Mody C. Boatright, Wilson M. Hudson, and Allen Maxwell, 270–272. Dallas: Southern Methodist University Press, 1954.

________. "The Weeping Woman." In *Texas Folk and Folklore*, edited by Mody C. Boatright, Wilson M. Hudson, and Allen Maxwell, 127–130. Dallas: Southern Methodist University Press, 1954.

Phillips, Juanita Stroud. *Hispanic Folklore in the Rio Grande Valley of Texas*. Bloomington, Ind.: 1st Books Library, 2001.

________. "The Spanish Folklore of Cameron County, Texas." Master's thesis, University of Texas, Austin, 1950.

Ramírez, Emilia Schunior. *Ranch Life in Hidalgo County after 1850*. Edinburg, Tex.: New Santander Press, 1971.

Reyna, José R. *Raza Humor: Chicano Joke Tradition in Texas*. San Antonio: Penca Books, 1980.

________. "Chicano Folklore: Raza Humor in Texas." *De Colores* 1.4 (1975): 58–65.

Richard, J. A. "Riddles of Texas Mexican Children." In *Backwoods to Border*, edited by J. Frank Dobie, 181–187. Dallas: Southern Methodist University Press, 1940.

Roach, Joyce Gibson. "The Legend of El Tejano, the Texan Who Never Was." *Western Folklore* 27 (1968): 33–42.

Robinson, G. C. "Mustangs and Mustanging in Southwest Texas." In *Mustangs and Cow Horses*, edited by J. Frank Dobie, Mody C. Boatright, and Harry H. Ransom, 3–21. Dallas: Southern Methodist University Press, 1940.

Russell, Rubye S. "Folklore of South Texas and Mexico." Master's thesis, Sul Ross State College, 1952.

Scott, Florence Johnson. "Customs and Superstitions among Texas Mexicans on the Rio Grande Border." In *Coffee in the Gourd*, edited by J. Frank Dobie, 75–84. Austin: Publications of the Texas Folklore Society, 1923.

Seriff, Suzanne Katherine. "'Este Soy Yo': The Politics of Representation of a Texas-Mexican Folk Artist." Ph.D. dissertation, University of Texas at Austin, 1989.

Shotwell, Clayton Moore Jr. "The Chicano Popular '*Corrido*' in Texas (1955–1985): A Musical Study of Commercially Produced '*Corrido*' Tunes." Ph.D. dissertation, University of Minnesota, 1987.

Shumard, Malnor Jr. "Mexican Folk-Escapades and Tales." In *Coyote Wisdom*, edited by J. Frank Dobie, Mody C. Boatright, and Harry H. Ransom, 234–240. Dallas: Southern Methodist University Press, 1938.

Smith, Honora DeBusk. "Mexican Plazas Along the River of Souls." In *Southwestern Lore*, edited by J. Frank Dobie, 69–84. Dallas: Southwest Press, 1931.

Sonnichsen, Charles L. "Mexican Ghosts from El Paso." In *Texas Folk and Folklore*, edited by Mody C. Boatright, Wilson M. Hudson, and Allen Maxwell, 118–123. Dallas: Southern Methodist University Press, 1954.

________. "Mexican Spooks from El Paso." In *Straight Texas*, edited by J. Frank Dobie and Mody C. Boatright, 120–129. Austin: Texas Folklore Society, 1937.

Spielberg, Joseph, and Antonio N. Zavaleta. "Historic Folk Sainthood along the Texas-Mexico Border." In *Studies in Matamoros and Cameron County History*, edited by Milo Kearney, Anthony Knopp, and Antonio Zavaleta, 347–375. Brownsville, Tex.: The University of Brownsville and Texas Southmost College, 1997.

Stoker, Catherine J. "The Flaming Flower." In *Puro Mexicano*, edited by J. Frank Dobie, 143–152. Austin: Texas Folklore Society, 1935.

Storm, Dan. "The Little Animals of Mexico." In *Coyote Wisdom*, edited by J. Frank Dobie, Mody C. Boatright, and Harry H. Ransom, 18–35. Dallas: Southern Methodist University Press, 1938.

________. "The Little Animals." In *Texas Folk and Folklore*, edited by Mody C. Boatright, Wilson M. Hudson, and Allen Maxwell, 39–45. Dallas: Southern Methodist University Press, 1954.

________. "The *Pastor* and the Serpent." In *In the Shadow of History*, edited by J. Frank Dobie, Mody C. Boatright, and Harry H. Ransom, 122–133. Hatboro, Penn.: Folklore Associates, 1966.

________. "The Wonderful *Chirrionera*." In *Puro Mexicano*, edited by J. Frank Dobie, 88–100. Austin: Texas Folklore Society, 1935.

Storm, Joe. "Sons of the Devil." In *Puro Mexicano*, edited by J. Frank Dobie, 190–193. Austin: Texas Folklore Society, 1935.

Sutherland, Mary A. "Pedro and Pancho." In *Coffee in the Gourd*, edited by J. Frank Dobie, 85–86. Dallas: Southern Methodist University Press, 1923.

________. "Treasure Chest on the Nueces." In *Legends of Texas*, edited by J. Frank Dobie, 49–51. Hatboro, Penn.: Folklore Associates, 1964.

Sutherland, Tucker. "Ghost Stories from a Texas Ghost Town." In *Singers and Story Tellers*, edited by Mody C. Boatright, Wilson M. Hudson, and Allen Maxwell, 115–122. Dallas: Southern Methodist University Press, 1961.

Taylor, Hugh McGehee. "How the Tehuana Women Became Handsome." In *Puro Mexicano*, edited by J. Frank Dobie, 135–142. Austin: Texas Folklore Society, 1935.

________. "The Little White Dog." In *Puro Mexicano*, edited by J. Frank Dobie, 201–210. Austin: Texas Folklore Society, 1935.

Torres, Eliseo. *The Folk Healer: The Mexican American Tradition of Curanderismo*. Kingsville, Tex.: Nieves Press, 1983.

Van Stone, Mary R., and E. R. Sims. "Canto del Niño Perdido." In *Spur-of-the-Cock*, edited by J. Frank Dobie, 48–89. Dallas: Southern Methodist University Press, 1933.

Ward, Hortense Warner. "Yellow Flower of Death." In *The Sky is my Tipi*, edited by Mody C. Boatright, 155–167. Dallas: Southern Methodist University Press, 1949.

Washington, Ann Reed. "Christmas Folklorico." In *Roots by the River*, by Valley By-Liners, 321–324. Mission, Tex.: Border Kingdom Press, 1978.

Wesley, Howard D. "Ranchero Sayings of the Border." In *Puro Mexicano*, edited by J. Frank Dobie, 211–220. Austin: Texas Folklore Society, 1935.

West, John O. *Mexican-American Folklore: Legends, Songs, Festivals, Proverbs, Crafts, Tales of Saints, of Revolutionaries, and More*. Little Rock: August House, 1988.

________. "*La Llorona*." In *The New Handbook of Texas*, edited by Ron Tyler, Douglas E. Barnett, Roy R. Barkley, Penelope C. Anderson, and Mark F. Odintz, vol. 4, 36–37. Austin: Texas State Historical Association, 1996.

________. "*Mal Ojo*." In *The Folklore of Texas Cultures*, edited by Francis Edward Abernethy, 82–83. Austin: Encino Press, 1974.

________. "The Weeping Woman: *La Llorona*." In *Legendary Ladies of Texas*, edited by Francis Edward Abernethy, 30–36. Second edition. Denton: University of North Texas Press, 1994.

Whatley, W. A. "The Mexican Folk Version of King Midas." In *In the Shadow of History*, edited by J. Frank Dobie, Mody C. Boatright, and Harry H. Ransom, 134–136. Austin: Texas Folk-Lore Society, 1939.

________. "A Mexican Popular Ballad." In *Happy Hunting Ground*, edited by J. Frank Dobie, 10–17. Austin: Texas Folklore Society, 1925.

________. "Mexican Munchausen." In *From Hell to Breakfast*, edited by Mody C. Boatright and Donald Day, 42–56. Dallas: Southern Methodist University Press, 1944.

Wood, Ben D. "A Mexican Border Ballad." In *Round the Levee*, edited by Stith Thompson, 55–57. Austin: Texas Folk-lore Society, 1916.

Woodhull, Frost. "Juan García Goes to Heaven." In *Puro Mexicano*, edited by J. Frank Dobie, 152–158. Austin: Texas Folklore Society, 1935.

Woolley, Bryan. "La Vida del Charro." In *Charreada: Mexican Rodeo in Texas*, edited by Francis Edward Abernethy, 17–36. Denton: University of North Texas Press, 2002.

17. LITERATURE

In this chapter we include works of poetry, drama, fiction (novels and short stories) as well as literary criticism. The works must be written about Tejanos or set in the Lone Star State. For literary criticism, authors are included if they are Tejanos, even though their works are broader in scope or set in some other state or nation. As a reminder, we define Tejanos as persons of Mexican descent who reside in Texas.

Doroteo Maldonado as a boy of about 8;
studio portrait of him standing on a new moon studio prop, ca. 1910.
A resident of San Diego, Texas.
The Institute of Texan Cultures at UTSA, No. 96-127
Courtesy of Maria E. Garza

Abernethy, Francis Edward. "The Spanish on the Moral." In *The Folklore of Texan Cultures*, edited by Francis E. Abernethy, 27–39. Austin: Encino Press, 1974.

Ables, L. Robert. "Adina Emilia de Zavala." In *The Handbook of Texas: A Supplement*, edited by Eldon Stephen Branda, vol. 3, 242–243. Austin: Texas State Historical Association, 1976.

________. "Adina Emilia de Zavala." In *The New Handbook of Texas*, edited by Ron Tyler, Douglas E. Barnett, Roy R. Barkley, Penelope C. Anderson, and Mark F. Odintz, vol. 6, 1146–1147. Austin: Texas State Historical Association, 1996.

Acosta, Teresa Palomo. *Nile and Other Poems*. Austin: Red Salmon Press, 1999.

________. *Passing Time*. Austin: privately printed, 1984.

________. "Chicano Literary Renaissance." In *The New Handbook of Texas*, edited by Ron Tyler, Douglas E. Barnett, Roy R. Barkley, Penelope C. Anderson, and Mark F. Odintz, vol. 2, 71–72. Austin: Texas State Historical Association, 1996.

________. "Sara Estela Ramírez." In *The New Handbook of Texas*, edited by Ron Tyler, Douglas E. Barnett, Roy R. Barkley, Penelope C. Anderson, and Mark F. Odintz, vol. 5, 424. Austin: Texas State Historical Association, 1996.

________. "Work." In *Texas Short Stories 2*, edited by Billy Bob Hill and Laurie Champion, 217–219. Dallas: Browder Springs Books, 2000.

Aguilar-Henson, Marcella. *The Multi-faceted Poetic World of Angela de Hoyos*. Austin: Relámpago Press, 1985.

________. "Angela de Hoyos and Ricardo Sánchez: A Thematic, Stylistic, and Linguistic Analysis of Two Chicano Poets." Ph.D. dissertation, University of New Mexico, 1982.

Akers, John. "From Translation to Rewriting: Rolando Hinojosa's *The Valley*." *The Americas Review* 21 (Spring 1993): 91–102.

Alarcón, Justo. "Las metamorfosis del diablo en *El Diablo en Texas* de Aristeo Brito." *De Colores* 5 (1980): 30–44.

Alarcón, Norma. "Interview with Pat Mora." *Third Woman* 3.1 (1985–1986): 121–126.

Alonzo, Adela. "*Sabor a Mí*/Savor Me." In *Common Bonds: Stories By and About Modern Texas Women*, edited by Suzanne Comer, 177–178. Dallas: Southern Methodist University Press, 1990.

Andrus, Pearl. *Juana, A Spanish Girl in Central Texas*. Burnet: Eakin Press, 1982.

Anzaldúa, Gloria. *Borderlands/La Frontera: The New Mestiza*. San Francisco: Aunt Lute, 1987.

________. "La Prieta." In *This Bridge Called My Back: Writings By Radical Women of Color*, edited by Cherríe Moraga and Gloria Anzaldúa, 198–209. Watertown, Mass.: Persephone Press, 1981.

Arrizón, Alicia. "Josefina Mona Niggli." In *The New Handbook of Texas*, edited by Ron Tyler, Douglas E. Barnett, Roy R. Barkley, Penelope C. Anderson, and Mark F. Odintz, vol. 4, 1013–1014. Austin: Texas State Historical Association, 1996.

________. "The Mexican American Stage: La Chata Noloesca and Josefina Niggli." In *Latina Performance: Traversing the Stage*, by Alicia Arrizón, 29–72. Bloomington: Indiana University Press, 1999.

Barrera, Aida. *Looking for Carrascolendas: From a Child's World to Award-Winning Television.* Austin: University of Texas Press, 2001.

Barsun, Helen W. "Los Pastores: A Remnant of Medieval Drama in San Antonio." Master's thesis, St. Mary's University, 1943.

Bertrand, Diane Gonzales. *Close to the Heart.* Houston: Arte Público Press, 2002.

________. *The Last Doll/La última muñeca*. Houston: Arte Público Press, 2000.

________. *Trino's Choice*. Houston: Arte Público Press, 1999.

________. *Trino's Time*. Houston: Arte Público Press, 2001.

Brito, Aristeo. *El Diablo en Texas*. Originally published Editorial Peregrinos (Tuscon), 1976. Tempe, Ariz.: Bilingual Review/Press 1990.

Broyles, Yolanda Julia. "Hinojosa's *Klail City y sus alrededores*: Oral Culture and Print Culture." In *The Rolando Hinojosa Reader*, edited by José David Saldivar, 109–132. Houston: Arte Público Press, 1984.

Bruce-Novoa, Juan. "Who's Killing Whom in Belken County: Rolando Hinojosa's Narrative Production." *Monographic Review/Revista Monográfica* 3 (1987): 288–297.

Calderón, Hector. "The Novel and the Community of Readers: Rereading Tomás Rivera's . . . *y no se lo trago la tierra*." In *Criticism in the Boderlands: Studies in Chicano Literature, Culture, and Ideology*, edited by Hector Calderón and José David Saldivar, 97–113. Durham: Duke University Press, 1991.

Canales, Viola. *Orange Candy Slices and Other Secret Tales*. Houston: Arte Público Press, 2001.

Candelaria, Nash. "The Border." *Bilingual Review/La Revista Bilingüe* 21.3 (1996): 241–253.

Cantú, Norma Elia. *Canicula: Snapshots of a Girlhood en la Frontera*. Albuquerque: University of New Mexico Press, 1995.

________. "The Offering and the Offerers: A Generic Illocation of a Laredo 'Pastorela' in the Tradition of Shepherds' Plays." Ph.D. dissertation, University of Nebraska, Lincoln,1982.

________. "Pastoras and Malinches: Women in a Traditional Folk Drama of Laredo, Texas." In *Recovering the U. S. Hispanic Literary Heritage*, edited by José F. Aranda Jr. and Silvio Torres-Saillant, vol. 4, 172–183. Houston: Arte Público Press, 2002.

Cárdenas de Dwyer, Carlota. "Chicano Literature: A Convergence of Cultures." *English in Texas* 10 (Winter 1978): 29–31.

Cárdenas, Reyes. *Get Your Tortillas Together.* San Antonio: M&A Editions, 1976.

________. "Anti-carnalismo." *Caracol* 3 (November 1976): 10.

________. "The Machismo Manifesto." *Caracol* 2 (April 1976): 7.

Carrillo, Leonardo, ed. *Canto al Pueblo: An Anthology of Experiences*. San Antonio: Penca Books, 1978.

Carr, Pat. "An El Paso Idyll." In *Her Works: Stories by Texas Women*, edited by Lou Halsell Rodenberger, 34–49. Bryan, Tex.: Shearer Publishing, 1982.

Castillo, Rafael. *Distant Journey*. Tempe, Ariz.: Bilingual Review/Press, 1991.

________. "The Penitent of Guadalupe Street." In *New Growth/2: Contemporary Short Stories by Texas Writers*, edited by Mark Busby, 17–28. San Antonio: Corona Publishing, 1993.

Castro, Donald F. "Chicano Literature: A Bibliographical Essay." *English in Texas* 7 (Summer 1976): 14–19.

Catacalos, Rosemary. *Again for the First Time*. Santa Fe: Tooth of Time Press, 1984.

________. *As Long As It Takes*. Springfield, Mo.: Iguana Press, 1984.

Chabrán, Richard, and Rafael Chabrán, eds. "Aristeo Brito." In *The Latino Encyclopedia*, edited by Richard Chabrán and Rafael Chabrán, vol. 1, 200. New York: Marshall Cavendish, 1996.

________. "Américo Paredes." In *The Latino Encyclopedia*, edited by Richard Chabrán and Rafael Chabrán, vol. 4, 1204. New York: Marshall Cavendish, 1996.

________. "Philip D. Ortego y Gasca." In *The Latino Encyclopedia*, edited by Richard Chabrán and Rafael Chabrán, vol. 4, 1184. New York: Marshall Cavendish, 1996.

________. "Ricardo Sánchez." In *The Latino Encyclopedia*, edited by Richard Chabrán and Rafael Chabrán, vol. 5, 1434. New York: Marshall Cavendish, 1996.

________. "Rolando Hinojosa." In *The Latino Encyclopedia*, edited by Richard Chabrán and Rafael Chabrán, vol. 3, 759. New York: Marshall Cavendish, 1996.

________. "Tomás Rivera." In *The Latino Encyclopedia*, edited by Richard Chabrán and Rafael Chabrán, vol. 5, 1397. New York: Marshall Cavendish, 1996.

Chávez, Denise. *Face of an Angel.* Houston: Arte Público Press, 1991. Reprint, New York: Farrar, Straus, and Giroux, 1994.

________. "The Closet." *The Americas Review* 14 (Spring 1986): 7–18.

________. "The McCoy Hotel." In *North of the Rio Grande: The Mexican-American Experience in Short Fiction*, edited by Edward Simmen, 413–428. New York: Mentor Book, 1992.

________. "The Wedding." In *Daughters of the Fifth Sun: A Collection of Latina Fiction and Poetry*, edited by Bryce Milligan, Mary Guerrero Milligan, and Angela de Hoyos, 27–39. New York: Riverhead Books, 1995.

Chávez, John R. "The Image of the Southwest in the Chicano Novel, 1970–1979." *Bilingual Review/La Revista Bilingüe* 14.3 (1987–1988): 41–56.

Cisneros, Sandra. *Woman Hollering Creek and Other Stories*. New York: Random House, 1991.

________. "Cactus Flowers: In Search of Tejana Feminist Poetry." *Third Woman* 3 (1986): 73–80.

________. "Do You Know Me?: I Wrote *The House on Mango Street*." *The Americas Review* 15 (Spring 1987): 77–79.

________. "Eyes of Zapata." In *Daughters of the Fifth Sun: A Collection of Latina Fiction and Poetry*, edited by Bryce Milligan, Mary Guerrero Milligan, and Angela de Hoyos, 147–178. New York: Riverhead Books, 1995.

Cole, M. R. *Los Pastores: A Mexican Miracle Play*. New York: Publications of the American Folklore Society, 1907.

Contreras, Sheila Marie. "A Mestizo Account: Teresa Palomo Acosta's Questions to a Spanish Grandmother." In *Reflexiones 1998: New Directions in Mexican American Studies*, edited by Yolanda C. Padilla, 103–122. Austin: CMAS Books, 1999.

Cortéz, Emiliano Carlos. "Teaching the Short Story in Spanish: Literary Analysis and Commentary." Ph.D. dissertation, University of North Texas, 1995.

Cortéz, Sarah, and Naomi Shihab Nye. *How to Undress a Cop: Poems*. Houston: Arte Público Press, 2000.

Cotera, María Eugenia. "Engendering a 'Dialectics of Our America': Jovita González's Pluralist Dialogue as Feminist Testimonio." In *Las obreras: Chicana Politics of Work and Family*, edited by Vicki L. Ruiz, 237–248. Los Angeles: UCLA Chicano Studies Research Center Publications, 2000.

Degollado, Rubén. "Not the Truth (I John 1:6–9)." In *Texas Short Stories*, edited by Billy Bob Hill, 289–297. Dallas: Browder Springs Publishing, 1997.

________. "Romanos 6:23." *Bilingual Review/La Revista Bilingüe* 22.1 (1997): 69–70.

De Herrera, Luis. "A Spin of the Zodiac Wheel." In *Texas Short Stories 2*, edited by Billy Bob Hill and Laurie Champion, 887–900. Dallas: Browder Springs Books, 2000.

de Hoyos, Angela. *Arise, Chicano! And Other Poems*. San Antonio: M&A Editions, 1975.

________. *Chicano Poems for the Barrio*. Bloomington, Ind.: Backstage Books, 1975.

________. *Selected Poems/Selecciónes*. San Antonio: Dezkalzo Press, 1979.

________. *Woman, Woman*. Houston: Arte Público Press, 1985.

de la Fuente, Patricia. "Invisible Women in the Narrative of Tomás Rivera." *Revista Chicano-Riqueña* 13 (1986): 81–89.

de la Garza, Beatriz. *The Candy Vendor's Boy and Other Stories*. Houston: Arte Público Press, 1994.

________. *Pillars of Gold and Silver*. Houston: Arte Público Press, 1997.

de la Torre, Alfredo. *Caracoleando*: *Poesia*. San Antonio: M&A Editions, 1979.

de Mireles, Jovita González. See Jovita González.

Detweiler, Louise. "The Question of Cultural Difference and Gender Oppression in Estela Portillo Trambley's *The Day of the Swallow*." *Bilingual Review/La Revista Bilingüe* 21.2 (1996): 146–152.

De Zavala, Adina. *History and Legends of the Alamo and Other Missions in and around San Antonio*, edited by Richard Flores. Houston: Arte Público Press, 1996.

Díaz, Gwendolyn. "Angela de Hoyos." In *The Chicano Writers First Series, Dictionary of Literary Biography*, edited by Francisco A. Lomelí and Carl R. Shirley, vol. 82, 140–144. Detroit: Gale Research, 1989.

Esparza, Laura. "An Unreasonable Woman." *The Americas Review* 23 (Fall 1995): 75–80.

Esparza, Phylis. "La Llamada." In *Corazón del Norte: A Selection of North Texas Latino Writing*, edited by Bryce Milligan, 11–15. San Antonio: Wings Press, 1996.

Espinoza, Mary Louise. "Rolando Hinojosa's Klail City Death Trip Series as a Historical Novel of Place." Master's thesis, California State University at Long Beach, 1991.

Fast, Robin Riley. "Nature and Creative Power: Pat Mora and Patricia Hampl." *San José Studies* 14.2 (1989): 29–40.

Fernández, Roberta. *Fronterizos: Una Novela en Seis Cuentos*. Houston: Arte Público Press, 2001.

________. *Intaglio: A Novel in Six Stories*. Houston: Arte Público Press, 1990.

________. "Amanda." In *Short Fiction by Hispanic Writers of the United States*, edited by Nicolás Kanellos, 31–38. Houston: Arte Público Press, 1993.

________. "Fermina." In *Barrios and Borderlands: Cultures of Latinos and Latinas in the United States*, edited by Denis Lynn Daly Heyck, 97–111. New York: Routledge, 1994.

________. "Latino Literature in the United States: A Resource Guide and Selected Bibliography for Teachers, Librarians and General Readers." *Texas Journal of Ideas, History and Culture* 17 (Fall/Winter 1994): 48–58.

Flores, Carlos Nicolás. "Friend of a Minor Poet." In *Texas Short Fiction: A World In Itself*, edited by Mike Hennech and Billy Bob Hill, 43–65. Fort Worth: ALE Publishing, 1993.

________. "Smeltertown." In *North of the Rio Grande: The Mexican-American Experience in Short Fiction*, edited by Edward Simmen, 390–411. New York: Mentor Book, 1992. Also printed in *Pieces of the Heart: New Chicano Fiction*, edited by Gary Soto, 63–80. San Francisco: Chronicle Books, 1993.

________. "Yellow Flowers." *Cuentos Chicanos: A Short Story Anthology*, edited by Rudolfo Anaya and Antonio Márquez, 69–91. Albuquerque: University of New Mexico Press, 1984.

Flores, Guadalupe. "By Baby, the Chupacabra." In *Texas Short Stories 2*, edited by Billy Bob Hill and Laurie Champion, 71–80. Dallas: Browder Springs Books, 2000.

Flores, Noé E. "A Study on the Status of Chicano Literature in Selected Texas Secondary Schools." Ed.D. dissertation, Texas A&I University, 1979.

Fox, Linda C. "From *Chants* to *Borders* to *Communion*: Pat Mora's Poetic Journey to *Nepantla*." *Bilingual Review/La Revista Bilingüe* 21.3 (1996): 219–230.

Fredericksen, Brooke. "Cuando lleguemos/When we arrive: The Paradox of Migration in Tomás Rivera's ' . . . *y se lo tragó la tierra*.'" *Bilingual Review/La Revista Bilingüe* 19 (May-August 1994): 142–150.

Galaviz, Victoria García. "Victoria García Galaviz." In *This Promiscuous Light: Young Women Poets of San Antonio*, edited by Bryce Milligan, 15–28. San Antonio: Wings Press, 1996.

Galindo, Mary Sue. *Icy Watermelon/Sandía Fría*. Houston: Arte Público Press, 2001.

Gámez, Rocky. "Enedina Pascasio." In *Common Bonds: Stories By and About Modern Texas Women*, edited by Suzanne Comer, 179–182. Dallas: Southern Methodist University Press, 1990.

García-Camarillo, Cecilio. *Selected Poetry*. Houston: Arte Público Press, 2000.

García, Edward H. "Joseph's Bones." In *Texas Short Stories 2*, edited by Billy Bob Hill and Laurie Champion, 841–848. Dallas: Browder Springs Books, 2000.

García, Lionel G. *Hardscrub*. Houston: Arte Público Press, 1989.

________. *I Can Hear the Cowbells Ring*. Houston: Arte Público Press, 1994.

________. *Leaving Home*. Houston: Arte Público Press, 1985.

________. *A Shroud in the Family*. Houston: Arte Público Press, 1987.

________. *To a Widow with Children*. Houston: Arte Público Press, 1994.

________. "The Apparition." In *North of the Rio Grande: The Mexican-American Experience in Short Fiction*, edited by Edward Simmen, 279–310. New York: Mentor Book, 1992.

________. "The Day They Took My Uncle." In *Short Fiction by Hispanic Writers of the United States*, edited by Nicolás Kanellos, 53–61. Houston: Arte Público Press, 1993.

________. "The Ringing of the Bell." *Texas Journal of Ideas, History and Culture* 20 (Fall/Winter 1997): 28–31.

________. "Three A.M." *¡Tex!* (1999).

________. "Tutoring Amnesty." In *New Growth: Contemporary Short Stories by Texas Writers*, edited by Lyman Grant, 133–136. San Antonio: Corona Publishing, 1989.

________. "Mr. Tyrone." In *Texas Short Stories 2*, edited by Billy Bob Hill and Laurie Champion, 819–828. Dallas: Browder Springs Books, 2000.

García-Zapata, Victoria. *Peace in the Corazón*. San Antonio: Wings Press, 1999.

Garza, Carmen Lomas. *Family Pictures/Cuadros de familia*. San Francisco: Children's Book Press, 1990.

________. *In My Family/En mi familia*. San Francisco: Children's Book Press, 1996.

Garza, Cheo. *Capirotada*. San Antonio: Trucha Publications, 1980.

Garza, Daniel L. "Saturday Belongs to the Palomía." In *North of the Rio Grande: The Mexican-American Experience in Short Fiction*, edited by Edward Simmen, 154–159. New York: Mentor Book, 1992.

________. "Stripper Whirlwind: The *Pizcadores* and the Machines." In *The Chicanos: Mexican American Voices*, edited by Ed Ludwig and James Santibañez, 31–36. New York: Penguin Books, 1971.

________. "A Rosary for Santos." In *Yearnings: Mexican-American Literature*, edited by Albert C. Chávez, 110–124. West Haven, Conn.: Pendulum Press, 1972.

Garza-Falcón, Leticia M. *Gente Decente*. Austin: University of Texas Press, 1998.

________. "Américo Paredes' Narratives of Resistance: Property, Labor, Education, Gender, and Class Relations." In *Gente Decente: A Borderlands Response to the Rhetoric of Dominance*, by Leticia M. Garza-Falcón, 156–197. Austin: University of Texas Press, 1998.

________. "Cycles of Solitude in the Narratives of the Texas-Mexican Borderlands." *Journal of the West* 40 (Spring 2001): 42–49.

________. "The Historical Fiction of Jovita González: Complex and Competing Class Identities." In *Gente Decente: A Borderlands Response to the Rhetoric of Dominance*, by Leticia M. Garza-Falcón, 74–132. Austin: University of Texas Press, 1998.

________. "María Cristina Mena's 'Elite', Fermina Guerra's 'Folk': The Struggles of Their Distinct and Converging Worlds." In *Gente Decente: A Borderlands Response to the Rhetoric of Dominance*, by Leticia M. Garza-Falcón, 133–155. Austin: University of Texas Press, 1998.

________. "The Texas History of Beatriz de la Garza's Narratives: Sustaining Women, Hispanic Heroes, and a Sense of Place." In *Gente Decente: A Borderlands Response to the Rhetoric of Dominance*, by Leticia M. Garza-Falcón, 215–238. Austin: University of Texas Press, 1998.

Gaspar de Alba, Alicia. *The Mystery of Survival and Other Stories*. Tempe, Ariz.: Bilingual Review/Press, 1993.

________. "Beggar on the Cordoba Bridge." In *Three Times a Woman: Chicana Poetry*, edited by Alicia Gaspar de Alba, María Herrera-Sobek, and Demetria Martínez, 1–50. Tempe, Ariz.: Bilingual Review/Press, 1989.

Gilb, Dagoberto. *The Magic of Blood*. Albuquerque: University of New Mexico Press, 1993.

________. "Getting a Job in Dell City." In *New Growth: Contemporary Short Stories by Texas Writers*, edited by Lyman Grant, 15–25. San Antonio: Corona Publishing, 1989.

________. "I Danced with the Prettiest Girl." In *New Growth/2: Contemporary Short Stories by Texas Writers*, edited by Mark Busby, 91–99. San Antonio: Corona Publishing, 1993.

Glover, Joyce Lee. *Rolando Hinojosa and the American Dream*. Denton: University of North Texas Press, 1997.

Gómez, Rogelio R. "The Aztecs are Coming." In *North of the Rio Grande: The Mexican-American Experience in Short Fiction*, edited by Edward Simmen, 350–356. New York: Mentor Book, 1992.

________. "The Way It Is." In *New Growth: Contemporary Short Stories by Texas Writers*, edited by Lyman Grant, 219–232. San Antonio: Corona Publishing, 1989.

Gómez-Vega, Ibis. "La Tortillera." *Bilingual Review/La Revista Bilingüe* 25 (2000): 306–314.

Gonzales, Rebecca. *Slow Work to the Rhythm of Cicadas*. Fort Worth: Prickly Pear Press, 1985.

González, Barbara Renaud. "Mother's Day." In *Living Chicano Theory*, edited by Carla Trujillo, 435–437. Berkeley: Third Woman Press, 1998.

________. "To My Unborn Daughter: Tejana Poetry." *La Voz de Esperanza* (March 1999): 7, 9.

González, D. Scott. "Manantial." In *Corazón del Norte: A Selection of North Texas Latino Writing*, edited by Bryce Milligan, 26–34 . San Antonio: Wings Press, 1996.

González, Genaro. *Only Sons*. Houston: Arte Público Press, 1991.

________. *The Quixote Cult*. Houston: Arte Público Press, 1998.

________. *Rainbow's End*. Houston: Arte Público Press, 1988.

________."Un hijo del sol." In *The Chicano: From Caricature to Self-Portrait*, edited by Edward Simmen, 308–316. New York: New American Library, 1970.

________. "Too Much His Father's Son." In *Short Fiction by Hispanic Writers of the United States*, edited by Nicolás Kanellos, 65–70. Houston: Arte Público Press, 1993.

González, John M. "Terms of Engagement: Nation or Patriarchy in Jovita González's and Eve Raleigh's *Caballero*." In *Recovering the U.S. Hispanic Literary Heritage*, edited by José F. Aranda, Jr. and Silvio Torres-Saillant, vol. 4, 264–276. Houston: Arte Público Press, 2002.

González, Jovita Guerra (de Mireles). *Dew on the Thorn*, edited by José Limón. Houston: Arte Público Press, 1997.

________. *The Woman Who Lost Her Soul and Other Stories*, edited by Sergio Reyna. Houston: Arte Público Press, 1997.

________. "America Invades the Border Towns." *Southwest Review* 15 (1930): 468–477.

________. "Among My People." *Southwest Review* 17 (1932): 179–187.

________. "The Bullet-Swallower." In *Puro Mexicano*, edited by J. Frank Dobie, 107–114. Austin: Texas Folklore Society, 1935.

________. "The Devil in Texas." In *A Treasury of Western Folklore*, edited by B. A. Botkin, 699–702. New York: Crown Publishers, 1951.

________. "Stories of My People." In *Texas Folk and Folklore*, edited by Mody C. Boatright, Wilson M. Hudson, and Allen Maxwell, 19–24. Dallas: Southern Methodist University Press, 1954.

González, Jovita, and Eve Raleigh. *Caballero: An Historical Novel*, edited by José E. Limón and María Cotera. College Station: Texas A&M University Press, 1996.

Grajeda, Ralph. "Tomás Rivera's Appropriation of the Chicano Past." In *Modern Chicano Writers: A Collection of Critical Essays*, edited by Joseph Sommers and Tomás Ybarra-Frausto, 74–85. Englewood Cliffs, N.J.: Prentice-Hall, 1979.

Granado, Ramón Roberto. "Green Guaraches." In *The Bicentennial Collection of Texas Short Stories*, edited by James P. White, 86–90. Odessa, Tex.: privately printed, 1974.

Grevel, Laura Hawkins. "La Vida de Eduardo." In *New Texas 95*, edited by Kathryn S. McGuire and James Ward Lee, 189–194. Denton: Center for Texas Studies, 1995.

Griffith, Albert J. "The Scion, the Señorita, and the Texas Ranch Epic: Hispanic Images in Film." *Bilingual Review/La Revista Bilingüe* 16 (January-April 1991): 15–22.

Guerra, Victor J. "Con Su Pluma en la Mano: The Legacy of Américo Paredes." *Hopscotch: A Cultural Review* 2.1 (2000): 86–91.

Gurasich, Marj. *Benito and the White Dove: A Story of José Antonio Navarro*. Austin: Eakin Press, 1989.

Guzmán, Celeste. *Cande, te estoy llamando*. San Antonio: Wings Press, 1999.

Hart, Elva Treviño. *Barefoot Heart: Stories of a Migrant Child*. Tempe, Ariz.: Bilingual Press/Editorial Bilingüe, 1999.

Hatch, Sheila Sánchez. *Guadalupe and the Kaleidoscopic Screamer*. San Antonio: Wings Press, 1996.

________. "Sin Palabras." In *Daughters of the Fifth Sun: A Collection of Latina Fiction and Poetry*, edited by Bryce Milligan, Mary Guerrero Milligan, and Angela de Hoyos, 138–143. New York: Riverhead Books, 1995.

________, ed. *Tierra Norte: A Collection of Works from North Tejas*. San Antonio: M&A Editions, 1994.

Hazlerig, Jack O. "Conde." In *Texas Short Fiction: A World In Itself*, edited by Mike Hennech and Billy Bob Hill, 3–15. Fort Worth: ALE Publishing, 1993.

Hernández, Guillermo. "Rolando Hinojosa: Klail City Death Trip Series." In *Chicano Satire: A Study in Literary Culture*, by Guillermo Hernández, 85–111. Austin: University of Texas Press, 1991.

Hernández, Irene Beltrán. *Across the Great River*. Houston: Arte Público Press, 1989.

________. *Heartbeat, Drumbeat*. Houston: Arte Público Press, 1992.

________. *The Secret of the Brothers*. Houston: Piñata Books, 1995.

Hernández, Jo Ann Yolanda. "White Bread Competition." In *New Texas 95*, edited by Kathryn S. McGuire and James Ward Lee, 167–174. Denton: Center for Texas Studies, 1995.

Hernández-Tovar, Inés. "Sara Estela Ramírez: The Early Twentieth Century Texas-Mexican Poet." Ph.D dissertation, University of Houston, 1984.

________. *Con razón Corazón*. San Antonio: M&A Editions, 1987.

________. "Sara Estela Ramírez, Sembradora." *Legacy: A Journal of Nineteenth Century Women Writers* 6 (1989): 13–26.

________, ed. *Hembra: Hermanas en movimiento brotando raices de Aztlán*. Austin: Center for Mexican American Studies, University of Texas at Austin, 1976.

Herrera-Sobek, María. *Chicana Creativity and Criticism: Charting New Frontiers in American Literature*. Houston: Arte Público Press, 1988.

________. *The Mexican Corrido: A Feminist Analysis*. Bloomington: Indiana University Press, 1990.

________. "Américo Paredes: A Tribute." *Mexican Studies* 16 (Summer 2000): 239–266.

________. "The Devil in the Discotheque: A Semiotic Analysis of a Contemporary Legend." In *Monsters with Iron Teeth: Perspectives on Contemporary Legend*, edited by Gillian Bennett and Paul Smith, 147–158. Sheffield, Eng.: Sheffield Academic Press, n.d.

________. "Naked Moon/Luna desnuda." In *Three Times a Woman: Chicana Poetry*, edited by Alicia Gaspar de Alba, María Herrera-Sobek, and Demetria Martínez, 51–100. Tempe, Ariz.: Bilingual Review/Press, 1989.

Hinojosa-Smith, Rolando R. *Los amigos de Becky*. Houston: Arte Público Press, 1991.

________. *Ask a Policeman: A Rafe Buenrostro Mystery*. Houston: Arte Público Press, 1998.

________. *Becky and Her Friends*. Houston: Arte Público Press, 1989.

________. *Claros varones de Belken: Fair Gentlemen of Belken County*. Tempe, Ariz.: Bilingual Review/Press, 1986.

________. *Dear Rafe*. Houston: Arte Público Press, 1985.

________. *Estampas del valle y otras obras: Sketches of the Valley and Other Works*. Berkeley: Quinto Sol, 1973.

________. *Generaciones y semblanzas*, translated by Rosaura Sánchez. Berkeley: Editorial Justa Publications, 1977.

________. *Klail City: A Novel*. Houston: Arte Público Press, 1987.

________. *Klail City y sus alrededores*. La Habana: Casa de las Américas, 1976.

________. *Korean Love Songs*. Berkeley: Justa, 1978.

________. *This Migrant Earth*. Houston: Arte Público Press, 1987.

________. *Mi querido Rafa*. Houston: Arte Público Press, 1981.

________. *Partners in Crime: A Rafe Buenrostro Mystery*. Houston: Arte Público Press, 1985.

________. *Rites and Witnesses: A Comedy*. Houston: Arte Público Press, 1982.

________. *Useless Servants*. Houston: Arte Público Press, 1993.

________. *The Valley*. Ypsilanti, Mich.: Bilingual Review/Press, 1983.

________. "Borges's Dagger." In *Texas Short Stories 2*, edited by Billy Bob Hill and Laurie Champion, 253–255. Dallas: Browder Springs Books, 2000.

________. "In the Pit with Bruno Cano." In *North of the Rio Grande: The Mexican-American Experience in Short Fiction*, edited by Edward Simmen, 230–235. New York: Mentor Book, 1992.

________. "Es el Agua." In *Reflexiones 1999: New Directions in Mexican American Studies*, edited by Richard R. Flores, 149–152. Austin: CMAS Books, 1999.

________. "Sweet Fifteen." *Texas Monthly* 16 (1988): 96–99. Reprinted in *Barrios and Borderlands: Cultures of Latinos and Latinas in the United States*, edited by Denis Lynn Daly Heyck, 35–36. New York: Routledge, 1994.

________. "Tomás Rivera." In *The New Handbook of Texas*, edited by Ron Tyler, Douglas E. Barnett, Roy R. Barkley, Penelope C. Anderson, and Mark F. Odintz, vol. 5, 597–598. Austin: Texas State Historical Association, 1996.

________. "A Sense of Place." *Texas Journal of Ideas, History, and Culture* 17.1 (1994): 18–21.

________. "A Voice of One's Own." In *The Rolando Hinojosa Reader: Essays Historical and Critical*, edited by José David Saldivar, 11–17. Houston: Arte Público Press, 1985.

________. "This Writer's Sense of Place." In *The Texas Literary Tradition: Fiction, Folklore, History*, edited by Don Graham, James W. Lee, and William Pilkington, 120–124. Austin: College of Liberal Arts, University of Texas at Austin, Texas State Historical Association, 1983.

Hixon, Adelyn. "The Superbly Encompassing 'Arte Público' Publications and Mission Earn Great Press." *Hispanic Outlook in Higher Education* 10 (May 5, 2000): 39–41.

Hughes, Mary Gray. "The Deserter." In *Her Works: Stories by Texas Women*, edited by Lou Halsell Rodenberger, 126–136. Bryan, Tex.: Shearer Publishing, 1982.

________. "The Judge." In *North of the Rio Grande: The Mexican-American Experience in Short Fiction*, edited by Edward Simmen, 196–211. New York: Mentor Book, 1992.

________. "Luz." In *Common Bonds: Stories By and About Modern Texas Women*, edited by Suzanne Comer, 228–238. Dallas: Southern Methodist University Press, 1990.

Hunter, Mai Francis. "*Los Pastores*, Spanish American Play of the Nativity Preserved in the Vicinity of Corpus Christi, Texas." Master's thesis, Texas College of Arts and Industries, 1940.

Islas, Arturo. *Migrant Souls*. New York: Morrow, 1990.

________. *The Rain God*. Palo Alto, Calif.: Alexandrian Press, 1985.

________. "Rain Dancer." In *North of the Rio Grande: The Mexican-American Experience in Short Fiction*, edited by Edward Simmen, 330–349. New York: Mentor Book, 1992.

Jackson, Guida. "The Evil Eye." In *New Growth: Contemporary Short Stories by Texas Writers*, edited by Lyman Grant, 170–180. San Antonio: Corona Publishing, 1989.

________. "The Umbilical Cord." In *New Texas 91: Poetry and Fiction*, edited by James Ward Lee, 79–84. Denton: Center for Texas Studies, 1991.

Jason, Philip K. "A Conversation with Rolando Hinojosa." *Bilingual Review/La Revista Bilingüe* 25 (2000): 298–305.

Jones, Nancy Baker. "Leonor Villegas de Magnón." In *The New Handbook of Texas*, edited by Ron Tyler, Douglas E. Barnett, Roy R. Barkley, Penelope C.

Anderson, and Mark F. Odintz, vol. 6, 753–754. Austin: Texas State Historical Association, 1996.

Juárez, Tina. *Call No Man Master.* Houston: Arte Público Press, 1995.

________. *South Wind Come*. Houston: Arte Público Press, 1998.

Kanellos, Nicolás, and Luis Davila, eds. *Los Tejanos*. Special issue of *Revista Chicano Riqueña* 8 (Autumn 1980).

Keller, Gary D. (El Huitlacoche). "A Chicano FBI Searching for Carmen Loca in ¡Sal Si Puedes!." *Bilingual Review/La Revista Bilingüe* 16 (1991): 197–210.

________. "The Mojado Who Offered Up His Tapeworms to the Public Weal." In *Zapata Rose in 1992 and Other Tales*, by Gary D. Keller, 12–33. Tempe, Ariz.: Maize Press, 1992.

________. "Papi Invented the Automatic Jumping Bean." In *Zapata Rose in 1992 and Other Tales*, by Gary D. Keller, 1–11. Tempe, Ariz.: Maize Press, 1992.

Kreneck, Thomas H. "Recovering the 'Lost' Manuscripts of Jovita González." *Texas Library Journal* 74 (Summer 1998): 76–79.

Lattin, Vernon E. "Novelist Structure and Myth in '. . . *y no se lo tragó la tierra*.'" *Bilingual Review/La Revista Bilingüe* 10 (September-December 1982): 220–226.

Lattin, Vernon E., Rolando Hinojosa, and Gary D. Keller, eds. *Tomás Rivera, 1935–1984 The Man and His Works*. Tempe: Bilingual Review/Press, 1988.

Lea, Aurora Lucero-White. *Literary Folklore of the Hispanic Southwest*. San Antonio: Naylor Company, 1953.

Leal, Luis. "Américo Paredes and Modern Mexican American Scholarship." *Ethnic Affairs* 1 (Fall 1987): 1–11.

Lee, Joyce Glover. *Rolando Hinojosa and the American Dream*. Denton: University of North Texas Press, 1997.

Libretti, Tim. "'We Can Starve Too': Américo Paredes' *George Washington Gómez* and the Proletarian *Corrido*." In *Recovering the U.S. Hispanic Literary Heritage*, vol. 2, edited by Erlinda Gonzales-Berry and Chuck Taylor, 118–130. Houston: Arte Público Press, 1996.

Limón, José. "Folklore, Gender Repression, and Cultural Critique: The Case of Jovita González." *Texas Studies in Literature and Art* 35 (Winter 1993): 453–473.

________. "Perspective from the South." *Discovery: Research and Scholarship at the University of Texas at Austin* 8 (Winter 1983): 25–29.

________. "With a Corrido in His Heart: Américo Paredes is the Top Chicano Scholar." *Nuestro* 3 (September 1979): 40–42.

Lomelí, Francisco A. "Tomás Rivera: The Writer as Creator of Community." *Vortex: A Critical Review* 1 (Spring 1986): 5–6, 13–14.

Martínez, Eliud. "Personal Vision in the Short Stories of Estela Portillo Trambley." In *Beyond Stereotypes: The Critical Analysis of Chicana Literature*, edited by María Herrera-Sobek, 71–90. Binghamton, N.Y.: Bilingual Press/Editorial Bilingüe, 1985.

Martínez, Manuel Luis. "Visiting the Dead." *Bilingual Review/La Revista Bilingüe* 23.1 (1998): 50–60.

Martínez, Max. *The Adventures of the Chicano Kid and Other Stories*. Houston: Arte Público Press, 1982.

________. *Layover*. Houston: Arte Público Press, 1997.

________. *A Red Bikini Dream*. Houston: Arte Público Press, 1990.

________. *Schoolland*. Houston: Arte Público Press, 1988.

________. *White Leg*. Houston: Arte Público Press, 1996.

________. "Faustino." In *Short Fiction by Hispanic Writers of the United States*, edited by Nicolás Kanellos, 83–121. Houston: Arte Público Press, 1993.

Martín-Rodríguez, Manuel M. *Rolando Hinojosa y su "cronicón" chicano: Una novela del lector*. Sevilla: Universidad de Sevilla, 1993.

________. "Klail City Death Trip Series de Rolando Hinojosa: La novela del lector." Ph.D. dissertation, University of California at Santa Barbara, 1990.

________. "Rolando Hinojosa y su 'Klail City Death Trip Series': Una Novela del lector." *The Americas Review* 21 (Summer 1993): 89–101.

McKenna, Teresa. "Engendering the Border: Toward a Chicana Literary Aesthetic." In *Migrant Song: Politics and Process in Contemporary Chicano Literature*, edited by Teresa McKenna, 104–125. Austin: University of Texas Press, 1997.

________. "Power Reversals and the Comic: Rolando Hinojosa as a Political Writer." In *Migrant Song: Politics and Process in Contemporary Chicano Literature*, edited by Teresa McKenna, 72–103. Austin: University of Texas Press, 1997.

Meier, Matt S. with Conchita Franco Serri and Richard A. García. "Américo Paredes." In *Notable Latino Americans: A Biographical Dictionary*, by Matt S. Meier, 293–296. Westport, Conn.: Greenwood Press, 1997.

________."Sandra Cisneros." In *Notable Latino Americans: A Biographical Dictionary*, by Matt S. Meier, 87–91. Westport, Conn.: Greenwood Press, 1997.

________."Rolando Hinojosa Smith." In *Notable Latino Americans: A Biographical Dictionary*, by Matt S. Meier, 198–202. Westport, Conn.: Greenwood Press, 1997.

________."Tomás Rivera." In *Notable Latino Americans: A Biographical Dictionary*, by Matt S. Meier, 317–320. Westport, Conn.: Greenwood Press, 1997.

Mena, María Cristina. "The Education of Popo." In *North of the Rio Grande: The Mexican-American Experience in Short Fiction*, edited by Edward Simmen, 68–84. New York: Mentor Book, 1992.

Meyer, Nicholas E. "Tomás Rivera." In *The Biographical Dictionary of Hispanic Americans*, by Nicholas E. Meyer, 189–191. New York: Facts on File, 1997.

Milligan, Bryce, ed. *Corazón del Norte: A Selection of North Texas Latino Writing*. San Antonio: Wings Press, 1996.

________. "Ever Radical: A Survey of Tejana Writers." In *Texas Women Writers: A Tradition of Their Own*, edited by Sylvia Ann Grider and Lou Halsell Rodenberger, 207–246. College Station: Texas A&M University Press, 1997.

Milligan, Mary Guerrero. "Lotería: La Rosa." In *Daughters of the Fifth Sun: A Collection of Latina Fiction and Poetry*, edited by Bryce Milligan, Mary Guerrero Milligan, and Angela de Hoyos, 248–253. New York: Riverhead Books, 1995.

Mohr, Nicholasa. "An Awakening in Summer 1956." *The Americas Review* 20 (Fall/Winter 1992): 14–19.

Morales, Alejandro. *La verdad sin voz*. Mexico City: Editorial Joaquín Mortiz, 1979.

Mora, Pat. *Agua, Agua, Agua*. Glenview, Ill.: Good Year Books, 1994.

________. *Agua santa: Holy Water*. Boston: Beacon Press, 1995.

________. *All My Family*. Columbus, Ohio: McGraw-Hill, 1995.

________. *A Birthday Basket for Tía*. New York: Macmillan, 1992.

________. *Borders*. Houston: Arte Público Press, 1986.

________. *Chants*. Houston: Arte Público Press, 1984.

________. *Communion*. Houston: Arte Público Press, 1991.

________. *Confetti*. New York: Lee and Low Books, 1996.

________. *The Desert Is My Mother: El desierto es mi madre*. Houston: Arte Público Press, 1994.

________. *The Gift of the Poinsettia: El regalo de la flor de nochebuena*. Houston: Piñata Books, 1995.

________. *Listen to the Desert: Oye al desierto*. New York: Clarion Books, 1994.

________. *Nepantla: Essays from the Land in the Middle*. Albuquerque: University of New Mexico Press, 1993.

________. *Tomás and the Library Lady*. New York: Knopf, 1997.

________. *Uno, dos, tres: One, Two, Three*. New York: Clarion Books, 1996.

________. *Voices from the Garden*. Boston: Beacon Press, 1996.

Morton, Carlos. *The Many Deaths of Danny Rosales*. Houston: Arte Público Press, 1983.

Morton, Susana Nevarez. "Conjunto Memories." In *Puro Conjunto, An Album in Words and Pictures*, edited by Juan Tejeda and Avelardo Valdez, 403–407. Austin: CMAS Books, Guadalupe Cultural Arts Center, 2001.

Muirhead, Eric. "Carmen." In *Texas Short Fiction: A World In Itself*, edited by Mike Hennech and Billy Bob Hill, 67–71. Fort Worth: ALE Publishing, 1993.

Muro, Amado (Chester Seltzer). *The Collected Short Stories of Amado Muro*. Austin: Thorp Springs Press, 1979.

________. "Cecelia Rosas." In *South by Southwest: 24 Stories from Modern Texas*, edited by Don Graham, 133–144. Austin: University of Texas Press, 1986.

________. "Mala Tores: A Story." In *The Chicanos: Mexican American Voices*, edited by Ed Ludwig and James Santibañez, 37–42. New York: Penguin Books, 1971.

________. "María Tepache." In *North of the Rio Grande: The Mexican-American Experience in Short Fiction*, edited by Edward Simmen, 161–165. New York: Mentor Book, 1992.

Neate, Wilson. "The Function of Belken County in the Fiction of Rolando Hinojosa: The Voicing of the Chicano Experience." *The Americas Review* 18 (Spring 1990): 92–102.

Niggli, Josefina. *Mexican Folk Plays*. Chapel Hill: University of North Carolina Press, 1938.

________. *Mexican Silhouettes*. Originally published 1928. San Antonio: Silhoutte Press, 1931.

________. *Mexican Village*. Chapel Hill: University of North Carolina Press, 1945.

________. *A Miracle for Mexico*. Greenwich, Conn.: New York Graphic Society, 1964.

________. *Step Down, Elder Brother: A Novel*. New York: Rinehart, 1947.

________ "Call Them Dreams." *Pax: A Journal for Peace through Culture* 3 (1985–1986): 98–102.

________. "The Engagement." In *Mexican American Authors*, edited by Américo Paredes and Raymund Paredes, 61–67. Boston: Houghton Mifflin, 1976.

________. "The Street of the Cañon." Reprinted in *Mexican American Authors*, edited by Américo Paredes and Raymund Paredes, 68–75. Boston: Houghton Mifflin, 1976.

________. "The Street of the Three Crosses." In *Mexican American Authors*, edited by Américo Paredes and Raymund Paredes, 53–60. Boston: Houghton Mifflin, 1976.

________. "Sunday Costs Five Pesos." In *Mexican American Authors*, edited by Américo Paredes and Raymund Paredes, 76–92. Boston: Houghton Mifflin, 1976.

Norquest, Carrol. *Rio Grande Wetbacks: Mexican Migrant Workers*. Albuquerque: University of New Mexico Press, 1972.

Nye, Naomi Shihab. "Tomorrow We Smile." In *New Growth: Contemporary Short Stories by Texas Writers*, edited by Lyman Grant, 252–257. San Antonio: Corona Publishing, 1989.

Olivares, Julián. *Tomás Rivera: The Complete Works*. Houston: Arté Público Press, 1991.

________. "Seeing and Becoming: Evangelina Vigil, *Thirty an' Seen a Lot*." In *The Chicano Struggle: Analyses of Past and Present Efforts*, edited by John A. García, Theresa Córdova, and Juan R. García, 152–165. Binghamton, N.Y.: Bilingual Press/Editorial Bilingüe, 1984.

________, ed. *Houston Hispanic*. Special Issue of *The Americas Review* 16 (Spring 1988).

________, ed. *International Studies in Honor of Tomás Rivera*. Houston: Arté Público Press, 1986.

Olsson, Karen. "The Border According to Guerra." *Texas Observer* (February 18, 2000): 12–14, 27.

Ornelas, Berta. *Come Down from the Mound*. Phoeniz: Miter Publishing, 1975.

Orozco, Cynthia E. "Fermina Guerra." In *The New Handbook of Texas*, edited by Ron Tyler, Douglas E. Barnett, Roy R. Barkley, Penelope C. Anderson, and Mark F. Odintz, vol. 3, 368. Austin: Texas State Historical Association, 1996.

________. "María Elena Zamora O'Shea." In *The New Handbook of Texas*, edited by Ron Tyler, Douglas E. Barnett, Roy R. Barkley, Penelope C. Anderson, and Mark F. Odintz, vol. 4, 1176–1177. Austin: Texas State Historical Association, 1996.

Orozco, Cynthia E., and Teresa Palomo Acosta. "Jovita González de Mireles." In *The New Handbook of Texas*, edited by Ron Tyler, Douglas E. Barnett, Roy R. Barkley, Penelope C. Anderson, and Mark F. Odintz, vol. 3, 236–237. Austin: Texas State Historical Association, 1996.

Ortego, Philip D. "The Coming of Zamora." In *The Chicano: From Caricature to Self-Portrait*, edited by Edward Simmen, 292–298. New York: New American Library, 1971.

Ortego y Gasca, Felipe de. "Brands, Bandits, and Ballads: Eiconia Images of Tejanos in the Literature of the Borderlands." *Journal of South Texas* 15 (Fall 2002): 86–107.

________. "The Chicano Renaissance." *Social Casework* (May 1971): 294–307.

________. "Life and Literature of the Mexican American Southwest: The Beginnings and the Nineteenth Century." *Borderlands Journal* 5 (Fall 1981): 45–94.

________. "Literacy and Literature in South Texas Ranching Country—1836–1910." *Journal of South Texas* 13 (2000): 116–135.

________. "Twentieth Century Hispanics in Texas Letters: A Bibliographical Essay." *Journal of South Texas* 14 (2001): 5–21.

Osborn, Carolyn. "Mexicans and Gringos." In *New Growth/2: Contemporary Short Stories by Texas Writers*, edited by Mark Busby, 115–119. San Antonio: Corona Publishing, 1993.

________. "Overlappings." In *North of the Rio Grande: The Mexican-American Experience in Short Fiction*, edited by Edward Simmen, 358–379. New York: Mentor Book, 1992.

O'Shea, Elena Zamora. *El Mesquite, A Story of the Early Spanish Settlements Between the Nueces and the Rio Grande as Told by "La Posta del Palo Alto."* Dallas: Mathis Publishing, 1935.

Paredes, Américo. *Between Two Worlds*. Houston: Arte Público Press, 1990.

________. *George Washington Gómez: A Mexicotexan Novel*. Houston: Arte Público Press, 1990.

________. *The Hammon and the Beans and Other Stories*. Houston: Arte Público Press, 1994.

________. *Uncle Remus con chile*. Houston: Arte Público Press, 1993.

________. *"With His Pistol in His Hand": A Border Ballad and Its Hero*. Austin: University of Texas Press, 1958.

________. "El Corrido de Gregorio Cortéz: A Ballad of Border Conflict." Ph.D. dissertation, University of Texas, Austin, 1956.

________. "The Hammon and the Beans." In *The Chicano: From Caricature to Self-portrait*, edited by Edward Simmen, 274–278. New York: New American Library, 1971.

________. "The Legend of Gregorio Cortéz." In *Mexican American Authors*, edited by Américo Paredes and Raymund Paredes, 35–50. Boston: Houghton Mifflin, 1976.

________. "Mi Tía Pilar." In *Reflexiones 1998: New Directions in Mexican American Studies*, edited by Yolanda C. Padilla, 147–151. Austin: CMAS Books, 1999.

________. "Over the Waves Is Out." In *North of the Rio Grande: The Mexican-American Experience in Short Fiction*, edited by Edward Simmen, 142–152. New York: Mentor Book, 1992.

________. "A Sense of Place." *Discovery: Research and Scholarship at the University of Texas at Austin* 8 (Winter 1983): 21–24.

Paredez, Deborah. "Deborah Paredez." In *This Promiscuous Light: Young Women Poets of San Antonio*, edited by Bryce Milligan, 89–106. San Antonio: Wings Press, 1996.

________. "Tía María." In *Daughters of the Fifth Sun: A Collection of Latina Fiction and Poetry*, edited by Bryce Milligan, Mary Guerrero Milligan, and Angela de Hoyos, 98–102. New York: Riverhead Books, 1995.

Perales, Alonso M. *La Lechuza: Cuentos de mi Barrio*. San Antonio: The Naylor Company, 1972.

Peregrino, José Flores. *Mesquitierra*. Albuquerque: Pajarito Publications, 1977.

Perezdíaz, Roberto. "La Migra's Here." *Bilingual Review/La Revista Bilingüe* 23.3 (1998): 270–274.

Pérez, Hector. "Voicing Resistance on the Border: A Reading of Américo Paredes' *George Washington Gómez*." *Melus* 23.1 (Spring 1998): 27–48.

Pérez, Ramón "Tianguis." *Diary of an Undocumented Immigrant*. Houston: Arte Público Press, 1991.

Pino, Frank. "The Outsider and 'El Otro' in Tomás Rivera's 'y no se lo tragó la tierra.'" *Books Abroad* 49 (Summer 1975): 453–458.

Pollentier, Nicole. "Nicole Pollentier." In *This Promiscuous Light: Young Women Poets of San Antonio*, edited by Bryce Milligan, 107–122. San Antonio: Wings Press, 1996.

________. "For Ryan, Thanks for the Offer." In *Daughters of the Fifth Sun: A Collection of Latina Fiction and Poetry*, edited by Bryce Milligan, Mary Guerrero-Milligan, and Angela de Hoyos, 115–116. New York: Riverhead Books, 1995.

Purdy, Andrea R. "Jovita González de Mireles." In *American Women Writers, 1900–1945: A Bio-Bibliographical Critical Sourcebook*, edited by Laurie Champion, 142–146. Westport, Conn.: Greenwood Press, 2000.

Ramírez, Arturo. "Reconfiguring a Classic Chicano Novel: Severo Pérez'. . . *and the Earth did not Swallow Him*." In *Aztlán, Chicano Culture and Folklore: An Anthology*, edited by José 'Pepe' Villarino and Arturo Ramírez , 149–158. New York: McGraw Hill, 1998.

Ramírez, Elizabeth Cantú. *Footlights Across the Border: A History of Spanish-Language Professional Theatre on the Texas Stage*. New York: Peter Lang, 1989.

________. "A History of Mexican American Professional Theatre in Texas: 1875–1935." Ph.D. dissertation, University of Texas at Austin, 1982.

________. "Carlos Villalongín Dramatic Company." In *The New Handbook of Texas*, edited by Ron Tyler, Douglas E. Barnett, Roy R. Barkley, Penelope C. Anderson, and Mark F. Odintz, vol. 1, 978. Austin: Texas State Historical Association, 1996.

________. "Compania Juan B. Padilla." In *American Theatre Companies: 1888–1930*, edited by Weldon Durham, vol. 2, 353–358. Westport, Conn.: Greenwood Press, 1987.

________. "Compania Teatro Solórzano." In *American Theatre Companies: 1888–1930*, edited by Weldon Durham, vol. 2, 413–416. Westport, Conn.: Greenwood Press, 1987.

________. "Compania Villalongín." In *American Theatre Companies: 1888–1930*, edited by Weldon Durham, vol. 2, 449–453. Westport, Conn.: Greenwood Press, 1987.

________. "Concepción Hernández." In *The New Handbook of Texas*, edited by Ron Tyler, Douglas E. Barnett, Roy R. Barkley, Penelope C. Anderson, and Mark F. Odintz, vol. 3, 572. Austin: Texas State Historical Association, 1996.

________. "Estela Portillo Trambley." *Latin American Theatre Review* (Spring 1984): 103–104.

________. "Francisco E. Solórzano." In *The New Handbook of Texas,* edited by Ron Tyler, Douglas E. Barnett, Roy R. Barkley, Penelope C. Anderson, and Mark F. Odintz, vol. 5, 1142–1143. Austin: Texas State Historical Association, 1996.

________. "Hispanics and Mexican Women on the Texas Stage, 1875–1900." In *Women and Texas History: Selected Essays*, edited by Fane Downs and Nancy Baker Jones, 34–41. Austin: Texas State Historical Association, 1993.

________. "A History of Mexican American Professional Theatre in Texas Prior to 1900." *Theatre Survey* 24 (1983): 99–116.

________. "Mexican American Theatre." In *The New Handbook of Texas*, edited by Ron Tyler, Douglas E. Barnett, Roy R. Barkley, Penelope C. Anderson, and Mark F. Odintz, vol. 4, 679–680. Austin: Texas State Historical Association, 1996.

________. "Spanish-language Combination Companies on the American Stage: Organization and Practice in Texas." *Theatre History Studies* (1989): 77–91.

________. "Solsona Dramatic Company." In *The New Handbook of Texas*, edited by Ron Tyler, Douglas E. Barnett, Roy R. Barkley, Penelope C. Anderson, and Mark F. Odintz, vol. 5, 1143. Austin: Texas State Historical Association, 1996.

Ramón, Alberto M. *On Both Sides of the River: A Tale of the Magnificent Whitetail Bucks of South Texas and Northern Coahuila*. Carmel, Ind.: Guild Press of Indiana, 1996.

Ramos, Luis Arturo. *Angela de Hoyos: A Critical Look*. Albuquerque: Pajarito, 1979.

________. "Review: 'y no se lo tragó la tierra.'" *Caracol* 5 (January 1979): 10–11.

Rebolledo, Tey Diana. "Witches, Bitches, and Midwives: The Shaping of Poetic Consciousness in Chicano Literature." In *The Chicano Struggle: Analyses of*

Past and Present Efforts, edited by John A. García, Theresa Córdova, and Juan R. García, 166–177. Binghamton, N.Y.: Bilingual Press/Editorial Bilingüe, 1984.

Rechy, John. *City of Night*. New York: Grove Press, 1963.

________. *This Day's Death: A Novel*. New York: Grove Press, 1969.

________. *The Fourth Angel*. New York: Viking Press, 1975.

________. *Numbers*. New York: Grove Press, 1967.

Reed, Michael. "Structural Motif in the Stories of Tomás Rivera." *Journal of the American Studies Association of Texas* 18 (1987): 40–46.

Reyna, Sergio. "Jovita González y su obra folklórico-literaria: Reconstrucción de la historia cultural méxico-americana." In *Recovering the U.S. Hispanic Literary Heritage*, edited by José F. Aranda Jr. and Silvio Torres-Saillant, vol. 4, 184–200. Houston: Arte Público Press, 2002.

Rice, David. *Give the Pig a Chance and Other Stories*. Tempe, Ariz.: Bilingual Press, 1996.

________. "Heart-Shaped Cookies." *Bilingual Review/La Revista Bilingüe* 19 (1994): 155–157.

________. "El Sapo." *Bilingual Review/La Revista Bilingüe* 19 (1994): 151–155.

Rico, Manuel. "Vicente." In *Yearnings: Mexican-American Literature*, edited by Albert C. Chávez, 74–77. West Haven, Conn.: Pendulum Press, 1972.

Rivera, Jana. "Rolando Hinojosa-Smith." *Hispanic Outlook in Higher Education* 7 (August 30, 1996): 9–10.

Rivera, Tomás. *Always, and Other Poems*. Sisterdale, Tex.: Sisterdale Press, 1973.

________. *And the Earth Did Not Devour Him/ Y no se lo tragó la tierra*, translated by Evangeline Vigil-Piña. Houston: Arte Público Press, 1992.

________. *The Harvest: Short Stories*, edited by Julián Olivares. Houston: Arte Público Press, 1989.

________. *This Migrant Earth: Rolando Hinojosa's Rendition in English of Tomás Rivera's* " . . . y no se lo tragó la tierra." Houston: Arte Público Press, 1987.

________. *The Searchers: Collected Poetry*, edited by Julian Olivares. Houston: Arte Público Press, 1990.

________. *Y no se lo trago la tierra/And the Earth Did Not Part*. Berkeley: Quinto Sol Publisher, 1971.

________. "Chicano Literature: Fiesta of the Living." *Books Abroad* 49 (Summer 1975): 439–452.

________. "Mexican-American Literature: The Establishment of Community." *The Texas Literary Tradition: Fiction, Folklore, History*, edited by Don Graham, James W. Lee, and William Pilkington, 124–130. Austin: College of Liberal Arts, University of Texas at Austin, Texas State Historical Association, 1983.

________. "On the Road to Texas." In *Voices of Aztlán: Chicano Literature of Today*, edited by Dorothy E. Harth and Lewis M. Baldwin, 52–58. New York: New American Library, 1974.

________. "The Salamanders." In *Short Fiction by Hispanic Writers of the United States*, edited by Nicolás Kanellos, 205–207. Houston: Arte Público Press, 1993.

Robinson, Cecil. "A Kaleidoscope of Images: Mexicans and Chicanos as Reflected in American Literature." In *Bilingualism in the Southwest*, edited by Paul R. Turner, 107–129. Tucson: University of Arizona Press, 1975.

Rodríguez Aranda, Pilar E. "On the Solitary Fate of Being Mexican, Female, Wicked, and Thirty-three: An Interview with Writer Sandra Cisneros." *The Americas Review* 18 (Spring 1990): 64–80.

Rodríguez, Blanca. "Fronteras y literatura: El periódico *La Patria* (El Paso, Texas, 1919-1925)." *Mexican Studies/Estudios Mexicanos* 19 (Winter 2003): 107–125.

Rodríguez, José R. "Tramps." In *New Texas 95*, edited by Kathryn S. McGuire and James Ward Lee, 125–139. Denton: Center for Texas Studies, 1995.

Rodríguez, Juan. "Acercamiento a cuatro relatos de . . . *y no se lo tragó la tierra*." *Master* 5 (November 1974): 16–24.

________. "The Problematic in Tomás Rivera's . . . *y no se lo tragó la tierra*." *Revista Chicano-Riqueña* 6 (Summer 1978): 42–50.

Rodríguez, Mary Grace. *Long Short Story*. San Antonio: Wings Press, 1999.

Rodríguez, Salvador del Pino. "Lo mexicano y lo chicano en *El Diablo en Texas*." In *The Identification and Analysis of Chicano Literature*, edited by Francisco Jiménez, 365–373. New York: Bilingual Press/Editorial Bilingüe, 1979.

Rojas-Urista, Xelina. *Ku: poemas de Xelina*. La Jolla, Calif.: Maize Press, 1977.

Rosaldo, Renato. "Politics, Patriarchs, and Laughter." In *The Nature and Context of Minority Discourse*, edited by Abdul R. JanMohamed and David Lloyd, 124–145. New York: Oxford University Press, 1990.

________. "Race and Other Inequalities: The Borderlands in Arturo Isla's *Migrant Souls*." In *Race*, edited by Steven Gregory and Roger Sanjek, 213–225. New Brunswick, N.J.: Rutgers University Press, 1994.

Rosales, Veronica. "He Reminds Me of the Good Things in Life." *Bilingual Review/La Revista Bilingüe* 22.1 (1997): 71–73.

Ruiz-Flores, Lupe. *Lupita's Papalote/El Papalote de Lupita*. Houston: Arte Público Press, 2002.

Sáenz, Benjamín Alire. *Calendar of Dust*. Seattle: Broken Moon, 1991.

________. *Carry Me Like Water*. New York: Hyperion Press, 1995.

________. *Dark and Perfect Angels: A Collection of Poems*. El Paso: Cinco Puntos Press, 1995.

________. *Elegies in Blue: Poems*. El Paso: Cinco Puntos Press, 2002.

________. *The House of Forgetting: A Novel*. New York: HarperCollins, 1997.

________. "Exile: El Paso, Texas." In *The Late Great Mexican Border: Reports from a Disappearing Line,* edited by Bobby Byrd and Susannah Mississippi Byrd, 199–210. El Paso: Cinco Puntos Press, 1996.

Salazar, Anthony. "Ricardo Sánchez: Pachuco, Poet, Ph.D." *Caracol* 4 (June 1978): 14–15.

Saldaña, René. "El Soñador." In *Texas Short Stories 2*, edited by Billy Bob Hill and Laurie Champion, 165–172. Dallas: Browder Springs Books, 2000.

Saldívar, Joe. "Body by Fisher." In *Puro Conjunto, An Album in Words and Pictures*, edited by Juan Tejeda and Avelardo Valdez, 389–401. Austin: CMAS Books, Guadalupe Cultural Arts Center, 2001.

Saldívar, José David. "Chicano Border Narratives as Cultural Critique." In *Criticism in the Borderlands: Studies in Chicano Literature, Culture, and Ideology*, edited by Héctor Calderón and José David Saldívar, 167–180. Durham: Duke University Press, 1991.

________. "The Ideological and the Utopian in Tomás Rivera's . . . *y no se lo tragó la tierra* and Ron Arias' *The Road to Tamazunchale*." In *Missions in Conflict: Essays on U.S.-Mexican Relations and Chicano Culture*, edited by Renate von Bardeleben, Dietrich Briesemeister, and Juan Bruce-Novoa, 203–214. Tubingen: Narr, 1986.

________. "Rolando Hinojosa's Klail City Death Trip Series: A Critical Introduction." In *The Rolando Hinojosa Reader*, edited by José. D. Saldívar, 44–63. Houston: Arte Público Press, 1984.

________, ed. *The Rolando Hinojosa Reader: Essays Historical and Critical*. Houston: Arte Público Press, 1984.

Saldívar, Ramón. "The Borderlands of Culture: Américo Paredes' *George Washington Gómez*." In *Mexican Americans in Texas History,* edited by Emilio Zamora, Cynthia Orozco, and Rodolfo Rocha, 175–185. Austin: Texas State Historical Association, 2000.

________. "Bordering on Modernity: Américo Paredes' *Between Two Worlds* and the Imagining of Utopian Social Space." *Stanford Humanities Review* 3 (Winter 1993): 54–66.

________. "The Borders of Modernity: Américo Paredes' *Between Two Worlds* and the Chicano National Subject." In *The Ethnic Canon: Histories, Institutions, and Interventions*, edited by David Palumbo-Liu, 71–87. Minneapolis: University of Minnesota Press, 1995.

________. "The Form of Texas-Mexican Fiction." In *The Texas Literary Tradition: Fiction, Folklore, History*, edited by Don Graham, James W. Lee, and William Pilkington, 139–144. Austin: College of Liberal Arts, University of Texas at Austin, Texas State Historical Association, 1983.

________. "Introduction." In *The Hammon and the Beans and Other Stories*, by Américo Paredes, vii–li. Houston: Arte Público Press, 1994.

________. "Texas-Mexican Fiction." In *The New Handbook of Texas*, edited by Ron Tyler, Douglas E. Barnett, Roy R. Barkley, Penelope C. Anderson, and Mark F. Odintz, vol. 6, 361. Austin: Texas State Historical Association, 1996.

________. "View of Short-Handled Hoe." *Discovery: Research and Scholarship at the University of Texas at Austin* 8 (Winter 1983): 25–29.

Salinas, Marta. "The Scholarship Jacket." In *Nosotras: Latina Literature Today*, edited by María del Carmen Boza, Beverly Silva, and Carmen Valle, 68–70. Binghamton, N.Y.: Bilingual Review/Press, 1986.

Salinas, Omar. "Robstown." In *Voices of Aztlán: Chicano Literature Today*, edited by Dorothy E. Harth and Lewis M. Baldwin, 188–189. New York: New American Library, 1974.

Sánchez, Rosaura. "From Heterogeneity to Contradiction: Hinojosa's Novel." In *The Rolando Hinojosa Reader*, edited by José David Saldivar, 76–100. Houston: Arte Público Press, 1985.

Sánchez, Saul. *Hay Plesha Lichans tu di Flac*. Berkeley: Justa Publications, 1977.

________. "Untitled." *Caracol* 2 (March 1976): 16–17.

________. "Untitled." *Caracol* 2 (April 1976): 16–17.

San Miguel, Susan. "La Llorona of Leon Creek." In *Texas Short Stories*, edited by Billy Bob Hill, 482–497. Dallas: Browder Springs Publishing, 1997.

________. "Snake Woman." In *Texas Short Stories 2*, edited by Billy Bob Hill and Laurie Champion, 427–437. Dallas: Browder Springs Books, 2000.

Santos, E. D. *Mesquite Sighs*. Hondo, Tex.: La Sombra, 1991.

________. *On The Road, Too*. Hondo, Tex.: La Sombra, 1988.

Santos, John Philip. *Places Left Unfinished at the Time of Creation: A Memoir*. New York: Penguin Books, 1999.

Sauvageau-Pro, Juan. *A pesar del río/In Spite of the River*. Kingsville, Tex.: Twin Palms Editorial, 1977.

Schedler, Christopher. "Inscribing Mexican-American Modernism in Américo Paredes's *George Washington Gómez*." In *Recovering the U.S. Hispanic Literary Heritage*, edited by José F. Aranda Jr. and Silvio Torres-Saillant, vol. 4, 240–263. Houston: Arte Público Press, 2002.

________."Inscribing Mexican American Modernism in Américo Paredes' *George Washington Gómez*." *Texas Studies in Literature and Language* 42 (Summer 2000): 154–176.

Smylie, Vernon. *A Noose for Chipita*. Corpus Christi, Tex.: New Syndicate Press, 1970.

Sommers, Joseph. "Interpreting Tomás Rivera." In *Modern Chicano Writers: A Collection of Critical Essays*, edited by Joseph Sommers and Tomás Ybarra–Frausto, 94–107. Englewood Cliffs, N.J.: Prentice–Hall, 1979.

Southwell, Sam. "Lionel García, American Novelist." *The Americas Review* 22 (Fall/Winter 1994): 110–113.

Spencer, Laura Gutiérrez. "The Desert Blooms: Flowered Songs by Pat Mora." *Bilingual Review/La Revista Bilingüe* 20.1 (1995): 28–36.

Swift, Edward. "The Spanish Lesson." In *New Growth: Contemporary Short Stories by Texas Writers*, edited by Lyman Grant, 82–92. San Antonio: Corona Publishing, 1989.

Szumowski, Margaret. "Poems (Memory of Summer: The Rio Grande Valley; the Woman Who Loves the Valley: Borders)." *Bilingual Review/La Revista Bilingüe* 13 (September-December 1986): 62–66.

Tafolla, Carmen. *Curandera*. San Antonio: M&A Editions, 1983.

________. *Patchwork Colcha*. Flagstaff: Creative Educational Enterprises, 1987.

________. *Sonnets and Salsa*. San Antonio: Wings Press, 2001.

________. *Sonnets to Human Beings and Other Selected Works by Carmen Tafolla*. Santa Monica: Lalo Press, 1992.

________. *To Split a Human: Mitos, Machos y la Mujer Chicana*. San Antonio: Mexican American Cultural Center, 1984.

________. "Chencho's Cow." In *Daughters of the Fifth Sun: A Collection of Latina Fiction and Poetry*, edited by Bryce Milligan, Mary Guerrero Milligan, and Angela de Hoyos, 232–241. New York: Riverhead Books, 1995.

________. "Federico y Elfira." In *Common Bonds: Stories By and About Modern Texas Women*, edited by Suzanne Comer, 26–32. Dallas: Southern Methodist University Press, 1990.

________. "La Isabela de Guadalupe y otras chucas." In *Five Poets of Aztlán*, edited by Santiago Daydí-Tolson, 165–210. Binghamton, N.Y.: Bilingual Press/Editorial Bilingüe, 1985.

________. "I Just Can't Bear It." In *Texas Short Stories*, edited by Billy Bob Hill, 519–522. Dallas: Browder Springs Publishing, 1997.

________. "The Pot Has Eyes." In *Texas Short Stories 2*, edited by Billy Bob Hill and Laurie Champion, 907–911. Dallas: Browder Springs Books, 2000.

Tafoya, Jesús L. *Aquí Estuvieron*. Ciudad Juárez: Universidad Autónoma de Ciudad Juárez, 2000.

________. *Desde la ausencia*. Ciudad Juárez: La Nave de Saidah, 2002.

Taylor, Pat Ellis. "What Cecilia Reveals." In *New Growth: Contemporary Short Stories by Texas Writers*, edited by Lyman Grant, 211–218. San Antonio: Corona Publishing, 1989.

Testa, Daniel P. "Narrative Technique and Human Experience in Tomás Rivera." In *Modern Chicano Writers: A Collection of Critical Essays*, edited by Joseph Sommers and Tomás Ybarra-Frausto, 86–93. Englewood Cliffs, N.J.: Prentice-Hall, 1979.

Torres-Metzgar, Joseph V. *Below the Summit*. Berkeley: Tonatiuh International, 1976.

Torres, Olga Beatriz. *Memorias de mi viaje/Recollections of My Trip*, translated by Juanita Luna-Lawhn. Originally published 1918. Albuquerque: University of New Mexico Press, 1994.

Trambley, Estela Portillo. *Rain of Scorpions and Other Writings*. Berkeley: Tonatiuh-Quinto Sol International, 1975.

________. *Sor Juana and Other Plays*. Ypsilanti, Mich.: Bilingual Review/Press, 1983.

________. *Trini*. Binghamton, N.Y.: Bilingual Review/Press, 1986.

________. "Day of the Swallows." In *Contemporary Chicana Theater*, edited by Robert J. Garza, 207–245. Notre Dame: Notre Dame University Press, 1976.

________. "La Jonfontayn." In *Short Fiction by Hispanic Writers of the United States*, edited by Nicolás Kanellos, 187–197. Houston: Arte Público Press, 1993.

________. "Village." In *Her Works: Stories by Texas Women*, edited by Lou Halsell Rodenberger, 298–304. Bryan, Tex.: Shearer Publishing, 1982.

Treviño, Jesús Salvador. *The Fabulous Sinkhole and Other Stories*. Houston: Arte Público Press, 1989.

Urieste, Donaldo W. "The Child's Process of Alienation in Tomás Rivera's '... *y no se lo tragó la tierra*." In *The Chicano Struggle: Analyses of Past and Present Efforts*, edited by John A. García, Theresa Córdova, and Juan R. García, 178–191. Binghamton, N.Y.: Bilingual Press/Editorial Bilingüe, 1984.

Vásquez, Enedina Cásarez. *Recuerdos de una niña.* San Antonio: Centro de Comunicación Misioneros Oblatos de María, 1980.

Vigil-Piñón, Evangelina. *The Computer is Down*. Houston: Arte Público Press, 1987.

________. *Nade y Nade*. San Antonio: M&A Editions, 1978.

________. *Thirty an' Seen a Lot*. Houston: Arte Público Press, 1982.

________. *Woman of Her Word*. Houston: Arte Público Press, 1984.

Villanueva, Tino. *Chronicle of My Worst Years=Crónica de mis años peores*. Evanston, Ill.: Northwestern University Press, 1994.

________. *Hay otra voz: Poems, 1968–1971*. Staten Island: Editorial Mensaje, 1972.

________. *Scene from the Movie* Giant. Willimantic, Conn.: Curbstone Press, 1993.

________. *Shaking off the Dark*. Houston: Arté Público Press, 1984.

Villa, Raúl Homero. "Of *Corridos* and Convicts: *Gringo* (In)justice in Early Border Ballads and *Pinto* Poetry." In *Chicanas and Chicanos in Contemporary Society*, edited by Roberto M. DeAnda, 113–126. Boston: Allyn and Bacon, 1996.

Villegas de Magnón, Leonor. *The Rebel: Leonor Villegas de Magnón*, edited by Clara Lomas. Houston: Arte Público Press, 1994.

Viramontes, Helena María. "The Moths." *Texas Journal of Ideas, History and Culture* 20 (Fall/Winter 1997): 50–53.

Yáñez, R. "La Paz Groc." *Bilingual Review/La Revista Bilingüe* 23.3 (1998): 260–269.

Young, Elliott. "Before the Revolution: Catarino Garza as Activist/Historian." In *Recovering the U.S. Hispanic Literary Heritage II*, edited by Erlinda Gonzales-Berry and Chuck Tatum, 213–236. Houston: Arte Público Press, 1996.

Yzquierdo, Rosa Elena. "Abuela." *Texas Journal of Ideas, History and Culture* 20 (Fall/Winter 1997): 3.

Zamora, Emilio Jr. "Fighting on Two Fronts: José de la Luz Saenz and the Language of the Mexican American Civil Rights Movement." In *Recovering the U.S. Hispanic Literary Heritage*, edited by José F. Aranda Jr. and Silvio Torres-Saillant, vol. 4, 214–239. Houston: Arte Público Press, 2002.

________. "Sara Estela Ramírez: Una rosa en el movimiento." In *Mexican Women in the United States: Struggles Past and Present*, edited by Magdalena Mora and Adelaida del Castillo, 163–169. Los Angeles: Chicano Studies Research Center Publications, 1980.

Zavala, Ricardo I. "It No Looky Too Good." *Bilingual Review/La Revista Bilingüe* 16 (1991): 211–213.

________. "The Prayer." *Bilingual Review/La Revista Bilingüe* 18 (1993): 48–52.

Zilles, Klaus. *Rolando Hinojosa: A Reader's Guide*. Albuquerque: University of New Mexico Press, 2001.

18. MUSIC

One of the primary cultural attributes of a people is music, and the vibrancy and range of types and styles of Texas Mexican music is an indication of the contributions made by that culture to the Texas experience. We include works that are obviously (from the titles or contents) about Tejano music, whether historical or contemporary, and which cover such Texas Mexican music as conjuntos, orquesta, La Onda Chicana, folksongs, and Tejano or Norteño—what Manuel Peña refers to as *música tejana*.

Group of musicians, with their instruments, posed in yard of residence in San Antonio's "West Side."
The Institute of Texan Cultures at UTSA, No. 84-68

Acosta, Teresa Palomo. "Armando Marroquín." In *The New Handbook of Texas*, edited by Ron Tyler, Douglas E. Barnett, Roy R. Barkley, Penelope C. Anderson, and Mark F. Odintz, vol. 4, 516–517. Austin: Texas State Historical Association, 1996.

________. "Narcisco Martínez." In *The New Handbook of Texas*, edited by Ron Tyler, Douglas E. Barnett, Roy R. Barkley, Penelope C. Anderson, and Mark F. Odintz, vol, 4. 537–538. Austin: Texas State Historical Association, 1996.

________. "Tejano Conjunto Festival." In *The New Handbook of Texas,* edited by Ron Tyler, Douglas E. Barnett, Roy R. Barkley, Penelope C. Anderson, and Mark F. Odintz, vol. 6, 239. Austin: Texas State Historical Association, 1996.

________. "Tejana Singers." In *The New Handbook of Texas*, edited by Ron Tyler, Douglas E. Barnett, Roy R. Barkley, Penelope C. Anderson, and Mark F. Odintz, vol. 6, 237–238. Austin: Texas State Historical Association, 1996.

________. "Texas-Mexican Conjunto." In *The New Handbook of Texas*, edited by Ron Tyler, Douglas E. Barnett, Roy R. Barkley, Penelope C. Anderson, and Mark F. Odintz, vol. 6, 5–6. Austin: Texas State Historical Association, 1996.

Barbash, Louis, and Frederick P. Close. "Lydia Mendoza: The Voice of a People." *Texas Humanist* (November/December 1983): 18–20.

Benibo, Bilayne R., Pamela S. Meyer, and Javier Villarreal. "Anglo- and Mexican-American Attitudes Toward Selena's Memorialization." *Hispanic Journal of Behavorial Sciences* 21 (February 1999): 78–88.

Broyles-González, Yolanda. *Lydia Mendoza's Life in Music: Norteño Tejano Legacies*. New York: Oxford University Press, 2001.

________. "Ranchera Music(s) and the Legendary Lydia Mendoza: Performing Social Location and Relation." In *Chicano Traditions: Continuity and Change,* edited by Norma E. Cantú and Olga Nájera-Ramírez, 183–206. Urbana: University of Illinois Press, 2002.

Burr, Ramiro. *The Billboard Guide to Tejano and Regional Mexican Music*. New York: Watson-Guptill Publications, 1999.

________. "The Accordian: Passion, Emotion, Musicianship." In *Puro Conjunto, An Album in Words and Pictures*, edited by Juan Tejeda and Avelardo Valdez, 121–125. Austin: CMAS Books, Guadalupe Cultural Arts Center, 2001.

________. "Women in Conjunto Music." In *Puro Conjunto, An Album in Words and Pictures*, edited by Juan Tejeda and Avelardo Valdez, 85–95. Austin: CMAS Books, Guadalupe Cultural Arts Center, 2001.

Calderón, Ricardo E. "Tejano Music Awards Founder: Rudy R. Treviño." *Eagle Pass Business Journal* 4 (1997): 3, 22–23.

Calderón, Roberto R. "All Over the Map: *La Onda Tejana* and the Making of Selena." In *Chicano Renaissance: Contemporary Cultural Trends*, edited by David Maciel, Isidro D. Ortiz, and María Herrera-Sobek, 1–47. Tucson: University of Arizona Press, 2000.

Cantú, Tony. "Cashing in on Selena: How the Tejano Queen's Murder Caused an Economic Phenomenon." *Hispanic* (June 1996): 18–24.

Chabrán, Richard, and Rafael Chabrán, eds. "Conjunto." In *The Latino Encyclopedia*, edited by Richard Chabrán and Rafael Chabrán, vol. 2, 378. New York: Marshall Cavendish, 1996.

________. "Freddy Fender." In *The Latino Encyclopedia*, edited by Richard Chabrán and Rafael Chabrán, vol. 2, 587. New York: Marshall Cavendish, 1996.

________. "Leonardo 'Flaco' Jiménez." In *The Latino Encyclopedia*, edited by Richard Chabrán and Rafael Chabrán, vol. 3, 814. New York: Marshall Cavendish, 1996.

________. "Little Joe and the Latinaires." In *The Latino Encyclopedia*, edited by Richard Chabrán and Rafael Chabrán, vol. 3, 912. New York: Marshall Cavendish, 1996.

________. "Pachuco." In *The Latino Encyclopedia*, edited by Richard Chabrán and Rafael Chabrán, vol. 4, 1189. *New York: Marshall Cavendish, 1996.*

________. "Selena." In *The Latino Encyclopedia*, edited by Richard Chabrán and Rafael Chabrán, vol. 5, 1480. New York: Marshall Cavendish, 1996.

________. "Tejano Conjunto Festival." In *The Latino Encyclopedia*, edited by Richard Chabrán and Rafael Chabrán, vol. 6, 1587. New York: Marshall Cavendish, 1996.

________. "Tex-Mex." In *The Latino Encyclopedia*, edited by Richard Chabrán and Rafael Chabrán, vol. 6, 1587. New York: Marshall Cavendish, 1996.

Coronado, Raúl Jr. "Selena's Good Buy: Texas Mexicans, History, and Selena Meet Transnational Capitalism." *Aztlán* 26 (Spring 2001): 59–100.

Council, Kay Francine. "Exploratory Documentation of Texas *Norteño-Conjunto* Music." Master's thesis, University of Texas at Austin, 1978.

Cuéllar, José B. "El Saxofon in Tejano and Norteño Music." In *Puro Conjunto, An Album in Words and Pictures*, edited by Juan Tejeda and Avelardo Valdez, 135–154. Austin: CMAS Books, Guadalupe Cultural Arts Center, 2001.

Dickey, Dan W. "Corridos." In *The New Handbook of Texas,* edited by Ron Tyler, Douglas E. Barnett, Roy R. Barkley, Penelope C. Anderson, and Mark F. Odintz, vol. 2, 337–338. Austin: Texas State Historical Association, 1996.

________. "Música Norteña." In *The New Handbook of Texas*, edited by Ron Tyler, Douglas E. Barnett, Roy R. Barkley, Penelope C. Anderson, and Mark F. Odintz, vol. 4, 909–911. Austin: Texas State Historical Association, 1996.

Dovalina, Ismael. "Confessions of an Accordian Abuser." In *Puro Conjunto, An Album in Words and Pictures*, edited by Juan Tejeda and Avelardo Valdez, 355–358. Austin: CMAS Books, Guadalupe Cultural Arts Center, 2001.

Durán, Gustavo. *14 Traditional Spanish Songs from Texas*. Washington, D.C.: Pan American Union, 1942.

Flores, Carlos Jesús Gómez. "The Accordian on Both Sides of the Border." In *Puro Conjunto, An Album in Words and Pictures*, edited by Juan Tejeda and Avelardo Valdez, 71–80. Austin: CMAS Books, Guadalupe Cultural Arts Center, 2001.

Flynn, Ronald, Edwin Davison, and Edward Chávez. *The Golden Age of the Accordion*. Schertz, Tex.: Flynn Associates Publishing, 1992.

García, Ignacio. "Beto Villa's Chicano Big Band." *Nuestro* 4 (June/July 1980): 77–79.

Gil, Carlos B. "Lydia Mendoza: Houstonian and First Lady of Mexican American Song." *The Houston Review* 3 (Summer 1981): 249–260. Reprinted in *Chicano Border Culture and Folklore*, edited by José Villarino and Arturo Ramírez, 181–194. San Diego: Marin Publications, 1992.

Guerra, Carlos. "Accordian Menace . . . Just Say Mo!" In *Puro Conjunto, An Album in Words and Pictures*, edited by Juan Tejeda and Avelardo Valdez, 115–120. Austin: CMAS Books, Guadalupe Cultural Arts Center, 2001.

________. "The Unofficial Conjunto Primer for the Uninitiated Music Lover." In *Puro Conjunto, An Album in Words and Pictures*, edited by Juan Tejeda and Avelardo Valdez, 3–9. Austin: CMAS Books, Guadalupe Cultural Arts Center, 2001.

Gutiérrez, José Angel. "Chicano Music: Evolution and Politics to 1950." In *The Roots of Texas Music*, edited by Lawrence Clayton and Joe W. Specht, 146–174. College Station: Texas A&M University Press, 2003.

Henderson, Tim. "Ballad of Doña María Del Carmen Calvillo." *Journal of South Texas* 13 (2000): 322–324.

Hernández, Ramón Jr. "An Informal History of the Bajo Sexto." In *Puro Conjunto, An Album in Words and Pictures*, edited by Juan Tejeda and Avelardo Valdez, 127–129. Austin: CMAS Books, Guadalupe Cultural Arts Center, 2001.

________. "Three of the Greatest Bajo Sexto Players in the History of Conjunto." In *Puro Conjunto, An Album in Words and Pictures*, edited by Juan Tejeda and Avelardo Valdez, 81–84. Austin: CMAS Books, Guadalupe Cultural Arts Center, 2001.

Jones, Jan Lynn. "The History and Development of Casa Mañana Musicals, 1958–1980." Master's thesis, University of North Texas, 1981.

Kerr, Marianne Bachman. "*Corridos*: Reflections of Acculturation Along the Border." *Journal of Big Bend Studies* 7 (1995): 203–216.

Kreneck, Thomas H. "Eligio Roque Escobar." In *The New Handbook of Texas,* edited by Ron Tyler, Douglas E. Barnett, Roy R. Barkley, Penelope C. Anderson, and Mark F. Odintz, vol. 2, 890. Austin: Texas State Historical Association, 1996.

Limón, José E. *Dancing with the Devil: Society and Cultural Poetics in Mexican American South Texas*. Madison: University of Wisconsin Press, 1994.

________. *Mexican Ballads, Chicano Epic: History, Social Dramas, and Poetic Persuasions*. Stanford, Calif.: Stanford Center for Chicano Research, 1986.

________. *Mexican Ballads, Chicano Poems: History and Influence in Mexican-American Social Poetry*. Berkeley: University of California Press, 1992.

________. "El Baile: Culture and Contradiction in Mexican American Dancing." In *Puro Conjunto, An Album in Words and Pictures*, edited by Juan Tejeda and Avelardo Valdez, 241–252. Austin: CMAS Books, Guadalupe Cultural Arts Center, 2001.

________. "Selena, Sexuality, Greater Mexico and the Song-and-Dance with Hegemony." *ETNOFOOR* 10 (1997): 90–111.

________. "Texas-Mexican Popular Music and Dancing: Some Notes on History and Symbolic Process." *Latin American Music Review* 4 (Fall/Winter 1983): 229–246.

________. "With a *Corrido* in His Heart: Américo Paredes is the Top Chicano Scholar." *Nuestro* 3 (September 1979): 40–42.

Lindstrom, Naomi. "Four Representative Hispanic Women Poets of Central Texas: A Portrait of Plurality." *Third Woman* 2.1 (1984): 64–70.

López, Jesús Ignacio. "Arnoldo Ramírez: A Pioneer in *Conjunto* Music." *South Texas Studies* 9 (1998): 114–140.

López, Joey. "Música Chicana." *Caracol* 1 (June 1975): 8.

Luevanos, Carmen. "The Tejano Conjunto Festival en San Antonio: Eight Years of Change." In *Puro Conjunto, An Album in Words and Pictures*, edited by Juan Tejeda and Avelardo Valdez, 107–111. Austin: CMAS Books, Guadalupe Cultural Arts Center, 2001.

Martínez, Andy. "Talkin' 'Bout Baldemar." *Nuestro* 1 (April 1977): 60–61.

Martínez, Max. "El Conjunto Bernal: Style and Legacy." In *Puro Conjunto, An Album in Words and Pictures*, edited by Juan Tejeda and Avelardo Valdez, 97–105. Austin: CMAS Books, Guadalupe Cultural Arts Center, 2001.

________. "Valeria Longoria." In *Puro Conjunto, An Album in Words and Pictures*, edited by Juan Tejeda and Avelardo Valdez, 279–294. Austin: CMAS Books, Guadalupe Cultural Arts Center, 2001.

McDowell, John Holmes. "The *Corrido* of Greater Mexico as Discourse, Music, and Event." In *"And Other Neighborly Names": Social Process and Cultural Image in Texas Folklore*, edited by Richard Bauman and Roger D. Abrahams, 44–75. Austin: University of Texas Press, 1981.

McNeil, Norman Laird ("Brownie"). "Mexican Border Ballads." Master's thesis, University of Texas, Austin, 1944.

________. "El Contrabando del Paso." In *Texas Folk and Folklore*, edited by Mody C. Boatright, Wilson M. Hudson, and Allen Maxwell, 152–156. Dallas: Southern Methodist University Press, 1954.

________. "Corrido de Kansas." In *Texas Folk and Folklore*, edited by Mody C. Boatright, Wilson M. Hudson, and Allen Maxwell, 150–151. Dallas: Southern Methodist University Press, 1954.

________. "Corridos of the Mexican Border." In *Mexican Border Ballads and Other Lore*, edited by Mody C. Boatright, 1–34. Dallas: Southern Methodist University Press, 1946.

McNutt, James C. "Miguel Acosta: *Instrumentista*." In *Hecho en Tejas: Texas-Mexican Folk Arts and Crafts*, edited by Joe S. Graham, 172–187. Denton: University of North Texas, 1991.

Mendoza, Lydia. *Lydia Mendoza: A Family Autobiography*, compiled by Chris Strachwitz and James Nicolopulus. Houston: Arte Público Press, 1993.

________. "The Lark of the Border." In *Ethnic Recordings in America: A Neglected Heritage*, by American Folklife Center, 119–132. Washington, D.C.: Library of Congress, 1982.

Mendoza, Vicente T. "Some Forms of the Mexican *Canción*." In *Singers and Storytellers*, edited by Mody C. Boatright, Wilson M. Hudson, and Allen Maxwell, 46–55. Dallas: Southern Methodist University Press, 1961.

Miles, Elton. "The Corridos of the Big Bend." In *Sonovagun Stew: A Folklore Miscellany*, edited by Francis E. Abernethy, 36–47. Dallas: Southern Methodist University Press, 1985.

Miller, W. "Latin American Child and Music." *Texas Outlook* 31 (October 1947): 26.

Morthland, John. "Border Music: A Veteran Filmmaker's New Documentary Looks at the Rich History of Tejano." *Texas Monthly* (September 1993): 98, 103.

________. "Elida Reyna." *Texas Monthly* (September 2000): 152–153.

Paredes, Américo. *A Texas-Mexican Cancionero: Folksongs of the Lower Border*. Urbana: University of Illinois Press, 1976.

________. *"With His Pistol in His Hand": A Border Ballad and Its Hero*. Austin: University of Texas Press, 1958.

________. "Ballads of the Lower Border." Master's thesis, University of Texas, Austin, 1953.

________. "The Ancestry of Mexico's *Corridos*: A Matter of Definitions." *Journal of American Folklore* 76 (1963): 231–235.

________. "The *Corrido*: Yesterday and Today." In *Ecology and Development of the Border Region*, edited by Stanley R. Ross, 293–297. Mexico City: Asociación Nacional de Universidades e Institutos de Enseñanza Superior, 1983.

________. "'El corrido de José Mosqueda' as an Example of Pattern in the Ballad." *Western Folklore* 17 (1958): 154–162.

________. "The Mexican *Corrido*: Its Rise and Fall." In *Madstones and Twisters*, edited by Mody C. Boatright, Wilson M. Hudson, and Allen Maxwell, 91–105. Dallas: Southern Methodist University Press, 1958.

________. "The Mexico-Texan Corrido." *Southwest Review* 27 (1942): 470–481.

Patoski, Joe Nick. *Selena: coma la flor*. Boston: Little, Brown, 1996.

________. "Is Tejano Music Dead?" *South Texas Studies* 10 (1999): 82–93.

Peña, Manuel H. *The Mexican American Orquesta*. Austin: University of Texas Press, 1999.

________. *Música Tejana: The Cultural Economy of Artistic Transformation*. College Station: Texas A&M University Press, 1999.

________. *The Texas-Mexican Conjunto: History of a Working-Class Music*. Austin: University of Texas Press, 1985.

________. "The Emergence of Texas-Mexican Conjunto Music, 1935–1960: An Interpretive History." Ph.D. dissertation, University of Texas at Austin, 1987.

________. "Conjunto Music: The First Fifty Years." In *Puro Conjunto, An Album in Words and Pictures*, edited by Juan Tejeda and Avelardo Valdez, 61–69. Austin: CMAS Books, Guadalupe Cultural Arts Center, 2001.

________. "The Emergence of Conjunto Music, 1935–1955." In *"And Other Neighborly Names": Social Process and Cultural Image in Texas Folklore*, edited by

Richard Bauman and Roger Abrahams, 280–299. Austin: University of Texas Press, 1981.

________. "Folksong and Social Change: Two Corridos as Interpretive Sources." *Aztlán* 12 (Spring/Fall 1982): 13–42.

________. "From *Ranchero* to *Jaitón*: Ethnicity and Class in Texas-Mexican Music." *Ethnomusicology* 29 (Winter 1985): 29–55. Reprinted in *Between Two Worlds: Mexican Immigrants in the United States*, edited by David G. Gutiérrez, 149–174. Wilmington, Del.: Scholarly Resources, 1996.

________. "Latino Music in the United States." In *The Hispanic Almanac*, edited by Nicolás Kanellos, 595–620. Detroit: Gale Research, 1993.

________. "Música frontera/Border Music." *Aztlán* 21 (1996): 191–225.

________. "Music for a Changing Community: Three Generations of a Chicano Family *Orquesta*." *Latin American Music Review* 8.2 (1987): 230–245.

________. "Ritual Structure in a Chicano Dance." *Latin American Music Review* 1.1 (1980): 47–73.

Ragland, Cathy. *Reclaiming Texas: The Tejano Music Explosion*. Washington, D.C.: Smithsonian Institution Press, 2003.

________. "La Voz del Pueblo Tejano: Conjunto Music and the Construction of Tejano Identity in Texas." In *Puro Conjunto, An Album in Words and Pictures*, edited by Juan Tejeda and Avelardo Valdez, 211–227. Austin: CMAS Books, Guadalupe Cultural Arts Center, 2001.

Reyna, José R. "Notes on Tejano Music." *Aztlán* 13 (Spring/Fall 1982): 81–94.

________. "Tejano Music as an Expression of Cultural Nationalism." In *Chicano Border Culture and Folklore*, edited by José Villarino and Arturo Ramírez, 175–180. San Diego: Marin Publications, 1992. Reprinted in *Puro Conjunto, An Album in Words and Pictures*, edited by Juan Tejeda and Avelardo Valdez, 191–198. Austin: CMAS Books, Guadalupe Cultural Arts Center, 2001.

Richmond, Clint. *Selena: The Phenomenal Life and Tragic Death of the Tejano Music Queen*. New York: Pocket Books, 1995.

Robb, John Donald. "The Music of Los Pastores." *Western Folklore* 16.4 (1957): 263–280.

Romero, Maritza. *Selena Pérez: Queen of Tejano Music*. New York: PowerKids Press, 1997.

Rosales, Francisco Arturo. "La Música en Houston: Fifty Years of Mexican-American Music." *The Americas Review* 16 (Spring 1988):12–25.

Ruiz, Geraldo. *Selena: La Ultima Canción*. New York: El Diario Books, 1995.

San Miguel, Guadalupe Jr. *Tejano Proud: Texas-Mex Music in the Twentieth Century*. College Station: Texas A&M University Press, 2001.

________. "Música Tejana: Nuestra Música." *Journal of Texas Music History* 1 (Spring 2001): 24–35.

________. "The Rise of Recorded Tejano Music in the Post-World War II Years, 1946–1964." *Journal of American Ethnic History* 19 (Fall 1999): 26–49.

Scruggs, Thomas Mitchell Jr. "*Ay, Te Dejo en San Antonio: Conjunto*, Anglos, and the Jiménez Family of San Antonio." Master's thesis, University of Texas at Austin, 1985.

Seeber, Jill S. "Santiago Jiménez, Sr." In *The New Handbook of Texas,* edited by Ron Tyler, Douglas E. Barnett, Roy R. Barkley, Penelope C. Anderson, and Mark F. Odintz, vol. 3, 941. Austin: Texas State Historical Association, 1996.

Shannon, Kelly. "San Antonio's Premier Singer Rosita Fernández Still Charms Texas Listeners After 65 Years." *Corpus Christi Caller-Times*, December 25, 1995.

Shorkey, Clayton T. "Bruno Villarreal." In *Puro Conjunto, An Album in Words and Pictures*, edited by Juan Tejeda and Avelardo Valdez, 301–314. Austin: CMAS Books, Guadalupe Cultural Arts Center, 2001.

Shotwell, Clayton Moore Jr. "The Chicano Popular 'Corrido' in Texas (1955–1985): A Musical Study of Commercially Produced 'Corrido' Tunes." Ph.D. dissertation, University of Minnesota, 1987.

Spencer, Laura Gutiérrez. "The Desert Blooms: Flowered Songs by Pat Mora." *Bilingual Review/La Revista Bilingüe* 20.1 (1995): 28–36.

Strachwitz, Chris, and James Nicolopulos, comps. *Lydia Mendoza: A Family Autobiography*. Houston: Arte Público, 1994.

Tatum, Charles M. "Música Tejana." In *Chicano Popular Culture/Que Hable el Pueblo*, by Charles M. Tatum, 22–31. Tucson: University of Arizona Press, 2001.

Taylor, Paul S. "Mexicans North of the Rio Grande." *Survey Graphic* (May 1931): 201–202.

________. "Songs of the Mexican Migration." In *Puro Mexicano*, edited by J. Frank Dobie, 221–245. Austin: Texas Folklore Society, 1935.

Tejano Roots: The Women (1946–1964). El Cerrito, Calif.: Arhoolie Records, 1991.

Tejeda, Juan. "Eva Ybarra." In *Puro Conjunto, An Album in Words and Pictures*, edited by Juan Tejeda and Avelardo Valdez, 295–300. Austin: CMAS Books, Guadalupe Cultural Arts Center, 2001.

________. "!Conjunto! Estilo y Clase: Narciso Martínez, Valerio Longoria, Tony de la Rosa, Paulino Bernal, Flaco Jiménez y Esteban Jordan." In *Puro Conjunto, An Album in Words and Pictures*, edited by Juan Tejeda and Avelardo Valdez, 315–351. Austin: CMAS Books, Guadalupe Cultural Arts Center, 2001.

________. "An Odyssey through the Magical Land of Conjunto, El Movimiento Xicano, and the Tejano Conjunto Festival." In *Puro Conjunto, An Album in Words and Pictures*, edited by Juan Tejeda and Avelardo Valdez, 359–377. Austin: CMAS Books, Guadalupe Cultural Arts Center, 2001.

________. "Santiago Jiménez, Sr." In *Puro Conjunto, An Album in Words and Pictures*, edited by Juan Tejeda and Avelardo Valdez, 255–278. Austin: CMAS Books, Guadalupe Cultural Arts Center, 2001.

Tejeda, Juan, and Avelardo Valdez, eds. *Puro Conjunto, An Album in Words and Pictures: Writings, Posters, and Photographs from the Tejano Conjunto Festival en San Antonio, 1982–1998*. Austin: CMAS Books, Guadalupe Cultural Arts Center, 2001.

Treviño, Adrián. *Tejano Music, 1830–1930: An Informal History*. Albuquerque: Trellis Publishing, 1990.

Treviño, Rudy R. "Tejano Music: A Historical Perspective." *Music World Magazine* (February 1997): 30–33.

Valdez, Avelardo, and Jeffrey A. Halley. "Career and Identity in Mexican American Conjunto Musicians." In *Current Research on Occupations and Professions: Creators of Culture,* edited by Muriel Cantor, vol. 8, 223–246. Greenwich, Conn.: JAI Press, 1993.

________. "Gender in the Culture of Mexican American Conjunto Music." *Gender and Society* 10 (1996): 148–167.

________. "The Popular in Conjunto Tejano Music: Changes in Chicano Class and Identity." In *Puro Conjunto, An Album in Words and Pictures*, edited by Juan Tejeda and Avelardo Valdez, 199–209. Austin: CMAS Books, Guadalupe Cultural Arts Center, 2001.

________. "Why Are There So Few Women Conjunto Artists?" In *Puro Conjunto, An Album in Words and Pictures*, edited by Juan Tejeda and Avelardo Valdez, 229–239. Austin: CMAS Books, Guadalupe Cultural Arts Center, 2001.

Vargas, Deborah R. "Cruzando Frontejas: Remapping Selena's Tejano Music 'Crossover.'" In *Chicana Traditions: Continuity and Change*, edited by Norma E. Cantú and Olga Najera-Ramírez, 235–236. Urbana: University of Illinois Press, 2002.

Weaver, Neal. *Abraham Chávez: El Paso's Maestro*. El Paso: The Musical Friends of the Maestro, 1992.

Whatley, W. A. "A Mexican Popular Ballad." In *Happy Hunting Ground*, edited by J. Frank Dobie, 10–17. Austin: Texas Folk-lore Society, 1925.

Wood, Ben D. "A Mexican Border Ballad." In *Round the Levee*, edited by Stith Thompson, 55–57. Austin: Texas Folk-lore Society, 1916.

Young, Ron. "Macías: The Stradivarius of Bajo Sextos." In *Puro Conjunto, An Album in Words and Pictures*, edited by Juan Tejeda and Avelardo Valdez, 131–134. Austin: CMAS Books, Guadalupe Cultural Arts Center, 2001.

19. RELIGION

A particularly vital element in the construction of Tejano identity and livelihood is religion. We have selected items which relate, from Spanish colonial times to the current epoch, to the religious life of people of Mexican descent living in Texas. Because the Catholic church is so integral to the identity of the majority of Tejanos, many of the studies relate to Catholicism. However, other Tejanos turned to Protestantism and studies of that development are included in this compendium as well.

Women inside Mission Espada, San Antonio, Texas, 1941.
The Institute of Texan Cultures at UTSA, No. L-2760-E
The San Antonio Light *Collection*

Acosta, Teresa Palomo. "Bishops' Committee for Hispanic Affairs." In *The New Handbook of Texas*, edited by Ron Tyler, Douglas E. Barnett, Roy R. Barkely, Penelope C. Anderson, and Mark F. Odintz, vol. 1, 554. Austin: Texas State Historical Association, 1996.

________. "Home Altars." In *The New Handbook of Texas,* edited by Ron Tyler, Douglas E. Barnett, Roy R. Barkley, Penelope C. Anderson, and Mark F. Odintz, vol. 3, 677–678. Austin: Texas State Historical Association, 1996.

________. "Nuestra Señora de Guadalupe." In *The New Handbook of Texas*, edited by Ron Tyler, Douglas E. Barnett, Roy R. Barkely, Penelope C. Anderson, and Mark F. Odintz, vol. 4, 1064–1065. Austin: Texas State Historical Association, 1996.

________. "Sociedades Guadalupanas." In *The New Handbook of Texas*, edited by Ron Tyler, Douglas E. Barnett, Roy R. Barkley, Penelope C. Anderson, and Mark F. Odintz, vol. 5, 1131–1132. Austin: Texas State Historical Association, 1996.

________. "Texas Mexican Industrial Institute." In *The New Handbook of Texas*, edited by Ron Tyler, Douglas E. Barnett, Roy R. Barkley, Penelope C. Anderson, and Mark F. Odintz, vol. 6, 361–362. Austin: Texas State Historical Association, 1996.

Alexander, Bobby C. "A Pentecostal-Styled Mexican Mission in Dallas: An Illustration of Religious Diversity among New Latino Immigrants." *Listening* 33.3 (Fall 1998): 175–187.

Alfaro, Juan. "The Spirit of the First Franciscan Missionaries in Texas." *U.S. Catholic Historian* 9 (Spring 1990): 49–66.

Almaráz, Félix D. Jr. *Crossroad of Empire: The Church and State on the Rio Grande Frontier of Coahuila and Texas, 1700–1821*. San Antonio: Center for Archaeological Research of the University of Texas at San Antonio, 1980.

________. *The San Antonio Missions and Their System of Land Tenure*. Austin: University of Texas Press, 1988.

________. "Franciscan Evangelization in Spanish Frontier Texas: Apex of Social Contact, Conflict, and Confluence, 1751–1761." *Colonial Latin American Historical Review* 2 (Summer 1993): 253–287.

________. "Harmony, Discord, and Compromise in Spanish Colonial Texas: The Rio San Antonio Experience, 1691–1741." *New Mexico Historical Review* 67 (October 1992): 329–356.

________. "The Return of the Franciscans to Texas, 1891–1931." *Catholic Southwest* 7 (1996): 91–114.

________. "San Antonio's Old Franciscan Missions: Material Decline and Secular Avarice in the Transition from Hispanic to Mexican Control." *Americas* 44 (July 1987): 1–22.

Alvírez, David. "The Effects of Formal Church Affiliation and Religiosity on Fertility Patterns of Mexican Americans in Austin, Texas." Ph.D. dissertation, University of Texas at Austin, 1971.

________. "The Effects of Formal Church Affiliation and Religiosity on the Fertility Patterns of Mexican American Catholics." *Demography* 10.1 (February 1973): 19–36.

Atkinson, Ernest E. "Hispanic Baptist Theological Seminary." In *The New Handbook of Texas,* edited by Ron Tyler, Douglas E. Barnett, Roy R. Barkley, Penelope C. Anderson, and Mark F. Odintz, vol. 3, 631. Austin: Texas State Historical Association, 1996.

Ayala-Scheuneman, María de Jesús. "A Brief History of Three Presbyterian Educational Institutions in South Texas." *Journal of South Texas* 3 (1991): 66–82.

Azpiazu, Joseph. "Virgen de San Juan del Valle Shrine." In *The New Handbook of Texas*, edited by Ron Tyler, Douglas E. Barnett, Roy R. Barkely, Penelope C. Anderson, and Mark F. Odintz, vol. 6, 760. Austin: Texas State Historical Association, 1996.

Badillo, David A. "Between Alienation and Ethnicity: The Evolution of Mexican American Catholicism in San Antonio, 1910–1940." *Journal of American Ethnic History* 16 (Summer 1997): 62–83.

Baird, Robert. *The Life of Ramón Monsalvatge, a Converted Spanish Monk of the Order of the Capuchins*. New York: 1845.

Barrón, Clemente. "Racism and Religious Life." *Review for Religious* 55.5 (September-October 1996): 494–505.

Barsun, Helen W. "Los Pastores: A Remnant of Medieval Drama in San Antonio." Master's thesis, St. Mary's University, 1943.

Barton, May Wilson. "Methodism at Work among the Spanish-Speaking People of El Paso, Texas." Master's thesis, Texas Western College, 1950.

Barton, Paul Thomas. "In Both Worlds: A History of Hispanic Protestantism in the United States Southwest." Ph.D. dissertation, Southern Methodist University, 1999.

Barton, Paul, and David Maldonado, eds. *Hispanic Christianity within Mainline Protestant Traditions: A Bibliography*. Decatur, Ga.: Asociación para la Educación Teológica Hispana, 1998.

Bayard, Ralph Francis. *Lone Star Vanguard: The Catholic Re-Occupation of Texas, 1838–1848*. St. Louis: Vincentian Press, 1945.

Benson, Nettie Lee. "Bishop Marin de Porras and Texas." *Southwestern Historical Quarterly* 51 (July 1947): 16–39.

Berlant, Jeffrey L. "Protestants and Mexicans." In *The Mexican-American People: The Nation's Second Largest Minority*, by Leo Grebler, Joan W. Moore, and Ralph C. Guzmán, 486–512. New York: Free Press, 1970.

Brackenridge, R. Douglas. "José María Botello." In *The New Handbook of Texas*, edited by Ron Tyler, Douglas E. Barnett, Roy R. Barkely, Penelope C. Anderson, and Mark F. Odintz, vol. 1, 659. Austin: Texas State Historical Association, 1996.

________. "Mexican American Presbyterians." In *The New Handbook of Texas*, edited by Ron Tyler, Douglas E. Barnett, Roy R. Barkley, Penelope C. Anderson, and Mark F. Odintz, vol. 4, 662–663. Austin: Texas State Historical Association, 1996.

Brackenridge, R. Douglas, and Francisco O. García-Treto. *Iglesia Presbiteriana: A History of Presbyterians and Mexican Americans in the Southwest.* San Antonio: Trinity University Press, 1974.

________. "'Not Quite a Standard Judicatory': Texas-Mexican Presbytery, 1908–1960." In *Iglesia Presbiteriana: A History of Presbyterians and Mexican Americans in the Southwest*, by R. Douglas Brackenridge and Francisco O. García-Treto, 87–126. San Antonio: Trinity University Press, 1974.

________. "Presbyterian Missions to Mexican Americans in Texas in the Nineteenth Century." *Journal of Presbyterian History* 49 (Summer 1971): 103–132.

Bronder, Saul E. "Robert Emmet Lucey." In *The New Handbook of Texas*, edited by Ron Tyler, Douglas E. Barnett, Roy R. Barkely, Penelope C. Anderson, and Mark F. Odintz, vol. 4, 328–329. Austin: Texas State Historical Association, 1996.

________. *Social Justice and Church Authority: The Public Life of Archbishop Robert E. Lucey*. Philadelphia: Temple University Press, 1982.

Buck, Carlos. "A Study on the History of the Mexican-American Presbyterian Church in Texas." Master's thesis, Austin Presbyterian Theological Seminary, 1969.

Calleros, Cleofas. *El Paso's Missions and Indians*. El Paso: McMath, 1953.

________. *Historia de la Parroquia de San Ignacio de Loyola, El Paso, Texas*. El Paso: American Printing, 1935.

Campbell, T. N. "The Indians of the San Antonio Missions: Their Origin and Acculturation." In *Proceedings of the 1984 and 1985 San Antonio Missions Research Conferences*, edited by Gilberto R. Cruz, 35–38. San Antonio: LEBCO Graphics, 1986.

Cantú, Norma Elia. "The Offering and the Offerers: A Generic Illocation of a Laredo Pastorela in the Tradition of Shepherds' Plays." Ph.D. dissertation, University of Nebraska-Lincoln, 1982.

________. "Matachines." In *The New Handbook of Texas*, edited by Ron Tyler, Douglas E. Barnett, Roy R. Barkely, Penelope C. Anderson, and Mark F. Odintz, vol. 4, 552–553. Austin: Texas State Historical Association, 1996.

Carrera, Richard. "Mexican American Baptists' Dependency on Anglo Baptist Institutions in South Texas: A Case Study in Bee County." Master's thesis, University of Texas–Pan American, 2000.

Castañeda, Carlos E. *Our Catholic Heritage in Texas, 1519–1936: The Finding of Texas, 1519–1693*. Austin: Von Boeckmann-Jones, 1936.

________. *Our Catholic Heritage in Texas, 1519–1936: The Winning of Texas, 1693–1731*. Austin: Von Boeckmann-Jones, 1936.

________. *Our Catholic Heritage in Texas, 1519–1936: The Missions at Work, 1731–1761*. Austin: Von Boeckmann-Jones, 1938.

________. *Our Catholic Heritage in Texas, 1519–1936: The Passing of the Missions, 1762–1782*. Austin: Von Boeckmann-Jones, 1939.

________. *Our Catholic Heritage in Texas, 1519–1936: The End of the Spanish Regime, 1780–1810*. Austin: Von Boeckmann-Jones, 1942.

________. *Our Catholic Heritage in Texas, 1519–1936: The Fight for Freedom, 1810–1836*. Austin: Von Boeckmann-Jones, 1950.

________. *Our Catholic Heritage in Texas, 1519–1936: The Church in Texas Since Independence, 1836–1950*. Austin: Von Boeckmann-Jones, 1958.

________. "Don Carlos de Sigúenza y Góngora." *Catholic Historical Review* 16 (April 1930): 86–89.

________. "The Early Missionary Movement in Texas." *Missionary* 35 (December 1921): 360–361.

________. "Fr. Antonio Margil de Jesús." *Missionary* 38 (1924): 163–164, 197–199.

________. "Fray Juan de Zumárraga and Indian Policy in New Spain." *The Americas* 5 (1949): 296–310.

________. "God's Work in the Southwest." *Extension* 48 (November 1953): 18–19, 56.

________. "Pioneers in Sackcloth." *Preliminary Studies of the Texas Catholic Historical Association* 3.5 (October 1939): 309–326.

________. "Pioneers of the Church in Texas." In *Diamond Jubilee, 1874–1949: Archdiocese of San Antonio*, edited by M. J. Gilbert, 1–16. San Antonio: Schneider Printing Company, 1949.

________. "The Sons of St. Francis in Texas." *The Americas* 1 (January 1945): 289–302.

________. "Sources for Spanish American Church History." *Catholic Literary World* 10 (December 1938): 99–102.

Chabrán, Richard, and Rafael Chabrán, eds. "Patricio Fernández Flores." In *The Latino Encyclopedia*, edited by Richard Chabrán and Rafael Chabrán, vol. 2, 607. New York: Marshall Cavendish, 1996.

Chappelle, A. M. "Local Welfare Work of Religious Organizations in San Antonio." Master's thesis, University of Texas, Austin, 1939.

Chávez, Tomás Jr. *Quinceañera: A Liturgy in the Reformed Tradition*. San Angelo, Tex.: Presbytery of Tres Ríos, 1983.

________. *Texas American Presbyterians*. Midland: First Presbyterian Church Press, 1980.

Chipman, Donald E. "José Francisco Mariano Garza." In *The New Handbook of Texas,* edited by Ron Tyler, Douglas E. Barnett, Roy R. Barkley, Penelope C. Anderson, and Mark F. Odintz, vol. 3, 107–108. Austin: Texas State Historical Association, 1996.

________. "Juan José de Ganzabal." In *The New Handbook of Texas,* edited by Ron Tyler, Douglas E. Barnett, Roy R. Barkley, Penelope C. Anderson, and Mark F. Odintz, vol. 3, 81. Austin: Texas State Historical Association, 1996.

Cohen, Jan Hart. "To See Christ in Our Brothers: The Role of the Texas Roman Catholic Church in the Rio Grande Valley Farm Workers' Movement, 1966–1967." Master's thesis, University of Texas at Arlington, 1970.

Cole, M. R. *Los Pastores: A Mexican Play of the Nativity*. Boston: Houghton, Mifflin, 1907.

Connally, Ernest A. "The Ecclesiastical and Military Architecture of the Spanish Province of Texas." Ph.D. dissertation, Harvard University, 1955.

Cook, Joy. "Bishop Patrick Flores: A Barrio Bishop." *La Luz* 1.4 (August 1972): 18–21.

Crabbe, Rita. "Mariano Simon Garriga." In *The New Handbook of Texas,* edited by Ron Tyler, Douglas E. Barnett, Roy R. Barkley, Penelope C. Anderson, and Mark F. Odintz, vol. 3, 100–101. Austin: Texas State Historical Association, 1996.

Cruz, Gilberto R. "San Antonio Missions Declared Property of the Church by the Republic of Texas." In *Proceedings of the 1984 and 1985 San Antonio Missions Research Conferences*, edited by Gilberto R. Cruz, 8–12. San Antonio: LEBCO Graphics, 1986.

________. "The San Antonio Missions During the Texas Revolution." In *Proceedings of the 1984 and 1985 San Antonio Missions Research Conferences*, edited by Gilberto R. Cruz, 3–7. San Antonio: LEBCO Graphics, 1986.

________. "The Vicariate Apostolic of Brownsville, 1874–1912: An Overview of Its Origins and Development." In *From the Mississippi to the Pacific: Essays in Honor of John Francis Bannon, S.J.*, edited by Russell M. Magnaghi, 79–104. Marquette, Mich.: Northern Michigan University Press, 1982.

Cruz, Gilberto R., and Marta Cruz. *A Century of Service: The History of the Catholic Church in the Lower Rio Grande Valley*. Harlingen, Tex.: United Printers and Publishers, 1979.

Dawson, J. M. "Among the Mexicans in Texas." *Missionary Review of the World* 50 (October 1927): 757.

Day, James M. *Six Missions of Texas*. Waco: Texian Press, 1965.

de la Teja, Jesús F. "José Refugio Guadalupe de la Garza." In *The New Handbook of Texas,* edited by Ron Tyler, Douglas E. Barnett, Roy R. Barkley, Penelope C. Anderson, and Mark F. Odintz, vol. 3, 108. Austin: Texas State Historical Association, 1996.

________. "St. James at the Fair: Religious Ceremony and Civic Boosterism on the Colonial Mexican Frontier." *The Americas* 57.3 (2001): 395–416.

De León, Arnoldo. "Tejano Holy Days in the Nineteenth Century." *South Texas Journal of Research and the Humanities* 2 (Spring 1978): 35–44.

de Luna, Anita. "Spirituality, Theological Aesthetics, and Catechesis: Religiosidad Popular in the Tejano Catechetical Journey." Ph.D. dissertation, Graduate Theological Union, 2000.

________. "*Evangelizadoras del Barrio*: The Rise of the Missionary Catechists of Divine Providence." *U.S. Catholic Historian* 21.1 (Winter 2003): 53–71.

De Zavala, Adina. *History and Legends of the Alamo and Other Missions in and Around San Antonio*. San Antonio: privately printed, 1917.

Díaz, Benjamín. *Compendio de Historia de la Convención Bautista Mexicana de Texas*. San Antonio: Casa Evangélica de Publicaciones, 1961.

Díaz-Stevens, Ana María. "The Saving Grace: The Matriarchal Core of Latino Popular Religion." *Latino Studies Journal* 4 (September 1993): 60–78.

Diekemper, Barnabas C. "The Catholic Church in the Shadows: The Southwestern United States during the Mexican Period." *Journal of the West* 24.2 (April 1985): 46–53.

Dixon, John Henry. "Hallelujah's: A History of Hispanic Protestantism in El Paso." Master's thesis, University of Texas at El Paso, 1989.

Domenech, [Emmanuel]. *Missionary Adventures in Texas and Mexico: A Personal Narrative of Six Years' Sojourn in Those Regions*. London: Longman, Brown, Green, Longmans, and Roberts, 1858.

Donahue, William H. "The Missionary Activities of Fray Antonio de Jesús Margil in Texas, 1716–1727." *The Americas* 14 (July 1959): 45–55.

Doyon, Bernard. *The Cavalry of Christ in the Lower Rio Grande Valley, 1849–1883*. Milwaukee: Bruce Press, 1956.

Dragostin, Sigmund. "The Cursillo as a Social Movement." In *Catholics/U.S.A.: Perspectives on Social Change*, edited by William T. Liu and Nathaniel J. Pallone, 479–490. New York: John Wiley and Sons, 1970.

Dunigan, Joseph L. Jr. "The Religious Socialization of Mexican Americans: A Function of Analysis of Catholic Education." Master's thesis, University of Texas at El Paso, 1970.

Elizondo, Virgilio P. *Christianity and Culture: An Introduction to Pastoral Theology and Ministry for the Bicultural Community*. San Antonio: Mexican American Cultural Center Bookstore, 1975.

________. *The Future is Mestizo: Life Where Cultures Meet*. San Antonio: Mexican American Cultural Center Press, 1998.

________. *The Galilean Journey: The Mexican American Promise*. Maryknoll, N.Y.: Orbis Books, 1983.

________. *Mestizaje: The Dialectic of Cultural Birth and the Gospel*. 3 vols. San Antonio: Mexican American Cultural Center Press, 1978.

________. "*Mestizaje* as a Locus of Theological Reflection." In *Frontiers of Hispanic Theology in the United States*, edited by Allan Figueroa Deck, 104–123. Maryknoll, N.Y.: Orbis Books, 1995.

________. "The Mexican American Cultural Center Story." *Listening* 32.3 (Fall 1997): 152–160.

Elizondo, Virgilio, and Timothy M. Matovina. *San Fernando Cathedral: Soul of the City*. Maryknoll, N.Y.: Orbis Books, 1998.

Estrada, Isabel A., Ruby H. Vargas, and Judith L. Bishop. *Fieles al Maestro: Bordadoras del Diseño Misionero*. Dallas: Women's Missionary Union of Texas, 1992.

Fernández, Eduardo C. "The Contributions of the Jesuit Order in the New Mexico–Colorado–West Texas Area as the Rocky Mountain Mission, 1867–1919." In *Seeds of Struggle/Harvest of Faith: The Papers of the Archdiocese of Santa Fe Catholic Cuatro Centennial Conference*, edited by Thomas J. Steele, Paul Rhetts, and Barbe Awalt, 135–148. Albuquerque: LPD Press, 1998.

Fitzmorris, Mary Angela. *Four Decades of Catholicism in Texas, 1820–1860*. Washington, D.C.: Catholic University of America, 1926.

Flores, María Eva. "Las Hermanas." In *The New Handbook of Texas*, edited by Ron Tyler, Douglas E. Barnett, Roy R. Barkley, Penelope C. Anderson, and Mark F. Odintz, vol. 4, 89–90. Austin: Texas State Historical Association, 1996.

________. "PADRES." In *The New Handbook of Texas*, edited by Ron Tyler, Douglas E. Barnett, Roy R. Barkley, Penelope C. Anderson, and Mark F. Odintz, vol. 5, 9–10. Austin: Texas State Historical Association, 1996.

________. "St. Joseph's Parish, Fort Stockton, Texas, 1875–1945: The Forging of an Identity and Community." *U.S. Catholic Historian* 21.1 (Winter 2003): 13–31.

Flores, Richard R. "Los Pastores: Performance, Poetics, and Politics in Folk Drama." Ph.D. dissertation, University of Texas at Austin, 1989.

Flying Chips: Latin-American Presbyterianism in Texas. n.p.: Executive Committee of Home Missions, Synod of Texas, Presbyterian Church U.S. [1947].

Foik, Paul J. "Fray Juan Padilla." *Mid-America* 13.2 (1930): 132–140.

Foppe, Regina E. "The Response of the Roman Catholic Church to the Mexican Americans in West Texas, 1839 into Post-Vatican II." Master's thesis, Texas Tech University, 1976.

Forrestal, Peter P. "The Venerable Fray Antonio Margil de Jesús." *Mid-America* 14 (April 1932): 305–334.

Fowler, Sheri. "Tested by Fire: A South Texas Town Rebuilds Its Church with Faith, Hope, and Lots of Charity." *Texas Monthly* (August 1993): 72–73.

García, Juan Carlos. "Predictors of Participation in Continuing Education by Hispanic Pastors in Texas." Ph.D. dissertation, Southwestern Baptist Theological Seminary, 1998.

García, Mario T. "Catholic Social Doctrine and Mexican American Political Thought." In *El Cuerpo de Cristo: The Hispanic Presence in the U.S. Catholic Church*, edited by Peter Casarella and Raul Gómez, 292–311. New York: Crossroad, 1998.

________. "The Chicano Southwest: Catholicism and its Meaning." *U.S. Catholic Historian* 18.4 (Fall 2000): 1–24.

García, Richard A. "The Catholic Church." In *Rise of the Mexican American Middle Class: San Antonio, 1929–1941*, by Richard A. García, 151–174. College Station: Texas A&M University Press, 1991.

García, Rogelia Olga. "A History of the Catholic Church in Laredo." Master's thesis, Texas A&I College, 1953.

Garza, Minerva. "The Influence of Methodism on Hispanic Women through Women's Societies." *Methodist History* 34.2 (1996): 78–89.

George, Eugene. "An Architectural Overview of the Spanish Missions of Texas." In *Proceedings of the 1984 and 1985 San Antonio Missions Research Conferences*, edited by Gilberto R. Cruz, 60–63. San Antonio: LEBCO Graphics, 1986.

Gerald, Rex E. "An Introduction to the Missions of the Paso del Norte Area." *Password* 20 (Summer 1975): 47–58.

Gibson, Delbert L. "Protestantism in Latin-American Acculturation." Ph.D. dissertation, University of Texas, Austin, 1959.

Gifford, David R. "Presbyterian Pan American School." In *The New Handbook of Texas*, edited by Ron Tyler, Douglas E. Barnett, Roy R. Barkley, Penelope C. Anderson, and Mark F. Odintz, vol. 5, 328–329. Austin: Texas State Historical Association, 1996.

Glazer, Mark. "Faith and Saints in Mexican-American Folk Religion." In *More Studies in Brownsville History*, edited by Milo Kearney, 275–283. Brownsville, Tex.: Pan American University at Brownsville, 1989.

González, Anibal A. "José Antonio Díaz De León." In *The New Handbook of Texas,* edited by Ron Tyler, Douglas E. Barnett, Roy R. Barkley, Penelope C. Anderson, and Mark F. Odintz, vol. 2, 631–632. Austin: Texas State Historical Association, 1996.

Gosnell, Lynn, and Suzanne Gott. "San Fernando Cemetery: Decoration of Love and Loss in a Mexican American Community." In *Cemeteries and Gravemarkers: Voices of American Culture*, edited by Richard E. Meyer, 217–236. Ann Arbor: UMI Research Press, 1989.

Grebler, Leo, Joan W. Moore, and Ralph C. Guzman, eds. "Protestants and Mexicans." In *The Mexican-American People: The Nation's Second Largest Minority*, edited by Leo Grebler, Joan W. Moore, and Ralph C. Guzman, 486–512. New York: Free Press, 1970.

Grijalva, Joshua. *A History of Mexican Baptists in Texas, 1881–1981*. Dallas: Baptist General Convention of Texas, 1982.

Guthrie, Keith. "Presbyterian School for Mexican Girls." In *The New Handbook of Texas*, edited by Ron Tyler, Douglas E. Barnett, Roy R. Barkely, Penelope C. Anderson, and Mark F. Odintz, vol. 5, 329. Austin: Texas State Historical Association, 1996.

Gutiérrez, Blanca M. "The Shrine of La Virgen de San Juan del Valle." In *Border Life in the Rio Grande Valley: Essays of Remembrance and Research*, edited by Hal Kopel, 105–109. Edinburg, Tex.: Hidalgo County Historical Society, 1996.

Habig, Marion A. *The Alamo Chain of Missions: A History of San Antonio's Five Old Missions*. Chicago: Franciscan Herald Press, 1968.

________. *The Alamo Mission: San Antonio de Valero, 1718–1793*. Chicago: Franciscan Herald Press, 1977.

________. *San Antonio's Mission San José: State and National Historic Site, 1720–1968*. San Antonio: The Naylor Company, 1968.

________. "Benito Fernández de Santa Ana." In *The New Handbook of Texas,* edited by Ron Tyler, Douglas E. Barnett, Roy R. Barkley, Penelope C. Anderson, and Mark F. Odintz, vol. 2, 984–985. Austin: Texas State Historical Association, 1996.

________. "Joseph Antonio González." In *The New Handbook of Texas,* edited by Ron Tyler, Douglas E. Barnett, Roy R. Barkley, Penelope C. Anderson, and Mark F. Odintz, vol. 3, 234. Austin: Texas State Historical Association, 1996.

________. "Mission San José y San Miguel de Aguayo, 1720–1824." *Southwestern Historical Quarterly* 71 (April 1968): 496–516.

Hamburg, Earl G. *The Shrine of Our Lady of San Juan: San Juan, Texas*. Alamo, Tex.: The Alamo News, 1971.

Harrison, David C. "A Survey of the Administrative and Educational Policies of the Baptist, Methodist, and Presbyterian Churches Among Mexican American People in Texas." Master's thesis, University of Texas, Austin, 1952.

Hasdorff, James C. "The *Southern Messenger* and the Mexican Church-State Controversy, 1917–1941." Master's thesis, St. Mary's University, 1968.

________. "The *Southern Messenger* and the Mexican Church-State Controversy, 1917–1941." *Journal of Texas Catholic History and Culture* 5 (1994): 25–46.

Hendricks, Rick. "Antonio Severo Borrajo: Hispano-Mexican Patriot Priest." *Southern New Mexico Historical Review* 9.1 (January 2002): 1–5.

________. "The Church in El Paso del Norte in the Eighteenth Century." In *Seeds of Struggle/Harvest of Faith: The Papers of the Archdiocese of Santa Fe Catholic Cuarto Centennial Conference*, edited by Thomas J. Steele, Paul Rhetts, and Barbe Awalt, 101–118. Albuquerque: LPD Press, 1999.

________. "Santa María de las Caldas and the Hacienda de San Antonio: Diligencias Matrimoniales from the Lost Curacy, 1733–1739." *Nuestras Raices* 6 (Fall 1994): 115–125.

Hinojosa, Gilberto M. "The Enduring Hispanic Faith Communities: Spanish and Texas Church Historiography." *Journal of Texas Catholic History and Culture* 1 (March 1990): 20–35.

________. "Mexican-American Faith Communities in Texas and the Southwest." In *Mexican Americans and the Catholic Church, 1900–1965*, edited by Jay P. Dolan and Gilberto M. Hinojosa, 1–125. South Bend, Ind.: University of Notre Dame Press, 1994.

________. "Past and Present Perspectives on the Texas Missions." In *Proceedings of the 1984 and 1985 San Antonio Missions Research Conferences*, edited by Gilberto R. Cruz, 49–51. San Antonio: LEBCO Graphics, 1986.

Hinojosa, Juan-Lorenzo. "Culture, Spirituality, and United States Hispanics." In *Frontiers of Hispanic Theology in the United States*, edited by Allan Figueroa Deck, 154–164. Maryknoll, N.Y.: Orbis Books, 1995.

Hodges, B. A. *A History of the Mexican Mission Work Conducted by the Presbyterian Church in the United States of America in the Synod of Texas*. Waxahachie, Tex.: Woman's Synodical of Texas, 1931.

Holden, William Curry. *Teresita*. Owings Mill, Tex.: Stemmer House Publishers, 1978.

Holworthy, Mary Xavier. *Father Jaillet: Saddlebag Priest of the Nueces*. Austin: Von Boeckmann-Jones, 1948.

Hough, Richard L. "Religion and Pluralism Among the Spanish-Speaking Groups of the Southwest." In *Politics and Society in the Southwest: Ethnicity and Chicano Pluralism*, edited by Z. Anthony Kruszewski, Richard L. Hough, and Jacob Ornstein-Galicia, 169–195. Boulder, Colo.: Westview Press, 1982.

Hutton, Mittie. "Early Religious Activities of the Spanish in Texas." Master's thesis, Southwestern University, 1933.

Icaza, Rosa María. "Prayer, Worship, and Liturgy in a United States Hispanic Key." In *Frontiers of Hispanic Theology in the United States*, edited by Allan Figueroa Deck, 134–153. Maryknoll, N.Y.: Orbis Books, 1995.

Juárez, José Roberto. "La Iglesia Católica y el Chicano de Sud Tejas, 1836–1911." *Aztlán* 4 (Fall 1973): 217–256.

________. "Los Padres Rancheristas: The Nineteenth Century Struggle for Mexican American Catholicism in South Texas." In *Ranching in South Texas: A Symposium*, edited by Joe S. Graham, 15–43. Kingsville, Tex.: Texas A&M University-Kingsville, 1994.

Kennedy, Edward. *A Parish Remembers: Fifty Years of Oblate Endeavor in the Valley of the Rio Grande*. Mercedes, Tex.: Mercedes Enterprise, 1959.

Kilgore, Dan. "The Spanish Missions and the Origins of the Cattle Industry in Texas." In *Proceedings of the Second Annual Mission Research Conference*, edited by Gilberto R. Cruz, 62–67. San Antonio: Missions National Historical Park, 1984.

Kinsall, Al. "The Lady in Blue: María De Agreda of Spain." *Journal of South Texas* 8 (1995): 80–96.

Kress, Margaret Kenny. "Diary of a Visit of Inspection of the Texas Missions Made by Fray Gaspar José Solis in the Year 1767–68." *Southwestern Historical Quarterly* 35 (July 1931): 28–76.

Larralde, Carlos. "Chicano Jews in South Texas." Ph.D. dissertation, University of California, Los Angeles, 1978.

________. "Santa Teresa: A Chicana Mystic." *Grito del Norte* 3 (April-June, 1978): 9–114.

Leutenegger, Benedict, ed. *Life of Fray Antonio Margil, O.F.M.* Washington, D.C.: Academy of American Franciscan History, 1959.

________, trans. *Nothingness Itself: Selected Writings of Ven. Antonio Margil, 1690–1724*, edited by Marion A. Habig. Chicago: Franciscan Herald Press, 1976.

Lickteig, Franz B. "Commissariate of the South, Chapter VI: The Big Bend Missions." *The Sword* 26.3 (October 1966): 38–59.

Littlejohn, E. G. "The Holy Spring of Father Margil at Nacogdoches." In *Legends of Texas*, edited by J. Frank Dobie, 204–205. Hatboro, Penn.: Folklore Associates, 1964.

Machado, Daisy Lucrecia. "Of Borders and Margins: Hispanic Disciples in Texas, 1888–1945." Ph.D. dissertation, University of Chicago, 1996.

________. *Of Borders and Margins: Hispanic Disciples in Texas, 1888–1945.* New York: Oxford University Press 2003.

________. "Kingdom Building in the Borderlands: The Church and Manifest Destiny." In *Hispanic/Latino Theology: Challenge and Promise*, edited by Ada María Isasi-Díaz and Fernando F. Segovia, 63–72. Minneapolis: Fortress, 1996.

Maldonado, David J. *Crossing Guadalupe Street: Growing Up Hispanic and Protestant*. Albuquerque: University of New Mexico Press, 2001.

Markides, Kyriakos S., and Thomas Cole. "Change and Continuity in Mexican American Religious Behavior: A Three-Generation Study." In *The Mexican American Experience: An Interdisciplinary Anthology*, edited by Rodolfo O. de la Garza, Frank D. Bean, Charles M. Bonjean, Ricardo Romo, and Rodolfo Álvarez, 402–409. Austin: University of Texas Press, 1985.

Martin, Carlos G. "Evangelistic Strategies of Seventh-Day Adventists to Reach Recent Hispanic Immigrants to Texas: A Critical Evaluation." Ph.D. dissertation, Southwestern Baptist Theological Seminary, 1992.

Martínez, Joel N. "The South-Central Jurisdiction." In *Each in Our Own Tongue: A History of Hispanic United Methodism*, edited by Justo L. González, 39–64. Nashville: Abingdon, 1991. Translated as "La Jurisdicción Central del Sur." In *En Nuestra Propia Lengua: Una Historia del Metodismo Unido Hispano*, edited by Justo L. González, 43–70. Nashville: Abingdon, 1991.

Martínez, Juan Francisco. "Origins and Development of Protestantism among Latinos in the Southwestern United States, 1836–1900." Ph.D. dissertation, Fuller Theological Seminary, 1996.

Matovina, Timothy M. *Tejano Lay Initiatives in Worship, 1830–1860*. Notre Dame: Cushwa Center for the Study of American Catholicism, University of Notre Dame, 1993.

________. *Tejano Religion and Ethnicity: San Antonio, 1821–1860*. Austin: University of Texas Press, 1995.

________. "San Antonio Tejanos, 1821–1860: A Study of Religion and Ethnicity." Ph.D. dissertation, Catholic University of America, 1993.

________. "Guadalupan Devotion in a Borderlands Community." *Journal of Hispanic/Latino Theology* 4 (August 1996): 6–26.

________. "Lay Initiatives in Worship on the Texas *Frontera*, 1830–1860." *U.S. Catholic Historian* 12 (Fall 1994): 107–120.

________. "New Frontiers of Guadalupanismo." *Journal of Hispanic/Latino Theology* 5 (August 1997): 20–36.

________. "No Melting Pot in Sight." In *Perspectivas: Hispanic Ministry*, edited by Allan Figueroa Deck, Yolanda Tarango, and Timothy Matovina, 35–39. Kansas City, Mo.: Sheed and Ward, 1995.

________. "Our Lady of Guadalupe Celebrations in San Antonio, Texas, 1840–1841." *Journal of Hispanic/Latino Theology* 1 (November 1993): 77–96.

________. "Religion and Ethnicity in San Antonio: Germans and Tejanos in the Wake of United States Annexation." *Catholic Southwest: A Journal of History and Culture* 10 (1999): 29–49.

________. "Representation and the Reconstruction of Power: The Rise of PADRES and Las Hermanas." In *What's Left? Liberal American Catholics*, edited by Mary Jo Weaver, 230–237. Bloomington: Indiana University, 1999.

________, ed. *Beyond Borders: Writing of Virgilio Elizondo*. Maryknoll, N.Y.: Orbis Books, 2000.

Matovina, Timothy M., and Gerald E. Poyo, eds. *¡Presente! U.S. Latino Catholics from Colonial Origins to the Present*. Maryknoll, N.Y.: Orbis, 2000.

McCracken, Ellen. "Reterritorialized Spirituality: Material Religious Culture in the Border Space of San Fernando Cathedral." *Arizona Journal of Hispanic Cultural Studies* 4 (2000): 193–210.

McMurtrey, Martin. *Mariachi Bishop: The Life Story of Patrick Flores*. San Antonio: Corona Publishing, 1987.

McNeely, John H. "Holding Institute." In *The New Handbook of Texas*, edited by Ron Tyler, Douglas E. Barnett, Roy R. Barkely, Penelope C. Anderson, and Mark F. Odintz, vol. 3, 660–661. Austin: Texas State Historical Association, 1996.

Meier, Matt S. with Conchita Franco Serri and Richard A. García. "Patrick Flores." In *Notable Latino Americans: A Biographical Dictionary*, by Matt S. Meier, 152–155. Westport, Conn.: Greenwood Press, 1997.

Mendoza, Manuel. "The Hispanic Missions of Texas: An Interpretation." In *Proceedings of the Second Annual Mission Research Conference*, edited by Gilberto R. Cruz, 81–83. San Antonio: Missions National Historical Park, 1984.

Messing, Francis Alfred. "Dominic Manucy, Vicar-Apostolic of Brownsville, Texas, and Third Bishop of the Diocese of Mobile, Alabama, 1823–1885." Master's thesis, Notre Dame Seminary, New Orleans, 1964.

Missena, Esteban Guillermo. "A Study of Learning Styles and Related Factors of Adults in Selected Hispanic Baptist Churches in Tarrant County." Ph.D. dissertation, Southwestern Baptist Theological Seminary, 1997.

Mongeau, Gerard. "The Mexicans—A Rural Problem of the Catholic Church in the Southwest." *Mary Immaculate* (March 1938): 78–81, 94–95.

________. "Mexicans in Our Midst." *Mary Immaculate* (December 1933): 325–327, 345.

Montalvo, Carmela. "The Pastorela: The Missionary's Medium for Religious Instruction." *Tejidos* 2 (Fall 1975): 17–46.

Moore, James Tallmadge. *Acts of Faith: The Catholic Church in Texas, 1900–1950.* College Station: Texas A&M University Press, 2002.

________. *Through Fire and Flood: The Catholic Church in Frontier Texas, 1836–1900.* College Station: Texas A&M University Press, 1992.

Mounger, M. A. "Mission Espiritu Santo of Coastal Texas: An Example of Historic Site Archeology." Master's thesis, University of Texas, Austin, 1959.

Náñez, Alfredo. *History of the Rio Grande Conference of the United Methodist Church.* Dallas: Bridwell Library, Southern Methodist University, 1980.

Náñez, Clotilde Falcón. "Hispanic Clergy Wives: Their Contribution to United Methodism in the Southwest, Later Nineteenth Century to the Present." In *Women in New Worlds: Historical Perspectives on the Wesleyan Tradition*, edited by Hilah E. Thomas and Rosemary Skinner Keller, 166–168. Nashville: Abingdon, 1981.

Nieto, Leo D. "The Chicano Movement and the Gospel: Historical Accounts of a Protestant Pastor." In *Hidden Stories: Unveiling the History of the Latino Church*, edited by Daniel R. Rodríguez-Díaz and David Cortés-Fuentes, 143–157. Decatur, Ga.: A.E.T.H., 1994.

Novo-Peña, Sylvia, and Roberto Flores. *Interiors: Secular Aspects of Religion.* Houston: D. H. White, 1982.

Novosal, Paul. "The Tenure of the Brothers of Mary at Concepción Mission, 1855–1911." In *Proceedings of the Second Annual Mission Research Conference*, edited by Gilberto R. Cruz, 57–61. San Antonio: Missions National Historical Park, 1984.

Nunley, Carol Elaine. "Translation of Spanish Documents Pertaining to Mission Nuestra Señora del Rosario." Master's thesis, Texas Woman's University, 1975.

O'Rourke, Thomas P. *The Franciscan Missions in Texas, 1690–1793*. Washington, D.C.: Catholic University of America, 1927.

Orozco, Cynthia E. "Texas IAF Network." In *The New Handbook of Texas*, edited by Ron Tyler, Douglas E. Barnett, Roy R. Barkely, Penelope C. Anderson, and Mark F. Odintz, vol. 6, 344. Austin: Texas State Historical Association, 1996.

Parisot, P. F. *The Reminiscences of a Texas Missionary*. San Antonio: St. Mary's Church, 1899.

Parisot, Pierre Fourier, and C. J. Smith. *History of the Catholic Church in the Diocese of San Antonio, Texas*. San Antonio: Carrico and Bowen, 1897.

"A Prelude to Hispanic Church Leadership in the '80s: Patrick F. Flores. *La Luz* 8 (August-September 1979): 9.

Privett, Stephen A. *The U.S. Catholic Church and Its Hispanic Members: The Pastoral Vision of Archbishop Robert E. Lucey*. San Antonio: Trinity University Press, 1988.

________. "Robert E. Lucey: Evangelization and Catharsis among Hispanic Catholics." Ph.D. dissertation, Catholic University of America, 1985.

Puckett, Fidelia Miller. "Ramón Ortiz." In *The New Handbook of Texas*, edited by Ron Tyler, Douglas E. Barnett, Roy R. Barkely, Penelope C. Anderson, and Mark F. Odintz, vol. 4, 1171. Austin: Texas State Historical Association, 1996.

Pulido, Alberto L. "Mexican American Catholicism in the Southwest: The Transformation of a Popular Religion." In *Emerging Themes in Mexican American Research*, edited by Juan R. García, 93–108. Tucson: Mexican American Studies and Research Center, 1993.

Quezada, J. Gilberto. "Father Carmelo Tranchese, S.J.: A Pioneer Social Worker in San Antonio, Texas, 1932–1953." Master's thesis, St. Mary's University, 1972.

________. "Toward a Working Definition of Social Justice: Father Carmelo A. Tranchese, S.J., and Our Joy of Guadalupe Parish, 1932–1953." *Journal of Texas Catholic History and Culture* 4 (1993): 44–64.

Quirarte, Jacinto. *The Art and Architecture of Texas Missions*. Austin: University of Texas Press, 2002.

Rankin, Melinda. *Texas in 1850*. Waco: Texian Press, 1966.

________. *Twenty Years Among the Mexicans: A Narrative of Missionary Labor*. Cincinnati: Chase and Hall, 1875.

Rayburn, John C. "Melinda Rankin—Crusader of the Rio Grande." *Journal of Presbyterian History* 40 (September 1962): 160–180.

Remy, Martha Caroline Mitchell. "Protestant Churches and Mexican-Americans in South Texas." Ph.D. dissertation, University of Texas at Austin, 1970.

Rivas, José. "A Study to Determine the Role of the Ethical and Socio-Cultural Background as Influence Forces in the Religious Education of Baptist Students of Mexican Descent in Texas." Ph.D. dissertation, Southwestern Baptist Theological Seminary, 1967.

Roberts, Kathryn. "The Contribution of the Southern Presbyterian Church to the General Education of Latin-American Youth through Its Texas Mission Schools." Master's thesis, Southwest Texas State University, 1950.

Rodríguez, Edmundo. "The Hispanic Community and Church Movements: Schools of Leadership." In *Hispanic Catholic Culture in the U.S.: Issues and Concerns*, edited by Jay P. Dolan and Allan Figueroa Deck, 206–239. Notre Dame: University of Notre Dame, 1994.

Rodríguez, José Policarpo. *"The Old Guide," Surveyor, Scout, Hunter, Indian Fighter, Ranchman, Preacher: His Life in His Own Words*. Nashville/Dallas: Publishing House of the Methodist Episcopal Church, South, 1897.

Rodríguez, Moisés. "The Cultural Context of Southern Baptist Work among Mexican Americans in Texas." Ph.D. dissertation, Baylor University, 1997.

Rollin, María F. "The Champion of Zapata: Father Edward Bastien and the Fight for Just Compensation." *Catholic Southwest: A Journal of History and Culture* 12 (2001): 107–118.

________, ed. *The Fighting Padre of Zapata: Father Edward Bastien and the Falcon Dam Project*. Southwestern Studies No. 110. El Paso: Texas Western Press, 2003.

Romero, Juan."Charisma and Power: An Essay on the History of PADRES." *U.S. Catholic Historian* 9.1–2 (Winter/Spring 1990): 147–163.

________. "Mexican American Priests: History of PADRES 1969–1989." In *Hispanics in the Church: Up from the Cellar*, edited by Philip E. Lampe, 71–94. San Francisco/London: Catholic Scholars Press, 1994.

Rowland, Thomas H. "The Search for the Old Socorro Mission." Master's thesis, University of Texas at El Paso, 1984.

Ryan, Stephen P., "*Revista Católica*." In *The New Handbook of Texas*, edited by Ron Tyler, Douglas E. Barnett, Roy R. Barkely, Penelope C. Anderson, and Mark F. Odintz, vol. 5, 552–553. Austin: Texas State Historical Association, 1996.

Sandoval, Moisés. "The Future of the Hispanic Church." In *Barrios and Borderlands: Cultures of Latinos and Latinas in the United States*, edited by Denis Lynn Daly Heyck, 134–138. New York: Routledge, 1994.

________, ed. *Fronteras: A History of the Latin American Church in the USA since 1513*. San Antonio: Mexican American Cultural Center, 1983.

Santos, Richard G. "Chicanos of Jewish Descent in Texas." *Western States Jewish Historical Quarterly* 15 (July 1983).

Schmitz, Joseph W. *Six Missions of Texas*. Waco: Texian Press, 1965.

________. *The Society of Mary in Texas*. San Antonio: The Naylor Company, 1951.

Scotford, John R. "Mexico in Texas." In *Within These Borders: Spanish-Speaking Peoples in the U.S.A.* by John R. Scotford, 31–55. New York: Friendship Press, 1953.

Sekul, Joseph D. "Communities Organized for Public Service: Citizen Power and Public Policy in San Antonio." In *The Politics of San Antonio: Community, Progress, and Power*, edited by David R. Johnson, John A. Booth, and Richard J. Harris, 175–190. Lincoln: University of Nebraska Press, 1983.

________. "COPS: The Catholic Church and Grass Roots Organizing." *South Texas Studies* 1 (1991): 88–123.

Shirley, Dennis. *Valley Interfaith and School Reform: Organizing for Power in South Texas*. Austin: University of Texas Press, 2002.

Simons, Helen, and Roni Morales. "Churches, Chapels, and Shrines: Expressions of Hispanic Catholicism in Texas." In *Hispanic Texas: A Historical Guide*, edited by Helen Simons and Cathryn A. Hoyt, 107–119. Austin: University of Texas Press, 1992.

Sisneros, Samuel E. "El Paseño, Padre Ramón Ortiz: 1814–1896." *Password* 42 (Summer 1997): 55–77.

Slattery, Margaret Patrice. *Promises to Keep: A History of the Sisters of Charity of the Incarnate Word*. San Antonio, Tex.: n.p., 1995.

Stanford, Lois. "Religious Cofradías in El Paso's Lower Valley: Remembering the Hijas de María." *Password* 39 (Fall 1994): 113–124.

________. "Local Devotion to St. Michael: Examining Expressions of Popular Catholicism in Socorro, Texas." In *Seeds of Struggle/Harvest of Faith: The Papers of the Archdiocese of Santa Fe Catholic Cuatro Centennial Conference*, edited by Thomas J. Steele, Paul Rhetts, and Barbe Awalt, 119–134. Albuquerque: LPD Press, 1999.

________. "Persistence in Religious Faith and Practice: Traditional Holy Week Observances in Socorro, Texas." *Catholic Southwest: A Journal of History and Culture* 9 (1998): 75–98.

Stecker, Sister Mary of Providence. "The History of San Fernando Cathedral." Master's thesis, Catholic University of America, 1940.

Sweeney, Mary Frances. "The Social and Religious Customs of the Spanish-Indian Population of San Antonio, Texas." Master's thesis, Southwest Texas State Teachers College, 1938.

Tafoya, Carmen. "Expansion of the Church in Texas." In *Fronteras: A History of the Latin American Church in the USA since 1513*, edited by Moisés Sandoval, 225–237. San Antonio: Mexican American Cultural Center, 1983.

Tatum, Inez. "Mexican Missions in Texas." Master's thesis, Baylor University, 1938.

Taylor, Anna J. "New Mexican Pastores and Priests in the Texas Panhandle, 1887–1915." *Panhandle Plains Historical Review* 57 (1984): 65–80.

Taylor, Charles J. "The Mexicans of Texas." *Mary Immaculate* (December 1915): 7–8.

________. "Our Mexican Problem in Texas." *Mary Immaculate* (June 1923): 30–32.

Taylor, Mary D. "Cura de la Frontera, Ramón Ortiz." *U.S. Catholic Historian* 9.1–2 (Winter/Spring 1990): 67–85.

Taylor, Mrs. Thos. F. "Texas for Mary." *Mary Immaculate* 11.3–8 (March-August 1928): 53–54, 76–78, 105–106, 124–125, 148–150.

Thrash, James C. "Spanish-Speaking Presbyterians in South Texas." Master's thesis, Texas A&I University, 1969.

Tijerina, Andrés. "A Tejano Prayer." In *Tejano Empire: Life on the South Texas Ranchos*, by Andrés Tijerina, 107–121. College Station: Texas A&M University Press, 1998.

Timmons, William H. "The Church of Isleta—Recent Documentary Discoveries." *Password* 28 (Fall 1983): 113–117.

Torres, Irene Calderón. "The Church-State Conflict in Mexico and Its Effects in the El Paso Area after 1910." Master's thesis, University of Texas at El Paso, 1983.

Treviño, Roberto R. "*La Fe*: Catholicism and Mexican Americans in Houston, 1911–1972." Ph.D. dissertation, Stanford University, 1993.

________. "Facing Jim Crow: Catholic Sisters and the 'Mexican Problem' in Texas." *Western Historical Quarterly* 34 (Summer 2003): 139–164.

________. "In Their Own Way: Parish Funding and Mexican American Ethnicity in Catholic Houston, 1911–1972." *Latino Studies Journal* 5 (September 1994): 87–107.

________. "Mexican Americans and Religion." In *The New Handbook of Texas*, edited by Ron Tyler, Douglas E. Barnett, Roy R. Barkley, Penelope C. Anderson, and Mark F. Odintz, vol. 4, 672–676. Austin: Texas State Historical Association, 1996.

Turner, Kay F. "Mexican American Home Altars: The Art of Relationship." Ph.D. dissertation, University of Texas at Austin, 1990.

________. "Mexican American Home Altars: Towards Their Interpretation." *Aztlán* 13.1–2 (Spring/Fall 1982): 309–326.

Ulmer, Dwayne Craig. "A Comparative Analysis of Hispanic Youth and Anglo Youth Ministries in Churches of the Southern Baptist Convention." Ed.D. dissertation, Southern Baptist Theological Seminary, 2001.

Valdez, Mary Paul. *Hispanic Catholics in the Diocese of Dallas, 1890–1990 / Hispanos Católicos en la Diócesis de Dallas, 1890–1990*. [Dallas: Diocese of Dallas, 1990.]

________. *The History of the Missionary Catechists of Divine Providence*. San Antonio: Missionary Catechists of Divine Providence, 1978.

________. "Missionary Catechists of Divine Providence." In *The New Handbook of Texas*, edited by Ron Tyler, Douglas E. Barnett, Roy R. Barkely, Penelope C. Anderson, and Mark F. Odintz, vol. 4, 774. Austin: Texas State Historical Association, 1996.

Vález, María Luisa. "The Pilgrimage of Hispanics in the Sisters of Charity of the Incarnate Word." *U.S. Catholic Historian* 9 (Spring/Winter 1990): 181–194.

Vernon, Walter N. "Alfredo Nuñez." In *The New Handbook of Texas*, edited by Ron Tyler, Douglas E. Barnett, Roy R. Barkley, Penelope C. Anderson, and Mark F. Odintz, vol. 4, 935–936. Austin: Texas State Historical Association, 1996.

________. "Lydia Patterson Institute." In *The New Handbook of Texas*, edited by Ron Tyler, Douglas E. Barnett, Roy R. Barkely, Penelope C. Anderson, and Mark F. Odintz, vol. 4, 343. Austin: Texas State Historical Association, 1996.

Vidaurri, Cynthia Lee. "The Mexican-American Religious Folk Arts Tradition in South Texas." Master's thesis, Texas A&I University, 1991.

Wagner, John A. "The Role of the Christian Church." In *La Raza: Forgotten Americans*, edited by Julian Samora, 27–45. Notre Dame: University of Notre Dame Press, 1966.

Walsh, Albens. "The Work of the Catholic Bishops' Committee for the Spanish-Speaking People in the United States." Master's thesis, University of Texas, Austin, 1952.

Warren, Mark Russell. "Social Capital and Community Empowerment: Religion and Political Organization in the Texas Industrial Areas Foundation." Ph.D. dissertation, Harvard University, 1995.

Warton, Mary Wilson. "Methodism at Work among the Spanish-Speaking People of El Paso, Texas." Master's thesis, Texas Western College, 1950.

Watt, Alan J. "The Religious Dimensions in the Farm Worker Movement." Ph.D. dissertation, Vanderbilt University, 1999.

Weber, David J. "The Church in Jeopardy." In *The Mexican Frontier, 1821–1846: The American Southwest under Mexico*, by David J. Weber, 69–82. Albuquerque: University of New Mexico Press, 1982.

________. "Failure of a Frontier Institution: The Secular Church in the Borderlands under Independent Mexico." *Western Historical Quarterly* 13 (1981): 125–143.

Weddle, Robert S. "Cross and Crown: The Spanish Missions in Texas." In *Hispanic Texas: A Historical Guide*, edited by Helen Simons and Cathryn A. Hoyt, 25–36. Austin: University of Texas Press, 1992.

Wheat, John. "'Los Pastores': Continuity and Change in a Texas-Mexican Nativity Drama." *Journal of Texas Catholic History and Culture* 5 (1994): 47–64.

Wright, Pearl Couser. "Religious *Fiestas* in San Antonio." Master's thesis, St. Mary's University, 1946.

Wright, Robert E. *The Oblate Cavalry of Christ*. Rome: O.M.I. General Postulation, 1998.

________. "Popular and Official Religiosity: A Theoretical Analysis and a Case Study of Laredo-Nuevo Laredo, 1755–1857." Ph.D. dissertation, University of California, Berkeley, 1992.

________."Anglo Protestant Denominations and Mexicans in the Border Zone, 1836–1875." In "Popular and Official Religiosity: A Theoretical Analysis and a Case Study of Laredo-Nuevo Laredo, 1755–1857," by Robert E. Wright, 279–331. Ph.D. dissertation, Graduate Theological Union, Berkeley, 1992.

________. "Building Churches and Communities in 19th Century South Texas." *Heritage: A Publication of the Texas Historical Foundation* 17.1 (Spring 1999): 16–20.

________. "The Catholic Church in Laredo-Nuevo Laredo, 1858–1881." In *San Agustín Parish of Laredo: Abstracts of Marriage Book II, 1858–1881*, by Angel Sepúlveda Brown and Gloria Villa Cadena, ix–xxxiii. San Antonio: privately printed, 1993.

________. "Catholic Diocesan Church of Spanish and Mexican Texas." In *The New Handbook of Texas,* edited by Ron Tyler, Douglas E. Barnett, Roy R. Barkley,

Penelope C. Anderson, and Mark F. Odintz, vol. 1, 1030. Austin: Texas State Historical Association, 1996.

________. "The Hispanic Church in Texas under Spain and Mexico." *U.S. Catholic Historian* 20.4 (Fall 2002): 15–33.

________. "José Antonio Valdez." In *The New Handbook of Texas*, edited by Ron Tyler, Douglas E. Barnett, Roy R. Barkely, Penelope C. Anderson, and Mark F. Odintz, vol. 6, 688–689. Austin: Texas State Historical Association, 1996.

________. "José Darío Zambrano." In *The New Handbook of Texas*, edited by Ron Tyler, Douglas E. Barnett, Roy R. Barkely, Penelope C. Anderson, and Mark F. Odintz, vol. 6, 1140–1141. Austin: Texas State Historical Association, 1996.

________. "Local Church Emergence and Mission Decline: The Historiography of the Catholic Church in the Southwest During the Spanish and Mexican Periods." *U.S. Catholic Historian* 9 (Winter/Spring 1990): 27–48.

________. "The Parish of San Agustín, Laredo, 1760–1857." In *San Agustín Parish of Laredo, Abstracts of Marriage Book I, 1790–1857*, by Angel Sepúlveda Brown and Gloria Villa Cadena, 1–46. San Antonio: privately printed, 1989.

________. "San Agustín Church, Laredo." In *The New Handbook of Texas*, edited by Ron Tyler, Douglas E. Barnett, Roy R. Barkely, Penelope C. Anderson, and Mark F. Odintz, vol. 5, 791–792. Austin: Texas State Historical Association, 1996.

________. "San Fernando Cathedral Parish." *The New Handbook of Texas*, edited by Ron Tyler, Douglas E. Barnett, Roy R. Barkely, Penelope C. Anderson, and Mark F. Odintz, vol. 5, 842–843. Austin: Texas State Historical Association, 1996.

Xavier [Holworthy], Mary. *Father Jaillet, Saddlebag Priest of the Nueces*. Austin: Von Boeckmann-Jones, 1948.

Zelman, Donald L. "Carmelo Antonio Tranchese." In *The New Handbook of Texas*, edited by Ron Tyler, Douglas E. Barnett, Roy R. Barkley, Penelop C. Anderson, and Mark F. Odintz, vol. 6, 547. Austin: Texas State Historical Association, 1996.

20. SOCIAL CONSTRUCTS

This chapter includes the studies that show the development and inter-relationships of the Tejano community from the perspectives of the social sciences including geography, sociology, psychology, linguistics, and political science. The studies investigate daily living, politics, self-concept, identity, language, class, and environmental concerns.

Five men wearing aprons of Masonic Order, Conception, Texas, ca. 1890.
L-R: ? Palacios, Eduardo García, others unknown.
The Institute of Texan Cultures at UTSA, No. 96-235

Acosta, Teresa Palomo. "Alianza Hispano-Americana." In *The New Handbook of Texas*, edited by Ron Tyler, Douglas E. Barnett, Roy R. Barkley, Penelope C. Anderson, and Mark F. Odintz, vol.1, 104. Austin: Texas State Historical Association, 1996.

________. "Association for the Advancement of Mexican Americans." In *The New Handbook of Texas*, edited by Ron Tyler, Douglas E. Barnett, Roy R. Barkley, Penelope C. Anderson, and Mark F. Odintz, vol.1, 269. Austin: Texas State Historical Association, 1996.

________. "Confederación de Organizaciones Mexicanas y Latino Americanas." In *The New Handbook of Texas,* edited by Ron Tyler, Douglas E. Barnett, Roy R. Barkley, Penelope C. Anderson, and Mark F. Odintz, vol. 2, 263–264. Austin: Texas State Historical Association, 1996.

Acuña Patrick, Ida Hilda. "Quality of Life Perceptions Among Residents of Rural Unincorporated Subdivisions in Hidalgo County, Texas." Ph.D. dissertation, Texas A&M University, 1990.

Adkins, Patricia Guynes. "An Investigation of the Essentiality of Idioms and Figures of Speech in the Education of Bilingual Students in the Ninth Grade in Texas and New Mexico." Ph.D. dissertation, University of Colorado, 1966.

Aguirre, Lydia. "Alternative Health Practices Along the Western Texas Border." In *Modern Medicine and Medical Anthropology in the United States-Mexico Border Population*, edited by Boris Velimirovic, 60–66. Washington, D.C.: Pan American Health Organization, 1978.

Ainslie, Ricardo C. *No Dancin' in Anson: An American Story of Race and Social Change*. Northvale, N.J.: Jason Aronson, 1995.

Alarcón Cantú, Eduardo. "Nuevo Laredo, Tamaulipas: Cincuenta años de crecimiento urbano (1940–1990)." *Río Bravo* 2 (Spring 1993): 1–23.

Alcalá, Joyce Lynn. "Validation of Measures of Depression with Hispanic Children: A Multimethod Investigation." Ph.D. dissertation, Texas A&M University, 1990.

Álvarez, Salvador. "The Influence of Phonological Characteristics Upon Orthography in Mexican-American Second Graders." Ph.D. dissertation, University of Texas at Austin, 1973.

Amastae, Jon. "The Use of Phonology in the Study of Bilingualism." In *Southwest Area Linguistics Then and Now: Proceedings of the Fifth Southwest Area Language and Linguistics Workshop*, edited by Bates Hoffer and Betty Lou Dubois, 229–246. San Antonio: Trinity University, 1976.

________. "Official English and the Learning of English." In *Chicano Studies: Survey and Analysis*, edited by Dennis J. Bixler-Márquez, Carlos F. Ortega, Rosalía Solórzano Torres, and Lorenzo LaFarelle, 229–233. Dubuque, Iowa: Kendall/Hunt, 1999.

Anderson, Martha Davis. "Latin-American Teenagers and the News in Ten Rio Grande Valley Districts." Master's thesis, University of Texas, Austin, 1966.

Andrulus, S. "Ethnicity as a Variable in the Utilization and Referral Patterns of a Comprehensive Mental Health Center." *Journal of Community Psychology* 5 (1977): 231–237.

Armour, Basil W. "Social Problems of the Mexicans in the Rio Grande Valley of Texas." Master's thesis, Texas A&M University, 1932.

Arreola, Daniel D. "Beyond the Nueces: The Early Geographical Identity of South Texas." *Río Bravo* 2.2 (1992): 46–60.

Arreola, David Robert. "Psychotherapists' Perceived Differences of Locus-of-Control Assertiveness, Self-Disclosure, and Psychological Adjustment for Mexican- and Anglo-Americans." Ph.D. dissertation, Michigan State University, 1991.

Artean, Delfina Brown. "Rural Elderly Mexican-Americans: An Assessment of Functioning in Daily Living." Ph.D. dissertation, University of Maryland, 1982.

Atkinson, Rosa M. "The Educational Retardation of the Spanish-speaking Child and Recommendations for Remediation." Master's thesis, University of Texas, Austin, 1953.

Atwood, E. Bagby. *The Regional Vocabulary of Texas*. Austin: University of Texas Press, 1962.

Atwood, Patricia Beaty. "Self-Concept and Its Relation to Acculturation and Oral Language Acquisition among Secondary Mexican-American Students." Ph.D. dissertation, Texas Woman's University, 2001.

Austin, Alfredo López. "Medical Anthropology in a Border Context." In *Modern Medicine and Medical Anthropology in the United States-Mexico Border Population*, edited by Boris Velimirovic, 43–48. Washington, D.C.: Pan American Health Organization, 1978.

Bailey, Stanley, Karl Eschbach, Jacqueline Hagan, and Nestor Rodríguez. "The Human Costs of Border Enforcement: Migrant Deaths at the Texas-Mexico Border." *Migration World* 24.4 (1996): 16–20.

Baker, Margaret T. "An Analysis of Significant Factors Related to Incapacity of Parents in Families Receiving Aid to Dependent Children in Texas on the Basis of Deprivation of Parental Support Through Physical or Mental Incapacity." Master's thesis, University of Texas, Austin, 1956.

Bath, C. Richard, Janet Tanski, and Roberto Villarreal. "The Politics of Water Allocation in El Paso County: A Case Study of the *Colonias*." *Journal of Borderlands Studies* 9.1 (1994): 15–38.

Bath, C. Richard, and Victoria Rodríguez. "Comparative and Binational Air Pollution Policy in El Paso, Texas and Ciudad Juárez, Chihuahua." *Borderlands Journal* 6.2 (1983): 171–197.

Baumel-Schreffler, Sandra. "Mexican-Spanish in Houston, Texas: A Study of Language Contact and Its Effects on Overt Subject Pronouns." Ph.D. dissertation, University of Florida, 1995.

Bayley, Robert. "Consonant Cluster Reduction in Tejano English." *Language Variation and Change* 6.3 (1994): 303–326.

________. "Variation in Tejano English: Evidence for Variable Lexical Phonology." In *Language Variety in the South Revisited*, edited by Cynthia Bernstein, Thomas Nunnally, and Robin Sabino, 197–209. Tuscaloosa: University of Alabama Press, 1997.

Beasley, R. M., and G. Antunes. "The Etiology of Crime: An Ecological Analysis." *Criminology* 1.4 (1974): 439–461.

Benefiel, Patricia Ann. "Life Satisfaction, Leisure Satisfaction, and Leisure Participation among Anglo, Black, and Hispanic Older Adults." Ph.D. dissertation, Texas Woman's University, 1987.

Berberfall, Lester. "Some Linguistic Problems of the Spanish-speaking People of Texas." *Modern Language Journal* 42 (1958): 87–90.

Bernal, Ernesto M. "Psychometric Inadequacies on the TAAS." *Hispanic Journal of Behavorial Sciences* 22 (November 2000): 481–507.

Berrios, Lizardo S. "*Colonias* in the Lower Rio Grande Valley of South Texas: A Survey Report." *Policy Research Project Report*. Austin: LBJ School of Public Affairs, 1977.

Betts, Dianne C., and Daniel J. Slottje. *Crisis on the Rio Grande: Poverty, Unemployment, and Economic Development on the Texas-Mexico Border*. Boulder, Colo.: Westview Press, 1994.

Blanton, Carlos Kevin. "'They Cannot Master Abstractions, But They Can Often Be Made Efficient Workers': Race and Class in Intelligence Testing of Mexican Americans and African Americans in Texas During the 1920s." *Social Science Quarterly* 81 (December 2000): 1014–1026.

Boldt, Joanne Shuhi. "Patterns of Intergenerational Helping among Mexican-Americans: A Three Generational Study." Ph.D. dissertation, University of Kentucky, 1985.

Borg, Eva D. "A Study of the Maternity Homes' Services for the Unmarried Mother in the San Antonio, Texas Area." Master's thesis, Our Lady of the Lake College, 1960.

Bradshaw, Benjamin S., and Edwin Fonner. "The Mortality of Spanish Surnamed Persons in Texas: 1969–1970." In *The Demography of Racial and Ethnic Groups*, edited by Frank D. Bean and W. Parker Frisbie, 261–282. New York: Academic Press, 1978.

Bradshaw, Benjamin S., and Frank D. Bean. "Some Aspects of the Fertility of Mexican Americans." In *Demographic and Social Aspects of Population Growth*, edited by Charles Westoff and Robert Parke Jr., 139–164. Washington, D.C.: U.S. Government Printing Office, 1972.

________. "Trends in the Fertility of Mexican Americans: 1950–1970." *Social Science Quarterly* 53 (March 1973): 688–696.

Bray, Nancy Gail. "South Texas La Raza, a Fulcrum for Revolt? The Political Socialization Experience in Two Texas Towns." Master's thesis, University of Texas at Austin, 1975.

Brennan, James Edward. "A Study of the Channels of Communication Used by Spanish-named Residents of San Antonio, Texas." Ph.D. dissertation, Louisiana State University, Baton Rouge, 1968.

Briody, Elizabeth Kathleen. "Household Work/Subsistence Strategies Among Mexican Americans of the Lower Rio Grande Valley." Ph.D. dissertation, University of Texas at Austin, 1985.

Briones, Ernestina Handy. "Self-esteem and Leadership Aspiration of Registered Nurses in the Rio Grande Valley." Ed.D. dissertation, University of Houston, 1995.

Brookshire, Marjorie S. "Some Notes on the Integration of Mexican-Americans since 1929, Nueces County, Texas." *Industrial Relations Research Association Annual Proceedings* 8 (December 1955): 356–361.

Brown, R. L. "Social Distance Perceptions as a Function of Mexican American and Ethnic Identity." *Sociology and Social Research* 57.3 (1973): 273–287.

Brown, Robert W., R. Todd Jewell, and Jeffrey J. Rous. "Abortion Decisions among Hispanic Women along the Texas-Mexico Border." *Social Science Quarterly* 81.1 (March 2000): 237–252.

Broyles, Harvey Lloyd. "Some Phases of Spanish-Culture Segregation in South Texas." Master's thesis, Texas A&I University at Kingsville, 1949.

Bruhn, J. G., et al. "Follow-up of Minority Premedical Students Attending Summer Enrichment Programs in a Medical Setting." *Texas Medicine* 72.8 (1976): 87–90.

Buchanan, Anne, and Kenneth M. Weiss. "Infant Mortality in a Mexican-American Community: Laredo, Texas, 1950–1977." *Social Biology* 38 (Fall/Winter 1991): 233–241.

Buitron, Richard Arthur Jr. "Who Are We? The Quest for Tejano Identity in San Antonio, Texas, 1913—the Present." Ph.D. dissertation, Florida State University, 2002.

Bunn, Susan. "Case Studies of Mexican-American Adults who have obtained Prominence in Texas." Ph.D. dissertation, Texas A&M University, 1997.

Bussell, Robyn Ellen. "Battered Latinas and Law Enforcement: An Analysis of Their Experience." Master's thesis, University of Texas at Arlington, 2001.

Caldwell, Nicole Latysha. "The Assessment of the Influence of Ethnicity, Acculturation, and Explanatory Models of Pain Perception and the Resulting Impact on Primary Care Patients with Fibromyalgia." Ph.D. dissertation, University of Texas Southwestern Medical Center at Dallas, 2000.

Cantú, Norma Elia. "La Quinceañera: Towards An Analysis of a Life Cycle Ritual." *Southern Folklore* 56 (1999): 73–101.

Cárdenas, Amparo Amalia Galván. "Mexican American and Anglo-American Attitudes Towards Spanish and English as a Function of Social Factors in South Texas." Ph.D. dissertation, University of Texas at Austin, 1981.

Cárdenas, José A. "Chicano Self-Determination and Mental Health: Cristal as Pioneer." In *Chicano Mental Health: The Case of Cristal: An Evaluation of the Zavala County Mental Health Outreach Program*, by Sally Jones Andrade, 161–170. Austin: Hogg Foundation for Mental Health, 1978.

Carlson, Paul Edward. "Investigation of Bias in the Diagnosis of Behaviorally-Disordered Mexican-American Children Using the Social Behavior Assessment Scale." Ph.D. dissertation, Ohio State University, 1983.

Carrell, Theresa, and Traxel Stevens. "Leaping the Language Barrier." *Texas Outlook* (September 1961): 19–20, 44.

Carter, David Lee. "Hispanic Attitude toward Crime and Justice in Texas: A Study of Perceptions and Experiences." Ph.D. dissertation, Sam Houston State University, 1980.

Castro, Allen. "Mexican-American Values and Their Impact on Mental Health Care." Ph.D. dissertation, University of Texas at Austin, 1996.

Cavazos, Alonzo M. Jr. "A Measure of Bachelor of Social Work Students' Learning in Field Instruction at the University of Texas–Pan American." Ed.D. dissertation, University of Houston, 1994.

Cavazos, Esperanza. "A Study of the Effect of Birth Order on Intelligence." Master's thesis, Texas A&M University–Kingsville, 2000.

Cázares, Ralph B., Edward Murguía, and W. Parker Frisbie. "Mexican American Intermarriage in a Nonmetropolitan Context." In *The Mexican American Experience: An Interdisciplinary Approach*, edited by Rodolfo O. de la Garza, Frank D. Bean, Charles M. Bonjean, Ricardo Romo, and Rodolfo Álvarez, 393–401. Austin: University of Texas Press, 1985.

Cerda, Gilberto, Berta Cabaza, and Julieta Farios. *Vocabulario español de Texas*. Austin: University of Texas Press, 1970.

Champion, Carol Esparza. "Face-ism in Texas and Mexico." *Borderlands Journal* 3 (Spring 1980): 121–130.

Chandler, Sue Ann. "The Use of Alternate Health Resources in a South Texas Town." Master's thesis, University of Houston, 1978.

Chapa, J. "The Question of Mexican American Assimilation: Socio-economic Parity or Underclass Formulation?" *Public Affairs Comment* 35.1 (1988): 1–7.

Chaston, John Malcolm. "Aspect Choice in Preterit and Imperfect Usage in the Speech of Mexican-American College Students in Texas: A Sociolinguistic Approach." Ph.D. dissertation, University of Texas at Austin, 1987.

________. "Imperfect Progressive Usage Patterns in the Speech of Mexican American Bilinguals from Texas." In *Sociolinguistics of the Spanish-Speaking World,* edited by Carol A. Klee and Luis A. Ramos-García, 299–311. Tempe, Ariz.: Bilingual Press/Editorial Bilingüe 1991.

Chávez, Leo R. "The Power of the Imagined Community: The Settlement of Undocumented Mexicans and Central Americans in the United States." *American Anthropologist* 96.1 (1994): 52–73.

Christiansen, John R. "Estimation of Socioeconomic Status of Spanish-Americans in Atascosa and Bexar Counties, Texas." *Rocky Mountain Social Science Journal* 2.1 (1965): 215–222.

Cisneros, René, and Elizabeth Leone. "Becoming Literate: Historias de San Antonio." In *Spanish in the United States: Sociolinguistic Issues*, edited by John J. Jergen, 86–109. Washington, D.C.: Georgetown University Press, 1990.

Clegg, J. Halvor. "Fonética y fonología del español de Texas." Ph.D. dissertation, University of Texas, Austin, 1969.

Cobas, J. A. "Status Consciousness and Leftism: A Study of Mexican American Adolescents." *Social Forces* 55.4 (1977): 1028–1042.

Coleman, Jeffrey Alan. "Language Contact in the Inner City: The Acquisition of AAVE Features by Bilingual Hispanic Adolescents." Master's thesis, University of North Texas, 1998.

Coltharp, Lurline H. "Invitation to the Dance: Spanish in the El Paso Underworld." In *Texas Studies in Bilingualism*, edited by Glenn Gilbert, 7–17. Berlin: de Gruyter, 1970.

Colwell, Brian, Dennis Smith, and James J. Zhang. "Cambio en las escuelas: Mexican-American Parent Attitudes Toward School Health Education." *Journal of Community Health* 25 (October 2000): 427–437.

Connell, Earl Monroe. "The Mexican Population of Austin, Texas." Master's thesis, University of Texas, Austin, 1925.

Conner, Ruth. "Some Community, Home, and School Problems of Latin American Children in Texas." Master's thesis, University of Texas, Austin, 1949.

Cornejo, R. J. "The Acquisition of Lexicon in the Speech of Bilingual Children." In *Bilingualism in the Southwest*, edited by P. R. Turner, 67–93. Tucson: University of Arizona Press, 1973.

Costello, R. M., et al. "Mexican American Behavioral Adjustments in an Anglo Hospital." *Psychiatric Annals* 7.12 (1977): 82–85.

Crasilneck, Harold Bernard. "A Study of One Hundred Latin-American Juvenile Delinquents in San Antonio, Texas." Master's thesis, University of Texas, Austin, 1948.

Crawford, Ann Fears, and Crystal Sasse Ragsdale. "First Chicana Legislator: Irma Rangel." In *Women in Texas: Their Lives, Their Experiences, Their Accomplishments*, 330–339. Burnet, Tex.: Eakin Press, 1982.

Cruz, Adrián. "The Battle to be Mayor: A Case Study of Interethnic Conflict in the Lower Rio Grande Valley." Master's thesis, University of Texas–Pan American, 2001.

Davidson, C., and C. M. Gaitz. "Are the Poor Different?: A Comparison of the Work Behavior and Attitudes Among the Urban Poor and Non-Poor." *Social Problems* 22.2 (1974): 229–245.

Davidson, Randy. "Outmarriage Among Hispanics: Cameron County, 1870–1970." In *Still More Studies on Brownsville History*, edited by Milo Kearney, 49–56. Brownsville, Tex.: University of Texas at Brownsville, 1991.

Davies, Christopher S. "Colonia Settlements: Working-class Refuge Stations along the Texas-Mexico Border." *Planning Forum* (1995): 33–53.

Davies, Christopher S., and Robert K. Holtz. "Settlement Evolution of 'Colonias' along the U.S. Mexico Border: The Case of the Lower Rio Grande Valley of Texas." *Habitat International* 16 (1992): 119–142.

Davila, Guillermo H. "Joint Air Pollution Monitoring Program Developed in the Cities of Juárez, Chihuahua, Mexico, El Paso, Texas, and Las Cruces, New Mexico." In *Air Pollution Along the United States-Mexico Border*, edited by Howard G. Applegate and C. Richard Bath, 155–160. El Paso: Texas Western Press, 1974.

Davis, Ethelyn Clara. "Little Mexico: A Study of Horizontal and Vertical Mobility." Master's thesis, Southern Methodist University, 1936.

Davis, James Alston. "'Do People Like Me Have Any Control Over Politics?': A Study of the Locus of Political Control as Perceived by Mexican-American Adolescents of South Texas." Ph.D. dissertation, Miami University, 1977.

Dearman, Cecil J. "A Socio-economic Study of Latin American Farm Migrants in Texas." Master's thesis, Texas A&M College, 1947.

De Juana, Ana Cristina Downing. "Intermarriage in Hidalgo County, 1860–1900." Master's thesis, University of Texas at Pan American, 1998.

de la Garza, Rodolfo O. "Voting Patterns in Bi-Cultural El Paso." *Aztlán* 5 (1974): 235–260.

de la Garza, Rodolfo O., and Claudio Vargas. "The Mexican-Origin Population of the United States as a Political Force in the Borderlands: From Paisanos to Pochos to Potential Political Allies." In *Changing Boundaries in the Americas*, edited by Lawrence A. Herzog, 89–111. San Diego: Center for U.S.-Mexican Studies, 1992.

Díaz De León, Efren. "Code-switching as a Strategy for Communication by Third-grade Students in Bilingual Classrooms." Ed.D. dissertation, Texas A&I University, 1986.

Dingus, Anne. "Adios, Bandito." *Texas Monthly* 14 (January 1986): 186–187.

Dodson, Jack E. "Differential Fertility in Houston, Texas, 1940–1950: A Study of Recent Trends." Ph.D. dissertation, University of Texas, Austin, 1955.

________. "Minority Group Housing in Two Texas Cities." In *Studies in Housing and Minority Groups*, edited by Nathan Glazer and Davis McEntire, 84–109. Berkeley: University of California Press, 1960.

Dodson, Ruth. *Don Pedrito Jaramillo: Curandero*. San Antonio: Casa Editorial Lozana, 1934.

________. "Don Pedrito Jaramillo: The Curandero of Los Olmos." In *The Healer of Los Olmos and Other Mexican Lore*, edited by Wilson M. Hudson, 9–70. Dallas: Southern Methodist University Press, 1951.

Doggett, Elizabeth Belk. "A Linguistic and Cultural Profile of First Grade Mexican American Children in Austin, Texas." Master's thesis, University of Texas at Austin, 1970.

Doran, Amanda R. "Language Use and Identity in a Bilingual Community: Re-Examining the English of Mexican Americans." Ph.D. dissertation, University of Texas at Austin, 2001.

Dunn, Edward Wesley Jr. "A Factor Analysis of Communication Habits and Attitudes among Mexican-Americans in Austin and San Antonio, Texas." Ph.D. dissertation, University of Texas at Austin, 1973.

Dwyer, Augusta. *On the Line: Life on the U.S.-Mexican Border*. London: Russell Press, 1994.

Earle, Duncan. "Defining *Colonias*: Perspectives and Solutions on the 'Problem' in Texas." In *Memoria of the Bi-national Conference: Housing Production and Infrastructure in the Colonias of Texas and Mexico*, edited by Peter Ward, et al., 11–12. Austin: Mexican Center of ILAS, 1995.

Earle, Duncan, and Chang-Shan Huang. "Building Identity on the Border: Texas Colonias as Cultural Texts." In *Permeable Boundaries and the Construction of Space*, edited by Nezar al Sayyad, 77–96. Berkeley: IASTE, 1996.

Elías De Mounce, María Elena. "Mexican Elites in the United States: An Introductory Investigation of Privileged Mexicans in South Texas." Master's thesis, University of Texas–Pan American, 1996.

Elías-Olivares, Lucía Ernestina. "Ways of Speaking in a Chicano Community: A Sociolinguistic Approach." Ph.D. dissertation, University of Texas at Austin, 1976.

________. "A Study of the Oral Spanish Vocabulary of Ten High School Mexican-American Students in Austin, Texas." Master's thesis, University of Texas at Austin, 1970.

Elías-Olivares, Lucía, and G. Valdes. "Language Diversity in Chicano Speech Communities: Implications for Language Teaching." In *Bilingual Education for Hispanic Students in the United States*. New York: Teachers College Press, 1982.

Ellis, Christine Evangeline. "The Relation of Socioeconomic Status to the Intelligence and School Success of Mexican Children." Master's thesis, University of Texas, Austin, 1932.

Ellis, John M. "Spanish-Surname Mortality Differences in San Antonio, Texas." *Journal of Health and Human Behavior* 3.2 (1962): 125–127.

Ellwells, Gladys. "Factors Influencing the Assimilation of the Mexican in Texas." Master's thesis, Southern Methodist University, 1941.

Embry, John Edgar. "Adolescents' Perception of Deviance: A Study of Delinquent and Nondelinquent Mexican American Adolescents' Perceptions of Alcohol-Related and Nonalcohol-Related Peer Problem Behaviors." Ph.D. dissertation, University of Nebraska-Lincoln, 1986.

Evans, Carol Anne. "The Transmission of Spanish as a Family Language." Ph.D. dissertation, University of Texas at Austin, 1989.

Fabrega, H. Jr. "Mexican Americans of Texas: Some Social Psychiatric Features." In *Behavior in New Environments: Adaptation of Migrant Populations*, edited by E. G. Brody, 249–273. Beverly Hills: Sage Publications, 1970.

Fabrega, H. Jr., and C. A. Wallace. "Acculturation and Psychiatric Treatment: A Study Involving Mexican Americans." *British Journal of Social Psychiatry* 4.2 (1970–1971): 124–136.

________. "Value Identification and Psychiatric Disability: An Analysis Involving Americans of Mexican Descent." *Behavioral Science* 35.5 (1968): 362–371.

Farris, B. E., and Norval D. Glenn. "Fatalism and Familialism among Anglos and Mexican Americans in San Antonio." *Sociology and Social Research* 60 (1976): 393–402.

Ferry, Barbara. "Following Jaime." In *The Late Great Mexican Border: Reports from a Disappearing Line*, edited by Bobby Byrd and Susannah Mississippi Byrd, 139–145. El Paso: Cinco Puntos Press, 1996.

Finney, Floy C. "Juvenile Delinquency in San Antonio, Texas." Master's thesis, University of Texas, Austin, 1932.

Firestone, Juanita M., and Richard J. Harris. "Hispanic Women in Texas: An Increasing Portion of the Underclass." *Hispanic Journal of Behavioral Sciences* 16 (May 1994): 176–185.

Flanagan, Sammy Lee Jr. "Gender Identity Development in Self-disclosed Gay Men in Hidalgo County, Texas." Master's thesis, University of Texas–Pan American, 2000.

Flores, Darlene. "Computational and Statistical Applications to the Project at the Language and Linguistics Research Center at Pan American University." In *Southwest Areal Linguistics Then and Now: Proceedings of the Fifth Southwest Areal Language and Linguistics Workshop*, edited by Bates Hoffer and Betty Lou Dubois, 264–268. San Antonio: Trinity University, 1976.

Flores, Elena. "Sexual Attitudes and Behavior among Mexican-origin Adolescent Females." Ph.D. dissertation, The Wright Institute, 1992.

Flores, Estevan T. "Dealing in Marijuana: An Exploratory Story." *Hispanic Journal of Behavioral Sciences* 3 (June 1981): 199–212.

Fody, Michael III. "A Glossary of Non-Standard Spanish Words and Idioms Found in Selected Newspapers of South Texas during 1968." Master's thesis, Southern Illinois University, 1969.

Foley, Douglas E. "Decolonization and Mental Health in South Texas." In *Chicano Mental Health: The Case of Cristal: An Evaluation of the Zavala County Mental Health Outreach Program*, by Sally Jones Andrade, 151–160. Austin: Hogg Foundation for Mental Health, 1978.

________. "The Legacy of the *Partido Raza Unida* in South Texas: A Class Analysis." *Ethnic Affairs* 2 (Spring 1988): 47–73.

________. "The Politics of Studying Raza Unida Politics: Reflections of a White Anthropologist." In *Reflexiones 1999: New Directions in Mexican American Studies*, edited by Richard Flores, 51–80. Austin: Center for Mexican American Studies Books, 1999.

Foley, Douglas E., Clarice Mota, Donald E. Post, and Ignacio Lozano. *From Peónes to Politicos: Ethnic Relations in a South Texas Town, 1900–1977*. Austin: University of Texas Press, 1977.

Foley, Neil. "'The Little Brown Man in Gringo Land': The 'Second Color Menace' in the Western South." In *The White Scourge: Mexicans, Blacks, and Poor Whites in Texas Cotton Culture*, by Neil Foley, 40–63. Berkeley: University of California Press, 1997.

Folse, Kimberly A. "Hispanic Fathers and the Child Support Enforcement Experience." *Journal of Multicultural Social Work* 6 (1997): 139–158.

Fong, Robert S. "A Comparative Study of the Organizational Aspects of Two Texas Prison Gangs: Texas Syndicate and Mexican Mafia." Ph.D. dissertation, Sam Houston State University, 1987.

Fraga, Feliz, and John J. Kennedy. *A Study of the Recreational Needs of the Senior Latin American in San Antonio, Texas*. San Antonio: Our Lady of the Lake College, 1954.

Frausto, Manuel H. "Vocabulario español de San Marcos, Texas." Master's thesis, Southwest Texas State University, 1969.

Fredrickson, Signe Kay. "Suicidal Factors Profiling Mexican American Youth in Rural South Texas Counties." Master's thesis, Texas A&M University-Kingsville, 1999.

Freeman, Donald M. "Party, Vote, and the Mexican American in South Texas." In *La Cause Politica*, edited by F. Chris García, 55–60. Notre Dame: University of Notre Dame Press, 1974.

Fukumoto, Mary Nancy. "Perceptions of Ethnic Distinctiveness by a Group of Mexican-Americans: Case Study in a Housing Project in East Austin." Ph.D. dissertation, University of Texas at Austin, 1983.

Fuller, Roden. "Occupations of the Mexican-Born Population of Texas, New Mexico, and Arizona." *Journal of the American Statistical Association* 23 (March 1928): 64–74.

Galindo, D. Letticia. "Linguistic Influence and Variation on the English of Chicano Adolescents in Austin, Texas." Ph.D. dissertation, University of Texas at Austin, 1988.

________. "Caló and Taboo Language Use Among Chicanas: A Description of Linguistic Appropriation and Innovation." In *Speaking Chicana: Voice, Power, and Identity*, edited by D. Letticia Galindo and María Dolores Gonzales, 175–193. Tucson: University of Arizona Press, 1999.

________. "Language Attitudes toward Spanish and English Varieties: A Chicano Perspective." *Hispanic Journal of Behavioral Sciences* 17 (February 1995): 77–99.

________. "The Language of Gangs, Drugs, and Prison Life among Chicanas." *Latino Studies Journal* 4 (1993): 23–43.

________. "A Sociolinguistic Study of Spanish Language Maintenance and Linguistic Shift towards English among Chicanos." *Lenguas Modernas* 18 (1991): 107–116.

Galván, José L. "Marble Terminology in a Bilingual South Texas Community: A Sociolinguistic Perspective on Language Change." In *Spanish in the United States: Sociolinguistic Aspects*, edited by John Amastae and Lucía Elías-Olivares, 413–430. Cambridge: Cambridge University Press, 1982.

Galván, Roberto A. "El Dialecto Español de San Antonio, Texas." Ph.D. dissertation, Tulane University, 1955.

________."Un Estudio Geográfico de Algunos Vocablos Usados por Los Habitants De Habla Español de San Antonio, Texas." Master's thesis, University of Texas, Austin, 1949.

________. "'Chichecano' neologismo jergal." *Hispania* 53 (1970): 86–88.

________. "More on 'frito' as an English Loan-word in Mexican Spanish." *Hispania* 54 (1971): 511–512.

García, Anita H. "Identification and Classification of Types of Common Deviation from Standard Spanish made by Representative Native Speakers in South Texas." Master's thesis, Texas A&I University, Kingsville, 1969.

García-Camarillo, Cecilio. "Food Stamps are Playing Hard to Get." *Caracol* 3 (October 1976): 11.

García, Homer Dennis Calderón. "Chicano Social Class, Assimilation, and Nationalism." 2 vols. Ph.D. dissertation, Yale University, 1980.

García, Lucy. "Vocabulario selecto del español de Brownsville, Texas." Master's thesis, Southwest Texas State University, 1972.

García, Maryellen. "Pa(ra) in Locative Phrases in the Spanish of El Paso–Juárez." Ph.D. dissertation, Georgetown University, 1981.

García, Nelda C. "Language Factors in the Employment of Bilingual Mexican Americans: A Case Study Analysis." Ph.D. dissertation, Michigan State University, 1971.

Garza, Eugenio Davila. "Adolescent Mexican-American Student Attitudes of Self-Concept, Locus-of-Control and Family Ideology in the Lower Rio Grande Valley of Texas." Ph.D. dissertation, Georgia State University, 1977.

Garza-Falcón, Leticia M. *Gente Decente: A Borderlands Response to the Rhetoric of Dominance*. Austin: University of Texas Press, 1998.

Garza, Fernando Villerreal. "Personality Factor Comparisons of Anglos and Mexican-Americans of Driving While Intoxicated Offenders and Nonoffenders." Ed.D. dissertation, Texas Tech University, 1990.

Garza, Refugio S. "En el Nombre de Dios y Don Pedrito Jaramillo (In the Name of God and Don Pedrito Jaramillo)." Master's thesis, Texas College of Arts and Industries, 1952.

Gingiss, Peter, and Valerie Sheppard. "Stress Variation in Texas English." In *Southwest Areal Linguistics Then and Now: Proceedings of the Fifth Southwest Areal Language and Linguistics Workshop*, edited by Bates Hoffer and Betty Lou Dubois, 152–161. San Antonio: Trinity University, 1976.

Gómez, Daniel Parra. "Discouragement, Encouragement, and At Risk Hispanic Elementary Students' Self-esteem: An Ethnographic Case Study." Ed.D. dissertation, Texas Tech University, 1994.

Gómez, Ernesto Alvarado. "The Evaluation of Psychosocial Casework Services to Chicanos: A Study of Process and Outcome." Ph.D. dissertation, University of Texas at Austin, 1982.

González, Blanca N. "Attitudes Toward Psychotherapy and Willingness to Seek Psychotherapy of Mexican-Americans of Low and High Acculturation Levels." Ph.D. dissertation, Boston University, 1996.

González, Gustavo. *The English of Spanish-speaking Migrant Children: Preliminary Report.* Austin: Southwest Educational Development Laboratory, 1969.

________. "The Acquisition of Spanish Grammar by Native Spanish Speakers." Ph.D. dissertation, University of Texas at Austin, 1970.

________. "Some Characteristics of the English Used by Migrant Spanish-Speaking Children of Texas." *Aztlán* 7 (Spring 1976): 27–49.

González, Shon Asención. "The Prejudiced Attitude within the Hispanic Culture between Light-skinned and Dark-skinned Hispanics." Master's thesis, Texas A&M University-Kingsville, 2000.

Goodman, Paul Wershub, and Kathryn Renner. "Social Factors and Language." In *Problems in Applied Educational Sociolinguistics: Readings on Language and Culture Problems of United States Ethnic Groups*, edited by Glenn G. Gilbert and Jacob Ornstein, 55–62. The Hague: Mouton Publishers, 1978.

Goodwin, Kathryn Michele. "An Educational Tool to Help Mexican-Americans Identify Food Label Information." Master's thesis, Texas Woman's University, 1997.

Gossett, J. T., et al. "Extent and Prevalence of Illicit Drug Use as Reported by 56,745 Students." *JAMA: Journal of the American Medical Association* 216 (1971): 1464–1470.

Grossman, Beth. "Ethnic Identity and Self Esteem: A Study of Anglo, Chicano, and Black Adolescents in Texas." Ph.D. dissertation, New School for Social Research, 1981.

Grossman, Beth, R. Wirt, and A. Davids. "Self-Esteem, Ethnic Identity, and Behavioral Adjustment Among Anglo and Chicano Adolescents in West Texas." *Journal of Adolescence* 8 (1985): 57–68.

Guerra, Anna María. "Depressive Symptomatology in Mexican-Americans." Ph.D. dissertation, University of Houston, 1992.

Guerra, Irene. "The Social Aspirations of a Selected Group of Spanish-name People in Laredo, Texas." Master's thesis, University of Texas, Austin, 1959.

Guinn, Bobby. "Anthropometry of Mexican American Children in the Lower Rio Grande Valley." *Hispanic Journal of Behavioral Sciences* 10 (June 1988): 139–147.

Guinn, Bobby, Tom Semper, and Layne Jorgensen. "Perceived Leisure Freedom and Activity Involvement Among Mexican American Adolescents." *Hispanic Journal of Behavioral Sciences* 18 (August 1996): 356–366.

Gurnack, Anne Marie. "Access to Health Care in a West Dallas Community." Ph.D. dissertation, University of Texas at Arlington, 1979.

Gutiérrez, Armando. "The Politics of the Texas Border: An Historical Overview and Some Contemporary Directions." In *Views Across the Border: The United States and Mexico*, edited by Stanley R. Ross, 117–137. Albuquerque: University of New Mexico Press, 1978.

Gutiérrez, Carl. "Legislating Languages: 'The Ballad of Gregorio Cortéz' and the 'English Language Amendment.'" *The Americas Review* 17 (Winter 1989): 61–72.

Gutiérrez, Félix. "Spanish-Language Media in America: Background, Resources, History." *Journalism History* 4 (Summer 1977): 34–67.

Hagan, Jacqueline, and Nestor Rodríguez. "Resurrecting Exclusion: The Effects of the 1996 Immigration Reform on Families and Communities in Texas, Mexico and El Salvador." In *Latinos: Remaking America*, edited by Marcelo Suárez-Orozco and Mariela Paez, 190–201. Los Angeles: University of California Press, 2002.

Hamilton, James. "Mexican American Problems and Trends in Corpus Christi, Texas." Master's thesis, St. Mary's University, 1970.

Hardt, Annabelle. "Bi-cultural Heritage of Texas." Doctoral dissertation, University of Texas, Austin, 1968.

Harris, James Kilbourne. "A Sociological Study of a Mexican School in San Antonio, Texas." Master's thesis, University of Texas, Austin, 1927.

Harris, Mary Catherine. "Relationships between Ethnicity and Measures of Career Decision-making Behavior in a Comprehensive Texas High School." Ph.D. dissertation, Texas A&M University, 1998.

Harris, Richard J., and Juanita M. Firestone. "Ethnicity, Family Change, and Labor Force Patterns in Texas, 1980–1990." *Hispanic Journal of Behavioral Sciences* 19 (August 1997): 268–280.

Harrison, Helene W. "A Methodological Study in Eliciting Linguistic Data from Mexican American Bilinguals." Ph.D. dissertation, University of Texas, Austin, 1967.

Hasselmo, Nils. "Code-Switching and Modes of Speaking." In *Texas Studies in Bilingualism*, edited by Glenn Gilbert, 179–210. Berlin: de Gruyter, 1970.

Hayes, Alice Frazer. "Acoustic Vowel Charts: Spanish Vowels of One Idiolect." Master's thesis, University of Texas, Austin, 1961.

Hecht, Ilse H. "Folk Practices of the Childbearing Period among Mexican American Women." Master's thesis, Texas Woman's University, 1976.

Heiler, Barbara. "An Investigation of the Causes of Primary Stress Mislocation in the English Speech of Bilingual Mexican-American Students." Master's thesis, University of Texas at El Paso, 1966.

Hensey, F. "Grammatical Variables in Southwestern American Speech." *Linguistics: An International Review* 108 (1973): 5–26.

Hernández, Arthur E. "Do Role Models Influence Self Efficacy and Aspirations in Mexican American At-Risk Females?" *Hispanic Journal of Behavioral Sciences* 17 (May 1995): 256–263.

Herrick, Earl M. "Spanish Interference in the English Written in South Texas High Schools." In *Southwest Areal Linguistics Then and Now: Proceedings of the Fifth Southwest Areal Language and Linguistics Workshop*, edited by Bates Hoffer and Betty Lou Dubois, 162–169. San Antonio: Trinity University, 1976.

Hidalgo, Margarita. "Language and Ethnicity in the 'Taboo' Region: The U.S.-Mexico Border." *International Journal of the Sociology of Language* 114 (1995): 29–45.

Hinojosa, Irma. "Increasing the Consent Rate for Organ Donation in the Hispanic Population." In *U.S.-Mexico Border Health: Issues for Regional and Migrant Populations*, edited by J. Gerard Power and Theresa Byrd, 24–31. Thousand Oaks, Calif.: Sage Publications, 1998.

Holbert, Jerry Edward. "Rural/Urban Conflict over Water Control in the Lower Rio Grande Valley of Texas." Ph.D. dissertation, Texas A&M University, 1984.

Holmes, Malcolm D. "Perceptions of Abusive Police Practices in a U.S.-Mexico Border Community." *Social Science Journal* 35 (1998): 107–118.

Holmes, Malcolm D., and Howard C. Daudistel. "Ethnicity and Justice in the Southwest: The Sentencing of Anglo, Black, and Mexican Origin Defendants." In *The Mexican American Experience: An Interdisciplinary Anthology*, edited by Rodolfo O. de la Garza, Frank D. Bean, Charles M. Bonjean, Ricardo Romo, and Rodolfo Álvarez, 301–313. Austin: University of Texas Press, 1985.

Hoppe, S. K., and P. L. Heller. "Alienation, Familialism, and the Utilization of Health Services by Mexican Americans." *Journal of Health and Social Behavior* 16.3 (1975): 304–314.

Horton, Frances. "Food Habits and Living Conditions of Mexicans Dwelling in the Rio Grande Valley between Roma and Mercedes." Master's thesis, University of Texas, Austin, 1936.

Hotvedt, Mary Eleanor. "Family Planning among Mexican-Americans of South Texas." Ph.D. dissertation, Indiana University, 1976.

Howard, Raymond G. "Acculturation and Social Mobility Among Latin-Americans in Resaca City." Master's thesis, University of Texas, Austin, 1952.

Hunt, Thomas Lynn. "The Equity and Impact of Medicare and Medicaid with Respect to Mexican Americans in Texas." Ph.D. dissertation, University of Texas at Austin, 1978.

Hutchison, James. "Teenagers and Contraception in Cameron and Willacy Counties." *Borderlands Journal* 7 (Fall 1983): 75–90.

Hwang, Sean-Shong, and Steven H. Murdock. "Ethnic Enclosure or Ethnic Competition? Ethnic Identification among Hispanics in Texas." *Sociological Quarterly* 32 (1991): 469–476.

Jacobson, Rodolfo. "Intrasentential Code-switching and the Socioeconomic Perspective." In *Spanish in the United States: Sociolinguistic Issues*, edited by John J. Jergen, 59–66. Washington, D.C.: Georgetown University Press, 1990.

________. "The Social Implications of Intra-sentential Code-switching." In *Spanish in the United States: Sociolinguistic Aspects*, edited by John Amastae and Lucía Elías-Olivares, 182–208. Cambridge: Cambridge University Press, 1982.

Janis-Towey, Andrea Phyllis. "Hispanic Culturally Sensitive Assessment of Parent-Adolescent Conflict." Ph.D. dissertation, University of Wisconsin, Milwaukee, 1995.

Jerome, Annette Corrine. "An Investigation of the Effects of a Structured Group to Enhance Self-esteem, Internal Locus of Control Orientation and Career Aspirations of Hispanic Adolescent Females." Ph.D. dissertation, Brigham Young University, 1995.

Johnson, Carmen Acosta. "Fertility Differentials Among Mexican Americans of Five Southwestern States," Ph.D. dissertation, University of Texas Health Center at Houston, 1975.

________. "Breast-feeding and Social Class Mobility: The Case of Mexican Migrant Mothers in Houston, Texas." In *Twice a Minority: Mexican American Women*, edited by Margarita B. Melville, 66–82. St. Louis: C.V. Mosby Company, 1980.

Johnson, L. V., and M. Matre. "Anomie and Alcohol Use; Drinking Patterns in Mexican American and Anglo Neighborhoods." *Journal of Studies on Alcohol* 39 (1978): 894–902.

Johnson, Michael Gregory. "Discourse Markers in Tejano Speaking: Code Switching as a Resource in Spanish-English Conversation." Ph.D. dissertation, University of Texas at Austin, 1995.

Jones, B. D., and R. Shorter. "The Ratio Settlements of Social Status: Some Cross Cultural Comparisons." *Social Forces* 50.4 (1972): 499–511.

Juárez, Anna. "The Historical Development of Social and Ethnic Stratification in Laredo, Texas, 1750–1900." Master's thesis, University of Texas at Austin, 1983.

Karcher, Michael Justin. "Descriptive Operationalizing of Racial/Ethnic Awareness (DORA): A Study of Intergroup Understanding and Identity among Youth in South Texas." Ed.D. dissertation, Harvard University, 1997.

Kelley, Arthur Randolph. *Physical Anthropology of a Mexican Population in Texas: A Study in Race Mixture*. New Orleans: Middle American Research Institute, Tulane University, 1947.

Keyes, Grace G. "Mexican American and Anglo Midwifery in San Antonio, Texas." Ph.D. dissertation, University of Wisconsin, Milwaukee, 1986.

Kiev, Ari. *Curanderismo: Mexican American Folk Psychiatry*. New York: Free Press, 1968.

King, Genevieve. "The Psychology of a Mexican Community in San Antonio, Texas." Master's thesis, University of Texas, Austin, 1936.

Klapp, Orrin E., and L. Vincent Padgett. "Power Structure and Decision-Making in a Mexican Border City." *American Journal of Sociology* 65 (1960): 400–406.

Klee, Carol A. "Differential Language Usage Patterns by Males and Females in a Rural Community in the Rio Grande Valley." In *Language and Language Use: Studies in Spanish*, edited by Terrell A. Morgan, James E. Lee, and Bill VanPatten, 125–145. Lanham, Md.: University Press of America, 1987.

Kresselman, Harold B. "A Study of 100 Male Latin-American Juvenile Delinquents in San Antonio." Master's thesis, University of Texas, Austin, 1948.

Krueger, D. "The Relationship of Ethnicity to Utilization of Community Mental Health Centers." Ph.D. dissertation, University of Texas at Austin, 1974.

Kuvlesky, W. P., and Victoria M. Patella. "Degree of Ethnicity and Aspirations for Upward Social Mobility Among Mexican American Youth." *Journal of Vocational Behavior* 1.3 (1971): 231–244.

Kuvlesky, W. P., et al. "Status Projections and Ethnicity: A Comparison of Mexican Americans, Negro, and Anglo Youth." *Journal of Vocational Behavior* 1.2 (1971): 137–151.

Lampe, Philip E. "The Acculturation of Mexican Americans: Public and Parochial Schools." *Sociological Analysis* 36 (1975): 57–66.

________. "Mexican American Self-Identity and Ethnic Prejudice." *Cornell Journal of Social Relations* 10.2 (1975): 223–237.

Lance, Donald M. "Dialectical and Nonstandard Forms in Texas Spanish." In *El Lenguaje de los Chicanos: Regional and Social Characteristics used by Mexican Americans*, edited by Eduardo Hernández-Chávez, Andrew D. Cohen, and Anthony F. Beltramo, 37–51. Arlington, Va.: Center for Applied Linguistics, 1975.

________. "Spanish-English Code Switching." In *El Lenguaje de los Chicanos: Regional and Social Characteristics used by Mexican Americans*, edited by

Eduardo Hernández-Chávez, Andrew D. Cohen, and Anthony F. Beltramo, 138–153. Arlington, Va.: Center for Applied Linguistics, 1975.

Lane, John Hart Jr. "Voluntary Associations among Mexican Americans in San Antonio, Texas: Organization and Leadership Characteristics." Ph.D. dissertation, University of Texas, Austin, 1968.

Langewiesche, William. *Cutting for Sign: One Man's Journey along the U.S.-Mexican Border*. New York: Vintage Books, 1993.

Langston, Edward L. "The Impact of Prohibition on the Mexican-United States Border: The El Paso-Cuidad Juárez Case." Ph.D. dissertation, Texas Tech University, 1974.

Larralde, Carlos Montalvo. "Chicano Jews in South Texas." Ph.D. dissertation, University of California, Los Angeles, 1978.

Laurel, Noel Fernando. "An Intergenerational Comparison of Attitudes toward the Support of Aged Parents: A Study of Mexican-Americans in Two South Texas Communities." D.S.W. dissertation, University of Southern California, 1976.

Lawrence, Patricia A. "Psychological Risk Factors and Substance Abuse Among Young Adults: A Comparison of Non-Hispanic Whites and Mexican Americans." In *U.S.-Mexico Border Health: Issues for Regional and Migrant Populations*, edited by J. Gerard Power and Theresa Byrd, 32–51. Thousand Oaks, Calif.: Sage Publications, 1998.

Lazos, Hector. "A Study of the Relationship of Language Proficiency in the Mother Tongue and Acquisition of Second Language Reading Skills in Bilingual Children at Age Twelve." Ph.D. dissertation, University of Texas at Austin, 1981.

Lee, K. W. "Fundamental Attitudes of Mexican Americans in Edinburg, Texas Towards Political Participation." *South Texas Journal of Research and the Humanities* 1 (Fall 1977): 149–166.

Lee, Mathew T., Ramiro Martínez Jr., and Richard Rosenfeld. "Does Immigration Increase Homicide? Negative Evidence from Three Border Cities." *Sociological Quarterly* 42 (Fall 2001): 559–580.

Lee, Mathew T., Ramiro Martínez Jr., and S. Fernando Rodríguez. "Contrasting Latinos in Homicide Research: The Victim and Offender Relationship in El Paso and Miami." *Social Science Quarterly* 81 (March 2000): 375–388.

Lehman, Donald J. "Modern *Jacales* of Presidio (Texas)." *El Palacio* 46 (1939): 183–186.

Liebowitz, Stephen W. "Factors that predict Sexual Behavior among Young Mexican American Adolescents: An Exploratory Study." *Hispanic Journal of Behavioral Sciences* 21 (November 1999): 471–479.

Limón, José E. "El Meeting: History, Folk Spanish, and Ethnic Nationalism in a Chicano Student Community." In *Spanish in the United States: Sociolinguistic Aspects*, edited by John Amastae and Lucía Elías-Olivares, 301–322. Cambridge: Cambridge University Press, 1982.

Lipski, John M. "Sabine River Spanish: A Neglected Chapter in Mexican-American Dialectology." In *Spanish in the United States: Sociolinguistic Issues*, edited by John J. Jergen, 1–13. Washington, D.C.: Georgetown University Press, 1990.

Liu, Samuel T. "Essays on the Effects of Immigration on Education and Crime." Ph.D. dissertation, Massachusetts Institute of Technology, 2000.

Logan, Donald Moody. "Need Affiliation of Mexican-Americans and Anglo-Americans of South Texas." Ph.D. dissertation, Texas Tech University, 1971.

Lope Blanch, Juan M. "Problemas de morfología dialectal en el español de Tejas." In *El Español hablado en el Suroeste de los Estados Unidos*, by Juan M. Lope Blanch, 33–42. México: Universidad Nacional Autónoma de México, 1990.

López, Pedro. "Perceptions of Fear of Crime: A Comparative Analysis of White, Black, and Hispanic Texas Residents." Ph.D. dissertation, Sam Houston State University, 1983.

Lorimer, Carolyn Buxton Smith. "An Experiment in the Peer-Teaching of Spanish at the Elementary Level." Master's thesis, University of Texas at Austin, 1972.

Lozano, Amparo Augusta. "An Experiment in Teaching Spanish and English to Spanish-speaking Children." Master's thesis, University of Texas, Austin, 1932.

Lujan, Juan R. "Fourteen-Year-Old Drop-Outs in the Harlingen School System." Master's thesis, University of Texas, Austin, 1956.

Lundberg, David John. "A Comparison of Career Maturity and Personality Preferences Between Mexican-American and Anglo-American Adolescents." Ph.D. dissertation, University of North Carolina at Greensboro, 1995.

Lynch, Linda. "Beauty and the Beast, Trashing the Texas/Mexico Border." In *The Late Great Mexican Border: Reports from a Disappearing Line*, edited by Bobby Byrd and Susannah Mississippi Byrd, 186–198. El Paso: Cinco Puntos Press, 1996.

Lynch, Michael J. III. "The Role of J. T. Canales in the Development of Tejano Identity and Mexican American Integration in Twentieth Century South Texas." *Journal of South Texas* 13 (2000): 220–259.

Macías, José Carlos. "Violent Crime in Texas: An Indepth Look at Counties with a Population above 100,000." Master's thesis, University of Texas–Pan American, 1995.

Maciel, David R., and James B. Speer Jr. "Related Studies on the Chicano in Texas." *Aztlán* 6 (Fall 1975): 459–462.

Madsen, William. "Anxiety and Witchcraft in Mexican-American Acculturation." *Anthropology Quarterly* (1966): 110–127.

________. "Value Conflicts and Folk Psychotherapy in South Texas." In *Magic, Faith, and Healing*, edited by Ari Kiev, 420–440. New York: Free Press, 1964.

Mahoney, Mary. "Spanish and English Language Usage by Rural and Urban Mexican American Families in Two South Texas Counties." Master's thesis, Texas A&M University, 1967.

Mahon, Joan Deatly. "A Study to Assess the Relationship between Organizational Factors of Service Delivery and Utilization of Title III Programs by Older Hispanics in Dallas County, Texas." Master's thesis, University of Texas at Arlington, 1988.

Malina, Robert M., and Antonio N. Zavaleta. "Secular Trend in the Stature and Weight of Mexican American Children in Texas Between 1930 and 1970." *American Journal of Physical Anthropology* 52 (May 1980): 453–462.

Marambio, Juan. "Vocabulario español de Temple, Texas." Master's thesis, Southwest Texas State University, 1970.

Marcum, John P. "Minority Group Status and Fertility in a Neighborhood Context." Ph.D. dissertation, University of Texas at Austin, 1976.

Maril, L. M., and A. N. Zavaleta. "Drinking Patterns of Low-income Mexican-American Women." *Journal of Studies on Alcohol* 40 (1979): 480–484.

Maril, Robert Lee. *Living on the Edge of America: At Home on the Texas-Mexico Border*. College Station: Texas A&M University Press, 1992.

________. *Poorest of Americans: The Mexican Americans of the Lower Rio Grande Valley of Texas.* Notre Dame: University of Notre Dame Press, 1989.

________. "Towards a Media Theory of the Lower Rio Grande Valley." *South Texas Journal of Research and the Humanities* 1.1 (1976): 32–41.

Markides, Kyriakos S., and Harry W. Martin. *Older Mexican Americans: A Study in an Urban Barrio*. Austin: CMAS, University of Texas at Austin, 1983.

Marrocco, M. A. W. "The Spanish of Corpus Christi, Texas." Ph.D. dissertation, University of Illinois at Urbana-Champaign, 1973.

Márquez, Benjamín. *Constructing Identities in Mexican American Political Organizations: Choosing Issues, Taking Sides*. Austin: University of Texas Press, 2003.

________. *Power and Politics in a Chicano Barrio: A Study of Mobilization Efforts and Community Power in El Paso*. Lanham, Md.: University Press of America, 1985.

Marshall, Carolyn Emmett. "Evaluation of a Bilingual Video-Novella Method to Teach Elderly Mexican American Non-readers how to decrease their Risk of Diabetic Complications." Ph.D. dissertation, Texas A&M University, 1994.

Marshall, María Sandra González. "The Childbearing Beliefs and Practices of Pregnant Mexican-American Adolescents Living in Southwest Border Regions." Master's thesis, University of Arizona, 1987.

Martínez, Armando. "Acculturation, Self-Concept, Anxiety, Imagery and Stress as Related to Disease in Mexican-Americans." Ph.D. dissertation, University of North Texas, 1981.

Martínez, Glenn Andrew. "Topics in the Historical Sociolinguistics of Tejano Spanish, 1791–1910: Morphosyntactic and Lexical Aspects." Ph.D. dissertation, University of Massachusetts, Amherst, 2000.

Martínez, José Villarreal Jr. "Internal Colonialism and Decolonization in El Centro: A Sociohistorical Analysis of Chicanos in a Texas City." Ph.D. dissertation, University of Texas at Austin, 1981.

Matre, Marc, and Tatcho Mindiola Jr. "Residential Segregation in Southwestern Metropolitan Areas: 1970." *Sociological Focus* 14 (January 1981): 15–31.

Maunder, Marvel Lee. "Job Satisfaction of Hispanic Food Service Workers." Ph.D. dissertation, Texas Tech University, 1990.

Maurer, R., and J. C. Baxter. "Images of the Neighborhood and City Among Black, Anglo, and Mexican American Children." *Environment and Behavior* 4.4 (1972): 351–388.

May, Darlene Rae. "Notas sobre el tex-mex." *Noticias culturales del Instituto Caro y Cuervo* 70 (1966): 17–19.

McCary, Mallie M. "These Minorities in Our Midst: With Emphasis on Latin-Americans in Texas." Master's thesis, University of Texas, Austin, 1953.

McClendon, Juliette Jane Canfield. "Spanish-speaking Children of Big Springs: An Educational Challenge." Ph.D. dissertation, University of Texas, Austin, 1964.

McCleskey, Clifton, and Bruce Merrill. "Mexican-American Political Behavior in Texas." *Social Science Quarterly* 53 (March 1973): 785–799.

McClinton, Johnnie W. "Effectiveness of a Bilingual Vocational-Technical Program." Ph.D. dissertation, University of Missouri, Columbia, 1972.

McDonald, Jason John. "Race Relations in Austin, Texas, c. 1917–1929." Ph.D. dissertation, University of Southampton, 1993.

McDowell, John H. "Sociolinguistic Contours in the Verbal Art of Chicano Children." In *Spanish in the United States: Sociolinguistic Aspects*, edited by John Amastae and Lucía Elías-Olivares, 333–353. Cambridge: Cambridge University Press, 1982.

McFarlane, J., and J. Fehir. "*De Madres a Madres*: A Community, Primary Health Care Program Based on Empowerment." *Health Education Quarterly* 21.3 (1994): 381–394.

McGarry, Francesca. "A Study of Cultural Patterns among Three Generations of Mexicans in San Antonio, Texas." Master's thesis, University of Texas, Austin, 1957.

________. "Variations of Selected Cultural Patterns Among Three Generations of Mexicans in San Antonio, Texas." *American Catholic Sociological Review* 19 (March 1958): 24–34.

McKee, Nancy Patricia. "Living in *La Fabrica*: Environment, Opinion, and Strategies for Survival among Low Income Mexican-Americans in Laredo, Texas." Ph.D. dissertation, Washington State University, 1985.

McKee, Okla Markham. "Five Hundred Non-dictionary Words Found in the El Paso-Juárez Press." Master's thesis, Texas Western College, 1955.

McLemore, S. Dale. "The Origins of Mexican-American Subordination in Texas." *Social Science Quarterly* 53 (March 1973): 656–670.

McMillen, Jay Ben. "The Social Organization of Leisure among Mexican-Americans in Houston, Texas." Ph.D. dissertation, Texas A&M University, 1980.

McReynolds, Veon. "Variables Related to Predicting Absconding Probationers." Ph.D. dissertation, University of Texas at Austin, 1987.

Megargee, E. I. *Delinquency in Three Cultures: Project Followup Summary*. Austin: Hogg Foundation for Mental Health, 1968.

Merrill, Celia Dale. "Mexican-American English in McAllen, Texas: Features of Accentedness in the English of Native Spanish Bilinguals." Ph.D. dissertation, University of Texas at Austin, 1987.

Michel, Joseph. "A Pilot Project for Recording the Speech of the Five-Year Old Texas Spanish-English Pre-School Bilingual Child." *Florida Language Reporter* 20 (Fall 1969): 15–17.

Miller, Lawrence W. "A Note on Cultural Assimilation in South Texas." *Borderlands Journal* 6 (Fall 1982): 93–98.

Miller, Michael V. "Poverty, Development, and Quality of Life in a Texas Border City." Ph.D. dissertation, Texas A&M University, 1981.

________. "Chicano Community Control in South Texas: Problems and Prospects." *Journal of Ethnic Studies* 3.3 (1975): 70–89.

________. "Implications for Quality of Life on the Texas-Mexico Border: Interdependence, Inequality, and Sociocultural Diversity." In *Politics and Society in the Southwest: Ethnicity and Chicano Pluralism*, edited by Z. Anthony Kruszewski, Richard L. Hough, and Jacob Ornstein-Galicia, 105–129. Boulder, Colo.: Westview Press, 1982.

________. "Mexican Americans, Chicanos and Others: Ethnic Self-Identification and Selected Social Attitudes of Rural Texas Youth." *Rural Sociology* 41.2 (1976): 237–247.

________. "Vehicle Theft Along the Texas-Mexico Border." *Journal of Borderland Studies* 2.2 (1987): 12–32.

Miller, Michael V., et al. "The Impact of the 1982 Peso Devaluations on Crime in Texas Border Cities." *Journal of Borderland Studies* 1.2 (1986): 1–23.

Miller, S. O. "Current Status of Hispanic Social Workers." In *Hispanic Mental Health Professionals*, edited by E. L. Olmedo and S. López, 13–21. Los Angeles: University of California, Spanish Speaking Mental Health Research Center, 1977.

Miller, Tom. "Discreets of Laredo." In *The Late Great Mexican Border: Reports from a Disappearing Line*, edited by Bobby Byrd and Susannah Mississippi Byrd, 108–121. El Paso: Cinco Puntos Press, 1996.

Mindiola, Tatcho Jr. *The Mexican American Legislative Caucus*. Houston: Mexican American Studies Research Report, University of Houston, 1984.

________. *A Profile of Hispanic Voters in Houston, Texas*. Houston: Center for Mexican American Studies Research Report, University of Houston, 2001.

________. "The Cost of Being Mexican American and Black in Texas, 1960–1970." Ph.D. dissertation, Brown University, 1978.

________. "Age and Income Discrimination against Mexican Americans and Blacks in Texas, 1960 and 1970." *Social Problems* 27 (1979): 196–208.

________. "Core-Periphery Distinctions in Discrimination against Spanish Surnamed Males in Houston, Texas." *Borderlands Journal* 4 (Spring 1981): 293–307.

________. "A Personal Comment on Assimilation." *The Houston Review* 3 (Summer 1981): 261–266.

Mindiola, Tatcho Jr., and Armando Gutiérrez. *Voters and Non Voters: A Case Study of Mexican Americans in Houston.* Houston: Mexican American Studies Research Report, University of Houston, 1983.

Mindiola, Tatcho Jr., and Max Martínez. "Introduction to Chicano–Mexicano Relations." In *Chicano-Mexicano Relations*, edited by Tatcho Mindiola Jr. and Max Martínez, 1–7. Houston: Mexican American Studies Program, University of Houston, 1986.

Mindiola, Tatcho Jr., Nestor Rodríguez, and Yolanda Flores Nieman. *InterGroup Relations Between Hispanics and African Americans in Harris County.* Houston: Center for Mexican Studies Research Report, University of Houston, 1986.

Mirowsky, John II. "Mental Symptoms and Their Meaning: Patterns of Agreement and Mutual Influence among Mexicans, Mexican Americans, and Anglos." Ph.D. dissertation, Yale University, 1981.

Moffett, Linda Nance. "An Evaluation of Selected Variables of the Truancy Reduction Impact Program." Ed.D. dissertation, Texas A&M University-Kingsville, 1996.

Montgomery, Gary T., and S. Orozco. "Valediction of a Measure of Acculturation for Mexican Americans." *Hispanic Journal of Behavioral Sciences* 6 (March 1984): 53–63.

Morin, Kenneth Noah. "Attitudes of Texas Mexican-Americans toward Mental Retardation: A Guttman Facet Analysis." Ph.D. dissertation, Michigan State University, 1969.

Mote, Thomas A. Jr., Luiz F. S. Natalicio, and Fernando Rivas. "Comparability of the Spanish and English Editions of the Spielberger State-Trait Anxiety Inventory." *Journal of Cross Cultural Psychology* 2.2 (1971): 205–206.

Mrak, Norma Ariana. "Cambios en el paradigma pronominal acusativo de tercera persona: los efectos de la simplificación en el español de hablantes de origen mexicano de Houston." Ph.D. dissertation, University of Houston, 2000.

Mucchetti, Emil Anthony. "The Prevalence of Love Addiction among Undergraduates at Texas A&M University-Kingsville." Master's thesis, Texas A&M University-Kingsville, 1999.

Mugerauer, Robert. "Porous Boundaries: Fence Patterns and Mexican-American Identity in San Antonio, Texas." In *Hybrid Urbanism: On the Identity Discourse and the Built Environment*, edited by Nezar Al Sayyad and Ananya Roy, 206–228. Westport, Conn.: Praeger, 2001.

Murphy, L. F. "Experiment in Americanization." *Texas Outlook* 23 (November 1939): 23–24.

Murray, Mary John. *A Socio-cultural Study of 118 Mexican Families living in a Low Rent Public Housing Project in San Antonio, Texas*. Washington, D.C.: Catholic University of America Press, 1958.

Nall, Frank C. II, and Joseph Spielberg. "Social and Cultural Factors in the Responses of Mexican-Americans to Medical Treatment." In *Hispanic Culture and Health Care: Fact, Fiction, Folklore*, edited by Ricardo Arguijo Martínez, 51–64. St. Louis: C. V. Mosby Company, 1978.

Natalicio, Diana S. "Formation of the Plural in English: A Study of Native Speakers of English and Native Speakers of Spanish." Ph.D. dissertation, University of Texas, Austin, 1969.

Nathan, Debbie. "Project Change El Paso." In *Chicano Studies: Survey and Analysis*, edited by Dennis J. Bixler-Márquez, Carlos F. Ortega, Rosalía Solórzano Torres, and Lorenzo LaFarelle, 181–192. Dubuque, Iowa: Kendall/Hunt, 1999.

Navarro, Ana Cecilia. "Understanding the Mexican American Voter: Legacy and Potential of the Mexican American Community of El Paso." Master's thesis, University of Texas at El Paso, 1986.

Newton, Ada L. "The History of Architecture along the Rio Grande as Reflected in the Buildings around Rio Grande City, 1749–1920." Master's thesis, Texas A&I University, 1964.

Nieman, Yolanda Flores, Andrea J. Romero, Jorge Arredondo, and Victor Rodríguez. "What Does It Mean to Be 'Mexican': Social Construction of An Ethnic Identity." *Hispanic Journal of Behavioral Sciences* 21 (February 1999): 47–60.

Nies, Charles M. "Social Psychology Variables Related to Family Planning Among Mexican American Females." Ph.D. dissertation, University of Texas at Austin, 1974.

Noonan, Dana. "Inter-Generational Differences in the Social and Geographical Mobility of Mexican Americans in the Urban Southwest." Ph.D. dissertation, University of Minnesota, 1983.

O'Brennan, Junius, and Nopal Smith. *The Crystal Icon*. Austin: Galahad Press, 1981.

O'Connor, Robert Mark. "Binational Urbanization and Urban Planning on the United States-Mexico Border: A Comparative Analysis of Ciudad Juárez–El Paso." Master's thesis, University of Washington, 1982.

Okeze, Ignatius Onuoha. "An Analysis of African American and Hispanic Parents' Attitudes Toward Child-rearing Practices of Learning Disabled Children." Ed.D. dissertation, Texas Southern University, 1993.

Orozco, Cynthia E. "Texas IAF Network." In *The New Handbook of Texas*, edited by Ron Tyler, Douglas E. Barnett, Roy R. Barkely, Penelope C. Anderson, and Mark F. Odintz, vol. 6, 344. Austin: Texas State Historical Association, 1996.

Ortiz, Lorelei Amanda. "Cruzando las fronteras de la comunicación profesional entre México y los Estados Unidos/A Descriptive Context-Sensitive Rhetorical Text Analysis of the Form, Function, and Emerging Hybrid Discourse of Professional Communication on a United States/Mexico Border: El Paso/Juárez (Texas)." Ph.D. dissertation, New Mexico State University, 2001.

Paine, H. J. "Attitudes and Patterns of Alcohol Use Among Mexican Americans: Implications for Service Delivery." *Journal of Studies on Alcohol* 38 (1977): 544–553.

Paramo Ricoy, María Teresa. "Social Identity, Telenovelas and the Reading Process: Ten Case Studies among Hispanics in Texas." Ph.D. dissertation, University of Texas at Austin, 1999.

Parietti, Ellen M., Joáo B. Ferreira-Pinto, and Theresa Byrd. "Easy Access to Contraceptives Among Female Adolescents in a U.S.-Border City." In

U.S.-Mexico Border Health: Issues for Regional and Migrant Populations, edited by J. Gerard Power and Theresa Byrd, 119–138. Thousand Oaks, Calif.: Sage Publications, 1998.

Patella, Victoria M. "A Study in the Validity of Language Usage as an Indicator of Ethnic Identification." Master's thesis, Texas A&M University, College Station, 1971.

Patella, Victoria M., and W. P. Kuvlesky. "Situational Variation in Language Patterns of Mexican American Boys and Girls." *Social Science Quarterly* 53.4 (1973): 855–864.

Patrick, J. Michael, and Armando C. Alonzo. "Improving Living Conditions in *Colonias* in the Rio Grande Valley of South Texas." *Río Bravo* 2 (Spring 1993): 85–103.

Patterson, Jean Scarborough. "The Influence of English on the Spanish Syntax of El Paso–Juárez." Master's thesis, University of Texas at El Paso, 1953.

Patterson, Maurine. "Some Dialectical Tendencies in Popular Spanish in San Antonio." Master's thesis, Texas State College for Women, 1946.

Peck, R. F., and Rogelio Díaz-Guerrero. "Two Core-Culture Patterns and the Diffusion of Values Across Their Border." *International Journal of Psychology* 4.2 (1967): 272–282.

Peña, Albar Antonio. "Spanish-Speakers." In *Reading for the Disadvantaged: Problems of Linguistically Different Learners*, edited by Thomas D. Horn, 157–160. New York: Harcourt, Brace, and World, 1970.

Peña, Devón G. *The Terror of the Machine: Technology, Work, Gender, and Ecology on the U.S.-Mexico Border*. Austin: CMAS Books, 1997.

Perales, Daniel Patricio. "Patterns of Homicide: Houston, Texas, 1987." Dr. P.H. dissertation, University of Texas Health Science Center at Houston, 1989.

Peregrino, Santiago. "The Political Ideology of the Mexican-American in a Southwest City: El Paso." Master's thesis, University of Texas at El Paso, 1970.

Pérez, Anita Méndez. "Mexican-American Mothers' Perceptions and Beliefs about Language Acquisition among Toddlers with Language Disabilities." Ph.D. dissertation, University of Texas at Austin, 1998.

Pfaff, Carol W. "Constraints on Language Mixing: Intrasentential Code-Switching and Borrowing in Spanish/English." In *Spanish in the United States: Sociolinguistic Aspects*, edited by John Amastae and Lucía Elías-Olivares, 264–298. Cambridge: Cambridge University Press, 1982.

Phillips, Rebecca K. "Spanglish as a Marker of Identification among Hispanics in the United States: A Case Study of Two Tejano Radio Stations." Master's thesis, Rice University, 2002.

Pierce, James Alfred. "Sociolinguistic Relationships in Attitudes toward Anglo and Mexican-American Varieties of English in Corpus Christi, Texas." Ph.D. dissertation, University of Texas at Austin, 1989.

Polinard, J. L., Robert D. Wrinkle, and Norman E. Binder. "Ethnicity and Political Participation in Cameron and Hidalgo Counties: Mexican American Voters and Nonvoters." In *Studies in Matamoros and Cameron County History*, edited by Milo Kearney, Anthony Knopp, and Antonio Zavaleta, 89–106.

Brownsville, Tex.: University of Texas-Brownsville and Texas Southmost College, 1997.

Porter, Charles Jesse. "Recreational Interests and Activities of High School Boys of the Lower Rio Grande Valley of Texas." Master's thesis, University of Texas, Austin, 1940.

Poulter, Virgil Leroy. "A Phonological Study of the Speech of Mexican-American College Students Native to Fort Worth-Dallas." Ph.D. dissertation, Louisana State University and Agricultural and Mechanical College, 1973.

________. "A Comparison of Voiceless Stops in the English and Spanish of Bilingual Natives of Fort Worth-Dallas." In *Texas Studies in Bilingualism*, edited by Glenn Gilbert, 42–49. Berlin: de Gruyter, 1970.

Powell-Griner, Eve. "Differences in Infant Mortality among Texas Anglos, Hispanics, and Blacks." *Social Science Quarterly* 69.2 (1988): 452–467.

Pycior, Julie Leininger. "La Raza Organizes: Mexican American Life in San Antonio, 1915–1930: As Reflected in Mutualista Activities." Ph.D. dissertation, University of Notre Dame, 1979.

Queen, Rae Wyatt. "Characteristics Related to Career Decision Making for Hispanic Adolescents in Texas." Ph.D. dissertation, Texas A&M University, 1999.

Quezada, J. Gilberto. "Father Carmelo Tranchese, S. J.: A Pioneer Social Worker in San Antonio, Texas, 1932–1953." Master's thesis, St. Mary's University, 1972.

Quiroga, I. R. "The Use of a Linear Discriminant Function of the Minnesota Multiphasic Personality Inventory Scores in the Classification of Psychotic and on Psychotic Mexican American Psychiatric Patients." Ph.D. dissertation, University of Illinois, 1972.

Quiroz, Rudolph Anthony. "Claiming Citizenship: Class and Consensus in a Twentieth Century Mexican American Community." Ph.D. dissertation, University of Iowa, 1998.

Ralph, Paige Heather. "Texas Prison Gangs." Ph.D. dissertation, Sam Houston State University, 1992.

Ramírez, Carina. "Lexical Usage of and Attitude Toward Southwest Spanish in the Ysleta, Texas Area." Master's thesis, University of Texas at El Paso, 1971.

Ramírez, Manuel Bernardo. "El Pasoans: Life and Society in Mexican El Paso, 1920–1945." Ph.D. dissertation, University of Mississippi, 2000.

Ramírez, Manuel Ceballos. "El curso del Río Bravo en Tamaulipas y en su frontera con Texas: una reflexión histórica." *Río Bravo* 4 (1995): 113–120.

Ramos, Irma N., Marlynn May, and Kenneth S. Ramos. "Environmental Health Training of *Promotoras* in *Colonias* along the Texas-Mexico Border." *American Journal of Public Health* 91.4 (2001): 568–570.

Rechy, John. "Jim Crow Wears a Sombrero." *The Nation* 10 (October 1950): 210–213.

Redlinger, L. J., and J. B. Michel. "Ecological Variations in Heroin Abuse." *Sociological Quarterly* 11.2 (1970): 219–229.

Reed, Patricia Menghini. "The Relation among Attachment, Style, Emotional Dependency, and Machismo in Hispanic Males." Ph.D. dissertation, The Fielding Institute, 2001.

Relethford, John H., Michael P. Stern, Sharon P. Gaskill, and H. P. Hazuda. "Social Class, Admixture, and Skin Color Variation in Mexican-Americans and Anglo-Americans Living in San Antonio, Texas." *American Journal of Physical Anthropology* 61 (May 1983): 97–102.

Reséndiz, Rosalva. "International Auto Theft: An Exploratory Research of the Property Offender and the Organizational Crime Process in the United States/Mexico Border." Master's thesis, University of North Texas, 1996.

Rhoades, Cecilia Claudine. "The Poison Crop: South Texas Farmers Versus Toxwaste Hazardous Waste Storage Facility." Ph.D. dissertation, University of Texas at Austin, 1997.

Richardson, Chad. "Social Class on the South Texas-Mexico Border." In *Batos, Bolillos, Pochos, and Pelados: Class and Culture on the South Texas Border*, by Chad Richardson, 95–122. Austin: University of Texas Press, 1999.

Richardson, Chad, María Olivia Villarreal-Solano, and Cruz C. Torres. "Anglo-Hispanic Relations in South Texas from 1945 to 1993: A Triangulated Profile." *Río Bravo* 3.2 (1994): 114–134.

Rips, Geoffrey. "Mexican Americans *Jalaron la Palanca*, Democrats Say *Olé*." In *Practicing Texas Politics: A Brief Survey*, edited by Eugene W. Jones, Joe E. Ericson, Lyle C. Brown, Robert S. Trotter Jr., and Eileen M. Lynch, 86–88. Boston: Houghton Mifflin, 1984.

Robinson, Robin. "Accommodation to Domination: Demise of the Tejano Elite in the Lower Rio Grande." *Journal of South Texas* 10 (1997): 69–87.

Rodríguez, Nestor, and Jacqueline Hagan. "Transborder Community Relations at the U.S.-Mexico Border: Laredo/Nuevo Laredo and El Paso/Ciudad Juárez." In *Caught in the Middle: Border Communities in an Era of Globalization*, edited by Demetrios G. Papademetriou and Deborah Waller Meyers, 88–116. Washington, D.C.: Carnegie Endowment for International Peace, 2001.

Rodríguez, Nestor, and Rogelio T. Nuñez. "An Exploration of Factors that Contribute to Differentiation Between Chicanos and *Indocumentados*." In *Mexican Immigrants and Mexican Americans: An Evolving Relation*, edited by Harley L. Browning and Rodolfo O. de la Garza, 138–156. Austin: CMAS, University of Texas Press, 1986.

Rodríguez, Salvador Fernando. "Patterns of Homicide in Texas: A Descriptive Analysis of Racial/Ethnic Involvement by Crime-Specific Categories." Ph.D. dissertation, University of Texas at Austin, 1990.

Rogers, Thomas Guy. "The Housing Situation of Mexicans in San Antonio, Texas." Master's thesis, University of Texas, Austin, 1927.

Romano, Octavio Ignacio. "Don Pedrito Jaramillo: The Emergence of a Mexican American Folk Saint." Ph.D. dissertation, University of California at Berkeley, 1964.

________. "Donship in a Mexican-American Community in Texas." *American Anthropologist* 62 (1960): 966–977.

Romano-V., Octavio Ignacio. "Charismatic Medicine: Folk Healers and Folk-Sainthood." *American Anthropologist* 67 (1965): 1151–1173.

Romero, Andrea Jean. "The Impact of Ethnic Identity on Sociopsychological Stress and Mental Well-being in Adolescents from a Rural Setting." Ph.D. dissertation, University of Houston, 1997.

Romero, Yolanda García. "The Mexican American Frontier Experience in Twentieth Century Northwest Texas." Ph.D. dissertation, Texas Tech University, 1993.

Rosales, F. Arturo. "Shifting Self Perceptions and Ethnic Consciousness among Mexicans in Houston, 1908–1946." *Aztlán* 16 (1985): 71–94.

Rosales, Rodolfo. "The Rise of Chicano Middle Class Politics in San Antonio, 1951–1985." Ph.D. dissertation, University of Michigan, 1991.

________. *The Illusion of Inclusion: The Untold Political Story of San Antonio*. Austin: University of Texas Press, 2000.

Rosales, Sylvia Méndez. "A Study of the Relationship between Oral Language Proficiency and Reading Readiness/Achievement of Selected Mexican American Children in Corpus Christi, Texas." Ed.D. dissertation, Texas A&I University, 1980.

Rosen, Daniel Allan. "Mexican Americans and the Broadcast Media: A Study of San Antonio's Bilingual Bicultural Coalition on Mass Media." Master's thesis, University of Texas at Austin, 1976.

Rubel, Arthur J. *Across the Tracks: Mexican-Americans in a Texas City*. Austin: University of Texas Press, 1966.

________. "La Envidia como proceso casual de enfermedad en un vecindario del estado de Texas, E.U.A." *Memorias del XI Congreso Intreamericano de psícologia* 2 (1967): 146.

________. "The Mexican American *Palomilla*." *Anthropological Linguistics* 7 (April 1965): 92–97.

________. "Some Cultural Aspects of Learning English in Mexican-American Communities." In *Schools in Transition: Essays in Comparative Education*, edited by Andreas M. Kazamias and Erwin H. Epstein, 370–382. Boston: Allyn and Bacon, 1968.

Ruiz, Esther Hope. "The Acquisition of Information among Functionally Illiterate Mexican-American Adults in a Large City in Texas." Ph.D. dissertation, Texas A&M University, 1999.

Ryan-Arredondo, Kim. "An Evaluation of Internal Bias as a Function of Hispanic Status on the Minnesota Multiphasic Personality Inventory-Adolescent Lie Scale." Ph.D. dissertation, Texas A&M University, 2002.

Saavedra, Rebecca. "Alienation of Latino Medical Students: The Effect of Acculturation, Ethnic Identity and Minority Student Stressors." Ed.D. dissertation, University of Houston, 1994.

Saegert, J., S. Kazarian, and R. K. Young. "Part/Whole Transfer with Bilinguals." *American Journal of Psychology* 86.3 (1973): 537–546.

Said, Sally Eugenia Sneed. "A Descriptive Model of Austin Spanish Syntax." Master's thesis, University of Texas at Austin, 1970.

Salazar, José María Jr. "Dilemma of a Gay Chicano: Parallels between Cultural and Sexual Identities." *Tejas* 2 (October 1990): 8–9.

Salazar, Martín. "Mexican Americans' Observed Perceptions of Counselor Credibility as a Function of Language." Ed.D. dissertation, Texas Tech University, 1994.

Salazar, Mauricio Eduardo, and David Briggs. "The Texas Department of Corrections Ignores Drug Addicts." *Caracol* 3 (October 1976): 9.

Saldaña, Delia, Albana M. Dassori, and Alexander L. Miller. "When is Caregiving a Burden?: Listening to Mexican American Women." *Hispanic Journal of Behavioral Sciences* 21 (August 1999): 283–301.

Salinas, E. *The Colonias Factbook: A Sumary of Living Conditions in Rural Areas of South Texas and West Texas Border Communities*. Austin: Texas Department of Human Services, 1988.

Sánchez, Raúl M. "Building Dams and Damning People in the Texas-Mexico Border Region: Mexico's El Cuchillo Dam Project." In *Fluid Arguments: Five Centuries of Western Water Conflict*, edited by Char Miller, 303–328. Tucson: University of Arizona Press, 2001.

________. "Mexico's El Cuchillo Dam Project: A Case-Study of Nonsustainable Development and Transboundary Environmental Harms." *University of Miami Inter-American Law Review* 28 (Winter 1996/1997): 425–436.

________. "To the World Commission on Dams: Don't Forget the Law, and Don't Forget Human Rights—Lessons from the U.S.-Mexico Border." *University of Miami Inter-American Law Review* 30 (Spring 1999): 629–639.

Sánchez-Rosado, Kevin Adolfo. "Levels of Acculturation of Children of Mexican Descent as Perceived in their Kinetic Family Drawings." Ph.D. dissertation, Andrews University, 2001.

Sánchez, Rosaura. "Nuestra Circunstancia Linguistica." *El Grito* 6 (Fall 1972): 45–74.

Santos, Richard G. "Chicanos of Jewish Descent in Texas." *Western States Jewish Historical Quarterly* 15 (1983): 327–335.

Sawyer, Janet Beck Moseley. "A Dialect Study of San Antonio, Texas: A Bilingual Community." Ph.D. dissertation, University of Texas, Austin, 1957.

________."Aloofness from Spanish Influence in Texas English." *Word* 15 (1959): 270–281.

________. "Social Aspects of Bilingualism in San Antonio Texas." *Publications of the American Dialect Society* 41 (1964): 7–15.

________. "Spanish-English Bilingualism in San Antonio, Texas." In *El Lenguaje de los Chicanos: Regional and Social Characteristics used by Mexican Americans*, edited by Eduardo Hernández-Chávez, Andrew D. Cohen, and Anthony F. Beltramo, 77–98. Arlington, Va.: Center for Applied Linguistics, 1975.

________. "Spanish-English Bilingualism in San Antonio, Texas." In *Texas Studies in Bilingualism*, edited by Glenn Gilbert, 18–41. Berlin: de Gruyter, 1970.

________. "The Speech of San Antonio, Texas." In *A Various Language: Perspectives on American Dialects*, edited by Juanita V. Williamson and Virginia Burke, 570–582. New York: Holt, Rinehart and Winston, 1971.

Schmidt, Samuel. "Planning a U.S.-Mexican Bi-National Metropolis: El Paso, Texas–Cuidad Juárez, Chihuahua." In *The North American Cities and the*

Global Economy: Challenges and Opportunities, edited by Peter Karl Kresl and Gary Gappert, 187–219. Thousand Oaks, Calif.: Sage Publications, 1995.

Schreiber, Janet M., and Loralee Philpott. "Who is a Legitimate Health Care Professional? Changes in the Practice of Midwifery in the Lower Rio Grande Valley." In *Modern Medicine and Medical Anthropology in the United States-Mexico Border Population*, edited by Boris Velimirovic, 127–138. Washington, D.C.: Pan American Health Organization, 1978.

Scott, Carmen Casillas. "Spanish Language Maintenance and Loyalty in El Paso-Juarez: A Socio-linguistic Study of the Contact Situation in a Highly Bilingual Area." Master's thesis, University of Texas at El Paso, 1969.

Scott, J., and C. M. Gaitz. "Ethnic and Age Differences in Mental Health Measurements." *Diseases of the Nervous System* 36.7 (1975): 389–393.

Selby, Maija Leena. "Infant Mortality in the Mexican American Community: An Analysis of Differentials in Infant, Neonatal, and Postneonatal Mortality by Ethnicity and Parental Nativity, 1974–1975 Single Live Birth Cohort, Harris County, Texas." Ph.D. dissertation, University of Texas Health Science Center at Houston, 1982.

Serna, Melissa S. "Gender and Educational Differences in the Psychic Phenomena Beliefs of Mexican-Americans." Master's thesis, Texas A&M University-Kingsville, 1997.

Sethuraju, Nadarajan Raj. "Race Relations on Campus: African Americans and Hispanics in Two Educational Institutions." Ph.D. dissertation, Texas Woman's University, 2000.

Shelton, Edgar G. "Political Conditions Among Texas Mexicans Along the Rio Grande." Master's thesis, University of Texas, Austin, 1946.

Simmons, Ozzie G. "The Mutual Images as Expectations of Anglo Americans and Mexican Americans." *Daedalus* 90.2 (1961): 289–299.

Sliwiak, Stanley Andrew. "A Comparative Study of Value Orientations in American Society, Mexican Society and High School Students." Ph.D. dissertation, Loyola University of Chicago, 1984.

Sloan, John W., and Jonathan P. West. "Community Integration and Policies among Elites in Two Border Cities: Los Dos Laredos." *Journal of Interamerican Studies and World Affairs* 128 (November 1976): 452–474.

Sobin, Nicholas. "On the Study of Syntax and Bilingualism: A Report of Work in Progress at the Language and Linguistics Research Center at Pan American University." In *Southwest Areal Linguistics Then and Now: Proceedings of the Fifth Southwest Areal Language and Linguistics Workshop*, edited by Bates Hoffer and Betty Lou Dubois, 247–263. San Antonio: Trinity University, 1976.

________. "Texas Spanish and Lexical Borrowing." In *Spanish in the United States: Sociolinguistic Aspects*, edited by Jon Amastae and Lucía Elías-Olivares, 166–181. Cambridge: Cambridge University Press, 1982.

Soldner, Doris Bridges. "Who Shall Protect the Silent Interest of the Child? A Multi-ethnic Study of Child Abuse in Dallas County." Ph.D. dissertation, Southern Methodist University, 1996.

Solís, Manuel. "Growing Up Tejano." *Latino Studies Journal* 7 (Fall 1996): 17–25.

Soto-Fulp, Sylvia. "Conflict Resolution Styles: Ethnic and Gender Differences." Ph.D. dissertation, New Mexico State University, 1996.

Sotomayor, Marta, et al. "Mutual Help Among the Elderly in the Barrio." *Agenda* 7.4 (July, August 1977): 32–35.

Sowards, Kathryn Ann. "Early Childbearing and the Epidemiology of Infant Death in the Mexican Ancestry and Anglo Populations of San Antonio, Texas: 1935–1984." Ph.D. dissertation, University of Texas at Austin, 1995.

The Status of Illiteracy in San Antonio. San Antonio: Intercultural Development Research Association, 1983.

Stenger-Castro, Earl M. "The Mexican-American: How His Culture Affects His Mental Health." In *Hispanic Culture and Health Care: Fact, Fiction, Folklore*, edited by Ricardo Arguijo Martínez, 19–32. St. Louis: C. V. Mosby Company, 1978.

Stephens, Richard C., George T. Oser, and Zena Smith Blau. "To Be Aged, Hispanic, and Female: The Triple Risk." In *Twice a Minority: Mexican American Women*, edited by Margarita B. Melville, 249–258. St. Louis: C. V. Mosby Company, 1980.

Stephens, Richard C., Zena Smith Blau, George T. Oser, and Melanie D. Millar. "Aging, Social Support Systems, and Social Policy." *Journal of Gerontological Social Work* 1 (1978): 33–45.

Stockwell, Rosa Veronica. "The Effects of Nutrition Education on the Nutrition Knowledge of Elderly Mexican Americans." Master's thesis, Texas A&M University-Kingsville, 1993.

Stoddard, Ellwyn R. *The Role of Social Factors in the Successful Adjustment of Mexican American Families to Forced Housing Relocation*. El Paso: Community Renewal Program, 1970.

________. "The Adjustment of Mexican American Barrio Families to Forced Housing Relocation." *Social Science Quarterly* 53 (1973): 749–759.

________. "Teen-age Pregnancy in the Texas Borderlands." *Journal of Borderland Studies* 8.1 (1993): 77–93.

Suárez, Lucina. "Neural Tube Defects in Mexican-Americans Living on the United States-Mexico Border: The Effects of Folic Acid and Dietary Folate." Dr. P.H. dissertation, University of Texas Health Science Center at Houston, 1998.

Sullivan, Teresa A., Francis P. Gillespie, and Michael Hout. "Alternative Estimates of Mexican American Mortality in Texas, 1980." *Social Science Quarterly* 65 (June 1984): 609–617.

Sweeney, Mary Frances. "The Social and Religious Customs of the Spanish-Indian Population of San Antonio, Texas." Master's thesis, Southwest Texas State Teachers College, 1938.

Swope-Marrs, Suzanne Rebecca. "Factors Influencing Minority Students' Selection of Teaching as a Career Choice." Ed.D. dissertation, Texas A&M University-Commerce, 1998.

Tan, P. Phillip, and Ellen Ryan. "Homeless Hispanic and Non-Hispanic Adults on the Texas-Mexico Border." *Hispanic Journal of Behavioral Sciences* 23 (May 2001): 239–249.

Taylor, Paul S. "Note on Streams of Mexican Migration." *American Journal of Sociology* 36 (September 1930): 287–288.

Teller, Charles H. "Physical Health Status and Health Care Utilization in the Texas Borderlands." In *Views Across the Border: The United States and Mexico*, edited by Stanley R. Ross, 256–279. Albuquerque: University of New Mexico Press, 1978.

Tenayuca, Emma, and Homer Brooks. "The Mexican Question in the Southwest." *Political Affairs* (March 1939): 257–268.

Teschner, Richard V. "Beachheads, Islands, and Conduits: Spanish Monolingualism and Bilingualism in El Paso, Texas." *International Journal of the Sociology of Language* 114 (1995): 93–105.

Teske, Raymond Herman Charles Jr. "An Analysis of Status Mobility Patterns among Middle-Class Mexican-Americans in Texas." Ph.D. dissertation, Texas A&M University, 1973.

Teske, Raymond H. C. Jr., and Bardin H. Nelson. "An Analysis of Differential Assimilation Rates Among Middle-Class Mexican Americans." *Sociological Quarterly* 17.2 (1976): 218–235.

________. "Middle Class Mexican Americans and Political Power Potential: A Dilemma." *Journal of Political and Military Sociology* 4.1 (1976): 107–119.

________. "Two Scales for the Measurement of Mexican American Identity." *International Review of Modern Sociology* 3.2 (1973): 192–203.

Thomas, Dorina Alaniz. "Reading Achievement of Chicano Children as a Function of Language Spoken and Language Preference." Ph.D. dissertation, University of Michigan, 1980.

Thomas, P. J. "Administration of a Dialectical Spanish Version and Standard English Version of the Peabody Picture Vocabulary Test." *Psychological Reports* 40 (1977): 747–750.

Thomforde, Duane W. "Political Socialization in South El Paso." Master's thesis, University of Texas at El Paso, 1969.

Thompson, Roger N. "Language Loyalty in Austin, Texas: A Study of a Bilingual Neighborhood." Ph.D. dissertation, University of Texas at Austin, 1971.

Tiefenbacher, John P. "Environmental Hazards of the Lower Rio Grande Valley." In *A Geographic Glimpse of Central Texas and the Borderlands*, edited by James F. Petersen and Julie A. Tuason, 85–94. Indiana, Penn.: National Council for Geographic Education, 1995.

Timmons, Patrick. "*La Abogada de México*: Sandra Babcock's Battle Against the Death Penalty." *Texas Observer* 94 (October 25, 2002): 8–9, 20.

Torres-Ayala, Buenaventura. "The Relationship of Spanish Language Usage and Exposure to Spanish Oral Proficiency among Mexican American College Students." Ph.D. dissertation, University of California, Los Angeles, 1994.

Torres, Maryann. "Happiness and Global Self-Worth among College Students: Ethnic and Gender Variables." Master's thesis, Texas A&I University, 1993.

Torres-Raines, Rosario. "*Casas Ricas y Pobres*: The Effects of Housing Market Expenditures on Residential Segregation of Mexican Americans in Texas and California." Ph.D. dissertation, Texas Woman's University, 1978.

Touliatos, J., and B. W. Lindholm. "Behavior Problems of Anglo and Mexican American Children." *Journal of Abnormal Child Psychology* 4.3 (1976): 299–304.

Towers, George William. "Colonia Formation and Economic Restructuring in El Paso, Texas." Ph.D. dissertation, University of Arizona, 1991.

Treviño, F. M., and J. G. Bruhn. "Incidence of Mental Illness in a Mexican American Community." *Psychiatric Annals* 7.12 (1977): 33–51.

Trook-White, Eve. "The Role of Complaining Parties in Court Use Patterns: A Case Study of South Texas Hidalgo County Courts during 1980." Ph.D. dissertation, Sam Houston State University, 1991.

Trotter, Robert Talbot II. "Cultural Barriers to the Delivery of Health Care to Mexican-Americans in the Lower Rio Grande Valley of Texas." Ph.D. dissertation, Southern Methodist University, 1976.

________. "Contrasting Models of the Healer's Role: South Texas Case Examples." *Hispanic Journal of Behavioral Sciences* 4 (1982): 315–328.

________. "Evidence of an Ethnomedical Form of Aversion Therapy on the United States-Mexico Border." *Journal of Ethnopharmacology* 1.3 (1979): 279–284.

________. "Ethnic and Sexual Patterns of Alcohol Use: Anglo and Mexican American College Students." *Adolescence* 17 (1982): 305–325.

________. "Mexican-American Experience with Alcohol: South Texas Examples." In *The American Experience with Alcohol: Contrasting Cultural Perspectives*, edited by Linda Bennet and Genevieve M. Ames, 279–296. New York: Plenum Press, 1985.

Trotter, Robert T. II, and Juan Antonio Chavira. *Curanderismo: Mexican American Folk Healing*. Athens: University of Georgia Press, 1981.

________. *The Gift of Healing*. Edinburg, Tex.: Pan American University, 1975.

Tubb, Verity Anne. "The Factor Structure and Psychometric Properties of the Psychopathy Checklist-Revised: Data from an Hispanic Federal-inmate Sample." Ph.D. dissertation, University of Texas at El Paso, 2001.

Tucker, Philip Alan. "Mexican American Male Drinking Patterns: A Study of Men in Fort Worth." Master's thesis, University of Texas at Arlington, 1990.

Turner, R. G., and J. M. Horn. "Personality Correlates of Holland's Occupational Types: A Cross Cultural Study." *Journal of Vocational Behavior* 6.3 (1975): 379–389.

Upham, W. Kennedy, and David E. Wright. *Poverty among Spanish Americans in Texas: Low-income Families in a Minority Group*. College Station: Texas Agricultural Experiment Station, 1966.

Urbina, Martín Guevara. "Capital Punishment: A New Perspective on Race and Ethnic Differences in Punishment and Death Sentence Outcomes." Ph.D. dissertation, Western Michigan University, 2000.

Urdaneta, María Luisa. "Chicana Use of Abortion: The Case of Alcalá." In *Twice a Minority: Mexican American Women*, edited by Margarita B. Melville, 33–51. St. Louis: C. V. Mosby Company, 1980.

Vaccaro, Georgiana Chenault. "Identifying and Acquiring Information Needed to Work Successfully without Formal Training: Perceptions of Selected Immigrant Latino Workers in Texas." Ph.D. dissertation, Texas A&M University, 1998.

Valdes, Guadalupe. "Bilingualism in a Mexican Border City: A Research Agenda." In *Bilingualism and Language Contact: Spanish, English, and Native American Languages*, edited by Florence Barkin, Elizabeth A. Brandt, and Jacob Ornstein-Galicia, 3–17. New York: Columbia University Teachers College, 1982.

Valdez, Avelardo. "Recent Increases in Intermarriage by Mexican American Males: Bexar County, Texas, From 1971 to 1980." *Social Science Quarterly* 64.1 (1983): 136–144.

________. "Residential Patterns of Chicanos, Undocumented Mexicans, and Anglos in San Antonio (Bexar County) Texas: An Assessment of Recent Change and Social Costs." In *Mexican Immigrants and Mexican Americans: An Evolving Relation*, edited by Harley L. Browning and Rodolfo O. de la Garza, 120–137. Austin: Center for Mexican American Studies Publications, 1986.

Valdez, Avelardo, and Alberto G. Mata Jr. "Life Histories of Four Chicano Heroin Injecting Drug Users in Laredo, Texas." In *Life, Death, and In-Between on the U.S.-Mexico Border/Así es la vida*, edited by Martha Oehmke Loustaunau and Mary Sánchez-Bane, 39–60. Westport, Conn.: Bergin and Garvey, 1999.

Valdez, Avelardo, G. Edward Codina, and Charles D. Kaplan. *A Needs Assessment of Mexican American Injecting and Other Drug Use in Laredo*. San Antonio: University of Texas at San Antonio, 1996.

Valdez, Avelardo, Zenong Yin, and Charles D. Kaplan. "A Comparison of Alcohol, Drugs, and Aggressive Crime among Mexican-American, Black, and White Male Arrestees in Texas." *American Journal of Drug and Alcohol Abuse* 23 (May 1997): 249–265.

Valenzuela, Angela. "'Checkin' Up on My Guy': Chicanas, Social Capital, and the Culture of Romance." *Frontiers: A Journal of Women's Studies* 20 (Spring 1999): 60–79.

________. "High Stakes Testing and U.S. Mexican Youth in Texas: The Case for Multiple Compensatory Criteria in Assessment." *Harvard Journal of Hispanic Policy* 14 (2002): 97–116.

________. "Mexican-American Youth and the Politics of Caring." In *From Sociology to Cultural Studies: New Perspectives*, edited by Elizabeth Long, 322–350. Malden, Mass.: Blackwell Publishers, 1997.

Van Der Kuip, Deirdre. "The Use of Invasive Myocardial Revascularization Procedures Following Myocardial Infarction and the Effectiveness of these Procedures in the Biethnic Community of Nueces County, Texas, 1988–1991." Ph.D. dissertation, University of Texas Health Science Center at Houston, 1995.

Van Derslice, James, Amy K. Liebman, and Theresa L. Byrd. "Community-University Partnerships Addressing Environmental Issues along the U.S.-Mexico Border." In *Life, Death, and In-Between on the U.S.-Mexico Border/Así es la vida*, edited by Martha Oehmke Loustaunau and Mary Sánchez-Bane, 209–220. Westport, Conn.: Bergin and Garvey, 1999.

Vila, Pablo Sergio. *Crossing Borders/Reinforcing Borders: Social Categories, Metaphors, and Narrative Identities on the U.S.-Mexico Frontier*. Austin: University of Texas Press, 2000.

________. "Everyday Life, Culture, and Identity on the Mexican-American Border: The Ciudad Juárez–El Paso Case." Ph.D. dissertation, University of Texas at Austin, 1994.

________. "Narrative Identities: The Employment of the Mexican on the U.S.-Mexico Border." *Sociological Quarterly* 38.1 (1997): 147–183.

Villamil Tinajero, Josefina, and Dee Ann Spencer. "Creating a Future for Hispanic Mothers and Daughters on the U.S.-Mexico Border." In *Life, Death, and In-Between on the U.S.-Mexico Border/Así es la vida*, edited by Martha Oehmke Loustaunau and Mary Sánchez-Bane, 95–112. Westport, Conn.: Bergin and Garvey, 1999.

Villarreal, Roberto E. "Mexican-Americans in South Texas: An Inquiry into Social and Political Change." Ph.D. dissertation, University of Oklahoma, 1975.

Walker, Deborah J. "Parental Investment and Grandparental Investment among Mexican Americans of Laredo, Texas." Ph.D. dissertation, Pennsylvania State University, 1990.

Ward, Peter M. *Colonias and Public Policy in Texas and Mexico: Urbanization by Stealth*. Austin: University of Texas Press, 1999.

Washington, Ann Reed. "South Texas' Greatest Folk Healer." In *Roots by the River*, by Valley By-Liners, 95–99. Mission, Tex.: Border Kingdom Press, 1978.

Waugh, Julia Nott. *The Silver Cradle: Las Posadas, Los Pastores, and Other Mexican American Traditions*. Originally published 1955. Austin: University of Texas Press, 1988.

Weaver, C. M. "Accidents as a Measure of the Cultural Adjustments of Mexican Americans." *Sociological Quarterly* 11 (1970): 119–125.

Weinman, Maxine L. "United States and Mexico-Born Hispanic Teen Mothers: A Descriptive Study of Factors that Relate to Postpartum Compliance." *Hispanic Journal of Behavioral Sciences* 16 (May 1994): 186–194.

Wells, Gladys. "Factors Influencing the Assimilation of the Mexican in Texas." Master's thesis, Southern Methodist University, 1941.

White, Jean. "Time Orientation as a Factor in the Acculturation of the Southeastern Spanish Speaking Groups." Master's thesis, University of Texas, Austin, 1955.

Wilkinson, William Van. "Alcohol Drinking Patterns in a South Texas Mexican American Community." Ph.D. dissertation, Sam Houston State University, 1985.

________. "The Influence of Lifestyles on the Patterns and Practices of Alcohol Use Among South Texas Mexican Americans." *Hispanic Journal of Behavioral Sciences* 11 (November 1989): 354–365.

Williams, F., and R. C. Naremore. "Language Attitudes: An Analysis of Teacher Differences." *Speech Monographs* 41.4 (1974): 391–396.

Williams, F., et al. "Ethnic Stereotyping and Judgments of Children's Speech." *Speech Monographs* 38.3 (1971): 168–170.

Williams, J. A., et al. "Voluntary Associations and Minority Status: A Comparative Analysis of Anglo, Black, and Mexican Americans." *American Sociological Review* 38.5 (1973): 637–646.

Williams, Norma. "Changes in Funeral Patterns and Gender Roles among Mexican Americans." In *Women on the U.S.-Mexico Border: Responses to Change*, edited by Vicki L. Ruiz and Susan Tiano, 197–217. Boston: Allen and Unwin, 1987.

________. "Role Making among Married Mexican American Women: Issues of Class and Ethnicity." *Journal of Applied Behavioral Science* 24 (1987): 203–217.

________. "Traditional Life-cycle Rituals among Mexican Americans in Texas." In *The Mexican American Family: Tradition and Change*, 18–40. Dix Hills, N.Y.: General Hall Publishers, 1990.

Wilson, Robert, and Peter Menzies. "The Colonias Water Bill: Communities Demanding Change." In *Public Policy and Community: Activism and Governance in Texas*, edited by Robert Wilson, 229–274. Austin: University of Texas Press, 1997.

Wright, David E., Esteban Salinas, and William P. Kuvlesky. "Opportunities for Social Mobility for Mexican-American Youth." In *Chicanos and Native Americans: The Territorial Minorities*, edited by Rudolph O. de la Garza, Z. Anthony Kruszewski, and Tomás A. Arciniega, 43–60. Englewood Cliffs, N.J.: Prentice-Hall, 1973.

Wright, Paul. "Ethnic Segregation in Two Early West Texas Towns." *Southwestern Historical Quarterly* 102 (1999): 294–320.

Yin, Zenong, Jesse T. Zapata, and David S. Katins. "Risk Factors from Substance Use Among Mexican American School-Age Youths." *Hispanic Journal of Behavioral Sciences* 17 (February 1995): 61–76.

Young, Elliott. "Deconstructing *La Raza*: Cultural Ideology of the *Gente Decente* of Laredo, 1904–1911." *Southwestern Historical Quarterly* 98 (October 1994): 227–259.

21. DEMOGRAPHY

Demography is the statistical science dealing with the distribution, density, and vital statistics of populations—especially as classified by age, sex, income, and ethnicity. We have included such studies along with those which look at Tejano population numbers and percentages, immigration and migration, vital statistics, the Bracero program, and repatriation.

"New Citizens" whose petitions were heard in the 83rd District Court of Presidio County are pictured. Alpine Avalanche, *July 2, 1959. Courtesy of Archives of the Big Bend, Bryan Wildenthal Memorial Library, Sul Ross State University, Alpine, Texas*

Ainslie, Ricardo C. "Cultural Mourning, Immigration, and Engagement: Vignettes from the Mexican Experience." In *Crossings: Mexican Immigration in Interdisciplinary Perspectives*, edited by Marcelo M. Suárez-Orozco, 285–300. Cambridge, Mass.: Harvard University Press, 1998.

Baker, Susan González. "Many Rivers to Cross: Mexican Immigrants, Women Workers, and the Structure of Labor Markets in the Urban Southwest." Ph.D. dissertation, University of Texas at Austin, 1989.

Balderrama, Francisco, and Raymond Rodríguez. *Decade of Betrayal: Mexican Repatriation in the 1930s*. Albuquerque: University of New Mexico Press, 1995.

Barker, E. Shannon. "Los Tejanos de San Antonio: Mexican Immigrant Family Acculturation, 1880–1929." Ph.D. dissertation, George Washington University, 1996.

Bean, Frank D., Elizabeth H. Stephen, and Wolfgang Opitz. "The Mexican Original Population in the United States: A Demographic Overview." In *The Mexican American Experience: An Interdisciplinary Anthology*, edited by Rudolfo O. de la Garza, Frank D. Bean, Charles M. Bonjean, Ricardo Romo, and Rodolfo Álvarez, 57–78. Austin: University of Texas Press, 1985.

Blevins, Audie Lee. "Rural to Urban Migration of Poor Anglos, Mexican Americans, and Negroes." Ph.D. dissertation, University of Texas at Austin, 1970.

Browning, Harley L., and Rodolfo O. de la Garza, eds. *Mexican Immigrants and Mexican Americans: An Evolving Relation*. Austin: Center for Mexican American Studies, 1986.

Browning, Harley L., and S. Dale McLemore. *A Statistical Profile of the Spanish Surname Populaton of Texas*. Austin: University of Texas Press, 1964.

________. "The Spanish-surname Population of Texas." *Public Affairs Comment* 10 (January 1964): 1–4.

Cárdenas, Gilberto. "Mexican Illegal Aliens in the San Antonio Labor Market." *Texas Business Review* 53 (1979): 187–191.

Cárdenas, Gilberto, and Estevan T. Flores. *Social, Economic, and Demographic Characteristics of Undocumented Mexicans in the Houston Labor Market: A Preliminary Report*. Houston: Gulf Coast Legal Aid Foundation, 1980.

Cárdenas, Gilberto, Rodolfo O. de la Garza, and Niles Hansen. "Mexican Immigrants and the Chicano Ethnic Enterprise: Reconceptualizing an Old Problem." In *Mexican Immigrants and Mexican Americans: An Evolving Relation*, edited by Harley L. Browning and Rodolfo O. de la Garza, 157–174. Austin: CMAS Publications, 1986.

Cavazos, Sylvia. "The Disposable Mexican: Operation Wetback, 1954, the Deportation of Undocumented Workers in California and Texas." Master's thesis, University of Texas–Pan American, 1997.

Coalson, George O. "The Development of the Migratory Farm Labor System in Texas, 1900–1954." Ph.D. dissertation, University of Oklahoma, 1955.

Connell, Earl Monroe. "The Mexican Population of Austin." Master's thesis, University of Texas, Austin, 1925.

De León, Arnoldo, and Kenneth L. Stewart. "Lost Dreams and Found Fortunes: Mexican and American Immigrants in South Texas, 1850–1900." *Western Historical Quarterly* 14 (July 1983): 291–310.

________. "Tejano Demographic Patterns and Socio-Economic Development." *Borderlands Journal* 7 (Fall 1983): 1–9.

Dunn, Timothy Joseph. "Immigration Enforcement in the United States-Mexico Border Region, the El Paso Case: Bureaucratic Power, Human Rights, and Civic Activism." Ph.D. dissertation, University of Texas at Austin, 1999.

Ellis, John M. "Mortality Differentials for a Spanish Surname Population Group." *Southwestern Social Science Quarterly* (1959): 316–318.

________. "Spanish Surname Mortality Differences in San Antonio, Texas." *Journal of Health and Human Behavior* 3 (Summer 1962): 125–127.

Erenburg, Mark Edward. "A Study of the Potential Relocation of Texas-Mexican Migratory Farm Workers to Wisconsin." Ph.D. dissertation, University of Wisconsin, Madison, 1969.

Farris, Buford Elijah. "A Comparison of Anglo and Mexican-American Stratification Systems in San Antonio and Their Effects on Mobility and Intergroup Relations." Master's thesis, University of Texas at Austin, 1972.

Firestone, Juanita M., and Richard J. Harris. "Hispanic Women in Texas: An Increasing Portion of the Underclass." *Hispanic Journal of Behavioral Sciences* 16 (May 1994): 176–185.

Flores, Estevan Tim. "Post-Bracero Undocumented Mexican Immigration to the United States and Political Recomposition." Ph.D. dissertation, University of Texas at Austin, 1982.

Flores, Roy, and Gilberto Cárdenas. *A Study of the Demographic and Employment Characteristics of Undocumented Aliens in San Antonio, El Paso, and McAllen, Texas*. San Antonio: U.S. Comission on Civil Rights, Texas State Advisory Committee, 1978.

Freeman, Gary, Luis F. B. Plascencia, Susan González Baker, and Manuel Orozco. "Explaining the Surge in Citizenship Applications in the 1990s: Lawful Permanent Resident in Texas." *Social Science Quarterly* 83 (December 2002): 1013–1025.

García, Juan Ramón. "Operation Wetback: 1954." Ph.D. dissertation, University of Notre Dame, 1977.

________. "The Texas Operation." In *Operation Wetback: The Mass Deportation of Mexican Undocumented Workers in 1854*, by Juan Ramón García, 206–223. Westport, Conn.: Greenwood Press, 1980.

Gonzales, Manuel G. *The Hispanic Elite of the Southwest*. El Paso: Texas Western Press, 1989.

González, Larry Justin. "Hispanic/Latino Empowerment in Houston." Ph.D. dissertation, University of Houston, 1994.

González, Rosalinda M. "Chicanas and Mexican Immigrant Families, 1920–1940: Women's Subordination and Family Exploitation." In *Decades of Discontent: The Women's Movement, 1920–1940*, edited by Lois Scharf and Joan M. Jensen, 59–84. Westport, Conn.: Greenwood Press, 1983.

Graves, Ruth. "A History of the Interrelationships between Imported Mexican Labor, Domestic Migrants, and the Texas Agricultural Economy." Master's thesis, University of Texas, Austin, 1960.

Guerrero, Andre L. "The Presence of Undocumented Mexican Children in Texas Public Schools." Ed.D. dissertation, Harvard University, 1990.

Gutiérrez, David Gregory. "Ethnicity, Ideology, and Political Development: Mexican Immigration as a Political Issue in the Chicano Community, 1910–1977." Ph.D. dissertation, Stanford University, 1988.

Ham-Chande, Roberto, and John R. Weeks. "A Demographic Perspective of the U.S.-Mexico Border." In *Demographic Dynamics of the U.S.-Mexico Border*, edited by John R. Weeks and Roberto Ham-Chande, 1–27. El Paso: Texas Western Press, 1992.

Handman, Max S. "Economic Reasons for the Coming of the Mexican Immigrant." *American Journal of Sociology* 25 (January 1930): 601–611.

________. "The Mexican Immigrant in Texas." *Proceedings, Conference of Social Work* (1926): 332–339.

________. "San Antonio." *Survey* 66 (May 1, 1931): 163–166.

Harrison, Helene W. "A Methodological Study in Eliciting Linguistic Data from Mexican American Bilinguals." Ed.D. dissertation, University of Texas, Austin, 1967.

Heller, Michelle A. "Too Many Immigrants." *Hispanic* 7 (April 1994): 27.

Idar, Edward, and Andrew McLellan. *What Price Wetback?* Austin: American G.I. Forum and Texas State Federation of Labor-AFL, 1953.

Jones, Dixie Lee Franklin. "The Plight of the Migrant Child in the Lower Rio Grande Valley." Master's thesis, University of Texas at Austin, 1969.

Jones, Richard C. "Changing Patterns of Undocumented Mexican Migration to South Texas." *Social Science Quarterly* 65.2 (1984): 465–481. Reprinted in *The Mexican American Experience: An Interdisciplinary Anthology*, edited by Rodolfo O. de la Garza, Frank D. Bean, Charles M. Bonjean, Ricardo Romo, and Rodolfo Álvarez, 101–117. Austin: University of Texas Press, 1985.

Juárez, Rumaldo Z., Rubén E. Sáenz, Armando López, Doreen D. Garza, Karen D. Fossom, and Alicia López-González. *Lower Rio Grande Valley Demographics and Health Statistics*. Edinburg, Tex.: Texas-Mexico Border Health Coordination Office, 1994.

________. *Texas-Mexico Border County Demographics and Health Statistics*. Edinburg, Tex.: Texas-Mexico Border Health Coordination Office, 1994.

King, Allen G., B. Lindsay Lowell, and Frank D. Bean. "The Effects of Hispanic Immigrants on the Earnings of Native Hispanic Americans." *Social Science Quarterly* 67.4 (1987): 673–689.

Kiser, George C., and David Silverman. "Mexican Repatriation during the Great Depression." *Journal of Mexican American History* 3.1 (1973): 139–164.

Koestler, Fred L. "Bracero Program." In *The New Handbook of Texas,* edited by Ron Tyler, Douglas E. Barnett, Roy R. Barkley, Penelope C. Anderson, and Mark F. Odintz, vol. 1, 658. Austin: Texas State Historical Association, 1996.

Latinos in Texas: A Socio-Economic Profile. Claremont, Calif.: Tomás Rivera Center, 1995.

Limón, José E. "Language, Mexican Immigration, and the 'Human Connection': A Perspective from the Ethnography of Communication." In *Mexican Immigrants and Mexican Americans: An Evolving Relation*, edited by Harley L. Browning and Rodolfo O. de la Garza, 194–210. Austin: CMAS Publications, 1986.

Lindsay, Marcia. "A Study of the Hispanic Population of Tom Green County, Texas, in 1910." *Fort Concho Report* 19 (Fall 1987): 3–18.

Manuel, Herschel T. "The Mexican Population of Texas." *Southwestern Social Science Quarterly* 15 (June 1934): 29–51.

________. "The Mexican Population of Texas." *Southwest Review* 17 (1932): 290–302.

Maril, Robert Lee. *Poorest of Americans: The Mexican Americans of the Lower Rio Grande Valley of Texas.* Notre Dame: University of Notre Dame Press, 1989.

Martínez, Oscar. "On the Size of the Chicano Population: New Estimates, 1850–1900." *Aztlán* 6 (Spring 1975): 43–59.

Massey, Leonard Ellis. "Migration of the Spanish-speaking People of Hidalgo County, Texas." Master's thesis, University of Texas, Austin, 1953.

McBride, John. *Vanishing Bracero: Valley Revolution*. San Antonio: The Naylor Company, 1963.

McConville, Lawrence J. "A History of Population in the El Paso–Ciudad Juárez Area." Master's thesis, University of New Mexico, 1966.

McKay, R. Reynolds. "Texas Mexican Repatriation during the Great Depression." Ph.D. dissertation, University of Oklahoma, 1982.

________. "The Federal Deportation Campaign in Texas: Mexican Deportation from the Lower Rio Grande Valley during the Great Depression." *Borderlands Journal* 5.1 (Fall 1981): 90–120.

________. "The Impact of the Great Depression on Immigrant Mexican Labor: Repatriation of the Bridgeport, Texas, Coal Miners." In *The Mexican American Experience: An Interdisciplinary Anthology*, edited by Rodolfo O. de la Garza, Frank D. Bean, Charles M. Bonjean, Ricardo Romo, and Rodolfo Álvarez, 91–100. Austin: University of Texas Press, 1985.

________. "The Texas Cotton Acreage Control Law of 1931 and Mexican Repatriation." *West Texas Historical Association Yearbook* 59 (1983): 143–155.

Meador, Bruce S. "'Wetback' Labor in the Lower Rio Grande Valley." Master's thesis, University of Texas, Austin, 1951.

Miller, Hubert J. "Mexican Migrations to the United States, 1900–1920, With a Focus on the Texas Lower Rio Grande Valley." *Borderlands Journal* 7 (Spring 1984): 165–205.

Miller, Michael V., and James D. Preston. "Vertical Ties and the Redistribution of Power in Crystal City." *Social Science Quarterly* 53 (March 1973): 771–784.

Morelos, Cynthia A. "A Survey of Leadership Activities and Community Involvement of Mexican American Women in San Antonio, 1920–1940." *Journal of South Texas* 13 (2000): 193–206.

Norquest, Carrol. *Rio Grande Wetbacks: Mexican Migrant Workers*. Albuquerque: University of New Mexico Press, 1972.

Plascencia, Luis F. B., Miguel Ceballos, and Robert W. Glover. *Texas Farm Worker Enumeration Project*. Austin: Center for the Study of Human Resources, 1989.

Powell, Eve Ellen. "The Relationship of Social-Demography Factors, Birth Weight, and Infant Mortality among Spanish Surname, Anglo and Nonwhite Populations in Texas." Ph.D. dissertation, University of Texas at Austin, 1985.

Rhinehart, Marilyn D., and Thomas H. Kreneck. "In the Shadow of Uncertainty: Texas Mexicans and Repatriation in Houston during the Great Deprssion." *The Houston Review* 10.1 (Spring 1988): 21–33.

Richardson, Chad, and Joe Feagin. "The Dynamics of Legalization: Undocumented Mexican Immigrants in the United States." *Research in Political Sociology* 3 (1987): 179–201.

Ríos McMillan, Nora E. "The Immigration Issue Between 1929 and 1954 as seen through *La Prensa*." *South Texas Studies* 6 (1995): 20–52.

Robledo, Amado. "The Impact of Alien Immigration on Public Policy and Educational Services on Selected Districts in the Texas Educational System." Ph.D. dissertation, University of Houston, 1977.

Robledo, Amado, and Barton R. Herrscher. "The Impact of Alien Immigration Education in Texas." In *Bridging Two Cultures: Multidisciplinary Readings in Bilingual Bicultural Education*, edited by Martha Cotera and Larry Hufford, 424–432. Austin: National Education Laboratory Publishers, 1980.

Rodríguez, Marc Simon. "Obreros Unidos: Migration, Migrant Farm Worker Activism, and the Chicano Movement in Wisconsin and Texas, 1950–1960." Ph.D. dissertation, Northwestern University, 2000.

Rodríguez, Nestor. "Chicano-Indocumentado Work Relations: Findings of the Texas Indocumentado Study." In *Chicano-Mexican Relations*, edited by Tatcho Mindiola Jr. and Max Martínez, 72–84. Houston: Mexican Americans Studies Program, 1986.

Rodríguez, Nestor, and Rogelio T. Nuñez. "An Exploration of Factors that Contribute to Differentiation between Chicanos and *Indocumentados*." In *Mexican Immigrants and Mexican Americans: An Evolving Relation*, edited by Harley L. Browning and Rodolfo O. de la Garza, 138–156. Austin: CMAS Publications, 1986.

Rosales, Francisco Arturo. "The Mexican Immigrant Experience in Chicago, Houston, and Tucson: Comparisons and Contrasts." In *Houston: A Twentieth-Century Urban Frontier*, edited by Francisco A. Rosales and Barry J. Kaplan, 58–77, 192–194. Port Washington, N.Y.: Associated Faculty Press, 1983.

Sánchez-Walker, Marjorie. "Migration Quicksand: Immigration Law and Immigration Advocates at the El Paso–Ciudad Juárez Border Crossing, 1933–1941." Ph.D. dissertation, Washington State University, 1999.

Saunders, Lyle, and Olen E. Leonard. *The Wetback in the Lower Rio Grande Valley of Texas*. Austin: University of Texas Press, 1951.

Scruggs, Otey M. "Texas and the Bracero Program." *Pacific Historical Review* 32 (August 1963): 251–264.

Sheridan, Clare. "Contested Citizenship: National Identity and the Mexican Immigration Debates of the 1920s." *Journal of American Ethnic History* 21 (Spring 2002): 3–35.

Skinner, Carolyn E. "Social Workers' Perceptions of Undocumented Immigrants and Immigration Law." Master's thesis, University of Texas at Arlington, 1987.

Smith, Ann Crowley. "Whites, Blacks and Hispanics as Candidates in Local Elections." Ph.D. dissertation, University of Texas at Arlington, 1988.

Spillman, Robert C. "A Historical Geography of Mexican American Population Patterns in the South Texas Hispanic Borderland." Master's thesis, University of Southern Mississippi, 1977.

Stoddard, Ellwyn R. "A Conceptual Analysis of the Alien Invasion: Institutionalized Support of Illegal Mexican Aliens in the United States." *International Migration Review* 10 (1976): 157–190.

Taylor, Paul S. "Note on Streams of Mexican Migration." *American Journal of Sociology* 36 (September 1930): 287–288.

Teske, Raymond, H. C. Jr., and B. H. Nelson. "An Analysis of Differential Assimilation Rates Among Middle-Class Mexican Americans." *Sociological Quarterly* 17.2 (1976): 218–235.

________. "Middle Class Mexican Americans and Political Power Potential: A Dilemma." *Journal of Political and Military Sociology* 4.1 (1976): 107–119.

________. "Two Scales for the Measurement of Mexican American Identity." *International Review of Modern Sociology* 3.2 (1973): 192–203.

Tjarks, Alicia V. "Comparative Demographic Analysis of Texas, 1777–1793." *Southwestern Historical Quarterly* 77 (January 1974): 291–338.

Valdez, Avelardo. "Residential Patterns of Chicanos, Undocumented Mexicans, and Anglos in San Antonio (Bexar County), Texas: An Assessment of Recent Change and Social Costs." In *Mexican Immigrants and Mexican Americans: An Evolving Relation*, edited by Harley L. Browning and Rodolfo O. de la Garza, 120–137. Austin: CMAS Publications, 1986.

Valerius, John Behner. "The Spanish-speaking Population of Texas, 1954–1955: Estimates and a Study of Estimation Methods." Master's thesis, University of Texas, Austin, 1956.

Vincent, Vern, and Ed Vento. "Population and Employment Forecasts for the Lower Rio Grande Valley of Texas to the Year 2000." *Borderlands Journal* 8 (Spring 1985): 81–100.

Weeks, John R., and Roberto Ham-Chande, eds. *Demographic Dynamics of the U.S.-Mexico Border*. El Paso: Texas Western Press, 1992.

Weintraub, Sidney, and Gilberto Cárdenas. *The Use of Public Services by Undocumented Aliens in Texas*. Austin: Lyndon Baines Johnson School of Public Affairs, 1984.

Weintraub, Sidney, and Stanley R. Ross. *The Illegal Alien from Mexico: Policy Choices for an Intractable Issue*. Austin: University of Texas at Austin, States Border Research Program, 1980.

Whittington, Lona Teresa. "The Road of Sorrow: Mexican Refugees Who Fled Pancho Villa through Presidio, Texas, 1913–1914." Master's thesis, Sul Ross State University, 1976.

Wilson, Foster W. "Demographic Characteristics of Texas White Persons of Spanish Surname." Master's thesis, Texas A&M University, College Station, 1966.

Wright, Linda C. "The Bracero Question, 1943–64: Congress, the Nation, and Texas." Master's thesis, Southwest Texas State University, 1980.

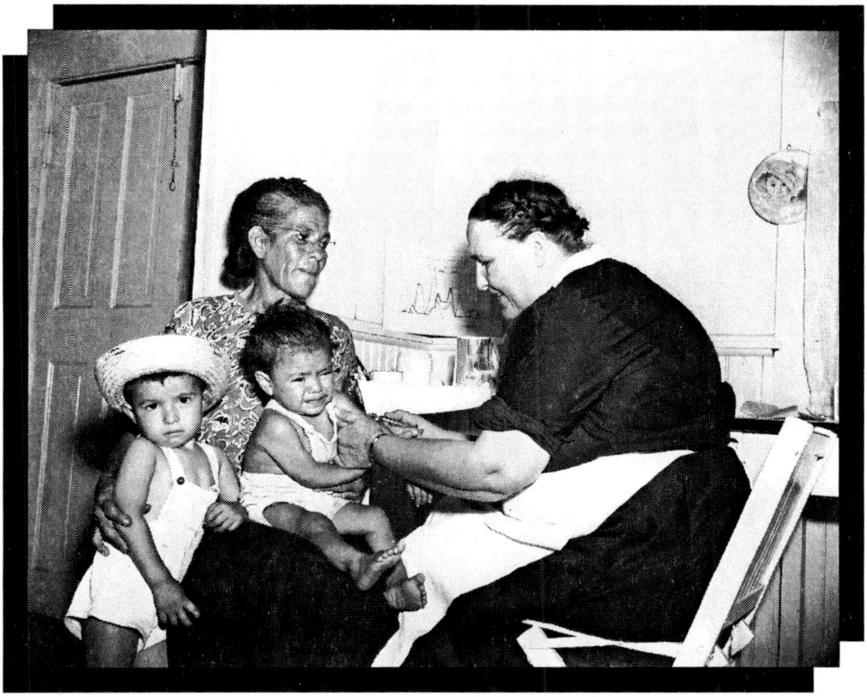

22. HEALTH/HEALING

As with any community, its survival depends heavily upon the availability of support for good health—the medical practitioners. For Tejanos, too often the normal (read Anglo) medical treatment and facilities were not available. So, within the community, faith healers as well as formally educated doctors and nurses emerged to deal with the health—mental as well as physical—of Tejanos. This section includes works covering the status of health and healing in the Hispanic community in the Lone Star state. Works discuss topics such as illness, wellness, methods of treatment, particular sickness problems, alcohol- and drug-related difficulties, and comparisons with Anglos. The presence in the Mexican-Texas community of *curanderos* is a vital aspect of many of these works.

Mrs. Esperanda Vasquez with her two children, Gilbert and Juan, receiving immunization shots at the St. Alphonsus Clinic, ca. 1943.
The Institute of Texan Cultures at UTSA, No. L-3079-H
The San Antonio Light *Collection*

Aceves, Melba Lucila. "Pregnancy Outcomes among Hispanic Adolescents in Relation to Uterine Growth, Weight Gain, and Prepregnant Weight." Master's thesis, University of Texas Graduate School of Biomedical Science at Galveston, 1988.

Agogino, George A., and Bobbie Ferguson. "*Curanderismo*: The Folk Healer in the Spanish-speaking Community." *Masterkey* 57.3 (1983): 101–106.

Aguilar, Lydia. "A Genetic Marker Study on Non-Insulin Dependent Diabetics in the Mexican-American Community from Starr County, Texas." Ph.D. dissertation, University of Texas Health Science Center at Houston, 1985.

Aguirre, Lydia. "Alternative Health Practices Along the Western Texas Border." In *Modern Medicine and Medical Anthropology in the United States-Mexico Border Population*, edited by Boris Velimirovic, 60–66. Washington, D.C.: Pan American Health Organization, 1978.

Alcalá, Joyce Lynn. "Validation of Measures of Depression with Hispanic Children: A Multimethod Investigation." Ph.D. dissertation, Texas A&M University, 1990.

Alegría, D., et al. "*El Hospital Invisible*: A Study of Curanderismo." *Archives of General Psychiatry* 34 (1977): 1354–1357.

Andrade, Erasmo Wilivaldo. "Comments on Mental Health Consultation in a Rural Chicano Community: Crystal City." *Aztlán* 6 (Fall 1975): 455–458.

Andrade, Sally Jones, ed. *Chicano Mental Health: The Case of Cristal; An Evaluation of the Zavala County Mental Health Outreach Program*. Austin: Hogg Foundation for Mental Health, 1978.

Andrulus, S. "Ethnicity as a Variable in the Utilization and Referral Patterns of a Comprehensive Mental Health Center." *Journal of Community Psychology* 5 (1977): 231–237.

Aranda-Navanjo, Barbara. "The Health-Seeking Experiences of Mexican-American Women with HIV/AIDS." Ph.D. dissertation, University of Texas at Austin, 1997.

Arreola, David Robert. "Psychotherapists' Perceived Differences of Locus-of-Control Assertiveness, Self-Disclosure, and Psychological Adjustment for Mexican- and Anglo-Americans." Ph.D. dissertation, Michigan State University, 1991.

Austin, Alfredo López. "Medical Anthropology in a Border Context." In *Modern Medicine and Medical Anthropology in the United States-Mexico Border Population*, edited by Boris Velimirovic, 43–48. Washington, D.C.: Pan American Health Organization, 1978.

Barrientos, Guido A. *Reaching Out/Dame La Mano: Utilization of Mental Health Resources in El Paso and Mexico: Utilización de cursos de salud mental en El Paso y en México*. El Paso: Texas Western Press, 1998.

Boesch, Jennifer E. "A Nutrition/Behavior Modification Intervention Program for Elderly Hispanic Persons." Master's thesis, Texas Woman's University, 1997.

Bourke, John G. "Popular Medicine, Customs, and Superstitions of the Rio Grande." *Journal of American Folklore* 7 (1894): 119–146.

Bradshaw, Benjamin S., and Edwin Fonner Jr. "The Mortality of Spanish Surnamed Persons in Texas: 1969–1971." In *The Demography of Racial and Ethnic*

Groups, edited by Frank D. Bean and W. Parker Frisbie. New York: Academic Press, 1978.

Bray, Molly Sue. "Linkage and Association of Candidate Obesity Genes in Mexican-Americans from Starr County, Texas." Ph.D. dissertation, University of Texas Health Science Center at Houston, 1998.

Brown-Pearson, Alice Dianne. "An Analysis of Alcohol Self-reported Use and Abuse Patterns in an Hispanic Serving Institution from 1991 to 1997." Ph.D. dissertation, Texas A&M University, 1999.

Bruhn, J. G. "Health Manpower Needs among Mexican Americans in Texas." *Texas Report on Biology and Medicine* 32 (1974): 633–647.

Bruhn, J. G., et al. "Follow-up of Minority Premedical Students Attending Summer Enrichment Programs in a Medical Setting." *Texas Medicine* 72.8 (1976): 87–90.

Buchanan, Anne, and Kenneth M. Weiss. "Infant Mortality in a Mexican-American Community: Laredo, Texas, 1950–1977." *Social Biology* 38 (Fall/Winter 1991): 233–241.

Butt, Leslie. "Health and Healing at Work: Social Negotiations in Families of Mexican American Migrant Farmworkers." Master's thesis, Simon Fraser University, 1991.

Byrd, Theresa. "Notes on Community Health on the Border from Theory and Practice." In *U.S.-Mexico Border Health: Issues for Regional and Migrant Populations*, edited by J. Gerard Power and Theresa Byrd, 195–207. Thousand Oaks, Calif.: Sage Publications, 1998.

Cárdenas, José A. "Chicano Self-Determination and Mental Health: Cristal as Pioneer." In *Chicano Mental Health: The Case of Cristal: An Evaluation of the Zavala County Mental Health Outreach Program*, by Sally Jones Andrade, 161–170. Austin: Hogg Foundation for Mental Health, 1978.

Carlson, Paul Edward. "Investigation of Bias in the Diagnosis of Behaviorally-Disordered Mexican-American Children Using the Social Behavior Assessment Scale." Ph.D. dissertation, Ohio State University, 1983.

Carrasco, Sara Margarita Campos. "Mexican American Folk Medicine: A Descriptive Study of the Different *Curanderismo* Techniques Practiced by *Curanderos* or *Curanderas* and Used by Patients in the Laredo, Texas Area." Ph.D. dissertation, Texas Woman's University, 1984.

Castillo, Julián. "Preference for and Utilization of Health Care Services by Mexican Americans in South Texas." Ed.D. dissertation, University of Houston, 1986.

Castro, Allen. "Mexican-American Values and Their Impact on Mental Health Care." Ph.D. dissertation, University of Texas at Austin, 1996.

Chandler, Sue Ann. "The Use of Alternate Health Resources in a South Texas Town." Master's thesis, University of Houston, 1978.

Codina, G. Edward, Charles D. Kaplan, Zenong Yin, Alberto G. Mata Jr., and Avelardo Valdez. "Readiness for Treatment: Predictors of Drug Abuse Help-Seeking in Mexican American, African American, and White San Antonio Arrestees." *Free Inquiry for Creative Sociology* 24 (1996): 17–24.

Colwell, Brian, Dennis Smith, and James J. Zhang. "*Cambio en las escuelas*: Mexican-American Parent Attitudes Toward School Health Education." *Journal of Community Health* 25 (October 2000): 427–437.

Costello, R. M., et al. "Mexican American Behavioral Adjustments in an Anglo Hospital." *Psychiatric Annals* 7.12 (1977): 82–85.

Cotter, John Vincent. "Mosquitoes and Disease in the Lower Rio Grande Valley, 1846–1986." Ph.D. dissertation, University of Texas at Austin, 1986.

Dever, Martha Esther Victoria. "A Study of Community Health Service Utilization by Hispanic Elderly." Master's thesis, University of Texas at Arlington, 1995.

Díaz De León, Cynthia Denise. "Influence of Cultural Variables on the Adjustment of Hispanic and Anglo Children with Cleft Conditions." Ph.D. dissertation, University of Texas at Austin, 1996.

Dodson, Ruth. *Don Pedrito Jaramillo: Curandero.* San Antonio: Casa Editorial Lozano, 1934.

________. "The Curandero of Los Olmos." In *Texas Folk and Folklore*, edited by Mody C. Boatright, Wilson M. Hudson, and Allen Maxwell, 264–269. Dallas: Southern Methodist University Press, 1954.

________. "Don Pedrito Jaramillo: The Curandero of Los Olmos." In *The Healer of Los Olmos and Other Mexican Lore*, edited by Wilson M. Hudson, 9–70. Austin: Texas Folklore Society, 1951.

________. "Folk Curing Among the Mexicans." In *Cultural Differences in Medical Care*, edited by Robert H. Gemmill, 59–76. Ft. Sam Houston, Tex.: Academy of Health Sciences, 1972.

________. "Folk-Curing Among the Mexicans." In *Tone the Bell Easy*, edited by J. Frank Dobie, 82–98. Austin: Texas Folklore Society, 1932.

________. "The Life of Don Pedro Jaramillo: Benefactor of Humanity." *Perspectives in Mexican American Studies* 1 (1988): 69–74.

Dunaway, Sherry S. "Folk Healing and Western Medical Practices in a Mexican-American Community." Master's thesis, University of Texas at Arlington, 1984.

Estrada, Antonio Luciano. "Health Services Utilization among Anglos, Mexican Americans and Mexicans." Ph.D. dissertation, University of California, Los Angeles, 1986.

Fabrega, H. Jr. "Mexican Americans of Texas: Some Social Psychiatric Features." In *Behavior in New Environments: Adaptation of Migrant Populations*, edited by E. G. Brody, 249–273. Beverly Hills: Sage Publications, 1970.

Fabrega, H. Jr., and C. A. Wallace. "Acculturation and Psychiatric Treatment: A Study Involving Mexican Americans." *British Journal of Social Psychiatry* 4.2 (1970–1971): 124–136.

________. "Value Identification and Psychiatric Disability: An Analysis Involving Americans of Mexican Descent." *Behavioral Science* 35.5 (1968): 362–371.

Fantini, Albino. "Illness and Curing among the Mexican Americans of Mission, Texas." Master's thesis, University of Texas, Austin, 1962.

Farabee, David, Lynn Wallisch, and Jane Carlisle Maxwell. "Substance Abuse among Texas Hispanics and Non-Hispanics: Who's Using, Who's Not, and Why." *Hispanic Journal of Behavioral Sciences* 17 (November 1995): 523–536.

Farge, E. J. *La Vida Chicana: Health Care Attitudes and Behaviors of Houston Chicanos*. San Francisco: R&E Research Associates, 1975.

________. "A Review of Findings from 'Three Generations' of Chicano Health Care Behavior." *Social Science Quarterly* 58.3 (1977): 407–411.

Foley, Douglas E. "Decolonization and Mental Health in South Texas." In *Chicano Mental Health: The Case of Cristal: An Evaluation of the Zavala County Mental Health Outreach Program*, by Sally Jones Andrade, 151–160. Austin: Hogg Foundation for Mental Health, 1978.

Forbes, Douglas. "Ethnic Variation in Infant Mortality, Bexar County, Texas, 1964–1984." Ph.D. dissertation, University of Texas at Austin, 1992.

García-Londono, Gloria. "Blood Pressure and Dietary Factors in Mexican-Americans of Starr County, Texas." Dr.P.H. dissertation, University of Texas Health Science Center at Houston, 1991.

Garza, Refugio S. "En el nombre de dios y Don Pedrito Jaramillo." Master's thesis, Texas A&I University, 1952.

Gebre, Gebreamlak. "Factors Affecting Prenatal Care Use and Pregnancy Outcome in Texas: A Comparative Study Among and Within Black, Anglo, and Hispanic Populations." Dr.P.H. dissertation, University of Texas Health Science Center at Houston, 1987.

Gibbs, C. E., et al. "Patterns of Reproduction Health Care Among the Poor of San Antonio, Texas." *American Journal of Public Health* 64 (1974): 37–40.

Gittins, Colleen Anne. "Case Studies of Selective Mutism in Hispanic Children." Master's thesis, University of Texas–Pan American, 1996.

Goff, David C. Jr. "Percutaneous Transluminal Coronary Angioplasty and Coronary Events in a Biethnic Texas Community, 1985–1990." Ph.D. dissertation, University of Texas Health Science Center at Houston, 1992.

Gómez, Ernesto Alvarado. "The Evaluation of Psychosocial Casework Services to Chicanos: A Study of Process and Outcome." Ph.D. dissertation, University of Texas at Austin, 1982.

Gómez, Sarah Ann. "Experiences and Opinions about Fiber and Breast Cancer in Older Hispanic Women in the Houston Area." Master's thesis, Texas Woman's University, 2001.

Gonzales, Clara Ann. "Indigent Health Care: Hispanics in Texas." *Texas Journal of Rural Health* (Summer 1987): 5–6.

González, Blanca N. "Attitudes Toward Psychotherapy and Willingness to Seek Psychotherapy of Mexican-Americans of Low and High Acculturation Levels." Ph.D. dissertation, Boston University, 1996.

González-Lima, Erika Musiol. "Characteristics and Stress Levels of Hispanic and Non-Hispanic Caregivers of Alzheimer's Disease Patients." Ph.D. dissertation, Texas A&M University, 1989.

Graham, Joe S. *Grandmother's Tea: Mexican Herbal Remedies—A Study Guide*. San Antonio: University of Texas Institute of Texan Cultures, 1979.

________. "Curanderismo." In *The New Handbook of Texas,* edited by Ron Tyler, Douglas E. Barnett, Roy R. Barkley, Penelope C. Anderson, and Mark F. Odintz, vol. 2, 452. Austin: Texas State Historical Association, 1996.

________. "Effectiveness of Traditional Folk Medicine." *South Texas Studies* 5 (1994): 104–130.

________. "Folk Medicine and Intracultural Diversity among West Texas Mexican Americans." *Western Folklore* 44 (1985): 168–193.

________. "The Role of *Curandero* in the Mexican-American Folk Medicine System in West Texas." In *American Folk Medicine: A Symposium*, edited by Wayland D. Hand, 175–190. Los Angeles: University of California Press, 1976.

Grimm, Agnes G. "Pedro Jaramillo." In *The New Handbook of Texas,* edited by Ron Tyler, Douglas E. Barnett, Roy R. Barkley, Penelope C. Anderson, and Mark F. Odintz, vol. 3, 910–911. Austin: Texas State Historical Association, 1996.

Guerra, Anna María. "Depressive Symptomatology in Mexican-Americans." Ph.D. dissertation, University of Houston, 1992.

Gunn, R. "Alcohol Use Among Mexican American Youth." *Journal of School Health* 48.2 (1978): 90–91.

________. "Characteristics of Drug Use Among Mexican American Students." *Journal of Drug Education* 5.3 (1975): 235–247.

Gunn, R., and R. S. Hurley. "A Comparison of Drug Use Among Houston and Lower Rio Grande Valley Secondary Students." *Adolescence* 6 (1976): 455–459.

Gu, Qin (KEN). "Sources of Familial Aggregation and Co-aggregation of Fasting Blood: Glucose and Nutritional Factors among Mexican-Americans in Starr County, Texas." Dr.P.H. dissertation, University of Texas Health Science Center at Houston, 1995.

Gurnack, Anne Marie. "Access to Health Care in a West Dallas Community." Ph.D. dissertation, University of Texas at Arlington, 1979.

Hanis, C., R. E. Ferrell, S. A. Barton, L. Aguilar, A. Garza-Ibarra, B. R. Tulloch, C. A. García, and W. J. Schull. "Diabetes Among Mexican Americans in Starr County, Texas." *American Journal of Epidemiology* 118 (1983): 272–277.

Hawkins, Nicole DeShaun. "Six-year Survival Analysis of African American and Hispanic Women with Breast Cancer in the State of Texas." Master's thesis, University of North Texas Health Science Center at Fort Worth, 1999.

Hearn, Charles John. "Texas Nurses' Perceptions of Health Care Barriers Experienced by Hispanics/Latinos." Master's thesis, University of North Texas, 1997.

Hecht, Ilse H. "Folk Practices of the Childbearing Period among Mexican American Women." Master's thesis, Texas Woman's University, 1976.

Higginbothan, John C. "Utilization of *Curanderos* by Mexican Americans." *American Journal of Public Health* 80 (December 1990): 32–35.

Hinojosa, Irma. "Increasing the Consent Rate for Organ Donation in the Hispanic Population." In *U.S.-Mexico Border Health: Issues for Regional and Migrant*

Populations, edited by J. Gerard Power and Theresa Byrd, 24–31. Thousand Oaks, Calif.: Sage Publications, 1998.

Holtzman, Wayne H. "Mental Health and Personality Development in the Border States." *Texas Psychologist* 27.1 (1975): 56–61.

________. "Personality Development and Mental Health of People in the Border States." In *Views Across the Border: The United States and Mexico*, edited by Stanley R. Ross, 308–329. Albuquerque: University of New Mexico Press, 1978.

Hoppe, S. K., and P. L. Heller. "Alienation, Famialism, and the Utilization of Health Services by Mexican Americans." *Journal of Health and Social Behavior* 16.3 (1975): 304–314.

Hudson, Wilson M., ed. *The Healer of Los Olmos and Other Mexican Lore*. Dallas: Southern Methodist University Press, 1951.

Hunter, Leslie Gene, and Cecilia Aros Hunter. "'Mother Lane' and the 'New Mooners': An Expression of *Curanderismo*." *Southwestern Historical Quarterly* 99 (January 1996): 291–325.

Hunt, Thomas Lynn. "The Equity and Impact of Medicare and Medicaid with Respect to Mexican Americans in Texas." Ph.D. dissertation, University of Texas at Austin, 1978.

Hurtado, Aida. "Midwife Practices in Hidalgo County, Texas." *Trabajos Monográficos: Studies in Chicana/Latina Research* 3 (1987): 1–30.

Jaco, E. Gartley. "Mental Health of the Spanish-Americans in Texas." In *Culture and Mental Health*, edited by Marvin K. Upler, 467–488. New York: Macmillan Company, 1959.

________. "Social Factors in Mental Disorders in Texas." *Social Problems* 4.4 (1957): 322–328.

Johnson, L. V., and M. Matre. "Anomie and Alcohol Use: Drinking Patterns in Mexican American and Anglo Neighborhoods." *Journal of Studies on Alcohol* 39 (1978): 894–902.

Joos, Sandra Kay. "Social, Attitudinal and Behavioral Correlates of Weight Change Among Mexican American Women." Ph.D. dissertation, University of Texas Health Science Center at Houston, 1984.

Juárez, Rumaldo Z., Rubén E. Sáenz, Armando López, Doreen D. Garza, Karen D. Fossom, and Alicia López-González. *Lower Rio Grande Valley Demographics and Health Statistics*. Edinburg, Tex.: Texas-Mexico Border Health Coordination Office, 1994.

________. *Texas-Mexico Border County Demographics and Health Statistics*. Edinburg, Tex.: Texas-Mexico Border Health Coordination Office, 1994.

Judd, Judith. "A Study of Food Habits and Medical-Nutrition Status of Spanish-Speaking Families of Low Socio-Economic Status Residing in Dallas, Texas." Ph.D. dissertation, Texas Woman's University, 1962.

Kay, Margarita Artschwager. "Health and Illness in a Mexican American Barrio." In *Ethnic Medicine in the Southwest*, edited by Edward H. Spicer, 99–168. Tucson: University of Arizona Press, 1977.

Kelly, Michael P. "Divine Resources: Health Education Activities at Churches Along the U.S.-Mexico Border." In *U.S.-Mexico Border Health: Issues for Regional and Migrant Populations*, edited by J. Gerard Power and Theresa Byrd, 215–223. Thousand Oaks, Calif.: Sage Publications, 1998.

Keyes, Grace Granger. "Mexican American and Anglo American Midwifery in San Antonio, Texas." Ph.D. dissertation, University of Wisconsin, Milwaukee, 1985.

Kiev, Ari. *Curanderismo: Mexican-American Folk Psychiatry*. New York: Free Press, 1968.

Kimber, Clarissa. "Plants in the Folk Medicine of the Texas-Mexico Borderlands." *Proceedings of the Association of American Geographers* (1973): 130–133.

Krueger, D. "The Relationship of Ethnicity to Utilization of Community Mental Health Centers." Ph.D. dissertation, University of Texas at Austin, 1974.

Laosa, Luis M., Alan G. Burstein, and Harry W. Martin. "Mental Health Consultation in a Rural Chicano Health Community: Crystal City." *Aztlán* 6 (Fall 1975): 433–454.

Lara, Jesusa. "Health Outreach Programs in the *Colonias* of the U.S.-Mexico Border." In *U.S.-Mexico Border Health: Issues for Regional and Migrant Populations*, edited by J. Gerard Power and Theresa Byrd, 208–214. Thousand Oaks, Calif.: Sage Publications, 1998.

Larson, L. B., et al. "Nutrition Status of Children of Mexican American Migrant Parents." *Journal of American Diet Association* 64.1 (1974): 29–35.

Lawrence, Patricia A. "Psychological Risk Factors and Substance Abuse Among Young Adults: A Comparison of Non-Hispanic Whites and Mexican Americans." In *U.S.-Mexico Border Health: Issues for Regional and Migrant Populations*, edited by J. Gerard Power and Theresa Byrd, 32–51. Thousand Oaks, Calif.: Sage Publications, 1998.

LeBlanc, Donna Marie. "Quality of Maternity Care in Rural Texas." Dr.P.H. dissertation, University of Texas Health Science Center at Houston, 1983.

Levin, Jeffrey Scott. "Socioethnic Differences in the Determinants of Prenatal Care Utilization and Birth Weight." Ph.D. dissertation, University of Texas Graduate School of Biomedical Science at Galveston, 1987.

Limón, José E. "Healing the Wounds: Folk Symbols and Historical Crisis." *Texas Journal of Ideas, History and Culture* 20 (Fall/Winter 1997): 44–49.

Lofstrom, Katina Marie. "Dietary Fat Intake and Fat Practices Among a Multiethnic Parent-child Population." Master's thesis, Texas Woman's University, 2000.

Longoria, Norma Linda. "Dietary Propensity among South Texas Mexican American WIC Participants." Master's thesis, Texas A&M University-Kingsville, 1997.

Luna Hollen, Mary Louise. "The Association Between and Among Food Patterns, Health Perceptions, and Stage of Self-identity Development in Predicting Health Perceptions Using a Newly Designed Cross-cultural Health Inventory Algorithm." Ph.D. dissertation, Texas Woman's University, 2001.

Macklin, June. "*Curanderismo* and *Espiritismo*: Complementary Approaches to Traditional Mental Health Services." In *Modern Medicine and Medical Anthropology in the United States-Mexico Border Population*, edited by Boris

Velimirovic, 155–162. Washington, D.C.: Pan American Health Organization, 1978.

________. "*Curanderismo* and *Espiritismo*." In *Modern Medicine and Medical Anthropology in the United States-Mexico Border Population*, edited by Boris Velimirovic, 155–162. Washington, D.C.: Pan American Health Organization, 1978.

Madsen, William. *Society and Health in the Lower Rio Grande Valley: A Guide for Medical and Welfare Workers among the Mexican-American*. Austin: Hogg Foundation for Mental Health, 1961.

________. "The Alcoholic Agringado." *American Anthropologist* 66 (1964): 355–361.

________. "Society and Health in the Lower Rio Grande Valley." In *Mexican Americans in the United States: A Reader*, edited by John H. Burma, 329–342. Cambridge, Mass.: Schenkman Publishing, 1970.

________. "Value Conflicts and Folk Psychotherapy in South Texas." In *Magic, Faith, and Healing*, edited by Ari Kiev, 420–440. New York: Free Press, 1964.

Mahnken, Jonathan David. "A Validation Study for Self-reported Data of Recent Mammography Use Among Older Mexican-American Women in Southeast Texas." Master's thesis, University of Texas Graduate School of Biomedical Science at Galveston, 2000.

Marcuse, E. K., and G. Grand. "Epidemiology of Diphtheria in San Antonio, Texas." *Journal of American Medical Association* 224 (1970): 305–310.

Maril, Robert Lee, and Antonio N. Zavaleta. "Drinking Patterns of Low-Income Mexican-American Women." *Journal of Studies in Alcohol* 40.5 (1979): 480–485.

Marshall, Carolyn Emmett. "Evaluation of a Bilingual Video-Novella Method to Teach Elderly Mexican American Non-readers How to Decrease their Risk of Diabetic Complications." Ph.D. dissertation, Texas A&M University, 1994.

Marshall, María Sandra González. "The Childbearing Beliefs and Practices of Pregnant Mexican-American Adolescents Living in Southwest Border Regions." Master's thesis, University of Arizona, 1987.

Marsh, Elizabeth F. "Dietary Studies of Families on Relief." Master's thesis, University of Texas, Austin, 1935.

Martin, Harry W., Cervando Martínez, Robert Leon, Chad Richardson, and Victor Reyes Acosta. "Folk Illnesses Reported to Physicians in the Lower Rio Grande Valley: A Binational Comparison." *Ethnology* 24 (July 1985): 229–236.

Martínez, Armando. "Acculturation, Self-Concept, Anxiety, Imagery and Stress as Related to Disease in Mexican-Americans." Ph.D. dissertation, University of North Texas, 1981.

Martínez, Cervando, and Harry W. Martin. "Folk Diseases Among Mexican Americans." *Journal of the American Medical Association* 196.2 (1966): 161–164.

________. "Folk Diseases Among Urban Mexican-Americans." In *Hispanic Culture and Health Care: Fact, Fiction, Folklore*, edited by Ricardo Arguijo Martínez, 131–137. St. Louis: C. V. Mosby Company, 1978.

Martínez, Gustavo Ricardo. "The Relationship of Social Support to Post-traumatic Stress Disorder Among Hispanic and White Vietnam Combat Veterans." D.S.W. dissertation, Catholic University of America, 1990.

Martínez, María Elena. "A Case Comparison Study of Dietary Factors and Risk of Colorectal Polyps." Ph.D. dissertation, University of Texas Health Science Center at Houston, 1993.

Mayers, Raymond Sánchez. "Use of Folk Medicine by Elderly Mexican American Women." *Journal of Drug Issues* 19 (Spring 1989): 283–295.

McClean, Cathy Heather. "Factors Affecting Compliance of Hispanic Women with Cervical Dysplasia." Master's thesis, University of Texas Graduate School of Biomedical Science at Galveston, 1990.

McFarlane, J., and J. Fehir. "*De Madres a Madres*: A Community, Primary Health Care Program Based on Empowerment." *Health Education Quarterly* 21.3 (1994): 381–394.

McLemore, S. Dale. "Ethnic Attitudes Toward Hospitalization: An Illustrative Comparison of Anglos and Mexican Americans." In *Hispanic Culture and Health Care: Fact, Fiction, Folklore*, edited by Ricardo Arguijo Martínez, 256–261. St. Louis: C. V. Mosby Company, 1978.

McNeil, Norman Laird ("Brownie"). "*Curanderos* of South Texas." In *And Horns on the Toads*, edited by Mody C. Boatright, Wilson M. Hudson, and Allen Maxwell, 32–44. Dallas: Southern Methodist University Press, 1959.

Mobley, Connie Chenevert. "Interaction Between Diabetes Educators and Clients of Low Socioeconomic Status: A Naturalistic Study." Ph.D. dissertation, Texas A&M University, 1993.

Nall, Frank C. II, and Joseph Spielberg. "Social and Cultural Factors in the Responses of Mexican-Americans to Medical Treatment." In *Hispanic Culture and Health Care: Fact, Fiction, Folklore*, edited by Ricardo Arguijo Martínez, 51–64. St. Louis: C. V. Mosby Company, 1978.

Nathan, Debbie. "Love in the Time of Cholera: Waiting for Free Trade on the U.S./Mexico Border." In *The Late Great Mexican Border: Reports from a Disappearing Line*, edited by Bobby Byrd and Susannah Mississippi Byrd, 43–63. El Paso: Cinco Puntos Press, 1996.

Omoloh, Wilfred J. "A Descriptive Analysis of Adolescent Pregnancy and Birth Outcomes in Tarrant County, Texas." Master's thesis, University of North Texas Health Science Center at Fort Worth, 1999.

Orozco, Cynthia E. "Clinica de la Beneficencia Mexicana." In *The New Handbook of Texas,* edited by Ron Tyler, Douglas E. Barnett, Roy R. Barkley, Penelope C. Anderson, and Mark F. Odintz, vol. 2, 162–163. Austin: Texas State Historical Association, 1996.

Paine, H. J. "Attitudes and Patterns of Alcohol Use Among Mexican Americans; Implications for Service Delivery." *Journal of Studies on Alcohol* 38 (1977): 544–553.

Paredes, Américo. "Folk Medicine and the Intercultural Jest." In *Spanish-Speaking People in the United States*, edited by June Helm, 104–119. Seattle: University of Washington Press, 1968. Reprinted in *Folk Groups and Folklore Genres: A*

Reader, edited by Elliott Oring, 63–77. Logan: Utah State University Press, 1989.

Philen, Robert Carleton. "This Is Where It All Comes Together: The Border, Gay Community, and HIV Prevention in El Paso/Juárez." Ph.D. dissertation, Cornell University, 2001.

Pulley, Leavonne. "Health Promotion and Smoking Cessation in Bicultural Communities in South Central Texas." Ph.D. dissertation, University of Texas at Austin, 1994.

Pursley, Virginia Williams. "Sociocultural Aspects of Mexican-American Adolescents Who Risk Pregnancy." Ph.D. dissertation, Texas Woman's University, 1989.

Quesada, Gustavo M., and Peter L. Heller. "Sociocultural Barriers to Medical Care among Mexican Americans in Texas: A Summary Report of Research Conducted by the Southwest Medical Sociology Ad Hoc Committee." *Medical Care* 15 (May 1977): 93–101.

Quiroga, I. R. "The Use of a Linear Discriminant Function of the Minnesota Multiphasic Personality Inventory Scores in the Classification of Psychotic and on Psychotic Mexican American Psychiatric Patients." Ph.D. dissertation, University of Illinois, 1972.

Ramírez, Amelie Gutiérrez. "Comparison of Health Behaviors of Mexican American and Non-Hispanic White Females: Implications for Health Promotion Programs." Dr. P.H. dissertation, University of Texas Health Science Center at Houston, 1992.

Ramírez, David Gaytan. "An Empirical Assessment of the Concept of Mexican American Underutilization of Mental Health Services." Ph.D. dissertation, University of Texas at Austin, 1982.

Ramírez, Olga M. "Some Factors Related to Mathematics Anxiety among Hispanic College Undergraduates." Ph.D. dissertation, Texas A&M University, 1985.

Ramos, Irma N., Marlynn May, and Kenneth S. Ramos. "Environmental Health Training of *Promotoras* in *Colonias* along the Texas-Mexico Border." *American Journal of Public Health* 91.4 (2001): 568–570.

Ready, Timothy Paul. "An Investigation of Biological, Psychosocial and Sociocultural Influences upon the Blood Pressures of Adolescents in Corpus Christi, Texas." Ph.D. dissertation, Michigan State University, 1981.

Rhoades, Cecilia Claudine. "The Poison Crop: South Texas Farmers versus Toxwaste Hazardous Waste Storage Facility." Ph.D. dissertation, University of Texas at Austin, 1997.

Rodríguez, Isabel Ann. "Identifying Barriers to Health Care Perceived by Hispanics in a West Texas Community." Master's thesis, Texas Tech University, 1996.

Rodríguez, María Elena. "Mary Dilley, *Curandera*: A Modern South Texas Folk Healer." Master's thesis, Texas A&M University-Kingsville, 1993.

Rodríguez, Reymundo, and Marion Tolbert Coleman, eds. *Mental Health Issues of the Mexican Origin Population in Texas: Proceedings of the Fifth Robert Lee Sutherland Seminar in Mental Health*. Austin: Hogg Foundation for Mental Health, University of Texas at Austin, 1987.

Romano-V., Octavio Ignacio. "Don Pedrito Jaramillo: The Emergence of a Mexican American Folk Saint." Ph.D. dissertation, University of California, Berkeley, 1964.

________. "Charismatic Medicine, Folk-Healing, and Folk-Sainthood." *American Anthropologist* 67 (1965): 1151–1173.

Rubel, Arthur J. "Concepts of Disease in Mexican-American Culture." *American Anthropologist* 62 (1960): 795–814.

________. "The Epidemiology of a Folk Illness: *Susto* in Hispanic America." In *Hispanic Culture and Health Care: Fact, Fiction, Folklore*, edited by Ricardo Arguijo Martínez, 75–91. St. Louis: C. V. Mosby Company, 1978.

Ruiz, Alberto. "The Predictability of Self-reported Physical Activity, Attitudes Toward Physical Activity, and Gender on Cardiovascular Endurance Status Among Sixth-grade Hispanic Students." Ed.D. dissertation, University of Houston, 2001.

Russell, A. Yvonne, Martha S. Williams, and Patricia A. Farr. "The Health Attitudes of Young Hispanic Women and the Health Status of their Children on the Texas-Mexico Border." *Journal of Community Health* 23 (June 1998): 165–179.

Saunders, Lyle. "Healing Ways in the Spanish Southwest." In *Patients, Physicians and Illness*, edited by E. Gartley Jaco, 189–206. New York: Free Press, 1958.

Sawyer-Morse, Mary Kaye. "Psychosocial and Behavioral Correlates of Disordered Eating among Young Adult Hispanic Females." Ph.D. dissertation, University of Texas at Austin, 1997.

Selby, Maija Leena. "Infant Mortality in the Mexican American Community: An Analysis of Differentials in Infant, Neonatal, and Post Neonatal Mortality by Ethnicity and Parental Nativity, 1974–75 Single Live Birth Cohort, Harris County, Texas." Dr.P.H. dissertation, University of Texas Health Science Center at Houston, 1982.

Schlesinger, Bill. "Project Vida: Community Health Models that Work." In *U.S.-Mexico Border Health: Issues for Regional and Migrant Populations*, edited by J. Gerard Power and Theresa Byrd, 165–172. Thousand Oaks, Calif.: Sage Publications, 1998.

Schreiber, Janet M., and Loralee Philpott. "Who is a Legitimate Health Care Professional? Changes in the Practice of Midwifery in the Lower Rio Grande Valley." In *Modern Medicine and Medical Anthropology in the United States-Mexico Border Population*, edited by Boris Velimirovic, 127–138. Washington, D.C.: Pan American Health Organization, 1978.

Scott, J., and C. M. Gaitz. "Ethnic and Age Differences in Mental Health Measurements." *Diseases of the Nervous System* 36.7 (1975): 389–393.

Shapiro, Harold A. "Health Conditions in San Antonio, Texas, 1900–1947." *Southwestern Social Science Quarterly* 34 (December 1953): 60–76.

Smithers, W. D. "Nature's Pharmacy and the *Curanderos*." In *Nature's Pharmacy and the Curanderos and The Border Trading Posts*, edited by W. D. Smithers, 15–40. Alpine, Tex.: Publications of the West Texas Historical and Scientific Society, 1961.

Smith, Grover H. (Dean). "*Curanderismo*: Mexican Folk Healing." *Journal of Big Bend Studies* 7 (1995): 217–227.

Smith, Helen P. "Health and Nutrition of Mexican Infants and Pre-School Children." Master's thesis, University of Texas, Austin, 1930.

Sorenson, Ann Marie. "Ethnicity and Fertility: The Fertility Expectations and Family Size of Mexican-American and Anglo Adolescents and Adults, Husbands and Wives." Ph.D. dissertation, University of Arizona, 1985.

Spielberg, Joseph. "Social and Cultural Configurations and Medical Care: A Study of Mexican-Americans' Response to Proposed Hospitalization for the Treatment of Tuberculosis." Master's thesis, University of Texas, Austin, 1959.

Steffen-Batey, Lyn. "Physical Activity and Survival after a First Myocardial Infarction: The Corpus Christi Heart Project." Ph.D. dissertation, University of Texas Health Science Center at Houston, 1998.

Stenger-Castro, Earl M. "The Mexican-American: How His Culture Affects His Mental Health." In *Hispanic Culture and Health Care: Fact, Fiction, Folklore*, edited by Ricardo Arguijo Martínez, 19–32. St. Louis: C. V. Mosby Company, 1978.

Stern, Michael P., Sharon Parten Gaskill, Clarence R. Allen Jr., Virginia Garza, José L. González, and Revel H. Waldrop. "Cardiovascular Risk Factors in Mexican Americans in Laredo, Texas." *American Journal of Epidemiology* 113 (May 1981): 546–555.

Stern, Michael P., Sharon Parten Gaskill, H. P. Hazuda, L. I. Gardner, and S. M. Heffner. "Does Obesity Explain Excess Prevalence of Diabetes among Mexican Americans? Results of the San Antonio Heart Study." *Diabetologia* 24 (1983): 272–277.

Stotts, Roger Craig. "Factors Influencing Access to Health Care among Mexican American Elderly in Texas." Dr.P.H. dissertation, University of Texas Health Science Center at Houston, 1998.

Tafolla, Carmen. *Curandera*. San Antonio: M&A Editions, 1983.

Tan, Joo Ean. "Mortality from Ischemic Heart Disease and Diabetes Mellitus in Bexar County: A Comparison of the Mexican Origin and Anglo Populations." Ph.D. dissertation, University of Texas at Austin, 1991.

Teller, Charles H. "Physical Health Status and Health Care Utilization in the Texas Borderlands." In *Views Across the Border: The United States and Mexico*, edited by Stanley R. Ross, 256–279. Albuquerque: University of New Mexico Press, 1978.

Thompson, Sharon Eileen. "An Analysis of Social Support and Prenatal Care among Low-income Women in a United States/Mexico Border City." Ph.D. dissertation, University of New Mexico, 1999.

Thornberrry, Spencer Lee. "Dental Health Care of Elementary School Students at Canutillo, Texas, Four Years after Their Participation in Head Start Dental Program." Master's thesis, University of Texas at El Paso, 1971.

Tijerina, Mary Sylvia. "Mexican-American Women's Perspectives of End-stage Renal Disease and the Hemodialysis Regimen: Psychosocial Influences on Compliance with Treatment Recommendations." Ph.D. dissertation, University of Texas at Austin, 2000.

Torres, Eliseo. *The Folk Healer: The Mexican-American Tradition of Curanderismo*. Kingsville, Tex.: Nieves Press, 1983.

________. *Green Medicine: Traditional Mexican American Herbal Remedies*. Kingsville, Tex.: Nieves Press, 1983.

Trotter, Robert Talbot II. "Cultural Barriers to the Delivery of Health Care to Mexican-Americans in the Lower Rio Grande Valley of Texas." Ph.D. dissertation, Southern Methodist University, 1976.

________. "Contrasting Models of the Healer's Role: South Texas Case Examples." *Hispanic Journal of Behavioral Sciences* 4 (September 1982): 315–328.

________. "Evidence of an Ethnomedical Form of Aversion Therapy on the United States-Mexico Border." *Journal of Ethnopharmacology* 1.3 (1979): 279–284.

________. "Ethnic and Sexual Patterns of Alcohol Use: Anglo and Mexican American College Students." *Adolescence* 17 (1982): 305–325.

________. "Mexican-American Experience with Alcohol: South Texas Examples." In *The American Experience with Alcohol: Contrasting Cultural Perspectives*, edited by Linda Bennet and Genevieve M. Ames, 279–296. New York: Plenum Press, 1985.

Trotter, Robert T. II, and Juan Antonio Chavira. *Curanderismo: Mexican American Folk Healing*. Athens: University of Georgia Press, 1981.

________. *The Gift of Healing*. Edinburg, Tex.: Pan American University, 1975.

Urrutia-Rojas, Ximena. "Hispanic Incorporation and Access to Health Care in Houston and Harris County, Texas: Adopting an Hispanic Perspective to the Aday and Andersen Model." Dr.P.H. dissertation, University of Texas Health Science Center at Houston, 1995.

Valdez, Avelardo, and Alberto G. Mata Jr. "Life Histories of Four Chicano Heroin Injecting Drug Users in Laredo, Texas." In *Life, Death, and In-Between on the U.S.-Border/Así es la vida*, edited by Martha Oehmke Loustaunau and Mary Sánchez-Bane, 39–60. Westport, Conn.: Bergin and Garvey, 1999.

Valdez, Avelardo, G. Edward Codina, and Charles D. Kaplan. *A Needs Assessment of Mexican American Injecting and Other Drug Use in Laredo*. San Antonio: University of Texas at San Antonio, 1996.

Valdez, Avelardo, Zenong Yin, and Charles D. Kaplan. "A Comparison of Alcohol, Drugs, and Aggressive Crime among Mexican-American, Black, and White Male Arrestees in Texas." *American Journal of Drug and Alcohol Abuse* 23 (May 1997): 249–265.

Valdez, Ramiro. "Chicano Value Orientations and Mental Health Policy." Ph.D. dissertation, Brandeis University, 1980.

________. "Chicano Health in Texas: Some Overviews and Recommendations." *Borderlands Journal* 4 (Fall 1980) 7–20.

Van Der Kuip, Deirdre. "The Use of Invasive Myocardial Revascularization Procedures Following Myocardial Infarction and the Effectiveness of these Procedures in the Biethnic Community of Nueces County, Texas, 1988–1991." Ph.D. dissertation, University of Texas Health Science Center at Houston, 1995.

Weiss, Nancy Sue. "The Epidemiology of Uterine Cervical Cancer among Anglo and Hispanic Women in Texas." Ph.D. dissertation, University of Texas Health Science Center at Houston, 1991.

Wilkinson, William Van. "Alcohol Drinking Patterns in a South Texas Mexican American Community." Ph.D. dissertation, Sam Houston State University, 1985.

________. "The Influence of Lifestyles on the Patterns and Practices of Alcohol Use Among South Texas Mexican Americans." *Hispanic Journal of Behavioral Sciences* 11 (November 1989): 354–365.

Williams, Coleen. "Cultural Differences and Medical Care of Ten Mexican Migrant Families in San Antonio, Texas." Master's thesis, University of Texas, Austin, 1959.

Williams, Vanessa Palestine. "A Six-year Analysis of the Distribution of Time to Death among Colorectal Cancer Patients in the State of Texas." Master's thesis, University of North Texas Health Science Center at Fort Worth, 2000.

Yin, Zenong, Jesse T. Zapata, and David S. Katins. "Risk Factors from Substance Use Among Mexican American School-Age Youths." *Hispanic Journal of Behavioral Sciences* 17 (February 1995): 61–76.

Youssef, Adel Abdelhamid. "Macular Edema in Hispanics with Non-Insulin Dependent Diabetes Mellitus in Starr County, Texas: Prevalence, Incidence and Risk Factors." Ph.D. dissertation, University of Texas Health Science Center at Houston, 1995.

Zavaleta, Antonio N. "Substance Abuse in the Rio Grande Valley." *Agenda* (May/June 1979): 4–7.

________. "Texas-Mexican Border Folk Medicine in the Midst of Change." *Borderlands Journal* 10 (Fall 1986): 161–172.

Zavaleta, Antonio N., and Robert M. Malina. "Growth, Fatness, and Leanness in Mexican American Children." *American Journal of Clinical Nutrition* 33 (September 1980): 2008–2020.

23. COMMUNITIES (URBAN AND RURAL)

Listed in this chapter are works dealing with Tejano communities, whether urban or rural. The coverage herein does not confine itself to specific histories of towns, cities, or farm communities with defined geographical boundaries, but offers a wider depiction of activities within those localities. Among the topics covered are social life, work, urban dynamics, religious contributions, and many more.

Women and girl laundering in acequia. Mission Espada, San Antonio, Texas, ca. 1942.
The Institute of Texan Cultures at UTSA, No. L-2969-D
The San Antonio Light *Collection*

Achor, Shirley. *Mexican Americans in a Dallas Barrio*. Tucson: University of Arizona Press, 1978.

Achor, Shirley Collidge. "Of Thorns and Roses: Variations in Cultural Adaptation Among Mexican Americans in an Urban Texas Barrio." Ph.D. dissertation, Southern Methodist University, 1974.

Adams, William L., and Anthony K. Knopp. *Portrait of a Border City: Brownsville, Texas*. Austin: Eakin Press, 1997.

Ainslie, Ricardo. *No Dancin' in Anson: An American Story of Race and Social Change*. Northvale, N.J.: Jason Aronsen, 1995.

Applegate, Howard G., and C. Wayne Hanselka. *La Junta de los Ríos del Norte y Conchos*. El Paso: Texas Western Press, 1974.

Arnold, Charles August. *The Folklore, Manners, and Customs of the Mexicans in San Antonio, Texas*. San Francisco: R&E Research Associates, 1971.

Arreola, Daniel D. "The Mexican American Cultural Capital." *Geographical Review* 77 (January 1987): 17–34.

Ballí, Cecilia. "Ciudad de la Muerte." *Texas Monthly* 31 (June 2003): 108–117, 170–173.

Barbee, William Clayton. "A Historical and Architectural Investigation of San Ygnacio, Texas." Master's thesis, University of Texas at Austin, 1981.

Barr, Alwyn. "Occupational and Geographic Mobility in San Antonio, 1870–1900." *Social Science Quarterly* 51 (September 1970): 396–403.

Barsun, Helen W. "Los Pastores: A Remnant of Medieval Drama in San Antonio." Master's thesis, St. Mary's University, 1943.

Barton, May Wilson. "Methodism at Work among the Spanish-Speaking People of El Paso, Texas." Master's thesis, University of Texas, Austin, 1950.

Berrios, Lizardo S. "*Colonias* in the Lower Rio Grande Valley of South Texas: A Survey Report." *Policy Research Project Report*. Austin: LBJ School of Public Affairs, 1977.

Black, F. Michael, ed. *Mirando City: A New Town in a New Oil Field*. Laredo: Laredo Publishing, 1972.

Bradshaw, Benjamin, David R. Johnson, Derral Cheatwood, and Stephen Blanchard. "A Historical Geographical Study of Lethal Violence in San Antonio." *Social Science Quarterly* 79 (December 1998): 863–878.

Byrd, Theresa L., James VanDerslice, and S. K. Peterson. "Variation in Environmental Risk Perceptions and Information Sources among Three Communities in El Paso." *Risk: Health, Safety and Environment* 8 (1997): 355–372.

Caram, Dorothy F., Anthony G. Dworkin, and Nestor Rodríguez, eds. *Hispanics in Houston and Harris County*. Houston: Houston Hispanic Forum, 1989.

Cárdenas, Cipriano. "Hispanic Journalism in Brownsville, Texas." In *Studies in Matamoros and Cameron County History*, edited by Milo Kearney, Anthony Knopp, and Antonio Zavaleta, 227–236. Brownsville, Tex.: University of Texas at Brownsville–Texas Southmost College, 1997.

Cárdenas, Gilberto, Jorge Chapa, and Susan Burek. "The Changing Economic Position of Mexican Americans in San Antonio." In *Latinos in a Changing U.S.*

Economy: Comparative Perspectives on Growing Inequalities, edited by Rebecca Morales and Frank Bonilla, 160–183. Newbury Park, Calif.: Sage Publications, 1993.

Chabrán, Richard, and Rafael Chabrán, eds. "King Ranch." In *The Latino Encyclopedia*, edited by Richard Chabrán and Rafael Chabrán, vol. 3, 827. New York: Marshall Cavendish, 1996.

Chaney, Gussie Scott. "The Mexican Element in San Antonio." *The Passing Show* 3 (June 13, 1908): 78.

Clark, John W. Jr., and Ana María Juárez. *Urban Archaeology: A Culture History of a Mexican American Barrio in Laredo, Webb County, Texas.* Austin: Texas State Department of Highways and Public Transportation, 1986.

Connell, Earl Monroe. "The Mexican Population of Austin, Texas." Master's thesis, University of Texas, Austin, 1925.

Crimm, Ana Carolina Castillo. "Founding Families: The Mexican Americans of Victoria." *South Texas Studies* 3 (1992): 1–25.

Crook, Elaine Carland. "San Antonio, Texas, 1846–1861." Master's thesis, Rice University, 1964.

Cuéllar, Carlos Eliseo. *Stories from the Barrio: A History of Mexican Fort Worth.* Fort Worth: Texas Christian University, 2003.

________. "Stories from the Barrio: A History of Mexican Fort Worth." Ph.D. dissertation, Texas Christian University, 1998.

Davis, Ethelyn Clara. "Little Mexico: A Study of Horizontal and Vertical Mobility." Master's thesis, Southern Methodist University, 1936.

de la Garza, Rodolfo O. "Voting Patterns in Bicultural El Paso." A Contextual Analysis of Chicano Voting Behavior." *Aztlán* 5 (Spring and Fall 1974): 235–260.

de la Garza, Rodolfo O., and Janet Weaver. "Does Ethnicity Make a Difference: Chicano-Anglo Public Policy Perspectives in San Antonio." *Social Science Quarterly* 66 (September 1985): 576–586.

De León, Arnoldo. *Ethnicity in the Sunbelt: A History of Mexican Americans in Houston.* College Station: Texas A&M University Press, 2001.

________. *San Angeleños: Mexican Americans in San Angelo, Texas.* San Angelo: Fort Concho Museum Press, 1985.

De León, Arnoldo, and Kenneth L. Stewart. "A Tale of Three Cities: A Comparative Analysis of the Socio-Economic Conditions of Mexican Americans in Los Angeles, Tucson, and San Antonio, 1850–1900." *Journal of the West* 24 (April 1985): 64–74.

De Wetter, Mardee. "Revolutionary El Paso, 1910–1917." Master's thesis, Texas Western College, 1946.

Dickens, E. Larry. "The Political Role of Mexican Americans in San Antonio, Texas." Ph.D. dissertation, Texas Tech University, 1969.

Dillman, Daniel. "The Functions of Brownsville, Texas, and Matamoros, Tamaulipas: Twin Cities of the Lower Rio Grande." Ph.D. dissertation, University of Michigan, 1968.

Donigan, Norma F. "An Occupational Study of Dallas Migratory Mexicans." Master's thesis, Southern Methodist University, 1950.

Dunn, Timothy Joseph. "Immigration Enforcement in the United States-Mexico Border Region, the El Paso Case: Bureaucratic Power, Human Rights, and Civic Activism." Ph.D. dissertation, University of Texas at Austin, 1999.

Edwards, Elmer J. "Randado, Texas." In *The Handbook of Texas*, edited by Walter Prescott Webb and H. Bailey Carroll, vol. 2, 436. Austin: Texas State Historical Association, 1952.

Elizondo, Virgilio P., and Timothy M. Matovina. *San Fernando Cathedral: Soul of the City*. Maryknoll, N.Y.: Orbis Books, 1998.

Epperson, Jean L. *Lost Spanish Towns: Atascosito and Trinidad de Salcedo*. Woodville, Tex.: Dogwood Press, 1996.

Eyde, David B. "Pluralism in El Paso, Texas." In *Politics and Society in the Southwest: Ethnicity and Chicano Pluralism*, edited by Z. Anthony Kruszewski, Richard L. Hough, and Jacob Ornstein-Galicia, 155–167. Boulder, Colo.: Westview Press, 1982.

Finke, Eugene Irving. "Aldermanic Redistricting in El Paso, Texas: A Case Study of Democratic Representation." Ph.D. dissertation, New Mexico State University, 1984.

Flores, María Eva. "The Good Life the Hard Way: The Mexican American Community of Fort Stockton, Texas, 1930–1945." Ph.D. dissertation, Arizona State University, 2000.

________. "St. Joseph's Parish, Fort Stockton, Texas, 1875–1945: The Forging of an Identity and Community." *U.S. Catholic Historian* 21.1 (Winter 2003): 13–31.

Fraley, Elizabeth. "A Chronological History of the San Antonio Fiesta de San Jacinto and the Battle of Flowers." Master's thesis, Southwest Texas State Teachers College, 1943.

Francesca, Sister M. "Variations of Selected Cultural Patterns Among Three Generations of Mexicans in San Antonio, Texas." *American Sociological Review* 21 (February 1956): 84–87.

Garabedian, Charles Albert. "The Wildcats vs. the Mustangs: The Consolidation of the San Felipe and Del Rio Independent School Districts." Master's thesis, Sul Ross State University, 1994.

García, Ignacio. "COPS: Policing the System." *Nuestro* 4 (August 1980): 22, 24.

García, María-Cristina. "Colonias." In *The New Handbook of Texas*, edited by Ron Tyler, Douglas E. Barnett, Roy R. Barkely, Penelope C. Anderson, and Mark F. Odintz, vol. 2, 221–222. Austin: Texas State Historical Association, 1996.

García, Mario T. *Desert Immigrants: The Mexicans of El Paso, 1880–1920*. New Haven: Yale University Press, 1981.

________. "The Chicana in American History: The Mexican Women of El Paso, 1880–1920: A Case Study." *Pacific Historical Review* 49 (May 1980): 315–337.

________. "Mexican Americans and the Politics of Citizenship: The Case of El Paso, 1936." *New Mexico Historical Review* 59 (April 1984): 187–204.

________. "Racial Dualism in the El Paso Labor Market, 1880–1920." *Aztlán* 6 (Summer 1975): 197–218.

García, Richard A. *Rise of the Mexican American Middle Class: San Antonio, 1929–1941*. College Station: Texas A&M University Press, 1991.

________. "The Making of the Mexican American Mind, San Antonio, Texas, 1929–1941: A Social and Intellectual History of an Ethnic Community." 2 vols. Ph.D. dissertation, University of California at Irvine, 1980.

________. "Class, Consciousness, and Ideology—The Mexican Community in San Antonio, Texas: 1930–1940." *Aztlán* 9 (Fall 1978): 23–70.

García, Rogelia O. *Dolores, Revilla and Laredo: Three Sister Settlements.* Waco: Texian Press, 1970.

Garza, Aida. *Feria en Benavides, September 14, 15, 16, 2001.* Benavides, Tex.: Task Force Committee for Benavides Feria, 2001.

Goldberg, Robert A. "Racial Change on the Southern Periphery: The Case of San Antonio, Texas, 1960–1965." *Journal of Southern History* 49 (August 1983): 349–374.

Goodman, Mary Ellen. *The Mexican American Population of Houston: A Survey in the Field, 1965–1970*. Houston: Rice University Studies, 1971.

Green, Stan, ed. *The Story of Laredo* (Volumes 1–15). Laredo: Border Studies, 1991.

Griswold del Castillo, Richard. "Literacy in San Antonio, Texas." *Latin American Research Review* 15 (April 1980): 180–185.

________. "'Only for My Family': Historical Dimensions of Chicano Family Solidarity—The Case of San Antonio in 1860." *Aztlán* 16 (1985): 145–176.

Guerra, Irene. "The Social Aspirations of a Selected Group of Spanish-Name People in Laredo, Texas." Master's thesis, University of Texas, Austin, 1959.

Guerra, Robert S. "Political Fragmentation in a Mexican American Community: The Case of Houston, Texas." Master's thesis, University of Houston, 1969.

Halla, Frank Louis Jr. "El Paso, Texas, and Juárez, Mexico: A Study of a Bi-ethnic Community, 1846–1881." Ph.D. dissertation, University of Texas at Austin, 1978.

Hamilton, James. "Mexican American Problems and Trends in Corpus Christi, Texas." Master's thesis, St. Mary's University, 1970.

Handman, Max Sylvius. "San Antonio: The Old Capital City of Mexican Life and Influence." *Survey* 66 (May 1, 1931): 163–166.

Harris, James Kilbourne. "A Sociological Study of a Mexican School in San Antonio, Texas." Master's thesis, University of Texas, Austin, 1927.

Haynes, Kingsley E. *Colonias in the Lower Rio Grande Valley of South Texas: A Summary Report.* Lyndon B. Johnson School of Public Affairs, Policy Research Report 18. Austin: University of Texas Press, 1977.

Heller, Dick D. Jr. "La Casita, Texas." In *The New Handbook of Texas*, edited by Ron Tyler, Douglas E. Barnett, Roy R. Barkely, Penelope C. Anderson, and Mark

F. Odintz, vol. 3, 1185–1186. Austin: Texas State Historical Association, 1996.

Hendricks, Rick, and W. H. Timmons. *San Elizario: Spanish Presidio to Texas County Seat*. El Paso: Texas Western Press, 1999.

Hernández, Mary Ester. "Some Connections Between San Antonio and the Mexican Revolution." Master's thesis, University of Texas at Austin, 1973.

Hollas, James, and Robert R. Bezdek. *Nueces County Elections: 1972–1980.* Corpus Christi, Tex.: Corpus Christi State University, 1980.

Hopkins, Kenneth N. "The Early Development of the Hispanic Community in Fort Worth and Tarrant County, 1849–1949." *East Texas Historical Journal* 38 (Fall 2000): 54–67.

Jiménez, Alfredo, and Beatriz Suñe. "Society and Culture in the Spanish Borderlands." In *Handbook of Hispanic Cultures in the United States*, edited by Nicolás Kanellos and Claudio Esteva-Fabregat, vol. 4, 228–258. Houston: Arte Público Press and Instituto de Cooperación Iberoamericana, 1994.

Johnson, Alvin S. "Mexico in San Antonio." *New Republic* (June 24, 1916): 190–191.

Kanellos, Nicolás. "San Antonio." In *A History of Hispanic Theatre in the United States: Origins to 1940*, by Nicolás Kanellos, 71–103. Austin: University of Texas Press, 1990.

King, Genevieve. "The Psychology of a Mexican Community in San Antonio, Texas." Master's thesis, University of Texas, Austin, 1936.

Knight, Lawrence Phillip. "Becoming a City and Becoming American: San Antonio, Texas, 1848–1861." Ph.D. dissertation, Texas A&M University, 1997.

Knowlton, Clark S. "Changing Patterns of Segregation and Discrimination Affecting the Mexican Americans of El Paso." In *Politics and Society in the Southwest: Ethnicity and Chicano Pluralism*, edited by Z. Anthony Kruszewski, Richard L. Hough, and Jacob Ornstein-Galicia, 131–154. Boulder, Colo.: Westview Press, 1982.

________. "Patterns of Accommodation of Mexican Americans in El Paso, Texas." In *Politics and Society in the Southwest: Ethnicity and Chicano Pluralism*, edited by Z. Anthony Kruszewski, Richard L. Hough, and Jacob Ornstein-Galicia, 215–236. Boulder, Colo.: Westview Press, 1982.

Knox, William John. "The Economic Status of the Mexican American Immigrant in San Antonio, Texas." Master's thesis, University of Texas, Austin, 1927.

Kohout, Martin Donell. "Benavides, Texas." In *The New Handbook of Texas*, edited by Ron Tyler, Douglas E. Barnett, Roy R. Barkely, Penelope C. Anderson, and Mark F. Odintz, vol. 1, 486. Austin: Texas State Historical Association, 1996.

Kreneck, Thomas H. *Del Pueblo: A Pictorial History of Houston's Hispanic Community*. Houston: Houston International University, 1989.

________. *Mexican American Odyssey: Félix Tijerina, Entrepreneur and Civic Leader, 1905–1965*. College Station: Texas A&M University Press, 2001.

________. "Documenting a Mexican American Community: The Houston Example." *American Archivist* 48 (Summer 1985): 272–285.

Landolt, Robert Garland. *The Mexican-American Workers of San Antonio*. New York: Arno Press, 1976.

________. "The Mexican-American Workers of San Antonio, Texas." Ph.D. dissertation, University of Texas, Austin, 1965.

Lane, John Hart Jr. *Voluntary Associations Among Mexican Americans in San Antonio, Texas*. New York: Arno Press, 1976.

Langston, Edward L. "The Impact of Prohibition on the Mexican-United States Border: The El Paso–Ciudad Juárez Case." Ph.D. dissertation, Texas Tech University, 1974.

Laquest, Katherine Watson. "A Social History of the Spaniards in Nacogdoches." Master's thesis, Baylor University, 1941.

Ledesma, Irene. "The New Deal Public Works Program and the Mexican Americans in McAllen, Texas, 1933–1936." Master's thesis, Pan American University, 1977.

Lee, Sylvia Anne. "Image of Mexican Americans in San Antonio Newspapers: A Context Analysis." Master's thesis, University of Texas at Austin, 1973.

Longoria, Mario D. "Revolution, Visionary Plan, and Marketplace: A San Antonio Incident." *Aztlán* 12 (Autumn 1981): 211–226.

"Lopeño, Texas." In *The Handbook of Texas*, edited by Walter Prescott Webb and H. Bailey Carroll, vol. 2, 81. Austin: Texas State Historical Association, 1952.

Luna, Jesús. "Francisco I. Madero's Organization of the Mexican Revolution in San Antonio, Texas." Master's thesis, East Texas State University, 1969.

Madera, Mark, Liliana Milani, Danny Samuels, and John Zona. *The Barrios: Mexican Americans in Houston*. Houston: Rice University, 1971.

Márquez, Benjamín. *Power and Politics in a Chicano Barrio: A Study of Mobilization Efforts and Community Power*. Lanham, Md.: University Press of America, 1985.

________. "Power and Politics in a Chicano Barrio." Ph.D. dissertation, University of Wisconsin-Milwaukee, 1983.

Martínez, Oscar J. *The Chicanos of El Paso: An Assessment of Progress*. El Paso: Texas Western Press, 1980.

Matovina, Timothy M. *Tejano Religion and Ethnicity: San Antonio, 1821–1860*. Austin: University of Texas Press, 1995.

McCaffery, Isias James. "Organizing *las Costureras*: Life, Labor, and Unionization among Mexican Garment Workers in Two Borderland Cities, Los Angeles and San Antonio, 1933–1941." Ph.D. dissertation, University of Kansas, 1999.

McConville, Lawrence J. "A History of Population in the El Paso–Ciudad Juárez Area." Master's thesis, University of New Mexico, 1966.

Melville, Margarita B. *Mexicans in Houston*. Houston: Houston Center for the Humanities, 1982.

________. "Mexicans." In *The Ethnic Groups of Houston*, edited by Fred R. von der Mehden, 41–61. Houston: Rice University Studies, 1984.

Miller, Michael V., and James D. Preston. "Vertical Ties and the Redistribution of Power in Crystal City." *Social Science Quarterly* 53 (March 1973): 772–784.

Mindiola, Tatcho Jr. "Core-Periphery Distinctions in Discrimination Against Spanish Surnamed Males in Houston, Texas." *Borderlands Journal* 4 (Spring 1981): 293–308.

________. "The Cost of Being a Mexican Female Worker in the 1970 Houston Labor Market." *Aztlán* 11 (Fall 1980): 231–247.

Mindiola, Tatcho Jr., Yolanda Flores Nieman, and Nestor Rodríguez. *Black-Brown Relations and Stereotypes*. Austin: University of Texas Press, 2002.

Moffatt, Lori. "Border Crossings: Exploring Los Dos Laredos." *Texas Highways* (May 2003): 22–29.

Mugerauer, Robert. "Porous Boundaries: Fence Patterns and Mexican-American Identity in San Antonio, Texas." In *Hybrid Urbanism: On the Identity Discourse and the Built Environment,* edited by Nezar Al Sayyad and Ananaya Roy, 206–228. Westport, Conn.: Praeger, 2001.

Nixon-Méndez, Nina L. "The Development of a City Preservation Plan Based on the Historical Analysis of Urban Settlement Patterns in Laredo, Texas." *Journal of Big Bend Studies* 9 (1997): 77–88.

________. "*Los Fundadores Urbanos* (Urban Pioneers): The Hispanics of Dallas, 1850–1940." *Journal of the West* 32 (October 1993): 76–82.

O'Connor, Robert Mark. "Binational Urbanization and Urban Planning on the United States-Mexico Border: A Comparative Analysis of Ciudad Juárez–El Paso." Master's thesis, University of Washington, 1982.

Odintz, Mark. "Crystal City, Texas." In *The New Handbook of Texas*, edited by Ron Tyler, Douglas E. Barnett, Roy R. Barkely, Penelope C. Anderson, and Mark F. Odintz, vol. 2, 430–431. Austin: Texas State Historical Association, 1996.

"Los Ojuelos." In *The Handbook of Texas*, edited by Walter Prescott Webb and H. Bailey Carroll, vol. 2, 82. Austin: Texas State Historical Association, 1952.

Pedescleaux, Desiree Selma. "Transition, Incorporation, and Governmental Responsiveness in Two American Cities. Ph.D. Dissertation, Yale University, 1991.

Piñon, Fernando. "Leadership and Mexican-American Politics: A Study of Two Texas Cities." Master's thesis, North Texas State University, 1971.

Polinard, J. L., Robert D. Wrinkle, and Norman E. Binder. "Ethnicity and Political Participation in Cameron and Hidalgo Counties: Mexican American Voters and Nonvoters." In *Studies in Matamoros and Cameron County History*, edited by Milo Kearney, Anthony Knopp, and Antonio Zavaleta, 89–106. Brownsville, Tex.: University of Texas-Brownsville and Texas Southmost College, 1997.

Prewitt, Steven W. "'We Didn't Ask to Come to This Party': Self-Determination Collides with the Federal Government in the Public Schools of Del Rio, Texas, 1890–1971." Ph.D. dissertation, University of Houston, 2000.

Quiroz, Rudolph Anthony. "Claiming Citizenship: Class and Consensus in a Twentieth Century Mexican American Community." Ph.D. dissertation, University of Iowa, 1998.

________. "Class and Consensus: Twentieth-Century Mexican American Ideology in Victoria, Texas." *Southwestern Historical Quarterly* 106 (July 2002): 31–54.

________. "Mexican American Struggles for Citizenship: Local Organizations in Twentieth Century Victoria, Texas." *South Texas Studies* 7 (1996): 108–130.

"Ramarito, Texas." In *The Handbook of Texas*, edited by Walter Prescott Webb and H. Bailey Carroll, vol. 2, 433. Austin: Texas State Historical Association, 1952.

Ramírez, Manuel Bernardo. "El Pasoans: Life and Society in Mexican El Paso, 1920–1945." Ph.D. dissertation, University of Mississippi, 2000.

"Ramírez, Texas." In *The Handbook of Texas*, edited by Walter Prescott Webb and H. Bailey Carroll, vol. 2, 433. Austin: Texas State Historical Association, 1952.

Ramos, Juan. "Spanish-speaking Leadership in Two Southwestern Cities: A Descriptive Study. Ph.D. dissertation, Brandeis University, 1968.

Raymond, Howard G. "Acculturation and Social Mobility Among Latin Americans in Resaca City." Master's thesis, University of Texas, Austin, 1952.

Remy, Caroline M. "Hispanic-Mexican San Antonio: 1836–1861." *Southwestern Historical Quarterly* 71 (April 1968): 564–582.

Rice, Gwendolyn. "Little Mexico and the Barrios of Dallas." In *Dallas Reconsidered: Essays in Local History*, edited by Michael V. Hazel, 158–168. Dallas: Three Forks Press, 1995.

Richardson, Chad. "Building Strengths from Within: *Colonias* of the Rio Grande Valley." *Journal of Borderland Studies* 11 (Fall 1996): 51–68.

Robinson Ellis, Leigh Ann. "The Place of Borders and Between: Little Mexico, 1900–1950, Dallas, Texas." Master's thesis, University of Texas at Arlington, 1996.

Rodríguez, Nestor P. "Economic Restructuring and Latino Growth in Houston." In *In the Barrios: Latinos and the Underclass Debate*, edited by Joan Moore and Raquel Pinderhughes, 101–128. New York: Russell Sage Foundation, 1993.

________. "The Growth of Houston's Hispanic Population." In *Hispanics in Houston and Harris County*, edited by Dorothy F. Caram, Anthony G. Dworkin, and Nestor Rodríguez, 49–54. Houston: Houston Hispanic Forum, 1989.

Rodríguez, Nestor P., Noelia Elizondo, David Mena, Ricardo Rojas, Adolfo Vásquez, and Frank Yeverino. "Political Mobilization in Houston's Magnolia." In *Barrio Ballots: Latino Politics in the 1990 Elections*, by Rodolfo O. de la Garza, Martha Menchaca, and Louis DeSipio, 83–114. Boulder, Colo.: Westview Press, 1994.

Rodríguez, Nestor P., and Jacqueline Hagan. "Transborder Community Relations at the U.S.-Mexico Border: Laredo/Nuevo Laredo and El Paso/Ciudad Juárez." In *Caught in the Middle: Border Communities in an Era of Globalization*, by Demetrios G. Papademetriou and Deborah Waller Meyers, 88–116. Washington, D.C.: Carnegie Endowment for International Peace, 2001.

Rogers, Thomas Guy. "The Housing Situation of the Mexicans in San Antonio, Texas." Master's thesis, University of Texas, Austin, 1927.

Romero, Mary. "El Paso Salt War: Mob Action or Political Struggle." *Aztlán* 16 (1985): 119–143.

Romero, Yolanda G. "The Mexican American Frontier Experience in Twentieth Century Northwest Texas." Ph.D. dissertation, Texas Tech University, 1993.

________. "From Rebels to Immigrants to Chicanas: Hispanic Women in Lubbock County." Master's thesis, Texas Tech University, 1987.

________. "Adelante Compañeros: The Sanitation Workers' Struggle in Lubbock, Texas, 1968–1972." *West Texas Historical Association Yearbook* 69 (1993): 82–87.

________. "Los Socios del Sementerio [*sic*]: A Mexican American Burial Society in Early Lubbock, Texas." *West Texas Historical Association Yearbook* 63 (1987): 123–130.

Romo, Ricardo. "The Urbanization of Southwestern Chicanos in the Early Twentieth Century." In *New Directions in Chicano Scholarship*, edited by Ricardo Romo and Raymund Paredes, 183–207. Santa Barbara: University of California, Santa Barbara, 1984.

Rosales, Francisco Arturo. "The Mexican Immigrant Experience in Chicago, Houston, and Tucson: Comparisons and Contrasts." In *Houston: A Twentieth-Century Urban Frontier*, edited by Francisco A. Rosales and Barry J. Kaplan, 58–77. Port Washington, N.Y.: Associated Faculty Press, 1983.

________. "La Música en Houston: Fifty Years of Mexican-American Music." *The Americas Review* 16 (Spring 1988): 12–25.

________. "Mexicans in Houston: The Struggle to Survive, 1908–1975." *The Houston Review* 3 (Summer 1981): 224–248.

________. "Shifting Self-Perceptions and Ethnic Consciousness Among Mexicans in Houston, 1908–1946." *The Americas Review* 16 (Spring 1988): 71–94.

Rosales, Rodolfo. *The Illusion of Inclusion: The Untold Political Story of San Antonio*. Austin: Univeristy of Texas Press, 2000.

________. "The Rise of Chicano Middle Class Politics in San Antonio, 1951–1985." Ph.D. dissertation, University of Michigan, 1991.

Rose, Victor M. *Some Historical Facts in Regard to the Settlement of Victoria, Texas: Its Progress and Present Status.* Laredo, Tex.: Daily Times Print, 1883.

Rubel, Arthur J. *Across the Tracks: Mexican-Americans in a Texas City.* Austin: University of Texas Press, 1966.

________. "Social Life of Urban Mexican Americans." Ph.D. dissertation, University of North Carolina, 1962.

Russell, James W. "Class and Nationality Relations on a Texas Border City: The Case of El Paso." *Aztlán* 16 (1985): 217–239.

San Miguel, Guadalupe Jr. *Brown, Not White: School Integration and the Chicano Movement in Houston*. College Station: Texas A&M University Press, 2001.

________. "Endless Pursuits: The Chicano Educational Experience in Corpus Christi, Texas, 1880–1960." Ph.D. dissertation, Stanford University, 1979.

________. "'The Community is Beginning to Rumble': The Origins of Chicano Educational Protest in Houston, 1965–1970." *The Houston Review* 13 (1991): 127–148.

________. "From a Dual to a Tripartite School System: The Origins and Development of Education Segregation in Corpus Christi, Texas." *Integrated Education* 17 (September/December 1979): 27–38.

Schmidt, Samuel. "Planning a U.S.-Mexican Bi-National Metropolis: El Paso, Texas–Ciudad Juárez, Chihuahua." In *The North American Cities and the Global Economy: Challenges and Opportunities*, edited by Peter Karl Kresl and Gary Gappert, 187–219. Thousand Oaks, Calif.: Sage Publicatoons, 1995.

Scogin, Russell Ashton. *The Sanderson Flood of 1965: Crisis in a Rural Texas Community*. Alpine, Tex.: Sul Ross State University, 1995.

Sloan, John W., and Jonathan West. "The Role of Informal Policy-making in the U.S. Border Cities." *Social Science Quarterly* 58 (September 1977): 270–282.

Strauss, Melvin P. "The Mexican-American in El Paso Politics." In *Urbanization in the Southwest*, edited by Clyde J. Wingfield, 56–74. El Paso: Texas Western Press, 1968.

Taylor, Paul S. "The Mexican Invaders of El Paso." *Survey* 36 (July 8, 1916): 380–382.

Tijerina, Andrés A. *The History of Mexican Americans in Lubbock County, Texas*. Lubbock: Texas Tech Press, 1979.

________. "A History of the Mexican Americans in Lubbock County, Texas." Master's thesis, Texas Tech University, 1973.

Towers, George William. "*Colonia* Formation and Economic Restructuring in El Paso, Texas." Ph.D. dissertation, University of Arizona, 1991.

Treviño, Roberto R. "La Fe: Catholicism and Mexican Americans in Houston, 1911–1972." Ph.D. dissertation, Stanford University, 1993.

Turk, Judy Van Slyke, Jim Richstad, Robert L. Bryson Jr., and Sammye M. Johnson. "Hispanic Americans in the News in Two Southwestern Cities." *Journalism Quarterly* 66 (Spring 1989): 107–113.

Ugalde, Antonio. *The Urbanization Process of a Poor Mexican Neighborhood*. Austin: University of Texas Press, 1974.

Vila, Pablo Sergio. "Everyday Life, Culture and Identity on the Mexican American Border: The Ciudad Juárez–El Paso Case." Ph.D. dissertation, University of Texas at Austin, 1994.

Villarreal, Roberto E., Norma G. Hernández, and Howard D. Neighbor. "EPISO and Political Empowerment." *Journal of Borderlands Studies* 3 (1988): 81–96.

Waddell, Paul Allen. "Factors Determining Household Choice of Residence, Workplace, and Housing Tenure: The Dallas-Fort Worth Metroplex, 1980." Ph.D. dissertaion, University of Texas at Dallas, 1989.

Ward, Peter M. *Colonias and Public Policy in Texas and Mexico: Urbanization by Stealth*. Austin: University of Texas Press, 1999.

Watson, Walter T. "Mexicans in Dallas." *Southwest Review* 22 (January 1937): 406–429.

West, Richard. "San Antonio: The Barrio." In *Richard West's Texas*, by Richard West, 53–88. Austin: Texas Monthly Press, 1981.

Wilkinson, Joseph B. *Laredo on the Rio Grande Frontier*. Austin: Jenkins Publishing, 1975.

Woods, Frances Jerome. *Mexican Ethnic Leadership in San Antonio, Texas*. Originally published in 1949. New York: Arno Press, 1976.

Woodward, Kenneth. "In Old San Antonio, *Mestizaje* Nurtures New American Way." *Smithsonian* 16 (December 1985): 115–127.

Wright, Robert E. "Popular and Official Religiosity: A Theoretical Analysis and Case Study of Laredo-Nuevo Laredo, 1755–1857." Ph.D. dissertation, Graduate Theological Union, Berkeley, 1992.

________. "San Fernando Cathedral Parish." In *The New Handbook of Texas*, edited by Ron Tyler, Douglas E. Barnett, Roy R. Barkely, Penelope C. Anderson, and Mark F. Odintz, vol. 5, 842–843. Austin: Texas State Historical Association, 1996.

Young, Elliott. "Deconstructing *La Raza*: Identifying the *Gente Decente* of Laredo, 1904–1911." *Southwestern Historical Quarterly* 98 (October 1994): 227–259.

Zavaleta, Antonio N. "'The Twin Cities': A Historical Synthesis of the Socio-Economic Interdependence of the Brownsville-Matamoros Border Community." In *Studies in Brownsville History*, edited by Milo Kearney, 125–173. Brownsville, Tex.: Pan American University at Brownsville, 1986.

Author Index

A

B

C

D

E

F

G

H

I

J

K

L

M

N

O

P

Q

R

S

T

U

V

W

X

Y

Z